THE DARK STREAM

Leon Gerdener Rousseau was born and educated in Cape Town. His journalistic career began with several years on the staff of *Die Burger.* In 1959, together with Koos Human, he co-founded Human & Rousseau Publishers.

His acclaimed biography of Eugène Marais, *Die Groot Verlange,* was published in 1974 and won the CNA Literary Award. In 1982 he translated the work into English under the title *The Dark Stream* and again received much praise for the work. This is the second edition and is available for the first time in paperback.

He is also the author of a number of other books, some of which have been translated and published in Holland.

He has five children and lives in a lakeside house at Zeekoeivlei near Cape Town.

THE DARK STREAM
THE STORY OF
EUGÈNE MARAIS

LEON ROUSSEAU

JONATHAN BALL PUBLISHERS
Johannesburg

First published in hard cover in 1982 by
Jonathan Ball Publishers (Pty) Ltd
P O Box 33977
Jeppestown
2043

This edition published in soft cover in 1999.

ISBN 1 86842 076 0

Cover design by Michael Barnett, Johannesburg
Cover reproduction by Ince (Pty) Ltd, Johannesburg
Design and phototypesetting of text by Book Productions, Pretoria
Printed and bound by National Book Printers, Drukkery Street, Goodwood, Western Cape.

For my Parents

O, Diep Rivier, O, Donker Stroom
hoe lank het ek gewag, hoe lank gedroom,
die lem van liefde wroegend in my hart?
– in jou omhelsing eindig al my smart.
Blus uit, O Diep Rivier, die vlam van haat –
die groot verlange wat my nooit verlaat.
Ek sien van ver die glans van staal en goud,
ek hoor die sag gedruis van waters diep en koud;
ek hoor jou stem as fluistering in 'n droom
Kom snel, O Diep Rivier, O Donker Stroom!

O, Deep River, O, Dark Stream,
how long have I waited, how long dreamed
the blade of love twisting in my heart?
– in your embrace is ended all my pain.
Blow out, O Deep River, the flame of hate –
the great longing which never leaves me.
I see from afar the gleam of steel and gold,
I hear the soft murmur of waters deep and cold;
I hear your voice like whispering in a dream
Come quick, O Deep River, O Dark Stream!

FOREWORD

One of my main aims in writing *The Dark Stream* was to create a readable story. In fact I would prefer the book to be read as a novel or *roman de vie* rather than as a scientific biography, although no doubt it has elements of all three.

I say this in spite of the soul-breaking amount of work that went into digging up the material. Many of the facts had been obscured by legend, many others had been suppressed by Marais himself, by his friends or relations and by those members of the Afrikaans establishment who thought that the full story might harm his reputation as a pioneer of the Afrikaans language and its literature.

Probably at least a hundred people have to be thanked for helping me to research the material – scores of them for long interviews, some for a single important fact or clue.

In the introduction to the Afrikaans edition I mentioned that the names of one company and two persons could not be left out, even in the briefest of forewords. This list has now to be expanded.

The firm was Shell South Africa (Pty) Ltd, which gave me a generous grant for research in South Africa and abroad, including a month in London. Without the assistance of Shell the project would have been far beyond my means. That the money did not last long was hardly Shell's fault.

The first person I want to thank is the late Mr. Eugène C.G. Marais, son of the poet, without whose assistance during the course of twelve years it would have been quite impossible to complete the book in its present form. "Oom Eugène" (that is, Eugène junior, for I never knew the father) was a lovable man and I retain only the fondest memories of our prolonged and perforce intermittent attempts to arrive at what he, in gentle satire, was wont to call "the soul of Eugène Marais".

I would like to thank Winie Rousseau for her constant moral support and for three words said at a time when I was close to despair. "There is such a thing as *Do or Die*," she told me mildly. These simple words helped me to keep going.

I thank my children, Pierre, Chris, Louise and Leontine, for matching their mother's patience and forbearance while I was working on the book.

I would also like to thank the late Rev. F.G.M. Du Toit, author of *Eugène N. Marais – Sy Bydrae tot die Afrikaanse Letterkunde* (1940) (Eugène N. Marais – His Contribution to Afrikaans Literature). Apart from unpublished biographical and other information which the author generously made available to me from time to time, this book – although not a biography – formed part of the foundations on which *The Dark Stream* was built.

Now, almost exactly seven years after writing the foreword to the Afrikaans edition, I must also thank Mr. Jonathan Ball of Johannesburg for persuading me to translate the work. I had always hesitated to attempt this, as my home language is Afrikaans. Even if someone else were to translate the book I would first have had to plough through the Afrikaans text, condensing material not essential in an English edition and expanding statements which many English-speaking readers might have found unintelligible. Then a translator would have had to be found to translate the revised manuscript into English. In the end, encouraged by Jon and his editor, Alison Lowry, I found that in some ways it was simpler to expand, condense and add new insights while translating the book myself.

Finally, my thanks to Professor Harvey of Stellenbosch, who translated most of the Afrikaans poems quoted in *The Dark Stream*, poems both by Marais and others (including the excerpts from Van Wyk Louw's "Ballade van die Bose" – "Ballad of Evil" – which head the eight main parts of the book).

Leon Rousseau

CAPE TOWN, OCTOBER 1981

CONTENTS

Part 4: A New Beginning

Part 5: The Waterberg

Part 6: Interludes

PART 1: YOUNG PRETORIA

... Van voor die daeraad se blank begin straal ek by albei jou oë in.	... Before the pale beginnings of sunrise I shine steadily into both your eyes.

1. Les Marais

Isolated in its encirclement of hills, Pretoria was a lonely little village in 1871.

In a simple cottage in the village forty-six-year-old Catharina Marais had just given birth to her thirteenth child – her thirteenth child and the first to be born in the Zuid-Afrikaansche Republiek (South African Republic), as the Transvaal was called.

A painting by Baines shows Pretoria and its environs in the same month, January. The scattered, thatch-roofed cottages and the surrounding farms are dominated by a menacing thundercloud. What the weather conditions actually were on the day of Eugène Marais's birth is not known. It was a primitive society, and no meteorological records were kept.

Catharina and her husband, Jan, who was fifty years old, were not Transvalers. Jan had grown up on his parents' beautiful farm Nectar in the Jonkershoek valley near Stellenbosch. Until eleven years before he and his wife had lived there with all the comforts of civilization at hand. But in that year tragedy had struck.

First the daughter named after Catharina had died at the age of eleven and little more than a year later Jan Christiaan Nielen's namesake, a small boy who was then just four and a half years old, suffered the same fate.

Two months later their baby, Sebastira, followed the others into death.

Taking their remaining six children with them, the Marais' left their paradise, which to them had become a place of sorrow. They moved to Bloemfontein, "a little *dorpie* (village)", as it was called, even though it was the capital of the recently founded Free State Republic. Here Jan Marais became Government Secretary in 1863, and the couple had three more children. In 1867, less than four years before young Eugène's birth, Jan Marais was discharged from office because of "gross irregularities in keeping the public accounts", as the local newspaper, *The Friend*, put it.

One misfortune now followed another. Hardly a month after his insolvency, late in 1869, Jan Marais was committed for trial. It must have been at about this time that the family fled to the Transvaal, following in the footsteps of Jan Marais's extremely successful brother, "Lang Piet". Near Pretoria, the capital, they went to live in a cottage on Piet's farm, Les Marais. Jan's romantically named farm near Bloemfontein, Gem of the Prairie, was put up for sale. Eventually, however, Jan Nielen Marais decided to return to Bloemfontein to take his medicine. He was sentenced to a year in gaol, of which he served only five months. Conditions in the Bloemfontein gaol were regarded as so intolerable – except, one presumes, for "kaffirs" – that Jan was allowed to serve his sentence in a room in the town. It was during the period of his imprisonment that Catharina Marais moved from Lang Piet's farm to an even simpler cottage in the village when her time approached. Jan Nielen returned to Pretoria only after the boy's birth.

What an unspeakable scandal for such refined gentlefolk from the Cape. One of Jan Nielen Marais's ancestors had been Baron Van Rheede van Oudtshoorn, who died on the ship which was bringing him to the Cape to take up his appointment as Governor. One of Catharina's ancestors had been Commissioner-General De Mist, one of the progressive, enlightened rulers of the Cape after the French Revolution.

Unfortunately, these were family fantasies. In fact recent genealogical research has indicated that there was no link whatever between Eugène's mother and Commissioner-General De Mist, while the relationship between Jan Christiaan Nielen and Baron Van Rheede van Oudtshoorn is uncertain and – if true – was certainly more tenuous than the Marais' thought.

The exaggerated, romanticized view of their own ancestry was by no means untypical of the Marais family. There was talk of a family crest somewhere in the archives of France, implying noble or at least gentle birth. The true circumstances surrounding Eugène

Marais's birth were kept a family secret, consciously or unconsciously, for more than a century, until they were revealed as a result of research by Karel Schoeman for his book, *Bloemfontein*, published in 1980.

At the time of his youngest son's birth, at any rate, Jan Nielen was regarded as a disgrace to his family. He had lost his namesake, the jolly little toddler of Nectar in the Jonkershoek valley and his thirteenth child was not named after the dead child to make good the loss. The boy was christened Eugène – Eugène Nielen, to keep the fashionable Nielen surname in the family.

On this day, 9 January 1871, in the little cottage in Pretoria, one finds the primary factors which were to shape the life and person of Eugène N. Marais. Ineradicably implanted in his genes by generations of ancestors were the versatility, the artistry, the flashes of genius, but then, too, the exaggerated delicacy of feeling and the imbalance which were to characterize Marais's life. He was to grow up fatherless, with all the incalculable consequences of such a condition, for after his return from Bloemfontein, old Jan Nielen, more than ever, was a lame duck, the "perfect invalid", as his daughters called him, the head of the family only in name, and no real father. As the "*laatlam*" (late lamb), the one born late and last, Eugène would, according to the old superstition, run the gauntlet between complete failure and great fame, and he was the mystic number thirteen. He would have to stand up to his six prudish older sisters, a formidable half dozen. He was to grow up with the acute consciousness of sin and evil which typified his era, his church, his nation and his family, elements which can hurl a man from side to side like dice in a glass. He was to grow up close to the animals of the veld, and to snakes of all kinds, here in the rugged new North.

And within reach – perhaps in that very cottage, certainly readily available – there were the medicines with which most educated people would treat their infants, soothing and tranquillizing syrups with such a high opium content that a careless dose could kill.

On a secondary level, too, the scene was being prepared for the newly born baby. Already some of his fellow-actors were on the stage, others in the wings. Sigmund Freud, fourteen years old, was a promising scholar in Vienna, and Maurice Maeterlinck a schoolboy in the town of his birth, Ghent. For half a century receptive young minds had been influenced by Thomas de Quincey's *Confessions of an English Opium Eater.* Paul Kruger was Commandant-General of the Transvaal Republic. In the Cape Colony the first hesitant writings in a new language, Afrikaans, had begun to appear about ten years earlier. Victoria had been Queen of England for thirty-three years. A young man, Cecil John Rhodes, had come to South Africa for reasons of health a short while before. In the Salpêtrière in Paris, a hospital for the treatment of psychological and nervous ailments, Dr. Jean-Martin Charcot was soon to start treating his patients with a new method – psychotherapy – and also by hypnosis.

2. A Dear Little Village

After the confinement Catharina and her newborn son returned to Oom Piet's farm. Only after Jan Marais's return from Bloemfontein did they move to the village itself.

Not that it made much difference. Pretoria, not quite twenty years old, was little more than a collection of smaller and larger farms. The Marais' house lay on the thickly wooded banks of the Apies river. Not until much later were real streets to be laid out here, streets with names, and only then would one be able to say that the house lay on the corner of Jacob Maré and Prinsloo Streets.

The front of the house, where Eugène was eventually to be given a small room of his own, was unimpressive. Only when one went to the back, to the huge garden between the house and the river, did one see how spacious it was.

Spacious but uncomfortable, with its thatched roof, its raw-brick walls, its manured floors, draughty rooms, and linen ceilings on which a leaking roof drew grotesque patterns. Gusts of wind would fill the house with red dust. The sanitation was of the most elementary kind.

Even so this house, too, was given an elegant name: Lynnwood House.

The French name of the farm, the English name of the house, the Anglo-American name of the farm near Bloemfontein were all characteristic.

Pretoria was by no means an "Afrikaans" village in those early days. "Of all the large towns in the Transvaal," F. Lion Cachet was to write about a time when Pretoria had become somewhat larger, "one is nowhere given the impression that the country is inhabited by the Boers to a lesser extent than in Pretoria, with its large foreign population of extremely questionable antecedents."

The Marais' friends were English-speakers, people from the Cape Colony and the small number of more refined Transvalers they had come to know there.

Eugène inherited a fragmented culture. The day-to-day language spoken by his parents and siblings was sometimes an early form of Afrikaans, which, however undeveloped, came naturally to the tongue, and sometimes a bastardized Dutch, which became more elegant and more Netherlands as soon as they received important visitors. They spoke English fluently, and they liked to speak it, partly to show their superiority, partly, perhaps, to remind them of the old Cape. The six daughters' names illustrated this as well. The eldest, christened Elizabeth, was called Lizzie; the second, Petronella, Polly; Gezina was changed to Jessie; Sophie Laetitia became Sophie, pronounced in the English manner; Catharina Mynhardina became Katie (or Kate) and Georgina was called Georgie.

It was a frontier town. Game was abundant. "Meintjeskop was infested with lions," one of the oldest inhabitants, a daughter of the Rev. H.S. Bosman, was to tell the author many decades later in an interview, referring to the hill on which the Union Buildings now stand. Eugène Marais himself was to write:

"We were completely isolated from the outside world. There was no railway or telegraph, no carriages, only a mail-coach which brought letters from the coast once a month and in the rainy season very irregularly. The nearest railway station was almost a thousand miles away."

From the Fountains to the Arcadia Drift, the Apies river was thickly wooded.

East of the river there were no plots or town houses at all, only a number of farms, like Muckleneuk, near the Poort, the property of the Walkers; Harmonie, where Jan Preller lived; Mr. Mears's farm, Sunnyside; Travenna, which for a time was the home of an English doctor, Lyle; and Arcadia, which belonged to Oom Fanie Meintjes.

To the west of the village there was only a single farm: Skinner's

Court, the property of Landdrost Skinner, who also had a town house in Market Street South.

The south-eastern outskirts of the village, where the Marais' lived, lay virtually in the veld. Closer to the only square, Market Square, the houses were rather more closely spaced. Simple, single-storied dwellings, some of them thrown together in an irregular manner, they lay like wooden blocks on a nursery floor between patches of acacias, shrubs and willows, orchards and the luxuriant, untrimmed rambling roses of the hedges.

In winter the Market Square, on which the Rev. Bosman's tiny church was built, was a big patch of dry ground dotted here and there with tufts of arid grass. Only during Nagmaal, the Holy Communion service, every three months, would it come to life. Then the farmers of the outlying districts would sit around the camp fires next to their outspanned wagons. Jukskeie – the yoke-pins with which the oxen were harnessed – lay scattered about. Here and there deep ruts could be seen in the soil, baked hard by the sun, where wagons had stuck fast in the rainy season.

Pretoria's main buildings were grouped around the square: all the shops, the long, single-storied Government Building with its thatched roof, the European Hotel, the Post Office, Barclay's Bank and the church, the Rev. Bosman's two-gabled manse, a scattering of houses, vacant lots, a large old oak tree in the south-western corner of the square where all auction sales were held.

Eugène grew up like a boy on a farm. In summer Pretoria teemed with mambas and puffadders, two of the deadliest snakes in the world. A whole nest of them was discovered under the President's porch. Eugène Marais's lifelong fascination with snakes began at a very early age. Even as a young boy he kept scorpions, and possibly tarantulas.

The dense trees and shrubs were alive with birds. One of the boy's earliest memories was of his mother feeding sparrows, yellowfinches, wagtails and other birds from her back door.

In this house the mother was the stronger vessel. What Eugène learnt, he learnt from her. Her family, the Van Niekerks of Malmesbury in the old Cape, were horse people, and her love of horses was transmitted to her son. When the aged Oom Jakob van Deventer, an infamous horse-thief, was gaoled in Pretoria, Eugène was frequently sent across to take him food. Oom Jakob stole horses because he loved them, said Eugène's mother; he wasn't a bad man.

Eugène himself learnt to ride at an early age. He grew to know the horses of Pretoria: the tough, salted Basuto ponies on which the Boers came to town; Captain Von Schlickmann's Arab mustang; the Percherons and Suffolks rumbling through the dusty streets with laden wagons behind them; the hunters and thoroughbreds of the English; the prancing Morgans of the mail coach. And the horses of Sunnyside, old Mr. Mears's farm, where horse races were regularly held.

The world belonged to him. He was learning something about life and creation which Sigmund Freud in Vienna and Maurice Maeterlinck in Ghent would never completely understand.

Easy years, in many respects. "Everyone knew everyone else intimately," Eugène Marais himself was to write later through the rose-coloured spectacles of time, for here, too – as we shall see – there were the socially untouchables, and for some people this may have applied to Eugène's father as well. "Everyone was called by their Christian names, or Oom or Tante So-and-So. One never knocked at a door. One simply went in and walked through to the back, where the kitchen was."

"A dear old village", one of Eugène's friends was to call it later.

Even so the tiny paradise was not as innocent as the child was to remember it. Jan Marais, Eugène's father, was a ruined man, almost a pauper. His profession was law, and in Bloemfontein he had been a civil servant. In the Transvaal he had for a time tried to earn a living transporting goods by ox-wagon and peddling his wares in the countryside. Now he simply did nothing. In the fifteen years since he had left the Cape Colony he had lost everything. Les Marais was the property of his brother and Lynnwood House was soon to belong to one of his sons, Melt. He was what his daughters might have called "genteelly poor".

Not that money was so important at the time. There was enough to live on. Even so, young Eugène soon realized that there were differences between their way of life and that of his father's younger brother, Oom Lang Piet Marais, soon to be known as Ryk Piet (Rich Piet).

From the earliest days of Pretoria comes a story about Oom Lang

Piet's enterprise. At a fair held on the Market Square he and a tiny black dwarf, King Coffee, were featured as "the Tallest and Shortest Men in the World" and photographs of the two were peddled. (Later, in his prosperity, Lang Piet tried to buy them all back – including the negatives – and destroy them.) Soon after this dubious beginning Oom Lang Piet opened a shop on Market Square and before long an estate agency as well. His clothes hung on his long frame with casual elegance, his gold watch-chain sparkled in the sun; his flowing beard was as neatly trimmed as his moustache; his light grey topper was of the latest design.

All his life Eugène would have the desire to make money as Oom Lang Piet did and all his life he would be foiled in this desire.

These were, on the face of it, happy years but even so, it frequently happened that the small boy would disappear into the bush during picnics or outings as if he no longer felt at home in company.

On Market Square stood the Rev. H.S. Bosman's primitive thatched church. There were no chairs or benches; the congregation had to arrange its own seating. The pulpit was a packing crate, covered in green baize. Every member of the congregation brought his or her own stub of candle to the evening service. There were no lights.

Eugène Marais went to school for the first time in the consistory of this little church. He was five years old. The teacher was Miss Pottger, who also ran a small shop. Some of his schoolfriends were children from the Zoutpansberg and the Waterberg whose parents had been murdered by savages.

A farm in the mountains: kloofs and krantzes, rivers and fountains, an abundance of game beyond imagining, a wonderland. But on the highest krantz: Mapela, the black eagle, cruel and powerful, sending out his warriors to loot and burn, murder and mutilate. The Boer who had to leave the farm for some days. The faithful servant who came to warn the mother and her child: "Mapela is coming to murder you tonight." The flight to the maize field, hiding there during the night, listening to the shrieking warriors burning down the house and driving off the cattle.

Horrors like these, deeply engraved in the consciousness of the Voortrekkers and their children, was one reason for the hardness of heart of which the Rev. Bosman complained: his congregation took no interest in missionary work among the heathens. To the Rev. Bosman, born and bred in the Cape Colony, such an attitude was inexplicable.

In this respect, too, Eugène was subjected to clashing influences – the Transvaal realities of the immediate past and the greater tolerance of the settled Cape society which he learnt from his parents and older sisters.

There were more important contradictions to confuse him. The attitude of the Marais family to their new fatherland revealed a certain dualism which could not fail to influence their youngest son. It was not that they despised all Transvalers. At a time when his health had been better, Eugène's father had got to know the Boers on his travels, peddling his wares in the Bushveld. Many a wide-eyed little Transvaal girl had seen a real doll for the first time in her life – a doll from the famous manufactory in Graaff-Reinet in the Cape Colony – on Oom Jan's wagon. On these journeys Jan Marais had learnt to know the Transvalers better than his wife and daughters knew them. Among them he even made some friends whom the rest of the family eventually came to accept. But the Marais' had no time for uneducated *takhare* (backvelders) in moleskin trousers – and least of all for Doppers, as members of the ultra-conservative Reformed Church were called.

With more Schadenfreude than embarrassment the Marais' would tell how Paul Kruger – then Commandant-General of the Republic – had come to visit them in Bloemfontein and how Mrs. Marais, taking one look at his unkempt appearance, had made him wait on the stoep until her husband came home. "Mother thought of him as a servant and treated him as such," one of the Marais girls was to relate in English, the language in which she was always to be most at home. "She wouldn't put a quilt on his bed."

The President of the Transvaal Republic, Tom Burgers, an educated and liberal man, was much more to the Marais' liking. In fact he was a good family friend. One morning after they had been playing Swart Piet (Black Pete) in Lynnwood House the previous evening, Eugène's older sister, Jess, was reprimanded by a civil servant. That morning, he told her, the President had had an unsightly red mark on his forehead. Couldn't she have let the burnt cork cool down before she marked him? Only that evening did Jess find out that no such thing had happened – the civil servant had only been pulling her leg.

President Burgers would often confide in his good friends the Marais' regarding questions which bothered him. The Transvalers distrusted him because he was too learned, too liberal in church matters, not enough of a Boer or a Dopper. That was why the taxes remained unpaid, why the Transvaal burghers took part so half-heartedly in punitive expeditions against rebellious native tribes and why the Republic had fallen into such chaos that England was considering its annexation.

Shortly after Eugène's sixth birthday, in 1877, Theophilus Shepstone, a British Special Commissioner, and a bodyguard arrived in Pretoria and began talks with President Burgers.

Only a few months later Shepstone ran up the British flag and annexed the Transvaal in the name of Britain. At this stage not even Paul Kruger advocated armed resistance. The Transvalers were still too uncertain of their rights as an independent state, and no one could deny that there was chaos in the Republic.

Burgers left the Transvaal and went to settle in the Cape. His feeling of personal defeat was so intense that, before his death four years later, he was to say: "Bury me in the entrance to a sheepfold, so that all signs of my existence may be wiped from the face of the earth."

Lang Piet Marais, Jan's brother, gave his full support to the pro-English elements by joining the Defence Committee which had been formed to protect Pretoria against Boers who might decide to invade the small town and drive Shepstone out.

Jan Marais and his family were not prepared to go to quite the same lengths. Melt, especially, who had just started work as a clerk in the shop of Field & Hofman, felt strongly pro-Republican. All the same, Shepstone and his officers were hospitably received in the Marais' home. The Administrator was especially fond of the delicious figs in Mrs. Marais's garden.

Eugène Marais was transferred to a thatch-roofed house outside Pretoria where Archdeacon A. Roberts, an English minister of the church, ran a small school. Eugène's schoolfriends included Johannes van Boeschoten, later to be knighted, and two Melville brothers, one of whom was eventually to become an important officer in the English army. It certainly seemed as if Eugène's parents were doing their best to give their youngest son the most "English" education which Pretoria could offer.

There were only eight scholars, and Eugène did not come first in class, although he wrote the best essays of them all. His academic achievements were always to remain little above average.

Archdeacon Roberts was a conscientious man. Naturally, they had to know the Anglican Catechism and Book of Common Prayer by heart. Naturally, they had to know the history and geography of the British Isles. But this was not all. In teaching them cricket and soccer, he brought the playing fields of Eton to the backveld. In the Hondekuil, a pool in the Apies river, they learnt to play water polo.

Like all scholars in English South Africa, but probably to an even greater extent, Eugène learnt to see the world through English eyes.

He learnt to know the English Tommies. He would see them when walking past Ulundi House, Shepstone's and later Lanyon's headquarters, where guards in their red, white and blue uniforms could always be seen, and near the military camp, and on Saturdays in the village itself. At first they were magnificent creatures: inhabitants of another, alien world, romantic figures from illustrated magazines and books. As he got to know them better he saw that they were very ordinary men, many of them rough and unrefined, some of them unwashed and lice-ridden, who frequently knew less about their own country than Archdeacon Roberts' scholars and who spoke with a variety of accents which would have sent Roberts into a fit if he had heard them in his classroom. Their pay was less than a shilling a day. They were the cannon-fodder of Imperial England.

Much more amenable, much more acceptable to Eugène's own people were the English officers and officials who came to visit at Lynnwood House. According to a family tradition the friendship between H. Rider Haggard, one of Shepstone's aide-de-camps, later to become famous as a writer, and Eugène's sister Jess soon developed into a love affair.

Jess was as pro-English as Melt, her brother, was a Republican. Only a few years before she had married one of the Rex's of Knysna in Oom Lang Piet's house. Now, although she was only 23, she seldom saw her carefree, faithless husband – a quadroon, and extremely fond of the bottle.

Rider Haggard was to write a novel called *Jess*, in which he sought to inject local colour by the profuse use of words which bear little resemblance to any in either Dutch or Afrikaans and in which *skellums* (rascals) abound, most of these being Boers. Jess, the heroine, is described as follows: "She was small and rather thin, with quantities of curling brown hair; not by any means a lovely woman, as her sister undoubtedly was, but possessing two very remarkable characteristics – a complexion of extraordinary and uniform colour, and a pair of the most beautiful dark eyes he had ever looked on. Altogether, though her size was almost insignificant, she was a striking-looking person, with a face one is not likely to forget."

This was a literary portrait, intentionally obfuscating: Eugène's sister was tall, not short, but in every other respect it was a fair enough likeness.

The story about the love affair may have been apocryphal. What was true, however, was that Rider Haggard had a cottage outside Pretoria which he mockingly called the "Palatial" and which was later to be known as Jess's Cottage. This, according to the story, was their rendezvous.

Although the English had come to maintain order, they did little better than the Transvalers. In March 1879 the alarm was given in the small town. A bloodthirsty black horde of warriors had reached Pienaar's river and was fast approaching Pretoria. That night Eugène and other members of his family took refuge in the house of Mr. Goosen Verdoorn – one of the richest men in Pretoria – on the south-western corner of Pretorius and Van der Walt Streets, a solid building with a flat roof and parapets, as if designed to serve as a fort in emergencies.

Not before the next day were the inhabitants of Pretoria told that the rumours had been exaggerated; the natives had retreated.

From this time, when Eugène was about nine, dates an apparently insignificant story.

Dusk at Lynnwood House. In the back garden a large number of young people were having a party. The garden was overgrown and the willows Jan Marais had planted on the banks of the river some years ago were now tall trees.

Suddenly two ghostly apparitions appeared from behind one of the willows – Eugène and a young friend, both draped in bedsheets. At the same time drawn-out, blood-curdling shrieks could be heard coming from across the river where, it was said, a madwoman lived. Eugène and his friend had timed their appearance to coincide with her lamentations, which came at dusk every evening.

Girls and boys fled in terror at the sight of them, and their fear was so infectious that Eugène and his friend themselves took fright, tripping over the willow-roots and causing even greater pandemonium by following the other children in their bloodied white gowns into the safety of the house.

This was how Eugène Marais was to tell the story to his son much later.

Here, for the first time, we see Marais the showman, the stage artiste, the magician, who liked to mystify others, especially by means of phenomena he would present as being supernatural.

In December 1879, Eugène's older sister, Lizzie Niemeyer, arrived from the Free State to visit her parents. She was the eldest of the Marais children, just this side of forty, with eight children of her own, three others having died. She may have come to Pretoria to discuss her financial problems, for her husband, the trading partner of her brother Charles in the Free State village of Boshof, had not been doing well lately.

However, Lizzie had not been in Pretoria for long when more important events overshadowed all family problems. There had long been rumours that armed Boers were to converge on Paardekraal in the month of January; now they suddenly decided to muster their forces almost at once.

Few people in Pretoria were aware that the British High Commissioner had also gone to Paardekraal for talks with Kruger, Pretorius and Piet Joubert, and of these even fewer expected to hear the outcome soon. After a Boer patrol was spotted near the military camp at Pretoria British cavalrymen regularly patrolled the vicinity of the village and the camp. On the very night of the discovery of the Boer patrol Boers cut the telegraph cable between Pretoria and Heidelberg.

In times of crisis the divisions in a family come to the fore. Eugène's brother Melt, now a twenty year old field-cornet, had already left for Paardekraal and Lizzie was hurriedly sent back to the Free State. The news that the burghers had proclaimed a republic at Paardekraal and that Frans Joubert had routed Colonel Anstruther's force at Hondespruit caused an uproar. There was talk of a Boer attack on Pretoria.

On Dingaan's Day, 16 December, the day the Voortrekkers had broken the might of the Zulu king Dingaan at the Battle of Blood River, the Boer forces began their siege of Pretoria.

Oom Jan Celliers, a good friend of the Marais' (and the father of the boy who was later to become a famous, pioneering Afrikaans poet) was gaoled for supporting the Boers. His newspaper, *De Volksstem (The Voice of the People*, as it was democratically called), was closed down.

Early in the new year all the inhabitants of Pretoria were put into three camps for their own safety: the Tronk (Gaol) Laager, a rectangular, walled area between the Loretto Convent and the gaol; the so-called Wagon Laager, a collection of tents, wagons and lean-to's near the shooting range; and the military camp itself, where Jan Marais and his family lived in tents.

Counting refugees from outside Pretoria, almost four thousand people were housed in the three camps.

Jan Marais and his family were obviously privileged inhabitants. Although nobody was allowed to leave the camp, an exception was made for Eugène. "I and the small Koranna who was my constant companion," he was to write much later, "had been given permission to leave the camp and were playing at the river when the Boers, led by Henning Pretorius, nabbed a number of cattle east of the Apies river in what is now Sunnyside. The English shot at them from the fort and some of the shells fell not far from us in the bush on the river bank. Soon after that the Koranna and I, watching from the bush, saw the fight at Skinner's Court, where Henning Pretorius was shot through the chest."

Before the end of that month came the report that General Colley and his force had been defeated at Majuba. The British dead included General Colley himself. In the military camp in Pretoria the Union Jack flew at half mast.

What the reactions in the Marais tent were one cannot tell. Perhaps they were mixed. But for the young boy, Eugène, these events were a turning point. He did not know exactly why, but his heart was on the side of the Boers.

Early in March, while constant heavy rains made life hard for the inhabitants of the camps, General Piet Joubert began negotiating with Colley's successor, and on 6 March an armistice was signed.

3. Big Brother Charles of Boshof

The wagon was a house, a fort, a ship. They lived in it. After dark its canvas sides were like walls against the night, and always it carried them further and further away: Daspoort, Hornsnek, Agter-die-Berg, Rustenburg, Marico.

Eugène Marais, ten years old, was travelling by ox-wagon in the company of a trader, one Van Heerden, to Boshof in the Free State, where he was to go and live with his eldest brother, Charles.

Several months had passed since the Boer victory. Eugène and his family had left the military camp and had moved back into Prinsloo Street. Melt had come back from the war, Oom Jan Celliers had been released and was again publishing *De Volksstem*. Many of the well known faces had disappeared from Pretoria. Once more there were picnics and outings to Sunnyside and other farms near the village, family gatherings, and swimming in the Hondekuil.

Even so, it was not the same as before. For months the English troops remained in the camp, and later behaved so badly that the military authorities declared the village out of bounds. The weekend of the soldiers' riots one could hear the noise as far as Prinsloo Street. And even after the Convention of Pretoria, when the troops had left, Transvaal was not completely free. Neither was there a president. The three war leaders, Joubert, Pretorius and Kruger, governed as a triumvirate.

Mr. Verdoorn, the owner of Koedoespoort and one of the richest men in Pretoria, in whose large house many people had taken shelter against the menacing black invasion two years before, had lost virtually all his money because of the cancellation of agreements due to the signing of the peace. Andries, the Verdoorn son who was attending a public school in England, had to look for a job to earn money for his journey home. There were similar cases among the

Marais' friends and acquaintances. Only Oom Lang Piet was richer than ever.

Jan Marais himself seems to have taken his final financial knock during the First Boer War. Lynnwood House now belonged to Melt, as Les Marais belonged to one of his other sons, Hennie. His wife and his daughters looked after him, his sons clothed him, fed him and gave him lodging. He was a rather pathetic King Lear, Transvaal style.

A century later, from the crow's nest of time, it seems as if the First Boer War was not only a watershed in Eugène Marais's attitude to his own people but also in his relationship with his father. His move to Boshof was symbolic. He was soon to regard his brother Charles as his real father.

There were, however, practical reasons for the move: in Boshof, which had an excellent school, Eugène would receive a better education than in Pretoria; and by paying for the boy's schooling and lodging, Charles would be doing his bit.

Of all these things Eugène was only vaguely aware. He was ten years old and this was his greatest adventure.

On the farm Wildebeesthoek, the property of Oom Josop Fourie – grandfather of Jopie Fourie, who was later to become one of the most famous Boer scouts – in Agter-die-Berg (Behind the Mountain) Van Heerden's "trek" spent two weeks. Eugène had been here many times before in the company of his parents, but he had never seen it look more beautiful. The mountain streams were overflowing, everything was cool and fresh, the oranges and tangerines an incredibly bright orange against the dark green orchards. There were outings with the children on the farm: to the watermill, where Oom Josop and his sons ground their own grain; to the vineyards and orchards; to the tobacco-shed, where Oom Josop's black "boys" would compress the yellow Magaliesberg leaves into rolls which would later turn as dark as stinkwood; to the great still where brandy was distilled from the farm's grapes, peaches and wild plums; possibly also to the krantzes and ravines of the Magaliesberg range.

This was Eugène Marais's last visit to the farm. No doubt the description he was to give of it and its environs more than fifty years later was a romanticized one.

> No one today can form the slightest idea of the abundant luxury of Agter-die-Berg then. This blessed land was so lush and fertile that fruit and usable crops of every kind literally grew wild. Magaliesberg tobacco was famed throughout South Africa as the finest yield the land could produce; and Magaliesberg's brandy grapes, peaches and wild plums were valued, at any rate in the Transvaal, far more highly than the products of the Cape Colony. It is hard to believe today that innumerable wagon-loads of oranges and naartjies (tangerines) were transported from Agter-die-Berg to Kimberley in the heyday of the diamond fields, when incredible prices for all Magaliesberg products were obtainable.
>
> In Agter-die-Berg we traded cattle and leather for a huge load of oranges, also dried fruit, tobacco, flour and brandy – all intended for the Kimberley market. But we did not travel directly to Kimberley. Mr. van Heerden first went on a long hunting trip through Marico, where we loaded a second "bare" wagon with biltong and hides. The load of oranges went everywhere with us. Every day it was the task of us children to sort through part of the load for oranges with rotten patches. These reject oranges were our reward for the work done.
>
> The hunting trip took months – how many I no longer recall; and yet the greater part of the load arrived in Kimberley sound, and Mr. van Heerden made a small fortune out of it. We sold the choicest out-of-hand at a shilling apiece.
>
> I remember how we children were filled with wonder by the speechless astonishment our oranges caused the Free State children, who had never seen an orange. We exchanged fowls and ducks – "one for one" – for oranges with rotten spots, which we were now collecting for this purpose instead of eating the fruit ourselves. I know the ownership of coops full of chickens and ducklings gave me a feeling of inexhaustible wealth.

On the same journey, it seems, Eugène was also to come into contact with an infinitely more ruthless kind of profiteering. In another article he was to write:

> As a child the author came into contact with the unrestricted liquor trade of the time among the Griquas, a people of mixed yellow blood. The arrival of a liquor wagon in a Griqua town always produced indescribable scenes. It was quite usual for several people to die. When their money ran out, the men offered tools, wagons, oxen, guns for liquor. It was by no means uncommon for parents to

> trade their chldren for drink, and many a Griqua "orphan" was "apprenticed" by the liquor dealer under such circumstances. Needless to say, the dealers practised all kinds of deceit against the unfortunate ones, the least abominable being the manufacture of counterfeit brandy by adding water to an extract of chewing tobacco.

These words cast little light on the young boy's own reactions to the harrowing scenes he witnessed. Elsewhere in the article, referring to the Hottentots' craving for tobacco, there are more significant words:

> From Tierra del Fuego to the icy plains of Greenland; from the Cape to Vladivostok, the traveller among primitive peoples hears only one beseeching word which echoes forever after in his nightmares: "Tobacco! Tobacco!"

In the light of his later life, the young boy was blissfully unaware of the symbolic significance of what he was witnessing in Griqualand.

In Boshof Eugène moved into Charles's unpretentious little house on Market Square. Charles, the oldest of the Marais sons, was 31. His wife, Emily, had borne him two daughters, four year old Amy and the baby, Kate. Not far from them lived Lizzie, Eugène's eldest sister – who had been staying in Pretoria just before the outbreak of the First Boer War the year before – and her husband, Emil Niemeyer. Emil was a wool-buyer and Charles Marais was his junior partner.

The Niemeyers had a larger house than Charles, and they needed it. There were eight children, of whom several were about the same age as Eugène: Elizabeth, Gustav, John and young Emil.

At the time it was said that the Free State educational system numbered among the best in the world. In any case Mr. David Field's school was much larger than any Eugène had attended in Pretoria, with four teachers and more than a hundred pupils. As in Pretoria, even though this was a Boer republic, the language of instruction was English, Dutch being taught only as a foreign language.

During his school years at Boshof Eugène came into contact with a remarkable old recluse, James Bain, who was spending the last years of his life in a vast house in the middle of a walled garden. Here the young boy saw a painting by Thomas Baines which Mr. Bain had commissioned more than twenty years before on his farm, Bainsvlei, near Bloemfontein: "The greatest hunt in history".

The painting showed a plain between koppies, and on the plain thousands and thousands of fleeing animals. In the foreground Basutos, some of them mounted, were shooting at wildebeest or stabbing springbuck to death.

The painting was done when Prince Alfred was on a visit to the country. Old Mr. Bain had arranged the hunt. The day before Basutos had organized a huge drive covering a vast area of the veld and on the day of the Prince's visit between twenty and thirty thousand head of big game were driven past his house. It was the greatest hunt in history, and it was never to be surpassed. Even now, in 1881, game was scarce around Bloemfontein.

In the apparently rather dull town of Boshof other matters aroused Eugène's lively interest.

"In rainy years," he was to write later, "when the pans (shallow lakes) filled up, the district was transformed. It became the sanctuary of millions of water-birds, including numerous visitors from Central Africa and as far north as the Nile – as naturalists established at the time. In one particularly rainy year the biggest of the pans – Karee Pan – joined hands with Prince Pan, and from there there was one broad waterway, stretching from pan to pan as far as the Vaal River."

Eugène's studies progressed fairly well. As always his essays were among the best in the class. He detested arithmetic. Fortunately, Seppie de Villiers, one of his schoolfriends, lived just across the way from Charles's house and Eugène could go to his window early in the morning to copy the day's sums.

Seppie worked hard. Either he or Anna van Ryneveld always came first in class and in the evenings he was always at his books. But in the afternoons and during the weekends he was pleasant company, and he and Eugène often went for walks together.

Independent Boer Republic or not, in the Free State, too, the intellectual world was largely English. In old Mr. Bain's house Eugène saw an original manuscript by the poet Shelley. Byron's poetry inspired him to try his own hand at poetry. "The Soldier's Grave", later to be published in the *Paarl District Advertiser*, was written on his twelfth birthday. Probably all the other famous 19th century names should be added to his reading matter: Coleridge, Keats, Wordsworth, Browning, Poe, Scott, Dickens – quite possibly also De Quincey, for at this time, sixty years after its first publication in book form, *The Confessions of an English Opium Eater* was regarded as a classic.

Although the twelve year old boy probably knew this only in regard to De Quincey, Coleridge and possibly Poe, virtually all these famous 19th century creative artists used opium, as an anodyne, as a stimulant or as a tranquilliser.

Due to the depression in the wool market, Lizzie and her husband, Emil Niemeyer, were finding it increasingly difficult to support their large family. Niemeyer and Charles Marais decided to get out of the wool trade and start a general agency, Niemeyer and Marais. To economize, some of the Niemeyer boys were brought back home from Grey College in Bloemfontein. At the end of 1884 Lizzie and her younger children went to live in Paarl, where the school was said to be excellent and the cost of living low. Her brother, Eugène, now almost fourteen, went with them.

It was a long journey, first by ox-wagon to Kimberley and then another hundred miles south to Potfontein, the extreme point reached by the railway line from Cape Town. However, such were the fabulous riches of the Kimberley diamond mines that the Cape Government was hoping to complete the line to the diamond city by the following year. On their way south the travellers frequently saw signs of the construction of the railway.

None of them had ever seen a train and when the locomotive's tall chimney stack and shiny copper boiler steamed into the little siding Eugène must have felt his throat tighten at the sight of so much beauty and power.

Incredibly rapidly – within two days – they had reached Paarl.

4. The Boland

Although Paarl was much larger than Pretoria, it reminded Eugène of the village of his birth. There was the same feeling of space, with large gardens and many trees. But there was one important difference: here everything was old. The thatch-roofed house into which they moved on Cedarberg Square had been built long before the founding of Pretoria.

Cedarberg Square was the social centre of Southern Paarl. Within a conveniently close distance lay the Paarl Public School, which Eugène and his cousins were to attend. Walking along the dirt road past Gribble's photographic studio, one would eventually reach the other side of town, which was dominated by the manse and church of Northern Paarl and the imposing buildings of the Paarl Gymnasium, founded some years before by the Rev. Van der Lingen.

One of Eugène's very first impressions was the difference between the Afrikaans spoken here and the language he had learnt in the Free State and Transvaal. People from the very best families would say: "Lat wiet vir djou ma ek sal kom," which was how the Coloureds spoke in the Transvaal. If Eugène disliked the accent, he disliked that totally unnecessary "vir" even more.

If Paarl was not exactly the melting pot in which the new language, Afrikaans, was being forged from Dutch, it was at least true that a number of revolutionary spirits in and around the town were acutely conscious of the transition. Dutch, a stilted language which most people spoke imperfectly, was being replaced by a much simplified version perfectly adapted to the needs of a still largely rural community. This was the town where the Genootskap van Regte Afrikaners (Society of True Afrikaners) had been founded some ten years before, thereby inaugurating the First Afrikaans Language Movement. The venerable founders of the movement, some of them most learned men, were hailed by a large part of the populace, but regarded as cranks by many scholars. Who wanted "kitchen Dutch", the bastardized language spoken by the Coloureds, as the language of a civilized people?

As always in South Africa, there were many cross-currents, causing a very involved situation. Many of those Afrikaners who despised Afrikaans and wanted to perpetuate Dutch as the other language of South Africa, next to English, spoke Dutch very badly indeed and readily lapsed into their despised home language, Afrikaans. Others, although Afrikaans-speaking, despised both Dutch and Afrikaans, preferring English, even if they spoke it atrociously. As a Paarl schoolboy Eugène Marais could not have failed to notice how many people were speaking a mixture of Afrikaans and English; how many pretended no longer to know Dutch or Afrikaans, speaking English only; and how many had so much contempt for their own language that they refused to speak it even in their own homes, or who attended only the evening church services because those were conducted in English.

The new school differed in many respects from the one in Boshof. The teachers were more dignified, perhaps a little pompous, but they treated the boys virtually like adults. When addressing the class they would not say "boys" as was the custom in Boshof, but "gentlemen", although they never hesitated to give their pupils six of the best when necessary. The staff even included two doctors – Drs. Zahn and Haarhoff.

Eugène's essays were better than ever. Mr. Inglis, the classics teacher, was also well satisfied. Over the weekends Eugène would polish his Latin by translating long extracts from the Vulgate into English. He was particularly fond of the Psalms in the Latin Bible.

Not long after his arrival in Paarl he visited Cape Town for the first time. It was smaller and not as busy as Kimberley; even so he gawked at the horse-drawn trams and elegant carriages, at the tall Victorian buildings and the ubiquitous Malay and Coloured hawkers.

If Paarl had created an impression of great age, this impression was even stronger here. The most modern buildings – like those in Sea Point, where elegant villas lay on Marine Drive in their spacious gardens – were Victorian, but most of the older houses were still in the Dutch style. Eighty years of English rule had by no means wiped out all traces of the Dutch period. In the Gardens and Tamboerskloof (Ravine of the Drums), a suburb against the lower slopes of Table Mountain, lay the estates of the oldest Cape families – the De Waals, the De Smidts, the Hofmeyrs, the Jurgenses, the Van Bredas. And here, although Eugène could not have known it, lived Jimmy Roos, his future newspaper partner, on his father's farmstead, Bellevue.

The sense of tradition and established values which Eugène had found in the Cape became even more striking and more personal when he visited the Marais family at Stellenbosch for the first time. Here the traditions were those of his own ancestors, the Marais', the Nielens and the Onkruyts.

Oom Charles Marais – the second eldest son of Charles Marais and Petronella Nielen, Eugène's own father being the eldest – lived on the farm Mostertsdrif, on the banks of the Eerste river. On the left bank of the river lay Coetzenberg, where some of Oom Charles's cousins farmed. Oom Charles, a handsome, tall man, was in his fifties, but youthful for his age.

Oom Charles had his own distillery and in the cellar huge vats were stacked in rows against the stone walls. In the wine-making season Coloured labourers would bring in mule-wagons full of grapes from the vineyards. Baskets of grapes would then be deposited in the huge wine-press, where eight or ten barefoot Coloured boys had the task of constantly treading the fruit. A stream of juice flowed from the press into a second vessel. The wine-treading would continue hour after hour, and hour after hour one would hear the boys chanting monotonously as they walked round and round in the press:

> Maak toe die hek,
> die os is in die brand,
> keer daar voor die ertjieland!
> Tiedel-diedel-die, tiedel-diedel-da,
> tiedel-diedel-die, tiedel-diedel-da,
> keer daar voor die ertjieland!

Oom Charles's wife, Tant Miemie, had given birth to twenty-one children. Of those fourteen had died at a very early age and three later. Of the entire family only four survived: Nielen, Katy, Nellie and Andries.

Nielen was about Eugène's age, and it may have been with him that Eugène formed the greatest friendship in the few years he spent in the Western Cape. On visits to Stellenbosch he usually went to stay with Oom Charles, but sometimes he stayed with Oom Mynhardus of Klein Gustro, a farm at the entrance to the Jonkershoek valley, which stretched from the slopes of the Sonklipberg to the Eerste river.

Now Eugène knew all his father's brothers: Oom Lang Piet of Pretoria, Oom Charles of Mostertsdrif and Oom Mynhardus of Klein Gustro.

Oom Mynhardus was younger than Oom Charles, but his hair had turned white at an early age and his beard, too, was almost completely white. Soft-spoken and elegant of manner, he was goodness itself, and even more than Oom Charles he reminded Eugène of his own father. When the boy visited Klein Gustro, he slept in the middle of a huge room on a Dutch featherbed eighteen inches thick which almost suffocated him.

Sometimes he and his cousins would explore the beautiful Jonkershoek valley, where birds were so abundant one could catch a cageful of them in a single morning. Using bird-lime, they brought home Cape canaries and a variety of starlings, only to release them again once they started making a nuisance of themselves in the chicken run – all except the starlings. To Eugène's consternation Oom Charles always had the necks of these birds wrung.

Eugène's second name was Nielen, and he had always been interested in the Nielen ancestry. He had been told that grandmother Nielen had been a granddaughter of Baron Van Rheede van Oudtshoorn tot Nederhorst, who had been sent to the Cape as Governor but had died on the voyage. Eugène had seen Van Oudtshoorn's official seal – a great silver tube which had his private coat of arms on one side and the crest of the Dutch East India Company on the other – in the house of his brother Charles in Boshof. (Where this had come from, as the story about the Marais' relationship to the baron is said to have been false, one can only guess.)

If Eugène had never heard the story of how the Nielens had married into the Marais family, he was to hear it in Stellenbosch. It was a romantic story.

Earlier in the century the Marais' of Nectar and Coetzenberg and the Onkruyts of Jonkershoek had their own Sunday houses in the village. Every Sunday they spent some time there before the service and again once the service was over to get together with acquaintances and friends from Stellenbosch. One Sunday when they were about to drive back to their farms, they found that Charles (Eugène's grandfather) was missing. He was a man of about thirty, and a widower. When they went to look for him, they found his horse in front of the house of Dr. Johan Christian Nielen, whose wife was a daughter of Baron Van Oudtshoorn. And in the house they found Charles himself. He had gone to call on Petronella, old Dr. Nielen's exceptionally attractive eighteen year old daughter.

Unfortunately old Dr. Nielen was a strict Catholic. As always the family stood together; threatened with disinheritance, Charles was persuaded to stay away from Petronella. According to the story this almost broke him. He became completely withdrawn and depressed and would talk to no one. But some months later, riding on his horse through Stellenbosch, deep in thought, he felt somebody grasp the reins. Looking down, he saw Petronella standing in front of him in the street. Softly but firmly she asked him: "Why are you staying away?"

Charles got off his horse and told her the whole story.

"If that is all," she replied, "it's no problem. I am quite prepared to become a Protestant."

This may well have been the story Eugène heard at Mostertsdrif, since it was obviously believed by Wilfred Marais, Eugène's cousin and contemporary who told it to the present author. Unfortunately, later research again showed that the Marais' had romanticized their own past.

According to the genealogist Dr. J.A. Heese, it seems highly unlikely that Dr. Nielen could have been a Roman Catholic, as he had married a daughter of the Dutch Reformed Minister (Rev. Harders). All the children, including Petronella, were baptized in the Dutch Reformed Church at Stellenbosch. As a baptized Protestant there would have been no need for her to become a Protestant in order to marry Charles. What the story may well indicate as a characteristic of some members of the family is love of an obsessional kind. Charles had embraced his pain over a lost love like a bride until a friendly fate had come to his rescue. Much later, in comparable circumstances, Eugène Marais, too, was to cosset his suffering.

Wilfred Marais tells another story about Charles Marais and Petronella Nielen. At the end of the 19th century, he says, their mortal remains lay in a family vault near Stellenbosch, the only two coffins in the vault.

Did Eugène Marais hear the story, visit the vault and see the two coffins by candlelight? And did he see the truth then, as suggested by the cynical poem "Skoppensboer" (Jack of Spades) he was to write later? That sunny afternoon in the Stellenbosch street, he on horseback and she standing before him, and again at their wedding and during their first night together and later watching their children at play in the sunshine at Nectar – always something lay in wait, relentless, stronger than life.

Soon after his arrival in Paarl Eugène again started writing poetry. His "Ode to the Paarl" was submitted to the *Paarl District Advertiser* and accepted for publication. Perhaps encouraged by this success, he also submitted "The Soldier's Grave", which he had written in Boshof, to the paper. It was published three weeks later. Thereafter the newspaper published two strongly patriotic poems: "Majuba" and "South Africa".

"But they stayed not, up they rushed," the young boy describes the Boers storming up the mountain in "Majuba", "... till the guarded top they reached, far on high; /There to free their loved land / From the Northern Tyrant's hand – /From ignoble slavery's band, /Or to die!"

Equally unequivocal are the sentiments in the last lines of "South Africa".

> And yet, sweet land, with all thy store
> Of peaceful treasures, yet thy sons are slaves!
> Descendants of those men, who from the waves
> Have snatched their home; brave men
> To whom vile bondage had been death ...
> Oh shame
> That they, who now bow to foreign thrones, should claim
> Descent so noble, and should bring such shame
> Upon our fathers' glorious, unstained name.

The quotations from these literarily insignificant, youthful poems show how strongly Eugène Marais's patriotism had developed in the five years since the First Boer War. The severe degree of anglicization he had found in the Western Cape may have contributed to this process. One of his teachers, a Miss White, was an American. It may not be far-fetched to surmise that she, thinking back to her own people's War of Independence against Britain in the previous century, encouraged him in this direction as well.

During the course of eighteen months nine of Eugène's poems were published in the *Paarl District Advertiser*. One need look at only a portion of one more, a poem he called "There shall be no more sea", of which each verse ends with the words of the title.

> (He) Who stilled the waters of stormy Galilee
> Is thy sole master; 'tis he that guides the fisher's bark,
> While night, with livid lightning lit, hangs dark
> Upon thy troubled waters, and to him we'll flee
> For refuge when there shall be no more sea.

Certainly not a great poem, but a majestic and, for a fifteen year old boy, remarkable theme which was to recur in his writings in a variety of aspects throughout the rest of his life: the drying up of rivers, of subterranean resources and eventually the disappearance of the sea itself.

Apart from his successes at school and the publication of his first poems, Eugène was also a member of the Union Debating Society, and friends were to remember his considerable wit. Swimming was still one of his great pleasures. His great triumph came when, following a challenge, he successfully swam the length of a small mountain lake four times.

In general, the period he spent in Paarl was one of strict moral self-control. An anecdote from that time is characteristic. One Saturday afternoon, after the heavy winter rains, he and Dawie Mostert, a good friend who lived on the other side of Cedarberg Square, walked to the banks of the Berg river. As the boys sat watching the surging water, Eugène produced a pipe he had recently acquired.

"It's bad for your health," Dawie told him. "It damages your brain." Eugène hesitated only for a moment. Without replying, he flung the pipe into the swirling water.

When Eugène was ready to write his final exams, so the story goes, he was still too young. The principal, Mr. Le Roux, had to obtain special permission from the Department of Education and the boy was hardly sixteen when he matriculated in the second class.

In the winter of 1887 Eugène returned to Boshof. Had he by this time begun to think of Charles's house as his parental home? One of the poems written in Paarl had in fact been published under the pseudonym "Eugène, O.F.S".

At about this time the Marais' existence in Boshof was completely disrupted by the death of Emil Niemeyer, Eugène's brother-in-law and his brother Charles's partner. Emil, a kind-hearted, meek-mannered man of forty-eight, had long had financial problems. Now, after further setbacks, he found himself facing bankruptcy. Taking a gun, he walked to a koppie outside the village and shot himself. It was three months before the birth of his youngest child.

A dark thread of instability, addiction and suicide runs through the lives of this branch of the Marais family and those of the men they married.

Lizzie's fourteenth child, whom she was expecting in September, was never to have a father. With his sister and her youngest children, Eugène travelled back to Pretoria by ox-wagon.

PART 2: FOR COUNTRY AND PEOPLE

en nou dat jy groei om die baasskap te hê, is ek die rooi naelstring waaraan jy lê.	and now that you are growing into mastery I am the red umbilical cord to which you are bound.

1. Going Home

Late in 1887 Eugène Marais arrived back in Pretoria to start his career. He was sixteen years old.

In the eight years of his absence his parents had aged considerably and his father – now 65 – had become even more eccentric. The first thing Eugène noticed when he came home were the cherry-red pillars of the verandah. Some years before, getting up at the break of day, the old man had painted them this colour – to his wife's almost hysterical consternation. Nobody had ever got around to repainting them.

Eugène's sister, Lizzie Niemeyer, and the children who had returned with her from Boshof, lived with her parents for the time being. She intended setting up a boarding-house as soon as possible to provide for her family.

Pretoria itself had changed even more than Eugène's parents. The centre of the small town was almost unrecognizable. The thatch-roofed church he remembered so well was gone, destroyed by fire. It had been replaced by a fashionable new church with a tall tower and transept. The square itself was no longer called Market Square but Church Square and the market was now held elsewhere, although auctions still took place under the oak tree in the south western corner.

The square was considerably smaller than before, as quite a number of new streets and alleys had been cut from it. Broderick's shop was no longer there, neither was Lys's, and in their places stood the big three-storied Alexandra Building and the Lys Building. Of the buildings he had known so well, virtually only the Raadzaal with its thatched roof was left, and even now there were plans to erect a new Government building in its place.

Eugène became an articled clerk with Kuranda & Marais, the firm of attorneys which belonged to his brother Melt and his partner. Kuranda was a fine man, very much in love with Eugène's sister Georgie, but because he was a Jew, the Marais' could not consent to the marriage.

Eugène was enjoying life. It was pleasant to have money, even only a few pounds a month, to buy one's own clothes and to smoke cigarettes (so much more progressive than a pipe) and – when he had some money left over – to buy a few of the books he had always wanted.

However, legal work bored him and when his work brought him into contact with the exciting things which were happening in the Republic since the discovery of gold, this only stimulated him to experience it all at closer quarters. In any case, he wanted to write. Not law, but journalism attracted him as a career – however disparagingly his more successful family, especially Oom Lang Piet's people, might talk about it.

In this he was supported by his oldest brother, called Henry by some of the family and Hennie by others, who wrote for the *Transvaal Advertiser* as "Amphy Bias".

With the help of an old family friend, Jan Celliers, editor of *De Volksstem*, Eugène obtained a job on the staff of the *Transvaal Advertiser*. It is possible that he wanted a job with *De Volksstem* and that Jan Celliers had no vacancies, but it seems equally likely that Eugène himself preferred the *Advertiser* to Celliers' paper.

For ten years or more English had been his language of instruction, and the last few years had been spent in a British colony. Of course he spoke Afrikaans fluently. Naturally he could write Dutch. But to an even greater degree than the semi-anglicised family he had left behind in Pretoria he had, in the Cape Colony, learnt to think in English. He was always to write more easily in English than in any other language; to count in English; to switch to English as soon as he wished to emphasize a point or wanted to convince someone.

Eugène Marais, one of the pioneers of the Afrikaans language, eventually learnt to write that language very well, but never without conscious effort.

The editor under whom Marais started working as a cub reporter at the *Advertiser* in 1888 was Dr. John Scoble.

From him and from his brother Henry Eugène learnt the principles of journalism as they were practised in the South African Republic at the time. This journalistic tradition seems to have been American rather than British or Dutch, as one might have expected.

It was journalism as depicted in the work of Mark Twain – whose best known books had been published by then – and it included violent personal attacks in the editorial columns, the horse-whipping of editors by infuriated readers, and an occasional duel between editors.

The column Henry wrote as "Amphy Bias" – articles about events of the day, competent and often to the point, but sometimes quite exaggerated, criticizing for the sake of criticism – indicates the principles the seventeen year old boy was now absorbing, as the Afrikaans saying goes, with his mother's milk.

Basically, the principles were simple: a newspaper had to criticize. If there were no real grievances, one had to dig up less important matters and pad them out a little. For a newspaper there was only one criterion, and that was whether the people were reading it. To be read, it had to be spiced, like food. Its salt and pepper? Gossip and criticism, and strong language, as strong as one could make the mixture without appearing in court.

Later Eugène would further refine this principle. The danger was not appearing in court, but losing a court case. There was a great difference. A successful libel case, especially if it concerned exposures, was one of the best investments a newspaper could make.

The *Advertiser* was published only twice a week. Eugène had plenty of free time but at times articles had to be written at tremendous speed to meet the press's deadlines. In America some newspaper offices were already using typewriters, but such refinements were a rarity in the Transvaal. Everything was written by hand, and it was probably at this time that Eugène learnt to write rapidly, flowingly and still legibly, an ability he was to retain all his life.

The relationship between him and Henry became closer. Apart from their love of journalism, they also shared an almost passionate interest in minerals, in the gambler's game of prospecting.

The goldfields of the Rand and the mining town which was developing with them at breathtaking speed, were part of the Pretoria journalist's beat. One can imagine Eugène's first visit to Johannesburg as a reporter shortly after he had started working for the *Advertiser*.

Communication between the two towns was regular and comfortable. Geo. Heys & Company's express coaches left for Johannesburg three times a day: at 7.15, at noon and at 2 p.m. If one caught the earliest carriage, one could be there in time for lunch. In such a carriage we can picture the seventeen year old Eugène Marais, sitting proudly in the expensive vehicle (£1 return), the cravat at his throat, his watch-chain draped casually over his waistcoat, the tip of his notebook just visible above his jacket pocket.

When the coach was full – eight passengers inside and another six on top – it was a fairly tight fit. But the ten horses trotted smartly along the gravel road and before one knew where one was, the coach had stopped at the Halfway House Bar. Occasionally a newcomer would start up in fright when the driver shouted *hokaai* (stop!), as several coaches had been robbed by highwaymen on this road. Here they all got down to stretch their legs, and some of them had a couple of quick ones in the bar before the express coach continued its journey.

Even those who visited Johannesburg regularly saw it growing like a toadstool. It was barely two years since the discovery of the ridge on old Oosthuizen's farm, Langlaagte. A year later five hundred ore-stamps were at work on the Witwatersrand, and another five hundred were on their way in ox-wagons.

Eugène's uncle, Lang Piet, had had a share in just about every gold discovery in the Transvaal. This was the one time he did not get in first. In fact he had missed his chance some years before. He and a number of Pretorians had been hunting near the main reef of the Witwatersrand. One of the Taylor brothers had struck an ore-bearing rock from a cliff, intending to test it at home, but his older brother impatiently knocked it from his hand. "You seem to think there's gold in everything," he remarked. "You'll start looking for it in bricks soon."

In the end it was Oom Lang Piet's friend Harry Struben who made the first fortune from Rand gold. He and his brother Fred pegged out a total of 760 morgen. But Oom Piet was hot on their heels, and soon a large part of the farm Paardekraal, next to Langlaagte, belonged to him.

Within weeks one farm after another had been cut up: Braamfontein, Doornfontein, Turffontein. Among these three the first village of tents sprang up, Ferreira's Camp; among them Landdrost Von Brandis read the proclamation of the diggings standing on an empty whisky-case in front of his tent one morning; and among them the first corrugated iron buildings were erected, the first streets surveyed, the first brick houses built. This was Johannesburg, not yet two years old and already bigger than Pretoria.

The express coach terminus was Market Square, a huge bare piece of veld, six street-blocks long, on which a number of wagons were outspanned. Of the dozens of empty lots available on the square eighteen months before, more than half had already been filled – mostly by corrugated iron buildings – and everywhere labourers were busy erecting new structures.

At the office of the Landdrost on the north-eastern corner of the square, visiting journalists would spend some minutes talking to the hopelessly overworked but ever courteous Landdrost Von Brandis to pick up any possible news items.

Across the square one could see the ugly red brick building of the *Transvaal Mining Argus*, the newspaper founded the previous year by Charles Deecker.

Eugène remembered Deecker from his childhood days, before the war of 1880 against the English, when both he and Jan Celliers had had to close their newspapers: Jan Celliers because the English had gaoled him on a charge of sedition and Deecker because they needed his assistance and his printing press to publish the military newspaper in the refugee camp. But after the war it was Celliers who was allowed to reopen *De Volksstem* without any delay – using a new printing press the Government had given him – and Deecker who struggled to get going once more. Later he and Henry were colleagues on the *Advertiser*.

The furthest diggings lay to the west. On the way there, walking along one of the rutted gravel streets, one would pass a spanking new building, extremely solid and elegant for Johannesburg, with a Greek gable and a Greek pediment across its portals: this was the Freemasons' Temple, rising above the corrugated iron hovels on either side. Many of the best known Pretoria families – including quite a number of the Marais' – were Masons.

Few claims still belonged to the original diggers; most of them had already changed hands half a dozen times, and each time the price had jumped. The streets were crowded. By the weekend they would be even more jammed: ox-wagons, Cape carts, landaus, spiders, buggies, men on horseback, men on foot, all of them in high spirits, boisterous and noisy, already anticipating the pleasures of the weekend which lay ahead, money jingling in their pockets, young and wealthy, with the certain expectation of even more treasures from the brown patch of earth to which they could return on Monday.

But there were others, and not a few, who scorned the pleasures of the weekend, jealous of every hour not spent in the greater pleasure of the treasure hunt, the ultimate fulfilment of childhood dreams in which shining coins would appear magically between fingers groping in the sand.

These were the people who bribed the mining boys to keep on working while the other boys went to the beer drink, who tried to keep the liquor peddlers away from their claims, who spent every moment at the diggings and followed every movement as the crushed ore was swept across the amalgam table, whose eyes shone as they scraped the gold-bearing mercury from the plates to be refined.

Beyond the last buildings lay the wonderland: deep ditches in the brown earth, unsightly piles of soil, hundreds of pulleys for hoisting up the ore, stamps thundering and hissing like weird locomotives – all part of the incredibly vast chain of diggings stretching for seventeen miles across the Highveld.

The mining techniques Eugène Marais saw here must have reminded him very much of those at Kimberley, except that these were much more dangerous. Now and again a white man and a gang of natives would emerge post-haste from one of the ditches; a match would spark, a fuse would sputter, there were cries of "Look out!" – and moments later masses of shattered rock would shoot into the air and fall back to earth like giant hailstones. Loads of ore would be dug out by the labourers, hauled to the surface in buckets and brought to the nearest mill by ox-wagon. As in Kimberley's early days, diggings often collapsed, occasionally with loss of life, and in the rainy season the water in the ditches would rise to a level of several feet, making work impossible. These were the methods which visiting experts had criticized so severely a short while before. The new technique, already being practised by the larger companies, was to sink vertical shafts and then to dig horizontal tunnels out from them. But towers and shafts cost money. The deeper one went, the more they cost. The pattern which had emerged in Kimberley was already forming here: the smaller digger would be pushed out and the big capitalist would grow ever more prosperous.

Eugène frequently visited Johannesburg in these years. Everything fascinated him, and he learnt a great deal. Partly through family connections, partly through his job as a journalist, he met a great many people. One imagines him listening to the stories told by an old prospector who had looked for tin and lead in the wild north. One finds him at a diggers' dinner, surrounded by gleaming cutlery and glassware, but soon annoyed and upset by the drunkenness and fisticuffs, which would eventually force the more civilized guests to retire. One sees him listening to a number of Uitlanders airing their grievances against Kruger, not the least of these being Kruger's concession policy. Back in Pretoria one sees him talking to supporters of Commandant-General Piet Joubert's opposition party.

For more than five years now, it had been Kruger against Joubert. For more than five years Kruger had been firmly in the saddle and, after the latest presidential election, in which he had beaten Joubert by five to one, now more firmly than ever. Even Pretorians of the old school like Eugène's friend and mentor, Jan Celliers, editor of *De Volksstem*, had supported Kruger in the election.

For other old Pretorians, including the Marais', the old *takhaar*, as they called him, the backvelder, still remained a thorn in the flesh. One had to admit, of course, that he had built up a powerful state – but how could he help doing so, given the revenue from the gold mines?

Their natural distrust and dislike were fed by a variety of real and imagined wrongs.

Their main objection was to Kruger's concession policy, which stipulated that the monopoly of producing a product or of trading in it would be given to individuals at a price. And the second, no less objectionable than the first, was Kruger's policy of appointing mainly Dutchmen in the civil service and only Dutchmen in the important governmental posts. Dutchman 1 to Dutchman 2 (according to a story doing the rounds in Pretoria at the time): "Do you want to tell me you've been in the country for six hours and you have not been given a position in the civil service yet?"

Governmental posts for Dutchmen, concessions for Jews and their proselytes: David Benjamin, Alois Nellmapius, Sammy Marks and, last but not least, E. Lippert, who monopolized the country's total dynamite production and of whom the wits were fond of saying: "Lippert E., Lippert E., what crimes have been committed in thy name?"

A dislike and suspicion of Jews were almost universal at the time. This was not quite the case in the Transvaal. Paul Kruger, although deploring the fact that they were not Christians, thought of the Jews as the chosen race, certainly as a very special breed of men. And the Hollanders he appointed to run his republic came from a country where for centuries Jews had enjoyed not only complete religious freedom but an exceptional degree of freedom from prejudice.

The Marais', like many other immigrants from the British Colony of the Cape of Good Hope, if not always rabid anti-Semites, certainly resented the favouritism Kruger seemed to show these men with their particular business acumen. And that was not all. His policies affected their pockets as well as their honour. They were old Pretorians. They had already been here a long time when the discovery of gold had shot the Transvaal economy into the air like a rocket. Part of these riches were their due. Instead of that they were prohibited by law from entering certain fields of investment. They did not ask for concessions; all they wanted was a just division of the millions the concession-holders earned from liquor, dynamite and other products.

As far as governmental posts were concerned: the Marais' and their friends knew very well why Kruger preferred giving important government posts to Dutchmen. "Landszoonen" (sons of the country), as he called born Transvalers, were usually not well educated enough. And to him Afrikaners from the Cape – this was the sting – even if they had lived in the Republic for twenty years, were politically unreliable.

With increasing indignation, the old Pretorians watched Hollanders receiving 65% of the votes in the newly founded railway company, while they controlled only 30% of the shares; how a Dutchman, S. Wierda, was appointed head of the Department of Public Works; how a Dutchman, Dr. W.J. Leyds, became State Secretary before his thirtieth year; and how the Government bought *De Volksstem* from Jan Celliers and made a Dutchman, Dr. Frans Engelenburg, its editor.

Given this atmosphere, a confrontation between the Government and the gifted, impetuous young reporter was just around the corner.

2. The First Clash

Winter 1889. On Church Square, dusty and criss-crossed by wagon wheels, the Volksraad was again assembling for a meeting in the dilapidated old thatch-roofed Raadzaal.

It may be that Eugène, covering the session for the *Advertiser*, spoke a few words to Oom Jan Celliers, for the older man had important things to say today.

They were good friends. Eugène respected Celliers as an honest man. Before the presidential elections, then still editor of *De Volksstem*, he had advised both Kruger and Joubert to stand down for a man of better education. However, when the choice was between Kruger or Joubert, he supported Kruger because he regarded the old warrior as the better statesman. In the Volksraad Eugène frequently found that he and Celliers shared the same views against the conservative members, the so-called Kruger yes-men.

Nevertheless there was no real opposition. Even men like Celliers, strongly opposed to the concession policy and the President's nepotism, usually supported the Government's stand. In spite of this, there was still ill feeling if dissidents occasionally ventured to criticize the Government.

One by one the members came in, dignified in their black frock coats and top hats: Frik Eloff, the President's son-in-law and private secretary, a man with his finger in many pies; Schalk Burger of Lydenburg, who had more than once sided with Jan Celliers when there were differences of opinion in the Raad; Bezuidenhout of Potchefstroom; De Beer of Waterberg: Wolmarans of Rustenburg; the Rev. Bosman, who was to open the proceedings with a prayer; the President himself.

Later, after the opening, Eugène pricked up his ears when Jan Celliers got up to discuss the Francis concession. The young reporter knew about this. It was yet another case in which the Government had sold itself short by granting a particular concession and where, moreover, there were rumours of bribery or gifts given to certain members of the Council.

Jan Celliers said nothing about bribery, but used some convincing examples to point out how ridiculous the concession was.

The Chairman, Mr. B.H. Klopper, rapped the table in front of him with his hammer. "I am sorry, Mr. Celliers, but I cannot allow you to continue making such charges."

"Mr. Chairman, may I know why not?"

"Order! You are deliberately misrepresenting the facts. You are telling untruths, Sir, and I have an idea that you are doing so only to make the Volksraad ridiculous in the eyes of the public."

"Mr. Chairman, could you please tell me which facts I have misrepresented?"

"Please, Mr. Celliers, we shall say no more about the matter."

"But I have not finished putting my side of the question yet."

"I am sorry, I can allow no further debate."

Eugène Marais himself now takes up the tale. In his political column in the *Transvaal Advertiser*, Glimpses from the Hoekie, he wrote the next day:

"Again I have to publish a little tale that was not intended for my ears. But I glory in revealing the duplicity of these men, although the world might deem the means dishonourable."

He describes what happened during the meeting and then continues:

"During the ten minute recess the Chairman and Mr. Stoop were standing near the reporters' table when the former said with great emphasis: 'From now I'll show Celliers. I'll sit on him (op zy tabernakel gé) as much as possible.' Mr. Stoop loudly applauded the noble resolution.

"The Chairman happening to turn around and seeing me writing said (with evident alarm) that he trusted reporters do not make notes of private conversations. I dangled with my golden chain and smiling put the question by.

"I was nevertheless greatly surprised. I had never thought that the Chairman, that religious man, with eyes turned up and mouth turned down, whose every word is oiled with the grace of God, whose every phrase is mingled with biblical allusions – I had never thought, I say, that this man could utter anything he would blush to see published."

The biting comment was partly journalistic cynicism. Marais was also, to some extent, showing off his control of the English language. After all, he was only eighteen. But the remarks also illuminate the contempt the perspicacious, free-thinking young man felt for many of the people who ruled his country. Not only were they pious, unctuously pious – they were also hypocrites.

The next afternoon, when there was no session of the Volksraad, a letter from the chairman, Mr. Klopper, was delivered to the *Advertiser*. For the sake of the truth and accuracy of the *Advertiser*'s reports, the letter said, the Chairman did not wish to see Marais in the Volksraad as a reporter again.

Scoble backed Eugène to the hilt. One did not find such bright young reporters "at the corner of every street" (Scoble's words from a leader published later). In a defiant five-point letter, Scoble completely rejected the Chairman's request.

Klopper's remarks were made while the Volksraad had adjourned, he wrote, and moreover in his capacity as a private person. It was a private matter, and Klopper could not make use of his position as Chairman of the Volksraad to remedy a private grievance. He could do so only through a court of law.

The next day there was an almost tangible hostility in the Raadzaal. In the press bench, Gluckstein, who represented the newly founded Government paper, the *Press*, must have soon made it clear to Eugène that both Klopper and the President himself were furious about the letter. They regarded it as an insult.

It would have been only natural for even a hard-boiled young reporter like Marais to feel ill at ease during the proceedings. That morning nothing happened. During the afternoon session, Marais occasionally glanced at the President. The broad-shouldered old man sat easily in his official chair, leaning slightly forward, the sharp eyes below the bushy eyebrows darting from one face to another. He was a hunter, a fighter, and in the Raadzaal he was as formidable an enemy as he had been in the hunting field or during battle. Whenever a daring member ventured to criticize him, Eugène was always reminded of a young dog trying to corner a lion, for behind that simple peasant's face lay a short temper and a sharp brain. He dominated the Volksraad. When he wanted to have his way, he would first brazenly pretend that acceptance of his proposals by the Raad went without saying. This ploy frequently worked. If it did not, he would start cajoling and coaxing, usually throwing in some of his famous animal proverbs. As a last resort he would lose his temper – some said he could switch on his anger – and when Kruger was wrathful it was a very courageous man indeed who dared stand up to him.

Finally, on that June afternoon, Eugène heard the Chairman say: "His Honour the President has something to say about a particular matter."

Paul Kruger got to his feet, at sixty-four amazingly agile for such a heavily built man. There was an important matter about which the Council had to come to a decision before resuming its ordinary activities, he said. The Chairman had been insulted by a newspaper reporter, as all the members knew. The Chairman had written a courteous letter to the editor of the newspaper requesting the removal of the reporter who had insulted him. Instead of an apology the Chairman had received an exceptionally ill-mannered reply. The Council could not proceed with its activities as a legislative body before this insult had been wiped out. They would be making fools of themselves if they did so. The person concerned should not be allowed in the Council, and the Council should adopt a motion to this effect if he should persist in returning. The reporter had been removed that morning, but here he was again.

Mildly but audibly Jan Celliers remarked: "Nobody was removed."

"Order! Order! It is Mr. Wolmarans' turn to speak."

The debate continued. Wolmarans demanded an immediate decision: they should ask the advice of the State Attorney. Jan Celliers tried to calm the feelings of the members, and the Chairman again put his case. The Volksraad was then adjourned so that Eugène's column and Dr. Scoble's letter could be translated into Dutch.

When the matter was reopened the next day, the Volksraad formally adopted a motion to prohibit the *Advertiser's* representative from sitting at the press table – a unique action in the Transvaal Republic.

It was a serious state of affairs, but Dr. Scoble reacted characteristically by writing a strongly worded leader on the matter and sending Eugène back to the Volksraad.

"... the Volksraad has passed a resolution excluding the *Advertiser* forever from the reporters' table. We may assure our readers that they will not lose much by this illegal stretch of authority."

Dr. Scoble was true to his word. Henceforth Eugène sat in the public benches, not at the press table. That was all, except that the name of his column was changed to "Glimpses from the benches".

Eugène soon found that the Volksraad's ban had made him very well known, and notorious in some quarters. But old Pretoria supported his actions almost to a man.

He was happy in his job, and he worked hard. Shortly after he joined the *Advertiser*, Dr. Scoble decided to publish three issues every week instead of two. Eugène had been in the paper's permanent employ for quite a while now. He went to the office every day and worked at home many evenings. He liked the office, but he liked his own room in his parents' house even more. It fitted him like an old glove. Sitting at his desk, with a view of the water furrow in which he had spent many hours fishing as a boy, a waste-paper basket on each side of his table to receive his crumpled attempts at writing, he could become so absorbed in his work that he would not even hear a knock at the door. The hours sped by.

On the shelf behind him one might expect to see, among numbers of others, books in which pantheism was glorified, perhaps the writings of Pope, with whom Eugène might have said during this period: "Slave to no sect, who takes no private road, / But looks through nature up to nature's God", or: "All are but parts of one stupendous whole, / Whose body Nature is and God the soul". (Not until much later would he also agree with Pope in saying:

"And, spite of pride, in erring reason's spite, / One truth is clear, / Whatever is, is right".)

His pen-holder, before him on the desk, was a human skull. In one corner of the room lived a family of spiders. Eugène liked studying their habits, and Nancy – his mother's almost white Cape Coloured servant, who had virtually become part of the family – had strict instructions not to disturb them.

Eugène's sister Lizzie Niemeyer and her children had not been living with her parents for some time. In an unpretentious house in Proes Street she eked out an existence by taking in boarders. But, like all the sisters, she frequently came to visit. His sisters and his mother did not like Eugène's pantheism, nor did they like that skull, nor the spiders, nor the snakes and scorpions he kept in the house and garden. He even kept a live python – and some of the sisters' children were still quite small.

Suddenly a sharp image of the nineteen year old young man swings into focus. He was in revolt. He was not an atheist, but he rejected the narrow dogma of his church, his sect. He delighted in provoking the highest authority in the country, the President. He took not the least notice of what his mother or his middle-aged sisters thought. And because most of his sisters had definite ideas and strong personalities, clashes were frequent. The estrangement between some of the Marais sisters and their youngest brother began even before his twentieth year.

In England – the intellectual source of Eugène Marais's ideas – it was a time of intellectual revolution, of new ideas, of an intense clash between the conservative old and the progressive new. Every new scientific theory which shook the Victorian world was enthusiastically investigated by Eugène Marais; every new literary work which the Establishment deplored, he read avidly and admiringly. George Moore's *Confessions of a Young Man* (1886) was read by every well-read progressive youth during the last few years of the nineteenth century; and George Moore's hero, too, had kept a python as a pet.

Lord Kitchener, Kitchener of Khartoum, was to shock Victorian England by simply mentioning the possibility that the skull of one of his slain enemies might make a fine pen-holder. In fact the remark harmed his reputation, "left a bad taste". Eugène Marais not only mentioned the possibility. His pen-holder *was* a skull.

The skull presented a challenge, to his mother, to his sisters, to his contemporaries in general. It said: "I ignore, and with impunity, the superstition that the bones of the dead have to be buried; I demand the right to study the characteristics of the human body; not only do I dare to examine that forbidden subject, evolution – this skull proves it."

"By about the nineties of the previous century," N.P. van Wyk Louw, the prominent Afrikaans poet and critic, was to write, "shall we say: when Kolbe, Eugène Marais, General Smuts and General Hertzog were very young, and Leipoldt, Totius and Celliers were boys, our people [the Afrikaners] – all, or a great many of them – 'started dreaming in a different key'; chiefly as a result of the advent of new scientific, mainly biological, concepts. And in all these figures the old peasant world was broken, the almost sixteenth-century world in which we had lived ..."

This was why Eugène Marais despised – hated and despised – the backvelders who governed *his* country so arrogantly: the members of the Volksraad who were in favour of abolishing experiments to produce rain because rain came from God; the members who condemned attempts to exterminate the huge swarms of locusts, which caused tens of thousands of pounds worth of damage in the Transvaal every year, because locusts were a visitation of the Lord; the member, De Beer, who had threatened to trek to Damaraland if more railways were built; the member, Taljaard, who had objected to the use of the word "participeen" (participate) in the Volksraad because he had never seen it in the Bible, which meant that it could not be Dutch; the President, who disapproved of dancing because it meant bowing the knee unto Baal (but unblushingly accepted a Government loan of £7 000 at less than half the current rate of interest).

His country, his beloved country. Of all his family Eugène was the only one who had been born here. He and the Transvaal had grown up together. Along with its history, so his love for the Transvaal had grown. The fact that those sentiments which in Eugène Marais had developed spontaneously, happened to correspond to the *avant garde* ideas of his intellectual world, was coincidental, but served to reinforce his own ideas: British radical opinion was anti-imperialist, pro-Boer.

At the centre of his love of fatherland lay a revolutionary image, that of Majuba. Dauntless, inspired young men storming up the mountain slopes, and hurling the mighty tyrant from his citadel. "Bliss was it in that dawn to be alive, and to be young was very heaven."

And now? The State which, since the discovery of gold, could have become one of the wealthiest, most progressive in the world, was being led (misled!) by petty old men, narrow-minded old men, dishonest old men, and especially by one old man who – precisely because he was so strong – concentrated and compounded in himself the vices of all the others.

During this time Eugène Marais gave many people the impression of being antisocial. He was a handsome young man, but the company of women did not interest him, and that of men only when they had something worthwhile to say. Small talk bored him to death. Journalism, his books, his animals, occupied all his time. His mother and friends did their best to persuade him to attend parties and picnics. Sometimes he did go along on outings but quite often – as in his childhood days – he simply disappeared into the bush, only reappearing when everyone had been waiting for hours to start eating.

His interest in plants and animals had grown since his early childhood days, and this went for his interest in mining as well. Much later a close friend was to say of Eugène Marais that he, better than anyone else, would be capable of writing the story of gold in South Africa. A great deal of the tremendous knowledge which he always retained on this subject was gained during these early years. From old prospectors, from the Johannesburgers, perhaps also from his uncle, Lang or Ryk Piet Marais, he heard, bit by bit, the entire fascinating story of the very first gold strikes; of Mauch's early prospecting; of the discovery of gold at Eersteling; of the gold rush to the Lydenburg diggings from Delagoa Bay, of diggers crossing first the Lebombo mountains and then a hundred mile long plain where malaria and sleeping sickness were more dangerous enemies than the lions and crocodiles; about the great days in the Cape Valley and near Barberton (also known as the Duiwelskantoor or Devil's Office) when the Diggers' Committee imposed fines of a few pounds for murder and homicide and when the waitresses got onto bar counters at closing time to auction their bodies for the night. He became an expert on the methods used by the old diggers: sluices, waterwheels, ovens, arrastras, panning, single stamps, primitive amalgam tables. And week after week, month after month, he witnessed the incredible growth of the Witwatersrand mining industry.

This was the time of Oom Ryk Piet's greatest triumph. For years he had owned the farm Varkensfontein (Pig's Fountain), north-east of Heidelberg, which he had won in a bet at the Pretoria Club. Now Eugène suddenly heard that he had sold the farm for £50 000.

As the story went, somebody had arrived in Pretoria and offered Oom Piet £1 000 for the "worthless" farm. The potential buyer intended fattening cattle there for the Johannesburg market. However, the amount was suspiciously high for a useless farm and Ryk Piet decided to investigate. On his last trip there he had left his own prospector behind on the farm to look for gold. Until now the man had had no success.

The old prospector was still there, but very close to the DT's. The people who had their eye on the farm had given him £50 and some cases of whisky to keep his mouth shut. For there *was* gold on the farm. Lots of gold. Lang Piet substituted the whisky for strong black coffee and gradually drew the story from the old prospector. He then went to the buyers' office in Johannesburg and told them that he was quite willing to accept £1 000 for the farm, excluding the mineral rights. After all, these were of no interest to them.

After interminable negotiations they gave Ryk Piet £50 000 in cash and another 50 000 £1 shares in the new goldmine they wanted to open there. Yet another mining town would soon rise up on the bare veld.

According to Mr. Wilfred Marais, a son of Ryk Piet, who supplied this information, the buyers decided that Varkensfontein would not be an attractive name for the new town. Lang Piet could choose his own name. It so happened that he had just read *The Fortunes of Nigel* by Sir Walter Scott, the story of a young man who is cheated of a fortune, and he decided to call the new town Nigel.

For Eugène this was just another example of Oom Piet's incredible luck, for nobody had ever expected gold to be discovered at such a distance from the Rand. However, on the Rand itself there were new developments, and new fortunes were being made. It was now clear that the optimists had been right and the pessimists wrong. Eckstein (in German literally "corner-stone") had secretly bought large tracts of ground near the main Reef only a short while before. According to the experts this ground was worthless, as no gold had ever been found close to the surface there. But Eckstein followed the predictions of his own experts, and at the unheard of depth of 580 feet they struck the southern reef. People were saying even now that equally rich lodes would be found at 2 000, even 3 000 feet.

In the meantime Eugène remained involved with his own job. It was hard work, and the competition was severe. In Pretoria there were now six newspapers, three having been founded in the past year: *The Transvaal Times* and the two Government papers, *De Pers* and *The Press*. Not that the established papers were very much older: the *Advertiser* and *Land en Volk* had both been founded when Eugène had been at school in the Western Cape, and even the old *Volksstem*, which Jan Celliers had sold to the Government the year before, was no older than about fifteen years. The new editor was a young Dutchman, Dr. Frans Engelenburg, said to be extremely gifted but rather arrogant. In fact Dr. Engelenburg was an excellent professional journalist and he soon made an enemy of Eugène Marais by describing Henry Marais's "Amphy Bias" column as cheap sensationalism. This was close to the bone, and Eugène regarded it as a personal affront. He wondered when he and Engelenburg would have their first clash. Since he had survived his argument with the President, he feared no one.

3. Country and People

The year 1890 had begun badly.

Early in the year gold shares suddenly took a sharp dip. Nobody could explain why, but there was no lack of rumours. Were the lodes petering out? Was somebody manipulating the shares?

It is quite probable that Eugène knew the truth before most people. His job and his family had by this stage brought him into contact with some of the mining magnates, including Percy Fitzpatrick of Corner House – at this time a suffocatingly hot two-storied corrugated iron building on the corner of Commissioner and Simmonds Streets. Later Fitzpatrick was to write *Jock of the Bushveld* and become a member of the Reform Committee. At the moment he, like all the other equally hard-boiled mining magnates of Johannesburg, was obsessed by only one thing: a deep despondency about the dark future which faced them. Fitzpatrick himself had lost all his money in the Barberton crash when the reefs had suddenly run out. Now it seemed that the same thing was about to happen to Johannesburg.

The catastrophe menacing them was the more unexpected as they had begun finding gold at great depths only a short while before. This was going to mean a new lease of life for the Rand. But at those great depths the engineers also started finding pyrites-sulphides in which iron, copper, lead, zinc and gold occur together. This meant a tough or refractory ore from which it was very difficult to extract gold. The gold was there all right, but the new ore consumed so much mercury that its exploitation became uneconomical. At the moment the mines extracted about seventy per cent of the gold from the ore. They would be able to take hardly half this amount from the deeper lying reefs. With the exception of the small number which lay right on the main reef, all the Rand mines would have to close down. For the 17 000 people in Johannesburg, whose very life depended on the mines, it would spell disaster.

During the following months Eugène saw gold shares dropping lower every day, some days by only a few pence, sometimes by shillings a share. Every week *The Star* carried reports of companies which had been liquidated and mines which had had to close down. By April, shares which had been worth 120 shillings could not be sold for six. Some shares were worth only a few pennies and the value of even the richest mine on the Rand had dropped by between 60 and 80 per cent. Within a few months, people said, Johannesburg would be a ghost town.

The slump soon spread to Pretoria. Speculators who had built houses to accommodate the capital's growing population, could not sell or let their properties. In Church Street East the empty and uncompleted houses stood like sad reminders of better times. The depression also had political consequences. In times of prosperity the Government could do more or less as it wanted. Now the anti-Kruger forces gradually started rallying. In this regard a strong new personality now appears in our story, a man who was to play an important part both in Transvaal politics and in Eugène Marais's life: Ewald Esselen.

Eugène had admired Ewald Esselen ever since the war against the English ten years before, when Esselen had interrupted his medical studies in Edinburgh and come home to tend the Boer wounded in the field. After the war he had become an advocate, practising in Cape Town, where he was soon elected a Member of the Cape Parliament. In the same year he was asked to join the Transvaal Bench, an office he had now occupied with great distinction for some time. The fact that he was a Judge of the Supreme Court did not prevent Esselen from expressing an increasing dissatisfaction with the Kruger regime in private and semi-private conversation. His outspokenness had nothing to do with his drinking habits – these were, for the time being, well under control – but stemmed from deep conviction. When he had arrived in the Transvaal, he said, he had been prepared to wade through rivers of blood for the President. This was no longer true.

The young reporter of the *Transvaal Advertiser* and the distinguished judge had exactly the same views about politics. They began seeing each other more frequently. They became friends.

Since the previous election increasing numbers of Transvalers had begun having doubts about the concession policy, about the appointment of Dutchmen and about Kruger's nepotism. After the "Leyds letter", the feeling against the Hollanders had intensified. Copies of this letter, in which F. W. Leyds, the Republic's State Secretary and a Hollander, had unflattering things to say about various Boer leaders, were distributed amongst members of the Volksraad in May 1890 in order to discredit Leyds.

Kruger's only effective antagonist still remained General Joubert. Eugène – like Jan Celliers and many others – would have preferred a better educated man to lead the opposition, but Joubert was all they had. In any case the General had lately shown encouraging signs of progressive thinking, like his recent plea for Transvaal's participation in the International Exposition in Chicago. He realised that the Republic would be able to resist real and potential enemies more effectively if it had more friends abroad.

But Kruger had a tremendous advantage over Joubert, as Ewald

Esselen and others well realised. The only way to eliminate this advantage was to give the Joubert party an efficient mouthpiece. And this mouthpiece would have to be published in the Dutch language, for the voters who now favoured Kruger and might be wooed to vote for Joubert were Afrikaans-speaking to a man. (There was no talk at this time in the Transvaal of an Afrikaans-language newspaper for Afrikaans-speakers; one might admit to speaking Kitchen Dutch (Afrikaans), but one at least read and wrote Dutch.) Kruger's Government had its own Dutch newspaper, *De Pers*. The *Volksstem*, too, was pro-Government. The only completely independent Dutch paper was *Land en Volk* (Country and People), which belonged to T.J. Meyer. Meyer was by no means the country's most enterprising editor. During the past year he had first been sued by Gluckstein of *De Pers* and then challenged to a duel by Dr. Engelenburg of the *Volksstem*. This had made him more timid than ever.

Meyer had to be replaced as editor. This was arranged behind the scenes by supporters of General Joubert, and their choice fell on the fiery, gifted young reporter of the *Advertiser*. True, Eugène Marais was still very young, hardly nineteen, but he had an extremely facile pen and his thinking was progressive. In addition, he was a "landszoon" – not an Afrikaner from the Cape Colony, but a born Transvaler.

Thus Eugène Marais, a precocious teenager, became editor of the only Dutch-Afrikaans opposition newspaper in the Transvaal in the first half of 1890.

For Eugène it was a great advancement, not only in prestige but in salary as well. All he had to do was guarantee that *Land en Volk* would continue to follow its present editorial policy. T.J. Meyer remained the proprietor, but was no longer to edit the paper. As *Land en Volk* was published only weekly, Marais not only had to write the copy for the entire paper himself but also sell his own advertising space. If, after all this, he still had the energy or time to take on extra work, he would be free to do so.

Enthusiastically, he moved into *Land en Volk*'s ramshackle office in Koch Street (later Bosman Street), where his only assistant was a Cape Coloured boy who made tea, swept the office and carried simple messages, his main route lying between the office in Koch Street and Flavell & Brown's printing works in St. Andrew Street, taking copy to be set to the printers and bringing back galleys which Eugène had to proof-read.

Scoble had taught Eugène a great deal. Criticism being the salt and pepper of a newspaper, Marais introduced a special column devoted to abuse. It was called "Swart Pilletjies" (Little Black Pills). Marais himself wrote the column under the pseudonym of "Apteker" (Apothecary). Eugène's inspiration was his brother's column "Amphy Bias", and it gave him great delight to attack all and sundry: faulty sanitation in Pretoria, abuses by the Zarps (Republican Police Force), Wierda's latest stupidity.

Wierda, a Dutchman, who had been appointed as head of the Department of Public Works some years before, was one of Eugène's favourite targets. According to one of his friends, a land surveyor, A.C. Vlok, Wierda's designs, judged by the latest continental developments, were completely out of date. "It is to be deplored that the insane asylum has not yet been completed," wrote Eugène in one issue of the column. "What on earth will the Government do with Wierda if he goes mad before they have accommodation for him?"

As his own reporter, leader-writer, proof-reader, advertising salesman, designer and bookkeeper, Eugène soon discovered how easily a paper's small profits can turn into a loss.

Land en Volk consisted of four large pages of fine type. Page 1 was devoted exclusively to advertisements, page 2 to advertisements, leaders and news reports, page 3 to reports only, page 4 again mainly to advertisements. The advertising tariff was two shillings per column inch and a shilling for repeats, which usually meant that the income from each full page of advertisements varied between £10 and £6. The paper was expensive – 3d. per copy, or more than a bulky newspaper was to cost eight decades later – but, as fewer than 2 000 copies were printed, the production price per copy was extremely high. The total expense was higher than the revenue from sales, making advertisements the only way to turn a profit.

In some of the large papers the trick was to maintain a balance between editorial matter and advertisements: enough advertisements to turn a profit, but not so few reports that the paper became tedious and lost readers. In the case of *Land en Volk* and the other small Pretorian publications, such problems were academic. As long as one's dead advertisements (such as those for stomach drops) were varied by some of topical interest (such as those for auctions and cattle sales), one could hardly have too many advertisements. Much more easily too few. But even for this there was a solution. The newspaper editor faced by a lack of advertisements had two ways out. As a special inducement to the advertiser, he could publish the advertisements on the news page in the form of reports. In the second place, he could apply for State advertisements, as the Government reserved about £6 000 a year for advertisements in struggling papers. The system was really quite simple. Eugène soon learnt the trick. When he had received permission to repeat a single column advertisement of perhaps ten inches deep from the *Staatscourant* (Government Gazette) in *Land en Volk*, he would cut the advertisement from the *Staatscourant*, paste it onto a sheet of paper and have it reset in larger type. This meant that the advertisement appeared in *Land en Volk* in a column depth of fifteen or sixteen inches, increasing the revenue by 50 - 60 per cent. This kind of liberty was overlooked, which did not mean that the Government lumped all papers together. Gluckstein of *The Press* could inflate the same copy to a double column advertisement of eighteen inches deep – a total of 36 inches, thereby increasing his revenue by 260 per cent without incurring the wrath of officialdom. Eugène was indignant but Meyer, the proprietor of *Land en Volk*, saw the matter more philosophically. *The Press* belonged to Nellmapius and Frik Eloff, Kruger's son-in-law, he explained, and possibly to the President as well. They could take such liberties; *Land en Volk* could not.

Even so, Eugène's moral protests were not so pronounced that they prevented him from accepting the assistant editorship of *The Press*, the Government newspaper, when Gluckstein asked him to help him out.

He now worked harder than ever. In the mornings he would attend the sessions of the Volksraad and in the afternoons, provided no important debates were expected, he would sell advertising space for *Land en Volk*, write leaders for *The Press*, contribute to *The Advertiser*, write leaders and columns for his own paper, write the Volksraad reports, collect local news items and not infrequently simply make clippings from other papers and have them typeset to supplement his own copy.

His duties as assistant editor of *The Press*, which in the meantime had become a daily, did not remain restricted to writing leaders. It was no easy task to fill a daily paper, even if it consisted of only four pages, like *The Press*. Each page of news consumed about ten thousand words in the fine newspaper type, or almost fifty of Eugène's handwritten quarto pages.

One of his most exciting assignments was the sensational news that a white man had murdered a woman at the brick-works.

The murder was committed in a corrugated iron hovel at the spot where the road to Johannesburg went through the brick-works. This assignment brought Eugène into close contact with Wilhelm (or William) Schröder, *The Press*'s brilliant cartoonist, who was to cover the case with him.

Eugène reported the story in full detail and Schröder supplied gruesome line drawings. After this it was again the Volksraad, now no longer the old thatch-roofed building, but the newly completed, imposing modern Raadzaal which had replaced it. Here he learnt more of the ways of the world.

At the time when Barend J. Vorster, the member for Zoutpansberg, was advocating the concession for the Selati Railroad, some people noticed that a strikingly large number of Members of Parliament were driving new spiders.

Making enquiries, Eugène established that at least eight members had been presented with spiders and at least five others with Cape carts. Money was involved too. One Baron Oppenheimer, who now found himself in Pretoria – thus went the story – had advanced a large amount to be used by Vorster to put the members into the right voting mood. As soon as Vorster's partners had obtained the concession they would re-sell it to Oppenheimer.

Eugène's natural inclination was to expose the story in *Land en Volk*, but his hands were tied. He was nothing more than the editor, and Meyer was a careful man. Eugène consoled himself to some extent by nicknaming Vorster "old spider-catcher".

During the same month, August, Ewald Esselen resigned as judge to join the Bar once more. To Eugène this was cheering news. Esselen would now be able to play a more active role in politics.

During this period, however, Eugène's political interests were overshadowed by questions which occupied his thoughts all day and most of the night. How could he increase *Land en Volk*'s circulation? The newspaper was only four years old and not well known outside Pretoria, while its main opponent, *De Volksstem*, was firmly entrenched.

What does a small paper do to gain new readers? What made *Di Patriot*, published in Paarl, expand so rapidly? Suddenly Eugène saw it all clearly: *Di Patriot* gave the people what they wanted by writing in *Afrikaans*, not Dutch.

But there were many problems. He could not use the language of *Di Patriot* in *Land en Volk*, as the *Patriot* wrote in Western Cape Afrikaans, the language associated in the Transvaal with Coloured people. When he had started school in Paarl, Eugène could hardly understand his schoolfriends, and to write the Afrikaans spoken in the Transvaal was a great deal more difficult than it sounded. For instance, what was the pronunciation of the word the *Patriot* spelt "beetje"? When the Transvaal Boers used the word, they would not say "tje", like the people of the Cape, but "kie". Perhaps it should be represented by a spelling like "beeki", Eugène thought. (The Transvalers eventually won, and by the 1980's the "kie" pronunciation had become universal, with the exception of a small minority of Cape Coloureds.)

Eugène decided to keep his ears open and work out a new system of spelling before he started publishing articles in Afrikaans.

In the meantime there was no lack of work. This was an important session, which kept him in the Volksraad for most of the day.

Before the end of that month a new man appeared in the press gallery. He was Jimmy Roos of the Johannesburg *Star* and he had just arrived in Pretoria to start a Pretoria office for his paper.

Roos was twenty-one, almost two years older than Eugène. He was a neat, distinguished young man with an elegant moustache and excellent manners, a member of one of the best Cape families. One of his cousins was Jan Hofmeyr, the leader of the Afrikanerbond, as the Cape opposition party was called. After having gained his B.A. with distinction at the South African College in Cape Town, he worked as a reporter on the staff of *De Zuid-Afrikaan* for some months before leaving for Johannesburg to help found the new paper for the Argus Group.

Eugène saw him daily, and they became fast friends. They spoke the same language, Afrikaans, and they shared memories: of the vineyards of the Western Cape, of the sea, of Tamboerskloof, where Jimmy had grown up on his father's estate, Bellevue, high up on the slopes of the mountain.

During these months at the end of 1890, in his office in the Marks Building, Jimmy spent his time working on a special supplement to the *Star* which also interested Eugène. It was an ambitious venture. Jimmy's goal was no less than to give a complete picture of Pretoria in 1890, with short illustrated articles about all the prominent Pretorians and all the town's important buildings. The supplement was to be published in November on Pretoria's thirty-fifth birthday and Jimmy had to work hard to meet the deadline.

The illustrations were done by William Schröder, the cartoonist with whom Eugène had covered the Whitlock murder. Schröder was one of the most able artists in South Africa. Recently he had made headlines when he was paid £600 for a portrait he had painted of the President, but B.J. Vorster, the man of the Selati railway concession, must have regarded it as a good investment. He had bought it, possibly using Oppenheimer's money, and presented it to the Volksraad. Now it hung in the new Government building.

Jimmy told Eugène more about the appalling events in Johannesburg during the past few months, where wealthy men became paupers overnight and sometimes committed suicide, and of those who had lost all hope and had gambled or drunk their last money away. Thousands had already left the town to start anew elsewhere.

It seemed like the old pattern: a rich find, a small number of people became millionaires or semi-millionaires, and then it all ended.

However, not long afterward, Eugène noticed to his surprise that the shares of a few of the mines which had been on the verge of insolvency suddenly started rising. And again he heard the story behind the story before most people did – possibly from his mining connections in Johannesburg, possibly from Oom Lang Piet, now living in Nigel House, the luxurious mansion he had built with some of the profits from the Nigel mine.

It sounded like a miracle. In Johannesburg the so-called Gold Recovery Syndicate had been engaged in experiments at the Salisbury mine for three months. The cause of the slump had been pyrites which consumed so much mercury that the extraction of gold had become uneconomical. By using a technique they called the MacArthur-Forrest process, the Gold Recovery Syndicate could successfully treat such recalcitrant pyrite-bearing ores. And by using the method, so it was said, they could take 85 to 90 per cent of the gold from the toughest ore. Could this be true? The claims sounded so exaggerated that in many circles the Syndicate was regarded as a bunch of crooks. Up to now nobody had ever extracted more than 75 per cent of the gold from the most amenable ores, and in unmanageable ores this might drop to 35 per cent.

Even so the crazy directors of the Syndicate were willing to enter into a "no cure no pay" agreement with any mine, meaning that the mine would not have to pay them a penny if they did not extract economic amounts of gold from the tailings. Before the end of 1890 an agreement was signed between the Gold Recovery Syndicate and the Robertson mine and soon all kinds of wild rumours began circulating.

The process really worked, and this meant not only that Johannesburg would be saved from disaster but that goldmining profits were to be even higher than before the slump.

Within the next month shares in the best known mines doubled and trebled. Hard work still lay ahead, but Johannesburg had once more become the City of Gold. Percy Fitzpatrick had been unnecessarily pessimistic when he had predicted that grass would grow in its streets within a year.

Nothing is known about Eugène Marais's share market transactions during these years. Taking into account his gambler's temperament and his journalistic and family connections – sources of both tips and financing – it is virtually certain that he must have frequently made his appearance in the Pretoria office of Driver & Filmer, the brokers, to buy or sell gold shares, and that he must have made at least a fair amount of money and possibly a great deal.

He was no longer visiting Johannesburg as frequently as before. His various activities kept him mostly in Pretoria. He was now editor of *Land en Volk*, assistant editor of *The Press* and he had recently been appointed assistant editor of *The Observer* as well.

Before the end of the year he began his experiment of using Afrikaans in *Land en Volk*.

When the first Afrikaans reports were printed in *Land en Volk*, they looked strange, even to Eugène, but he consoled himself by thinking how funny the Boland language of the *Patriot* must have looked when it was first published.

To his disappointment, there was virtually no reaction to the experiment during the first few weeks and, using the pseudonym "Hans", he himself wrote a letter which he published early in the new year to try and stimulate greater interest.

"Ek wens ook, meneer Editeur, om mijn groot blydschap uit te druk dat *Land en Volk* nou in Afrikaans, di ware taal van Suid Afrika, geskrywe word. Ik hoor dat jy al baing nuwe inteekenaars gekry het. Dit het ik verwag. Vir my part kon ik nooit di Hollans van di ander koerante verstaan het nie. Hulle skrywe net so hoog as di hemel, en dan spel hulle ook so snaaks daarby ..."

(I also wish, Mr. Editor, to express my great joy at the fact that *Land en Volk* is now written in Afrikaans, the true language of South Africa. I believe you have gained many new subscribers. This was what I expected. As far as I am concerned I could never understand the Dutch of the other papers. They write as high as heaven and then their spelling is so funny too.)

Eugène need not have worried. The paper's circulation soon began to rise. Some of the new subscribers may have read in the *Patriot* that *Land en Volk* was also to be published in Afrikaans, others had heard about it by word of mouth, while others had seen a copy by chance.

Jimmy Roos watched the experiment with critical interest. He and Eugène did not see eye to eye on this matter. Eugène did manage to convince Jimmy of the fact that even they, two educated young men, did not in fact speak Dutch, but Afrikaans. Jimmy was so struck by this new insight that at a meeting of the Vereeniging van Jong Zuid-Afrika (Society of Young South Africa), to which both of them belonged, he supported Eugène's point of view in a debate about Afrikaans. When the opponents were invited to state their argument in favour of Dutch *in the Dutch language*, nobody took up the challenge. However, Jimmy did not share Eugène's conviction that Afrikaans could become a written language. For that, he thought, Dutch should be used, if need be a simplified form of Dutch which approximated the Afrikaans manner of speaking but did not try to imitate it.

Shortly afterwards Eugène published a short poem in *Land en Volk* to illustrate his point.

Die sprinkaan en die droogte is zwaar op onze land en wat van ons zal worde is bowe mij verstant.	Locusts and drought weigh heavily upon our country and what will become of us is beyond my understanding.

"So," Eugène might have asked Jimmy, "how would you put that in good Dutch? What you want us to do is to translate ordinary spoken Afrikaans into Dutch before we publish."

And Jimmy conceded the point: if anything could be better expressed in Afrikaans than in Dutch, let it be published in Afrikaans. But, all things being equal, always give preference to Dutch.

Eugène took no notice of Jimmy. He continued to publish columns, letters, poems, news reports and political commentary in Afrikaans.

And two weeks later, following up a letter published in the *Patriot*, he replied to Jimmy indirectly in a leading article written in Afrikaans.

> Who are the enemies of the Afrikaans language? Are these the people who love our country and regard the "Afrikaans cause" as sacred? No – the enemies of the Afrikaans language are Jingo-Afrikaners – people who have sunk so low that one feels like rinsing one's mouth after having mentioned their names. In our time we have seen many bad nations and people, but never anything lower or more despicable than an English-minded Afrikaner who despises his mother tongue – the language spoken by his fathers.

Relations between the families of Ryk Piet and poor Jan Marais had long been less than cordial, and Eugène's leader did not improve them. Ryk Piet had both English sentiments and an English wife.

He had not felt completely at home in Pretoria for quite some time. He was fifty-six and he had made enough money. Why – the question his wife constantly put to him – should they stay here in the backveld if they could afford to live in civilisation? And so, at about the time of Eugène's latest leading article in Afrikaans, Ryk Piet decided to build himself a gentleman's residence in the rural surroundings of Mowbray in Cape Town and to retire there. Eugène's own brother, Henry, who wrote mainly in English, found the article unnecessarily bitter. Melt, the second youngest brother, applauded it wholeheartedly.

Melt was doing very well financially. He and his wife, Lenie Boshoff, a granddaughter of the old Free State president, lived in a house next to the old people (whose house – Lynnwood House – he owned). At night, when Eugène was working in his room in Prinsloo Street, he could sometimes hear the babies, Irene and Victor, crying.

Like Eugène, like Jimmy Roos, Melt was a supporter of Joubert. And to an increasing extent they all fixed their hopes on Ewald Esselen. Esselen was an educated man, as neither Kruger nor Joubert were, a brilliant jurist, an orator who could sweep an audience off its feet, a broad thinker – in short, a citizen of the world – but at the same time a man of the people who put the welfare of his own nation above all else. Only a few months after his resignation from the Bench he had stood as a candidate of the Volksraad in Potchefstroom and gained the seat without any trouble. Since then he had become the spokesman for the small number of members of the First Council who did not automatically agree with the President in everything. It was Ewald Esselen who united them and pointed out errors to the President on their behalf, for in an open clash Commandant-General Joubert had never yet been able to stand up to Kruger.

Eugène was not blind to Joubert's defects and Kruger's virtues. The Commandant-General was a brave warrior and an astute businessman (although nobody knew at this time of the huge fortune he was amassing by honest business acumen), but he lacked Paul Kruger's diplomacy, his ability to communicate with the people, his intellectual courage, his powers of perseverance and his extraordinary, albeit unschooled, mind. When Eugène had returned to Pretoria from the Western Cape, filled with patriotism and pride for the land of his birth, the Transvaal, he had been prepared to give the President a fair chance. But Kruger's nepotism, his apparent approval of fraud and the fact that he virtually always sided with his political supporters, right or wrong, had again kindled the decades long enmity between Eugène's family and Kruger. And Jimmy Roos's influence had accentuated this repugnance. Jimmy Roos was a Cape Colonial and a snob. He did not suffer uneducated backvelders gladly. In addition, absolute integrity was a way of life to him, and he despised the policy of concessions and the bribery that went with it.

Eugène desperately wanted to be able to say such things in *Land en Volk*. Time and again, when he was infuriated by Kruger's actions, he decided to write a violent attack on the President. But his hands were bound. Meyer and his advisers obviously thought it inadvisable to attack the Government too fiercely, and with good reason. The income *Land en Volk* derived from Government advertisements meant the difference between a profit and a loss.

Now supposing he did not write such an article himself but found someone to submit it as a letter written to the editor? No, such a procedure could not be kept secret. Then the solution struck him. He would write the letter himself, but pretend that it had been submitted by a reader, as he had done when he had written the anonymous letter about the Afrikaans articles in the paper. And to avoid suspicion and make the letters more convincing, he would create a pro-Kruger correspondent: someone who had fought in the Republic's wars, no longer very young, a born Transvaler (naturally!) who had always given Kruger his full support but was now becoming worried about his outrageous policy. Given these precautions, Meyer would suspect nothing. He would certainly not ask to see the original letters.

Taking great care, Eugène composed the first letter, signing it "Afrikanus Junior". He made it an open letter to "His Honour the State President S.J.P. Kruger", whom …

> I regard as the best statesman the people of the South African Republic could ever have chosen as their leader. Take note, Mr. President, I believe this to this day. My intention was only to show how deeply you have shaken our confidence in you. Be frank and open once more, Mr. President. Chase away the Jews and Hollanders. Become a true Afrikaner once more: forbid the granting of concessions and

thereby show the world that you personally have no interest in them. Be sincere in the church question. Declare yourself an open enemy of the United Church or be completely impartial. Push Leyds away from you and put an Afrikaner in his place. If you do all this, Mr. President, I can give you the firm assurance that you will never have a heartier supporter than

AFRIKANUS JUNIOR

The letter created an uproar. Soon the identity of Afrikanus Junior was the best kept secret in Transvaal journalism.

It is possible that Jimmy Roos played a part in this somewhat cunning practice of using *Land en Volk* as a voice against the Government and the President with impunity. In any case, during the first months of 1891, he and Eugène had frequent discussions on the freedom of expressing one's convictions. As long as Meyer remained proprietor of *Land en Volk*, Eugène would find this impossible.

What had started as a vague dream gradually became reality. Calculations were made and possibilities explored. In July 1891 Eugène Marais and Jimmy Roos bought *Land en Volk* for £500. Jimmy was twenty-two and Eugène had just turned twenty.

In their "Deed of Agreement of Partnership" they contracted to own and manage *Land en Volk* in equal parts. Each was to contribute £40 to the working capital. The amount paid for the paper was to be paid off in monthly instalments from their salaries.

Jimmy remained the *Star*'s representative in Pretoria and Eugène provided most of the copy for *Land en Volk*. The paper now became unashamedly pro-Joubert.

When F. Reginald Statham, editor of the *Observer*, departed on a trip abroad, Eugène became acting editor of that newspaper. There is also a story (not confirmed, seventy years later, by the records of that newspaper) that at about this time he was the Pretoria correspondent of the London *Times*. He was busier than ever.

On the important question about which Eugène and Jimmy could never quite agree, the use of Afrikaans in *Land en Volk*, they now maintained a kind of truce. Jimmy granted that those things which could be said best in Afrikaans might be published in Afrikaans, but to his mind such items were extremely rare. Leading articles, in any case, had to be written in Dutch. After all, a newspaper had its dignity. Nowadays the largest part of the Afrikaans matter in the paper consisted of poems and letters to the editor, as well as special columns and comment. Eugène had to battle to keep the percentage of Afrikaans at a level which would ensure a continuing rise in circulation.

Like the *Patriot*, *Land en Volk* received numerous poems. Most of it was doggerel, which Eugène was obliged to reject. Now and again he would write a poem or verse himself and publish it under a pseudonym.

For Eugène Marais 1892 became a remarkable year. At that time most prominent Pretorians were Freemasons. Eugène was admitted within three months of his 21st birthday. For such a young man it was a rare honour. His extremely successful older brother, Melt, had only joined the year before. After his initiation as an apprentice in March, Eugène was promoted to Fellow-craft in July and raised to Master as early as August.

This achievement was duly recorded in the family Bible his mother had given him some time before. It was a Netherlands State Bible which she herself had been given 48 years before, the year after her own coming of age and marriage. It must have been one of her most prized possessions, yet she gave it to the youngest of her ten living children, he who took after her in so many respects and about whose future she may already have felt a vague but terrifying premonition. Eugène's notes read:

> Took 3e in Masonry on August 30th 1892

After this two enigmatic lines follow:

> Vow & cross on Oct. 11, 1892
> Ring chastity on Oct. 12, 1892

Some months later, another (possibly even more personal) inscription appears on the first pages of the Bible, this time in code.

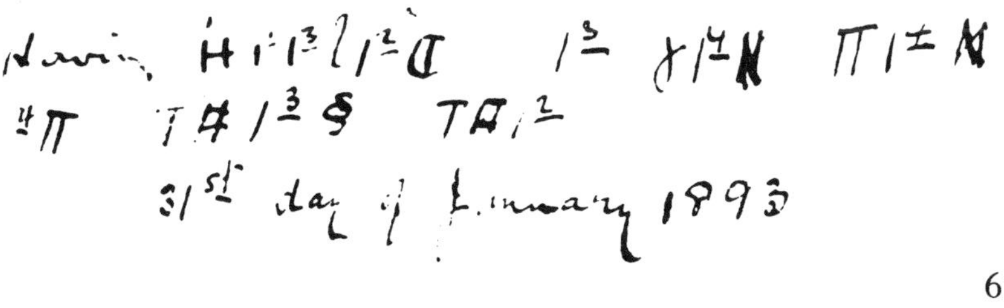

At that time codes were commonly used among Freemasons, but eighty years later an expert on Freemasonry, Mr. Julien M. Missak, could offer no explanation for this one. He suggested that it might have had something to do with astrological details concerning Marais's birth.

The two lines in connection with "Vow & cross" and "Ring chastity", he replied to the author's queries in a letter, certainly had nothing to do with Freemasonry and "are obviously concerned with something completely personal in Eugène Marais's life."

In the body of the Bible, too, the reference is repeated. Diagonally across the two first verses of Ecclesiastes 12 Marais wrote these words: *Took the vow of chastity ring on October 12/1892.*

The two verses from the Bible read as follows:

> Remember now thy Creator in the days of thy youth, while the evil days come not, nor the years draw nigh, when thou shalt say, I have no pleasure in them; While the sun, or the light, or the moon, or the stars, be not darkened, nor the clouds return after the rain.

If Eugène Marais had been clairvoyant he could hardly have chosen more prophetic words from the Bible – or had his mother chosen them? For desperately close by now were those years in his life of which he would say: "I have no pleasure in them –".

But this was 1892. The world was his oyster. He had come of age, he was a respected man in Pretoria. The praise and recognition he received made him, in the words of Milton, "scorn delights and live laborious days". In a strange way his romantic vow reminds one of the pipe which he had hurled into the swirling waters of the Berg river as a schoolboy.

In the first months after he and Jimmy Roos had bought *Land en Volk*, he enjoyed his work more than ever. He felt completely free, and his energy was boundless. But he was over-taxing his strength. The nervous energy he expended was not being replaced. He no longer slept well.

Land en Volk's financial problems were formidable. Circulation remained too low for the paper to make a profit.

Eugène was certain that he knew how to push up the circulation. They should use more Afrikaans and publish more reports which would make people sit up and take notice. But Jimmy was not in favour of Afrikaans, nor was he in favour of what he called "sensationalism". And in a partnership the rule of "when in doubt, don't", is usually upheld.

One thing about which Eugène could not complain was lack of attention. *Land en Volk* had become a power in the country – and it was being besieged from all sides.

Early in 1892 Eugène published a report about the dismissal of a prominent civil servant, Gert Ribbink, after a shortage of funds had come to light. Ribbink promptly sued the paper.

In May *De Pers* went for the jugular, accusing Jimmy Roos of having stolen State documents. The charge was false, and it was convincingly disproved in *Land en Volk*. An official had merely given Jimmy, as a reporter, some official documents to read. Even so *De Pers* then published a cartoon by Schröder in which the accusation was repeated. Jimmy, dignified as always, refused to prosecute.

Loftily, Dr. Engelenburg, editor of *De Volksstem* – or Volkssmet, "blemish of the people", as Eugène contemptuously called his main competitor in *Land en Volk* – now fired his first barrage. References to *Land en Volk* in *De Volksstem* were an exception, Dr. Engelenburg wrote in a leading article, and the reason for this was the contempt *De Volksstem* felt for *Land en Volk*.

> Why? We intend stating the facts once and for all. That our contemporary has constantly shown an inclination to adopt an improper attitude to other Dutch papers and to allow anonymous correspondents to do the same, leaves us completely cold ... Neither do we intend reproaching *Land en Volk* overmuch for the untruths it so frequently propounds, for we know that it is read but infrequently. But the fact that *Land en Volk* succeeds in being so persistently boring, is a constant source of annoyance to us as our position as newspaper editor obliges us to read many papers, including *Land en Volk*.

These facts combined, Dr. Engelenburg continued, did not provide sufficient reason to inflict the name of *Land en Volk* on readers of *De Volksstem*. After all, everybody knew that the young people who wrote the paper were still inexperienced. One required a good deal more to publish a newspaper than "a tiny bit of superficial school knowledge and vast lashings of effrontery". One might have said that the two young men could still become passable journalists if it were not for one thing, i.e. the fact that they served two masters, for while the one editor, Roos, also worked for the *Star* – "a well known British imperialist newspaper in Johannesburg ..." – the other, Eugène Marais, wrote not only for *Land en Volk* but also for the Government paper, *The Press*.

Dr. Engelenburg had not minced words. Among the several imputations that must have cut Marais and Roos to the quick was the one that few people read *Land en Volk*. Soon after Engelenburg's leader, Eugène announced in his newspaper that *Land en Volk*'s circulation had doubled. And he wrote:

> As far as our policy is concerned, we have only one – the truth. We shall expose, without fear or favour, all actions that to our mind seem dishonest ... We are hirelings of no person except the people of the South African Republic and in their interests we are prepared to sacrifice all the financial advantages we might have enjoyed if we had been prepared to adapt our policy slightly.

This was true. Of the £6 000 provided by the Government to subsidise newspapers by means of advertising, *Land en Volk* was now receiving nothing. It was expensive to speak the truth, in more senses than one.

The first libel case against *Land en Volk* since Eugène had started working there had begun, to his excitement and Jimmy's consternation.

Jimmy, with his meticulously ordered boxes and files filled with the historic writings he collected, with his meticulously ordered private life ("I purposely sleep under only a few blankets so as to wake up early in the morning") – Jimmy did not like disorder or disruption of any kind, and to him a libel case was the essence of disruption.

This was where they differed, Jimmy and Eugène. Eugène thoroughly enjoyed the Ribbink affair: writing and publishing the report about Ribbink's dismissal; the tension which preceded the court case (was he bluffing or would he really sue?); compiling the counter-plea, when for the first time Eugène saw how legal men could put biting sarcasm into strictly legal terms; the duel of the case itself, in which his advocates – Ewald Esselen and Advocate Wessels, leader of the Transvaal Bar, the two best legal men in the Republic – fought a bad case against Ribbink's three lightweights and lost it by the narrowest of margins.

To the nominal damages of £10 which Chief Justice J.G. Kotzé ordered, the legal costs had still to be added. Eugène and Jimmy could hardly afford them. Apart from the expense, it was always bad for a newspaper to lose a libel case, and salt was rubbed into their wounds by Schröder's cartoon in the *Press*: Chief Justice Kotzé giving *Land en Volk*, a squealing young boy, a thrashing with a bundle of twigs (£10 with costs).

On the credit side *Land en Volk* could count the cutting remarks Ewald managed to fire off in the course of his argument and especially the unexpected windfall B.J. Vorster gave them shortly after the case, when, speaking in the Second Council (the lesser chamber of the Volksraad), he demanded that Eugène be forced to provide the name of the civil servant who had given him the information regarding Ribbink. This rash proposal, withdrawn by Vorster only when he saw how little enthusiasm the members had for it, made the scales swing a short way in *Land en Volk*'s favour once more.

This was Eugène's first libel action – the first of many. The bug had bitten him.

For the time being, the Presidential election required all their efforts. To Eugène and his fellow Progressives it was clear that since the previous election public opinion was steadily swinging across to Joubert. However, Joubert still had a lot of ground to cover. To make up this leeway, they would have to throw every ounce of energy into the struggle.

Early in July Joubert's electoral committee was appointed, Ewald Esselen being elected chairman and Eugène and Jimmy both becoming members of the central committee for Pretoria. In August the Uitlanders, who had been airing their grievances for five years now without achieving a thing, founded the Transvaal National Union, and in the same month Chief Justice Kotzé entered the fray as the third Presidential candidate. This was bad news for Eugène and his friends as it meant that the votes against Kruger would be divided between Kotzé and Joubert. The Joubert committee would have to work even harder.

In the meantime, Ewald Esselen had been invited to give a speech at a meeting to be held by the National Union the following month. The Joubert committee was divided on whether or not to accept the invitation. There was a good chance that such a step might set a large portion of the electorate against Joubert, in which case much of their work would have been in vain.

In these turbulent, exhausting months during the second half of 1892 the insomnia and nervous exhaustion which had long plagued Eugène reached a climax.

And during this period, for the very first time, he used the new wonder drug of which he had read so much: morphine.

5. The Arms of Morpheus

Thirty-five centuries before Eugène Marais used morphine for the first time, the opium poppy – the plant from which opium and her daughter morphine are derived – had been cultivated in the Middle East. In Egyptian Thebes doctors had described opium as a tranquilliser for fretful children. Homer called it "the intoxicating poppy, the poppy impregnated in deadly sleep".

In the eighth century the Arabs had brought the opium poppy to Persia, and from there it had spread to India and China. By about 1500 the use of opium had become an everyday custom in Turkey. The first opium pipes appeared in China during the 17th century, and there the habit spread like wildfire.

In the meantime opium, which had disappeared in Europe after the fall of the Roman Empire, had been reintroduced there by the Arabs. The famous 16th century physician Dr. Paracelsus wrote: "I have a wonder drug, laudanon, which has no peer in cheating death."

By the 18th century it was commonly used as medicine, more especially in the form of laudanum (opium dissolved in alcohol). Dr. John Brown's *Elements of Medicine*, a medical handbook in which he strongly recommended opium, disseminated the medicinal use of laudanum among the intelligentsia of Europe.

In 1806, when Britain occupied the Cape for the second time, opium was generally not yet regarded as a dangerous drug in the English world but rather as an anodyne and tranquilliser which belonged in every well-equipped household medicine cabinet. It was used for pain, for nervous attacks, for hysteria. Mothers, governesses and children's nurses used a variety of opium syrups to lull the babies in their care: McMunn's Elixir, Batley's Sedative Solution, Godfrey's Cordial, Dalby's Carminative, Mother Bailey's Quieting Syrup and others. Some of these medicines contained up to half a grain of opium per ounce. This meant that two tablespoonsful of the medicine were enough to kill an adult. Such syrups, wrote a contemporary American doctor, "have soothed many and many a luckless infant into that state of quiet that knows no after-disturbing."

Hardly anyone who grew up during the first half of the 19th century in the Anglo-Saxon world was to escape these apparently inoffensive syrups and mixtures. Pure opium, too, and opium in the form of laudanum, were available freely and without a prescription. Charles Lamb drank it to break a cold, Shelley to combat headache, Southey to abate hayfever and insomnia. Others, like Sir Walter Scott and Keats, used more of it, so much in fact that it had a noticeable effect on their writings. A third group, of whom Coleridge was one, became completely dependent on it.

One of the best known members of the last mentioned group was Thomas de Quincey, whose *Confessions of an English Opium Eater* was published in a magazine in 1821 and was later to become one of the most discussed books of the 19th century. "The whole literature of opium addiction, French and American, is strewn with quotations from addicts who avowed that they were first led to experiment by reading De Quincey," writes Alethea Hayter in *Opium and the Romantic Imagination.*

There is no doubt that De Quincey romanticised the use of opium and elevated it to a cult. On the other hand his remarkable book was also the first to point out the awful dangers of the drug.

At the same time, Britain's power politics were to play a role. China's attempts to save her people from the destructive consequences of opium abuse led to the Opium War against England, for whose traders the opium trade was a profitable one, so profitable in fact that it had to be maintained by force of arms. China lost the Opium War and Britain lost the war against opium: in 1830 England imported opium to the value of £22 000; by 1850 this had risen to more than £80 000.

In the year of Eugène Marais's birth, and for many years thereafter, children's medicines with a high opium content were still freely available. In the year of his coming of age, 1892, every adult in the Transvaal could still buy opium without a prescription and it was an ingredient of a whole series of popular medicines for a variety of ailments.

By this time, all doctors and most educated people had become aware of the drug's dangers. Fortunately for those who had to endure pain or were troubled by nervous ailments or suffered insomnia, by now a new medicine was available, morphine – so called after Morpheus, Greek god of dreams, son of sleep and the night. Unlike opium, the scientists and doctors of the time believed, the new wonder drug – which was distilled from opium – was not habit-forming, while retaining all the benefits of opium.

It is against this background that one should reply to the question which has been asked so frequently in the past ninety years: why did Eugène Marais start using morphine?

During the course of Marais's life this question was also put to him *ad nauseam*, tactfully or less tactfully. Almost everyone who posed the question, as we shall see, was given a different explanation.

Marais was to tell his son that he had overtaxed his resources in his journalistic activities and had contracted neuritis, a painful inflammation of the nervous fibres.

If this explanation is not the exact truth, it may actually come fairly close.

From everything said in this chapter so far, it should be clear that the approach to opium and other drugs during the 19th century differed very much from that in the third quarter of the 20th century, when this book was first published. (At a later stage, in many countries, the pendulum was again swinging towards the 19th century attitude, and beyond.) The use of opium was legal, and within certain bounds, it was even socially acceptable. In view of all this, the question is not: what kind of people use drugs, but: what kind of people may have used opium in the nineteenth century?

One group of people used it purely as a medicine. Thus William

Wilberforce, champion of the slaves, used opium every day for the last 45 years of his life for a variety of ailments, but always managing to keep his consumption within strict limits.

A second group – usually sensitive, imaginative people like Eugène Marais – tried experimenting. They were interested in what was strange, what was bizarre, in unusual mental conditions. These were the people who, in the second half of the 19th century, were seduced by the descriptions of opium visions in the writings of such opium addicts as De Quincey and the French poet Charles Baudelaire. (Baudelaire had died by 1867, four years before Eugène Marais's birth, and his masterwork, *Les Fleurs du mal*, had been published ten years before.)

A much larger group used opium as a means of escape. These people tried to restore their self esteem, to wipe out the difference between their ideal vision of themselves and their real selves; they tried to escape from the tensions, disappointments and tedium of daily life. They were people who had not grown up, inadequate personalities.

A fourth, much rarer group, is depicted by Alethea Hayter in *Opium and the Romantic Imagination* as follows: "It is that element in personality which delights in secret rites and hidden fellowships, in being an initiate. French opium smokers talk of their drug in terms of sanctuaries and sacrileges, of 'une vie opiacée' in the same sense as 'une vie monastique', a vocation."

Where did Eugène Marais fit in?

It is possible that he started using morphine *as a medicine*, probably not (as he was to state later) as an anodyne but as a drug to alleviate nervous tension and insomnia, both of which may have been caused by overwork.

A strange footnote should be added to these observations. A well informed niece of Eugène Marais relates that enraged political opponents twice horsewhipped the fiery young newspaper editor. (It is just possible that illustration no. 19 contains an oblique reference to this.) The year or years of these events are unknown, neither was the story confirmed by anyone else. His son denies it. If true, it is conceivable that the mental and physical consequences would have driven a sensitive man like Eugène Marais to morphine – a bizarre possibility mentioned only in passing.

By way of experiment, following the example of De Quincey and others? One need only glance briefly at that image of Eugène behind his desk – always in the vanguard of any innovation, any new thought, with his human skull, his python, his pantheism, his challenge to accepted norms – to see how well such a hypothesis would fit the rash and impetuous young man.

The inadequate personality. At a later stage reluctance to accept responsibilities and the desire to escape from his own humiliations and shortcomings, were indeed to play an important part in Marais's morphine addiction. (By that time, in fact, the process had become a vicious circle.) There is no evidence that these tendencies were powerful enough in 1892 to have set him going.

The fourth possibility – which influences only a small minority of subsequent addicts to start using drugs – fits this exclusive young man like a glove. The secret society, the secret code, the obscure vow. How many other people kept a python as a pet in Pretoria in the nineties or used a skull as a pen-holder?

And if Marais had originally used morphine as a medicine, he soon elevated it to a source of pleasure, to a way of escaping reality, to part of the rites in an exclusive and mystical cult.

In the early nineties, according to a reliable member of the family, Eugène Marais, referring to De Quincey's *Confessions*, delivered an impassioned song of praise to the pleasures of opium at a meeting of the Vereeniging Jong Zuid-Afrika (Society of Young South Africa). Not only without shame, but proudly, he added: "I take it too. I have taken it – I am taking it still."

This may have been the supreme irony: as usual Marais may have been embroidering a little. While boasting that he was exposing himself to opium, he was using nothing more than the much safer, non-habit forming drug, morphine. That in actual fact morphine was far more dangerous and more addictive than opium, the world to its regret – and Eugène Marais to his even greater sorrow – was not to learn until much later.

In the next year, too, as we shall see, Eugène Marais was to describe, with the pride of the privileged initiate, the glories of his nights in letters to a friend.

Of the 19th century's two high priests of narcotics – De Quincey and Baudelaire – only De Quincey need concern us. Marais's intellectual world was formed in England.

Two-thirds of the way through his rather lengthy book, De Quincey describes how after twenty days of intense pain he turned to the "celestial drug" for the first time on a dreary, rainy Sunday:

> ... and in an hour, O heavens! what a revulsion! what a resurrection, from its lowest depths of the inner spirit! what an apocalypse of the world within me. That my pains had vanished was now a trifle in my eyes; this negative effect was swallowed up in the immensity of those positive effects which had opened before me, in the abyss of divine enjoyment thus suddenly revealed. Here was a panacea for all human woes; here was the secret of happiness, about which philosophers had disputed for so many ages, at once discovered; happiness might now be bought for a penny, and carried in the waistcoat-pocket; portable ecstasies might be had corked up in a pint-bottle; and peace of mind could be sent down by the mail.

And another fifteen pages along, even more lyrically:

> O just, subtle, and all-conquering opium! that, to the hearts of rich and poor alike, for the wounds that will never heal, and for the pangs of grief that "tempt the spirit to rebel," bringest an assuaging balm; – eloquent opium! that with thy potent rhetoric stealest away the purposes of wrath, pleadest effectually for relenting pity, and through one night's heavenly sleep callest back to the guilty man the visions of his infancy, and hands washed pure from blood; – O just and righteous opium! that to the chancery of dreams summonest, for the triumphs of despairing innocence, false witnesses; and confoundest perjury; and dost reverse the sentences of unrighteous judges; – thou buildest upon the bosom of darkness, out of the fantastic imagery of the brain, cities and temples, beyond the art of Phidias and Praxiteles – beyond the splendours of Babylon and Hekatómpylos; and, "from the anarchy of dreaming sleep," callest into sunny light the faces of long-buried beauties, and the blessed household countenances, cleansed from the "dishonours of the grave." Thou only givest these gifts to man; and thou hast the keys of Paradise, O just, subtle, and mighty opium!

What De Quincey describes so poetically here is euphoria (later Marais was to use the word in his own writings), the honeymoon of the opium addict, the first marvellous flights, when all pain, all worry, all anxiety disappear, when the dullest, most mundane man finds at least peace, and those with a poet's soul – like De Quincey and undoubtedly Eugène Marais – find not only peace but magnificent visions.

And for the gifted ones, the discerning ones, the original thinkers – like Eugène Marais – not only dreams and visions but deep insight, solutions to the secrets of life, a clear grasp of what used to be obscure and difficult.

When during these months Eugène Marais did not arrive for an appointment or left him in the lurch in other ways – thus Jimmy Roos was to tell his daughter much later – Jimmy usually ascribed it to the effects of morphine and shrugged it off.

Here he was mistaken. With or without morphine, ever since his earliest childhood, Eugène had resisted the tyranny of time and fixed appointments. In any case it would be a mistake to think that Marais's life was disrupted by morphine in these first months. In the manual he consulted so faithfully, De Quincey gives the safe instructions very clearly and not without humour:

> The late Duke of Norfolk used to say, "Next Monday, wind and weather permitting, I purpose to be drunk"; and in like manner I used to fix beforehand how often within a given time, when, and with what accessory circumstances of festal joy, I would commit a debauch of opium. This was seldom more than once in three weeks.

Many morphine addicts found it possible to lead an apparently completely normal life for many years. And, at least in these first few months, Marais's consumption was completely under control. His work, far from suffering from morphine, improved. The insight and understanding which morphine seemed to give him really did appear to help him solve the daily problems – if only because for the first time in many months he was getting enough sleep.

As though nothing at all had happened, the stormy year of 1892 continued on its normal, frenetic course.

There were only a few months to go before the most important election in the history of the Transvaal Republic. The pace accellerated, election fever was running higher than ever.

In September Ewald Esselen, chairman of Joubert's electoral

committee, spoke from the platform of the National Union.

Members of the committee had rightly doubted the wisdom of this step. General Joubert realized what negative results any association with the Uitlander movement could have for him. He therefore repudiated not only the National Union but Ewald Esselen and his electoral committee as well.

In October

Jimmy Roos told Eugène that he was very sorry, it had been pleasant to co-operate with him but they had offered him an excellent position in the Cape Legislative Assembly at £30 a month plus extras didn't Eugène want to buy his shares in the paper and Eugène got the money together and became full owner although Jimmy remained with the *Star* until the end of the year and offered to help where he could for which Eugène was grateful because

November

was such a busy month with the election so close and fisticuffs on Church Square and talk of war between the Krugerites and some Progressives because this was the only thing which would solve the matter they said and also the month of the Joubert congress stiflingly hot days in the hall and it became

December

even hotter and busier and in the meantime the campaign intensified and in his speeches Kruger referred to the lies told in *Land en Volk* meaning the Ribbink affair as a reason why the electorate should not vote for Joubert and the tension increased daily while fisticuffs broke out anew and Eugène increased his dose but mercifully

January

arrived unbearably hot but the end was in sight the election had begun and Eugène put in more hours every day in these last few days now without Jimmy's assistance and as editor of the *Observer* (Statham being still abroad) and of *Land en Volk* and assistant editor of *De Pers* but the election results came in slowly over the dusty Transvaal roads and not before early in

February
was it clear that Kruger would beat Joubert with a very small minority and that Chief Justice Kotzé had received almost no support and that in Potchefstroom Ewald Esselen had been beaten by *a mere seven votes.*

6. Lettie

On 2 March 1893, just after the election, Eugène's parents celebrated their golden wedding anniversary. On this Sunday at the end of summer almost the entire family gathered together. It was a great occasion. The photographer had to induce more than thirty people, including a dozen grandchildren, to sit still long enough for the time exposure, and he managed amazingly well.

Eugène had changed a great deal. Since the previous year he had lost weight and he was wearing his hair longer. In the photograph, perhaps by chance, he looks particularly run down.

Almost all Jan Marais's children were attending the celebration. A great deal had happened to them all during the past few years.

Lizzie Niemeyer, the eldest, now close to fifty, had lived in Pretoria with her children ever since her husband's suicide. She had moved from Proes Street to a more spacious house in Visagie Street where she could accommodate more lodgers.

Polly Clulee, close in age to Lizzie, still an attractive, dignified woman, had stayed behind with her children after her husband had left her.

Charles did not appear in the picture; he was in Boshof.

Henry, who had lost much of his hair, was reasonably happy with what some members of the family called his "exceptionally ugly, exceptionally lovable" wife, Bessie.

Jess Rex, close to forty, had become extremely prudish and mid-Victorian after her affair with Rider Haggard, if there had ever been such a thing. She, too, kept a boarding house. Her husband had left her so long ago that the youngest daughter, twelve year old Mabel, had never seen her father.

Melt, thirty-three, Commandant of the Pretoria Volunteer

Corps, had become prosperous by property transactions. On his large plot next to the old people's house he was soon to build one of Pretoria's first tennis courts.

Kate Dougall still had her humourless, church-bound, somewhat eccentric husband. As far as several of the Marais' were concerned, she might as well get rid of him.

Sophie Ueckerman's husband did not attend the golden wedding celebrations. They were on the point of divorce.

Georgie, the youngest of the children apart from Eugène, was twenty-five.

Five years before the old people had refused to allow Georgie to marry Kuranda. Now they had objections to her present suitor, Andries Verdoorn. It was in Andries' parental house that Eugène and other Pretorians had taken shelter when an attack by armed natives from the north had threatened the town. It was Andries who had had to find a job to pay for his return ticket to South Africa when his extremely wealthy father had been impoverished overnight as a result of the war against the English.

On this day of the golden wedding most of the guests were in a good mood. Johnny Niemeyer, Lizzie's twenty-four year old son, mustered up enough courage to corner Oupa Jan to talk to him. Couldn't Georgie and Andries marry? She was twenty-five. Was she to remain on the shelf because her parents denied her her second choice as well?

And the old man – perhaps foolishly – agreed. His wife was greatly upset when she heard this, for in Andries she recognized exactly the same kind of stick in the mud her own husband had become. But the promise had been made.

Eugène, too, the youngest of the brood, hardly twenty-two, met his beloved during this time, perhaps that very month.

Her name was Aletta Beyers. Friends called her Lettie. Her parents lived in Natal and she had come to Pretoria to visit her cousin, Lenie Boshoff, Melt Marais's wife. And Eugène's brother Melt lived next door to Lynnwood House.

Lettie was twenty years old and according to the standards of any age she was absolutely beautiful. She had magnificent dark brown, curly hair. Her mouth was full, her nose elegant, her neck graceful and proud, the kind of swan's neck most admired by the Victorians. Eugène, too, had become more attractive since the previous year. He looked more sophisticated. He was slimmer and there was a fascinating tiredness around his eyes. The enigmatic alchemy had been sparked.

He learnt to know her varying moods: at one moment she was happy, almost exuberant; a day later quiet and withdrawn. When she was depressed he was deeply concerned by the possibility that her mood might have been caused by something he had done wrong; in her merry phases – when sometimes it seemed to him as if she was teasing him and playing games with him – he could become light-headed from the desire to tell her how much he loved her.

But she was a lady (was there ever such a lady!) and he regarded himself as a gentleman. A declaration of love could not be made without an offer of marriage, and of this he was not so certain. Where would they live, how would he support her?

In a letter to Jimmy Roos, who had returned to the Cape the previous year, he wrote:

> My dear fellow, language becomes feeble when I attempt to describe to you the state of my heart while I am writing. Everything is drifting to the dogs – all thoughts and hopes and aspirations are overshadowed by one besetting presence. Miss Lettie Beyers from Natal is still here, and since her arrival I have been passing through a moral and physical hell on her account. I am just about as dead gone as a man can ever be and what is more I think I will be safe if I mentioned the fact to her. But, thank God! I have still too much instinctive honour for that. Imagine supporting a wife on "L & V". Horresco referens! Man, she is just about the most perfect female in body and mind that God ever planted in South Africa.

And a month later:

> There was a time when I dreamed that I would never be happy again – that my soul was no longer pregnable to any human influences whether for good or for evil – and behold, here comes a sweet little thing from Natal – a daughter of mine own people too! – and upsets all my most precious calculations, making a drivelling idiot of what was once a man or supposed itself to be a man. She has some of the

> elements of a flirt and more misery has she caused me than lies in all the massed villainy of the Government Buildings to do. The only respite I have is in the arms of the divine drug, which here, while the frost gathers dull and white on all that was alive without, nightly resuscitates for me the spring and "out of the anarchy of dreaming sleep and the fantastic imagery of the brain calls into sunny light" the presence of diviner beauties than eyes of flesh can ever behold.

The second letter clarifies various points. The quotation comes from De Quincey. The word "nightly" means that Eugène – granted the possibility that he may have exaggerated slightly, as was his fashion – was not, in the heart of the Transvaal winter, like De Quincey in the early stages of his addiction, restricting himself to a three-weekly "debauch".

The first sentence of the letter contains an even more ominous reference: the deadening of true feeling (for which the sufferer is then inclined to compensate by means of exaggerated feigned emotions) is one of the most terrible results of addiction to the opiates. This was why Coleridge had cried out in desperation: "I see, not feel, how beautiful they are!" That this could have happened to Eugène Marais at such an early stage, is hard to imagine. The condition was probably caused rather by over-exertion and nervous exhaustion.

Marais's reference to the "massed villainy of the Government Buildings" was by no means rhetoric, for though Lettie filled his thoughts he was busier than ever in the political field. To him Kruger and his Volksraad had really become the quintessence of evil. Stupid and shortsighted, but at the same time cunning; apparently pious, but in reality hypocritical and corrupt. The election had changed many things. After the tremendous excitement and exertion there was a spiritual let-down. The political fever had dropped and the pace of life returned to normal. But Eugène was embittered. Time and time again his thoughts would return to the results of the election:

Kruger	7 881
Joubert	7 009
Kotzé	81

Time and again he would think back to the story of the presidential election of 1863, thirty years before, in which Kruger was said to have "wrung the necks" of Pretorius' voting slips. This could have happened again. A majority of hardly 800 out of almost 15 000 was insignificant.

An almost equally bitter pill to swallow was Ewald Esselen's defeat in Potchefstroom by only seven votes. Eugène knew what a thorn in the flesh Ewald had become to the Government; he was the only man who could unite the Opposition in the Volksraad. In this case he had no doubt that there had been foul play. They could not yet prove it, but they were certain that Jan Kock, the electoral officer in the Volksraad elections in Potchefstroom, had watched the voting (which was public) very thoroughly and exerted considerable pressure on the voters to vote against Esselen. According to the stories, people who were known to be supporters of Esselen were disqualified on various pretexts, while the dead rose from their graves to support the Kruger candidate. And in the end Ewald had nevertheless been only seven votes short of victory. Seven! Jan Kock – they had to get at Jan Kock.

One arrives here at a turning point in the life of Eugène Marais. Without Jimmy Roos's conservative influence, his heart filled with hate, he was from this moment to wage a bitter, ruthless and merciless war against a corrupt government from his office in the Eendracht Building on the north-eastern corner of Church Square.

However, Kruger struck first. About the middle of the year Marais was arrested by the Zarps (members of the South African Republican Police) and only released when £100 bail could be found for him. The charge – criminal libel – arose from an article in *Land en Volk* in which a short time before he had claimed that the President, in spite of his salary of £7 000 a year, had submitted two different accounts for travelling expenses for a visit to Colesberg, when in fact he had been a guest of the Cape Government.

It was a long, drawn out case. In the meantime the feud outside the courtroom had become more violent, and Eugène no longer stood alone. *Land en Volk*'s editorial office in the Eendracht Building – two rooms in which all editorial duties were performed, including the folding of the newspapers – became a political rendezvous for the young progressives. There was talk that the Government intended closing down *Land en Volk*, and Eugène's fiery young supporters often arrived there armed with guns and bandoliers to protect the paper against a possible raid by the Zarps.

"While I am writing," Marais wrote to Jimmy Roos from his office, "there are about forty bloody-minded rebels in the front office, all describing in forcible if not elegant language the vials of wrath they are about to pour out on the heads of the government and the bench of the high court of justice. One fellow is shouting, evidently for me to hear: 'Laat hulle ver *Land en Volk* neem, ons skiet hulle dat hulle bars en vrek!'" (Let them take *Land en Volk*, we'll shoot them deader than a doornail.)

After a lengthy case in which Marais was defended by Ewald Esselen, he was found not guilty and discharged. Soon he wrote defiantly in his paper: "... Mr. Marais was arrested on a charge, brought by the President, of criminal libel. The court acquitted him, and in doing so suggested to the world *that the wrong person had been put into the criminal box*."

Miss Lettie Beyers had not yet returned to Natal. Eugène was madly in love with her, and he knew she loved him too. All that prevented their marriage was a lack of money. As it happened, these months were to bring a financial windfall.

After Joubert's near victory over Kruger in the previous election and as Marais's increasingly virulent and violent attacks on the Government persisted, the Uitlander movement in Johannesburg began considering the possibility of financial support for Joubert and his people in order to promote their own cause. Careful feelers were put out in regard to *Land en Volk*.

In his present mood – strongly anti-Kruger and strongly pro-Lettie – Marais agreed to listen to proposals and soon he began negotiating with a certain Vaylor, who was representing the Uitlanders' interests in the matter, about financial support for *Land en Volk*.

While these negotiations were in progress, Marais went to Johannesburg late in August and held a lengthy discussion with one of the Uitlander leaders, Charles Leonard, in his office.

Leonard accentuated the necessity of co-operation between the Uitlanders and the Boers.

Two forces were at work in the Transvaal, he told Marais. The Uitlanders and the Boers. By now Marais and his people knew all their grievances. They were legitimate ones, but the Uitlanders were powerless to restore them. Without the vote the Uitlanders' only solution would be to wage a struggle from within, just as William the Silent fought the King of Spain while he was His Majesty's stadthouder and the protector of His Majesty's subjects in Holland. Matters could not continue as they were. The two forces of the Republic either had to stand together or clash.

During the interview Marais does not seem to have said very much, but in a long, carefully worded letter written in reply to Leonard he expresses his understanding of the Uitlanders' position, while not doubting that in the event of a confrontation he would side with his own people – even with "this rotten thing which we call a republican government".

In the same letter he complains of a "despondent melancholy which I can't shake off" and continues: "I feel that I must get away to the seaside for a fortnight at least and I intend going as soon as this business with Mr. Vaylor is through. As the matter stands at present I cannot leave the business even for a week. If, therefore, you can do anything to hurry it through I shall esteem it an immense personal favour."

Charles Leonard was not a man to waste time. He had hardly received the letter when Eugène was told that the transaction had been approved in principle. Marais had only to meet a number of the mining magnates to discuss details.

For Eugène Marais the matter had been settled, and that is what he told his girlfriend. After several months in Pretoria, Lettie returned to her father's farm near Colenso, her mission accomplished.

Eugène accompanied her to Vereeniging, where she was to catch the night train to Natal. On that occasion he asked her formally to become his wife.

Later that evening he dined in Johannesburg with Leonard and some other Uitlander millionaires to clinch the *Land en Volk* deal.

In the end he sold *Land en Volk* for £2 500 to a company founded for the purpose by the Uitlanders. Marais undertook to stay on as editor for at least another two years, at a salary of £50 a month. The Johannesburgers were to provide a working capital of £2 000 as well as an annual subsidy of £600.

Marais was to retain the purchase price in the form of shares until his minimum term of office expired, and until that time he would be managing director of the company.

But the most important stipulation, the one which had clinched matters for him, was that he would be free to write what he wanted to, without interference from Johannesburg.

7. The Don Juan of Christiana

Two cartoons published after the election of 1893 illustrate the talents of two Transvaal artists.

One, by Eugène Marais's old friend and colleague, William Schröder, shows the three candidates on race-horses. The second, by Anton van Wouw, shows Kruger streaking past the winning post on his horse.

The difference between the two drawings is striking: Schröder's powerful and yet natural, that of Van Wouw – later to become one of the most favoured South African sculptors – rather stiff and amateurish. During that same year Schröder, who had just turned forty-one, died. South Africa had lost one of its most promising artists.

By chance, Commandant J. de la C. Schröder, who seems to have been William Schröder's brother, appears in the story at this stage. Commandant Schröder had been an officer in the State Artillery. He was now a private detective, and he was to play a part in Marais's feud against two other brothers, Jan and Frans Kock.

Ever since the Volksraad election, when Ewald Esselen lost the Potchefstroom seat by seven votes, Jan Kock, the electoral officer, had been a hated name to Marais. He did not doubt for a moment that Kock's irregularities had caused Ewald Esselen's defeat. And if the least doubt could remain, this was wiped out when a grateful President rewarded the electoral officer by appointing him a member of the Executive Council – even though Jan Kock did not meet the constitutional requirements for membership!

This did not deter Kruger in the least. He was a determined man. He circumvented the legal restrictions by making Jan Kock *Secretary* of the Executive Council – a completely new position for which he was not only to receive a thumping salary, but also the right to vote.

By giving the secretary the right to vote, Kruger was acting in accordance with his well known "iets voor niets" (something for nothing) policy. Not only had he rewarded a political favourite, in the event of an impasse in the Executive Council Jan Kock would give him the majority of one he might need.

The President was happy, Kock was happy. Ewald Esselen and Eugène Marais were anything but happy, and Marais was prepared to go to almost any lengths to avenge these wrongs.

Now, at the end of 1893, it seemed as if Schröder might be able to provide the means. Although Marais did have certain evidence against Jan Kock, he could prove nothing yet. But he did possess some damning facts against Jan Kock's brother, Frans Kock, which could seriously embarrass Jan Kock if they should become common knowledge.

Schröder had an excellent witness, Constable Willem Oberholzer, from whom Marais got the facts.

Constable Oberholzer was a member of the Mounted Police, stationed at Christiana. The landdrost of Christiana was Mr. Frans Kock, brother of Mr. Jan Kock, Secretary of the Executive Council.

During the past year Landdrost Kock had frequently sent the constable on all kinds of missions which had not seemed strictly necessary to Oberholzer. It had also struck him that Landdrost Kock was paying particular attention to Oberholzer's attractive wife.

One day Landdrost Kock sent Oberholzer once again to the border to take a hut count. He had left early that morning, but during the afternoon he had found a native in possession of a gun. Constable Oberholzer had arrested the man and brought him back to Christiana, where they arrived at nine o'clock that night. If it had not been for the native he would not have returned before the next day.

After he had charged the native and locked him in a cell, the constable went home to go to bed. Reaching his house, he knocked on the door, but no one came to open it. He knocked once more, and again nothing happened. The house was in darkness. When he knocked once again, his wife came to the door. He could see that she was trembling. Constable Oberholzer greeted her impatiently, pushing past her to the children's room. He was hungry and he was after the bread he had hidden beneath their bed. Under the bed he found Landdrost Kock, dressed only in a pair of trousers and a vest.

"Willem, what are you doing here?" asked the landdrost, obviously flustered.

A series of highly emotional scenes now followed. Constable Oberholzer was so furious that he hardly knew what he was saying. His wife ran out to fetch her brother and threw herself into his arms. Landdrost Kock, who had got dressed in the meantime, was threatening to commit suicide.

Not before the following morning at five o'clock did Landdrost Kock make his stealthy way back home, a deeply worried man.

Soon after these events Constable Oberholzer was approached by Frans Kock's brother, who offered him £150 if he would forget about the incident. But Constable Oberholzer was still in a vengeful mood. He wanted to divorce his wife, making Landdrost Kock the third party. Not until later, when his rage had calmed down, did he accept £75 damages and expenses from Landdrost Kock's family and friends.

Constable Oberholzer's testimony was not the only one that Commandant Schröder had. The constable's little nephew, who lived with them in the house, was willing to testify that Landdrost Kock had called on Mrs. Oberholzer more than once. One evening, on another occasion on which Constable Oberholzer had been out of town, Mrs. Oberholzer was dressed in only her night-gown when Landdrost Kock was there; the landdrost went into her room and only came out the next morning.

Marais felt uncertain. Should he publish the story in *Land en Volk*? Soon afterwards he saw a short report in the Government newspaper, *The Press*, according to which the malicious stories about Landdrost Kock of Christiana had arisen from a misunderstanding and the landdrost had been absolved from all blame.

Marais was furious. He knew the official report to be false, and he was convinced that Landdrost Kock was being protected only because he was a brother of one of President Kruger's most loyal senior officials. Without more ado he sat down at his desk, wrote out the whole story and published it in the next issue of *Land en Volk*.

Landdrost Kock of Christiana could not have wished for a worse Christmas present. For Eugène Marais himself, on the other hand, the festive season brought two lovely gifts:

Three chrysanthemums (yellow, white, purple) on a card, painted by her own hand and posted from Colenso with the message: "To Eugène from Lettie, a bright and happy Christmas."

A visit by Schröder, who showed him a line drawing of a collection of long poles and rolls of wire.

The drawing was part of Schröder's evidence against Jan Kock, Secretary of the Executive Council, and other prominent inhabitants of Potchefstroom. They had stolen telegraph poles and wire from the State in order to fence their own farms. Schröder could not yet prove this, but he was busy collecting additional evidence.

Marais's first reports were carefully worded, but as Schröder brought in more evidence they became fuller and more aggressive until by the end of February the State Attorney decided to prosecute Jan Kock, Secretary of the Executive Council, Dirk Tom, the new landdrost of Potchefstroom, and other inhabitants of the town on charges of theft or the possession of stolen goods.

Jan Kock's brother, the amorous landdrost of Christiana, had in the meantime sued *Land en Volk* for libel.

Before any of these cases could begin, Lettie had returned to Pretoria and Eugène forgot everything in the bliss of having her back. He even found time, in spite of his job, to see her quite frequently. Mrs. Bessie Findlay (a daughter of Eugène's sister, Lizzie Niemeyer) sometimes accompanied them as chaperone when they stayed overnight in Johannesburg or elsewhere outside Pretoria.

From this period dates Gustav Preller's classic image of Eugène Marais: distinguished and elegant at the opera, with his walking stick and red-lined cloak, a sophisticated citizen of the world.

To celebrate their engagement, Eugène and Lettie went to Johannesburg for a weekend. Eugène's youngest sister, Georgie, and Andries Verdoorn – whom she had married after all the previous June – went with them.

On the way there Lettie was boisterous. Later she became pensive, and she hardly said a word until they arrived at their hotel. There, she insisted on jumbling up all the shoes in front of the doors on their floor. The next week, when pictures were taken of the two couples, she could not stop laughing at the photographer, but by the time he was ready to take the picture, she had become so glum that he could not coax a smile out of her at all. Eugène found all her moods attractive. He was very much in love.

The case about the alleged theft of telegraph poles and wire began at about this time, under a special landdrost appointed by the Executive Council. After a trial of five days all the accused were found not guilty and the Executive Council decided not to dismiss any of them from their posts.

Eugène Marais was furious. "The end of the wire case has been an exceedingly surprising one," he wrote bitterly in *Land en Volk*. "Instead of allowing the case to be heard by a competent criminal court, the Executive Council itself sat as a criminal court and decided that all the accused should be not guilty, but that Tom and Debbes should be fined £100, *probably because they stole no wire*.

"In Potchefstroom two of Mr. Kock's witnesses, Heywood and Swanepoel, have been accused of perjury. Swanepoel has fled, but Heywood has been arrested."

To Eugène's indignation, Detective Schröder was also arrested at this time. Some of the accused had brought charges of theft against him because he had taken telegraph wire from certain properties to serve as exhibits. However, on the advice of the prosecutor, he was soon released.

For Eugène and for *Land en Volk* it was a triumph. That he was supported by a large part of the public became clear from the scores of letters of encouragement he received after the wire case. Some readers even sent financial contributions to help bear the costs of similar exposures.

Marais had never been so full of confidence in himself and in the eventual success of his battle against corruption in Government circles. When he read in *De Potchefstroomer* that one of his enemies intended instituting an action of libel against him, he replied defiantly in *Land en Volk*:

> *De Pers*, *Volksstem*, *Potchefstroomer* and other Dutch papers seem to take great delight in always egging people on to institute libel actions against *Land en Volk* and constantly to announce that Mr. So and So

> is on the point of starting a huge case against us. *Land en Volk* has never been scared by childish threats, and as far as these particular threats are concerned we are even less scared, as we know about more things than have been published.

In this year, the year of his marriage, he was well and truly on the war-path. Dr. Engelenburg of *De Volksstem* called him a "law-suit monomaniac" and not without some degree of justification, for there was something almost unnaturally intense about the summonses and counter-summonses in which he was constantly getting involved.

In July he sued one J.M.A. Wolmarans Jr. and *De Volksstem* for libel, with damages of £5 000, on the grounds of a statement by Wolmarans in *De Volksstem* that Marais was using detectives to obtain false evidence, was bribing people and was making lying statements against innocent people. Marais won the case and was awarded £10 damages. "That thoroughgoing young patriot, Mr. Eugène Marais, whose fate it usually is to be prosecuted," remarked the *Star*, "is varying the monotony of his journalistic experience by doing a little prosecution on his own account."

The favourable verdicts were encouraging, but all the court cases cost a great deal of time and money, even when he won them.

The Volksraad provided a new surprise by finding Marais guilty of criminal libel – outside the court – on the grounds of an article in which he had referred to "members of the Volksraad stupid enough or crooked enough" and "these swindlers". Marais reacted sharply in *Land en Volk* to this decision, at the same time submitting a petition to the First Volksraad in which he offered to prove his innocence. Without repealing their previous decision, the Volksraad replied that there had been no intention of pronouncing a sentence.

In the meantime, the libel action of Landdrost Frans Kock – the Don Juan of Christiana, as Marais mockingly called him in the newspaper – had started. Ironically, Charles Leonard, the Uitlander leader who had arranged financial support for *Land en Volk*, was one of Frans Kock's advocates. However, even this did not help the landdrost. Marais successfully defended himself against Kock's libel action by pleading "truth and justification" for the first time in the history of the Z.A. Republic.

In his verdict Mr. Justice De Korte did not doubt that adultery had been committed while Judge Morice – although to his mind actual adultery could not be proved – had no doubt about Kock's intentions. Consequently, he could not see how Kock's character could have suffered as a result of the report in *Land en Volk.*

That afternoon a report about the court case appeared in the *Star*. The second heading above the report read mockingly:

HE ASKED FOR SOME BREAD,
AND SHE GAVE HIM
A LANDDROST

The court case would be a severe blow to both Frans Kock and his pious brother.

For Eugène Marais it was a happy time. He was to marry within a fortnight.

8. A Vacant Lot

They married in Natal and spent their honeymoon there. It was a brief holiday. Eugène could not stay away from the newspaper for too long.

When they arrived back in Pretoria, they went to live in Lynnwood House for the time being.

Like a gem his beautiful young bride sparkled in her new setting. Lettie was not only beautiful, she was also kind. Everyone grew fond of her, and quite a number of young and older men fell in love with her from a distance. On the face of it she was completely happy. Even so – like Eugène – she could at times retreat into herself and become despondent. Accustomed to liberty and freedom of movement, she found the old house uncomfortable and although she got along with her in-laws well enough, the Marais' sometimes got on her nerves: the old people on the corner, she and Eugène in a room in the house, Melt in the house next door to support all the others and, some streets away, Sophie Ueckerman's boarding house. She wanted to get away, she wanted her own house. When Eugène made promises but did nothing about the matter she decided to buy a plot herself.

East of the town two new suburbs had been laid out on old Mr. Mears's farm Sunnyside: Sunnyside and Arcadia. Mr. Mears himself, the popular personality from Eugène's childhood days, had become a pathetic figure. When, after the discovery of gold, the price of land had started rising, he had decided not to sell – after all, the property would be even more valuable later – but to take a large bond on the farm. This money he took to Europe to enjoy life: London, Paris, Monte Carlo. At first he intended staying there for some months, but in the end it turned into years. The interest on the bond was not paid and when Mr. Mears ignored letters and cables, the creditors called up the bond. Sunnyside was cut up into plots.

Now Mr. Mears was back in Pretoria, trying to buy back Sunnyside. One could see him in the Palace of Justice every day. The judges were sorry for him, but they could do nothing for him. He was to die impoverished.

On the farm where as a child Eugène had gone on picnics and horse-riding, Lettie now bought a plot of just under 30 000 square feet for £45. It was plot 279, a tiny dot of ground in the rolling veld way outside the town. To the north, between the new extension and Meintjeskop, there were small farms, and not far from it Fairview, Ewald Esselen's sumptuous estate of fifty acres nestled against the slopes.

Beautiful and feminine she might be, but Lettie was also a practical, level-headed person. She did not buy the plot only because she herself wanted to leave Lynnwood House, but because she thought that in their own house she might be able to help Eugène more easily to get along without morphine. She put the plot in her own name not only to safeguard it in case of financial problems at *Land en Volk*, but also as an investment for the future – perhaps for herself, perhaps for her unborn progeny.

The reason for her anxiety was the drug. Eugène had been using it for two years, and addiction had set in. Shaking the habit at this relatively advanced stage would not be possible without the supervision of a doctor and then only if he could rest for a considerable time during the necessary treatment. A morphine syringe was not a pipe one could fling into the Berg river. Because he dearly loved Lettie and by exerting himself to the utmost, Eugène did indeed succeed in controlling his consumption, this in spite of the fact that the morphine addict needs increasing doses simply to obtain the same effect as before.

Eugène spoke openly to Lettie. He told her all – or almost all. She was the one person with whom he wanted to be completely honest. But as the months passed, white lies began slipping out. Later they became less white. Sometimes it seemed to him as if she had no understanding of the sacrifices he had already made for her sake. Next to Lettie morphine had become the most precious thing on earth. She was demanding the impossible from him. Ergo: she was being completely unreasonable. Ergo: he was morally justified in keeping a second syringe and a supplementary supply of tablets at the office. After all, what concern of hers was it how much he took?

And of course she found out all about it. It was a vicious circle.

There was also a second, less vicious circle in which morphine for the time being kept him at work and in which hard work for the time being prevented the worst excesses. His obsession – this was one of Lettie's lesser grievances – remained the newspaper and politics.

In October, when she was expecting her first baby, he wrote a letter under the pseudonym of Afrikanus Junior for the first time in three years. His target was again Dr. Leyds, the State Secretary. In his letter Marais purposely uses the word "gij", less polite than the formal "u", to express his contempt.

> Who are you? What is your position in the South African Republic? You are Mr. Kruger's ink-pot and pen, nothing more. If the Kruger regime should fall tomorrow you will find out that your personal and direct influence among the people is less than the shadow of a cobweb.

During this time the revelations in connection with the Selati railway concession were the talk of the town. Marais's information regarding bribery, four years before, had been completely correct. Via B.J. Vorster, members of the Volksraad had not only received American spiders and Cape carts as gifts, but also gold watches, shares in the proposed company and large cash amounts. The President himself was not involved, but now, after the exposures, he sided with the guilty ones by stating that he saw no evil in taking gifts.

What bothered Marais quite as much as the bribery was the enormous and totally unnecessary loss the Republic had suffered because of stupidity. An engineering firm which had contracted to build the two hundred mile long railway at £9 600 a mile, had farmed out the same contract to a sub-contractor two days later for £7 002 a mile, making a profit of more than £500 000 almost overnight – money which the Transvaal Treasury could have saved if the Government had approached the matter more circumspectly.

Marais also found it strange that none of these transactions had been brought to light during the two years that Dr. Leyds, anything but a fool, had handled the matter for the Government.

In the meantime, there were new developments in the attempts to effect a reconciliation between the Burgermag and the Volksvereniging – respectively the Kruger and Joubert parties. In October Marais attended a provisional meeting and helped to draft the circular convening a conference about the matter.

The conference was held in the Caledonian Hall the following month, and the delegates decided to nominate six Krugerites, six Joubert men and six neutral members to draft a constitution for a new reunited party.

Marais did not feel happy about the outcome of the meeting. In practice, he suspected, it would only mean that the principles of the Joubert party were to be swallowed up. But when a decision was taken soon afterwards on the principles of the new reunited group, the Volksmag (Power of the People), he was pleasantly surprised. In terms of section 4 of the Volksmag constitution the party's official language would be Afrikaans, not Dutch. In addition a reasonable attitude was adopted toward the Uitlanders, the party having pledged itself to "assist the government and the Volksraad in adopting and executing such laws regarding the new population as will be calculated to instil in them a sense of peace and satisfaction."

Marais decided to strike while the iron was hot. In the leader in which he commented on the congress, he again accentuated the necessity of Afrikaner unity, with particular though covert references to the Cape Afrikaners:

> The principle laid down by the Volksmag (the united front) is simply the recognition of the unity of the Afrikaner people throughout

> South Africa. The mission of the South African Republic in South Africa is to educate our people throughout South Africa to the ideal of national independence and liberty. We are a small republic surrounded by enemies – by our greatest enemy and persecutor in South Africa – and in that alone lies the danger to our independence. And how can we increase our size and strength? Only by closer links between all Afrikaners, and by acknowledging that the Afrikaans nation is one people, although separated from each other by rivers and borders. Every Transvaler feels that we have to strengthen ourselves by absorbing new arrivals; but every Transvaler also feels the danger of absorbing all new arrivals without more ado. A difference should be made, and who should be given preference? Should this not be given to our own people arriving here from elsewhere? The bonds between all Afrikaners are the bonds of blood and there is no power, no sword, no country, no money, no nation, no man who will cut these bonds.

In a certain sense the leader was a test for the sincerity of the Johannesburgers who were helping *Land en Volk* financially. True, they had promised him a free hand, but how would they react to his having called Britain "our greatest enemy and persecutor"? Marais realized that he was risking a great deal. If the Johannesburgers were now to withdraw their support, *Land en Volk* would have a deficit, for the huge legal expenses of the past few years had swallowed all the profits. Should one deduce from this that Marais had made substantial profits on the Stock Market and thought himself safe? In any case there does not seem to have been money for much besides the newspaper. Time and time again Lettie would ask him when he intended starting to build their house. Time and time again he was reminded of this when he passed along his prosperous brother's advertisement to be typeset:

> *Money! Money! Money!*
> *To borrow as a 1st bond on fixed property*
> *From £500 to £25 000.*
> At reasonable rates of interest, from Melt Marais

But time and time again he moved these prospects into the background of his thoughts. Right now he had far too much to do.

In the newspaper he was still lashing out in all directions without fear or favour. They were vicious attacks, and some were completely without political justification. Thus he published a report concerning a scandal in which Miss Pottger was involved, the same teacher whose classes he had attended as a five year old boy in the little thatch-roofed consistory on Market Square. And one can hardly imagine any detailed analysis of her sins which could have been worse than the innuendo of the report:

A SCHOOL IN SCANDAL

> The subsidy has been removed from Miss Pottger's school in Pretoria. Reports regarding education given in the school were false. To this an abominable event must be added. Moral considerations have made us decide to say nothing about it. Two years ago the matter of the school was also discussed by the Volksraad, again because of a transgression of the law.

This was but a foretaste. Before the end of the year the zealous Saint Eugène stormed the great Dragon himself. In *Land en Volk* he wrote:

> During a public meeting at Ermelo the President was asked why, if the newspaper disseminated untruths, *Land en Volk* was not prosecuted. His Honour replied that he could not instruct the State Prosecutor to prosecute the editor because the latter wrote so cautiously that the law could not be applied. Our reply to this is: truth is always so cautious that the law cannot be applied. And we hope soon to prove this to His Honour in a court of law.

Immediately after publication of the report, Marais notified the President via his attorneys of his intention to claim £10 000 damages on the grounds of various libellous statements made against *Land en Volk* by the President during his latest electoral trip. Friends, and possibly his wife, Lettie, eventually persuaded him not to take steps against the highest authority in the Republic.

In the meantime, however, he continued his attacks on Kruger and other members of the Government. Acrimonious letters signed by Afrikanus Junior, too, were published from time to time.

In the winter of 1895, when Lettie's time was very near, Eugène's foreman typesetter came to see him in his office. An assistant bookkeeper in the civil service, a certain Malan, had approached the typesetter and had tried to bribe him with Government money to reveal the identity of Afrikanus Junior. For the typesetter it was a tempting offer. For the true name of Afrikanus Junior and a sample of his handwriting Malan would pay the typesetter £120. For the name alone he would be paid £50. Apart from this Malan would also pay generously for any other information he could offer from the offices of *Land en Volk*.

Finally, he added, he need have no worries about doing these things, for if his actions came to light and he was dismissed, an appointment in the civil service awaited him.

The honesty of his foreman typesetter now enabled Marais to corner his enemies. Give Malan the name of Afrikanus Junior, he told his employee.

"No sir, I can't do that," replied the typesetter, who was well aware of Afrikanus Junior's identity. Marais quickly reassured him. He was not to tell Malan that Afrikanus Junior was Marais, he said. He could tell him that he was ... Well, let's say Smit – J. de V. Smit of the Waterberg. He was not to submit a sample of the handwriting, as this would unduly complicate matters.

The trick worked. *Land en Volk*'s foreman typesetter met the civil servant, told him Afrikanus Junior's name and received £50.

In the next issue of the paper Marais exposed the whole affair and asked Malan what he was to do with the £50. At the same time he advised the man to devote more of his time to his job, adding: "Your work leaves much to be desired."

It was June 1895. In a few weeks' time, on 8 July, a Monday, Paul Kruger's railway to Delagoa Bay was to be formally opened. Lettie was expecting her baby at about the same time. It would be ironic if Eugène Marais's first-born was to see the light of day during the festivities celebrating Paul Kruger's great triumph.

Some years before, the railway had been completed from Cape Town to Johannesburg. Kruger had hardly taken note of this achievement. But the completion of the eastern railway, giving the Transvaal an outlet to the sea, was another question. A huge sum, £20 000, had been set aside for the festivities in Pretoria.

4 July – four days before the opening:

In *Land en Volk* Eugène accepted the President's assurance that he had been unaware of the attempt to procure Afrikanus Junior's name.

7 July:

Eugène attended a press conference regarding the reporting of the official events.

8 July:

The day of the opening. Lettie's contractions had started the previous evening. In the early hours of the morning Dr. Kriel had been summoned to Lynnwood House. He eventually turned up, dead drunk – perhaps understandable during a time when Pretoria was celebrating the opening of the railway night after night. In the event, all went well with Lettie's confinement. Between two and three o'clock in the early hours of this winter night a baby boy was born.

Pretoria was bitterly cold before the break of dawn. Only later in the morning did it become another scintillating, sunny Highveld winter's day. By the afternoon, while thousands of spectators streamed to the station, it was almost hot. Eugène Marais too, as editor of *Land en Volk*, joined the crowd.

Zarps keeping back the mass of people. Annoying gusts of wind whipping dust from the loose gravel of the platform. The brass band playing bravely at the station building. The very important visitors on their decorated pavilion. The blue and gold of the uniforms worn by the guard of honour. Banners and streamers, flags and pennants. A quarter to three.

Dr. Kriel was drunk. How negligent had he been?

With a final flourish the brass band finished playing, and a single trumpet sounded a short fanfare. Voices were whispering: "The President", and the distant drumming of horses' hooves could be heard.

If only they had called another doctor, Dr. Veale for instance. He was older and more responsible. With him nothing would have gone wrong.

The escort – the Mounted Police and members of the Johannesburg Cavalry and Lancers – passed underneath the arch of honour at the entrance to the station and divided into two rows, to allow the black Presidential landau to pass between them. Almost soundlessly, the elegant carriage rolled past the guard of honour, turned parallel to the pavilion and stopped less than five yards from the side of the platform.

Nothing did go wrong. Lettie was completely healthy, the baby normal. Given good care there was no danger.

A uniformed official opened the door of the landau. The President and his travelling companions got out, while a roar from four thousand throats swept the polished rails.

No danger? That was self-delusion. He knew quite well how many apparently healthy young women died after apparently normal confinements.

On the platform on the opposite side, near the landau's back wheels, a group of officers and officials were waiting, but next to the black carriage and its two black horses, very close to the railway, Paul Kruger stood alone, straight and still, leaning on his walking stick. Alone, and perhaps Eugène Marais realised at this moment why it was right that he should be alone, why today he should not be with the others. This was his railway, his magic eastern rail, the route of freedom to the sea. It was his day of triumph. And while Marais watched the scene, a stark tableau dominated by black and white, everything he had learned to despise in Paul Kruger through the years was swept aside and for a moment the old man with the puffy face became a knight in search of the Holy Grail – glorious in every victory. (But would this Sir Percival find it?)

Only for a moment. The distant whistle of the train broke the spell and the knight turned back into an old man in a top hat, obstinate, gruff, unrefined, boorish, the kind of man who began ranting when he was frustrated and wept when ranting helped no more.

"The train! The eastern train!"

The train had been running for six months, but what was happening here today was much more than a ceremonial arrival. The thundering approach of the locomotive bearing the great Transvaal crest and the Vierkleur (the four-coloured Republican flag) on its bow from Delagoa Bay to Pretoria like a battleship was a kind of declaration of independence, and everyone who should know about it was here today to see it happen.

The parents who had lost three quarters of their children at an early age, the young widowers raising a single child – there were dozens of such people among his friends and family.

The steady thud of the locomotive's pistons was now very close. People cheered. The train came to a halt, hissing and blowing off steam.

Dr. Leyds. An excellent speaker (give the devil his due). He should be able to impress the important visitors.

The plot in Sunnyside, the house they intended building there. Would they ever live there?

"... an honour to have with us this afternoon the Honourable Sir Hercules Robinson, Her Majesty's High Commissioner in South Africa."

Two people in the sunlight, two coffins on a rocky ledge. Impossible. Such things happened to others.

"... Cape Colony. The Honourable Sir Walter Hely-Hutchinson, Governor of Natal."

Uncle Charles opening the iron door, looking back across his shoulder and saying: "I don't want you children to come in here."

"The Honourable Sir Graham Bower ..."

"*Promise me you will see to it that nothing happens to me.*"

"... play its justifiable role ..."

Two coffins seen dimly on a ledge. And something else. Something. Suddenly, very clearly, he was again aware of that musty odour.

"... the eastern rail."

"Eugène!"

At home all was well. His fears had been unfounded. There was nothing wrong with Lettie. He ought really to stay at her side tonight, but duty called. It was the night of the press dinner.

He went along and delivered his speech: early experiences in the Transvaal press. A brief report about it appeared in *The Press* the next day, lacking even the customary disparaging comment. Pretoria was celebrating. It was a time of goodwill.

The next day Eugène also attended the official banquet, one of 250 guests.

It was only some days later that Lettie's condition deteriorated. She had puerperal fever.

Saturday came. By two o'clock that afternoon, while Pretorians were driving to the races in their spiders, her fever had not yet broken.

It was Saturday evening and everywhere in Pretoria the parties began, and it was Sunday morning, Cape carts and landaus taking ladies and gentlemen to church in their best Sunday dress.

By Sunday afternoon, when the tables in the great houses were set with dainty cups and saucers, and dishes of cakes and pastries crowded the lace tablecloths, everyone in Pretoria who counted knew that there was virtually no hope for Mrs. Eugène Marais. Dr. Engelenburg of *De Volksstem* and Nathan of *The Press* went to Lynnwood House to inquire after her welfare personally and then wrote short reports about her condition for their newspapers.

Early in the new week her mind started wandering. Eugène, sitting next to her bed, heard snatches of episodes and conversations from her childhood days, things she herself may consciously have forgotten. He heard the names of people he had never known, women and men – cousins, friends, more than friends? Only very occasionally something from their short life together.

She died in the early hours of 17 July. She was not yet twenty-four.

The Rev. Bosman led the service in Lynnwood House. The coffin was covered in a multitude of wreaths. A procession of more than fifty carriages followed the hearse to the central cemetery, where she was buried in the Helde-akker, that part of the cemetery reserved for the heroes from Pretoria's past and its prominent people.

The established custom of the time among Afrikaners was that the first son should be named after his paternal grandfather. Eugène ignored this rule, having the baby christened Eugène Charles Gerard, his own name and the names of his brother Charles of Boshof, whom he had long adopted as his real father.

Eugène Marais was unable or unwilling to look after the child himself. His sister, Sophie Ueckerman, took the baby into her care.

The story has a footnote, which is mentioned because it was to play a part in Eugène Marais's life more than once in the future.

On 18 August, only five weeks after the birth of Lettie's baby, the wife of his old friend, the land surveyor A.C. Vlok, also gave birth to a son. Once more Dr. Kriel attended, and once again he was drunk. Within ten days the young mother died of puerperal fever.

At that time nobody knew what the illness was or what caused it. Some women got it, others did not. The people of Pretoria did know that it could strike even after the most careful treatment. But in the case of Mrs. Vlok – and possibly also Mrs. Marais – the doctor had not only been drunk, he had been grossly negligent.

Dr. Kriel was ordered, rather than requested, to leave Pretoria.

He was never to be tolerated there again. A quarter of a century was to pass before he visited the capital once more, and hardly had he moved into his hotel when a delegation of old Pretorians came to see him. He was told to leave the city at once.

But Lettie was dead.

9. The Cruellest Pain

One of the several legends surrounding Eugène Marais – one which he himself had helped to foster – was that the death of his wife had driven him to morphine. And although the legend is obviously false, it does contain an important grain of truth.

Without Lettie the anchor ropes had been cut; without Lettie there was grief to be submerged. In morphine (thus Marais was to put it later in a little known poem, without actually mentioning the drug by name) the most miserable mortal could find "heling vir die felste pyn" – "balm for the cruellest pain".

As repeatedly happened in times of great crisis, Eugène fled to his brother Charles in Boshof. A single letter which he wrote from Boshof has come down to us. It tells one virtually nothing about his condition, except perhaps that he was not thinking quite clearly:

> My dear Theo
> I thank you from the bottom of my heart for your kind letter. At the present moment I cannot write to you at length: when I find peace of aim I trust that I shall find opportunity to lay bare my heart to you …

It is not known who Theo was.

Three lines from a poem written at about this time and discovered some years later by Gustav Preller in one of the drawers of Marais's desk, may cast rather more light:

> A starless night is closing round.
> Farewell, my Love, for thou wert lost
> ere yet thy love I found.

Eugène Marais had had a marriage of less than eleven months to find Lettie's love – and to find his love for her.

Because of a series of circumstances already referred to, eleven months was far too short a time. Sorrow mixed with regret, self-reproach and feelings of guilt may develop barbs. The wounds they cause may fester.

To the other factors self-pity should be added, an element which was to play a considerable part in Marais's life. During the course of an intimate conversation with his son, he was later to supply one key to his tragedy in the words of the mid-Victorian Dutch poet, Jacques Perk: "I have embraced my pain and loved her as a bride. Now she has turned into an ogress."

In endlessly fretting about Lettie's death, in endlessly embracing his own pain, where did he put the blame?

He blamed himself.

He blamed his son – in the first weeks or months after the death of a beloved wife in childbirth probably not an unnatural reaction.

He blamed it on Dr. Kriel, who had been drunk. Better than most people Eugène Marais knew that puerperal fever was not caused by drunk doctors and that it could strike even after the most punctilious, most careful treatment. But who, in these circumstances, could think logically?

Marais's return from Boshof coincided with a certain report about Sammy Marks which goaded him into one of the most vicious attacks of his journalistic career.

Sammy Marks was a gnome-like Lithuanian Jew, one of Paul Kruger's many Jewish admirers and, in his case, with good reason. Kruger's concession policy had made him a millionaire.

Now, when Marais returned to Pretoria, he learnt that Marks had donated £10 000 to build a statue on Church Square in honour of the President. Marks had bought the monopoly to manufacture liquor for the entire Transvaal only a few years before for £120 000 from Eugène's arch-enemy Alois Nellmapius. The donation came from the profits on liquor.

All his hatred and resentment of Kruger rose up in him like a flame. And there were other factors to fan the blaze. He had been brought up to regard liquor as an evil, and he himself had little taste for it. He thought of the legacy of misery it had left in his own family. He thought of Ewald Esselen, now thirty-seven, who had lately been drinking more than even he could handle. He thought of all the young men who had made promising starts here in Pretoria and were now slowly drowning in the shandycafs and splits, the dog-noses and the cangoes of the canteens.

He thought of Dr. Kriel.

And now, only two months after Lettie's death, writing as Afrikanus Junior in *Land en Volk*, he launched perhaps the fiercest attack he had ever made on the President:

> Let our children be taught that the statue is not being erected by a grateful people to honour a great leader but by a Jew who obtained the money for it from selling liquor to our people, for which he had a monopoly. Let our children know that the price paid for the statue consists of the tears of widows, the lamentations of orphans and the poverty and misery of entire families. Once they know this, the influence of the statue will not be evil only.
>
> Let the children also be taught the significance of the statue in the political field. Let it stand as an image of the despicable speculation and concession policies that have done so much to destroy our country. Let it stand as an image of the domination by foreigners under which our people have suffered so long. Let it stand as an image of all that a Transvaal child should hate and let our children be taught to pass the statue with abomination in their hearts.

Old Pretoria had in the meantime made plans to help the two young friends – Eugène Marais and Christiaan Vlok – who had suffered so cruelly. And, typically of the time and place, it was decided *for* them that they should undertake a long sea voyage.

Late in 1895 they left for Mauritius on a Castle liner.

Eugène had been getting to know the increasingly doubtful joys of morphine for three years. Now he was to learn the pain of morphine. On the voyage Christiaan Vlok had watched his friend. He was deeply worried about him. Without foreseeing the consequences, he threw Eugène's morphine tablets into the sea.

By this time Eugène Marais knew a great deal about morphine. He knew about the American morphine addict – at that time it was a well known and much discussed case – who had departed on a voyage without morphine in a last desperate attempt to cure himself. Forty-eight hours later, unable to endure withdrawal any longer, he had jumped overboard and drowned.

Eugène knew the story. He knew the literature. But nothing he had read or heard had prepared him for the agony which followed. Chain-smoking hardly helped at all. Alcohol helped a little. No doubt the ship's doctor was consulted. He probably gave Eugène what he could: several popular medicines of the time contained a certain amount of opium.

Everything helped only temporarily. Time and time again the symptoms returned, time and time again in a more severe form. In the first twenty-four hours they were already extremely uncomfortable. A day later they seemed intolerable. The relief only set in after several days.

Mercifully, Eugène Marais was not yet a hardened morphine addict in 1895. By the time they reached land again – this was how A.C. Vlok was later to tell the story to his son – Eugène was cured of his morphine addiction. The suffering, the bitter reproaches, had now changed into gratitude. Eugène took his syringe from his pocket and looked into his friend's eyes.

"I no longer need it," he said. "Please take it as a memento, Christiaan, to remember that I shall be eternally grateful to you. On this voyage you have done nothing less than save my life."

That Vlok had thrown the morphine into the sea and that Marais had thanked him and had handed over his syringe as a gesture – these facts are quite probably correct. However, it is known that sudden forced withdrawal creates a resistance on the part of the patient, so that the "cure" is virtually always of short duration. If a period of total abstention followed the voyage, it could not have lasted for long.

At the end of November 1895 Eugène celebrated his return to Pretoria by instituting two actions for libel, one against the *Volksstem* and one against Tobias Smuts, commandant of Ermelo.

It was exactly a month before the Jameson Raid.

10. Doctor Jameson's Ride

More than two years before the Jameson Raid a British warship, the *Camperdown*, had sunk another British ship, the *Victoria*, in the Mediterranean by sailing into it amidships.

"Johannesburg is in the position of the *Victoria,*" Eugène Marais had warned one of the Uitlander leaders, Charles Leonard, by letter during that same year. "Your force is parallel. You are turned broadside onto us. I can foresee but one result in case of collision – the triumphant issue of my own people."

Now it had happened. By the end of 1895 there was open talk of revolution in Johannesburg. On 26 December Charles Leonard published a manifesto in which he demanded drastic reforms for the Uitlanders. For Leonard knew something the Government did not. At that stage Jameson and his eight hundred men were advancing on the Transvaal border.

From Johannesburg Landdrost Von Brandis notified the Government the same day that everything was in order. The President was still on his annual visit to the *platteland* (the country districts). Commandant-General Joubert was on his way to Pretoria from his farm.

When the General arrived in Pretoria the next day, a Friday, a letter from a Scottish carpenter awaited him. Writing from Johannesburg, the man warned him that the Uitlanders intended revolting on Old Year's Eve. British troops, he added, were waiting on the Bechuanaland border to come to their aid.

Armed burghers began arriving in Pretoria. Many Transvalers were spoiling for a fight. Many of them felt the same way as Oom Hans Botha, who had told the President that he already had five English bullets in his body dating from the first war against the English but that he could always make room for a few more.

Not only the burghers were in a belligerent mood; the Johannesburgers, too, were furious. The great franchise debate in August, which was a sequel to the latest Uitlander petition signed by 32 000 people, had raised tremendous expectations. In the end, nothing had come of it. In the meantime General Joubert had remained in contact with his most important supporters – Ewald Esselen, Eugène Marais and others. Early on Monday morning, less than four days after Leonard's manifesto, Joubert received a dramatic telegram from the commandant and landdrost of Marico: At that moment English troops were cutting the fence next to the telegraph wire inside the Transvaal border. There were about eight hundred men and a number of Maxim machine guns.

Rumours of a revolution in Johannesburg and an armed attack on Pretoria had meanwhile multiplied. It was hard to say where the greater danger lay: in Johannesburg or on the border.

Notifying the Government of the telegram, General Joubert sent instructions to the commandos of Rustenburg, Potchefstroom, Krugersdorp and other districts. At the same time he sent Eugène Marais and his own son-in-law, Abraham Malan, to Johannesburg to hold talks with the Uitlanders in order to establish how serious the situation was there.

Before his departure, Marais barely had enough time to write a report about the raid and hand it to his chief typesetter so that he and his men could rush a special edition of *Land en Volk*.

In Johannesburg the streets were full of excited people. In Commissioner Street there was a procession of several heavy canvas-covered vehicles, apparently gun-carriages. Marais and Abraham Malan were told of fortifications on the Pretoria side of the city and of rifles being distributed to the Uitlanders in front of the Consolidated Goldfields Building.

In the Rand Club they met Charles Leonard and another Uitlander leader, Abe Bailey, with whom they discussed the situation without coming to any conclusion. At that stage Marais and Malan did not yet have a mandate from the Transvaal Government to negotiate with the Uitlanders.

While the two of them were in Johannesburg, General Joubert was summoned to the Executive Council in Pretoria. He found this strange, as he had been there shortly before to outline his defence plans.

In the council hall Dr. Jorissen came up to him and asked without more ado: "General Joubert – do you know that your son-in-law Malan is in contact with the rebels in Johannesburg?"

Greatly surprised, Joubert replied: "Well, what about it?"

"Then it is high treason – and you will have to resign your post!" shouted Jorissen. "I demand it from you."

There was silence in the council chamber. Joubert looked around him, but nobody spoke. Eventually he told Jorissen contemptuously:

"But I will take no notice of you," using the insulting "jou".

"Don't you thee and thou me. I demand your resignation. This is high treason."

Again Joubert said: "I don't intend taking any notice of you" – and again he used the familiar "jou". Turning to the President, he asked: "Do you and the Executive Council want me to resign?"

"Brother Jorissen is being rash," Chief Justice Mr. Kotzé interrupted, and the President added: "Yes, he is jumping to conclusions, he should apologise."

Thus the matter was settled for the time being. Kruger, wise old man that he was in many ways, realised that it could be useful to preserve the contact with Johannesburg by means of people in whom the Uitlanders had confidence. When Marais and Abraham Malan returned to Pretoria, they were received by the Executive Council, which listened to their report about the conditions in Johannesburg and then empowered them to negotiate with the Uitlanders in the Government's name.

The situation seemed serious. Going by the information available to him, General Joubert had estimated that up to 20 000 Johannesburgers might now be armed. In the meantime Jameson's force was rapidly advancing on Johannesburg.

The deadline had arrived: it was the last day of the year, the day of the revolution.

Throughout Southern Africa the news of the Jameson Raid aroused unprecedented indignation in the hearts of almost everyone of Afrikaner descent. In the breakfast-room at Heathfield, his elegant estate in Mowbray near Cape Town, Ryk Piet Marais, regarded by all who knew him as an Anglophile, angrily paced the floor that morning, waving the *Cape Times* and shouting, "Damned blackguard! Infernal villain!"

On the same day his nephew, Eugène Marais, sent an urgent telegram from Pretoria to the Uitlander leaders in Johannesburg, in which he requested another meeting and beseeched them to avoid bloodshed at all costs. "For God's sake, let us meet and settle things like men."

The Government made available a special express train which carried Marais and Abraham Malan to Johannesburg for the second time within two days. At Johannesburg station they were met by Abe Bailey in person and taken to his carriage, where they were blindfolded and driven to an unknown destination.

One can imagine the scene: Marais in the carriage, listening to the shouting multitudes and the roar of traffic – unnaturally loud even for Old Year's Eve. To him it was a sign of the city's unbridled lust for life, its impatience and power. They were restless, he might have thought, because they were preparing themselves to fight for what they regarded as their birthright. It would be a mistake to underestimate the people – by now no fewer than 70 000 of them – who had built the biggest metropolis in Southern Africa on the bare veld within nine years. How would this mass of human life react when Jameson rode up Eloff Street?

In spite of the precautions, Marais recognized the place to which they had been brought. It was the Consolidated Goldfields Building.

At nine that night they met the Reform Committee – a name Marais now heard for the first time – in the company's General Committee Room. There were between fifty and sixty men and he recognized all the ringleaders: Abe Bailey, Charles Leonard, Percy Fitzpatrick, Max Langermann, Hays Hammond, Colonel Francis Rhodes (Cecil Rhodes's brother).

Eugène Marais and Abraham Malan listened to the Uitlanders' case and in turn gave them the Government's point of view. Marais, the more fluent in English, did most of the talking.

There was an ominous interruption – possibly pre-arranged – when George Farrar, a prominent Uitlander who had not attended the gathering, burst into the room in his shirtsleeves, his hands covered in oil, and shouted excitedly: "I say, fellows, come and give me a hand with the ammo!"

Charles Leonard and the others smiled embarrassedly at the interruption – or pretended to be embarrassed. Farrar departed with apologies and the discussion continued.

Not until shortly before midnight did the meeting decide to accept the Government's offer: a deputation would leave for Pretoria early the next morning to negotiate on the basis of the demands in the manifesto.

At five to twelve that night Marais sent a telegram to Pretoria to report the result of their negotiations. Hardly had the telegram been sent when church-bells began ringing somewhere, and at the twelfth stroke a tremendous tumult broke out from all directions: gun-shots, the cracking of the long whips with which the Johannesburgers delighted in disturbing the peace, the shouts and cries of thousands of men in all parts of the city.

The new year, 1896, had begun.

The next morning, 1 January, the Uitlander Commission which was to negotiate with the Government in Pretoria set off for the capital by train. Marais and Abraham Malan accompanied them.

On the same morning Dr. Jameson rejected the British High Commissioner's request to return to Bechuanaland.

That afternoon at three o'clock his force reached the Queen's Mine outside Krugersdorp, where the first serious clash with the commandos began.

General Joubert's plans were laid.

The next morning before the break of day, four hundred burghers of Potgieter and Malan's commandos advanced on Doornkop where they dug themselves in, while hundreds of others lay in wait all along the road from Krugersdorp to cut off Jameson's route to Johannesburg. As Commandant Cronjé's commando started closing the pincer in the west, Jameson was forced to move further south while the Boers evacuated one koppie after the other according to plan to allow him through – further south, ever closer to Doornkop, where the four hundred burghers were awaiting him in an impregnable position.

Now he could go no further. Rifle fire from Doornkop would make it impossible for him to reach the road to Johannesburg. Burghers surrounded him on all sides. He could expect no assistance from Johannesburg. His men were exhausted and hungry, his horses on their last legs.

When Jameson surrendered soon afterwards by hoisting the white apron of a black woman, Eugène Marais – as he was to state later – was one of the Transvalers who went to meet the invaders. Marais acted as an interpreter, and in this capacity also formed part of the guard which took Jameson and his officers to Pretoria.

Jameson and his men surrendered on 2 January and the Reformers were arrested. In the end it turned out that Johannesburg could hardly have carried off a revolution: only three thousand Uitlanders had been armed, not twenty thousand as General Joubert had thought. The vehicles seen in the streets of Johannesburg by visitors were not gun-carriages but mining machinery covered with canvas to give the impression of heavy artillery.

But there was no question about the Johannesburgers' intentions and the burghers were in a dangerous mood when members of the Reform Committee were brought to trial in Pretoria. At one stage there was even a petition that the advocates for the defence should be put over the border. The public mood became uglier still when Commandant Henning Pretorius, Eugène Marais's old friend and ally, returned from a holiday in the Cape Colony and brought a beam with him.

It was an ordinary thick wooden beam which had been built into a house near Cookhouse but it had ominous and highly emotional connotations. Seventy years before, during the Slachter's Nek Rebellion, the British authorities at the Cape had hanged six rebellious border farmers from that very beam – and had then hanged them again when the gallow-ropes had broken. This beam now came close to causing the deaths of the four Reform Committee leaders who had just been found guilty of high treason.

But Kruger acted wisely – in this case, as even Marais had to admit, much more wisely than General Joubert. He refused to give the English their own Slachter's Nek and all four Uitlanders were spared the death penalty. Lionel Philips, George Farrar, Francis Rhodes and Hays Hammond were as fortunate as Jameson and his fellow invaders, who had long been handed over to the British Government for punishment.

If Ryk Piet Marais was furious about the Jameson Raid, feelings ran very much higher still in the Transvaal. Faced by this kind of menace they had to have a strong leader. Consequently, Paul Kruger was more widely supported than ever, while Joubert's following declined. The burghers were still reproaching the Commandant-General – not without justification – for not having provided artillery at Doornkop and for having allowed the country to be caught off guard by the invaders. Some of them also reproached him for having sent his son-in-law and Eugène Marais of *Land en Volk* to negotiate with the Reform Committee. For them it smacked far too much of collusion with traitors.

The general feeling against General Joubert was not improved when he sued Dr. Jorissen for libel because of Jorissen's attack in the Executive Council.

Under the circumstances Marais had to break off his financial links with the gold magnates. The Johannesburg subsidy came to an end. Without this money he could hardly manage, but he had no choice. If it should now become known that *Land en Volk* was being financed by Uitlanders, the newspaper would lose all its influence. In the country's present mood even General Joubert would want nothing more to do with it, for he who had been so meek was terribly vengeful after the raid. This may have been a reaction to the criticism showered on him as a result of his negligence. In the end Ewald Esselen had to plead with him to vote for the motion in support of pardon for the Reformers in the Executive Council.

A direct consequence of all these factors was a decrease in *Land en Volk*'s circulation. Kruger was the man who had saved the Republic, and criticism of his Government had become unpopular – that is to say, as far as criticism was still allowed, for the "Hou-Jou-Bek-Wet" (Hold-Your-Tongue Act), as Marais disparagingly called the new Press Act in his leaders, was subjecting newspaper editors to irritating new restrictions. Thus the celebrated career of Afrikanus Junior had to come to a summary end, as the new Act prohibited the use of pseudonyms in letters to the press.

Marais was furious, but he could do nothing about it and he had to witness the beginning of the vicious circle which was to endanger the existence of the newspaper itself. The lack of the subsidy from Johannesburg, coupled with the dwindling circulation, forced him to canvass more advertising, so that the ratio between advertising and copy started to become extremely unhealthy - at its worst, one day in August, more than thirty columns of advertisements opposed to half a column of news.

It was a situation which could lead to a further decline in circulation and then even to the danger point where companies might stop advertising altogether. Money was scarce. The previous years' prosperity was no more. Shares had dropped and after the failure of the Jameson Raid, the big investors were keeping back their capital while studying the situation.

Early in the year something happened which many burghers, especially the older ones, regarded as divine retribution: the great explosion in Braamfontein near Johannesburg. In fact the crater was almost impressive enough to make one believe in the supernatural: 250 feet long by 50 feet deep. Some of the eighty dead were virtually pulverized: four crates of human remains were picked up in the vicinity.

A few trucks of dynamite which had been left in the hot sun too long had taken ten times more lives than the Jameson Raid.

There were other visitations. That summer the drought was so severe that water was sold by the pail in the streets of Johannesburg. In an attempt to make rain artificially, one of the mining companies shot explosives into the clouds above the Wanderers – to the shocked consternation of the conservative members of the Volksraad, who regarded this action as sacrilege.

In Eugène Marais's personal life destruction was reaching new heights; only morphine allowed him to forget. His mother had stopped discussing the subject with her son.

Aided by his foreman typesetter Marais tried to compensate for the decline in *Land en Volk*'s fortunes in other ways, for example by doing commercial printing – visiting cards, testament forms, deeds of transfer, price-lists. He bought new fonts and published increasingly larger advertisements for commercial printing in *Land en Volk*. In the end he also became, at a commission, the Pretoria agent of Dave Moss's huge lottery company in Johannesburg, which sold £30 000 worth of tickets for every horse-race.

Naturally, there were the wits who wondered why Eugène Marais, always so severely critical of Kruger's co-operation with the Jews, had now himself become the agent of a Jew.

It is not quite clear from all this whether Marais was making or losing money in this last year he spent in Pretoria before leaving for Europe. The former seems more likely. It does seem as if he still had the support of the Uitlanders, even if only indirectly in the form of advertising, commercial printing and agencies.

However, his reserves were weakened early in September when in the libel case he had instituted against Tobias Smuts shortly after his return from Mauritius, his advocates could not prove beyond doubt that Smuts had written the libellous letter. Marais had to fork out the legal costs, amounting to almost £500. The £50 damages received from *De Volksstem* earlier that year was swallowed up like one of the fat cows of Egypt.

Just a week after the financial blow of the libel case against Smuts, Eugène's father, Jan Christiaan Nielen, died. He was seventy-seven. There was no estate. The old man had long since lost every penny.

His mother, she who had been so strong – without her lame duck of a husband, whose whims and fancies, whose real and imaginary ills she had learned to know like the beating of her own heart – who would she care for now and for what would she live?

No longer for her youngest child. Only a month after her husband's death, Catharina Marais, too, lay on her deathbed.

Eugène Marais had loved her like few other people on earth. He held her in his arms. What was there in her dying eyes which made him ask: "Mother! Do you see something?"

And she replied, no longer of this world: "Nothing. There is nothing."

Now only the husk remained – Lynnwood House. The house was old and its walls seemed to echo many voices. Without those about whom it had grown like a shell, what purpose did it serve?

Melt was a good businessman. He decided to demolish the old place and build three smaller houses on the plot. It was quite large enough for that. Eugène could certainly not stay on there alone, said the family. Why couldn't he move into Sophie Ueckerman's boarding house, where he would be with his son?

The boy was fifteen months old now. That was how long Lettie had been dead.

It was a good thing that the house would be demolished. Eugène had been a child here, innocent and happy, and later a young bridegroom. Let oblivion come. Let them wipe it all out. Let them knock down the walls. Let them demolish the last remaining memory. And let him flee.

He was toying with the idea of following a course in medicine in Europe. Ewald Esselen advised against it.

"Forget about medicine, Eugène. I know you would make a good doctor, but the Republic needs advocates more urgently. Go to London, attend the Inner Temple – that's where I was. I can give you letters of introduction if you want them."

The decision was soon taken. It was becoming extremely cramped here, the struggle too hard. If all went according to plan he would be in London in six weeks' time, shortly after New Year.

Eighteen ninety-seven would be a great year, a new beginning.

PART 3: THE WIDE WORLD

O waar sal jy gaan en met watter skip? Die aarde is branding en oral is klip ...	Oh where will you go, in what ship fare? The world is all breakers and rocks everywhere ...

1. The Inner Sanctum

In December 1896 Eugène Marais appointed one J. Y. O'Brien, previously editor of *De Pers*, as editor of *Land en Volk* and sailed for London on the mailship, apparently travelling first class.

A fragment from one of Marais's uncompleted short stories may reflect his romantic impressions of the voyage:

> The first dinner on the Dunottar Castle was a clear compromise between convention and rank liberty. So few first class passengers were there on board that the captain's table alone was filled, and a small coterie of the lesser officers at another table constituted all the diners. They were all present because the ship had left the blustering south easter about the Cape of Storms and had only in the afternoon sailed into an almost airless calm ...

In London Marais at once went to the Transvaal Consul, Montagu White, arranging to collect his mail there. As early as 19 January of the new year he was admitted as a law student at the Inner Temple, one of the Inns of Court.

Marais had always been fond of embroidering. In his application to be admitted to the Inns of Court one finds, for the first time in his personal life, misrepresentations on a considerable scale – nothing criminal, but dishonesty to an extent which the average person would find reprehensible.

What Marais sought in London were escape and anonymity. Perhaps for these reasons – and perhaps because he did not find his residential address imposing enough – he gave his address as the "Transvaal Consulate, London". His successful application is recorded in the Inner Temple's Stamp Book:

"Let Eugène Marais (aged 26) of the Cape University and of the Transvaal Consulate, London, the youngest son of Jan Christiaan Nielen Marais, Pretoria, South African Republic, advocate, be generally admitted to this society ..."

Marais had never attended a college or university at the Cape (or anywhere else for that matter), nor did he have any connections with the Consulate, nor had his father ever been an advocate. But undergraduates were required to pass an examination in English, Latin and English history before their admission, and no doubt Marais found it below his dignity either to admit that he had never obtained a degree or to write elementary exams.

Conversations with Ewald Esselen and other Transvaal friends had acquainted Marais with the rather involved system of the Inns of Court. Each year contained four terms of 23 days, each ending with an examination: Hilary, Easter, Trinity and Michaelmas. Students had to write the finals for four subjects, but they were also required to "keep terms" by attending six of the twenty-three dinners in each term. Before being called to the Bar they had to complete twelve terms.

During the first three terms Marais found no trouble in complying with these regulations. But like many adults who have not studied for a long time, he had hopelessly underestimated the academic side of the course.

By the middle of the year he informed O'Brien, his acting editor, who duly reported it in *Land en Volk,* that he had successfully completed his first exam. In fact, he was not to write this exam until October, and he performed anything but brilliantly. Far more serious misrepresentations regarding his academic progress were soon to follow.

One imagines Marais going to the Inner Temple at year's end to see how he had fared in the Hilary exam, his second. London would have seemed gay in its covering of snow, like a scene from *A Christmas Carol.* In the Strand the densely massed cabs and carriages moved forward sluggishly. On top of the double-decker horse-drawn trams Marais could see the happy, beaming faces of rows of passengers. When two trams passed one another, the passengers would shout to one another exuberantly, their voices echoing in the frozen air.

On the notice-board in the Inner Temple Marais found a copy of the examination results:

> *Subj. II, Const. Law & Legal Hist. Pass:*
> *50/170.* His eyes scanned the list of names: *Khastgvi ... L'Estrange ...*
> *Lewis ... Marais. Marais, E.N. Terms kept:*
> *4. Oral & written exam.: 43/170.*

He had seven marks less than fifty; only seven below a pass. Just like Ewald Esselen in the election in Potchefstroom.

He could not bring himself to accept this. The report published in *Land en Volk* the next month gave the impression of a brilliant achievement.

Marais had just passed his third law examination at the Inner Temple, said the report. "The last two exams were passed within six weeks. This is a record for a South African student. But he had to work extremely hard to do so, and after the examination he was obliged to take a breather."

Should these words be seen as an attempt to present some indiscretion of which word had perhaps reached Pretoria, in a more favourable light? The report continued:

"He intends entering for the final exams in May, and hopes that the authorities of the Inner Temple will exempt him from a few terms so that he will be able to return to the country of his birth as soon as possible."

Nothing ever came of these plans. In May Marais did indeed write another exam, but it was nothing more than a supplementary exam to subject II. This time he passed it.

The next month *Land en Volk* dutifully reported that Marais had passed another exam – i.e. the fourth and last.

Nothing came of his intention to pass all his subjects within sixteen months and return to the Transvaal. Not before five years after his arrival in London was he to scrape through the last exam. In between, periods of up to eighteen months were to pass in which he wrote no exam at all.

What then did he do? We shall come to that. First, one should note that the more than five years Marais spent in Europe (mainly in London) are inordinately obscure. While during his editorship of *Land en Volk* his movements could be traced from month to month, week to week and occasionally even day to day, many months were to pass in London in which, biographically speaking, he simply disappeared and in which it is impossible to give an account of his life.

Sources are limited and unreliable. Most of Marais's own statements regarding his stay in London were made more than thirty years later, at a time of mental and physical degeneration, when he himself could hardly tell truth from fiction. His London "diary" – not a diary in the real sense, but loose, undated notes and observations – is a slim one. Letters dating from the period are rare. In 1962 the author of this life-story spent a month in London where, with the generous assistance of the British Council, he tried to follow up every possible clue of which he was aware. It seemed as if somebody had erased the spoor. It is also possible that the clues were false.

If it had been Eugène Marais's intention to lose himself among the six million inhabitants of London, he succeeded rather well in doing so – to this day.

Unless new discoveries are made, which seems highly unlikely, it will always remain impossible to give a coherent report of the five years Marais spent in Europe. As the outlines of a body which has long since fallen into dust can to some extent be guessed from the shape of the semi-fossilized clay in which it was embedded, certain deductions about Marais's stay in Europe can be made from the history of the era, from what we know about Marais's life before and after London, and also from the way in which his personality changed before and after those crucial five years. These chapters, then, contain much more conjecture than any other part of the life-story.

2. An Adopted Daughter

In the year of Eugène Marais's arrival in London we find him at 24 Lewisham Park, S.E.

It sounds like a suite of rooms, what was known at the time as "chambers". In actual fact it was the simplest kind of accommodation: a downstairs dining-room with a staircase leading to a bedroom in the attic.

Marais frequently called at the Transvaal Consulate, to collect mail or to have talks with Montagu White, who at this stage was collecting evidence for the House of Commons' Committee of Enquiry into the part played in the Jameson Raid by Rhodes's Chartered Company – "a committee of no enquiry" as it came to be called. There seems little doubt that Marais was doing his best to help the Consul promote the interests of the Transvaal.

Marais's entry into British society of the time was gained not only through Montagu White, but to an even greater extent through the Reformers who were now in London. There is no contradiction here. Marais was a Transvaal patriot for whom the Uitlanders had considerable respect.

Thus Percy Fitzpatrick, one of the members of the Reform Committee, wrote after the Jameson Raid: "Mr. Eugène Marais has worked consistently and honourably both for his people, the Transvaal Dutch, and for the cause of pure and enlightened government ... No one in the country has fought harder against the abuses which exist in Pretoria, nor has anyone risked more, nor yet is there a more loyal champion of the Boer."

A prominent Uitlander Marais knew in London was Hays Hammond, one of the four rebels sentenced to death and later pardoned.

As an American, Hammond may not have been completely acceptable in late Victorian London. On the other hand, he was one of the world's best known mining engineers, a member of that coterie to whom the great ones listened as avidly in London as in California or Johannesburg. More important: he had been condemned to death. That death sentence opened doors in the highest circles. Years later Hammond's wife was to tell how she had sat next to Eugène Marais at a dinner party and what refined and charming company he was.

It may have been through contacts of this kind that Marais was introduced to Marie Corelli, one of the most popular novelists of the time, whose *Mighty Atom* had been published the previous year. Marie Corelli never allowed her publishers to send out review copies; the critics were much too hostile. But so perfectly did her work reflect the spirit and taste of the age that she had become a popular idol. To the charming young man from the Transvaal she gave a signed picture of herself. In that year she was 43 years old and Marais 27. Even so, it sounds unlikely that – as he was to claim later – she wanted to marry him.

Henry Irving was another acquaintance of the time, the greatest actor of the period, then at the height of his fame, and manager of London's best known theatre, the Lyceum. Marais also met Gerald du Maurier, another theatre manager cum actor, but much younger than Irving. Gerald's father, George du Maurier, was the author of *Trilby*, one of the most famous novels of the nineties, which describes the romantic Bohemian life of the Parisian artists and in which the villain, Svengali, subjects a young girl to his will by hypnosis, turning her into a passive automaton. Striking echoes of this theme were to reappear in Marais's life years later.

At the Inner Temple, Marais's studies were not given the attention they required, but he did attend the dinners fairly faithfully. From his rooms he could get there by cab for a shilling, travelling into the City, then leaving Fleet Street by Whitefriar's Gate, crossing first the grounds of the Inns of Court and then those of King's Bench Walk. The cab would stop opposite the Terrace and in front of the massive series of grey buildings of the Inner and Middle Temples. From there it was only a short walk to the Hall, where the dinners were admittedly not up to Café Royal standards but where the tradition of centuries was a permeating and soothing one, the faded coats of arms on the walls overlooking the long oak table where the students would sit through the lengthy meals, getting to know one another rather less formally with the assistance of claret and port.

Quite a number of Marais's fellow students came from India, young men with names like Khastgvi, Ahmed, Patel, Singh, Sethu and Thakore. Marais might have been something of an impostor but a racist or snob he was not. He soon got to know the members of these "lesser breeds" of the British Empire. Meeting for a cup of tea in a tea-room or in their rooms, the young Transvaal widower would listen to the seditious talk of these dark young men. Their greatest ideal – and this was the most important bond between them and Marais – was to cast off the British yoke.

The Transvaal Consulate, the Uitlanders and the high society in which they moved, the world of the theatre, the aspirations of Indian students – for a student London had a thousand seductive faces.

In this year, 1897, the aged Queen Victoria had been on the throne for sixty years and during her reign London had become the greatest and richest city on earth. To anyone with an English background, like Marais, it was the capital of the world.

Not only was it incredibly huge; it was also new, modern, progressive, dynamic. In this century it had changed beyond all recognition. Scores and scores of the villages of half a century before had become suburbs or metropolitan neighbourhoods. In 1800 three bridges had spanned the Thames; there were now at least eight. The huge underground railway system was expanding constantly. Omnibuses were so abundant that steps were being considered to restrict their numbers. From fewer than a million people in 1800 the population had exploded to almost 4 500 000, or 6 500 000 in Greater London.

Nobody could get to know this macrocosmos completely. The visitor who tried exploring only a small part found himself with a full-time job on his hands.

Of all the hundreds of sights and experiences in London, Eugène Marais was attracted most powerfully to two: the British Museum in Great Russell Street and the Regent's Park Zoo.

To a foreign visitor of the late Victorian era, especially one from a state which until recently had been subservient to Britain, the primary impression left by the British Museum was one of a show of power. Here was stored the loot of Imperial England – Chinese porcelain, art treasures from India, friezes and statues from Babylon and Assyria, the marble of the Parthenon, the contents of Egyptian pyramids.

As suggested in his short story about the voyage, Eugène Marais had sailed to Britain around the west coast of Africa, not through the Suez Canal. In the British Museum he now saw the treasures of ancient Egypt for the first time – and nothing else in the museum fascinated and held him spellbound to a greater extent than this culture of thousands of years ago.

To what degree did Marais's interest in the opium cult spark and inspire his study of Egyptology? The question is not a far-fetched one. One of the great opium symbols of 19th century poetry held pride of place in the Museum's collection of Egyptian antiquities in the year of Marais's arrival in London. This was the enormous red granite bust of the young Memnon, better known as Ramses II.

Until early that century the statue of Ramses II had lain on its face among the temples of Thebes. When it was borne in triumph to Britain after the Napoleonic wars and given a place of honour in the British Museum, it had created a tremendous stir. For the next two generations it was to seize the imagination of English poets. It is the Ozymandias of Shelley's haunting poem; it appears repeatedly in the work of Keats; for De Quincey it symbolized the "breathlessness which belonged to a saintly trance", becoming, in one reference after another, the tangible expression of an opium reverie.

There is little doubt that Marais was aware of the statue's deep symbolic significance. One can picture the scene: the handsome twenty-six year old Transvaal burgher stands facing the massive statue in the year of his arrival in London, staring in wonder and amazement into the huge, apparently blind eyes, and being absorbed, for long moments, in the god-king's dream.

It is not hard to imagine an experience of this kind encouraging a young man like Marais to start studying the enigmatic civilization of ancient Egypt.

The papyrus Marais was to mention much later in connection with his studies of Egyptology was in the Museum at the time. Later it was to be called by another name, but by the end of the 19th century it was known as "The travels of an Egyptian". The huge papyrus, 8,25 m long and 20,5 cm high, consisted of letters written by a military scribe to another scribe in the 13th century B.C. By 1897 it was more than 3 000 years old.

Presumably using books which contained both facsimile reproductions and English translations of portions of this papyrus, Eugène Marais acquired the art of deciphering hieratic hieroglyphs, at least after a fashion. One need only look at some lines from the document to suspect that Marais was not only intrigued by the enigmatic symbols but also stirred by the Biblical manner of the existing translations: "A horse is harnessed for thee, swift as the jackal, red of ear; it is like a storm of wind when it goes forth. Thou loosest the rein and seizest the bow. Let us see what thy hand will do."

In the vast Regent's Park Zoo, Marais returned to other memories of his own continent, and here with an even greater longing. It was a pleasant outing: by train to Portland Road and across the park on foot, a distance of about three-quarters of a mile. For the thousands of child visitors the centre of attraction was the monkey house, a large building almost in the centre of the great zoo. So Marais found it too.

Later Marais was to state that the baby chimpanzee he reared and studied in his rooms during his stay in London was made available to him by the zoo itself. It is at least equally probable that he obtained it from a pet shop.

In the cold London winter the small animal contracted pneumonia. Marais lovingly nursed his adopted "daughter", Sally, but all his affection did not prevent her from crying bitterly. So human were the sounds she made that the neighbours in the adjoining rooms eventually began wondering where the young man had acquired a baby.

At a later stage he added a marmoset to his collection of pets, a South American monkey which was kept in a bird-cage to protect the tiny animal from the chimpanzee's attentions during Marais's absence.

Set against the improbable background of London, we see in this friendship between Marais and a couple of primates an almost equally revolutionary development as his later baboon studies. Marais not only kept the chimpanzee as a pet, he adopted her as a child in the house. Sally even had a high baby chair to sit on at table.

Studying primates by turning them into members of a family was not to become accepted practice until half a century later.

At the same time we have fascinating glimpses of the real beginnings of *My Friends the Baboons* and *The Soul of the Ape*. In his parental home, Lynnwood House, Marais had probably kept monkeys or baboons, perhaps both, but never had he studied a primate as intensively and at such close quarters as he studied Sally in London. Between the chimpanzee – the most intelligent of all primates – and the marmoset, he was beginning to acquire some insight into both the intellectual abilities and limitations of primates. He was beginning to sense something of their personality, their "soul".

What Eugène Marais should have done now – the hindsight of eight decades later – was to drop his half dozen interests, continue his legal studies and at the same time write a slim, readable little book about his adopted daughter, Sally – light and entertaining, as he was capable of doing, with no pretensions or philosophical speculation. It would have been the first book of its kind and it could have become a minor classic.

But for that he did not have the time.

3. "O for Excess!"

By this time it should be clear why Marais failed his second subject eleven months after his arrival in London, why in May of the next year he had not completed more than half his course – while he had hoped to leave London by that month – and why the Boer War was to trap him in London before he had managed to write a single further examination.

"Everything is drifting to the dogs," he had written to his friend and colleague Jimmy Roos three years earlier and these words had now become the complete truth. Half a dozen interests which had nothing to do with his course go a long way towards explaining his lack of success. But there were more subtle reasons for the condition into which he was lapsing.

Eugène Marais had grown up in an English literary and art tradition, a seductive one, as heady as champagne.

It was a tradition which went back to post-revolutionary France. The guillotine had wiped out the aristocracy; Napoleon's campaigns had killed off many of the courageous and adventurous ones who remained. The bourgeoisie – a money-grabbing lot, humourless, completely lacking in imagination – were firmly entrenched.

It was against this formidable, ubiquitous middle class that some thinkers began rebelling between ten and twenty years after the Battle of Waterloo. The writer and the artist no longer had patrons. Worse, there was no longer room for him, as his contribution to the economy was nil. He had to make do. No one was willing to help him. He was forced to live in the cheapest neighbourhood, and even there in an attic. Frequently he had no money to pay the rent or buy food.

Before the middle of the century the new way of life which had evolved from these circumstances was epitomized in a book which was to have a profound influence on the intellectual life of the 19th century. This was *Scènes de la Vie de Bohème* by Henri Murger. It reflected the artist's and the writer's resistance to the detested bourgeoisie and their petty values. The dingy attics in which they lived, the *grisettes* they kept because they could afford no other female company, eventually became the fashion, the norm. Bourgeois morals were suspect, sanctimonious, corrupt. It was more honest to be *amoral*. If one managed not to pay the bourgeois – the landlord, the restaurateur, the wine merchant – or if one managed to delude him, these were minor triumphs. From this rather naive Bohemian world – in fact little more than an extreme form of robust student merriment – eventually started emerging elements both more refined and more sinister.

Under the morbid influence of De Quincey and Edgar Allan Poe – both opium addicts – the French poet Charles Baudelaire soon began testing every possible sensation and pleasure for the sake of art. "The smoke of hashish rose in a blue cloud and hung over the decorative furniture of the Hôtel Pimodan," wrote William Gaunt in *The Aesthetic Adventure*, "and the court of the fantastic prince became a sort of opium den. In the sensual negress and the sexually aberrated he found, more inspiring to him than ideal beauty, the baneful attraction of the vampire, and the studies he pursued greatly to the detriment of his health and fortune resulted in the famous *Les Fleurs du Mal* of 1857."

Baudelaire, influenced by Anglo-Saxon culture, in turn started influencing the world of Anglo-Saxon art and writing.

In bourgeois London an oasis of moral freedom in Mother Grundy's desert was the house of Dante Gabriel Rossetti, who was later to become addicted to chloral, a soporific and anodyne. To this house came the artist Whistler, who had spent his student years in the Bohemian world on the Left Bank of the Seine and was now shocking his London contemporaries by openly keeping a mistress. Here came another artist, Burne-Jones, who is soon to appear briefly and indirectly in this story. Here came the poet Algernon Charles Swinburne – some of whose work Eugène Marais was later to translate into Afrikaans – and his Jewish artist friend Simeon Solomon, generally even more hopelessly drunk than Swinburne himself.

Swinburne, strongly influenced by Baudelaire, was soon to become the first great English exponent of a new approach to life and to art which by the late seventies had become known as aestheticism. The publication of his *Poems and Ballads* – which, as a Paarl schoolboy, Eugène Marais had quite possibly read under the blanket – caused such a storm of outrage that the publishers had to withdraw the book from circulation.

To the artists of the time, even those who had no natural bent in this direction, dissipation became a coveted way of life. "O for excess, for crime!" wrote George Moore, author of the book, *Confessions of a Young Man*, which might have inspired Eugène Marais to keep a live boa constrictor as a pet when he was a twenty year old journalist in Pretoria.

"O for crime!" These were more than words. Both across the English Channel and, when visiting London, in the citadel of Victorianism itself, two of the greatest French poets of the 19th century, Paul Verlaine and Arthur Rimbaud, were transforming Moore's *cri de coeur* into a way of life.

Alone or in each other's company they put to the proof virtually everything which the Victorian world found repugnant and disgusting – not excluding the bloodlust of bodily harm inflicted by stabbing and shooting.

In these final years of the 19th century a strikingly large number of English writers and artists were leading dissipated, unhappy lives, dying young or comparatively young in spite of the great progress made in medical science during the same period.

Such a one was Richard Middleton, dead before he was thirty. Such a one was the more gifted Ernest Dowson, born four years before Eugène Marais and dead before Marais was to leave London, whose most famous poem might contain a clue to Marais's own later love life: "I have been faithful to thee, Cynara, in my fashion."

Born in the same year as Dowson and also doomed to an early death was the far greater poet Lionel Johnson, author of the sombre, impressive verse "Dark angel", in which he sees the opiates as his menacing angel of doom.

The list is a long one. Francis Thompson, a consumptive and an opium addict – for whose poetry Eugène Marais was in later years to have the greatest admiration – lived the life of a drop-out in London, becoming the confidant of thieves and prostitutes, sleeping under bridges or in poor-houses like a beggar.

This was no longer naive Bohemianism. It was a compulsive urge, to the point of self-destruction, to drain both the sweet and bitter dregs of life. And the French found a word for it: *nostalgie de la boue*, a longing for misery, for the gutter.

Eugène Marais had grown up in this literary tradition; in fact he had grown with it. It explains that boa constrictor in Lynnwood House. It explains his defiant paean to the joys of opium when addressing the Vereeniging Jong Zuid-Afrika (Society of Young South Africa) in Pretoria. It may partly explain his misrepresentations regarding his legal studies in *Land en Volk*. What a delightful bit of deceit, straight from the pages of *La Vie de Bohème*, what a delightful trick to play the idiotic, self-satisfied bourgeois.

Now he had arrived at the fountain-head, in the capital of the world. There was now only a short way left to go. Seen against this background and tradition, it is irresistible to suppose that Eugène Marais, virtually lost among the six and a half million people of Greater London, recklessly practised the supreme art form, life itself, in his early years at the Inner Temple.

In the Marais family there was a story that Eugène's brother Charles – his father figure – was obliged to go and rescue him from an opium den in Hong Kong during his stay abroad. Like so many myths in connection with Marais's life, this one is false but it undoubtedly contains a grain of truth. Much nearer the mark may be a story told by a medical doctor who knew both Charles and his brother well. The story is basically the same, but the locale is not Hong Kong but London itself, the rescuer not Charles but – at Charles's insistence – Scotland Yard.

If Marais felt like visiting an opium den, he would not have had to leave London. Even in Johannesburg there were one or more at the time; in London there were scores, perhaps hundreds.

The Metropolitan Police were well aware of these places, but usually left them in peace. Now and again, in case of trouble, or to set an example, they would raid one of them. To one of these places, in the slums of Shadwell, Charles Dickens, escorted by the police, had ventured some years before to collect material for his uncompleted novel *Edwin Drood*, in which the murderer, John Jasper, frequents an opium den.

Of course Dickens could only take a murderer to such a terrible place. To present an author or artist or poet or student as going there – even if this happened in real life – would have shocked the confidence of his public.

The artist who drew the illustrations for *Edwin Drood* was rather less cautious. True, his opium den is repulsive enough, but the young man leaning against the bed-post, if rather unsteady, could be quite a decent chap at heart. This could well be nothing but a temporary aberration and the young man might be resuming his job or his studies before the week is out – perhaps even his studies at the Inner Temple.

4. Susanne

Woman as a goddess, woman as an object, as a possession – two opposite approaches which, through lack of more precise terms, may be called the chivalrous and the cynical view. The two ways of looking at a woman are often found in one and the same man – they may even be found in one man concerning the same woman, or they may overlap – and so it was with Eugène Marais. Even so, a subtle shift towards the more cynical approach seems to have entered Marais's sexual life in his London years.

The chivalrous or romantic approach is found in the oath of chastity Marais took in 1892, in the poem he wrote after his young wife's early death and in several inscriptions in his London diary.

"Indeed I should hardly have known that her hand rested on my arm at all," he quotes A.E.W. Mason in this diary, "did I not feel its touch more surely on the strings of my heart."

Elsewhere he describes a personal experience:

> Shortly after my arrival in England I went with Dot and Helen to a concert at Little Queen's Hall where a stout man sang the following charmingly. He affected me muchly.
>
> If thou wert blind I'd give my sight
> lest the darkness set me far from thee;
> If thou wert scorned I'd kill my pride

and outcast I would live with thee;
If thou wert dead I'd give my life
In the hope that I might pass to thee.

Although Victorian England was to become proverbial for its narrow-mindedness, a flourishing permissive society in which sex was freely available had been firmly established by the "naughty nineties" – at least underground.

For women of good families premarital intercourse was too dangerous, and the well-to-do student or bachelor either had to find a married woman – an almost equally risky business – or turn to prostitutes. Of these London had an estimated fifty thousand before the Boer War – more than the entire white population of Pretoria. Their fee varied from a few shillings to fifty pounds, and among the best there were refined and even educated girls from genteel but impoverished families.

If Eugène Marais slept with or befriended prostitutes during his stay in London he was in a sense merely keeping up the long tradition of the century which had spawned him – not least the literary tradition. In his *Confessions of an English Opium Eater*, De Quincey writes movingly about Anne, the sixteen year old prostitute who had taken pity on him in London and whom he was later to seek in vain. Francis Thompson, too, was befriended and aided by a girl of the streets. On the Left Bank in Paris prostitutes not only became artists' mistresses, but frequently their models.

In the nineties, for those seeking feminine company in London, there was yet a third solution.

These girls were children – they were sixteen, fifteen, sometimes fourteen years old – who occasionally sold their bodies to relieve the relentless, grinding poverty which was their lot at home. One of them, Kitty, is depicted with great animation in *My Secret Life*, the anonymous writings comprising eleven volumes and 4 200 pages in which a wealthy Victorian gentleman describes his endless amorous adventures.

Kitty was fifteen years old. She had to look after the younger children while her widowed mother went out to "char" but she sometimes left her younger sisters and brothers at home to go for a walk in the Strand, by day. This – as any connoisseur of London could tell one in one's club – was the time and the place to pick up the "little ones".

Kitty used her earnings to buy better food than the dry bread and thin gruel she and her siblings had at home. The author of *My Secret Life* paid her 3/6 at their first meeting. Nonetheless she did not regard herself as a prostitute.

Reading all the way through *My Secret Life* must be a tedious experience, yet the lively, natural dialogue in this part of the work perfectly conveys Kitty's world. In this prim Victorian era the word "fuck" is used unselfconsciously and in a completely functional way. On the other hand Kitty is shocked when the man asks her whether she is "gay" (professional). Not at all, she replies. She allows men to sleep with her, but the gay girls are those who dress specially for it, who come out in the evening and make a living from it.

He questions her about herself – her habits, her life at home. What does she do all day? She washes the two younger children, she replies. If there is food in the house, she feeds them. Then she scrubs the floor and washes down the entire house. There is no bath. There is not even a tub – nothing but a pail and basin. Even so, Kitty always washes herself carefully from head to toe. Her mother always said she was the most beautiful clean daughter a mother ever had.

The charm of these girls must have lain in their naivety and relative innocence. They had not yet been hardened, made cynical and embittered by what was perhaps to come later. For many men, too, their charm lay in their extreme youth.

The third female name to appear in Marais's London diary was that of a sixteen year old girl called Susanne. She and the Kitty of *My Secret Life* were not exact parallels but one is struck by certain similarities. Like Kitty, Susanne was a Cockney, and in London of the nineties, her accent branded her unmistakably, barring the way to middle class society. Perhaps her grandchildren, certainly her great-grandchildren, were to have little trouble in becoming models, movie stars, fashion designers, PRO's, editors and businesswomen, even though they spoke in virtually the same accents.

Might one of these descendants also have been a replica of a handsome young man from the Transvaal Republic?

For Susanne it was infinitely more difficult to follow a respectable career than it was to be for her descendants. She had been given her station in life and she had to accept it. If this worried her, she did not show it. She smiled easily, a charming smile, and if she became annoyed she soon regained her good humour. She liked men – and Eugène very much.

It was not a chance, fly-by-night meeting. Like an artist from the pages of *La Vie de Bohème*, he made a whole series of pencil sketches of her.

In one she is dressed in nothing but a Victorian ostrich-feather hat (feathers from Oudtshoorn?), hands sedately folded over her breasts; in another she is wearing a downy muff. Other sketches are captioned "Susanne in bed" and "Susanne doing her hair for bed". Was it she he remembered years later, or was it Lettie, or a third, or them all, when he was to write of the beauty that passes away:

> Die heerlikheid van vleis en bloed
> die hare wat die sonlig vang
> en weergee in 'n goue gloed!
>
> The loveliness of flesh and blood,
> of hair that catches up the sun
> and reflects it in a golden glow!

He liked to tease her good-naturedly. "What's the time?" he captioned a sketch of Susanne sitting on the bed and putting on her stockings. "Why am I awakened so early?"

He brought her gifts, generous as always. If he also gave her money, this did not make her a prostitute, and he did not regard her as such.

In one sketch he made light-hearted fun of her youth: "Sixteen's back view". She seems to have lived with a much older woman – her mother, she said. Apparently, Marais doubted this, for a sketch of a bespectacled old hag with a large nose and thinning hair was captioned: "Susanne's Ma (?)".

Did Marais live with them at one stage, or did he simply visit the house at times, Susanne spending nights in his rooms? Judging by the pattern of his later life, his relations with the older woman were probably cordial.

As far as Susanne is concerned, so much sophistication and worldly wisdom in a sixteen year old girl need not surprise one in the circumstances. Nor would it be surprising if under her easy laugh and apparent unconcern there was the heart of a frightened doe, nor if Marais saw this and if it aroused all his compassion for wild and bewildered children and animals.

One is too inclined to categorise relationships. No doubt their friendship was based on sex. But all that we know about Marais, both about his nature and about the conditions of his life in London, makes one surmise that it was also a deeper relationship, on her part perhaps one of love. His charm, which had not left him twenty years later, must have been irresistible by the turn of the century.

From Marais's point of view, again judging by later patterns, Susanne may have been the one person in London he really needed, for she was someone to protect.

But Susanne herself, Susanne at sixteen, asks us not to delve too deeply, although she asks it in her own way. Slim legs clad in black silk, holding her clothes in front of her, she tells Eugène – and maybe posterity as well – in one of the sketches: "Don't look."

5. This or Death

To persist systematically in a way of life which one feels to be evil and sinful, is neither easy nor pleasant, at least not in the long run.

In many of the writers and artists who had given themselves wholeheartedly to the cult, the pendulum swung back, frequently too late. Thus the despairing cry of Aubrey Beardsley, dying at 25: "Jesus is our Lord and judge. I implore you to destroy all copies Lysistrata and bad drawings ... By all that is holy all obscene drawings." Swinburne, who had shocked the Victorian era with both his poetry and his excesses, burnt himself out, spending his last days as a total abstainer in a drab suburban house. For his friend, Simeon Solomon, on the other hand, not even the spark could be saved: he died of chronic alcoholism shortly after the turn of the century.

Most tried to save themselves in time from the abyss. For those addicted to opium or other narcotics the way back was always a bitter one and in most cases impossible.

Yet it was they, the drug addicts, more than any others, whose only hope lay in taking the way back, however hard. The way ahead led through ever more densely entwining brambles and thorns. Daily the struggle became harsher, and only seldom, at this stage, was the suffering relieved by tantalizing glimpses of Sleeping Beauty's castle walls behind the hedge of thorns. For opium, and her daughter morphine, eventually have unpleasant surprises for their expectant subjects. The "faces of long-buried beauties called into sunny light" alternate with unexpected nightmares, reflections of guilt.

Many people, including doctors who treated him, were later to testify that Marais was troubled by dreams of fear and anxiety. We do not know what the nature of these dreams was. Unlike some of the great nineteenth-century opium addicts, Marais never described his. Clues to the terrifying visions of his nightmares were only to appear in certain short stories and diary entries shortly before his death. The evidence we do have about the 1890's is second hand.

In *Opium and the Romantic Imagination* Alethea Hayter partially summarizes an opium nightmare of the nineteenth-century poet, George Crabbe.

> And again and again returns the image of a woman, at first recognised as a fiend, a harlot image all too well remembered, with "tainted bosom bare"; then seen as a lost loved one, his dear affectionate wife, but the smiling mask shifts and there is a stranger's terrifying face beneath it; then again she comes as a brilliant fairy creature hung with gems – and in an instant is a shrivelled old corpse, stinking on a pauper's bed.

Was Marais troubled by comparable dreams as early as his student days in London – dreams in which tender memories of Lettie intermingled with images of Susanne, with those of a third, with those of a terrifying stranger?

Whatever the truth was, he would have to take the way back, the way to normality, to a world without morphine, for in morphine he had long recognised the quintessence of evil. In his London "diary" a single quotation allows us to glimpse something of his struggle.

> … like the scorched fly
> that spins in vain
> upon the axis of its pain
> then takes its doom to crawl
> blind and forgot from fall to fall …

In these pages, between quatrains, ironically, in which Omar Khayyám praises the earthly joys, Marais scribbled another fragment from the same poem.

> He sins in hope who sinning says:
> hatred of sin God's judgment stays.

Hatred of sin. This was no exaggeration. Every fibre in his body hated the white tablets, hated the syringe, hated and adored – and hated the more for the adoring.

Further clues to this struggle appear in a book-plate which Marais had designed and printed in 1898.

The singular and enigmatic engraving shows a prince kneeling at the gate of a garden (of Eden?) or park, or churchyard. In the foreground is an African ringhals – not an Indian cobra as it seems to be at first sight – hooded, tongue flickering, ready to strike. In the top right-hand corner are the words "Dit of Dood" – "This or Death".

The ringhals, combined with the fact that Marais himself practised drawing at the time, makes it virtually certain that he designed the book-plate himself and then had it copied by a professional artist. It was not simply thrown together from a number of hackneyed symbols fashionable at the time. Marais himself made the statements contained in the *ex libris*, consciously or not.

Explicit images and symbols played such a striking role throughout Marais's life that one is inclined to jump to the obvious conclusion: only prayer could save him from evil. And the nature of that evil is entirely clear – the flickering morphine syringe injecting a jet of venom into the veins, and in the end killing its victim, either in real death or in a living death in which all standards, all decency, all honour eventually vanished.

By what more concrete symbol could the syringe be represented than by the snake, age-old symbol of evil, whose venom enters the body of its victim via a hollow needle? And the age-old seducer, whispering to innocent man: "For God doth know that in the day ye eat thereof, then your eyes shall be opened, and ye shall be as gods, knowing good and evil." But the knowledge, the visions offered by opium and morphine, lead to a barren and lost paradise, a paradise of yesteryear.

Why a prince? Why prayer?

The Prince. This was what Marais had been called in Pretoria by Old Moes – that singular old hobo whose mixture of insight and insanity lent so much colour to Church Square and its vicinity in prewar Pretoria. Photographs of Marais at about the time of his marriage show a young man of princely appearance, and this, one must surmise, is how he saw himself when despondency or hardships had not robbed him of his self-confidence.

That he turned to prayer in London – although not frequently – and gave the matter serious thought, seems clear from notes in his London diary:

> Can you imagine anything more shocking than a young man to be caught at prayer – private prayer – by his friends? ... One suggests that the origin of this singular state of affairs is the idea of courage involved. It seems courageous to run all the risks of hell and somewhat cowardly to try and escape it by means of prayer.

In the lower left-hand corner of the book-plate appear initials which at first seem unreadable. A comparison with other prints in the British Museum's Department of Prints and Drawings has shown that they stand for "J.G.", or James J. Guthrie, a minor painter and book illustrator of the time.

Guthrie worked in the style of Burne-Jones, whose name was mentioned in a previous chapter as one of the pre-Raphaelite artists often seen in the house of Dante Gabriel Rossetti. James J. Guthrie may have been related to the far more distinguished Scottish artist, James Guthrie (1859-1930), who was knighted in 1903.

The Guthrie of the book-plate lived in Essex, in the peace of the English countryside (his full, unmistakably English address was Pear Tree Cottage, Ingrave, Under Brentwood). Possibly he and Marais met each other in London in June 1898, when a number of Guthrie's works formed part of a large exhibition.

The book-plate which Eugène N. Marais had designed and printed is reproduced here in its actual size.

A year after that Marais's book-plate was exhibited at the annual showing of the Ex Libris Society, the catalogue calling it simply: "Framed Book-plate, Eugène Nielen Marais".

This was only a few months before the outbreak of the Boer War, but in this ultra-English exhibition in the Westminster Palace Hotel in Victoria Street the motto on Eugène's book-plate was in Afrikaans!

The drawing was engraved on copper, and at Marais's request Guthrie made at least six sets of prints, two of them in a dark blue, two in a vibrant violet and two in black. It seems likely that three of the six book-plates, one in each colour, contained two additional words in the lower right-hand corner: Inner Temple. It is a piquant coincidence that the book-plate contains clues to Marais's own "inner sanctum".

The most inexplicable object in the book-plate is the phallus-like object in front of the prince. This cannot be simply the catch of the gate. It is too striking to be unintentional. And if it was intentional, whose idea was it: Marais's or the artist's? The catch of a gate usually signifies accessibility, not obstruction. Can it be that the prince can escape the snake (needle) only by entering the paradise of a woman's love by means of the phallus?

Later Marais was to tell his son: "People will look in vain for symbolic meanings in my book-plate."

In 1973 the book-plate was shown to a psychiatrist, a follower of the school of Jung. The psychiatrist knew little about Marais's life (little was known at the time). This was what he said:

> The book-plate is obviously a projection of Eugène Marais's own subjective. The prince is Marais himself. He looks into the future. The past, which lies behind him, is the snake, evil, morphine. The prince and the objects surrounding him are placed in an enclosed space, virtually a chamber. Thus the snake forms part of the frame surrounding the enclosed space in which the prince finds himself; it no longer forms part of his life. But inside the prince's own chamber plants of evil have started to grow, creeping over his robe. The menace has not been overcome.
>
> While evil lies behind him, he looks into the future to his salvation, which consists of various elements: his creative abilities (the book), his profession, and the crucifix, which may represent religion but in

the Jungian philosophy is also a symbol of sacrifice. This means that the prince has to sacrifice something to escape death, which lies behind him.

The phallic symbol in the gate is unmistakable. The gate is latticed and lattice-work is prominent in all parts of the drawing (e.g. top right). For Jung lattice represents what is feminine. The robe is a female symbol as well, and the drawing may represent a conflict between the male and female elements.

Sex, in many different forms, dominates this Ex Libris.

The prince represents youth – as we find it in all myths and legends – a youth which has to be preserved at all costs. This is why the prince wears a triple halo, like a bulwark. But the bulwark is not complete. It reminds one of a human foetus which has still to adopt its final shape.

Obviously there is no end to the speculation about a drawing of this kind. Two facts seem certain: that it had no symbolic significance to Marais is unthinkable; and the key to the meaning of the book-plate lies in the motto, This or Death.

To the author it seems likely that at this stage, at any rate, Marais did not envisage a choice between morphine and death, but the opposite: only by conquering morphine could he escape death, which was the wages of sin.

6. Serpents, Phantoms and Hypnotism

To the amoral artists, to the drunken or stupefied poets and writers of the late nineteenth century, there was one justification for their excesses: they *were* artists and writers. And this applied equally to the hundreds of nameless, forgotten men who destroyed themselves with drink, opium or women without ever completing a worthwhile painting or poem.

Eugène Marais, too, had no problem in justifying his existence in London. He saw himself as a student of life, and he lived as if both his time and his money were unlimited.

Like many gifted students of life before him, his interests were so wide that he could do justice to none of them. As one would expect, he tried, among other things, to write. There are several attempts in his London diary. Before the end of his first year in London he had the idea for a popular novel:

"Margaret de Roubaix. Scene opens Drakenstein in the valley of the Berg River. Love of Margaret and schoolmaster. She is previously engaged. Is seduced by her lover and censured by minister in church. Slagtersnek ends the story."

These notes were followed by a characteristic letter to Jimmy Roos:

> I am in very urgent need of some information and knowing the historical bent of your genius I appeal to you in the hope that it will not be in vain. Unfortunately I have no opportunity here of making any research and for you I do not think it will be any more trouble than dropping a note to some congenial spirit in your native city.
>
> Briefly I wish to know all about the *persons* of the six men executed on Slagter's Nek: their full names, ages and whether married or single ...

One can imagine the wry smile with which Jimmy Roos must have greeted this letter. It was just like Eugène. As a "small favour" he wanted Jimmy to do his research for him.

The letter ends with the words "Yours till death". It is the only known letter by Marais which contains these words and makes one suspect that he was preoccupied by death at the time, as confirmed by the motto on the book-plate he was to have designed some months later. It is not impossible that he was considering suicide even at this early age.

Many things occupied his thoughts. We have touched on his interest in theatre – from the music halls to the Lyceum. That he was dabbling in art is made clear by his sketches of Susanne and his acquaintance with James J. Guthrie, and possibly other artists.

All kinds of philosophical questions concerned him, some of them fairly radical. Thus he writes:

> It is easy to see the essential sanity of the anarchist cause if one is in a certain frame of mind. The present principles of human government then seem too utterly absurd for grown men to submit to ... The main business of the State is to protect the haves from the greed of the have-nots and to use and arm the have-nots for that very purpose.

> Charity if traced to its source is generally found to arise in the dark wood of human remorse.

Later on in the same uncompleted essay, he investigates the changes which the individual undergoes when he becomes part of a group. This may be seen as a prelude to his later theories regarding the termite nest and the baboon community.

> ... the unit ... has (become) an inert idiot like one in the trance of hypnotism, that obeys the words of one of its own puny atoms as the machine obeys the movement of its controlling lever. This is an army. Or again it becomes a raging maniac foaming at the mouth and setting at naught all the principles of right and wrong which any one of its atoms would readily subscribe to. And this is a human mob.

One of Marais's characteristics was the tendency to shy away from the restrictions placed on one's life by time. In fact the concept of time fascinated him. Here the name of Lewis Carroll should be mentioned for the first time. One of the most gifted mathematicians of the Victorian era, creator of *Alice in Wonderland*, Carroll's eccentric personality shows strange similarities to that of Marais – as we shall see at the end of Marais's life. Carroll, too, was intensely interested in time. Possibly in the year of Carroll's death, 1898, Marais wrote these words in his London diary:

> Time. Is time a fixed line or dimension along which we travel? Is it merely a creation of consciousness? If it be a creation of consciousness it would not exist without consciousness. Has every three-dimensional body to exist in the fourth dimension of duration or time? How then about its existence in the past? What is time? Finality is an essential. A contrast of time and eternity, if investigated and analysed, would open up great fields for enquiry. We can neither conceive finite space nor infinite space. Does the same principle apply to time? Does the past exist – or the future? Does time only exist in the present moment?

Marais had spent almost three years in Europe (mainly London) by the time the Boer War broke out. During this time he visited the

Continent several times. In Germany, he was to state much later in an interview: "I met a party of German students and acting on instructions from the Prussian Government we travelled to all the large European cities to study the question of immorality. Later some of them returned with me to London where we rented a house together."

Marais's son corrected this statement, which seems to have been bowdlerized in his first biography – "Not immorality, syphilis."

These German students, even though their names are not known, were to play an important part in Marais's life during the rest of his stay abroad, and it is they who now bring us to three of his most important interests in Europe, apparently contradictory, but in Marais's eyes closely related and complementary. These were medicine, psychology and the supernatural.

To understand the relationship between these three subjects in Marais's mind, one has to go back to the end of the eighteenth century, when an Austrian doctor, Franz Anton Mesmer, had Paris agog with his ability to cure diseases by means of "animal magnetism". In fact this was nothing but hypnotism – mesmerism – for which Mesmer had a great gift. Complaints about Mesmer's methods led to an investigation by a French Royal Commission. They were found to be dangerous. Mesmer disappeared from the scene, but his work was continued by others, some of them charlatans and frauds but others serious investigators. One of the latter was Dr. John Elliotson, who did his utmost to make the use of mesmerism in medical science acceptable. In this he did not succeed, and he is now remembered for little more than the fact that he taught Charles Dickens the techniques of hypnotism.

By the middle of the nineteenth century a new fad, spiritualism, wafted across the Atlantic from the United States to Britain and the Continent.

Many of the frauds who had made money from mesmerism now suddenly made a new debut as spiritualists. A great many people, including numbers of widows and neurotic personalities, attended séances, heard messages from "the other side" being transmitted by means of raps on the table, heard the dead talking in the voice of the medium or sensitive, later saw "ghostly hands" appear, and still later witnessed their deceased loved ones materialising partially or completely from ectoplasm. Other practitioners demonstrated telepathy, telekinesis, levitation and clairvoyance.

Apart from the frauds, there were those who commanded respect, like D.D. Home, who dominated the scene in the fifteen years before 1870 – the golden years of Victorian spiritualism. "Men and women who scorned the vulgarity of lesser mediums cultivated Home," states Ronald Pearsall in *The Table Rappers*. "He did not make spiritualism respectable, he made it fashionable."

Even so both mesmerism and spiritualism and associated phenomena remained somewhat suspect. Not before the eighties, when the highly regarded Society for Psychical Research was founded, were supernatural phenomena investigated in a scientific manner. Although numerous mediums and others were exposed, a number of phenomena remained for which no logical explanation could be given. Almost half a century before Dr. J.B. Rhine founded his Laboratory for Parapsychological Research at Duke University in North Carolina, a series of 246 experiments in telepathic transmission, similar to Rhine's, were conducted under the auspices of the Society in England. This reproduction was taken by Lyall Watson from the Society's report for 1884:

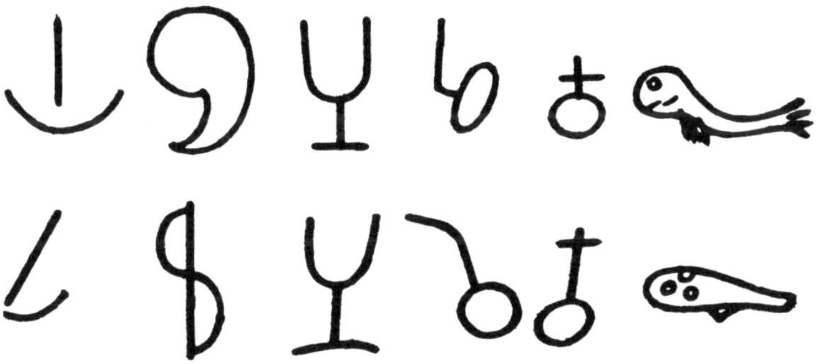

The first line contains symbols transmitted by telepathy to the receiver. The second line shows how the receiver transcribed the symbols. Marais was deeply interested in these experiments and tried to emulate them, as we shall see later.

In the same decade mesmerism, too, was applied really scientifically for the first time. In the Salpêtrière, a Parisian hospital for the mentally ill, Dr. Jean-Martin Charcot, a prominent neurologist, started applying mesmerism – as hypnosis was then still known – to cure or relieve physical defects of mental origin. A famous lithograph shows Charcot commanding a paralysed woman whom he had hypnotised, to walk.

In 1885 Sigmund Freud became one of Charcot's students. "No other person," he wrote to his fiancée, "has influenced me in this way." And after his return to Vienna Freud, too, began using hypnosis in treating mental illness. As early as 1893 he published a description of this treatment, *Studien über Hysterie* (Studies of Hysteria), which was to appear two years later, the year of Lettie Marais's death, in an English translation.

Marais had been conscious of many of these developments even before his departure from Pretoria. His real interest lay in medicine, but because Ewald Esselen and others thought that he would be able to do more for his country as a legal man, he had relinquished his intentions of following a medical course. It may be that Esselen, who himself had studied medicine in Scotland, also realised that Marais, as a morphine addict of four years standing, would find it easier to obtain a legal degree than a medical one.

Naturally, Marais was not prepared to acknowledge this, not even to himself. In fact it seems possible that he intended taking courses at the Inner Temple and at Guy's Hospital simultaneously. Certainly his idea was to attend lectures and demonstrations at a private clinic. Shortly before his death he was to state that he had studied at Guy's Hospital. The records of this institution do not confirm that he ever did so either full-time or part-time. The lack of evidence must not mislead one into underestimating the extent of his medical studies, however. In London he not only bought a set of medical instruments but also acquired considerable medical knowledge, as doctors in South Africa were to testify years later.

Judging by references in his writings, he certainly worked in a laboratory at the time or had the use of one. This work included experiments with snake venom. A number of guinea-pigs were injected with the venom and then treated with various antitoxins, never successfully. Possibly Marais met Dr. A.L.C. Calmette, the famous bacteriologist, during a visit to France. Calmette was then engaged in attempts to develop a serum. "When the writer was in Europe," Marais was to write later, "Calmette worked mainly with African and Brazilian snake venom. He was unfortunate enough to be bitten on the finger himself. His serum was applied immediately, but his colleagues were not entirely happy with this, and amputated the finger. There were no signs of poisoning."

It is possible that Marais visited the Salpêtrière in Paris in the company of his German student friends. The belief that he attended a demonstration by Charcot is obviously false, as the neurologist had died more than three years before Marais's arrival in Europe.

There is no doubt that he acquired Charcot's techniques – and not only in theory. Like Charles Dickens he had a particular bent in this direction, soon becoming an excellent hypnotist.

Hypnosis has its byways. Nineteenth-century mesmerists attested how frequently telepathic messages were involuntarily transmitted under the influence of hypnosis.

In "Laramie die Wonderwerker" (Laramie the Magician), one of Marais's longer short stories (this one contains revealing autobiographical details), Laramie relates: "A friend, a medical student, who then worked at the Salpêtrière, arranged for me to be invited to a séance at which the Italian medium Eusapia Palladina was to demonstrate her supernatural powers. About twenty people attended the demonstration, but they included some of the world's most important scientists. There was Prof. Flammarion, the French astronomer; there was the Italian psychologist Lombroso ... (and there was) Schiaparelli, the greatest astronomer of our century."

With the possible exception of Eusapia Palladina – a celebrated Italian medium who had reached the pinnacle of her fame by the end of the nineteenth century – Marais had probably never met any of the people mentioned in the extract quoted above. He may not even have attended any of their lectures or demonstrations. Even so the passage is of some importance, as the three names Marais mentions – Flammarion, Lombroso and Schiaparelli – were all important influences during the period of his stay in Europe and he was to refer to them repeatedly in his writings.

In the battle between the mediums – who maintained that they could call up ghostly voices and apparitions by means of supernatural powers – and the sleight-of-hand artists (like Houdini in a later decade), who claimed to expose the mediums by successfully matching their demonstrations on the stage, Marais may not have been quite certain where his loyalty lay.

Not all simulated pyschic phenomena could be explained or imitated. Even the mediums who were caught out had an ingenious explanation: the psychic phenomena were not constant, they said, and in order not to disappoint their public they were sometimes obliged to practise deception.

It is almost certain that Marais's own conjuring abilities (including card tricks and more rugged achievements like knife-throwing) were acquired in London. Anything that required skill and ingenuity interested him.

In the year before the Boer War the celebrated 64 year old German biologist Ernst Häckel visited Britain, lecturing at the University of Cambridge and elsewhere. It is improbable that Marais attended his lectures. He was well aware of Häckel's theories, however. This may have been partly because of his friendship with the German students. After all, next to Darwin and Lamarck, Häckel was the century's most prominent protagonist of the theory of evolution, and according to the German students he was the greatest of the three. It was certainly true that in several aspects he had been ahead of Darwin, as the Englishman himself admitted. And since resentment of Britain's Imperialist ambitions formed one of the bonds between Marais and the young Germans, the idea may have given them all a certain chauvinistic satisfaction.

Even so, if Marais and other Transvalers had thought that the German Empire would come to the aid of the South African Republic in the event of British aggression, these hopes were soon dashed by the Anglo-German treaty of 1898. There was now very little to prevent the British High Commissioner in South Africa, Lord Milner, from plotting war.

By February 1899 there was a boom on the Johannesburg Stock Exchange. Marais and other Progressive Transvalers hoped that the Volksraad would adopt a more liberal policy after the elections, and although the results did not entirely meet their expectations, Marais's hero, Lucas Meyer, did become a member of the Volksraad.

Marais had now been in England for more than two years and he had not lived frugally. It may be that at this stage he instructed his brokers to sell a number of shares and that he made a good profit.

In May there were talks between President Kruger and Lord Milner. The meeting did nothing to stem the tide. Kruger now realised what he was soon to state so tellingly: "It is not the vote you want – it is my country."

On 11 October Kruger demanded the withdrawal of the British troops massed near the Transvaal border in Natal. The ultimatum expired without the troops being withdrawn. Another war between Boer and Briton had begun.

7. The Golden Cross

On 12 October 1899 a number of young advocates and attorneys were discussing the ultimatum in Bureau Avenue, Pretoria. They were almost all "Cape" Transvalers, which meant that they had either been born in the Cape or were Progressives. What were they to do? The cousin who had been to school in Paarl with Eugène Marais, Johnny Niemeyer, said: "I am not prepared to fight for Paul Kruger and his Government. But I do intend fighting for my country."

Johnny Niemeyer did fight for his country – and fell on Talana Hill. Seventeen bayonet wounds were counted on his body.

Even the children of Ryk Piet Marais, at school in the Cape, now turned out to be pro-Boer. For this their heads were regularly rubbed full of dirt and held under the tap in the school-yard.

In the meantime a man from Scotland Yard had come to fetch Marais from the house in Teddington where he was living with his German friends. As a Transvaler he was naturally suspect. He was interviewed by the Earl of Selborne, Under-Secretary for the Colonies at the time. Selborne knew who Marais was and what role he had played in the Transvaal. He questioned him closely.

"I explained that there were no negotiations between me and the Government of the Republic," Marais said in an interview near the end of his life. And that is all we know of this conversation.

Marais had at one time helped the Transvaal Consul in London to collect evidence for the commission of inquiry into the Jameson Raid. Possibly Scotland Yard had made inquiries regarding the progress of his studies at the Inner Temple and had wondered whether he had been planted in London as a Boer spy. The fact was that he had not written an exam for eighteen months. Lord Selborne submitted his findings to the Government and Marais was released on parole. He had to undertake to do nothing against the interests of the British Government and to give fourteen days' notice before leaving England.

In London Marais excitedly read reports of how the Boers had not only countered the English, but were defeating them in one battle after another. By New Year's Day 1900 it was checkmate – but huge British reinforcements were on their way to South Africa.

Early in the new year Lord Roberts arrived in Cape Town. By the end of January the Boers recaptured Spioenkop, but on 27 February, the day of Majuba, four thousand Boers under Cronjé surrendered. This was a turning point in the war.

In March Roberts occupied Bloemfontein and in May first Kroonstad and then Johannesburg. In June Pretoria surrendered without a shot being fired.

Late in September President Kruger left for Europe, no doubt remembering De la Rey's bitter prediction following an accusation of cowardice in the Volksraad before the war: "When you have left the country, I shall still be fighting."

By November, little more than a year after the beginning of the war, it was all over, or so the English thought. Roberts left South Africa, leaving Kitchener in command.

This was the beginning, although the British could not have known it at the time, of a painfully protracted guerrilla war.

At about this time Marais succeeded in passing his third subject. He had not written an exam for two and a half years.

In the meantime, probably in order to support himself, he had apprenticed himself to a watch-maker where he learnt how to repair and reconstruct watches. Acquiring the art of working in precious metals, he made cigarette cases, snuff-boxes, rings, crucifixes, knife-hilts and cuff-links of gold and silver. This was one way of recapturing the elegance of yesteryear, of escaping the terrors of the war and of his dreams.

It may have been in Teddington that Marais started using perfume to disguise the odour of morphine, which not only permeated his room, but which he was beginning to detect on his own person.

In January 1901 he celebrated his thirtieth birthday. Sometimes he felt as if he had the experiences of a century behind him. Pretoria, his family, his own past seemed infinitely remote.

In South Africa Kitchener was applying a new programme to wipe out Boer resistance. In order to safeguard the railway links, all British troops were being recalled from unimportant areas. Women and children were being rounded up and put into concentration camps.

Soon afterwards the British started building the first of their block-houses. In April came the fall of Pietersburg, the Boers' last seat of government. Despair began to spread through the ranks of the burghers like an epidemic. Large numbers surrendered or joined the English in order to end the apparently hopeless struggle. Marais grew to hate them, these "hands-uppers" and joiners, just as he had hated and scorned Kruger and his followers. In his people's defeat and humiliation, more than in their victory – for such was his nature – he now felt impelled to go back and help his country. But how was he to get there?

In June he tried unsuccessfully to complete his course, failing Trinity Final (Subject IV) and obtaining only 81 marks out of 510 instead of the 210 required.

In South Africa tens of thousands of women and children were being transported to the camps. Thousands had died there already. Farmhouses were burnt down, crops destroyed, stock stabbed to death. In the towns and villages, too, there was widespread destruction.

For Eugène, his eldest brother, Charles, had been his real father ever since his early childhood. After the demolition of Lynnwood House, the house in which he had grown up, Charles's house in Boshof in the Free State, might have become the one house to which one day he hoped to return. Now this house, like hundreds of others in the Free State towns, was plundered and looted by British soldiers, stripped of all furniture and fittings and partially destroyed. The silver official seal of Baron Van Rheede van Oudtshoorn, whom the Marais' regarded as their ancestor, disappeared, never to be found again.

The English military leaders found the protracted war extremely annoying. Their plans to wipe out or remove all life in the Free State and Transvaal countryside, leaving only scorched earth behind them, had not yet broken the Boer forces. All leaders not willing to surrender, they now threatened, would be exiled for life.

In September of that year, 1901, Marais rewrote Subject IV in the Michaelmas examination. This time he managed to scrape through, obtaining 224 marks out of 510, only fourteen above the minimum required. He had another term still to complete, but from this he was exempted; the regulations of the Inner Temple seem to have allowed for such cases.

Now he could hardly wait to be off. He simply had to get involved.

Months went by. It was incredible that the Boers could last out so long. Rumours and reports said that thousands, perhaps tens of thousands of women and children had already died in the camps.

It was not before early in 1902 that Marais heard in a roundabout way of an expedition which was to leave Belgium and travel through East Africa to join General Beyers' forces in the Northern Transvaal. Marais reported at the Colonial Office and gave notice of his intention to travel to Belgium.

There were no objections, but there were delays, presumably not all of them caused by the bureaucrats. It took Marais some time to put his affairs in order.

Finally, he took ship for Europe. Around his neck, like a talisman, hung a Maltese cross he himself had made of gold.

8. A Secret Mission

Brussels, March 1902. In the Transvaal Legation in the Belgian capital, Dr. W.J. Leyds, Ambassador Extraordinary and Minister Plenipotentiary of the Transvaal Republic, was negotiating with two men who were on the point of departing on a dangerous mission. They were Dr. E. Schultz, a German doctor, and Piet Burger, a law agent from Middelburg, Transvaal. In those early days of 1902 the outcome of the war was still uncertain. The Boers in the field were in need of many things – not only ammunition and explosives, but doctors as well, as the British had refused to allow medical aid to pass through the lines.

While one expedition had been on its way to the Boer commandos through German South West Africa, Dr. Leyds had decided to send a second expedition through Mozambique.

It had not been easy to find a suitable leader for such an expedition. After several attempts his choice had fallen on a doctor who had worked in Prof. Von Leyden's clinic in Berlin – Dr. Schultz.

This Dr. Schultz could have been the hero of one of Karl May's adventure novels. He had had a great deal of experience in China. He was courageous and something of a diplomat. He was also arrogant and vehemently anti-British, with a healthy contempt for all nations except those of Western Europe. The manner in which he was to handle the expedition makes it seem as if the German Secret Service had given him a short but intensive course in espionage.

On this day in early 1902, Dr. Schultz and his assistant, Piet Burger, were receiving their final instructions. They were to leave Brussels at once for Paris, where they were to take possession of the equipment and explosives awaiting them there. They were then to sail for Dar-es-Salaam in East Africa, from where they were somehow to find their way to the Boer commandos.

At that stage Eugène Marais was still on his way to Brussels. Because of the delays in London, he arrived there after Schultz and Burger had left.

Within a day or two Schultz and Burger found themselves in an hotel in the Rue de Tremoelles, within sight of the world's highest construction, the Eiffel Tower, which had dominated the Paris skyline for the past thirteen years.

The first doubts about Burger began entering Dr. Schultz's mind even at this early stage. While the German was getting in touch with secret agents to arrange for taking possession of the explosives and equipment, Burger introduced him to émigré Boers for whom Schultz felt nothing but contempt. These people, he wrote in his report, "who brought their fortunes with them from their fatherland but have descended to the level of Bourse speculators in Paris, do not spend their money for the good of their own people, but swill it down in the company of prostitutes."

"I must request you not to introduce me to such men again," he told Burger primly.

The German's mistrust deepened when the equipment had to be selected. Burger insisted on taking along an expensive and heavy electric battery. When Dr. Schultz pointed out the problems of getting the battery through customs on the various borders, Burger took him aside and whispered: "Don't talk so loudly. We can sell the battery on board ship. If nobody wants it, we can throw it overboard. It's quite easy."

Dr. Schultz had other problems too. The whole of Europe was infested with wealthy English tourists, no doubt including a number of spies. He did not like the way in which the porter in the hotel questioned them about their destination.

The doctor now started applying the lessons which he might have learnt from the Secret Police. Leaving Piet Burger in Paris for the time being, he took the night train to Marseilles on 5 April, taking along all their luggage and equipment – but leaving Burger's famous battery behind.

In his compartment he came across another of the wretched Englishmen. Dr. Schultz was ill at ease. While the Englishman slept, he left the train at Lyons at three o'clock that morning, skipped the following train and arrived in Marseilles the next evening. Burger joined him there the following day. When they compared notes, Burger told Schultz that there had been an English spy in the compartment next to his on the train. The man looked so dangerous that he expected a bullet to be fired into his back through the wooden partition between the two compartments at any moment. "I outwitted him, though," he told Schultz triumphantly. "I asked the passenger sitting opposite me to exchange seats with me."

Unpleasantly surprised by such cowardice, Dr. Schultz questioned him more closely. Did he change trains as Schultz had suggested? No. Did he skip trains? No. But the English spy who was on the train was still hot on his heels. In fact there were two. They had followed him from the station to the hotel.

Dr. Schultz pricked up his ears. "Come and show me what they look like," he whispered, "but please be careful. They should not see us under any circumstances."

In front of the hotel Burger could see no one who even remotely resembled either of the two spies.

"We cannot risk anything," said the German doctor. "Pack your bags and tell the porter you're taking the night train to Nice at ten o'clock tonight."

Accompanying Burger to the station, Dr. Schultz left his luggage in the box-room. He then took him to another small hotel and ordered him to stay out of sight until the ship sailed for Dar-es-Salaam.

All went well. No further spies appeared on their trail and Piet Burger boarded the ship without mishap, carrying a false passport in the name of Richard Will, a Scottish attorney.

Meanwhile Eugène Marais had arrived in Brussels. Having heard about the expedition to the Transvaal, he said he would give anything to be able to accompany it.

To Dr. Leyds Eugène Marais was highly suspect. Not only President Kruger and the Transvaal Government but he himself had repeatedly and virulently been attacked by Marais in leading articles in *Land en Volk*. One can only surmise that he kept putting Marais off by offering excuses.

Marais was full of zeal. How best could he spend the time he had on his hands while waiting? Did he visit a hospital for children suffering from incurable diseases because he thought that he might be able to assist the children in the concentration camps? He had always been fond of children. He was never to forget the horrors he witnessed here. "Are there tears yet?" he was to ask in a poem years later.

Finally, he realised that he had missed the expedition.

In London Marais had kept up correspondence with an old friend from before the war, a certain Falconer, at one time manager of *Land en Volk*. After the British occupation Falconer had been made editor of the official British newspaper in Pretoria.

Not much is known about him. That he was really strongly pro-British seems unlikely.

When Marais realised that the expedition had left Europe, he decided to sail to Delagoa Bay on his own. (This was the bay in which Lourenço Marques lay – capital of Mozambique and later renamed Maputo – and the town itself seems often to have been called by this name at the time.) From there he would travel overland to join the Boer forces. He asked his friend Falconer by letter or cable to arrange for £1 000 to be transferred to the Standard Bank in Delagoa Bay.

In 1902 £1 000 was a sizeable sum. Where did it come from? It may be that Marais had made money in the pre-war Stock Exchange boom in Johannesburg – or from his newspaper – and that this money could not be transferred from the conquered Republic without the assistance of an old influential friend like Falconer. Even so it seems odd that the authorities had no objections.

The circumstantial evidence could lead one to believe that the British Government of occupation had financed Marais's expedition – and certainly not to go and help the Boers.

However, there is no evidence that Marais ever worked for the English and against his own people. Even in his confidential letter to Charles Leonard some years before, when he urgently needed the Uitlanders' money to keep *Land en Volk* going, he had made it quite clear that in the event of a clash he would remain on the Boer side. Later, too, as we shall see, his attitude was to be anything but pro-English.

Losing no further time, Marais sailed for Delagoa Bay aboard the *Admiral*. Falconer's £1 000 would be waiting for him there.

In the meantime Dr. Schultz, who was travelling to East Africa with Burger on another ship, had been having a hard time.

Not a few German and English passengers doubted whether Burger could really be British. He certainly spoke a remarkable English. Patiently and earnestly Dr. Schultz would explain that Mr. Will was a Scot, and the Scots simply did not speak English extremely well.

Unfortunately, Burger was no actor. He was fond of boasting, and many of his stories revealed an intimate knowledge of the Transvaal.

"This so-called Mr. Will is nothing but an Afrikaner," Dr. Schultz was told by a German passenger who had lived in the Transvaal and Rhodesia for seventeen years.

About this time the *Admiral* docked in Cairo. Marais took the opportunity of doing the tour of the Pyramids. They made an impressive spectacle.

Even so he felt a certain disappointment. In the British Museum he had seen so much that he had expected rather more here.

Aboard the first of the two ships, Dr. Schultz was now becoming seriously worried. The closer they got to Dar-es-Salaam, the more Burger seemed to be getting cold feet and when they went ashore in the East African city early in May he decided that they should part company for the time being once more. If they travelled on the same ship from Dar-es-Salaam to Beira, he reasoned, Burger might panic and throw the explosives overboard.

Leaving Burger in Dar-es-Salaam, Dr. Schultz took all the luggage with him on the ship to Beira. Burger was to stay behind until Schultz instructed him by telegram to follow.

Burger was by no means disinclined to relax in Dar-es-Salaam for some time. The Transvaal legation in Brussels had just cabled him £200 – the result of fraud, Dr. Schultz claims in his report. As a result of the Boer War there was a severe depression in Dar-es-Salaam and £200 was a fortune.

The marshes around the city teemed with wild duck. Burger hunted daily. Nor were his evenings spent in idleness. He lived like a king, and it was with regret that on 16 May he received a cable from Schultz instructing him to join him in Beira. Burger had to wait for the next available ship to Beira, and the next available ship was the *Admiral.*

On board Burger was overjoyed to meet a countryman, a certain Eugène Marais. During their short trip to Beira, Burger used every opportunity he got to spin the most unlikely tales about his own bravery and deprivations. And of course he lost no time in telling Marais all about the secret expedition.

Marais seems to have said nothing of his own futile attempts to join the expedition. At Burger's invitation he interrupted his journey to Lourenço Marques and went ashore in Beira, where he met Schultz and was accepted as a member of the expedition. The £1 000 waiting for him in the Standard Bank in Lourenço Marques was transferred to Beira.

While Burger had been enjoying himself thoroughly in Dar-es-Salaam, Schultz had been as busy as a bee in Beira. Having a smattering of Spanish and being a smooth talker, he had had no trouble at Customs. The explosives packed with the medicines and bandages and designated as "horse medicine and grease" had been brought to his room as his personal luggage.

As Schultz had lost all confidence in Burger, he had meanwhile recruited a certain Zimmerman, a Swiss, to join the expedition.

Now he was eager to continue the journey. Early in the year the

Boers had still had about 25 000 men in the field, but by February Kitchener had initiated his first drive. So successful had this systematic wiping-up operation been that the Boers' position was now extremely uncertain. The expedition seemed to have little time to lose.

To Schultz's annoyance Burger, useless even when in excellent health, fell seriously ill before they could leave Beira. His hunting trips around Dar-es-Salaam had resulted in a serious bout of malaria. Marais and Schultz nursed him day and night, but received so little thanks for it that Schultz said: "In the Fatherland I would have had no hesitation in kicking out a patient with this kind of approach. In Prof. Von Leyden's Berlin clinic we were accustomed to treating the dregs of society, but even there I was never a witness to such behaviour."

Marais, too, felt shame. Was this "the nation of courage" for whom foreigners like Schultz were risking their lives? Burger had told both Marais and Schultz that he had been wounded in battle. When Marais and Schultz compared notes, they found that Burger had got his stories mixed up. He had told Marais of a wound in his arm, Schultz of a leg wound.

"He showed me two wounds," the doctor told Marais. "They are nothing but blotches. He does have a scar below the knee, but that was caused by suppuration, and in any case it must be at least ten years old."

The unwanted delay gave Dr. Schultz time to compile a comprehensive report for the Transvaal Government about conditions in Beira. The town was in fact not controlled by the government of the Mozambique Company, he reported, but by the British Consulate and the British secret service.

The Portuguese secret service in Beira, he wrote, was completely innocuous. It consisted of three people. One patrolled the station, one guarded the brothels ("plus contents") and the third one "did not know what he was doing there himself."

The English secret service, on the other hand, had plenty of money and was willing to pay well for any information and assistance which might promote the war against the Boers. Beira was a dangerous place, and future agents should be warned to be careful.

By early June, when Burger seemed to have recovered sufficiently to continue the journey, Dr. Schultz had laid his plans. The expedition was to sail to the Save, an East African river some 150 miles further south. Pretending to be on a hunting expedition, they would sail up the Save as far as it was navigable. From there they would march up the northern bank, cross the river at the Oolarken Drift, continue on foot up to the Limpopo and then travel through the Northern Transvaal, hoping to meet the commandos in the vicinity of Pietersburg.

Marais helped Schultz hire a sailing boat from a West Indian half-caste, Captain Dicky, and buy equipment and supplies. Burger, Schultz complained in his report, did not lift a finger to help them. Zimmerman, too, seems to have been anything but zealous.

Even at this early stage the party had split up into two camps: Marais and Schultz on the one hand, Burger and Zimmerman on the other.

On the afternoon of 3 June 1902 all arrangements had been completed and all purchases made. Within the hour the English newspaper in Beira published a special edition, an enormous banner headline proclaiming:

PEACE SIGNED

The war had ended.

9. Chiloan and Machanga

"It was like a bolt from the blue," Dr. Schultz wrote in his report, but he soothed his companions by saying: "It must be a sham peace. This event cannot change the course of South African history." After discussing the matter, the party decided to continue their hunting expedition, both to gain time and to prevent suspicion.

The next day the party reached the island of Chiloan at the mouth of the Save in Captain Dicky's boat.

This was where Eugène Marais wrote or started working on "1902", one of the bitterest poems ever written in Afrikaans. His "inspiration" was Kipling's patriotic poem "Recessional": "God of our fathers, known of old, / Lord of our far-flung battle-line ..." Marais's poem, "1902", at least in the conventional sense of the word, was anything but patriotic. In June 1902 Marais was still unaware of the full extent of the British concentration camp policy, in which almost 40 000 women and children – about a third of them black or coloured – had died. On the other hand he had heard a great deal about the joiners, about the several thousands of National Scouts, of Boer officers who, in this so-called "white man's war", had led black commandos against their own people. In Europe he had met the émigrés who had earned Dr. Schultz's contempt. It may also have been self-reproach concerning his own passive role in the war which made him write:

God van ons Vaders, as U wil bestaan,
dat ons as Staat en Nasie moet vergaan,
– besoedel deur verraad, ontrou
aan alles deur ons vaders opgebou ...
(met) vuile hande, rooi bevlek,
met bloed van broer en vriend bedek;–
God van ons vaders, bly U wil bestaan,
leer ons genadiglik die dood blymoedig in te gaan.

God of our fathers, if it is Your will
that we must perish as State and Nation
– polluted by treachery, betraying
everything our fathers built up ...
(with) filthy hands, stained red
and covered in the blood of brother and friend; –
God of our Fathers, if that be Thy will,
then in Thy mercy teach us to meet our death with gladness.

The rest of the expedition was to reflect the spirit of this poem rather accurately. They were not marching to the Transvaal like heroes to supply the Boers with explosives and medicines. They were wasting long months in a tropical country, their energies sapped by disease, their spirits worn down by treason, fraud and discord.

On Chiloan the party had to show their documents to the Portuguese district commandant, one Bello. It may have been the heat, but it may also have been his disdain for all Portuguese, that made

Burger appear in his underpants at this interview, and it did not surprise Dr. Schultz that Bello treated them rather "off-handedly".

"Bello is an habitual drunkard of about thirty-five with a pointed beard and a pointed belly," Dr. Schultz wrote. "Bearing this in mind I bought twelve bottles of champagne at an auction sale in Beira for twenty-five shillings as a gift for him."

Cautious as always, the German doctor handed Bello only two of the twelve bottles of champagne at the first meeting.

After their short stay on the island of Chiloan, they travelled through the mouth of the Save and some way up the river to the village of Machanga, which Schultz wanted to make their temporary headquarters. As crocodiles were scarce here, the natives were skilled navigators.

Greater dangers lay in wait for them, however. In the room in Machanga in which Schultz and Marais slept, two Frenchmen had been killed by the murderous climate two years before. A third had fled in vain to Chiloan and died there.

Even now, in winter, the climate was unhealthy. If they stayed here too long they could easily catch malaria.

It was a wild, untamed country. In the rainy season the river was between five hundred and a thousand metres wide, but in winter, as the level of the water dropped, sand-banks and shallow islets would appear, breaking up the river into numerous water courses. The soil was exceptionally fertile, supporting bananas, oranges, cotton, sugar-cane, tobacco, coconuts, rice and vegetables. The river and the surrounding area teemed with game and birds.

Within a few days after their arrival in Machanga the four men departed on a hunting trip. As usual, Schultz and Marais did all the organizing. The worthy doctor could hardly stop talking about the high prices. Meat was scarce; even chickens cost an exorbitant sevenpence apiece. Many of the Save natives had been spoilt by working as "boys" on the Rhodesian and Transvaal mines, Schultz complained. Porters had to be paid a ridiculous ninepence a day.

At last all was ready. As the party marched west, the country became increasingly overgrown, and game more abundant. Frequently marshes and bogs barred their way. Buffalo had been wiped out here, but there were plenty of lions and leopards, hyenas and wild-cats. On this short safari Schultz and Marais became even more contemptuous of Burger. Almost every evening, the meticulous doctor noted in his diary, there was a quite intolerable stench next to their tent. At first he suspected "swinish Kaffirs," but one evening Schultz and Marais saw "our brave friend Burger" relieving himself between the crates of the provisions next to the tent. He had been too scared of the wild animals in the area to move further away.

By this time open enmity had developed between the two camps.

After some days on safari the party left the wilderness and began marching back to Machanga. Schultz was planning to sail to Beira in time to catch the German steamer to Delagoa Bay a few days later.

These plans were foiled by Burger. On the march back to Machanga he twice requested Schultz and Marais to make the final arrangements for hiring a sailing boat once they got there. This they agreed to do, travelling ahead to do so, but while they were trying to make a deal in Machanga they heard that Burger and Zimmerman had already left on the very boat they were trying to hire.

Hurrying to the river, they were just in time to see the two traitors sailing in the direction of the coast.

"What are you doing with our boat?" Marais called after them.

"Why didn't you wait for us?" Burger shouted back shamelessly.

Bitterly, Schultz wrote in his report: "He had left us behind in the wilderness virtually helpless" – for not only had he left without paying his share of the porters' wages, he had also taken the expedition's entire supply of ammunition with him. All that remained were the few rounds the two men had in their gunbelts.

"I think he is an English spy," Schultz now wrote in his report.

Apart from the ammunition, Burger had also absconded with the secret reports intended for the Boer leaders. Meanwhile, the explosives and components of instruments of sabotage were still lying in Dr. Schultz's hotel room in Beira. Supposing Burger was to send the Portuguese an anonymous letter to tell them about this illicit luggage?

The German doctor at once sent a messenger to the proprietor of the hotel in Beira: "No one may touch my bags without my permission. If anyone should insist on doing so, you are to summon the German Consul to prohibit any such interference."

"That will scare him," Schultz told Marais. "The Portuguese don't want to get into trouble with a great power like Germany."

At this stage there were differences of opinion between Schultz and Marais as well. Schultz wanted to get to Beira as soon as possible to continue the journey to the Transvaal. Marais saw no purpose in this. All was lost in any case. They might as well stay in this fascinating country for a while.

Schultz allowed himself to be persuaded.

Fascinating the country certainly was. The river teemed with hippopotamuses, which hid in the mangrove swamps on the river banks by day and at night went up the river to graze far above Machanga.

"It is undoubtedly one of the most incredible sights of Africa," Marais was to write later in a first-rate Afrikaans magazine article, "to watch the black procession moving up the centre of the river on a moonlit night from the high river bank at Machanga and to hear them snorting and blowing until long after midnight."

In Machanga Marais and Schultz soon had more company than they cared for. The presence of a doctor with a large supply of medicine drew sick natives to their hut from far and wide. Schultz treated them, performing occasional operations as well. Marais helped him enthusiastically. In his medical training the period in Machanga may be said to have formed part of his housemanship. It seems probable that he had learnt more than theory in Europe, but he was acquiring additional practical experience here, experience which was later to stand him in good stead in the Waterberg.

For Dr. Schultz the pressure eventually became too much. He and Marais left Machanga and went to live for a while on an island called Ma-em-Vu which was in the middle of the river. The native name, which meant Mother of Hippopotamuses, was an apt one. "Although the hippopotamuses and mosquitoes bothered us a great deal at night," Marais was to write later, "we still found it preferable to all the unpleasant diseases of Machanga."

During their stay on the island one of Dr. Schultz's erstwhile patients brought him, as a gift out of gratitude, a huge wicker-covered jar of Portuguese rum which had "the taste and flavour of sugar-cane and the potency of shrapnel", as Marais was to describe it. The visitor was a certain Coelho, a Spanish-speaking inhabitant of Machanga known as the capstao. He owned a covered trading vessel which had a crew of ten.

As they chatted, the capstao happened to mention a rich pearl-bed of which he knew. If the doctor and his friend would like to visit it, he would take them there in his boat. They could pick up a fortune from the sea-bed within a day.

This pearl-bed, he explained, had been fished out previously, but ten years ago the government had closed it and had been guarding it ever since to give the oysters a chance to grow again and to produce large pearls. However, the gunboat guarding the pearl-beds had been beached on the island of Chiloan a year ago. The crew had established a village there, laid out farmlands and taken black wives.

Marais found the Spaniard's story irresistible – "tales of pearls as large as a small tangerine, as bright as summer moonshine." And it was decided, so one surmises, that Marais would pay for the expedition.

"Three days later our squadron left Ma-em-Vu. It consisted of the capstao's large, covered sailing boat, with two canoes in tow and a crew totalling twelve men and two black girls.

"When the capstao was afloat the two young black girls formed part of his crew. Ashore they were the pride of his harem. We soon realised that they were by far the best sailors he had."

Sailing with reckless skill, the girls and their less gifted male companions reached the northern tip of Chiloan at noon.

Before them lay the open sea. It would be dangerous to continue the voyage before darkness fell, as the officials on Chiloan, however indolent, might still be on the look-out for illegal pearl-divers.

In the meantime one of the girls had gone ashore to gather a bundle of wood. Soon a huge fish, caught on the way there, was being grilled on deck.

For the first time Marais saw the contents of the boat's hold. Here the food was stored, the guns, the fishing lines, the barrels of water. He also saw two kid goats – "ewes no larger than scrub-hares. Both were tethered by a short rope and next to them were heaped the branches and leaves which were to keep them alive for ten days." This was the fresh meat which the capstao had promised to provide!

"Five or six jars of rum stacked next to the water barrels made me feel even more uneasy than before. One of the jars was immediately brought on deck, initiating a merry orgy.

"Before sunset our boat lay mastless. The capstao and all his men were sleeping a sleep which reminded one more of anaesthesia than of ordinary drunkenness. Night fell as suddenly as a black screen and there was a strong wind from the south-west ...

"We had to go to a great deal of trouble to wake the capstao and his sailors. I could not have imagined that a cloudless night could be so dark. One could literally not see one's hand before one's eyes. From all parts of the black river bank around us, tiny fires were shooting up, each indicating a Kaffir dwelling on Chiloan or on the mainland. These fires and the bright stars above us were the only compass by means of which the capstao intended to steer a course.

"I shall never forget that nocturnal voyage ... Under full sail the vessel shot through the water like an arrow, leaving two long, shiny wakes on each side. The capstao and his helmsmen stood on each side of the tiller while the rest of the sailors were gathered in the bow to look for the first signs of surf. It was one of the girls who caught the first glimpse of the distant reef, and judging by the general applause we could tell that the others had shared our feeling of unease.

"Again using some star to guide him, the capstao immediately changed course and shortly afterwards the boat was shooting ahead in still waters, although we could hear the pounding of the surf within ten yards of us.

"We were sailing along a reef which stretched for miles along the coast and which now served us as a breakwater ... the surf was so close to us that the least mistake at the helm might have caused our destruction.

"By midnight we were suddenly conscious of surf on three sides, the most dangerous being straight ahead. At once there was a great tumult of voices. The tiller was swung around by main force, the sail was dropped and we veered within a yard of the rock in front of us. At once the anchor was thrown overboard."

The boat was lying virtually on the pearl-bed and the next morning the divers set to work. Some pearls were found. Predictably, they were nothing special.

There was a stalwart turtle, though. "She came floating along the current which was flowing toward the mainland like a river, fast asleep on the surf, head and paddles outstretched. Rifles were whipped out, and at a distance of thirty yards two of us let her have it, while the sailors tumbled head over heels into one of the canoes to go and fetch her."

The enormous animal, six feet long and five feet wide, made a lengthy and entirely satisfying meal. She was full of eggs and well padded. "Never in my life have I enjoyed anything more than those grilled turtle chops and fried eggs."

These words end Eugène Marais's description of the expedition to the pearl-beds near the island of Chiloan. Again, as so often in his life, it was a mere fragment. What a stirring novel could he not have based on his stay along the East African coast.

This exciting and merry interlude, to which the austere German doctor makes no reference at all in his report, was to be succeeded by more difficult times. Back in Machanga, both Marais and Dr. Schultz contracted malaria. They took turns to nurse each other. Their spirits were low.

At that stage their quarters were raided.

"About eight o'clock (one evening) we heard a savage knocking on the door," Dr. Schultz wrote in his report. "'What drunken Kaffir is that?' I asked Marais angrily. And before us appeared Signor Bello, commandant of Chiloan, in all his dignity, obviously much the worse for wear even at this early hour."

He had come to search Dr. Schultz's luggage, Bello declared. (Had Burger sent anonymous letters after all?) The commandant was welcomed with great hospitality into the plain room. Dr. Schultz was in bed with malaria, but Marais was still up to producing champagne and port for the visitor. Would the commandant excuse them for the moment, Marais asked. His friend was ill. Of course the commandant could examine their luggage tomorrow. It would be a pleasure.

Bello failed to see through the deception. Drinking and chatting merrily, he neglected to insist on a search. When Marais started referring to the beautiful half-caste girls of Chiloan, Bello really got going, "pouring," as Schultz puts it in his diary, "a stream of words around our poor ears for hours on end." It was past midnight before the Portuguese staggered to his feet and managed to lurch through the doorway.

The next day Dr. Schultz ripped out the false bottoms of his suitcases, burnt the contents and scattered the ashes in the river. It was a close shave. A search of their luggage could have meant several months in gaol for both of them.

Marais and Schultz now awaited Bello's next call without trepidation. Perhaps because of his king-sized hangover, he did not call again.

More than a month had passed since Burger and Zimmerman had fled so treacherously. Schultz was becoming more impatient every day. To him the attitude of their landlord, a half-caste, made it clear that they were no longer welcome in Portuguese territory. But Marais had lapsed into complete lassitude. Nothing mattered any more.

Nothing, perhaps, but morphine. Dr. Schultz loyally records Marais's despondence in his diary. He does not mention drugs. Could Marais have successfully deluded him?

In any event Dr. Schultz thought they should be off at once. They were in danger. Burger had undoubtedly written anonymous letters advising Bello to arrest them. They were to leave without further delay.

Marais's nerves had long been close to snapping. The prudish, fastidious German doctor had been irritating him for weeks. His reply was uncharacteristically irascible:

"Go where you will. You certainly don't have to stay for my sake."

But Dr. Schultz stayed. As a medical man he felt a certain responsibility towards Marais, whose attacks of malaria had meanwhile become more severe. Even if he never refers to drugs in his diary, he may have become concerned about Marais's heavy use of opium and possibly also of laudanum – opium dissolved in alcohol, a blend still used at that time to suppress malaria. Our only clue is one sentence in his diary: "My conscience as a doctor, which is irrelevant here, made me stay after all."

In the meantime, Marais's condition had deteriorated. If Schultz had left after their quarrel, he might well have died here. The nightmares caused by severe attacks of malaria mingled with those of morphine. Even when he was not delirious, his thinking was by no means clear. One day he told a surprised Schultz: "I have come to a decision. I am simply going to walk to Pretoria from here and appear among my people."

Eventually Dr. Schultz succeeded in convincing him of his folly.

Late in July, with Marais still seriously ill, they left the hut and sailed down river, on their way to Beira. At three o'clock that afternoon, when they had gone about four miles, Marais's condition deteriorated so much that Schultz was obliged to go ashore. On the river bank the porters pitched a tent and cut grass to make a bed for Marais. Here, the German doctor was to write in his diary, Marais suffered such a heavy attack of malaria that he became semi-conscious, making Schultz fear for his life any moment.

It is just possible that Schultz was – perhaps unwittingly – describing morphine withdrawal symptoms but as there is no evidence for or against this, it must remain pure conjecture.

In spite of Marais's illness, they soon continued the journey. In the dangerous surf at the mouth of the Save they once again barely escaped death. Once again they landed on the island of Chiloan, spent a day there and then left for Beira, where they arrived on the evening of 3 August after an absence of seven weeks.

In the hotel their possessions had not been touched.

Shortly after their arrival, Schultz removed the smaller parts of time bombs and other instruments of sabotage from his trunks. He and Marais put the tiny objects in their pockets and, pretending to go for a walk, they buried everything in a mangrove swamp about three hundred metres from the lighthouse.

The 25 kilos of "horse medicine and wagon grease" which Dr. Schultz was still keeping in his room, not even showing it to Marais, was another matter.

In his report he writes: "Behind the hotel I discovered an unobtrusive exit for Kaffirs leading to the back of the hotel and the marsh. It was a very hot day, and everyone was bound to be asleep between one and three o'clock."

Marais, too, was asleep when the German cautiously took the trunk containing the remaining explosives and chemicals to the marsh. Some of it was burnt, some strewn about.

When Marais awoke that afternoon and realized what had happened, he felt hurt and mortified. Did Schultz not trust him after all?

That afternoon, after visiting the marsh, the doctor was struck down by a heavy bout of fever but by dusk he had recovered sufficiently to take his daily constitutional. Two Portuguese policemen tried to arrest him.

"Sirs," he cried defiantly, "I am walking on a public way. I am a German citizen. If you want to arrest me, you will have to bear the consequences."

Schultz was left in peace.

On 9 August he and Marais sailed for Lourenço Marques on a small coaster, the *Induna*, and here Marais met up with an old acquaintance from England: Amery, war correspondent of the London *Times*, now compiling the *Times History of the War*. Amery and Marais had been fellow students at the Inner Temple. Even though Amery was an outspoken imperialist, he made a good impression on Schultz. He was well bred and well informed and, having studied in Cologne for three years, he could speak fluent German.

Late in August Falconer, Marais's friend and erstwhile manager of *Land en Volk*, arrived in Lourenço Marques. Marais and Falconer were firm friends (in fact Marais was to tell Schultz that he had no better). Later, too, in conversations with his son, Marais was always to talk very highly of Falconer. They understood one another, he said.

He was bringing Marais news about *Land en Volk* which could be of great importance, Falconer told him. The situation was clear. There was martial law. An Afrikaans-Dutch newspaper could only be started or reopened in the Transvaal if the proprietor agreed to two conditions: the paper had to be pro-British or at least neutral, and its leading articles had to be submitted to the British military authorities for approval.

The two men negotiating in Delagoa Bay were doing so as friends, not as Boer and Briton.

In Pretoria Falconer had done everything in his power to obtain the best possible offer for Marais. Now again, in Delagoa Bay, he was leaning backwards to accommodate him. He may even have intimated that the English would be willing to overlook a great deal.

If Marais and Falconer could not come to a firm agreement at that stage, they must at least have reached a tacit understanding. As long as Marais was to adopt a neutral attitude, submitting his editorials to the authorities before publication – about this there was no room for negotiation – he could reopen *Land en Volk* as soon as he wished. What was more, the Colonial Government was prepared to subsidize his paper to an amount of £500 a quarter. It is not impossible that the £1 000 which Falconer had had transferred for Marais had been an advance payment on this subsidy.

For Marais the choice was a simple one: reopen *Land en Volk* on the British Government's conditions, with a subsidy, or keep it closed. In the event, he decided to reopen.

We shall see to what extent he kept his part of the agreement.

In Delagoa Bay both men were greatly relieved at having come to an understanding, and Falconer helped Marais as far as he could to put his affairs in order. He had less time for the German doctor.

"While Falconer lifted no finger to help me," Schultz writes somewhat peevishly in his report, "he swept all obstacles aside for Marais."

Falconer returned to Pretoria before Marais, but they must have remained in contact, for it was Falconer who was awaiting Marais on the station when he arrived in the Transvaal capital late in 1902.

PART 4: A NEW BEGINNING

Ek is jou wese se ondergrond en ek trap jou spoor soos 'n goeie hond	I am your being's underground and I follow your spoor like a faithful hound

1. The Homecoming

In an interview Eugène Charles Gerard Marais, Eugène Marais's only son, gave a description of his father's return to Pretoria which was almost as vivid and real as an ancient, flickering newsreel.

"One day in 1902," his son was to relate more than sixty years later, "Mr. Falconer came to fetch me at my godmother's house, took me by the hand and went with me to the old Pretoria station. I was seven at the time.

"We stood in front of the station, near the gate where we children used to go to give the commandos tins of rusks to take with them on the Natal campaign. To our right there were white railings, to our left the waiting rooms, and the tracks were in front of us. There were no platforms.

"When the Delagoa Bay train steamed into the station, Mr. Falconer at first looked for my father in vain. Then a tall man crossed the tracks, right in front of the locomotive. His first words were: 'Is this my son?'"

After Lettie Marais's death in 1895 the newly born baby had been adopted by Eugène Marais's sister, Sophie Ueckerman. In spite of the fact that father Ueckerman, an attorney, had left his wife and children years before, the home young Eugène grew up in was a happy one. He had no lack of friends. His cousin, Sonny, and his beautiful ten year old cousin, Fay, were more than friends – they soon became a beloved brother and sister.

"My mother possibly gave young Eugène more attention than her own children," says Norma, the third child, unreproachfully.

After Marais's return to Pretoria his son continued to live with the Ueckermans.

Sophie Ueckerman's house was on the corner of Prinsloo and Jacob Maré Streets, right opposite the large plot where Lynnwood House had stood on the banks of the Apies river. After the death of Eugène Marais's parents in 1896, some time before Marais left for Europe, his brother Melt had had the old house demolished. When Eugène returned after the Boer War he found three smaller houses instead of the rambling old dwelling where he had spent his childhood.

Only a few blocks from Sophie Ueckerman's house was the large boarding house which belonged to Jess Rex, one of his other sisters, now forty-eight years old.

This is where Eugène now went to live. Here, too, the father had long since left his family. The youngest daughter, Mabel, 23 years old, had in fact never seen her father, although at one stage they had corresponded. (Later on she was to become Mabel Malherbe, editor of the very first Afrikaans women's magazine, *Die Boerevrou*.)

What of Mabel's mother in this difficult year, 1902? In her youth Jess Rex had been regarded as rather a lively young girl, witness the story about her affair with Rider Haggard. Even before the war, perhaps by way of reaction, she had become completely mid-Victorian, extremely prim and proper – and so she was now, with an iron will and great perseverance and drive. In short: a formidable old girl.

Her boarding house reminded one rather of the house in which Eugène Marais had grown up. A huge old place with many rooms, it stood on a vast L-shaped plot, of which the short leg at the back bordered on the State Model School. From this establishment, which had served as a Boer P.O.W. camp during the war, Winston Churchill had escaped some years before. Now a row of stables stood on the boundary, for the energetic Jess also kept a small dairy.

What impression did the returning citizen of the world, Eugène Marais, make on his family and countrymen in 1902?

"The Pretorians of those days found my father's appearance somewhat unusual," relates his son. "His clothes were in accordance with the latest London fashions. He wore long, pointed shoes, and for some time he also sported a deerstalker cap like the one Sherlock Holmes used to wear. His suits were made of tussore silk, of which he was extremely fond, and they had buttons of pure gold. The buttons could be removed when the suits were washed and he had made them himself from golden coins: Kruger pounds for the jacket and half pounds for the waistcoat.

"He was always fond of precious metals and after his return he frequently worked in gold and silver. My godmother's house was not very far away and we saw each other regularly. Once he let me try on a golden ring which he had made, and we couldn't get it off. It was a terrible business, with Vaseline and bits of thread, before we managed it. It was the last time we tried that."

Eugène Charles Gerard must have been a delightful boy. He was certainly a charming man, then in his late sixties, when the author interviewed him for the first time, the first of many times. One could sense the admiration he must have had in 1902 for the father who had just returned from abroad. In 1902 Eugène Marais was not only a handsome man, a charming man and an extraordinarily talented man – he was also a man who had a natural love for children, all children, and an almost instinctive feeling for what mattered in their world.

"He very soon taught me and Sonny to play chess. On sunny Sundays we would sit and play on Mrs. Rex's garden path. And every evening he would tell us stories or read them to us, stories I can remember to this day. They were stories from all over the world, many of them from classical mythology. I remember that Hawthorne's *Twice Told Tales* was a great favourite.

"He was certainly not above playing the fool with us. Once he offered me sixpence if I could ride one of Mrs. Rex's young calves to the stables. I got there, but the calf rubbed me off against the manger."

If at this stage, seven years after Lettie's death, Eugène Marais still had mixed feelings about his son, he certainly did not show them, at least not to the boy himself. This was the more remarkable if one bears in mind how ill he was with malaria in these first months after his return to Pretoria, so ill that for the time being he could not work. Certainly his illness was not due entirely to malaria. He had always had the tendency to take things to heart. Now, after the war, he found himself in a slough of despond out of which he found it almost impossible to break. His people had not only been defeated – that would have been bad enough – they had been proven unworthy. And this, he felt, went for himself as well. On the East African expedition he had seen Burger through Dr. Schultz's cool Germanic eyes, and in a certain sense Burger was Eugène Marais.

He had little will to live and he was incapable of working. Even so, he had to start doing something. Even if for the time being he was too weak to practise, he was admitted to the bar as an advocate in October.

Marais had no inclination to become a newspaper editor again, possibly because he felt that in his personal capacity it would be difficult to keep to the spirit of his understanding with Falconer. He had to find an editor who could bring *Land en Volk* back to life. His choice fell on a young man named Gustav Preller. In the light of his agreement with Falconer, this was a revealing choice.

Gustav Preller was 27. Marais knew his background, as he knew that of just about every Pretoria-born Afrikaner. He also knew his young wife, Hannie, "as slim as a willow shoot", in Preller's own words.

Hannie was the daughter of one of the most prominent people in the capital: Commandant Henning Pretorius, until recently C.O. of the Transvaal State Artillery, the man who had brought the Slagtersnek beam to Pretoria shortly after the Jameson Raid.

Before the war Preller was first a shop assistant, then an articled clerk with a firm of attorneys, then a clerk in the Department of Mines in Pretoria. Educating himself by diligent study, he soon made it to chief clerk.

Preller had hero worshipped Marais for a long time. Apart from being editor of *Land en Volk*, Marais had also been assistant editor of *The Press* before the war.

In the nineties Preller had submitted a sketch to this paper, his "very first faltering step on the almost sacrosanct ladder of journalism. And some days later I received a short but friendly letter from Marais: 'I regret to say that your contribution, however interesting and suitable perhaps for the pages of a magazine, cannot be published in *The Press*.'"

Preller had privately preserved this note.

At the outbreak of war Preller was sent to the front. Besides being an artilleryman, he was also a war correspondent for *De Volksstem* and *De Zoutpansberg Wachter*.

By the middle of 1900 he found himself in Pretoria once more, where he helped the State Attorney, Jan Christiaan Smuts, to remove the Republic's bullion from the capital. Four months before the end of the war he was sent as a prisoner-of-war to a camp in India. By the middle of 1902 he returned to Pretoria and reapplied for his old job in the Department of Mining.

"I am sorry, Preller," the new, extremely pro-British head of the department is said to have told him, "you should have come back before the peace if you wanted your job back."

Preller was indignant and deeply disillusioned. He no longer saw any future in South Africa. In about August 1902 he decided to emigrate to Argentina with the Reverend Louis Vorster and a number of other Boers.

At about this time Eugène Marais returned to Pretoria and dissuaded Preller from leaving the country. If everyone fled, who would remain behind to reconstruct the Afrikaner nation?

Preller remained in Pretoria and accepted the editorship of *Land en Volk*.

One can see Marais and Preller going to the small press in Koch Street where *Land en Volk*'s printing machine had been waiting under canvas for several years. There, too, stood the handsome old mahogany desk at which Marais had written so many articles and leaders before the war.

Marais understood the restrictions under which they had to work. Years before he had complained bitterly about Kruger's Hold-Your-Tongue Act. He was now to learn what "hold your tongue" really meant. To Preller – perhaps not very firmly or insistently – he explained that *Land en Volk* was to be the only Afrikaans paper which was allowed to reopen, and that this could have happened only under strict conditions, including a rule of "no politics". "And I shall not be able to help you much at all," he added. "The fever still won't let go of me."

Preller, who had a single journeyman to attend to the technical side of publishing a newspaper, now received his first lessons in editorship. Marais could not stay with him for long. Future "editorial conferences" would have to be conducted in Marais's room in Jess Rex's boarding house.

Feeling his way, and rather grumpily, Preller set to work.

Throwing up partitions on one side of the printing press, he cleared a small office for himself. In the clearing-up process he came across a yellowed piece of paper in one of the drawers of Marais's old desk. Looking at it, Preller was both moved and surprised. Three lines, above all, caught his attention:

> A starless night is closing round.
> Farewell, my love, for thou wert lost
> ere yet thy love I found.

Lettie had now been dead for seven years. How often, in his feverish dreams in Jess Rex's boarding house, did she come to him still? There are longings, more especially if longing is bolstered by self-reproach, which die extremely slowly. Some never die.

While Preller was having a hard time at the paper, Marais was struggling with his attacks of malaria, taking his injections, dreaming his dreams – wonderful visions they were sometimes, at other times horrifying nightmares, and on occasion they mingled. But in spite of everything he was slowly returning to reality, the drab post-war reality of a conquered people.

There were days when he was not as ill as on others. Then he would play with young Eugène, with Sonny and with other children in the neighbourhood. He would talk to Jess's bright young daughter Mabel, who shared his own interest in journalism and in writing.

He would amuse her and the other lodgers by parodying the sentimental poems in Jess's birthday album. He had always delighted in writing parodies, even as a Paarl schoolboy.

There were quite a number of lodgers, and among them he soon discovered kindred souls. One of these was twenty-three year old Ben Tindall. Both Marais and Tindall were legal men, both had a great interest in literature, both had a wide general knowledge and a great love of nature. Ben Tindall opened new worlds for Marais. His father, an elderly Wesleyan missionary, had been a pioneer student of the dialects of the Hottentots and Bushmen of the Northern Cape and South West Africa. Tindall himself had learnt something of these peoples and their cultures. Quite likely it was he who now introduced Marais to the fascinating treasury of Bushman and Hottentot mythology, as recorded in the collections of Dr. W.H.I. Bleek, among others.

Gradually Marais again made contact with his own family.

Of Jan Marais's ten children who had been alive before the war not one had died. Some had lost a child or children during the war, others had been impoverished, others embittered, for during the war the family had been divided into two camps. But at least they were all still alive. One by one he got to see them again; of others he only heard.

There was Lizzie Niemeyer, at fifty-eight the oldest of the Marais children, whose husband had committed suicide as many as fifteen years before while he had been Charles Marais's partner in Boshof. Their son, Johnny, had fallen on Talana Hill. Lizzie, too, was keeping a boarding house in Pretoria – Donkerhoek in Schoeman Street.

There was Polly Clulee, only a year younger than Lizzie, another of the Marais sisters whose husband had deserted her.

There was Charles, now past fifty, back in his looted house in Boshof.

There was Henry, fifty, now living in style on Meintjeskop in Belvedere, one of the old corrugated-iron palaces which the British army had imported for its officers.

There was Jess Rex, forty-eight, in whose boarding house Eugène was staying.

There was Melt, forty-two, who had just returned from a prisoner-of-war camp and was slowly establishing himself as an estate agent in Pretoria once again.

There was Kate, forty, still married to accountant Dougall, a Jingo if ever there was one.

There was Sophie Ueckerman, thirty-seven, in whose house young Eugène was growing up.

There was Georgie, thirty-five, whose lovable, rather ineffectual husband, Andries Verdoorn, had returned from the war and was struggling to start anew on a small-holding at Grasfontein.

And there was Eugène – thirty-two – the youngest, still dreaming his dreams.

Preller had been moved by the poem he found in Marais's desk, but individual tragedy was being overshadowed by the greater tragedy of the war. How many thousands of men had returned to find that their wives had died in the camps? How many thousands more had returned only to learn of the death of a child and, all too often, in the poignant and understated words of Shakespeare's Macduff: "All my pretty ones? Did you say all?"

Despite all this the authorities kept insisting: "No politics."

"It was difficult to avoid the everyday realities of life," Gustav Preller was to write later. "The nameless sorrow one saw all around one, the destruction, the extermination, the apparent future plans for annihilation."

In other words, how could he remain silent when he had evidence that for Lord Milner the war, the real war for the possession of South Africa, was by no means over? As proprietor of *Land en Volk* and the person responsible for determining its policy, Eugène Marais was playing a singular role at this time – something like a double agent, a non-official spy employed by the Boers.

He had used English money to revive *Land en Volk*. He was now using his contacts in the English camp – including, possibly, the sympathetic Falconer himself, who felt guilty about England's role in the war – to obtain and publish secret information which Milner was extremely eager to suppress. Even before publication of the first issue of *Land en Volk* a copy of a letter Milner had written to Chamberlain, British Secretary of State for the Colonies, fell into Marais's hands. "After the peace the civil courts will be reopened," it said, more or less. "Many of the Boers' farms have been mortgaged. When the owners cannot pay, the mortgages will be called up and we can then buy the farms cheaply."

To Marais and Preller this was – in Preller's words – "a diabolical plot" to rob the Boers of their land.

"It was essential to warn the public against this," Preller was to write later. "Our people had to keep their land. For, as Roman history has taught us, in the long run the land does not belong to those who drench it in their blood in wars of conquest but to those who cultivate it and employ it usefully."

Land en Volk exposed the letter, pointing out the dangers. Technically they were completely correct in not submitting the article to the authorities, as it was a report and not a leader. The British authorities were furious. Marais – in spite of his instinct to protest against injustices, as he had done before the war – realised that it would do no good to have *Land en Volk* closed down. Lying ill in his boarding house room he pencilled a hurried note and sent it to Preller.

> Amice – Come and see me at once. The govt. want to close L & V down unless "no more opposition and ambiguous enmity" – E.N.M.

Thereafter everything, not only leaders, had to be submitted to the authorities.

Marais managed the paper from his bed and he did so laboriously, as his hurriedly scribbled notes to Preller show. By this time his bouts of fever had redoubled in vigour.

"He was often delirious when I visited him," Preller wrote about this time, "frightening me with the most amazing stories of pursuit I had ever heard. If it wasn't the English who were pursuing him in the fever marshes of East Africa, then the detectives here in Pretoria were on his track. In fact he had seen them in his room that very night. Thus he would rave, for weeks on end."

For the time being Preller would have to manage by himself, and in doing so he followed only his own head.

Below its masthead, *Land en Volk* was still printing the same defiant motto it had used before the war – "Truth, Liberty, Justice" – and Preller interpreted these words completely literally. To him it was a matter of pride to carry on Marais's fearless pre-war policy. This was to expose anything and respect no one's feelings – in fact, publish and be damned. In various editions he stated that "wretched methods of repatriation" were being used to bring people back from the camps.

The donkeys which were being handed to the Boers in terms of the peace treaty were sickening from some disease and they died by the score as soon as the Boers had signed the receipts.

The seed which was being distributed in terms of the agreement was sterilized seed-oats.

The purpose of the proposed expropriation of land previously exposed in *Land en Volk* was to make available enough land within a year for settling more than ten thousand "men and women of selected British race".

If any of these statements were true, it was certainly the last one, but to say so in 1902 was extremely dangerous.

Before the end of the year one of the issues of the paper was banned.

Meanwhile Marais's old friend, Ewald Esselen, and two of the Boer generals, Smuts and Botha, had approached him with an offer to buy *Land en Volk*. The sum of £6 000 – presumably to be provided by Mrs. Koopmans de Wet, a willing and patriotic Afrikaans lady in Cape Town, and Dr. Engelenburg in Europe – was mentioned.

Marais now found himself in a difficult situation. The offer was extremely tempting, being at least twice as much as the paper was worth. But his understanding with his friend Falconer was that he was not to sell *Land en Volk* to a third party without consulting the authorities.

At the same time enquiries were being made from the top – probably by Lord Milner himself – concerning the anti-British attitude adopted by a newspaper which was being financed by the Colonial Government.

Falconer, who was responsible for the agreement with Marais, was summoned to the office of the Colonial Secretary, W.E. Davidson, to offer some explanation.

Falconer took up the cudgels for his old friend as best he could. He did not believe that matters which endangered law and order were being published in *Land en Volk*. It was true that the newspaper reflected public opinion, and in the Transvaal public opinion was still anti-British.

In any case Marais had very little to do with the paper, he told Davidson soothingly. The editor was a certain Preller. He, Falconer, would personally see to it that no more irresponsible statements were made.

He kept this promise by visiting Preller in the *Land en Volk* office and talking it out with him.

Marais, on the other hand, was personally summoned to Lord Milner's mansion in Sunnyside, Johannesburg.

Lord Alfred Milner, High Commissioner for South Africa and Governor of the Transvaal and the Orange River Colony, energetic and conscientious, was busy trying to consolidate British supremacy in South Africa. Milner was a realist. For the first time South Africa was entirely under the British flag, but he well realised that no military conquest could guarantee permanent subjugation. The general drift of the *Land en Volk* leaders and reports which had so upset the authorities had been only too true. Milner wanted an energetic immigration policy to ensure the numerical superiority of English-speakers in South Africa. In addition, the Afrikaans-speaking population was to be systematically anglicised. This would be the only way to make South Africa remain within the British Empire voluntarily and permanently.

"Dutch should be used only to teach English," he had written before the end of the war in a memorandum regarding the future of South Africa, "and English to teach everything else."

When Eugène Marais went to lunch at Milner's mansion in Johannesburg, he was ill with malaria.

There were three of them: Milner, Marais and a senior official, a certain Somerset. Milner began sounding out his visitor during lunch, cautiously at first, then with increasing candour.

In South Africa, he said, the two population groups would have to find one another – Mr. Marais had said so in his paper himself – and everyone knew that. The situation showed certain similarities to that in Canada in earlier times. In Canada discord had been caused and perpetuated by the confrontation of two cultures and two languages. If Canada could have been made exclusively English-speaking, there would have been no problem.

That is what Lord Durham had tried to do, Eugène Marais remarked, and he had failed.

Milner granted this. Fortunately, the situation in South Africa was far less serious. In Canada the world's two most powerful cultures confronted one another. In South Africa the world's greatest language – not only the language of Shakespeare but the language of an empire on which the sun never set – had to contend with a lesser European language, Dutch. Nor was this the whole story. In the Cape Colony most people, educated people at any rate, preferred to speak English. And even those who still clung to Dutch, so he was given to understand, could no longer speak or write it correctly. Most of them spoke a broken *patois*.

Now and again Milner had to leave the room and then Somerset would encourage Marais. "You're doing well. I don't know why the Chief should worry so much about these things." But as soon as Milner returned, Somerset would become attentive and submissive once more.

The Governor pressed home his attack. Mr. Marais would concede that the English language already occupied a position of power in South Africa, that the cultural superiority of English in South Africa was probably at least as formidable as the British military superiority had been during the war. And it was not to end there. He would be frank – after all, *Land en Volk* had exposed the facts. The English-speaking population of South Africa was to be enormously enlarged by immigration from Britain within the next few years. Dutch would not be able to maintain itself for long. Its disappearance would either be painless or it could come about in an unpleasant and quarrelsome way. At a time when co-operation between the various population groups was so important, shouldn't they all help to let a natural process take its course in the least painful manner?

What was expected of him, asked Marais, who was feeling weaker by the minute.

Nothing but the obvious, Milner replied. The promotion of English. There was still time to decide on the best way of attaining this. It might be a good idea if Marais continued to publish *Land en Volk*, but devoted a good deal of its space to articles in which the Boer population was taught the principles of English. And next to teaching the Boers the language, this went without saying, the ideals of Empire should be promoted. Language was not enough. Thus *Land en Volk* might publish articles about history in which misunderstandings about past events were cleared up. As the Boer population was educated, an increasing percentage of the editorial matter could be published in English. At a later stage *Land en Volk* would either become an English paper or close down completely. That depended on Mr. Marais himself. The Imperial Government would not be ungrateful financially.

In the circumstances of 1903 this could have sounded like an acceptable and reasonable offer.

But Marais's instincts were against it, and he was too ill to react politely. "I can't do that," he replied bluntly.

And in truth he could not. *Land en Volk* had already stated its views against the acceptance of English as the sole language. In reply to the argument that apart from English there was no standard language in South Africa – only "kitchen Dutch, pulpit Dutch and high Dutch" – Marais (or possibly Preller) had written:

"However monstrous and despicable [our language] may seem to these strangers, they seem to forget that it is our mother tongue and the language in which we learnt to say our prayers at our mothers' knee ..."

Milner expressed his deep disappointment at Marais's negative reaction. The Government had generously assisted *Land en Volk* to resume publication in the hope that it would back the authorities. He was counting on Marais's help.

When Marais persisted in refusing, Milner asked him at least to say nothing of their interview and not to publicise the Government's aims for the Dutch language in his newspaper.

Marais was not willing to promise this either. In the end the Governor said: "Well, I want you to think about it. But please bear in mind that this is a question of policy. Opposition or enmity could have the most serious consequences for you and your paper."

By this time Marais was feeling so ill that he could not remain there for another moment. He only just made it to Jess Rex's boarding house, where he fell into bed, thinking, "Let Preller manage."

Later he was to tell Preller: "I was so ill that I would have promised anything if Milner had kept on nagging."

Marais came down with malaria once more. Everything was now left to Preller. After Falconer's sermon he was summoned to the office of the Colonial Secretary, Davidson. His Excellency was greatly upset about the irresponsible statements made in *Land en Volk*, Preller was warned.

The young editor defended himself cautiously: "Article 10 of the

Peace of Vereeniging gives my people the right to make demands," he said. "Are you trying to exclude us completely?"

Davidson shrugged. "I am sorry. These instructions come from His Excellency. In the end we shall simply have to close down *Land en Volk*."

"We either had to take in our sails or close down," Preller was to write later. "In the latter event we would have been unable to do anything for our public at all, so we decided to take in our sails."

Preller and Marais were not to prove over-zealous in doing so. Soon Marais was invited to Milner's mansion once more. This time the Governor complained about the disparaging way in which *Land en Volk* had lately been writing about joiners and hands-uppers.

"It is my duty to protect the people who helped us," said Milner.

Marais was no longer as ill as he had been. In spite of Milner's words he realised that the Governor felt only contempt for the Boer traitors. Every time Milner mentioned them, he did so in a snide manner.

Back in Pretoria Marais surprised his editor by turning up at the paper in person and immediately sitting down to write an eloquent leading article in which he opposed the proposed new Legislative Council, which the authorities intended packing with joiners and anglophiles.

An admiring Preller was never to forget the ease with which Marais could still do this in spite of his illness. "To me," he was to write later, "who was still struggling with high Dutch and would write a leading article at home at night, frequently retyping it again the next day, endlessly rephrasing and polishing it, for me it was a revelation and a pleasure to see him at work once more." And indeed the leading article Marais wrote without visible exertion in his little office in Koch Street was a clever piece of work, more damning and at the same time more cautious than many he had written before the war to criticize Paul Kruger's government. Without expressly attacking the British authorities as such, he condemned traitors in general – and, by implication, especially those who were willing to accept posts in the Colonial authorities' Legislative Council.

"What is to be done now? The hate is there, deep as the sea, and as wide as God's earth. We hate these people not so much because of what they did to make us lose the war; not so much because their hands are red with the blood of their brothers. We hate them from the depths of our hearts because they have sullied an honourable name."

"It was an article which tolled like a bell," Gustav Preller was to write. "That was how we all felt. Every day one met people in the street, pre-war acquaintances, whom one did not even want to see, let alone greet. The hate was there, and its aftertaste lingered in his words."

Adroitly, Marais tempered the severity of his words. Concerning the Boers' aversion to the traitors he said:

"The English can hardly expect anything else from us ... certainly they cannot expect their new subjects to make common cause with murderers and thieves, and in the moral code of nations the traitor who takes up arms against his own flesh and blood for money, lies far below these criminals. The English have a saying: 'We use but we despise the traitor.' They cannot expect more from us."

To this, he now knew, Milner could have no objection.

Rather like that East African capstao having to steer his shaky vessel between the coastal reefs, Eugène Marais now had to steer his paper between the reef of his own conscience and the mainland of the stern Colonial Government.

"Make the paper as tame as possible," reads another note which reached Preller from Jess Rex's boarding house. "Yesterday I was told for a fact from Milner's office that the additions to the Peace Act were occasioned expressly by the *Land en Volk* leader. It might help to say something *for* them in this and following issues – E.N.M."

Even so, he himself wrote a leading article of which Joseph Chamberlain, Secretary of State for the Colonies, no less, was the target.

At that stage the three Boer Generals, Botha, De la Rey and De Wet, had gone to England in an attempt to modify certain of the conditions of the peace treaty which they regarded as too harsh. The idea was entirely unacceptable to the British Government and reports from abroad constantly contained attempts to discredit the triumvirate.

At the same time Joseph Chamberlain announced that he intended visiting South Africa to make contact with the "leading Boers".

"The leading men he seeks," wrote Eugène Marais, "and who also wish to consult him, find themselves at his door in England at the moment – the beggars Botha, De la Rey and De Wet. We have no others here."

After this, according to Gustav Preller, the Colonial Government wanted to see not only proofs of leading articles and reports, but also copies of the printed paper.

3. The Avenging Angel

After the Boer War Eugène Marais was no longer the man he used to be, but he was by no means played out. The moment the malaria abated the old ardour returned – and it was directed not only at the English.

At the time ugly stories were circulating regarding the behaviour of a man Marais had once known, ex-Commandant A.H. Malan of Standerton. According to the rumours, Malan had cruelly whipped and otherwise maltreated a number of children in the prisoner-of-war camp on the island of Bermuda. Late in March 1903 *Land en Volk* published a letter, under a *nom de plume*, by one of the children who had been beaten. Marais added in a footnote that this was only one of a number of complaints he had received.

Malan soon wrote Marais an extremely courteous letter in which he asked whether Marais "held himself personally responsible for the statements in the letter." For the sake of truth and justice and also in the interests of his children and family, he would go to extremes to "purge myself of such defamation. As an erstwhile supporter of *Land en Volk* and one who still has a warm interest in its success, it would grieve me deeply to have to institute a claim for libel against your honour, (but) if you can suggest any other way which will enable me to refute the slander and to inform all the bodies concerned (parents, etc.) of the truth of the matter, your honour will always find me willing to meet him halfway."

Like an avenging angel Marais replied in an open letter which Preller, acting on Marais's instructions, published together with Malan's letter in *Land en Volk*.

As you (wrote Marais, intentionally using the insulting *gij*, more or less equivalent to German *du* or French *tu*) have known for many years, I am always responsible for everything published in *Land en Volk*. There were two reasons for publishing the letter. In the first place I believe that I have a certain obligation to the public. I may be wrong, but I have always acted on this supposition. In meeting this obligation I have never allowed anything in the world to stand in my way, no bonds of friendship nor any comparable considerations, as you yourself can testify.

The second reason is this. The whole country is full of rumours and talk about your behaviour on the island. My hands are full of documents which have a bearing on the matter. It was clear to me that unless an outspoken accusation could be made in a responsible manner or for which I could be personally responsible, the truth about this question might never have been made public. No amount of hearsay or rumours were sufficient for my purpose. I do believe, however, that the published letter will suffice in this respect. It is the only way in which you can clear your name of the stories repeated in all parts of the country every day.

The way in which you clear your name depends on yourself, of course, whether by means of a libel case or through the columns of *Land en Volk*, which paper is at your service now as always.

As far as is known, Malan never instituted a libel case.

Even so, all the problems considered, no one could say that *Land en Volk* was a paper worthy of its earlier fame. Few people in Pretoria realised this better and few people were scrutinizing the fortunes of *Land en Volk* more carefully than Dr. Frans Vredenrijk Engelenburg, pre-war editor of the *Volksstem* and Marais's old enemy and competitor.

Since Marais's departure for London Dr. Engelenburg had proved his mettle. During the period between the declaration of war and up to the occupation of Pretoria by the English, the *Volksstem* had continued publication under his leadership. There were numerous special editions and even a "campaign edition" printed in the field during the battle of Elandslaagte.

Dr. Engelenburg himself accompanied the commandos as a war correspondent while his paper was being published at home. Publication was only stopped when the English occupied the capital on 5 June 1900. Returning to Pretoria, Engelenburg found his office guarded by British soldiers. Adroitly, he slipped past them and removed certain valuable documents. However, when attempting to get away, he was arrested by the English.

He was sent to Stellenbosch on parole but made his way to Europe and eventually landed in Brussels, where he made himself useful to Dr. W.J. Leyds.

He, too, applied for permission to reopen his paper after the war but while the Colonial Government had looked upon Marais as a potential ally they saw Engelenburg – friend and confidant of President Kruger – as an enemy. Permission was withheld.

The reasons for the pre-war enmity between Marais and Engelenburg had now disappeared. During 1903 the Government reconsidered its decision, and granted Engelenburg permission to reopen *De Volksstem*. At the same time Marais, Engelenburg and certain Boer leaders seem to have started negotiating about the possibility of the two newspapers amalgamating, with Dr. Engelenburg as editor. Marais would be paid out for *Land en Volk* and he would be able to say goodbye to the newspaper world, which obviously no longer interested him.

From the Afrikaner point of view this could be an important step. One strong Afrikaans newspaper led by an experienced and able editor like Engelenburg, with the assistance of the best Afrikaans journalists in the country, would ensure a far more powerful voice to plead the Boer cause.

These plans were foiled by a British paper. The Pretoria correspondent of the London *Morning Post* heard of the negotiations and sent his paper an alarmist cable. According to him Generals Botha, Smuts and De la Rey wanted to buy the Afrikaans press in order to conduct a powerful, united press campaign against the Colonial Government.

Although the report was at least partially true, Marais denied it categorically and with characteristic scorn in *Land en Volk*.

"Needless to say," he wrote in a leading article entitled "Lies", "these slanderous and unworthy allegations … have not even received attention in the worst Jingo circles and have nowhere been taken seriously."

For Marais it was a dual setback. Not only did he miss the opportunity of getting rid of *Land en Volk* at a good price, but he would now be even more suspect in the eyes of the Colonial Government.

Permission to reopen *De Volksstem* was not withdrawn, however, and Dr. Engelenburg was looking for an able editor. What about Gustav Preller?

Preller felt a certain loyalty to Marais, but in all honesty he would have preferred to have been the assistant editor of *De Volksstem* under Dr. Engelenburg's editorship than editor of a struggling rag like *Land en Volk*, whose proprietor had obviously lost all interest in it.

The matter was settled amicably. Marais appointed an able Natal journalist, J.S.M. Rabie, as editor of *Land en Volk* and made things easier for Preller by telling him: "You must go where your future lies, Gustav. We can remain friends."

With Preller's departure to *De Volksstem*, Marais's interest in *Land en Volk* came to an end completely. Although he was only to sell it three years later, and although during this period he still occasionally used it as a platform for his opinions about the Afrikaans language, it was now to become more of a burden than a pleasure to him.

The year 1903 was a bad one for Marais.

In *Land en Volk* he could no longer say what he wanted to. Neither could he close it, as he was still hoping to find a buyer willing to pay a good price.

To an increasing extent the newspaper's losses made him dependent on the Government subsidy, and the English were paying more and more reluctantly. By the second half of 1903 payments were stopped completely. Marais's negotiations with Dr. Engelenburg may have been the last straw.

As Marais no longer took any interest himself, he was unable to inspire his editorial staff and after the resignation of Preller's successor, J.S.M. Rabie, there was a period of unending bother regarding editors and management.

Marais could, of course, practise as an advocate, but so soon after the war the legal profession was completely dead. He had rented an office in the Netherlands Bank building the previous year. Friends and family occasionally provided what the advocates called cat's meat – three guineas for an opinion, two guineas for a guinea-pig – but the large briefs did not materialize.

There were more serious problems, too. With enervating frequency malaria was still striking him down and, dominating the scene like a black avenging angel, the serpent now reared its hooded head once more.

In the first few months after his return to Pretoria, in spite of malaria, in spite of his own problems of addiction, he had resisted morphine with all his might.

He was no longer an anonymous atom among the millions in London, but one of the best known people in Pretoria. He would have to make a new beginning, and in this there could be no room for excess.

Eugène Marais was now thirty-three, and he was beginning to recognize his pattern. When in the past he had occasionally managed to force his consumption down to one or two grains a day, hoping that he would be able to live like a normal person, the craving would grow relentlessly week after week, and week after week the dose had to be increased, until, eventually, it reached four and five and six and seven grains a day.

Even when, by making sacrifices and exerting himself to the utmost, he managed to break this pattern, the moment he gave his body less than the amount it craved, that moment an evil time-bomb was activated somewhere in his being and then, relentlessly, there came a moment when the monotonous, daily, insufficient use of the drug, not for pleasure, but simply to keep away the worst deprivation, would become intolerable to his body, or spirit (or soul?) – and a binge would follow.

In the year of the Peace of Vereeniging, Eugène Marais had felt safe in the boarding house of his prudish sister Jess. When, after over-indulgence, he had to spend a day or two in bed, there was the convincing excuse that malaria had struck again, as in fact happened so frequently.

But Jess was no fool. Soon she knew the whole truth, and there may have been several other people who knew it as well. Superficially, the consequences of the immoderate use of morphine do not differ very much from that of alcohol, and of this Jess had had a great deal of experience, not only during her marriage but also as the keeper of a boarding house.

That Jess and some others knew about it, was bad enough. That they pestered him about it, was intolerable. So: still more morphine.

Was this the man who had so passionately praised the joys of opium when addressing the Vereeniging Jong Zuid-Afrika? It was he, but eleven years later.

For most morphine addicts the joys of the drug are shortlived. The pain it eventually produces is so overwhelming that even the memory of the original pleasure eventually disappears. This is why many morphine addicts deny that the drug ever gave them pleasure, even at the very beginning.

Judging by all the evidence, Eugène Marais did not follow this pattern. Even late in his life he would insist that morphine gave him great pleasure. Nevertheless, by 1903 the pain had become immeasurably greater than the joy.

That he should be tormented was bad enough. That people like his prudish sisters should worry over this entirely personal and private part of his life was unendurable. Eventually, every remark about it would become repulsive to him and finally the mere fact that people knew about it would offend him, as he knew that all of them, without exception, would allow their opinion of him to be coloured by this knowledge.

In the more than thirty years which were to remain for Eugène Marais early in the 20th century, there was to be another theme which, to an increasing extent, was to dominate his life: not only morphine, but the urge to flee from people who knew about his dependence and disapproved.

4. Winter Night

In 1904 *Land en Volk* carried a painfully ironic advertisement in one of its issues.

> EUCRASY
> *teen sterk drank*
> *misbruik van sterk drank*
> *Tabak en Droogerij*
> bedwelmende gewoonte
> en gevolgelijke senuweeagtig

Ziekten
Geheel veroverd, gekontroleerd
en genezen door
het gebruik van *Eucrasy*

EUCRASY
against strong liquor
abuse of strong liquor
Tobacco and Drugs
intoxicating habits
and consequent nervous
diseases
Completely conquered,
controlled and cured by
the use of *Eucrasy*

Apparently the worried mother was supposed to add a generous dose of Eucrasy to the food she served her son or husband. When the unsuspecting fellow again touched alcohol, tobacco or drugs, there would be such a strong reaction that he could never face them again.

One cannot guess how many Transvalers were cured of their weaknesses by Eucrasy, but there can be no doubt that it made many of them extremely ill.

Eugène Marais, at any rate, had to find more effective methods to combat his dependence. For this he went to live in Brooklyn.

"When we were schoolchildren in Pretoria," said his niece, Inez Verdoorn, in an interview, "he went to live there and tried to do without it."

Two of Marais's cousins, Rupert and Charles, sons of Oom Ryk Piet Marais, played a part in this decision.

These people may have felt something for the conquered Boers. However, they had never fought in the war, their businesses had not been shut down, their houses had not been destroyed, their lives had not been disrupted. They were the victors, and they were tremendously wealthy.

The elder of the two, Charles, had made a fortune selling property in Pretorian suburbs like Villieria, Mountain View and Pretoria

North. Some years before, their father, Ryk Piet, had paid Charles £5 000 to take Rupert in as a partner. In the Marais family Charles was known as the money-grabber. Rupert took life rather more easily. "He was rather a carefree kind of person," says a second cousin, George Findlay, "but his sense of justice was well developed, and he had an excellent sense of humour."

Even so, Ryk Piet had not invested his £5 000 unwisely. By 1904 Rupert, too, was a rich man.

Now the two brothers wanted to build houses worthy of their status in the new suburb of Brooklyn.

On Rupert's plot, on the corner of what were later to be called Brook and Williams Streets, he threw up a couple of rondavels in which he intended to live while supervising the construction of his house.

Although for the time being Brooklyn consisted mainly of vacant lots, it was obviously going to be a well-heeled neighbourhood. It was thickly wooded. Nothing but the wind pumps of proud owners who came to spend the weekends on their "plots" was visible above the tree-line.

At this stage somebody who was to play an important part in Eugène Marais's life during the next two decades made his appearance on the scene. His name was Charlie Pienaar.

Marais had family ties with just about every important person in Pretoria and Charlie was no exception. In his case there were not only marriage ties, but also financial ties with his family.

Charlie Pienaar, son of a Karoo farmer, had arrived in the Transvaal just before the war. He had joined the commandos, was captured near Murraysburg and exiled to Ceylon. After the war he had joined the attorneys Findlay and Niemeyer (both of whom were related to Eugène Marais).

Charles Marais and his brother gave his firm of attorneys all their property transactions, and at five guineas a transfer it was a lucrative business.

Charlie Pienaar, who used to be one of Eugène's circle of friends in Mrs. Rex's boarding house, was a young man, but he certainly did not lack intelligence.

He now used his contacts in the Marais family to obtain a plot in Brooklyn as well and he invited Eugène to join him in partnership.

They could build a simple little house there and share it.

No sooner said than done. The house was certainly simple. Although it was square and not round, it was little more than a rondavel, consisting of a passage, with a room on each side. A slate-covered stoep ran around the house, and the rustic thatched roof, which covered not only the house but the stoep as well, was supported by four-by-four wooden beams.

But it was a home.

Across the road, not yet named but later to be called Williams Street, Rupert and Charles were building their imposing mansions. North of this little group lay nothing but empty plots, and the nearest shop was three hundred yards to the south.

Eugène and Charlie would leave their bicycles on the stoep. There was room for them both to sleep, there was a fireplace with a handsome mantelpiece carved from wood, comfortable chairs, and no lack of books. Cured game hides covered the floor.

The part played by Eugène Marais in Brooklyn was primarily that of doctor and therapist – for himself. In 1905 medical science knew very little about morphine addiction. The way in which he treated himself here, trying to cure his addiction, at least proves that his intuition was sound.

Here in Brooklyn life became meaningful to him once more. A notebook dating from these years contains a rough diagram of the proposed garden, indicating the position for various roses: La France, Souvenir de Malmaison, Pearl d'Or, Blanche moreau, Kaiserin Victoria Auguste, Baron H. de Sacks, Sombreuil, and others.

He started a vegetable garden to supply him and Charlie with fresh vegetables. At one stage he also kept a cow. The chickens were so tame that they came to him to be stroked or to be rubbed under the wings. He planted fruit trees.

Using a foot-operated lathe on the side stoep, he and Charlie Pienaar made ash-trays and all kinds of wooden objects.

Eugène also made his own furniture.

He was surrounded by possessions which were dear to him. There was a variety of guns and revolvers, including a Colt and a Browning. On his desk lay four or five fountain pens – mostly Watermans – which he filled with a dropper. There was a beautiful barometer on the wall. The chronometer his employer, the watch-maker, had given him as a gift in London was so accurate that it lost no more than three seconds a year and on some of the furniture lay a variety of karosses, including some made from pelts of the rare silver fox.

For Eugène Marais this was a real home. For young Eugène – his first paternal home.

The boy was still living with Sophie Ueckerman but he spent most weekends and all the long vacations with his father in Brooklyn, usually accompanied by his cousin, Sonny. In Sophie Ueckerman's boarding house the two boys were growing up like brothers, and they were treated as such by Marais when they came to visit him in Brooklyn. To the boy these were unforgettable visits, unforgettable times. Seventy years later he was to remember them all in detail.

"Brooklyn was a suburb of windmills at the time. Each plot had its own, my father's as well. By getting on top of the windmill Sonny and I could count eighteen of them in the vicinity. Below our windmill my father rigged up a shower where we had to take baths under his supervision both in summer and winter. It was right under the tank. The icy cold blast stung like needles.

"That was the only water we had, and we had to carry it from there. My father always gave us a shilling for every tree we drenched thoroughly, which meant carrying three pails back and forth.

"Behind the house was a fenced off area with a vegetable garden, a cow-shed and a pen filled with fighting cocks. They were so accustomed to my father that they came to him to be stroked and scratched. Once, one of the cocks blinded another in a fight. After that he never allowed them to fight again.

"In front of the house there was a Japanese garden and in spring eight to ten varieties of violets would spread their fragrance all over the plot. In the middle of the garden there was an artificial pond. A huge toad lived in it. By day we boys had to catch flies and put them in a jar. In the evening we would gather on the front stoep and watch my father calling the toad, which would eventually come hopping along, take the flies from his hands and hop back contentedly to its home, where it would sit and grunt."

There were other animals too. George Findlay of Pretoria, who was a nephew of Marais and a young boy at the time, tells that the rough stone wall around the garden teemed with lizards. Marais could make them show themselves by knocking a pipe on a stone. He remembers that there were a number of tame tortoises in the garden. Once, when he and his mother went to visit Marais, he showed them a live puffadder in a perforated hat box.

Marais's fox-terrier, Gyppy, mostly slept on the bed with him.

In this virtually uninhabited suburb the smaller animals of the veld were still abundant. Scorpions, some of which Marais added to his collection, made a regular appearance. One of them introduced herself to Charlie Pienaar by killing a semi-grown chicken right before his eyes. "She grabbed the chicken by the leg, held it and used her deadly lance only once," Marais was to write in *The Soul of the Ant*. "The chicken was completely paralyzed within seconds, and death followed within ten minutes."

Marais now began patiently to rear this formidable lady of more than five inches in length. "She later knew me so well that I could bring my little finger suddenly in front of her and allow her to seize it with both pincers. She would arch her back until the tip of her sting pressed against my skin. Only then would she become conscious of my presence. The body would relax and the dangerous weapon would be laid to rest. I could handle her in any way I wished. She loved to be gently rubbed."

As he was to study the termites later, Marais now studied the habits of scorpions. His knowledge was limited, but he was learning fast. In his career as a zoologist this Brooklyn period may be regarded as a forerunner to his later researches in the Waterberg.

The two friends may have lived an isolated and peaceful life, but it was certainly not a monastic one. Copies of French magazines, including *Je sais tout*, lay on a coffee table in the sitting-room. In the cupboard other French magazines were kept which the children were not allowed to see.

Charlie enjoyed the reek of the great outside world which Eugène had brought with him. Although he helped his friend to get along without morphine, the phenomenon of opiates greatly interested him. Marais told Pienaar about the opium he had smoked in London. How, they wondered, would indigenous dagga (hashish) compare with it? It was no problem at all to obtain dagga in 1905.

Eugène and Charlie both tried it. For various reasons it gave them no pleasure, and both of them soon gave it up.

Charlie was something of a ladies' man. When Eugène told him about his amorous adventures in London and Paris he would listen attentively. He was shown the drawings of Susanne. Sometimes the two went courting together. When this happened over weekends or during a holiday, they told the boys: "Look out now, this place teems with scorpions and things at night."

"It was the only way to make us stay at home," said Marais's son. "We always went barefoot."

For the two boys, ten or eleven years old, the real fun would begin in winter. It was quite a routine. Sixty years later the boy, Eugène Charles, would remember this, too, in detail.

"First we had to shower – this was mandatory – and then jump into our pyjamas. Then we would dig up sweet potatoes and carry bundles of firewood into the house. As soon as the fire was blazing, we would sit down to eat in the warm and cosy sitting-room. It was often curry, for which at one stage my father specially kept an Indian cook. Nobody but he could make curry so strong that it made your eyes water."

Although at this stage the boy could not realise it, strongly flavoured foods, like curry, was one of the methods Marais used to tone down his withdrawal symptoms. It may be that he had acquired the taste for it from his Indian friends in London.

When the table had been cleared, they all sat down in front of the fireplace with its artfully carved wooden mantelpiece, and then Eugène Marais would read stories to the children in his soft, modulated voice: R.L. Stevenson, Conan Doyle, Hawthorne and Poe.

Then came the great moment: solemnly the sweet potatoes would be buried under the embers of the fire and left there.

"Most evenings games with my father's fox-terrier, Gyppy, would follow. He would hide his handkerchief under a cushion or in some other place, and then call the little bitch in to look for it. She always found it.

"Next, cards in front of the fire. This began as soon as Gyppy was tired. The stakes were a huge, gleaming, silvery heap of Callard & Bowser butterscotch which we children had gone to buy for that purpose at Rutowitz's shop in the afternoon. 'Sevens' – that's what we usually played.

"By the end of the game the sweet potatoes were dug from the fire and eaten with great gusto. Completely satiated, we boys would then creep under the pile of karosses which we used as blankets in my father's house."

While the children slept peacefully, no dreams disturbing their slumbers, Eugène Marais would often get up to look at them before going into the garden, where he would wander between his newly planted roses and cannas.

He would look at the stars, very bright above him, for Pretoria's night lights and street lights were few and far away. His thoughts would wander, like those of most Pretorians, to the war and its consequences, and what things could have been like had it not been for the war.

And it may have been on a Transvaal winter night like this that the idea came to him of writing an epic poem about the impressions of a sentry on commando – a poem he intended calling "Nagwag" – Night-watch.

From where the lonely burgher sat guarding his comrades he saw the vast expanse of veld lying before him in light and shadow. Against the ridges the grass moved in the cold, melancholy east wind.

Here, as he sat, the burgher was to ponder his people's past, the sorrows of war and the possibilities of the future.

But there were too many other things occupying Marais's time and he never wrote more than the first verse, a mere ten lines. This fragment he called "Winternag" – Winter Night.

It was to become one of the most famous poems in Afrikaans.

5. The Sandman

More than two years had passed since Eugène Marais had lunched with Lord Milner. What had his attitude to his mother tongue been during these two years as proprietor of *Land en Volk*?

The truth is that he had had nothing to say. In these two years one finds little more than an occasional reference to the language question in the paper, and it is almost certain that these articles were not written by Marais himself but by his editor, Dr. J. Vrolik.

Early in 1905 Marais himself wrote a leader about language. Preserving Dutch, he stated, should be one of the country's greatest priorities. The leader formed a prelude to a famous speech, "Is 't ons ernst?" (Are we in earnest?) which the famous Cape statesman, Jan Hendrik (Onze Jan – Our Jan) Hofmeyr, was to make at Stellenbosch some five weeks later.

Were the Afrikaners really in earnest when they said they were eager to preserve the Dutch language, Hofmeyr asked. Dutch was not even taught at most schools, and when it did form part of the syllabus it was taught so badly that hardly ten per cent of the scholars ever acquired the art of writing their parents an intelligible note in that language.

Only thirteen days later Gustav Preller replied to Onze Jan's question in *De Volksstem*: "Let us be in earnest about this". This was the first of a series of articles later to be called the Charter of the Second Afrikaans Language Movement. In these Preller advocated not only the survival of Dutch, but the systematic promotion of the new language, Afrikaans, which had a better chance of maintaining itself in the face of English.

Marais played an important part in this series of articles. As early as 1891 he had started publishing Afrikaans articles in *Land en Volk*. He and Preller must often have discussed the subject after the war, and it seems very likely that Preller's articles were inspired by these talks with his mentor. In fact, a combined campaign conducted from March to June 1905 in *Land en Volk* and in *De Volksstem* shows so many similarities and testifies to such a degree of agreement concerning basic principles that close consultation behind the scenes seems virtually certain.

Before the end of March Marais published an Afrikaans poem, "Die Afrikaanse Pop" (The Afrikaans Doll) which had originally appeared in *De Goede Hoop*. Five days later Preller printed the same poem in *De Volksstem*.

There was no lack of unpretentious poems and verses, but good stories were scarce. Marais decided to put up a prize of £3 for the best Afrikaans story published in *Land en Volk* every month.

He may have been thinking of the great success which Von Wielligh's "jakkals- en wolfstories" (wolf and fox – more correctly hyena and jackal – stories) had had in *Ons Klyntji* years before, when he decided to retell one of the idigenous folk tales himself by way of example. The story, "Die Tier en die Bokram" (The Leopard and the Billy-goat), appeared in *Land en Volk* as an early precursor of Marais's famous "Dwaalstories".

In the same issue he published "Piet van Snaar", a long epic poem, light in touch and without literary pretence.

The *nom de plume* he used, "Klaas Vakie" (The Sandman), may be significant. Later he was to write a child's poem using that sobriquet as the title. We know that a cradle song about Klaas Vakie was traditional in the Marais family and that Marais quite possibly learnt it as a child. In both the song and the later poem, Klaas Vakie is not the likeable little man who sets the child's mind at rest by making him sleep, but a somewhat menacing figure from the dark.

To the morphine addict, as we have seen, sleep may indeed be something menacing as it can bring nightmares in its wake. But there is a strong suspicion that Marais used the *nom de plume* "Klaas Vakie" with the poem "Piet van Snaar" as a sort of self-mockery or, at most, a little joke between him and one or two friends.

It may in fact be that the use of the name indicates a period of controlled morphine consumption, during which he thought that he could afford self-mockery. (In Afrikaans, "Klaas Vakie" can mean not only "the bringer of sleep", but also "the sleepy one".) At any rate we find him hard at work at this time.

Scores of stories had meanwhile been received for the competition. How many of these stories were written by Marais himself is a mystery, but his son relates:

"During this time my father wrote a number of fox and wolf stories for *Land en Volk*. He was ill with malaria, and the proofs were sent to his house in Brooklyn to be read. More than once I had to be his copy reader, and he just about killed himself laughing at my pedantic Dutch accent."

In these indigenous folk tales, which have been lost – probably because so many issues of *Land en Volk* were damaged or no longer exist – Eugène Marais was in fact preparing himself for writing his later "Dwaalstories" (Wandering Tales), some of the best stories ever written in Afrikaans prose.

At that stage, in any case, one has to accept that Marais and Preller often consulted about the next step in their campaign for the promotion of Afrikaans. In June 1905 Preller followed Marais's example by launching a competition for Afrikaans stories, and three days later his "Charter" for Afrikaans was published in *De Volksstem*. In the next two issues of *Land en Volk* Marais asked writers to build up an Afrikaans literature – for without a literature, he said, no language could hold its own for long. Among the "few pieces" he published to illustrate the possibilities of the language were the first ten lines of the long epic poem on which he had been working for quite a while, but could not complete. The fragment was published under the title "Winternag".

In one of Gustav Preller's subsequent articles about Afrikaans in *De Volksstem* he quotes the entire poem, using it as an example of the potential of the Afrikaans language. "The author," he said, "is an unlettered Boer who will never be able to write Dutch, but he is undoubtedly a poet. It is only a fragment, titled "A Winter Night", but one can listen to it."

(Three decades later Preller had become a great deal more positive: "If ten lines of all the poetry we have in Afrikaans *today* should still have survived a century hence, the ten lines of the poem "Winternag" will be among them.")

In July, and again in August, Marais devoted leading articles to the promotion of the Afrikaans language. But negotiations by an attorney, Hopley, regarding the sale of the paper, had been in progress for some time and pending this transaction Marais decided that very month to stop publication. Matters were to drag on for quite a while, however, for it was not before November that he wrote to Preller: "*Land en Volk* has finally been sold, and I believe it is to be published again this week. I do not know who the new owner is. It was bought by an agent, who is unwilling to divulge the name of his principals ..."

Land en Volk was to continue publication for another year or so before it was eventually closed down for good.

Saying goodbye to *Land en Volk* was not a great wrench for Marais. He had been trying to sell the paper for a long time, and although it seems that in the end he received only a modest amount for it, he could use the money well enough.

In the meantime there was a much more serious disruption. Charlie Pienaar had become engaged and intended marrying soon. He would have to leave the house and set up on his own. Eugène was perfectly welcome to move in with them, he said. Louise would welcome him.

Marais was grateful for the offer, but he was rather uncertain. The rustic little house in Williams Street had become part of his life.

About this time he took up a new hobby, or perhaps something more than a hobby. Breeding animals had long fascinated him, but now he began trying to breed a fox-terrier as closely as possible to the perfect ideal. In his notebooks he devotes almost a thousand words to the features of a show fox-terrier.

It was an expensive hobby. In January 1906 he paid £25 for a favourite bitch, Peggy, probably hoping to make money from breeding.

The only reference to income in his notes is the sale of one of Peggy's sons to Charlie Pienaar for £10. Proudly he compares the ideal measurements with those of Peggy and her daughter, Bonnie Greta:

> Length of head is 7½ to 8". Peggy 7½". Girth of muzzle before eyes 6½ to 7". Bonnie Greta 7¼". Hock to ground 3½ to 4". Peggy 4".

In June 1906 Bonnie Greta produced a bonny litter: four male puppies, Abd el Kadel, Mesrour, Ahmed Madrali, Israfel and two bitches, Al Sirat and Nour ed Deen.

But the tiny dogs were only a few months old when Marais pulled up his stakes once more. He had decided to go and practise in Johannesburg.

6. Hillbrow

The reasons for Marais's move to Johannesburg are unknown. Perhaps he soon realised that it would not do to live with Charlie and Louise Pienaar.

It may be that in Johannesburg he saw a far greater future as an advocate than in Pretoria, where briefs were still extremely scarce.

It may also be that a girl, Anne, was the cause of his move there.

Here we come to the first of the four or five great disrupting love relationships in Eugène Marais's life about which friends and family were always to refer in guarded terms. What might have happened in this relationship will not be obvious until later in the life story, when we deal with comparable relationships of which more is known.

It is true that Marais found financial success in Johannesburg. In one brief his knowledge of German enabled him to bank a fee of £800.

He had moved into Hillbrow, which in 1907 was not yet the concrete jungle it was later to become but a pleasant, fairly quiet suburb. He lived in a rented room or rooms and here, for the third time in three years, he was almost shot dead.

"The first time was in Brooklyn," his son was to say much later. "He had a .32 Browning on the desk in his room. One morning, when my father was sitting on his haunches next to a flower-bed in the garden, Charlie Pienaar was showing me and Sonny the pistol's mechanism. He had removed the magazine, but there was a bullet in the barrel and when he pulled the trigger the shot went through a window-pane, ricocheted from a rock in the garden and whistled across my father's head.

"Soon afterwards, while my father, Charlie Pienaar, Piet Marais and Rupert Marais went target-shooting at the block-house – this was north-east of his house in Brooklyn – he told them about the incident. Taking the pistol, Piet asked: 'Did it happen like this?' He then removed the magazine and pulled the trigger. My father was standing with his heels close together – a characteristic stance – and the bullet passed between his heels, cutting grooves in both of them.

"In Hillbrow he and a friend were dressing for the theatre one evening when my father told him about the previous cases and showed him the Browning. This time the shot went through the soft flesh of his hand, between the thumb and the index finger, grazing his breast. He exchanged the Browning for a Mauser and swore he would never buy a Browning again."

Three times, and each time a closer shave.

Marais practised law, he went to the theatre, he read, he was using too much morphine and he courted Anne – where and when he could.

Anne was attractive, perhaps beautiful. She was also young, extremely young. Her light, youthful sense of humour survives in a letter she wrote to Eugène Marais in her light, youthful handwriting: "Please don't think this is my natural voice. I have an awful cold."

The year which Marais spent in Hillbrow also saw the death of Francis Thompson, opium addict and inspired poet. In this year, although Marais had not yet read it, Thompson had written "Memorat Memoria", the disturbing poem from which Marais, in spite of all his admiration, was later to shrink back because so much of what he feared in himself found terrifying echoes there – the morphine dream, the dream of fear, in which the dead beloved appears in a variety of guises; the dream of guilt, in which the beloved woman, the beloved young girl, is a symbol of treason – treason by both the dreamer and the one dreamt about.

> Come you living or dead to me, out of the silt of the Past,
> With the sweet of the piteous first, and the shame of the shameful last?
> Come with your dear and dreadful face through the passes of Sleep,
> The terrible mask, and the face it masked – the face you did not keep?
> You are neither two nor one – I would you were one or two,
> For your awful self is embalmed in the fragrant self I knew ...

Some lines later there are the revealing words: "... how ... sad the songs we dare not sing!"

Almost seven decades later Marais's son was to say of him that a possible clue to the nature of his relationships with women may be found in the novel *Lolita*: the young girl as predator, the older man as her willing prey. Not everyone will agree with this interpretation of *Lolita*. Even so, rereading Nabokov's novel, one finds Humbert's strange love following a pattern reminiscent of that of De Quincey in his *Confessions* regarding opium. The first part of *Lolita* concerns itself mainly with the joys of conquest. In the second anxiety, humiliation, a sense of guilt emerge:

> ... I catch myself thinking today that our long journey had only de-

filed with a sinuous trail of slime the lovely, trustful, dreamy, enormous country that by then, in retrospect, was no more to us than a collection of dog-eared maps, ruined tour books, old tyres, and her sobs in the night – every night, every night – the moment I feigned sleep.

In the peaceful suburb of Hillbrow another half a century was to pass before the publication of *Lolita*. But as early as 1907 Francis Thompson, in the second half of "Memorat Memoria", had mercilessly dissected this aspect, too, of his own and Marais's inferno:

Ah, the ill that we do in tenderness, and the hateful horror of love!
It has sent more souls to the unslaked Pit than it ever will draw above.
I damned you, girl, with my pity, who had better by far been thwart,
And drove you hard on the track to hell, because I was gentle of heart.

Marais, too, had a kind heart. He could be gentle and compassionate. But no man is one man; every man has in him something of Mr. Hyde. And so, even in the gentle ones, the sensitive ones, perhaps even more so in them, self-regret eventually emerges, whether they be agnostics (even atheists) like Marais, or intensely religious like Thompson:

I shall have no comfort now in scent, no ease in dew, for this;
I shall be afraid of daffodils, and rose-buds are amiss;
You have made a thing of innocence as shameful as a sin,
I shall never feel a girl's soft arms without horror of the skin.
My child! what was it that I sowed, that I so ill should reap?
You have done this to me. And I, what I to you? – it lies with Sleep.

For Eugène Marais, in Hillbrow, in 1907, his love for Anne was soon to change, far too soon, into bitterness, self-regret and humiliation, until he could no longer stay in Johannesburg.

The few months in Hillbrow had been nothing but an interlude. Late in 1907 he moved to the Waterberg.

PART 5: THE WATERBERG

Wanneer jy wil vlug uit die stad wat brand, dan vlug ek saam soos 'n vrou aan jou hand.	When you wish to flee from the burning city, I shall flee on your arm like a woman you pity.

1. The Baboons of Doornhoek

There were several reasons for Marais's drastic decision to leave the city and to go and live in what, at the time, was an isolated and primitive part of the country. One was escape – not least from morphine – and in this Gustav Preller encouraged him.

In the Waterberg, so Marais thought, he would again be able to live a balanced life. He would also be able to forget the trauma of his relationship with Anne. In a less tense atmosphere, surrounded by none but good, simple countryfolk, he might learn how to get along without morphine, or at least how to reduce his intake. And he would be able to go prospecting.

"Like his brother Henry, my father was always most interested in minerals and prospecting," his son said later. "This may well have been the reason for his decision to go and live there."

It was more than an interest: it was a passion – the passion of the gambler and the digger.

Ever since his childhood days in Pretoria, the Waterberg – and the Waterberg's wealth – had fascinated him.

"It represented," he was to write later (in *The Road to Waterberg*), "the ideal theatre of manly adventure, of great endeavours and the possibility of princely wealth. Ivory was then what gold and diamonds became afterwards, and stories were told of bold and lucky hunters killing twenty tuskers in one morning – the value of a principality of land in a few hours."

And now, in the years after the war, there were again riches in the Waterberg – true, there was no longer ivory, but there was tin and platinum.

Marais had not visited the Waterberg until after the Boer War –

possibly in 1905 or 1906. This is how he saw it:

> An old acquaintance, Dolf Erasmus, met me in Nylstroom with a cart and four horses and for the first time in my life I was to enter Waterberg, the mystery region of my boyhood.
>
> Dolf's horses had to be rested and fed before we started. It was decided that we should travel by night so as to reach our destination in the central hills of Waterberg somewhere about sunrise.
>
> While we waited darkness succeeded dusk and the little village sank to dreamy quietness. Lights began to twinkle through the windows. From one cottage came the notes of a piano and across the river the jackals howled incessantly.
>
> Dolf and I inspanned at midnight and the four horses at once fell into the steady pace which meant that they knew a long journey and the road home lay before them. It was an intensely dark night and when we drove down to the drifts it seemed as if we were sinking into a gulf of impenetrable darkness.

The Dolf Erasmus who had come to meet Marais in Nylstroom was a tin prospector. He was the discoverer of the platinum deposits in the Waterberg and of tin in Doornhoek, or more accurately (to believe an old Waterberger): "It was old Isak, a Kaffir from Wilgeponder, who discovered the tin in Doornhoek. At the time one could still see it on the outside of the rock. The old Kaffir then told Dolf Erasmus about it, so Dolf became the discoverer."

Dolf Erasmus took Marais to Doornhoek, where a number of prospectors were living and working.

Marais looked around him. His childhood dreams had not been exaggerated. Even on a taped interview dating from 1973 the coo and chirrup of scores of species of birds may clearly be heard in the background. In 1905 or 1906 it must have been a magic world. Marais returned to civilization, but the memories would not leave him. He decided to settle there permanently.

Some time during 1907 – we do not know exactly when – Marais moved to the Waterberg, settling on the farm Doornhoek and buying prospecting rights from the owner, Van Staden.

It was no longer sparsely populated bushveld. When Niklaas van Heerden, a Voortrekker, had reached that part of the Waterberg in 1859 there were no whites further north, and the nearest people to the south lived at Doornfontein. In the next half a century, however, many descendants and new brides and bridegrooms joined the clan, and in 1907, the year of Marais's arrival, there was a white population of 103 (as opposed to seventeen in 1963, and only a few in 1973!) on the Van Heerden farm Kromkloof, which bordered on Doornhoek. There was also a large farm school and a shop, the property of "Oom Flip" Cohen, who was no doubt related to the "Oom Piet" Cohen of Nylstroom on whom several characters in Marais's short stories were based.

Later Marais was to become well acquainted with the people of Kromkloof, but at first he stayed with Dolf Erasmus on Doornhoek, until he joined up with one of the other prospectors, Alec Austin. Within a short time he and Austin had built themselves huts in the deep rift valley which dominated the farm Doornhoek, the so called Baboon Kloof.

In *My Friends the Baboons* he describes it as follows:

> A few years after the Anglo-Boer War, Mr. Alec Austin – a Transvaler who grew up on the veld – and I built a permanent residence in the high-lying valley between the double row of mountains of the well-known farm Doornhoek ...
>
> The whole region was a delightful one for the purpose we had in mind, and I do not think that I ever passed a happier time in my life than the three years we spent in the mountains of Doornhoek.

The ravine was an imposing natural phenomenon, bordered on one side by a precipice of more than two hundred feet in height and on the other by a steep ridge. Huge blocks of rock lay in heaps in the kloof, changing the river into a series of cascades and rocky pools in the rainy season. The entire ravine was densely covered in indigenous trees and shrubs, including ferns and a number of huge wild fig trees.

In 1907 a troop of baboons, estimated by Marais to number about three hundred, occupied the kloof. On the eastern side of the kloof there was a high rocky ledge, and behind the ledge a shallow cave which was protected in front by one of the large wild fig trees. Here the baboons spent their nights.

Marais and Austin's huts were within a few hundred yards of the upper entrance to the kloof. At the bottom of the kloof lived Willem van Staden, owner of the farm. Here Eugène Marais would leave his Cape cart and horses – Blackie and Sunlight – before walking up the kloof to the huts. Here, too, he left most of his possessions, most of them still packed in trunks and boxes.

Using stale bread bought from a baker in Nylstroom and bags of maize, Eugène Marais succeeded within a matter of weeks in accustoming the troop to him and Alec Austin.

The year 1907 had been preceded by some years of excellent rainfall and nature was at its most beautiful. Wild plums, wild peaches, "Kaffir oranges", medlars, red milkwood and other veld fruit grew abundantly in the kloofs, and insects abounded. "We had to become intimately acquainted with huge scorpions and spiders which, on rainy days, made a gruesome appearance from the thatched roofs of our huts. Snakes of all types we met every day."

Soon the baboons were so tame that Eugène Marais could move among them – although always keeping his Mauser within reach. He learnt how to tell the leaders apart, even giving the largest males nicknames, and he made notes of what he observed.

In these few months Marais gained the basic knowledge on which he was later to base his book *My Friends the Baboons* and large parts of *The Soul of the Ape*. For another nine years he was to observe the baboons of the Waterberg, frequently at Doornhoek, but these were to be the last intensive and systematic observations he made.

Early in 1908 a newly founded Johannesburg mining company obtained options on Doornhoek's mineral rights. All prospecting by other persons would have to cease. Eugène Marais would have to find a new home.

He was travelling in his Cape cart some miles north-west of Doornhoek when the road he was following ran through a farmyard. He had just been laid low by another bout of malaria, and was not feeling at all well. Reining in the horses, he stepped down from the cart and knocked at the farm-house door. Could he have some water?

Eugène Marais was wearing the riding breeches and leggings which were his uniform at the time, all according to the latest fashion. His Cape cart was shiny, his horses well groomed. In the Waterberg he was regarded as a rich and important man.

The Boer woman who invited him in and introduced him to her

husband, was a skilled midwife. She also had considerable nursing experience and she quickly noticed that there was something wrong with him. He should come inside and have something to eat, she insisted, and then rest a little.

Thus began a friendship which was to last for nine years.

The farm, one of the most beautiful in the Waterberg, was Rietfontein. The Boer and his wife were Gys and Maria van Rooyen.

By this time Eugène knew that he could not carry on prospecting on Doornhoek. He soon came to an agreement with the Van Rooyens. He was to live on Rietfontein. He could keep cattle there – one of his great interests as a lover of animals – he could prospect for minerals on the farm, and he could practise as a doctor. In these negotiations, although "Oom Gys", as head of the household, technically had the last word, "Tant Maria" played an important part. In spite of all her hospitality and compassion she also had considerable business acumen.

Eugène Marais's possessions – including a heavy, padlocked box with wrought-iron handles – were brought from Doornhoek to the stoepkamer (a room built to one side of the veranda) which Tant Maria had prepared for him. There was a wardrobe with some suitcases on top of it, a chair, a table and a beech bookcase filled with his books. The wooden bed, like most of the other furniture, was Oom Gys's handiwork. It had a matting of leather thongs, a coir mattress and a featherbed filled with down from Rietfontein's own ducks and geese.

2. Oom Gys and Tant Maria

Marais's possessions included a collection of medical instruments and a variety of medicines. In his diary he wrote:

> Rietfontein 4 March 1908. (Lukas G.C. Scheepers, Doorndraai, P.O. Nylstroom, husband not ill) Mrs. J.E. Scheepers wife (Iron and Quin. tonic) (31). J.E. Scheepers small daughter bad digestion. Costive pain (6). W.N. Prinsloo, same farm 20. Consumptive. Emulsion cod-liver oil.

This was the first and last time that Marais's "diary" was to contain such extensive medical notes, but the inscriptions leave little doubt that at that stage he intended establishing a medical practice.

The story that Marais gave his medical services free of charge to the whole district was later told by Gustav Preller. It is true that the inscription in the notebook contains no fee, but he knew the old Boers. According to their code of honour they were obliged to compensate a doctor who had treated them or their children, whether or not he asked for it, either in money or in kind.

Tant Maria and Oom Gys van Rooyen were a remarkable couple. In Afrikaans writing they were to live on in one of Marais's poems, "Wanneer dit reën op Rietfontein" (When it rains on Rietfontein):

Wanneer dit reën op Rietfontein
En deur die stof 'n straal van
groen verskyn,
Wanneer die wolke, swart en
swaar belaai,
In voue oor die berge
pak en swaai,
Dan sit oom Gysbert
op die stoep alleen;
Hy asem sag die geur
gemeng van stof en reën ...
Van agter uit die groot kombuis
Kom daar aanhoudend die gesuis
Van kole op die vuurherd
aangeblaas
Van pot en pan die
klinkende geraas –
Dis net so seker as die boek,
Tant Malie bak nou
pannekoek!

Oh, when it rains on Rietfontein
And streaks of green gleam on the
dusty plain,
And when the swollen clouds,
all black and grey
In folds over the mountains
clutch and sway,
Oom Gysbert sits out
on the stoep, quite calm
Breathing the smell of
dust and rain like balm ...
Sounds filter from the kitchen
grand
And when he hears the coals
being fanned
With constant hiss, and all
the while
The clink of pots and pans –
he'll smile
It's just as certain as the Book
Tant Malie's baking
"pannekoek"!

The lines tell us little more than that Tant Maria was an energetic farmer's wife and that one could frequently see Oom Gys sitting on the stoep – accurate but slender facts.

They were simple farming people, hardworking enough to make

quite a success of their farm in that fertile country. But the Boer War had deeply scarred them, in more ways than one. The Rietfontein of the previous century may have been a happier farm than the one which Marais learnt to know in 1908, and certainly it had been a more prosperous one.

Oom Gys was a wagon-builder and smith by trade as well as a competent bricklayer. When building a wagon he did not have to buy any parts at all. All these – in fact virtually anything at all – could be made on the farm. He had been forty-one when he acquired Rietfontein in 1893. In the six years before the outbreak of the Boer War in 1899, he had turned it into a beautiful and virtually self-sustaining farm. He had built the farm-house himself, assisted by four of his children – Maria, Cornelia, Piet and Adriaan. They had to make themselves equally useful when wagons had to be built or when there was carpentry to be done.

"When I was in my teens I often had to help him," his daughter, Cornelia, said later. "You know, the tree-trunks first had to be adzed to make them more or less straight and level. When that had been done he blackened a long string in some powdered charcoal, tied a leaden weight to the string and let the string twang against the tree-trunk, where it would leave a thin black line. The tree trunk was put on trestles and, using a double-handed saw, we had to saw all along the fine black line. If I happened not to follow the line exactly, he would roar: 'Moerneuker!'" (It is unlikely that Oom Gys, in that pious community, knew the meaning of this ancient oath, which had possibly come down the generations from his earliest Dutch sea-faring ancestors and meant nothing less than "motherfucker".)

There were few things which the master of Rietfontein could not make himself or which the farm could not produce. Certain products could be bought more cheaply from Jewish or "Coolie" (Indian) hucksters, it was true, and for a few things one might even have to drive to the shops in Naboomspruit or Nylstroom, but these were exceptions. Before the farm was burnt down by enemy troops, it had even boasted a sugar plantation, and sugar was "turned out" on a lathe which Oom Gys had made for the purpose.

Using nothing but a pocket knife and a hatchet he fashioned items of furniture from lilac trees (maksering) which grew on the farm.

He made the family's own shoes on hand-turned lasts of marula wood. To supplement his supply of cash, always scarce in those days, he built covered wagons, shod horses, shrank on the iron tires of carts or wagons, or repaired vehicles. Rietfontein's smithy was a busy place.

The couple had fourteen children (five more had died at birth or at an early age), of whom eight were still in the house.

Then the war came. The farm was partially burnt down, the women and children sent to concentration camps. In the Van Rooyen family Bible the consequences are grimly and starkly recorded.

> Katarina Petronella, born 1892 – died in camp
> Susara Aletta, born 1893 – died in camp
> Daniël Pieter, born 1895 – died in camp
> Anna Katarina, born 1898 – died in camp
> Wilhelmina, born 1900 – died in camp
> (11 months)

They were the five youngest children. Several of the survivors, too, never completely recovered from their experiences.

The oldest son, Gys, who lived one and a half miles from the main farm in his own house, was a twenty-seven year old married man when war broke out. He went on commando, was taken prisoner and sent to Bermuda. When he came back to Rietfontein after the war, not one of his children was alive. This was a shock from which he was never to recover entirely. In the third generation, too, – the grandchildren of Oom Gys and Tant Maria – the death toll was horrifying.

When Eugène Marais came to live on Rietfontein in 1908 the Van Rooyens had apparently largely surmounted these catastrophes. Most of the war damage had been repaired, and the farm was in excellent condition after some fine years of rain.

The poem "Rietfontein", some lines of which were quoted above, to some extent characterises the difference between husband and wife. Oom Gys was still tremendously agile for a man close to sixty. "When hunting," Eugène Marais's son was to relate later, "he could chase and overtake a kudu, jump from his horse, shoot at it, jump back in the saddle and gallop on."

Even so, he was fond of stoep-sitting and telling tall tales. Tant Maria, although only two years younger than her husband, was by far the more energetic of the two. Her personality, too, was the stronger. Naturally, she grieved for the children and grandchildren she had lost; naturally, she herself had been weakened by almost twenty pregnancies and the time she had spent in the concentration camp. But she was tough, and when her energies failed her, her will kept her going.

Apart from her work as a midwife and nurse, she was an excellent farmer's wife. In spite of the plentiful supply of black labour which was always available on the farm, she herself worked extremely hard. Her entire house was regularly given a new floor. To do so the floor had first to be covered in stink-oil leaves "to make it shine" and then given a new layer of "green" manure (cattle manure which was still runny, and could be worked easily) on which all kinds of rectangular, striped and curved patterns would then be drawn.

One factor which hampered the farmer's wife at that time was the almost universally held belief that all blacks had some kind of venereal disease, making them unfit to handle or work with food. This was particularly trying in view of the huge masses of food processed on a farm like Rietfontein. From the orchards oranges, bananas, walnuts, almonds, tangerines, peaches, guavas, apricots and a variety of fig species were brought to her pantry to be processed or bottled. Tant Maria was particularly famous for her prickly-pear jam. In the fireplace in her spacious kitchen she not only prepared simple dishes like grilled sheep's head, Oom Gys's favourite, but also huge meals for a multitude of guests. Twenty people for Sunday dinner was nothing unusual.

Clothes she mostly made herself. Bed-sheets were made from very tough calico which she bought for fourpence a yard from Indian peddlers from Nylstroom.

She was also a trained nurse and she could "doctor" well. She was the midwife for the entire region. Two of her house's eight rooms were outside rooms used exclusively for deliveries. Itinerant derelicts would sometimes just manage to make it as far as her house, where they would be nursed back to health, while many people visited the hot springs on the farm, hoping that this would cure their ills.

"Mother of strangers" one of her descendants was to call her much later. Even her enemies were to tell of the famished, half-crazed Jewish hobo who once appeared on Rietfontein and whom she conscientiously but unsuccessfully tried to nurse back to health. After his death she had the beautifully finished tambuti wood coffin taken down from the boekenhout beams where Oom Gys had stored it for his own funeral. Extremely indignant though he was, Tant Maria did not budge an inch and the hobo was laid to rest in the elegant coffin.

Virtually everyone who knew her called her Tant Maria, pronouncing it as one word, Tamária, the accent being on the second syllable, to such an extent that some visitors from the outside world thought Tamaria to be her name. She was a respected, well liked woman.

This did not mean, however, that she would refuse payment for her services. Those who were able were free to give her what they could afford: an ox, a sheep, a chicken, whatever they had.

She was certainly well pleased with the prestige she and Rietfontein would gain by having a wealthy, refined medical and legal man like Marais as a lodger. She was also well pleased with Eugène Marais as a man. In fact she grew very fond of him. As a nurse she soon realised that malaria was not his only problem. He told her about the morphine, calling it "morphia" after the fashion of the time (and almost seventy years later unlettered, Afrikaans-speaking Waterbergers were still to use this word when referring to Eugène Marais). What he told her was not the truth, for about this most intimate, most secret part of his personality he was never again to tell anyone, with the possible exception of his son, the whole truth. He did tell her that he needed morphine as a medicine but that he was only allowed to have a certain amount per day – for at that stage he was determined to restrict his consumption to the absolute minimum. Tamaria expressed no moral judgement and agreed to keep the supply under lock and key and to give him only small quantities at a time.

The arrangement seems to have worked well, at least for a time.

In fact, here on Rietfontein Marais had found all the elements which might possibly have made him happy.

"Who were his friends?" someone who had known him well at the time was asked, and the reply came: "Everybody!"

Everybody with whom he came into contact liked and respected him. He was an important and very learned man. He was a handsome man, a courteous man, and one, moreover, who could converse most entertainingly – not loftily like some other learned people, but unaffectedly, like one of themselves.

In these happy early years in the Waterberg Marais continued to visit Doornhoek to study the baboons and to see the friends he had made there. He made new acquaintances in Naboomspruit, where he went to collect his mail; frequently he also travelled to Nylstroom, about twenty-five miles to the south-west and he was a visitor on numerous farms.

He went to see his new friends, accompanying them on hunting expeditions and questioning them for hours on end about the customs and peculiarities of the veld animals they knew so well.

And he treated them. He was not just another "tannie" with a tin box full of Dutch patent medicines – however welcome these could be – but a man who had studied medicine abroad. He could cure all kinds of illness. He could even make the lame walk by "mesmerizing" them. ("Mesmerize" was another word introduced into the Afrikaans of the Waterberg by Marais; it soon became part of the vocabulary of the area and was stamped with a local flavour by accenting the last syllable.)

Soon Marais was known to a great many of the unsophisticated people of the Waterberg as "the Miracle Doctor".

3. The Miracle Doctor

Before the Boer War a young Dopper, a member of the stern and narrow-minded Reformed Church to which Paul Kruger had belonged, Jossie van Deventer, lived on a farm near Rietfontein. He had fallen in love with a lively young teacher.

Not only was Jossie a typical old-time Dopper, he also dressed like one, wearing a short jacket and carrying a knife, fork and spoon at his belt. His dress reflected his attitude to life, and his father, old

Oom Gert, was a good deal worse. Old Gert wanted nothing whatsoever to do with the attractive young teacher. She was a wild woman, he said. Why, she was even given to horse-riding. She also had a shrewish nature, talking when she should be silent.

When Jossie married the young teacher, who was called Hessie, Old Gert continued to bear her a grudge. On a trek to Natal, carrying a wagon-load of hides and tusks to sell there, Hessie van Deventer and her surly old father-in-law found themselves involved in their umpteenth argument around the camp-fire one evening. Losing his temper completely, the old man grabbed his sjambok and lashed her across the shoulders.

Hessie would not be silenced. From that moment on she avoided her father-in-law but there was no lack of arguments between her and her husband, Jossie. The climax came after the trip to Natal.

It was the custom of the Boers in the remote outlying districts to trek by ox-wagon to the nearest town once every three months to attend Nagmaal, the Holy Communion service. One day Jossie and Hessie were returning from Nagmaal in Nylstroom to their farm, Rooiwal, when they started to quarrel violently. Hessie was raging at her husband as the ox-wagon clattered over the pebbles of a ford.

"If you want to behave like a she-devil, why don't you get down?" Jossie roared back.

This was too much. Furiously Hessie got off the wagon. It took her only seconds to realise that this was exactly what he wanted, but when she tried to climb back up again the long whip cracked across the backs of the oxen and the wagon moved ahead so rapidly that she was left behind.

Many, many miles did Hessie trudge along the dusty roads before she reached Rooiwal, and when she finally sank down into a chair she said:

"I shall not walk again."

For seventeen years Hessie van Deventer was partially paralyzed. Everyone in the Waterberg knew about the case. Even the ford through which they had passed was named after her: Hessie-se-water (Hessie's water).

Jossie's conscience may have worried him a little. He certainly tried to cure his wife's paralysis by calling in all kinds of doctors, quacks and herbalists. Nobody could help her. Then they heard about the Miracle Doctor who had come to live with the Van Rooyens on the farm Rietfontein.

Hessie van Deventer spent her days in a small push-cart which somebody had built for her. Jossie now bodily hoisted his wife and the push-cart onto a wagon and took her to Rietfontein, where he told Eugène Marais a modified version of the story in one of Tamaria's maternity rooms. Examining her, Marais found that her legs still showed a reflex movement: it was functional paralysis. He was at once reminded of the experiments conducted by the Parisian neurologist Jean-Martin Charcot, Freud's mentor. Charcot had shown that certain physical defects, like paralysis, could be cured by using hypnosis to relieve the mental causes of the condition.

This is exactly what Marais now tried to do, and to the superstitious amazement of an entire community Hessie got up and walked for the first time in seventeen years. In a little known book, *Natuurkundige en Wetenskaplike Studies* (Natural and Scientific Studies), Marais describes the treatment in some detail:

> It was soon clear that Mrs. Van Deventer was highly susceptible to hypnosis. She was hypnotised three times to accustom her to the condition. The fourth time she was made to sleep very deeply, and it was then suggested to her that, as soon as she awoke, she would have a strong desire to walk, that she would try to walk at once and that she would again have the power to move her paralysed legs. After an hypnotic sleep lasting three hours (to strengthen the suggestion) she was awakened, and to her own surprise and extreme joy she started walking at once. The paralysis never reappeared.

There could not have been many qualified doctors in South Africa capable of this cure at the time.

Mrs. Hotine, a district nurse, who witnessed the treatment, states that Marais also massaged Mrs. Van Deventer's legs and gave her a bottle of coloured water which she was told to take regularly, all as additional means of suggestion.

Tant Hessie's cure caused the Miracle Doctor's fame to spread throughout the entire Waterberg – and to fill people with a great respect for him.

"When my husband went to look for him on Rietfontein to come

1. Painting by J.T. Baines showing Pretoria at about the time of Eugène Marais's birth. The date was January 1872 – the month of Marais's birth but a year later.

2

3

4

2,3. Eugène Marais's parents, Jan and Catharina Marais, at about the time when Marais was a young boy.

4. Market Square (later Church Square) in the early seventies of the nineteenth century during *Nagmaal* (Holy Communion). The picture was taken at about the time of Eugène Marais's parents' move from a farm outside Pretoria to the village itself.

5

5. "The shortest and tallest men in the world". Eugène Marais's famous uncle, Lang Piet (later "Ryk Piet") Marais, demonstrated his business acumen from an early age by selling prints of this photograph of himself and a black midget, "King Coffee", posing on Pretoria's Market Square. Later, during the years of his prosperity, he tried to buy back and destroy all copies of the photograph.

6

7

6. Lynnwood House in Eugène Marais's childhood days. This picture shows the house as seen from the Apies river, which ran behind it.

7. Front view of the house in which Eugène Marais grew up with his parents in Prinsloo Street, Pretoria. On the left is the room in which Eugène slept.

8. President Burgers (far left) and his family on the porch of their house in Prinsloo Street – the same street in which the Marais' lived. While the Marais' welcomed educated and refined people like President Burgers in their home, they – like most "old" Pretorians – felt nothing but contempt for Paul Kruger and other "Doppers" (members of the ultra-conservative Reformed Church).

9

9. Sir Theophilus Shepstone, Administrator of the Transvaal during the British occupation, and his staff. Next to Shepstone (front row, third from left) is the youthful H. Rider Haggard, one of Shepstone's deputies and later a famous writer. Haggard's books included *King Solomon's Mines* and *Jess.* According to an old Pretoria tradition Rider Haggard had a love affair with Eugène Marais's sister Jess Rex, whose husband had deserted her not long after their marriage.

10. Eugène Marais as a young schoolboy.

11. Jan Celliers, father of Jan F.E. Celliers, who was later to become a famous Afrikaans poet. Celliers *père* played a prominent part in Transvaal politics. His revelations about a concession during a Volksraad debate caused Eugène Marais to write scathingly about certain pro-Government members of the Volksraad in his column "Glimpses from the Hoekie". The resulting furore eventually led to his perpetual banishment from the Press Bench.

12. Dr. Frans Vredenrijk Engelenburg, editor of *De Volksstem* and one of Marais's greatest political enemies during the Kruger regime. However, in the years after the Boer War he became an ally against what were seen as injustices practised by the British Colonial administration.

13. Eugène Marais as a youthful journalist.

10

11

12

13

14

15

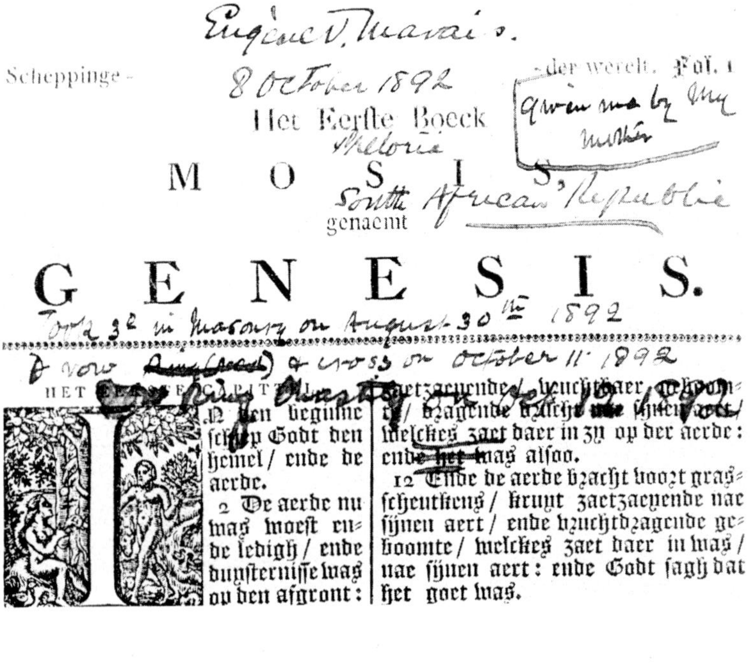

Eugène N. Marais.

Scheppinge - 8 October 1892 - der wereld. Fol. 1

Het Eerste Boeck

Pretoria

M O S I S, South African Republic

genaemt

Given me by my mother

G E N E S I S.

Took 3e in Masonry on August 30th 1892

A vow & cross on October 11 1892

HET EERSTE CAPITTEL.

IN den beginne schiep Godt den hemel / ende de aerde.

2 De aerde nu was woest ende ledigh / ende duysternisse was op den afgront:

zaetzaeyende / vruchtbaer geboomte / dragende vrucht nae sijnen aert / welckes zaet daer in zy op der aerde: ende het was alsoo.

12 Ende de aerde bracht voort grasscheutkens / kruyt zaetzaeyende nae sijnen aert / ende vruchtdragende geboomte / welckes zaet daer in was / nae sijnen aert: ende Godt sagh dat het goet was.

14. The golden wedding celebration of Eugène Marais's parents, Jan and Catharina Marais, 2 March 1893. Back row (left to right): Nancy, the Marais' Coloured domestic servant; Eugène Marais's two sisters Georgie and Kate; his brother Melt; Eugène Marais; his sister Jess; his sister-in-law Bessy (Henry's wife); his sister Sophie Ueckerman; his sister-in-law Lenie (Melt's wife); his niece Bessie Findlay; his brother-in-law John Dougall (Kate's husband); his brother Henry; Jess van der Byl (relationship unknown). Front row: Cecil Minnaar; Fay Ueckerman; Robbie and Katie Dougall; Fred Niemeyer; Leslie Marais; Arthur Clulee; Marguerite Niemeyer; Irene and Victor Marais; another of the Clulee children; Norma Ueckerman; Hilda, Katie and Lance Clulee; "Aunt" Polly Clulee; identity unknown; "Aunty" Bekker.

15. The first page of the Dutch Authorised Version of the Bible which Eugène's mother gave him as a present in 1892. His notes (written partly over the Bible text) concern his membership of the Freemasons and his "vow of chastity". It was the year in which he came of age.

16. Marais's signature and the date 1 June 1893 in Volume III of the collected works of Thomas de Quincey. The fact that Marais possessed the set of books was not confirmed until after the publication of *Die Groot Verlange*, the Afrikaans edition of *The Dark Stream*, and strengthens the supposition that in the early nineties he was influenced by De Quincey to start experimenting with drugs.

16

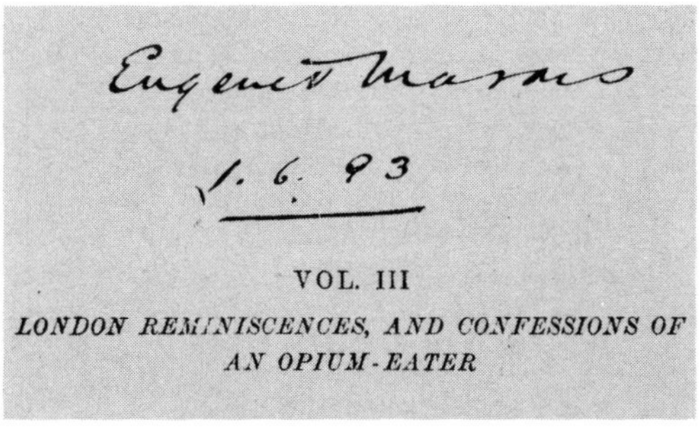
Eugène Marais

1. 6. 93

VOL. III

LONDON REMINISCENCES, AND CONFESSIONS OF AN OPIUM-EATER

17

1

19

17. Eugène Marais (right) and Justice Ewald Esselen, one of the prominent leaders of the opposition party to Paul Kruger's ruling party.

18. Eugène Marais and his newspaper partner Jimmy Roos when they were co-proprietors of *Land en Volk*. The picture was taken in 1892, the year of Marais's "vow of chastity" and also the year in which he started taking morphine.

19. Cartoon by William Schröder in *De Pers* following Ribbink's successful libel action against *Land en Volk* (1892). Justice Kotzé is chastizing the howling schoolboy with a bundle of twigs. However, compare the last paragraph on p.69 regarding Marais's alleged horse-whipping by enraged political opponents. Was the cartoon intentionally ambiguous? The caption reads: WELL DESERVED!

20. " ... the most perfect female in body and mind that God ever planted in South Africa," Eugène Marais describes his wife-to-be, Aletta Beyers of Natal, in a letter to a friend in 1893.

21

2.

23

24

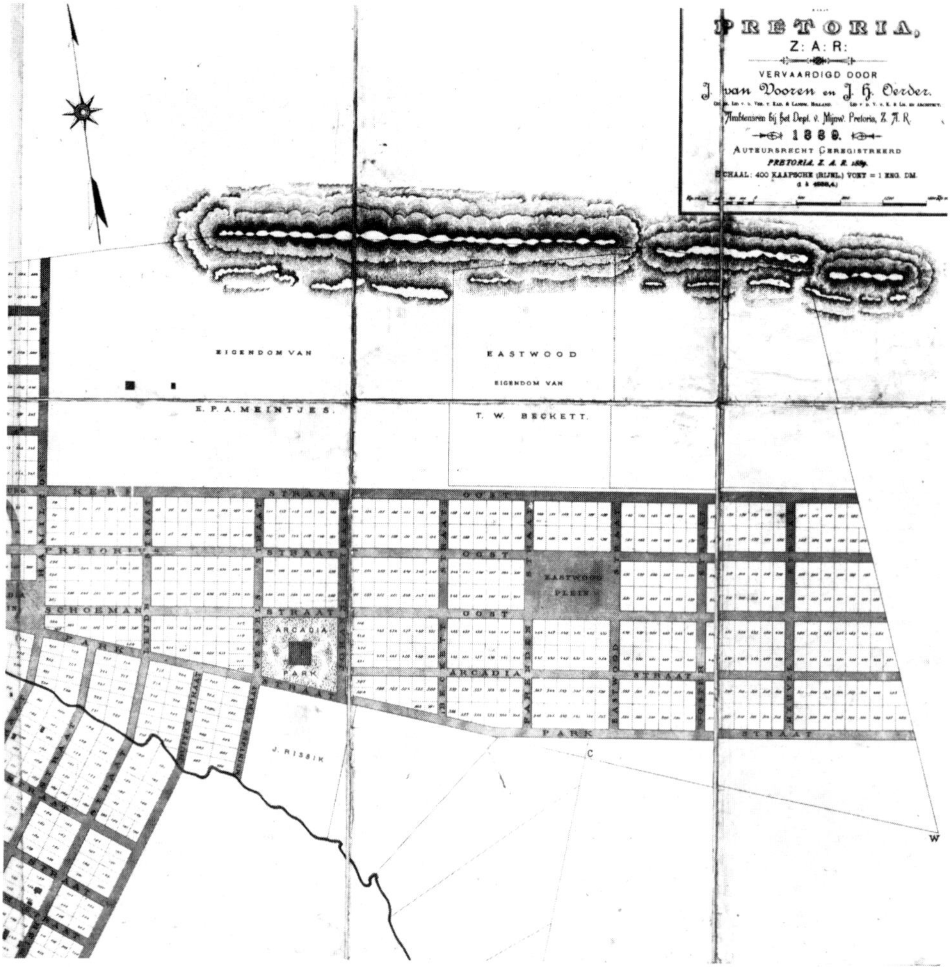

21. Eugène Marais's sister Jess Rex and her children: Percy, Mabel (later Mabel Malherbe, editor of *Die Boerevrou*, the first Afrikaans magazine for women) and Herbert.

22. Eugène Marais and Aletta Beyers (at the back) shortly before their marriage in 1894. Front row: Marais's brother-in-law Andries Verdoorn and his sisters Lizzie Niemeyer and Georgie Verdoorn.

23. The day when Eugène Marais's only son was born, 8 July 1895, was also the day of Paul Kruger's greatest triumph: the official opening of the Delagoa Bay railway-line. In this picture, taken during the opening, Kruger is seen standing by his coach

24. Newly laid out plots east of Church Square, Pretoria, from a city plan published in 1889. The plot which Marais's wife was to buy some years later lies in Arcadia Street, between Beckett and Farenden Streets.

25

26

25. One of the first industries in the South African (Transvaal) Republic was the Hatherley Distilleries Ltd. at Eerste Fabrieken (First Factories) near Pretoria. At ten shillings a gallon "Hatherley Gin" – and other brands of liquor – not only wreaked tremendous havoc in the Transvaal but also reaped huge profits for its producers. The monopoly (called a concession) to produce liquor in the Republic was originally allocated to Eugène Marais's arch-enemy Alois Nellmapius and was later sold to Sammy Marks. When Marks donated £10 000 for erecting a monument to Paul Kruger on Church Square, Marais attacked it virulently in *Land en Volk*, branding it "the Liquor statue".

26. The Rand Club in Johannesburg during the Jameson Raid. Here Eugène Marais and Commandant-General Joubert's son-in-law, Abraham Malan, met two of the Reformers – Charles Leonard and Abe Bailey – to discuss the menacing situation. The picture shows Sir Jacobus de Wet, British agent in Pretoria, asking the people of Johannesburg to lay down their arms and to proceed peacefully with their work.

27. "James I with the compliments of his Baas", is the inscription in Marais's handwriting on this photograph, taken shortly before his departure for Europe. He left the dog behind to protect his baby son.

28. The Crystal Palace in London, a symbol of the progressive, humming, dynamic "capital of the world" where Eugène Marais went to study in 1897 and stayed for five years – a period which had a profound influence on the rest of his life.

29. One of the most important influences on Eugène Marais during the time he spent in Europe was that of the Parisian neurologist Jean-Martin Charcot, who used hypnosis to cure functional paralysis. This famous lithograph shows Charcot persuading a paralyzed woman to "walk". Much later, in exactly the same way, Marais was to cure Tant Hessie van Deventer in the Waterberg after she had been partially paralyzed for seventeen years.

30. Marais could never agree with the theories of Charcot's student, Sigmund Freud, the most famous psychologist of all time.

29

30

31

32

31. Not the kind of hypnosis Charcot would have condoned: In George du Maurier's novel *Trilby*, exceptionally popular during the time of Marais's sojourn in London, the evil Svengali subjects a beautiful girl to his will by hypnosis.

32. The only known photograph from the time of Marais's expedition through East Africa at the end of the Boer War. The hunting seems to have been excellent. The picture shows the horns of kudu, gnu, impala, gemsbok, eland, sable and a Cape buffalo. At the top: the skin of a cheetah.

33. The unpretentious thatched cottage in Brooklyn where Eugène Marais and his friend Charlie Pienaar lived early in the century. The picture may have been taken in about 1906.

34

35

34. The Marais brothers, presumably shortly after Eugène Marais's return to Pretoria from Europe in 1902: Charles, Henry, Eugène and Melt.

35. Panoramic view of Hillbrow in the early years of the twentieth century. Eugène Marais lived there for some time while he was practising as an advocate in Johannesburg.

36. "An old acquaintance, Dolf Erasmus, met me in Nylstroom with a cart and four horses and for the first time in my life I entered Waterberg, the mystery region of my boyhood." Thus Eugène Marais began his classic essay "The road to Waterberg". In this picture, taken at the Pretoria Zoo well after the Waterberg period, Dolf Erasmus (right) and his son are shown with Marais.

37

37b

38

37. Gys and Maria van Rooyen, Marais's hosts and benefactors during the eight years he spent on their farm, Rietfontein, in the Waterberg. Photographs of this couple are extremely rare. This dour, retouched portrait was found hanging in a house in Pietersburg.

37b. A watercolour painting by Erich Mayer of Rietfontein's farmyard, dating from 1913. It shows the large alhambra tree in front of the farmhouse as well as the thatched out-house left of it in which Old Hendrik (grandfather of the Wandering Tales) and other migrant visitors used to spend the night.

38. Street scene in Nylstroom dating from the Waterberg period. The house of Marais's friend Emil Tamsen is on the extreme right.

39. Hans Purekrans van Rooyen, one of Marais's greatest friends, who lived on a farm on the Palala plateau, is shown at the extreme top right in this picture of a Boer commando.

39

40. Self-portrait of Erich Mayer, presented to Eugène Marais after a visit the artist paid Rietfontein in 1912.

41. Old Hendrik, from whom Eugène Marais heard the stories he was later to write down as the Wandering Tales, after a pen-drawing by Erich Mayer.

42. Ebrahim Ravat, Marais's Indian friend in Nylstroom, at an advanced age. Relatives of Ravat say that he himself was addicted to opium, which may explain the exorbitant prices at which he sold the drug to Marais.

43. On the balcony of Sophie Ueckerman's house in Maré Street, Pretoria, after Eugène Marais's return from the Waterberg in 1917. At the back is Sophie Ueckerman and in front (right) is her son, Carl (Sonny), who was later to die tragically.

42

3

44. On the farm Wellington on the Springbok Flats during World War I in 1917. Left to right: Eugène Marais; Helen Fichardt (later Mrs. Holtzhausen); madame Mona Rapacki-Warnia, whose husband had been interned by the authorities; Marais's nephew Carl (Sonny) Ueckerman; Gustav Fichardt (in pith helmet); Marais's niece, Norma Fichardt (born Ueckerman); and the Fichardts' son Juan.

45. Five of Eugène Marais's six sisters fairly advanced in age (probably taken in the early twenties): Jess Rex, Sophie Ueckerman, Lizzie Niemeyer, Georgie Verdoorn and Kate Dougall. Polly Clulee is not present.

45

46

47

46. Tielman Roos. During the time of his friendship with Eugène Marais (about 1920) he was the leader of the Transvaal National Party and a prominent legal man.

47. Fanie van Wyk, an attorney, and Eugène Marais in front of the legal partnership they founded in Erasmus (later Bronkhorstspruit).

48. The house in Brits in which Eugène Marais's son went to live in 1924 at the age of twenty-nine. Fifty years later, when this life-story was first published in the original Afrikaans edition, he was still there.

48a. The elegant silver holder in which Marais kept his syringe, an extra needle and, presumably, a supply of morphine tablets when available. These objects, as well as many others of a personal nature, such as suits made for Marais from the hides of game during his Waterberg period, and his medical instruments, were kept in his son's house from at least the time of Eugène Marais's death in 1936 for more than forty years. They were shown to almost no one. Although the author of this book established a most cordial relationship with Marais's son, he was shown only the medical instruments, certainly never the syringe. The existence of the latter did not become known until some years after his son's death, when it was auctioned by Sotheby's in Johannesburg in 1981. The syringe and other confidential possessions were probably kept in one of the most chaotic rooms the author had ever seen: an outside room lined with bookcases and filled with hundreds of dusty volumes and an incredible welter of other paraphernalia.

49

50

51

52

53

49. "I think of him daily with tears and unavailing regret," Eugène Marais wrote about the Afrikaans poet A.G. Visser in a letter to a friend. While Visser gave Marais friendship and medical care, Marais inspired him to write the four volumes of poetry published during the last years of Visser's life.

50. Connie Pistorius, another friend and benefactor from Eugène Marais's Heidelberg years.

51 and 52. On the veranda of the farm-house at Steenkampskraal, near Heidelberg, probably early in 1927, after Marais had undergone a withdrawal cure there. On the left is Mrs. Corrie Meyer. Her daughter, "Koekie", about ten, is with Marais. As a matter of interest a still from the Ross Devenish film *The Guest* is reproduced on the right. Eugène Marais was played by Athol Fugard, who also wrote the script, while Wilma Stockenström took the part of Tant Corrie. Apart from this film, works inspired by Marais's life include a British play (an extremely unflattering one) and an ambitious Afrikaans television series.

53. Gustav and Hannie Preller's spacious, comfortable house in Pretoria, 176 Blackwood Street, in the late twenties. The picture was taken after Marais's return to Pretoria. By this time part of the stoep had been enclosed to serve as his bedroom. On the stoep: Hannie Preller and two of the several dogs Marais kept there over the years.

DIE HUISGENOOT

VERENIG MET ONS MOEDERTAAL

Geillustreerde Weekblad

Onder Redaksie van Dr. H. G. Viljoen. *Uitgewers: Nasionale Pers, Bpk., Bus 692, Kaapstad.*

Deel XII No. 301.] 6 JANUARIE 1928 [Geregistreer aan die Hoofposkantoor as 'n Nuusblad. Prys 4d.

„Die Siel van die Mier" en Maurice Maeterlinck.

Deur Eugène N. Marais.

EK het verskeie briewe in die laaste tyd ontvang in almal waarvan my aandag bepaal word op die feit dat daar 'n bewys van 'n merkwaardige koïnsidens voorkom in resensies van die onlangs uitgegewe boek van Maeterlinck *The Life of the White Ant*. Dit is natuurlik 'n vertaling uit die oorspronklike Frans, en is 'n paar maande gelede deur die firma George Allen en Unwin, Ltd., in Engeland uitgegee.

Die gemelde koïnsidens bestaan hierin dat Maeterlinck presies dieselfde hipotese uiteensit wat in my artiekels *Die Siel van die Mier* gebesig word as 'n teoretiese uitleg van al die „onuitlegbaarhede" in termietgedrag—die hipotese, naamlik, van die dierlike eenheid van die miershoop. Dit het my so merkwaardig voorgekom dat twee mense gelyktydig en onafhanklik van mekaar tot dieselfde gevolgtrekking in hierdie opsig kan geraak, dat ek so spoedig moontlik Maeterlinck se boek in hande gekry het. Te meer merkwaardig het hierdie koïnsidens my voorgekom, daar Maeterlinck geen oorspronklike ondersoeker is nie. In sommige resensies word duidelik gemaak dat hy al sy feite uit die werk van praktiese ondersoekers geput het. Ek wis natuurlik dat geen ander bekende ondersoeker ooit 'n sweem van so 'n teorie had nie. In my artiekel maak dit die middelpunt uit van my teoretiese uitleg van termietgedrag en -morfologie.

In sommige van die gemelde briewe deur my ontvang, kon ek merk dat die skrywers as 'n feit aanneem dat ek op een of ander manier my teorie aan Maeterlinck ontleen het, of altans uit dieselfde bron waaruit Maeterlinck geskep het. Nou, ek is nie in die minste oor die eer van prioriteit begaan nie; maar ek is bang dat die meeste lesers as 'n feit hierna sal aanneem dat, indien daar plagiaat plaasgevind het, ek van Maeterlinck en nie Maeterlinck van my gebuit het nie. Die gewone leser bemoei hom selde met vergelyking van datums van uitgawe; en selfs waar hy sulks doen, is in hierdie geval die verskil in tyd so gering—slegs 'n paar jaar—dat die gewone leser gemaklik tot 'n verkeerde gevolgtrekking kan kom. Daarom is dit dat ek graag dadelik die feite in DIE HUISGENOOT wil uiteensit.

Dit moet duidelik verstaan word dat ek geen aanklag teen Maeterlinck wens te maak nie; ek wil hom nie van letterdiewery beskuldig nie, al blyk dit ook al duidelik dat hy sy teorie aan my *Siel van die Mier* ontleen het. Hy het sy informasie—soos hy self erken—uit 'n verskeidenheid van bronne geput. Dat hy nalatig was om in my geval die gewone erkenning te doen, is miskien verstaanbaar en vergeeflik. Nieteenin kan dit gemaklik 'n onherstelbare onreg teenoor my in die toekoms veroorsaak. Alreeds blyk dit uit sommige van die briewe met betrekking tot die saak deur my ontvang. Enkel om die moontlikheid van die onreg te vernietig, sit ek die feite hier uiteen.

Die eerste uiteensetting of, liewer, suggestie van die teorie van die dierlike eenheid van die miernes het plaasgevind in 'n artiekel deur my vir die Nuwejaarsuitgawe van DIE HUISGENOOT van Januarie 1923 geskrywe. Daarna is dit meer breedvoerig uiteengesit in die reeks van artiekels *Die Siel van die Mier*, wat begin het op 16 Okt. 1925. Die eerste paar artiekels het verskyn onder die hoof *Wondere van die Insektewêreld*. Die artiekel van 1923 had die opskrif *Verskynsels van die Dieresiel*.

Die boek van Maeterlinck *The Life of the White Ant* het in Engeland in November 1927 verskyn. Dit was waarskynlik gelyktydig met die oorspronklike Franse uitgawe. Van dié, egter, kon ek geen eksemplaar in Suid-Afrika in hande kry om seker te maak nie. Daar is derhalwe in enig geval 'n tydverskil van ongeveer twee jaar tussen my artiekels en die Engelse uitgawe.

In sy inleiding skryf Maeterlinck:

„So much for the facts. I have unearthed them from all kinds of places: they were confused and vague, obscure, often meaningless in their isolation . . . . . It is only the interpretation that is more or less my own . . . . . Interpretation, indeed, is the one exclusive property of the historian." (Blss. 15 en 16.)

Hieruit sou die leser geregtig wees om af te lei dat die gemelde hipotese deel uitmaak van sy eie interpretasie.

Vroeër in dieselfde inleiding skryf hy:

„It would have been easy, in regard to every statement, to allow the text to bristle with footnotes and references. In some chapters there is not a sentence but would have clamoured for these; and the letterpress would have been swallowed up by vast masses of comment, like one of those dreadful books we hated so much at school. There is a short bibliography at the end of the volume which will no doubt serve the same purpose." (Bls. 15.)

Dus word sy verontskuldiging vooraf gemaak. My naam kom in die bibliografie nie voor nie.

By die deurlees van die boek het ek dadelik die sterkste bewyse teëgekom dat Maeterlinck van my *Siel van die Mier* gebruik gemaak het. In sommige gevalle is daar woordelike sitate wat nooit die gevolg van koïnsidens kon gewees het nie—die besiging van die woord *Nasicornie* (p. 78, *Life of the White Ant*), by voorbeeld; die toepassing van hierdie woord was, wat my betref, oorspronklik. Dit was 'n vertaling van die Afrikaans *horingmier* of *eenhoringmier*. (DIE HUISGENOOT, 22 Jan. 1926. *Die Siel van die Mier.*)

Ek dink nie dat dit nodig sal wees om al die woordelike ooreenkomste aan te haal om te bewys dat Maeterlinck gebruik gemaak het van *Die Siel van die Mier* nie. Ek sal hier alleen in parallel laat volg twee uittreksels: een uit sy boek en een uit my artiekels, en die leser oordeel dan self of koïnsidens voldoende is om 'n uitleg te verskaf. En altyd moet in die oog gehou word, ten eerste, dat die gelyktydige „ontdekking" van so 'n teorie

54. Within months after Marais's return to Pretoria Maurice Maeterlinck's alleged plagiarism of the Afrikaans original of *The Soul of the White Ant* brought the South African writer great fame, at least in his own country. This portion of an article by Marais himself, which was published on the leader page of *Die Huisgenoot* on 6 January 1928, shows how much prominence was given to the incident in South Africa.

55

55. Outings in the Transvaal countryside formed part of the Prellers' way of life. Gustav Preller's majestic tourer, "Nog-'n-Nash" (Another Nash), dominates this scene of an expedition to the Bushveld. The picture was taken near Nylstroom. Left to right: Hannie and Gustav Preller, Carl, Young Gustav ("Tol") and Eugène Marais. The Prellers lived well. The family had several cars and they frequently bought in quantity as the formidable tin of Bakers Ltd. Biscuits (left) attests.

56

57

5

56. On the Prellers' farm Welgegund (later renamed Pelindaba) the family and their friends spent many weekends. This picture shows Carl and his fiancée (Marie Jacobs) and Eugène Marais on the banks of the Crocodile river. The picture refutes the supposition that Marais, because of the numerous scars on his upper arms from the morphine injections, never bathed. It also indicates the intimacy of his relationship with the Prellers.

57 and 58. The two doctors who treated Eugène Marais with considerable success during the last years of his life in Pretoria: Gideon Nel (left) and Hendrik Louw.

59. About two years before his death Eugène Marais sold a number of shares and enjoyed short-lived prosperity. This two-seater, with its characteristic dickey-seat, dates from that time. For a short time Marais also kept a chauffeur, John. The identity of the lady in the dickey-seat is not known.

9

60

61

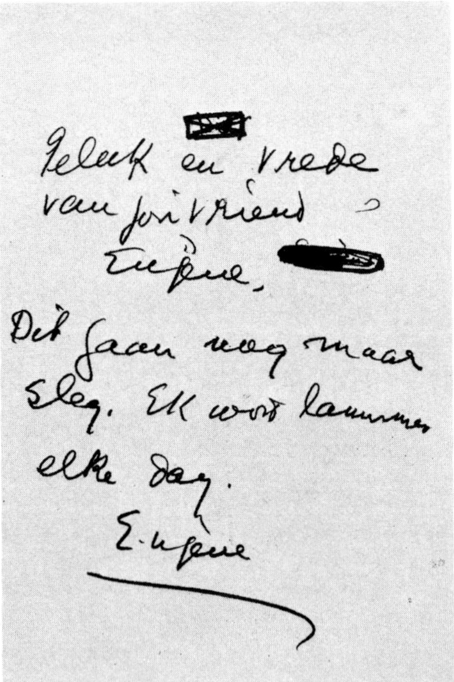

[redacted]
Geluk en vrede
van jou vriend
Eugène [redacted]

Dit gaan nog maar
sleg. Ek word lammer
elke dag.
Eugène

60. Eugène Marais with Edna (left) and Hettie Cross, probably 1934. The picture was taken at their house in Vermeulen Street.

61. Eugène Marais in Mrs. Cross's garden in Vermeulen Street, Pretoria, probably 1934. He is leaning on the "walking stick of heavy black wood with a cross handle of silver" to which he refers in his long last letter to Edna.

62. "I am becoming lamer every day," Eugène Marais wrote in this note to his friend and physician, Dr. Gideon Nel, probably in the year before his death, while he was undergoing his last withdrawal treatment on Gustav Preller's farm, Pelindaba.

63. Marais during the last years of his life. The picture is said to have been taken in a photographic automat in Pretoria.

64. One of the two busts Joan Couzyn made of Marais. The other was destroyed at the request of Gustav Preller.

63

4

65

65. Eugène Marais and Edna Cross late in 1935.

66. Gustav and Hannie Preller's new house at Pelindaba. They were still putting the finishing touches to the house when Eugène Marais moved into the rondavels some way below the house for the last time.

67. The rondavels on Pelindaba, in which Marais spent the last twenty-four hours of his life.

6

7

68. The house, at that time the property of Lood Pretorius (a brother of Hannie Preller), where Eugène Marais borrowed a shotgun on the afternoon of Sunday, 29 March 1936. He then walked a hundred yards into the wet veld and fired the two shots which ended his life.

Pictures 67 and 68 were taken by the author during the 60's.

and treat us in Swaershoek," Mrs. Annie van Heerden of Steenboksvlei, Swaershoek, was to say later, "they asked me: 'But aren't you afraid of him?'"

And indeed, for simple people there was something supernatural about his hypnotic abilities. He could paralyze birds at will, making them drop from the twigs on which they were perched. When, while he and his friends were idly chatting on Rietfontein's stoep, some chickens chanced to walk onto the stoep from the farm-yard, he could make them drop down next to his chair with a couple of gestures.

More than once he managed to do what was generally regarded as impossible, i.e. to hypnotise people against their will.

While Marais was amusing or impressing the Waterbergers with his hypnotic power, he was refining it into an instrument with which he was later to conduct some remarkable experiments. In the Waterberg his favourite subject was a young girl, Jane Brayshaw.

"Jane, a slender girl, grew up with us," one of the Van Rooyen daughters said in an interview. "After her mother's death her father married Ella van Heerden of Kromkloof, and that one gave her a pretty hard time. So we adopted her and she was married out of our house."

Eugène Marais was also to conduct experiments in hypnosis on Jane's sister, Mary, and on many other people, but it seems clear that a special relationship developed between him and Jane. She was a lively, intelligent girl, nervous by temperament and heredity – as Marais himself was later to describe her in a magazine article without mentioning her name. Her childhood had been a difficult one and it seems fair to surmise that she fell in love with, or at least became very attached to, the charming, understanding man who devoted so much time and attention to her.

Hypnosis gave this relationship an additional dimension. He could put her to sleep with a single gesture. Once he made her dance with a broomstick like a witch. On another occasion he stuck pins into her leg. She seemed to feel nothing. Like Trilby in Du Maurier's novel under Svengali's evil spell, she was completely in his power, the difference being that she was a willing prey.

Years later, after her marriage and long after Marais had left the Waterberg, she was to arrange a meeting between them on which occasion she beseeched him to hypnotize her again, only one more time.

There seems little doubt that Marais was aware of the hold which hypnosis gave him over Jane, and that he also realised how such a relationship could be abused. Twenty years later he was to warn a young girl he had befriended against ever allowing herself to be hypnotized.

Possibly a love affair developed between them. It is also possible that their relationship was a quasi-sexual one, based on hypnosis and, from her side, with masochistic undertones. Marais would not only have known the reaction but the term as well. He was acquainted with both the works of Havelock Ellis, whose first book about sexual behaviour was published in the year of his arrival in London, and with the *Psychopathia Sexualis*, those parts of R. von Krafft-Ebing's writings which for years were published in Latin only in order to make them inaccessible to the non-medical public.

Hessie van Deventer was Marais's most famous cure by hypnosis, but there were several other, less spectacular, successes.

"Now, when a woman got this fainting sickness," says Mrs. Annie van Heerden of Swaershoek, "he would mesmerize her and tell her never to get it again. She would recover completely and never come back either."

There was also the woman who suffered from "suffocation" and saw the trees approaching like Birnam wood in *Macbeth*. After she had been hypnotized by the Miracle Doctor she was cured for good – so she was to tell Marais's colleagues at *De Volksstem* in Pretoria more than twenty years later.

All the cures mentioned here had one thing in common. According to the witnesses, they seem to have been permanent.

They also show that Marais acted not only as a medical doctor but also as a psychiatrist, for what he cured in the three cases mentioned above were not physical ailments but mental conditions. Not only his hypnotic abilities but his entire personality, which was powerful and yet sympathetic and understanding, made him an excellent psychologist.

It would be a mistake to assume that the white inhabitants of early twentieth century Waterberg had few psychological problems. Traumatic experiences in the concentration camps and on the battlefield, impoverishment and deprivation as a result of the war, the inevitable inbreeding in a small population and plain backwardness (with dire consequences for children like Jane Brayshaw), all contributed to the evil harvest.

Naturally, not everyone who had such problems consulted the Miracle Doctor as a later generation would go and see a psychiatrist. Even so, Marais helped people who had mental problems in the Waterberg, as he did later in Pretoria, by questioning them and listening objectively to their replies, i.e. by analysis. Psychotherapy interested him at least as much as did medicine.

One of the medical apparatuses which Marais had brought from London was a machine which could administer shocks. Although it must have been a recognized medical technique of the time, its exact name could not be established. Mrs. Annie van Heerden remembers this about it:

"And then he had his old people, those who had rheumatism as I still have in this hand. Then he had an electrical thing, but we called it a shock-fish. He would put it in a basin of water. Then we all touched hands and then we all twitched, you know. It was electric shocks, you see. Then the people would touch hands and they would twitch all round, oh, it was great fun for the old people."

The electric discharge was caused by cranking a handle. In the Waterberg Marais often used this to amuse or impress his friends. It must have administered quite a shock, as he was always prepared to pay half a crown to any black man willing to touch it.

It may also be that Eugène Marais used this "shock-fish" as part of a sophisticated method of treatment.

In 1965 Dr. L. Wilson, assistant editor of the *British Medical Journal*, wrote: "Shock does not cure a patient. It simply relieves his symptoms temporarily, bringing him back to reality so that he can be receptive to various forms of psychotherapy."

Could Marais have tried to use electric shocks as part of his psychiatric treatment?

These were not the strangest of his psychological experiments, however.

A famous interpreter of dreams, tant Francina du Toit, lived near Nylstroom at the time. Marais spent several weeks in her house, apparently to study her philosophy and methods. Descendants of this woman state that Marais treated patients psychologically by questioning them about their dreams and then discussing basic themes which had appeared in them.

We shall see later that Marais also conducted experiments to determine whether supernatural abilities bore any relationship to the dream state.

4. The Ark

The Ark – this was Marais's name for the house on the farm Rietfontein which he had made his home.

It was a poet's name. Marais did not christen the farm the Ark only because of the variety of animals he was to keep as pets there over the years. Here, in the two maternity rooms, a nation was being reborn after the deluge of war. From here, like a dove, he himself could fly out over the waters for longer or shorter periods – sometimes for six months at a time – but to this haven he could always return.

He learnt to know it like that other ark of his childhood, the oxwagon in which as a ten year old boy he had travelled from Pretoria to Boshof. The house was built against a hill. From the stoep, past the huge alhambra tree, one could see the farm sloping downhill. To the right stood the boekenhout trees on which raw-hide thongs were curried.

To the left was the thatch-roofed outhouse, built of raw bricks like the main house. Hawkers like Sammy Coolie slept here when they arrived in the farm-yard with their wares. Here any tramp or wanderer might be put up for the night, even itinerant Bushmen like old Hendrik, whose name was to survive in Afrikaans literature as the man who told Marais his "Dwaalstories", or wandering tales.

Just below the ridge, in front of the house, Oom Gys had built a smithy. This was no longer the hive of industry it had been before the war, but it was still a popular rendezvous. Still farther down lay the gardens, the dam and the hot spring which fed it. In the distance the Springbok Flats stretched away into what seemed infinity.

Using an old barrel and some planks, Marais later constructed an ingenious bathing seat between the tall reeds in which he could bathe comfortably in what people who lived on the farm at the time were to remember as steaming water. They were amazed at how long he managed to stay in it.

Behind the farm-house, to the north-east, lay some hills where Marais would stroll between the numerous termitaries to watch the termites at work. He was not to study them intensively until much later.

The road which ran across the farm-yard, passing directly in front of the house, led to Welgevonden, two and a half miles away, where Hessie van Deventer's boorish old father-in-law lived, and in the opposite direction, past the spring, the gardens and the cultivated lands, it brought one to the crossroads, where one turned left for Naboomspruit and right for Nylstroom.

If one rode past Welgevonden, and passed through Bokpoort (Goat Pass) – but on horse- or muleback, certainly not with a cart and horses – one would reach the true Waterberg, a deeply scarred region of ravines and krantzes. Here, at the foot of the Hangklip (Hanging Rock) mountain, lived Piet van Rooyen, Gys's brother, on the farm Purekrans (Nothing but krantzes), not far from the source of the Palala river. Marais was not to visit this isolated area until later.

Hardly five miles from Rietfontein, on the road to Nylstroom, lay Doornhoek, where the tin mine had come into operation since Marais had moved to Rietfontein. Heavy mining equipment loaded on ox-wagons could be seen moving towards the mine from the nearest station. Gangs of blacks worked underground, and unsightly corrugated iron buildings were springing up everywhere; there was even a butchery, a shop and a small hotel. Marais must have watched the despoilation of the farm with mixed feelings, as mining, too, was close to his heart.

The "Tin islands" was what the Ancient Romans called Britain. The tin came mainly from Wales. Not only were the founding directors of the tin mining company on Doornhoek Welshmen, but many of the miners themselves were too. Marais got on very well with them. When the mine manager, Fred Thomas, offered him a job he accepted it. His salary was £30 a month.

The workers regarded him as the mine doctor and although he was unqualified this was certainly the work he did.

An old Waterberger, Hannes de Beer, was to talk about this more than six decades later (there is little doubt that he means Welshmen when he refers to Scotsmen): "I was driving the tin-stamp when the belt of the fly-wheel slipped off. One of the Scotsmen was there, and he tried to press back the belt with a small plank of deal while it was running, but the belt ripped the wood to pieces and dragged the Scotsman in between the belt and the wheel. He was mangled, man. Afterwards Eugène Marais came there with his kaffirs to wipe up the blood and stuff."

The work was certainly dangerous. Not long afterwards twenty blacks were to be buried in a rockfall. Marais himself twice narrowly escaped death in dynamite explosions.

Even so, mine doctor was not a full-time occupation. Marais gave some assistance with the administration of the mine – in this regard his knowledge of law was a great help – and, in the capacity of chief engineer, he even undertook the construction of a road down the ridge to the mine.

At Doornhoek, as in Johannesburg years before, two worlds met: the Afrikaans world of the Voortrekker and the farmer, and the international, largely English, world of mining. In this engagement there was an admixture of two cultures, but also of two languages. Hannes de Beer relates how an Irish mine-worker, a certain O'Brien, fell out with the mine manager. Peering into his umpteenth whisky in the bar that night, he muttered: "I have never seen such neukerij in all mijn levensdagen!" (I have never seen such buggery in all the days of my life.)

Surnames proved nothing. Jane Brayshaw knew hardly a word of English. Alec Austin, whose home language was most probably Afrikaans, often spoke English to Eugène Marais.

If Marais and Jane Brayshaw did have a relationship, he was not faithful to her. At Doornhoek he also courted O'Brien's young daughter, Gerty. The Irishman had a double rondavel. While he was sleeping in one of them Marais and Gerty would chat by candle light in the other. This was the *opsitkers*, the "sitting-up" candle, an age-old Boer custom. If the young girl welcomed her suitor, she would have a long candle ready. If she wanted to be rid of him soon, there would be only half a candle or less. They were not, apparently, supposed to blow out the candle. "I wouldn't say it was very serious," Hannes de Beer remarked about this relationship. "He was simply taking his pleasure, like any young man."

Some years later, after Jane Brayshaw had left Rietfontein, Marais was also involved with a girl called Nakkie de Beer. The only evidence about this relationship is a letter from her which surfaced in the Sotheby collection in the late seventies. When she wrote the letter, Nakkie seems to have been on the point of leaving the district. It is the naive and moving letter of a young girl leaving her beloved behind and Marais, too, must have attached a good deal of importance to the relationship to have kept the letter so long.

For the sake of convenience Marais stayed in the hotel at Doornhoek. Most of his possessions remained on Rietfontein, however, and he frequently went back to the farm to inspect the small span of oxen he kept there, or to supervise the ditches his labourers were digging on various parts of the farm in their search for minerals.

In the Baboon Kloof, where Marais and Alec Austin had previously studied the baboons, an old black man caught a newly born baboon and sold it to Marais. Marais called it Piet and took it everywhere with him. Piet would sit next to Marais on the driving seat of his Cape cart. As soon as he stopped, the baboon would jump off and take the horses' reins like a *touleier* (the leader of a team).

Now that he was staying at Doornhoek, Marais could continue his baboon studies. Again we have Hannes de Beer's testimony. "The kloof – it was steep on both sides, and on the other side there was a great krantz. Now, Eugène Marais would go at night after work to pass the time, he'd go to the kloof to watch them. Then he'd sit on the krantz and he'd sit there and watch them through his binoculars. He would go, man, even taking bags of sweets, so late at night, then he'd go there and throw them down ... to look at them, I mean.

"Many nights we'd go to the kloof with the lanterns, then we would sit on the krantz and see the big ones sit with their backs to each other and the little ones between them. He got to know them well, you know. He had a book in which he wrote it all down."

Hannes de Beer could not have understood very much of what Marais was trying to do, but this interview does confirm a fact which has been questioned, that Marais made notes about the baboons' behaviour.

An intensive, sustained investigation into nature had in fact long been one of his ideals – "an experiment in life", he had called it, in his notes, writing in English. In the fragment of a short story, probably written before he moved to the Waterberg, the main character dreams of a "long and absorbing term of investigation under ideal conditions". This was Marais's dream too, but because he was always trying to do half a dozen things at the same time, because his financial resources were limited and, last but not least, because of morphine, this ideal was never to be realized.

Many of the people who worked on the mine at Doornhoek lived on the densely populated neighbouring farm, Kromkloof, which had a white population of more than a hundred at the time.

One of these people was Jan Wessel Wessels, and he and Marais soon became good friends. For a time he spent nights in the observation huts in the Baboon Kloof with Marais, and they were to go on hunting expeditions together for years to come.

Ironies abound in Marais's life. Jan Wessel Wessels' wife, Drina, seems to have been a daughter of Jan Kock, the detested electoral official of Potchefstroom who had made Ewald Esselen lose the Volksraad election by seven votes years before. It was against him – and against his brother, the "Don Juan of Christiana" – that Marais had conducted such a bitter campaign in *Land en Volk*.

If Jan Kock had been guilty he had wiped out his debts and shamed Marais by falling in the Battle of Elandslaagte early in the Boer War.

Drina Wessels was probably unaware of the earlier feud between Marais and her father. She was a pioneering woman of the old type. "She grew up with the crack of rifles in her ears," Marais was to write in a magazine article. "Her husband was a famous warrior and hunter and he had spent his entire life in the wilder parts of South Africa. Very few people know as much about the veld as he does. According to Tant Drina she spent less than half her life under a roof. To this day she feels more at home on a buck-wagon in the open veld than in any house.

"For years Wessel Wessels took part in all the strife on our western borders and in the neighbouring Kaffir countries, where he was always accompanied by his young wife. She was almost as good a shot as he was, and was certainly as fearless."

What Marais did not mention in the article was that the couple's lives had been embittered for years as a result of superstition. They were childless, and this worried them both. One day they heard about an old Waterberg midwife who was said to be capable of curing the condition. Inspanning their oxen, they went to the old witch's farm, where Tant Drina was examined thoroughly. That night, by flickering candlelight, she and her husband were told the sombre news that she was a "white liver" and that the husbands of such women never lived for more than five years.

"Is there nothing we can do?"

The verdict was awesome: "The only way is never to sleep in the same bed."

Of course they believed her, they believed her implicitly. One can picture their predicament. Was Drina helping to hasten her husband's death? When they did have intercourse, it was with fear and trembling. It was years before Wessels decided to bear the consequences, and by the time Marais met him and assured him that their superstitious belief could have no foundation in fact, he still felt intensely indignant about the old wife whose stories had spoilt their nights for so many years.

5. Naboomspruit and Beyond

As the mine doctor Eugène Marais lived in two worlds, perhaps more. He felt equally at home in the company of Jan Wessels as in that of the foreigners who managed the mine. He and a certain Ford, who succeeded Fred Thomas as mine manager, became good friends. To some extent they were birds of a feather. Ford's habit of smoking only cigarettes specially made for him in the Cairo Club would not have been out of place in Marais himself.

Another friend was Armstrong, the owner of the hotel, a great thickset fellow with a singular past. Many years before, when Armstrong was little more than a baby, his parents tried to trek across the Limpopo to Bechuanaland. On the way they were murdered. The young boy was brought up by blacks, and he stayed with them until he was discovered by whites at the age of eleven and brought back to civilization.

Armstrong soon introduced Marais to a quite different breed of men from the Waterberg farmers. At that time the Waterberg was full of prospectors and remittance men, the black sheep of prominent English families who were paid a sizeable allowance just to keep them somewhere in the colonies.

Two of these whom Marais came to know best were Leroyd and Graves. Leroyd came from one of the best English families. Marais was much impressed by Leroyd's statement that he had been a member of the Athenaeum, the exclusive literary club in Pall Mall. Graves, a man of less distinguished heritage and more dissolute habits, had felt a debt of honour to Marais ever since Marais had successfully treated his attractive young wife.

Apart from the small hotel at Doornhoek, Armstrong also owned the hotel in Naboomspruit, where he and his wife lived. One could often see Marais's elegant Cape cart heading in that direction on a Friday or Saturday evening.

The hotel itself was not much to look at, although its drabness was to some extent relieved by two or three enormous eucalyptus trees. But inside the hotel the nights were frequently gay.

"They often played poker until two o'clock in the morning," said Marais's son. "Apart from Armstrong, Graves and Leroyd there was also a police sergeant, a certain De Beer. I remember De Beer always having a water glass full of brandy for every tot the others ordered."

Eugène Marais had exchanged the Inner Temple for a rather dreary little hotel in Naboomspruit, Leroyd the Athenaeum. Their conversations revived the elegant splendour of London's social life in the nineties. Neither was ever to see the capital of his world again.

Naboomspruit, the village closest to Rietfontein, was Marais's postal address. He was also frequently to be seen in Nylstroom, a larger village, where the Waterbergers went for commodities they could not obtain in Naboomspruit.

Here Marais made several new friends. One was Emil Tamsen, who had immigrated to South Africa from Germany as a sixteen-year old boy in 1885 and now had a shop in the village where, among other things, he also sold curios. A stuffed twelve foot long crocodile mounted over his shop front gave some idea of the commodities he had for sale.

Emil Tamsen was a nature lover, and he was fortunate enough to make a living from his hobby. Wild animals from all parts of the

Waterberg were brought to his farm, Tweefontein, about eight miles from Nylstroom, where hunting was strictly prohibited, and then shipped to the famous game park Carl Hagenbeck had established near Hamburg, Germany, in 1907. Later he was also to have one of the ten largest collections of postage stamps in the world.

"Oom Eugène and my father could talk for hours on end," says Emil Tamsen's son, Boetie, a young assistant in his father's shop at the time. "They always spoke about nature – baboons, spiders, snakes, scorpions and things like that."

Marais also became friends with one of Emil Tamsen's competitors in Nylstroom, "Oom Piet" Cohen, probably the same Cohen whose name was later to appear quite regularly in his writings.

A third friend of Marais's was in turn a competitor of Piet Cohen's, an Indian known throughout this part of the Waterberg simply as "Abraham Coolie".

According to the Waterbergers, there used to be three itinerant Indian traders in the area in the time before Marais's arrival: Abraham, Sammy and Jacob. Abraham – his real name was Ebrahim Ravat – was about forty years old when Marais got to know him in Nylstroom. By this time he had long since left to Sammy the tedious job of travelling around the district, confirmed by Marais's poem "Wanneer dit reën op Rietfontein" (When it rains on Rietfontein):

> Wanneer dit reën op Rietfontein,
> dan skielik op die werf verskyn
> ou Sammie met sy bondels groot en klein …
> Die meisies om hom dig vergaar,
> betas verlangend al die skone waar.
> Geduldig word elk stuk ontvou,
> van lowergroen tot bafta-blou;
> en krale skoner as die môredou
> versier elk' hals van sag satyn
> wanneer dit reën op Rietfontein

> Oh, when it rains on Rietfontein
> then suddenly comes out of the rain
> old Sammy with his bundles once again …
> The girls crowd round with longing stares

to finger all his lovely wares.
He unfolds everything to view
from vivid green to brightest blue;
and beads more lovely than the morning dew
each neck, so satin soft, enchain,
oh, when it rains on Rietfontein.

In the faint, yellowed snapshot which the poem is one must surely be able to discern the slim, seventeen year old figure of Jane Brayshaw among the other girls. For her "satin soft neck", one surmises, Marais would have bought not only beads but also the best perfume old Sammy could offer. None knew better than he the importance of bodily fragrance as a sexual trigger in man and beast.

Eugène Marais knew all three Indian traders, but he and Ebrahim, who was about his age, seem to have become close friends. As we have seen, many of Marais's fellow students in London had been Indians.

In Ebrahim Ravat, a herbalist, he now found a man of greater refinement and certainly of greater sophistication than many of the simple Waterberg farmers who were also his good friends.

When he arrived in Nylstroom, he would often have supper at Ebrahim's house, and he frequently spent nights there.

What did the people of Nylstroom – during a time and in a region where one would expect severe colour prejudice – have to say about this? Apparently, they said nothing. In these years the Waterberg presented a strange contrast between the extreme narrow-mindedness of people like old Gert van Deventer and great freedom to do as one wished. (Years later, an impoverished Waterberg farmer, whose account at an Indian shop had become extremely high, told the Indian that he could simply not pay. "Never mind," the Indian replied. "Just give me your daughter and I'll write off what you owe me." No sooner said than done. One cannot imagine that this endeared the people of the Waterberg to the shopkeeper, but he was certainly not lynched. On the contrary, his business flourished.)

If Eugène Marais chose to have supper or spend the night in a "Coolie house" one shrugged one's shoulders, and that was that.

One by one the clues appear which tell us that Eugène Marais, even in his early years in the Waterberg, was seldom free of the problems caused by his particular affliction.

The steaming hot bath in Rietfontein's spring helped to alleviate the worst withdrawal symptoms.

Alcohol helped too. "My father was not a drinker," states his son, "but when he could not get morphine he took brandy to alleviate the symptoms."

The strongly flavoured curry Ebrahim Ravat's wife served him – so strong that it made him perspire freely – served the same purpose.

And when Marais referred to opium one day, Ravat caught on immediately.

Oh yes, he could get some. It would be expensive, of course.

Ever since 1894 it had been illegal in the Transvaal to buy opium or any opium derivative, like morphine, without a doctor's prescription. But there was no ordinance, proclamation or act which prevented one from importing it, even if it was illegal in its country of origin.

Marais could not exploit this loophole. He was dependent on doctors for his supply or, in extreme cases, on easily obtainable popular medicines which contained a small amount of opium. The nearest doctor was Dr. Corkery in Warmbaths, and doctors were not supposed to supply morphine freely, but to try and cure their patients of the addiction.

According to one of his grandchildren, Ebrahim Ravat himself was addicted to opium, and he had no problem importing opium from the Far East for his own use.

"For his own use" – there lay the rub. As soon as he sold it to anyone else, he would be breaking the law. For an old friend like Eugène he would do it, of course, but then he would have to be rather well compensated for his risk.

No doubt the price was exorbitant, but for Marais this made no difference. From now on he would be able to count on a constant supply of opium in case his morphine ran out.

Morphine is injected; opium is smoked, eaten or – à la de Quincey – dissolved in alcohol and taken as laudanum. One should not jump to the conclusion that Marais wanted opium to lend a new, exotic dimension to his use of drugs. It was morphine on which he was dependent, and in this addiction the syringe, the prick of the needle, played an important and more than symbolic part. As a substitute for morphine, opium was the most desirable because they were most closely related, but it was still a substitute. (It is possible – although there is no direct evidence – that Marais distilled morphine himself from raw opium, not an involved process for someone who has some pharmaceutical knowledge.)

Moralists may deplore this, but the two or three years in the Waterberg during which Eugène Marais had enough morphine or opium to keep his body normal, were among the happiest in his life.

6. The Great Laboratory

It was not only his studies of baboons and termites which made Eugène Marais transform the farms Doornhoek and especially Rietfontein into great zoological laboratories from time to time. "There was no natural phenomenon," his son was to write fifty years later in his foreword to *The Road to Waterberg*, "no facet of human behaviour, no form of animal behaviour whose underlying causes Eugène Nielen Marais did not seek to probe." And of all the hundreds of studies which he undertook during the course of his life, a large number were done in the Waterberg.

It is true that Marais was a pioneer in the field of zoology by being the first man to observe intensively a group of primates in their natural surroundings, but this is not the whole truth. These observations were supplemented by studying and observing baboons in captivity. The following conclusions from *Natuurkundige en Wetenskaplike Studies* (Natural and Scientific Studies) were probably based on experiments carried out on the Van Rooyen farm:

> Rear a baboon, for example, in captivity from birth, and protect him artificially against rain and cold. Let him never see an insect or the natural fruits or roots of his own environment, and then take him to the mountains where he was born.
>
> He will be inexpressibly stupid. A live scorpion will scare him to death. He might starve, but he will not know how to pick up a stone to look for food. He will eat a poison-leaf apple as readily as a sand-apple. In other words, if you do not teach him, he will starve to death in the midst of plenty. But there is another factor: he can learn quickly. Persuade him only once to eat an insect, let him discover how

tasty a scorpion is but that it can sting, and show him that there are scorpions under every stone – and he is saved.

By way of comparison, Marais reared an otter in the same artificial way and then took the grown animal to the river:

> ... before long he will jump into the water and dive and swim as if he has never done anything else. If he is hungry, he will soon catch a crab and go and sit on the river bank to eat it. He knows what kind of food to eat and where to look for it without ever having learnt to do so.

Thus in the early years of the century, Marais arrived experimentally at his important theory of the phyletic and causal memory, respectively in the otter and the baboon (which had lost its instincts but had been compensated by a remarkable ability to learn).

Observations of both the baboons and other wild animals brought him to the conclusion that the onset of dusk causes feelings of melancholy and anxiety. After questioning a large number of people, he developed the theory of "hesperian depression", to which he estimated one out of twenty people were subject. (The term seems to have been coined by Marais himself; "hesperian" was derived from the Greek word for the west, where the sun sets.)

Eugène Marais may have been the first man to write about a phenomenon which, two generations later, has not yet been adequately examined or accounted for. Thus, to mention only one example, in her authoritative book, *Baby and Child*, first published in 1977, Penelope Leach states categorically that colic, a very well defined syndrome in babies "occurs exclusively during a particular period of the early evening."

On the farms Doornhoek and Rietfontein Marais kept a number of young and older baboons for observation and experiments.

Piet, the baboon who shared the driver's seat of his Cape cart with him, became amazingly clever. In the hot sun he would put on his "hat", a gourd which had been cut in half. In cold weather he would hang a sack around his shoulders. His achievements, as Marais was to describe them later, remind one of a chimpanzee.

> He could easily untie a series of knots to open a bag of fruit. He learnt

> to drink from a cup and from a bottle without having been taught to do so. He befriended all the domestic animals. He would carry kittens and pups in his arms for hours. Over a long period he was fond of riding a large sow. With no instruction whatsoever, he learnt how to drag objects which were out of reach towards him by using a hooked stick ... When he was threatened with punishment, he learnt how to stand on his head in order to put the antagonist in a good mood. He was fond of waking his master by carefully drawing apart the eyelids with one finger. He immediately fell head over heels in love with a human baby. The pram containing the baby would be pushed within his reach and left there. He would spend hours on the edge of the pram looking after the child. Any animal, including his own friends, who ventured too close would be furiously attacked. Now and again he would softly and lovingly touch the baby, pressing his lips to the tender cheeks. As soon as the child began to cry his own cries of alarm and lamentation would move the entire farm to pity ...

At a time when the supply of his own drugs was abundant Marais began to experiment with baboons and other animals to see how prone they were to opium and alcohol addiction. He found that the baboon easily became addicted to tobacco and other drugs, but that lower mammals – like his pet warthog, Jas – showed no similar tendency. Near the source of the Palala he was given information which to him suggested euphoric poisoning in animals. "An extremely poisonous berry is found in the region ... The baboons like eating these berries. According to the natives they are paralysed by the poison, reeling like drunkards. This they do even in times of plenty."

Marais's experiments on Rietfontein seem almost infinite: to prove the persistence of the phyletic memory in birds, he bred four generations of yellow weaver birds by hatching the eggs under canaries; he proved experimentally that one cicada could hear the signals of another for a distance of at least eight miles; he studied the tapping-beetles' morse code during the mating season; to prove that the winged termite queen lures the male to her by means of odour, he trained a fox-terrier who could follow a termite queen for almost a hundred yards against the wind – but could hardly trace the king over a distance of a yard; surgically or by means of acid he removed the olfactory abilities of smaller mammals, proving that they would never again become sexually excited; he witnessed the tortoise's long journey to find its mate and the sexual frenzy of the kudu.

A long series of experiments was devoted to pain alone. Other experiments were connected to the light signal in animals. By experiment he refuted Fabre's theory that emanation of light in the firefly was nothing but oxidation. Twice he witnessed illumination in the huge centipede, a rare phenomenon: "The animal is about twelve inches long ... and usually extremely agile and wary, but while illumination lasts it is in a state of cataleptic paralysis. (Its light) is so bright that fine print may easily be read in a completely dark room at a distance of about two feet from the animal."

Using acetylene lamps which he borrowed from the tin mine, Marais and his friends watched a particular species of grass, aristida, until the early morning hours to see how fertilization came about. He studied pollination by means of wind-borne seeds. He investigated the amazing phenomenon of certain black road-making ants (not termites) which seem able to prevent the germination of plant seeds stored in the humid nest.

Apart from Marais's books about termites and baboons there was a third, never to be written work which he might have called *The Soul of the Snake*, for next to baboons and termites no other creature excited his interest more. He had grown up knowing all about snakes in untamed, subtropical Pretoria; as a boy and later as a young man he had kept them as pets; in Europe he may have conducted experiments with snake venom.

Possibly by way of comparison, he also studied a variety of other reptiles. On the farm Nagwag, on the Palala, he managed to capture three baby crocodiles which were fleeing from the bank, and he kept them on Rietfontein for some years. Hannes de Beer tells of a hunting trip on which Marais captured an "alikruk", a regional word for what was probably a water leguan, which reaches a length of up to two metres.

The Waterberg teemed with snakes in the early years of the century. On Rietfontein Marais helped to kill three or four snakes which old Hendrik had discovered under the hessian bags on the floor of the outhouse during one of his visits. When Marais and Oom Gys opened one of the termite nests on the hills behind the farm-house, an eight foot long cobra emerged and spat poison at them. "Both of us got it full in the face," Marais was to write in *The Soul of the Ant*, "but luckily our eyes escaped." He studied the venom fangs of the puffadder – the perfection in nature of the hypodermic syringe. The experiments with snake venom which he seems to have begun in London were continued on Rietfontein.

Were certain animals more resistant to snake venom than others, Marais wondered? He determined experimentally that 10 mg of dried mamba venom, dissolved in alcohol, was sufficient to kill a dog weighing twenty pounds very quickly. He had been told by Waterbergers that the honey-badger – a notorious honey thief – could survive an amount of the poison sufficient to kill a large ox. (The animal needs to be resistant to poison, as it may be stung by scores of African bees during a single honey-raid.) What about snake venom? Marais started experimenting with two badgers which had grown up on the farm, one of which weighed 17½ pounds. After 10 mg of dried mamba venom had been injected into its artery, the badger showed signs of extreme pain for some time, but three minutes after the injection it calmed down and began eating the food which was given to it.

The second badger weighed eighteen pounds. Marais doubled the dose. After the injection there were signs of greater pain than in the first badger. It took twenty minutes for the animal to start calming down. An hour later its pulse and respiratory rates had returned to normal. Both badgers recovered without deleterious results.

These experiments illustrate Marais's attitude towards animals. He was a lover of animals, and he could become deeply attached to individual animals, but he was by no means sentimental.

Marais began questioning people about antidotes, a subject about which he knew more than any Waterberger. "Pull the skin of a black chicken over the wound," said one. A second was willing to bet on leguan fat, a third on hyena dung. After further experiments, Marais himself came to the conclusion that the only treatment in these years (long before the development of an efficient serum) was to cut into the wound as deeply as possible and to tie up the veins.

Even so, it was not scientific interest but his fame as a doctor which was soon to take him to the one place in the Waterberg where at that time it was possible to study snakes intensively and at close quarters. This was Swaershoek (literally: the valley of the brothers-in-law).

Picturesque Swaershoek, at the foot of the Sand river mountains, about forty miles west of Rietfontein, contained about ten farms at that time. Swaershoek had not been given its name for nothing. All the farms belonged either to the Van Heerdens or to their brothers-in-law – Eloffs, Van der Merwes and De Beers. To make things even more complicated, a total of nine Piets or Pieters were living in the valley.

Until the end of the first decade of the century nobody had ever seen a mamba on Rietvlei, old Piet van Heerden's farm. And then, suddenly, the place teemed with them.

Oom Piet's favourite grandson, Fanie, sixteen years old, was the first victim. One day as he was taking their lambs to the ewes which had come in from the veld, a hidden mamba struck with such violence that the boy had to exert all his strength to extract the fangs from his leg.

As the snake slithered away, the boy walked back to the house, where his parents were chatting to visitors, and calmly told them: "A mamba has bitten me and I shall die." A rider was sent to the nearest shop to fetch eau-de-luce, and in the meantime various well known remedies were applied: brandy in milk, tarred bandages above the wound, an ointment made from indigenous shrubs. Nothing helped. Soon the last symptoms made their appearance and shortly afterwards the boy died in convulsions on the stoep of the farm-house.

Oupa Piet swore there and then to burn alive the first mamba he came across. But, walking through the vlei on his way to the lands one day, he somehow dislocated (this is how the people described the phenomenon) his hip-bone and fell to the ground, where he lay helplessly. "And while he was lying there," says a relation, Pieter Pistorius, "as he looked up, two of the snakes, two of these mambas, were swaying above him, their mouths wide open. And later on Oom Piet said that it had been the Lord who had shown him that one did not have the right to take revenge, not even on a snake which had bitten one's grandson. They were extremely religious old people."

At about this time the dead boy's father, Andries van Heerden of

Steenboksvlei, undertook the journey to Rietfontein where the Miracle Doctor lived. He was troubled by his kidneys, and he was in desperate need of help. "The doctor is ill," Tant Maria told him. "Come again in two or three weeks."

By this time Marais no longer had a firm job as mine doctor. He was free to travel around the district. When he was well again, Gys van Rooyen took him to Swaershoek.

It did not take Marais long to realize that Andries van Heerden's kidney trouble would require lengthy treatment. Fortunately, he soon felt almost as at home in Swaershoek as he did on Rietfontein. They were mainly cattle farmers, but they also grew maize and some tobacco. In Steenboksvlei's orchard there were twenty-nine species of peaches, the biggest tangerines imaginable and various kinds of oranges. The veld, too, produced its edible products: Kaffir-thorn, wild plums, red milkwood, medlars, sour plums, wild peaches, monkey oranges, waterberries and wild grapes. Firewood was plentiful. There were sugar-bush, South African beech, wild lilac trees, ochnas (lekkerbreek) and karree. They had water from a fountain, from dams, from the river.

Here, too, there was a multitude of baboons – and, because of the baboons, there were many leopards as well. "They used to start roaring quite late," says Tant Annie van Heerden about the time when Marais stayed there. "Then one would hear the leopard's roar moving past a certain baboon cave and as soon as they heard the leopard, they began shouting with it all down the mountain. Then the ribboks would reply – they would whistle like mad. And the rock-rabbits screeched, and other things we did not know."

Marais's baboon experiment in Swaershoek included attempts to establish how high they could count. We shall deal later with his experiments to create apparently supernatural abilities by means of hypnosis, with which he may have begun in Swaershoek.

The Van Heerdens were quite aware of the fact that the Miracle Doctor himself was not altogether well. He had had an appendix, he told them, which had deteriorated to such an extent that part of his stomach had had to be cut away. This caused constant pain, for which he had to take flat, white tablets.

The farm next to Steenboksvlei was Rietvlei, old Piet van Heerden's property, Andries' father. This was where Marais came face to face with a black mamba for the first time.

It was a beautiful farm. "The house was picturesquely situated against a steep, overgrown koppie," Marais was to write in *'n Paradys van Weleer* (A Paradise of Yesteryear), "and had a high veranda from which there was a magnificent view across the orchard and lands. At the bottom of the orchard there was a reedy marsh and a large clump of poplars. An avenue of quince trees bordered the orchards on one side and left of the house, between the quince trees and the large water-furrow, the main road led to the north."

In view of the recent tragedy, Marais referred guardedly to mambas; but when Oom Piet heard that he had never seen one, he immediately sent two of his labourers to fetch a specimen. They were armed with a shotgun and some long staves.

"About two hours later – just before sunset – the two of them arrived at the farm-house with a black mamba of about ten feet three inches. It was the first time that I could admire the beautiful lines and magnificent colours of the black makopa."

For reasons Marais could only guess at, the multitude of snakes restricted themselves to a small corner of the vlei just below the ridge. From here they would slither across the road every day to go and catch rock-rabbits in the krantzes.

It was here that Marais sat waiting to observe them at close quarters in their natural surroundings. He had a rifle, and one of the younger Van Heerden children was armed with a double-barreled shotgun.

On the road they could see the trails of three fairly large snakes which had crossed it that day. When an hour had passed and the man and the boy had not seen another snake crossing the road, they walked down it again and found to their astonishment that three more snakes had crossed over during that time. On the way back they found a fourth trail. "At that moment Mr. Van Heerden himself came along to find out what luck we had had," Marais wrote in *Natuurkundige en Wetenskaplike Studies*. "We again walked down the sixty yards of the road and found two more trails. It seemed impossible that so many snakes could have crossed the road in this short time without being visible either in the furrow or on the bank. At my suggestion we again walked down the road to examine the bank thoroughly. Mr. Van Heerden was in front, a *kierie* (walking-stick) in his hand, I followed and the boy brought up the rear. In the green grass at our feet one makopa had hidden itself so well that we all passed it, nearly stepping on it, without seeing it. The boy must have missed it too narrowly for the snake's liking. He had just passed the spot when the snake reared, hissing loudly. I was still busy cocking my gun when Mr. Van Heerden had knocked it down with his *kierie*. It was a young male."

This was Marais's first encounter with a menacing mamba – the first of many. There were so many mambas on the farm at the time that Marais's patient, Andries van Heerden, shot fifty-two snakes in the avenue of quince trees next to the vlei in the course of three months.

In the Waterberg the mamba could grow to a length of about twelve feet according to Marais. It was, he wrote, South Africa's largest venomous snake, and probably the largest venomous snake in the world, with twenty times as much venom as a puffadder. "Muriti wa lesu" the Sesutos called it: Shadow of death.

In London a ringhals had featured prominently in Marais's ex libris. During the months he spent on the farm he got to know the ringhals's cousin, the black mamba, at close quarters. He describes the reptile in terms of almost poetic admiration:

> The head is long and narrow; the eyes as bright as jewels, and it is capable of keeping erect more than half its body – the position it usually adopts before attacking. The fangs are a shiny white. They are large, slightly curved backwards, and make a fine show against the dark black of the body. In a menacing attitude this snake is as terrifying as the black ringhals. There is perhaps no faster snake on earth. To see a mamba making its way across shrubs or through the branches of a tree, or even across level ground, reminds one more of the flight of an arrow than of the movement of an unwinged animal.

One surmises that Eugène Marais did not begin his experiments regarding the effect of snake venom on various animals which he conducted on Rietfontein until after his visit to Swaershoek.

After three months on the farm Marais's patient was cured. The Miracle Doctor did not ask for payment, but a grateful Andries van Heerden gave him nine head of cattle to take back to Rietfontein.

One of the labourers on the farm was a young black man named Daman. He was a year Kaffir, which meant that he was given a heifer for every year's work he did. To earn Marais's fee would have taken him nine years.

7. The Seventy-Second Hour

The few months spent in Swaershoek had been a pleasant interlude. Even so Marais was thankful to be back on Rietfontein. Nowhere did he feel more at home than in the Ark.

But now came a serious setback. That winter, as always, he accompanied Gys van Rooyen on a hunting trip to the Bushveld. There were a number of younger men in the party as well. Marais had packed his supply, but he must have underestimated his requirements. In the middle of the Bushveld he used up the last of his tablets.

Marais did not act at once. Perhaps he had forgotten how terrifying sudden withdrawal really was. It may be that he wanted to see the trip through without morphine. But as the symptoms became ever more severe he asked Oosthuizen, one of the young men with them, to go to Rietfontein and ask Tamaria for more tablets.

The nearest farm belonged to a man called Hamman. Oosthuizen went there as fast as he could and borrowed a horse to ride to Rietfontein. It was a long trip.

Eugène Marais had now been a morphine addict for at least sixteen years. The venom had become part of his body, part of his soul, and when suddenly deprived of the drug no suffering was spared him.

To the morphine addict accustomed to regular doses, discomfort is felt only a few hours after withdrawal. Later the patient becomes extremely restless. He throws himself down on a bed, asks for blankets, curls up and draws the blankets tightly around his shoulders. He might bury his head in the pillow, toss and turn for a few minutes, then get up and start walking around. He will then try to stay warm at all costs. He might lie in the hot sun, but this will not satisfy him either. He will seek out his bed and again wrap himself in the thickest blankets. Soon he might start pacing up and down once more. By now there will be severe shivering, as in ague and the patient's breathing will be like that of someone dying of cold, coming in short, powerful bursts. He will break out in goose-pimples. Besides the feeling of intense cold he might find that he cannot breathe through his nose, which runs excessively.

The first phase of withdrawal frequently ends in a merciful drowsiness. The patient falls into a deep sleep, the "yen", which might last from eight to ten hours and from which only a loud noise will wake him. This sleep brings no relief, however. When he wakes up, he is even more restless than before. The old symptoms return, and now there is also a feeling of suffocation. At this stage there are usually cramps, mostly stomach cramps. This is followed by vomiting and diarrhoea. His clothes are drenched in sweat. He has to keep his hands around his knees to control the violent convulsions of his legs. His hands may shake so badly that he can hardly light a cigarette.

Serious symptoms appear within the first twenty-four hours. After seventy-two hours – the Biblical "three days and three nights" – the symptoms reach a climax, and if morphine is withheld beyond this stage, death may follow.

To Marais's companions it certainly seemed as if he was dying. Oom Gys and the remaining two young men watched the reactions, which to them looked like a drawn-out, painful death struggle. When Hermanus Oosthuizen brought the tablets, they witnessed a miracle: "He was dying, man," one of the young men in the party said later. "And as soon as he got those pills, as soon as he started using them, he was as right as rain. That's how we found out."

That is how they found out. That is how the whole district found out. The Miracle Doctor could not live without the pills Tamaria kept for him.

Some of his friends were severely disapproving. They were tired of dipsomaniac prospectors; they knew the remittance men and other dregs of civilization who had come to hide out here in the Waterberg. Drunkards, impostors, frauds – they all had a crack of one kind or another. Marais was just one more.

Moral judgement was the exception. For most Waterbergers morphine was a totally alien concept. His prestige did suffer a serious blow however. He was now known to have feet of clay.

But the damage done to his good name was insignificant compared to the effects of the experience on his own mind. Even the wide Waterberg had become too narrow for him.

Even the Ark was no longer safe.

8. Purekrans

North of Doornhoek and Rietfontein, the Waterberg range barred the way to the more rugged interior. From Rietfontein there were two roads through the mountains, the wagon road through Tarentaalstraat (Guineafowl Street), a detour of almost a day, and the footpath through Bokpoort.

Beyond the mountains, at the foot of the Hangklipberg, lived Piet van Rooyen, Gys's brother, on the farm Purekrans, not far from the source of the Palala. One day Marais was urgently summoned to Oom Piet's bedside. The old man was seriously ill.

Marais made the journey to Purekrans, examined Oom Piet and concluded that nothing but an operation could save his life. Travelling back to Rietfontein he succeeded in contacting the nearest doctor, Dr. Corkery of Warmbaths. Marais now accompanied Dr. Corkery through the dangerous ravines of Bokpoort. At one stage the doctor's horse fell some way down a precipice, both horse and rider narrowly escaping death, but in the end they reached Purekrans safely. The doctor operated successfully the next day.

When Dr. Corkery had returned to Warmbaths, Eugène Marais remained behind on the Palala plateau, ostensibly to nurse Oom Piet van Rooyen back to health, but perhaps also because he hoped to find, in this even more remote part of the country, peace of mind once more.

On this occasion he stayed away from the Ark for at least six months. Here, on the rugged plateau, where farm names like Buffelshoek, Makoupan, Duikerfontein, Kwaggahoek and Elandsbos gave one an idea of how recently this was game country, a man could still disappear in the wilderness.

And that is exactly what Marais did. Travelling alone in a donkey-cart, he penetrated the Middleveld, that part of the Bushveld between the Palala and Magalakwêna rivers. On the banks of the

Magalakwêna he bought a plot of land and planted some indigenous trees.

Did he see this as a final sanctuary, a place of refuge for the day when the world would collapse around him and even the Ark would become hostile?

After a lengthy journey east of the Magalakwêna as far north as the Zoutpansberg, he eventually returned to Purekrans. He did not go back to Rietfontein. The Palala plateau was a new world to discover.

He spent some days on the farm of Dolf Snyder, east of Purekrans, and went with him when Snyder visited the kloofs of the Hangklip mountain to cut down droppers for building. One day, while they were working at the outer end of the narrow kloof, Marais suddenly caught sight of a troop of extremely excited baboons on the highest krantz. Looking down, he could see a large leopard creeping along a rocky ledge below the baboons, obviously on its way to its cave at the end of the ledge. Two strong male baboons had meanwhile followed the leopard from a higher ledge and before it could reach its lair, both of them jumped down on the predator from the highest krantz, which at this spot was only twelve feet above the ledge.

The struggle was short. The great canines of the baboon soon did their work, and within a few minutes the huge leopard lay motionless beneath them. But the first hero had sacrificed his life in the attack. On both flanks the claws of the leopard had exposed his lungs and the baboon managed to struggle only a few yards away from its enemy before it, too, died on the ledge.

Marais and Snyders joined in spontaneously when the baboons started cheering their fallen warriors.

Marais pondered the strange incident. What would induce a baboon to endanger its own life by recklessly attacking the troop's arch enemy? Was it instinct? But instinct should promote self-preservation, not destroy it. Only much later was Marais to stumble on a theory which explained the phenomenon to his satisfaction.

It was in this part of the Waterberg, too, one surmises, that Marais got to know the remarkable old character whom in a later magazine article he was to call simply "Oom Dirk".

This old man, he wrote, had bought a farm in the central part of the Waterberg and went to live there when the entire region was still uninhabited.

> An old hunter had to show me the way. We had to ride through the mountains on horseback; there were no roads for carts or wagons at the time ...
>
> Oom Dirk had built his house at the exit of a small kloof known as Geelhoutgrag (yellow-wood moat). There were six or seven gigantic yellow-wood trees at the top of the kloof and a sparkling stream bubbled merrily from the sandstone rocks down the kloof and past the house. In front of the house the water ran across tumbled rocks from one pool to another, eventually reaching lower ground across a rockfall of twelve feet high. The house had been built of stone in the mouth of the kloof. It was thatched and was surrounded on all sides by a wide verandah. The most singular aspect of the house was that it had been built entirely on a smooth sheet of rocks, which meant that the floors of all the rooms consisted of living rock.
>
> Never have I seen anything more beautiful in my life than the lonely little house in its natural environment ...
>
> At night – it was winter and bitterly cold in the mountains – we would sit around a great stone hearth in which lead-wood logs were blazing. A flask of wild plum brandy would be kept close at hand, and then Oom Dirk would tell us all about birds and animals – everything he had had the privilege of witnessing in nature – until the small hours.
>
> One could sense that everything he told one was gospel truth. In this simple soul there was no room for lies and exaggeration.

Marais describes how he and his companion had arrived at the house late at night and, after a hearty meal, had made up their beds near the fire-place on the rock floor. The following morning he was awakened by a chorus of bird calls which could be heard above the roar of the waterfall.

When they stepped outside, an incredible scene met their eyes.

> The whole verandah, the railings, the window sills, the chairs and couches were simply covered in live birds. On the floor vari-coloured wings fluttered in all the colours of the rainbow. The birds [were so tame that] they refused to give way, and one was afraid of putting one's foot down for fear of stepping on one of them. On a

settee, in the midst of the hubbub, sat Oom Dirk, calm and collected, as if this was nothing out of the ordinary. His hat, his shoulders, his lap, even his *veldskoens* were covered in tiny birds fighting for a seat. Next to him on the couch there were a number of dishes and tins containing all kinds of seed and meal-worms which he bred himself. In his hand was a long switch which he constantly used to stop bloody fights among the birds, for sad to say, his darlings were anything but peaceable.

It took two hours to feed all the birds, and then one species after another flew away. Eventually only two kinds remained: the flycatchers and twelve different species of sunbirds – "each a flying gem in the sparkling sunshine" – for whose food Oom Dirk cultivated a large number of plants.

On the same farm there were a number of tame klipspringers which the good old man could call to him by whistling with the shell of a spent cartridge.

One mother had twins. Occasionally they would appear unexpectedly by day. Then Oom Dirk had to rush around closing windows and doors, for once inside the little ones would dash glasses and mugs and mirrors to the ground. There was no table or shelf they did not examine, and they could jump from the floor to the highest shelf of the pantry with the greatest of ease.

Then, in one brief paragraph, Eugène Marais provides the key to this remarkable old Waterberger's ability to win the love of animals: "And the secret of his wonderful power? Here is Oom Dirk's own explanation: 'I am very fond of animals. This makes me observe them closely. I know their likes and dislikes. I know what they will do in particular circumstances, and I act accordingly.'"

Regarding his own abilities, Marais was later to put the matter even more succinctly: "If one loves nature, one learns automatically."

Not until after Piet van Rooyen's death, months later, was Marais to leave the farm Purekrans and return to Rietfontein.

From the events during this period, one feels, one begins to approach more closely an understanding of what Marais's son was later to call, in mild satire: "The Soul of Eugène Marais".

Was there really an Oom Dirk?

During various visits to the Waterberg, it was possible to check most of Marais's important references to his stay in this part of the country by questioning old inhabitants. But Marais's description of the old hermit and bird-lover – surely a remarkable figure – seemed familiar to no one.

Even so, there are small kloofs like Geelhoutgrag in the vicinity of Purekrans. Geelhout*kop* is only a few miles west of Purekrans and some miles to the north-east the farm Geelhout*kloof* lies on the slopes of the Hangklip mountain. The farm-house of Dielof Jordaan's farm Vlakfontein (also close to Purekrans) was built on a huge slab of rock which reminds one of the way Oom Dirk built his house. Even the stamvrugte brandy is typical of the area. Virtually every farm had its smoking still, for no excise officer ever ventured this far north.

Could Geelhoutgrag have been a thinly veiled name for Geelhoutkloof? Or was it – at least partly – a dream, a synthesis of all that Marais longed for, and did he see his own ideal self in "Oom Dirk"?

The primitive little house presents an exact parallel, in South African terms, to the remote country cottage De Quincey saw as his ideal abode.

First consider the countryside, beyond an almost impassable gorge. Here one could lose oneself completely. Then the "simple little house", strategically situated in a rock-piled kloof, and protected by a "moat" like a medieval castle. The floors of solid rock accentuate this impression.

This is an escape into the womb, albeit the womb of the earth. Escape and withdrawal from the confrontations of the outside world, at any rate, with the feeding and care of winged brothers as sole responsibility. The association with St. Francis of Assissi leads one's thoughts away from a fort towards a monastery, another symbol of safety and retreat.

Be it fact or fiction, here, one feels, is what Marais would have wanted if the choice had been his.

"Daar sal ek vrede weer besef ..." begins one of his best known poems – "I shall know peace there once again ..."

With what we know of this visit to the Palala plateau and of Marais's isolated flight into the wilderness to the north, it may be revealing to look once more at some lines of the poem:

Daar sal ek vrede weer besef
waar Tebes in die stil woestyn
sy magtig' rotswerk hoog verhef
en Mara in die sand verdwyn.
Waar smôrens van die hoogste krans
die berghaan draaiend opwaarts spoed
om uit die gloeiend' hemeltrans
met groot geroep die son te groet;
waar treurig nog die wolfgehuil
weerklankend in die klowe dwaal
en grootwild om die syferkuil
as skadu's in 'n stofwolk maal ...
O land van al ons liefde, daar
sou ek aanbiddend weer
die kloppe van u hart gewaar,
u moederlike skoonheid eer ...

I shall know peace there once again
where Thebes its mighty rampart rears
silent above the desert plain
wherein the Mara disappears.
Where every morning from the krantz
the eagle spiralling upwards flies
into the glowing vault of heav'n
to greet the sun with its shrill cries;
where sadly still the howl of wolves
wanders through kloofs, and echoes loud,
and game mills round the waterhole
like shadows in a dusty cloud ...
O land of all our love, oh, there,
while worshipping I would once more
your soft maternal heartbeats hear,
your beauty honour and adore ...

Mara is a river near Louis Trichardt, at the foot of the Zoutpansberg. Thebes, according to Eugène Marais's son, used to be the name of a koppie in the same part of the country.

The poem need not refer to any specific region. It might be composed of images from various times and places from the nine years which Marais spent in the Waterberg. However, both the Palala plateau and the Middleveld offer this kind of contrast between sheer krantzes and level plains – in times of drought a true desert – to which "Thebes" refers, and in the few months he spent there, he could have seen everything mentioned in the poem – the mountain eagle or bateleur on its krantz, the hyenas, the leopard (not quoted above), the big game around the drinking hole.

Here is another portion of the poem which might give one an insight into Marais's attitude to the several months of his flight into the wilderness:

> Met al U vrede om my heen
> sal nagt'liks uit die hemelstraat
> sag neerskyn op my laaste huis
> die vonkelend' sterrebeeld van U kruis.
>
> With all Your peace around me
> nightly from the Milky Way
> will shine down on my last home
> the sparkling, starry image of Your cross.

He longed for peace. He longed for the stars, old and dear friends. He longed for God in creation. And here, in his "last home" he wished to die.

Sporadically, over the two decades between his departure from the Waterberg and his death, Marais was to maintain his contact with Hans "Purekrans" van Rooyen. And during the last desperate weeks before his suicide it was to Hans he appealed, first by letter and then by telegram, to save and harbour him – not to the children of Oom Gys van Rooyen of Rietfontein.

"I shall know peace there once again ..." This dream was to endure.

He was to remember the few months spent at Purekrans all his life. After Piet van Rooyen's death there was no longer any excuse to stay away from his obligations on Rietfontein.

He had been away for about six months. Perhaps he himself did not realise how rapidly the time had passed. Even in Pretoria friends were beginning to worry about his prolonged absence.

Like a voice from another world one suddenly comes across a letter dating from the time, containing inexorable comment on such irresponsible escapism. And suddenly, too, one realises the intensity of Marais's longing for the "peace", the "loneliness" of the poem.

On 29 April 1910 Charlie Pienaar wrote to Gustav Preller:

> Regarding Eugène, I fear we can do nothing with the man. He undoubtedly has a powerful and brilliant intellect, but the fellow lives in a child-like state. Now and again I get a letter from him, but then he relapses once more into this inexplicable, unnatural condition of lethargy or dullness. I have tried hard to make him take an interest in the world and humanity once more, but he replies that since life has no purpose it is a matter of complete indifference to him where or how or how long he lives, or what he can do on earth or in any other place. He prefers to be where he need see as little of humanity as possible. I am told that he is apt to disappear into the bush on a donkey cart for six months at a time without anyone hearing from him.

"Life is real, life is earnest," Charlie seems, in the words of Longfellow, to be reprimanding Eugène. "Life is not an empty dream."

The sober words of the letter, with more than a hint of impatience at the old friend who simply refuses to do what is best for him, reveals how far Eugène and Charlie had moved away from each other in their intellectual worlds.

Sixty years later a French drug addict and hippy, Charles Duchaussois, found himself in Katmandu, capital of Nepal, after a long period of drifting. Deciding that he had nothing more to live for, he packed his last possessions and a supply of drugs in his rucksack and left the city to seek death in the mountains of Nepal – like many addicts before him in that country where so many of them were washed up in the late 1960's. In a bizarre, repulsive and yet largely convincing book, *Flash, ou le grand voyage*, he tells his story:

> I was 29 and I weighed 48 kilos.
> I was a junkie and I was going to end it all in the mountains.
> I was neither happy nor unhappy, neither scared or excited.
> I had at my disposal the fatalism of the East.
> I gave myself three weeks to live.

The mountains of Nepal – the plateau of Purekrans. Is there a connection? And does this connection contain the real explanation for Marais's attempts to get back to Purekrans during the last weeks before his death? Did he want to live there, or did he want to die there?

But from the time of Charlie's letter to those last weeks he would first have to struggle through another long quarter of a century.

9. The Comet

As usual Charlie Pienaar was very well informed, and not only regarding his friend's peregrinations. His suspicions that there was something drastically wrong were well founded.

Marais was approaching a crisis.

It was May 1910. It was the month in which the first Governor-General of the Union of South Africa, Lord Gladstone, asked General Botha to form the country's first Cabinet.

It was the month in which Hans "Purekrans" van Rooyen brought his wife, Babe, through Bokpoort to Rietfontein to have a baby under Tamaria's care.

It was also the month of Halley's comet.

Babe was put to bed in one of Rietfontein's maternity rooms. The intervals between her contractions were growing very short.

"I suppose you'll be getting up tonight, Hans," Marais told the young father-to-be. "Please call me when you wake up. The comet is due tomorrow morning."

By one o'clock that morning Babe's contractions were coming so regularly that Hans screwed up enough courage to call Tamaria. She had not been in the room for long when she said: "Hans, we shall not go to bed again tonight. In the meantime you can go and see whether Eugène's star has appeared yet."

"A son was born," Hans van Rooyen was to say later in an interview. "And Tamaria asked me to go and make coffee."

Hans had the kettle in his hand when he saw the comet rising above the horizon in the east. He hurried to Marais's room to wake him. They stood next to each other, Marais with his binoculars pressed to his eyes.

He remained standing for a long while without saying a word. Later Hans Purekrans fetched chairs for them. The comet was quite high in the sky when Marais eventually handed Hans the binoculars, saying:

"Hans, do you know what you are seeing? You are seeing something which millions of people never saw because they died too soon. But Halley predicted this centuries ago and when the little boy who was born to you and Babe this morning is in his seventies one day, the comet will appear once more.

"If this comet were to approach our earth as far as England is from us, it would scorch everything with its terrible heat. How great are the wonders of the heavens, Hans, and how great must their Creator be!"

Having said this, Hans Purekrans told the interviewer, Marais got up and went back to bed and never again showed the slightest interest in the comet.

At that stage there were very few things which did interest him. He had just about reached the end of his tether. The endless struggle to obtain enough morphine, but not to take too much of it, had become too much for him.

When he had returned from Purekrans the year before, he had again attempted to resume a normal way of life. Partly by way of therapy, partly to supplement his dwindling income, he had started breeding horses. Now this, too, no longer interested him.

Eighteen years before, shortly after his coming of age, he had marked the first two verses of the twelfth chapter of Ecclesiastes in the Bible his mother had given him: "Remember now thy Creator in the days of thy youth, while the evil days come not, nor the years draw nigh, when thou shalt say, I have no pleasure in them. While the sun, or the light, or the moon, or the stars, be not darkened, nor the clouds return after the rain."

Eugène Marais knew these words by heart. In the remote Waterberg, in the weariness of life which had crept up on him even before his fortieth birthday, they constantly returned to him, constantly milled in his besieged mind: "And fears shall be in the way, and the almond tree shall flourish, and the grasshopper shall be a burden, and desire shall fail ... Or ever the silver cord be loosed, or the golden bowl be broken, or the pitcher be broken at the fountain, or the wheel broken at the cistern. Then shall the dust return to the earth as it was: and the spirit shall return unto God who gave it.

Vanity of vanities, saith the Preacher; all is vanity."

Charlie Pienaar now arranged for Eugène's elder brother, Senator Charles Marais of Boshof, to be informed of his condition. It was decided that Eugène should spend some months in Boshof to recover.

Marais left everything in Oom Gys and Tamaria's hands. He would not be away long. They should take particular care of Angelier (Carnation), one of his mares, which had broken a leg. Bessie had just been served by a stallion belonging to Cornelis van der Merwe. He would be back on Rietfontein long before she foaled.

In Pretoria, his brother Charles met him at the station and took him to Boshof. Almost nothing had changed there. Charles was still living in the same house. Although the British troops had looted it, it had not been burnt down.

"He spent quite a while with us," one of Charles's daughters, Mrs. Kate Hurley (whose husband was Charles's legal partner at the time), was to say later. "He was terribly weak and he did nothing – only rested and read a little. He was reading Darwin."

Eugène recovered slowly. He was treated by Charles's own doctor, Dr. Stofberg.

This is the first withdrawal treatment about which we have direct evidence, even if the evidence is extremely scant. Mrs. Hurley mentions severe insomnia. No doubt there were also the customary nightmares and dreams of anxiety which accompany withdrawal.

We do not know what procedure was followed. Until only a few years before, the only treatment was to lock the patient in a room and keep morphine away from him. This caused almost unbearable suffering and would occasionally result in the patient's death. The most up-to-date treatment of the time, i.e. keeping the patient in a virtual coma by administering massive doses of hyoscine hydrobromide until the craving abated, had been tried for the first time in England shortly before (1908). We shall hear more about this drastic treatment with its repulsive side-effects later. It is highly unlikely that Dr. Stofberg would have attempted it in 1910.

Quite possibly, the treatment was determined in consultation with the patient, who would have known more about it than most doctors. It probably consisted of a gradual decrease of the dose, sufficient rest, some exercise and time spent peacefully in the house of an older brother with whom Marais had always felt very much at home.

And it worked. Gradually his interest in the world returned. Kate Hurley was to remember that he often spoke about the supernatural. He had probably started doing experiments concerning supernatural phenomena in the Waterberg by that time, and was planning further experiments.

By reading Darwin's *Origin of Species*, published more than fifty years earlier, he was also preparing himself for another aspect of his researches in the Waterberg.

Regarding his general state of mind, Kate Hurley added significant words.

"He was extremely embittered. He wanted nothing to do with his son."

Marais himself was later to quote the words of the Dutch poet, Perk: "I have embraced my pain, and loved her as a bride. Now she has turned into an ogress."

By this year, 1910, Marais's beloved wife, Lettie, had been dead for fifteen years. Even now he was still mourning the silver cord that had been loosed. Can it be that this grief had remained so fresh that he wanted to avoid anything which could remind him of it – even his own son? In this regard the son tells a revealing story. Shortly after the Boer War, he and his father were walking on Church Square in Pretoria when they saw a down and out hobo reading a paper on one of the benches.

"Now that we no longer have old Moes, we shall have to make do with this one," the son remarked.

"Who is he?"

"Van Voren."

"Is that Van Voren?" the older man asked in amazement, and he then told his son how Van Voren, a civil servant, had in the previous century refused to give the evidence which Marais needed to incriminate the President in court. And now, while they walked on Church Square, he pensively added Longfellow's words:

"Though the mills of God grind slowly, yet they grind exceeding small."

Did the irony of the words, and of the situation, not strike the father (as they certainly did not strike the son)?

For Paul Kruger and everything in connection with him he was never to have a kind word, right up until his death.

It may be valid to say that Marais's memory for real or imagined wrongs and for his own grief was unnaturally long, and that in this, perhaps as much as in his morphine addiction, lay the key to his tragic life.

Not his own alone. Every generation sees the comet once. Jan Christiaan Nielen when he was thirteen, in the old Cape Colony; Eugène Marais shortly after his thirty-ninth birthday in the Waterberg; and Eugène Charles as a fifteen year old schoolboy in Pretoria.

And there, like a line drawn below the last name in a family Bible, it all ended.

10. Patterns

Early in 1911 Marais was back on Rietfontein. He was full of newly found self-confidence, yet he remained quite willing to proceed according to the old pattern. This was a pattern of life which had begun much earlier, but which was consolidated in the Waterberg and, with only minor deviations, would be maintained for the rest of his life.

This pattern was as follows: Marais always lived with friends (sometimes with family) or with people he could befriend – usually a family with children – and almost always in a stoep room, outside room or rondavel. He very seldom had a permanent job, he seldom worked hard and sometimes not at all. He would devote a great deal of time to observing nature. To an increasing extent, he veered away from criticism of his morphine addiction, which restricted his social intercourse to those he had known for a long time, strangers who knew nothing about him, and especially children.

Finally, he always had to find actors to play four crucial roles in his life: the supplier of morphine; his host; an influential patron; and a protégé – a young person or animal – to whom in turn he could give his love and care.

It may sound far-fetched and simplistic to assume a rigid framework of this kind relatively early in a man's life. Even so, Marais seldom deviated from this pattern during the last thirty years of his life.

Some of the roles sometimes overlapped, and more than one part was frequently played by the same person. He would more often than not obtain his drugs from more than one source, but whoever gave them to him at that moment became the most important person in Marais's life. On Rietfontein, the sources were Ebrahim Ravat and especially Tamaria. His host was Oom Gys. Among his protégés during the ten or so years he spent in the Waterberg were Oom Gys's grandson, Barend (son of young Gys, who had built a primitive little cottage about one and a half miles from Rietfontein's farm-house), a young Bushman whose name has been forgotten and a five year old girl he was to recall as Marie in one of his poems.

One of his favourite pets was Jas – "the naughtiest warthog in the Bushveld", Hans Purekrans van Rooyen called him. When the people on the farm were infuriated by his misdeeds and tried to punish him, he would run to his master as fast as he could and hide there. Frequently he got into bed with Marais, muddy and dirty though he might be.

Marais's patron – always an old friend who had subsequently made his mark in the world, financially or otherwise – was Charlie Pienaar in the Waterberg period, the same Charlie Pienaar with whom he had shared a house in Brooklyn some years before and who had since become Secretary of Justice.

When tick-fever broke out in the Waterberg, the magisterial district of Nylstroom was divided into a number of "quarantine blocks" to keep the dreaded disease from spreading. Farmers who took their cattle outside their own block were heavily fined. A Resident Justice of the Peace had to be appointed for the quarantine block in which Rietfontein lay and Marais wrote a rather transparent letter about this to Charlie Pienaar:

> They want an R.J.P. appointed for the Block and they are all at me to get myself appointed – including old Boshoff (the Member) who came to see me yesterday for the purpose. There is a rumour that a rank Afrikaner-hater, Captain Groves, will be appointed. This they all dread. I am not pining for the honour but you would really do us a lot of harm if you appoint this man ... The other candidate is Gert Smit, also an energetic and able man, but with a still worse political record since he was a "joiner". I am the third person spoken of, but

> for Heaven's sake Charlie do use your influence that neither of these men be appointed.

To indicate the importance of the appointment, Marais writes, he could mention that since the demarcation of the quarantine lines, farmers in that particular block had to pay fines amounting to £600. He writes indignantly about the part played in this by one Blankenberg, assistant resident magistrate of Nylstroom:

> In many of these cases there were rank miscarriages of justice and a breach of all principles of law – manoeuvered by that other damned Boer-hater and general beast Blankenberg the A.R.M. of Nylstroom. If you could only be present to see that man interview a "Boer" it would make your blood boil and see red. For Heaven's sake old chap don't give us a duplicate of this within the block. Such a man could make these poor devils suffer hell ...
>
> I know you will do your best and let me know what you have done.

Charlie Pienaar could hardly have misunderstood the letter. To the best of his knowledge Eugène was "all right" again after his stay in Boshof. Charlie took the necessary steps. In June 1911 Eugène Marais was appointed Resident Justice of the Peace.

Apart from the fact that the farmers had begun shooting the destructive troop of baboons which lived at Doornhoek, this appointment made it virtually impossible for Marais to resume his baboon studies in the Baboon Kloof, however intermittent these had become. This may be why he always refers in his writings to an observation period of three years.

He had two constables serving under him and his office was within a mile of Rietfontein's farm-house. His salary was £7 a month.

It was not much, but at least it was a fixed and regular income. Marais reacted in characteristic fashion, buying a new pair of binoculars, and a leather bag.

Using steenbuck hides which Oom Gys tanned for him and which Tamaria treated with the boiled, broad leaves of a certain veld plant in order to give it a particularly rich, attractive colour, Marais got a tailor in Kromkloof to make him a handsome suit. Oom Gys made him a pair of leguan skin shoes. His belt was cut from the skin of a boa constrictor he had shot; he made the impressive buckle himself.

For his son, who came on a visit soon afterwards, he bought a coat of otter skins.

Marais had been living in the Waterberg for three or four years before his son came to visit him for the first time. The young adolescent, who had grown up in a refined and predominantly English-speaking world at Sophie Ueckerman's, found his first encounters with the Waterbergers somewhat startling.

"One night a blood-curdling sound awoke me," he relates. "It was a kind of lament which I had never heard in my life before. Only later did I realise that it was Oom Gys and Tamaria who were singing hymns in their bedroom before retiring."

The young boy found it strange to see his father living among these rough and ready people. Telling tall tales was nothing unusual in the Marais family – Oom Charles of Boshof was well known for it – but it was his first experience of a genuine Waterberg line-shooter like Oom Gys.

"Once on the Limpopo I saw an elephant dragging a crocodile from the water," Oom Gys would relate. "Holding the crocodile in its trunk, it then walked to the nearest thorn-tree, broke off a branch and impaled the crocodile on it."

"And what did he do with the crocodile while he was breaking off the branch?" asked young Eugène's father.

"Oh," Oom Gys replied glibly, "he kept his one foot on the crocodile's tail."

His father's comments on Oom Gys's omniscience would sometimes give the boy great satisfaction.

"Once we were sitting on the alhambra roots and looking across the Springbok Flats," the son says. "It was extremely dry. Clouds of dust hung over the plain and there was a peculiar veil across the sun."

On the stoep Oom Gys was chatting to a visitor. Pointing at the veil, the visitor asked: "Where does that stuff come from?"

"From the sun," Oom Gys replied without hesitation.

Marais's comment was to whisper into his son's ear: "Then it's come a bloody long way."

However, on this visit at the end of 1911, father and son did not stay on Rietfontein for long. Marais wanted to introduce the boy, who had just turned sixteen, to less artless friends. In the hotel at Naboomspruit young Eugène met people – remittance men, his father whispered later – who had known London at the turn of the century, the exciting capital of the world where his father had then been studying.

"Let's go and visit Du Bouillay," somebody proposed late one evening.

"My father, I, Leroyd and Sergeant De Beer got onto a wagon and left for Du Bouillay's ostrich farm on the Springbok Flats. Leroyd did not know the way at all and De Beer – well, all those water-glasses of brandy. We must have missed a gate somewhere, so we had to go through the bush. There was no other way out: I had to lead the oxen while my father drove. When eventually I was so tired that I could hardly put one foot in front of the other, we exchanged places."

But the famous Du Bouillay was not at home.

"There we played bridge until the early hours with an old woman who could hardly see a thing," the son relates. "In my otter-skin coat I eventually had to spend the night on a pile of maize husks in the farm-yard. My father came to see whether I was still alive early the next morning."

Marais's financial resources had been running low for some time. All his prospecting on Rietfontein had hardly produced a significant sign of tin, platinum or (as he might have secretly been hoping) gold.

He had also tried cattle-farming on Rietfontein, but this had never been a success. As a stock-buyer he had even travelled around the district to try and buy slaughter oxen for Cohen's butchery in Nylstroom. This, too, had not been lucrative. His only remaining hope lay in horse-breeding, with which he had begun after his stay on the Palala plateau.

On the face of it there was no reason why horse-breeding should not have succeeded. Marais had a natural love of horses, and he painstakingly studied his subject, noting everything in his diary. These notes appear under the heading "perdefokkerij", which means horse-breeding in Dutch but something quite different and somewhat obscene in Afrikaans. One need not deduce from this that the pioneering Afrikaans poet thought in Dutch rather than in his mother-tongue but rather that Afrikaans was still in an early stage of its development.

Marais learnt how to predict the birth date of a foal. He learnt how to tell a horse's age from its teeth. He grew fond of them all.

There is something heroic about a horse. In the yellowed pages of Marais's notebook, the names of many horses conjure up images of the patch of green lucerne he sowed for them, of muscles rippling under shiny, curry-combed skin, of mares grazing with their foals: Bessie, Angelier, Geluk, Spinnekop, Bakkop, Twyfelaar, Valkyrie, Kousband, Kappill, Sieraad, Baby, Valk, Snork – and all the foals which had died too soon to be named, for in this part of the world horse-sickness was a merciless killer.

In Nylstroom horses could be injected against the disease, but in practice this measure did not help much. All one could do was to bring a horse to a place where it was sure to contract the disease. If it died, one could do nothing. If it lived, one had to find witnesses to certify in writing that it had been ill.

Such a horse was then said to be salted (immunized). A good salted horse was worth £60 to £70, at least four times as much as an unsalted horse of the same quality.

It sounded easy enough: buy up unsalted horses cheaply, salt them and sell them at four times the price. But it did not work that way. In order to breed, one first had to buy salted horses. For Bessie, the salted six year old brown blazed mare which had, as Marais had predicted, foaled shortly after his return from Boshof, he had had to pay Andries van Heerden of Swaershoek £65. One of his great favourites, the stallion Bakkop, had been born on Rietfontein, true enough, but his other favourite, Baby, also had to be paid for. The seller in this case was Koos van der Merwe of Suikerbosfontein. The price was £60, payable in monthly instalments of at least £5.

To this day the balance sheet in Eugène Marais's notebook is heavily in Mr. Van der Merwe's favour.

	Dr	Cr	
Feb. 1913: medicine		£60	
For Sannie	12.6		7.6

In the Waterberg a horse could be bought on the condition that it did not die of horse-sickness within a certain time. But this was not always the case, and Marais's horse notes make it clear that he must have lost a great deal of money.

"Horses which have died at Rietfontein 1638 since 1911," he writes bitterly at one stage, and then gives a list of ten names. Every death upset him, but it is clear that the deaths of some horses moved him more than those of others. His notes on the course of Sieraad's illness have something of an *In Memoriam* about them:

> 28 Feb. 1913 morning 8 o'clock noticed it was not eating did not look very ill
> 8.30 gave him a purgative – a horse-ball dissolved in water
> 10 a.m. Fever 106 starts jerking slightly
> 5.30 p.m. Foam gall begins both nostrils
> 6 p.m. severe gall and falls down
> 6.30 p.m. dead
> 20 months old
> An outstanding horse

All his cash had been put into enterprises which were now failing – his prospecting, the cattle-farming, the horse-breeding.

While Marais was in London, his family had arranged to have the plot his wife had bought in Sunnyside transferred into his son's name. Now, in March 1912, seventeen years after Lettie's death, an application was made in the Pretoria Supreme Court to sell the plot in order to pay for young Eugène's maintenance. The master of the Supreme Court found that the father was unable to contribute to the boy's maintenance and education, and permission was consequently granted.

One fifth of the plot was sold for £130, and the remaining four-fifths was valued at £500. Sophie Ueckerman would now receive £5 a month for keeping and educating the seventeen year old boy. Lettie had made a fine investment for her son's future when she had bought the plot for £45 in 1894.

Eugène Marais had now spent four years in the Waterberg, and he had no intention of ever returning to Pretoria.

Once, when Hans Purekrans van Rooyen and his wife, Babe, were visiting Rietfontein again, Babe helped Tamaria in the house.

"Babe, do put some naphthalene in the trunk in which Oom Eugène keeps his suits of clothes," Tamaria said.

And he replied: "Oh, Tamaria, why worry? I won't ever wear those clothes again. Give them to the farm people."

He hardly ever saw newspapers or magazines and the books on his shelves had long been read at least once. In order to keep his mind occupied, he took to learning by heart numerous Dutch psalms and hymns while walking in the veld, as well as long passages from Shakespeare. Could it have been his longing for Lettie – or remorse – which led him, seventeen years after her death, to recite, greatly moved, the murder scene from *Othello* while walking among the thorn-trees in the veld?

> Put out the light, and then put out the light:
> If I quench thee, thou flaming minister,
> I can again thy former light restore,
> Should I repent me: but once put out thy light,
> Thou cunning'st pattern of excelling nature,
> I know not where is that Promethean heat
> That can thy light relume. When I have pluck'd the rose
> I cannot give it vital growth again ...

In the theme of *Othello* Marais must have recognized his own obsession: the needless death of a beloved wife because of tragic misunderstanding. And *Othello* – the most pessimistic of all Shakespeare's plays – happens to contain a clear reference to the use of the opium poppy as a way of soothing anxiety. After planting the seeds of the first fatal suspicion about Desdemona, Iago whispers offstage:

> Not poppy, not mandragora
> Nor all the drowsy syrops of the world
> Shall ever medicine thee to that sweet sleep
> Which thou owedst yesterday.

Eugène Marais, too, seldom found the rest he was seeking.

Occasionally, he wrote to his son, occasionally, too, to Charlie Pienaar and Gustav Preller, but to them mainly when he needed a favour.

Now and again visitors from the outside world would make their appearance on Rietfontein, and be amazed by the hundreds of cigarette stubs dotting the ground outside Marais's room, for even then he was smoking fifty or sixty a day. One of the visitors was the thirty-six year old Erich Mayer, German painter and nature lover. They got to know each other fairly well, and Mayer stayed on the farm for a while. When he left, he gave Marais a self-portrait as a gift.

In the same year, 1912, Marais's life was to be influenced by a conference held in Holland.

In the Hague representatives from a large number of countries attended a convention about the international opium trade.

All the member countries, including South Africa, agreed to adopt, within twenty-four months, legislation which would restrict the distribution and consumption of opium and other drugs.

For various reasons, it took some time for this legislation to be adopted in South Africa. However, the convention had drawn people's attention to the dangers of drugs, and as a result it soon became clear that the existing measures restricting the importation of opium would henceforth be applied far more strictly in South Africa.

Ebrahim Ravat would no longer be able to import opium from India in his personal capacity.

11. Wandering Tales and Supernatural Phenomena

Where there's a will there's a way. If Eugène liked, Ebrahim Ravat told him one day after having considered the matter, he could still obtain opium from India.

"How?"

"We'll ask our friends over there to pack it in ghee."

Marais knew ghee well. The Indians imported large quantities from India. Ghee was prepared by melting buffalo butter, causing most of the water to evaporate. The semi-liquid ghee which remained would then remain edible for months, even in hot weather.

Marais returned to Rietfontein feeling far more at ease and resumed his obligations as Justice of the Peace.

At about this time a mysterious spectral figure, a man on horseback, appeared at full moon near the police post on three different occasions. Years later Marais was to describe the apparition in considerable detail, using a sketch map of the vicinity:

> These events happened about twelve years after the Boer War. I was a special justice of the peace at the time and lived on the farm indicated with the letter N on the attached map. The farm-house was about one and a half miles from the police station where I held court once a week ...
>
> It is extremely important in judging this story to remember that no rider could leave the high road once he had passed the scattered rocks, since no horse could ride up the ridge marked M-M or pass through the donga marked K-K. For somebody stationed at the rocks marked G a horserider on the main road H-H would be visible over a distance of three miles in bright moonlight. This was confirmed experimentally ...

There was much more in the same vein.

Three times, always at full moon, the mysterious apparition appeared in the middle of the road – and there was no natural explanation.

It is quite true that a horseman was seen by several greatly alarmed eyewitnesses on Rietfontein. But it was not a ghost. Advocate E.N. Marais, Resident Justice of the Peace, had faked the phenomenon himself (a fact which he fails to mention in the article he wrote about it later).

Marais, at forty-two, was playing the same game – this time using all the authority and assistance he commanded as a special Justice of the Peace – as he had done as a ten year old boy in Pretoria.

The carefully arranged supernatural phenomena reveal Marais in his well known role of showman or magician, impressing, mystifying or deluding others.

On the other hand, as we have seen, Marais had over a long period been engaged in hit and miss experiments regarding supernatural phenomena. One aim of the game at the police post may have been to determine to what extent normal people might be persuaded by suggestion to believe that they have seen a ghost. Information of this kind is of obvious importance when determining the authenticity of other so-called apparitions.

Another series of experiments – some of them conducted in jest, others no doubt in all seriousness – which struck the Waterbergers as supernatural, was based on hypnosis.

These experiments were an extension of his baboon observations, on which he had now been engaged for some years, not only in nature but also, as we have seen, on the farm Rietfontein itself, where there were always a number of tame baboons. He may have watched them with the patience of a scientist, but it was the intuition of a poet which eventually enabled him to gain some insight into the true personality, the soul of the baboon. To his amazement he began discovering elements of this baboon personality in human beings under hypnosis. At a later stage in his experiments, he came to the conclusion that the so-called soul or personality operative in the higher primates like the baboon still existed in man, although in a latent form; that this soul was in fact the subconscious; and that under hypnosis it was possible to conjure forth the old animal soul.

And not the soul only but also the ancient sensory abilities which man had to sacrifice in exchange for his developing intellect and causal memory.

The human beings employed in this last phase of his experiment were Jane Brayshaw, who was always to hand, and her sister, Mary, who lived on Kromkloof. In his writings he refers to them by their initials, using a scientific style faintly reminiscent of Krafft-Ebings' *Psychopathia Sexualis*.

> J.B., Afrikaans girl, 18 years old, not fully developed, naturally lively and intelligent. Nervous by temperament and genetically. M.B., Afrikaans girl, 21 years old, fairly well developed, sister of the above; neurotic.

In a series of experiments he compared their sensory abilities to those of a number of baboons. Under hypnosis, he found, Mary's sense of hearing became eight times more acute than that of a normal person, and almost four times more acute than that of a baboon. In the hypnotic state her sense of smell, too, surpassed that of the baboon.

Jane was used to test the possible accentuation of the senses of touch and taste under hypnosis. Blindfolded, she succeeded in identifying by touch twenty virtually identical snail-shells which Marais had previously numbered and of which he kept changing the sequence. Her sense of taste was greater than that of the baboon.

Only in the acuity of her vision, he found, could Jane not beat the baboons. Even so, under hypnosis she could see as well as a normal person with a pair of good Zeiss binoculars.

There can be little doubt that Marais used Jane, and possibly Mary, in experiments to determine whether abilities like telepathy and clairvoyance were induced by hypnosis. He himself at least accepted the possibility of omens and telepathy.

One surmises that it was Jane of whom Eugène Marais's second cousin, George Findlay, relates the following:

"While he was at Rietfontein the aunts (Eugène Marais's sisters) wanted us to go there and save him. They had heard all kinds of stories. I did not like their attitude at all, but in the end we went there and met him in the hotel at Nylstroom.

"He had a girl with him, and everybody wanted him to hypnotise her. He then performed three tricks.

"First he took the sergeant's spurs and tossed them onto an empty lot next to the magistrate's court. She could not see him doing this. It was dark and the grass was tall. She found the spurs without hesitation.

"She then had to take up a position at the end of a long corridor between the back-yard and the bar. He would stand around the corner in the bar, putting a pin into the watch's flywheel to stop it. And every time, at that very moment, she would say: 'It's come to a stop.'

"He also had fifteen to twenty white cards with golden borders with which he transmitted a series of telepathic messages to her."

As George Findlay remembers it, Marais presented the entire demonstration as a series of tricks, not as proof of supernatural powers. Secret signs between Marais and Jane could have explained at least the second and third tricks.

However, there is evidence of other demonstrations of apparently supernatural powers under hypnosis in which there can be no question of co-operation between Marais and his subject.

Two stories illustrate this.

Hannes de Beer: "Yes, old Tamaria where he stayed, she had an avenue of banana trees and there was such a beautiful bunch of bananas. Well, she left the bunch of bananas there to ripen and she had a Bushman, called Jantjie, a young Bushman, as we say a *poon* (pony), and now he stole the bunch. And near to the house there were furrows and there was a wild olive-wood tree, hollowed out, you know, and there he hid it. Well, now, she told Eugène Marais about it. And while she was telling him, two Kaffir girls whom he did not know came past, and he called them. They came there and he said, you stand there. The two girls stood there, and both fast asleep. He did nothing to them, he simply sat looking at them. And he told the one girl about the bunch of bananas and so. He said, do you know where it is. Yes, said the girl, and he told the girl, he said, well now, you hurry up and go and get that bunch for me. Crikey, and the girl in her sleep she went and she walked and she brought that bunch back."

The implication here is that the woman did not know before being hypnotised where the bunch was. This is even clearer from the following story told by Mrs. Annie van Heerden of Swaershoek.

"Our horses were missing, and we needed them, because we had a cart there. You know, at the time we used a cart and horses. He also had a cart and horses there. Now the horses were gone. Now nobody knew where they were. My husband had sent Kaffirs to look for them, but they couldn't find them. And now they came back. He said and now let Daman come again. He said, come Daman, then he made like this and then Daman would sit down. He said, now you must quickly dream where the horses are, we are in a great hurry. But I must say, he had to sit for a while, about ten minutes. Then he snapped his fingers. Then Daman woke up and he said: 'Baas, I know where the horses are. I've seen them standing.' Then he would say where they were and mention the horses' names and everything. So my husband said, well run, go fetch those horses for us, and hurry up. And not very long, and the horses were there and we could drive off."

When a Czech, Rezl, managed to accentuate extra-sensory perception by means of hypnosis in 1966 this was regarded as a breakthrough in the world of parapsychology. Eugène Marais, if we are to accept the stories of eyewitnesses, seems to have managed this half a century before.

That Eugène Marais never committed these experiments – if one can in fact call them systematic experiments – to writing, is understandable. Who would have believed him?

Of particular interest in Mrs. Van Heerden's story are Marais's words to the black boy:

" ... now you must quickly *dream* where the horses are."

Several examples of Marais's interest in the possibility of clairvoyance in dreams date from the Waterberg period. In his horse-breeding notes he wrote: "15 April 1911 I dreamt that she (the mare Bessie) would give birth to a bay stallion foal with a white foot and a blaze. I told all of them. 1 May 1911 foal born bay stallion white right hind foot and blaze left front foot with white ring."

Tamaria must have been grateful to Marais for finding her magnificent bunch of bananas. For once Eugène had not been wasting his time. But what on earth possessed him to spend hours in the company of old Hendrik, an itinerant Bushman, listening to his stories like a child?

We do not know when Marais met old Hendrik for the first time. He seems to have visited Rietfontein every year. Certainly he was there in 1913, when Erich Mayer came to see Marais for the second time. Mayer, too, was fascinated by the old Bushman, and it seems possible that he encouraged Marais to write down the most important "wandering tales" in this year.

Decades later, N.P. van Wyk Louw (probably the most highly regarded Afrikaans poet) described these "wandering tales" (called Dwaalstories in Afrikaans) as "some of the greatest prose in our language". And indeed these remarkable tales, to be published eight years later in *Die Boerevrou*, a prominent Afrikaans cultural magazine, so outshine the rest of Marais's prose (apart from containing some of his most beautiful poems) that a literary critic, Ernst Lindenberg, once said during the course of a conversation: "I can't believe that Marais wrote them himself."

The words may have been said in jest, but they bring us to an interesting possibility. At least up to the thirties of the present century there used to be a flourishing underground sub-culture in all parts of South Africa: the dagga (marijuana) smokers. The smokers were virtually all of Hottentot or Bushman descent. Social norms were to change drastically during the next half a century, but at that time only the most degenerate "poor white" would admit to habitually smoking dagga. There is no evidence that dagga – and South African dagga is the most potent on earth – did the indigenous population of South Africa more harm than alcohol. (Eugène Marais, who had the opportunity of comparing the two by his own observations over a long period, was in fact very emphatic in claiming that brandy was much more dangerous than dagga.) On most farms dagga smoking, if frowned upon, was at least not prohibited. Children were usually allowed to visit the dagga smokers and listen to their tales. Among these smokers were many of the best-known story-tellers, but the most famous were the dagga rhymes. It was quite a ritual. First the smoker would suck deeply and gratefully at his pipe several times. A great coughing and clearing of the throat would follow. The smoker would then launch immediately into the first of the rhymes, and these rhymes are among the most remarkable and impressive in South African folk poetry.

Could it be that the Wandering Tales were told under the influence of dagga (by old Hendrik) and adapted later under the influence of morphine (by Eugène Marais)? This does not mean that they were given their final form under the influence of morphine. As a great many authors have found to their cost, the poetic process requires strict sobriety. In fact, we know that the Wandering Tales were finally written by Marais during a period of complete abstention.

It would be interesting to know in what form the stories were originally written down. According to his son, Marais prided himself on his ability never to have to make notes; he would rely completely on his memory. However, his baboon notes indicated that this was no fixed rule.

Thanks to Erich Mayer's visit, there is an excellent pen-sketch of the grandfather of the Wandering Tales in which old Hendrik, in spite of his tattered hat and clothes, still creates a dignified, patriarchal impression.

That this dignified, undoubtedly highly intelligent old man had to sleep in Gys van Rooyen's dingy, vermin-infested outbuilding, worried no one except Marais, and it is fair to surmise that he was not greatly put out either. That was simply how it was.

Even so, his attitude towards non-whites differed greatly from that of the average Waterberger and the average South African at the time. There was a time – and in some parts of the country this was to hold good sixty or seventy years later – when many whites never addressed a non-white in anything but a harsh and domineering manner. After all, they had to know their place. There is ample evidence to show that Marais never acted in this manner. He never referred to "Coolies" – the common word used by virtually all South Africans at the time – but spoke of them as Indians. After all, they were his friends. It is true that he used the word Kaffir, not only in everyday conversations but in his writings as well. But then Kaffir did not come to be regarded as an objectionable word until much later. To use a latterday cliché, he acknowledged the human dignity of all men.

In the early years of the century the Hereros, harassed by relentless German troops, fled across the desert to Bechuanaland. Some of them even reached the Transvaal. Here, a farm, Nagwag, on the banks of the Palala river, was allotted to them. Later, when white greed forced them to leave the farm, it was to Marais they appealed to find them a new place to live, dignified figures in their long military reject overcoats. In the event, he could give them no more than understanding and sympathy. The Government, as Marais was to put it delicately in an article much later "did not want (yet) another location to be formed". The Hereros were scattered and absorbed into the Waterberg's feudal system.

Interviewing the leader of the refugees, Captain Samuel, and the schoolmaster, Julius, who was also a preacher, Marais heard the details of their sad story. Both sympathy and realism emerge from the article he wrote about the desert flight of the Hereros, in which he compares their deprivations to those of those Voortrekkers who had inadvertently trekked into the desert.

> There is much in this great flight to remind one of the Mossamedes trek, except that everything in this one happened on a much larger scale. Thus more than seven hundred wagons were left behind in the desert and more than three thousand people died of thirst. The fact that this great catastrophe made no impression on the South African public is undoubtedly because the sufferers belonged to a Black people.

At this time the Waterberg, like so many other parts of South Africa, was a melting pot of various indigenous cultures and races. On a hunting expedition between the Magalakwêna and the Palala, Marais and Jan Nel, the famous, or infamous, hunter, met "old Klaas", one of the very few "Vaalpense" (yellow-bellies), "a pure black dwarf with peppercorns (woolly hair) and Kaffir features, but who had the ways and disposition of a Bushman." Old Klaas, like all members of his race, was an excellent tracker and hunter. He was also, surprisingly, adept at working with metals. He was about "four feet in height and obviously extremely old, the skin of his face being completely covered in wrinkles. His face was exceptionally broad and flat, his nose being probably the broadest and flattest I have ever seen. His mouth was huge, and the lips Negroid ..."

Marais and Jan Nel visited old Klaas's smithy and lair "in thick bush, right in the middle of a patch of the dreaded blue-thorn mimosa, impenetrable to both man and beast."

They saw the old gentleman's assistant grinding a quantity of iron-ore in a hollow stone. Then old Klaas himself deftly extracted pure iron from the ore in a furnace and allowed it to run into a mould shaped like a "Kaffir pick-axe" (a pick-axe in which the metal portion fits into the haft, not the other way round). Old Klaas's "wire-plate", which he used to make wire, and which Marais could not tell from the manufactured product, was an ingenious device apparently derived from an older indigenous culture. It was certainly not of European origin. Even old Klaas, who could repair rifles which baffled an able white blacksmith, could not have made it.

Marais's description of the "midget Vulcan", as he calls him, reveals his sympathy with primitive man. "Poor old Klaas ... This paradise he had carved from the wilderness when it had belonged to no one, where he had lived before the white man had arrived in that part of the world, to which he was bound by the deep feelings which bind an animal to its lair – the soil, the trees, his shack, his well – all this belonged to a Hebrew gentleman in London who had never seen the place, who had never been within six thousand miles of it. Eventually his representatives, supported by all the forces of civilisation, will come and drive old Klaas from the thorn-bush or extract a heavy rental from him. I did not want to spoil his last days by telling him this. I still have hopes that he has found a final resting place in the haak."

The contact Marais made during this time with a great variety of indigenous "races" brought him quite naturally to another field of investigation: anthropology, and specifically a comparison between the physical and intellectual abilities of various "races". Although he accepted the human dignity of all men, he was not blind, with the ideological blindness of a later generation of American scientists, to the realities of differences between groups of people.

What does surprise one is that Marais does not flinch from the extreme consequences of his findings. In an unpublished (and in our time virtually unpublishable) article, "The Yellow Streak in South Africa", he in fact seems to agree to some extent with those who have wondered whether the Bushman can really be called a human being.

> The psychologist finds so many ape-like mental attributes that it is difficult to avoid the conclusion that nothing more than the skeleton of an articulate language separates them from the anthropoids. And to the comparative anatomist the thing seems beyond question. The profound somatic differences between the Bushman and the lowest human race precludes all idea of a common species ... Everything points to a near ape-ancestry and to an ape-ancestry different from that of the rest of the human race.

However, as befits the author of the Wandering Tales, Marais adds:

> And it is a singular thing that this ape-like being ... the first cousin to the chimpanzee, should yet be the only true native South African artist. He was the first and only engraver and painter; the only musician; a poet and story-teller whose genius would compare favourably with that of any human race of a far higher degree of culture. And wherever the yellow streak has polluted the stream of "higher" South African blood it has prepotently carried with it this masterful strain of artistry. The so-called Bushman is our true and only Bohemian. With a broken-backed fiddle, a hoarse concertina and a bottle of virulent brandy he can still at will transform the wilderness into a joyous paradise. And withal, a sense of humour always proof against all miseries and vicissitudes.

The scientific accuracy of Marais's findings may be said to be of less significance than the philosophical content of his view. This is an antipode to that anthropological snobbery and arrogance which made the Victorians react to Darwin's theories in such a highly emotional way. "The Bushman," Marais seems to say, "is so like an ape that he can hardly be called a man, but this does not make me respect him any the less." Seen from a certain point of view, this view is not reactionary, but radical to the nth degree.

Not only his prose writings, but the atmosphere and spirit of his "native poetry" have made critics wonder to what extent Marais lived among the blacks in the Waterberg, accepting their way of life. The blacks are described "so lovingly", one prominent Afrikaans literary critic told the author, that he must have had intimate relations with them. This theory can neither be refuted nor confirmed. All that can be stated with certainty is that there is no evidence for it.

12. The Fruit of Infinite Suffering

A Saturday afternoon in the middle of the Transvaal summer. A primitive donkey cart came crawling across Rietfontein's farmyard and stopped in front of the house. It was driven by a Boer woman dressed in black, a large black kappie or bonnet shielding her face completely from the sun. She was bringing her husband to the Miracle Doctor to be cured.

In his room on the stoep Marais made the man lie down and started unravelling the bandages which had been wound around his leg. An unmistakable odour confirmed his suspicions.

When he had put the bandages back, he told the woman: "I can do nothing for you. You will have to go to Pretoria, to the big hospital there."

The man and his wife were dismayed, but they had long learnt to bear their setbacks in silence. Creaking, the donkey cart moved off. Marais stood on the stoep and watched them depart. They had been gone for only a short while when a thunderstorm broke over the area, covering everything in a grey curtain of rain. The man and his wife were lost to sight. Marais knew that he would never see the man again. Advanced gangrene could not be cured in Pretoria either.

The good doctor, if only for the sake of self-preservation,

tempers his compassion with a certain toughness, a certain cynicism. In the Waterberg Marais learnt to do this too. But there was a secondary reaction, born of his own nature, born of his own suffering and everything he had witnessed in the Waterberg, which was gradually to emerge to an ever-increasing degree during his stay in this part of the world. Marais was a compassionate man. He hated suffering. He hated suffering in children even more. In the Belgian hospital for incurably ill children which he had visited before the Boer War, he could hardly bear what he saw. Now, in the Waterberg, he visited the graves of the countless children who had died in the Nylstroom concentration camp and found, ironically, a certain consolation. They, at least, of all those who had been on the Boer side, had been pure and untainted. None of them had been traitors, none of them had been joiners, none of them had fought for a blemished, corrupt cause. They were the true victors, protectors of a people's honour. In an infinitely melancholy and yet inspiring procession he saw the tens of thousands of dead children before him, and he wrote:

> But you, o pale little ghosts, crying out in pain and suffering,
> come to us from the past to aid and protect us.
>
> Maar u, o bleke spokies, in u kermend', klagend' wee,
> staan voor ons ewiglik beskermend – uit die lang verlee.

But what about those who died in vain and in torture?

He had befriended a little girl, Marie, a beautiful child with brown tresses and shining eyes. "Mahlo-a-naledi" the blacks called her: "Starry Eyes". On the footpath between the trees she would come running to him at dusk, plump little arms held out to embrace him. She was five years old.

One day she got the croup. The Miracle Doctor had to treat her. Her death struggle lasted for eight days, eight days and eight nights. The Miracle Doctor, who had to witness it all, was powerless. Powerless but embittered. Later he was to write a moving poem about her death. Was it left out of his collected poems because it did not show the necessary acceptance of God's will?

> Farewell Marie!
> I do not know
> To whom it could afford such great pleasure
> To stretch your innocence upon that
> terrible rack ...

There can be no doubt about the meaning of these lines: If there was a God, he was a God of unimaginable sadism.

Eugène Marais had always loved children. It is impossible to say whether there is a connection between these events, but henceforth, for the rest of his life, more than to any others, his heart was to warm to little girls of five years old.

In his revolt against Marie's death he came face to face with a God for whom it was an everyday experience to torture little girls like Marie to death. Who or what was this God? It was a God who allowed an obscene poison, quintessence of evil, to dominate a man's life. And when that man fled from evil, when he found himself without supplies in the isolated bushveld, that God would start torturing him, hour after hour, day after day.

It was a God who had made fear and suffering the theme of creation, not as an exception but as the rule: the fear, night after night, of the baboons on their rocky ledge; the fear of the doe for the hunter, for the lion. Much later he was to summarise the impressions of these years in an article he wrote in English:

> One recalls a dark night in the drought; the fearful and trembling approach to the drinking-pool. Lips and throats are parched to silence by fear and thirst. The darkness pulsates with terror. Well do the helpless denizens of the wild know that the toll for water is death. The sudden alarm, the frenzied rush of terrified feet; a momentary silence and then the lonely cry of agony under the unheeding stars.

Coming from Eugène Marais these were terrible words: he who was always to regard the stars as the crown of creation, the last consolation. Even they were dispassionate, cruel, remote.

The God of these stars was no kindly light, no lode-star. He was a will-o'-the-wisp, hovering above poisonous marshes. It was He who was to make men, women and children – especially children – lose their way in the vastness of the bushveld, who made them wander around in circles until they died of hunger or thirst (a theme about which Marais was later to write repeatedly).

Marais reproaches this God only once or twice – as in "Mahlo-a-naledi" – for what good would it do to resist such relentless cruelty? This God was nature; there was no other.

His poem "Die Lied van Suid-Afrika" (The Song of South Africa) was born from this view of God as nature. It is an ironic antithesis to the national anthem, "The Voice of South Africa" (and poetically on a much higher level):

> Sy sê: Ek vorder as 'n heilige reg
> Die vrug van eindelose pyn
> Ek smyt hulle oor die berge weg
> En smoor hulle in die sandwoestyn.
>
> She says: I demand as a sacred right
> The fruit of endless pain
> I hurl them away over the mountains
> I smother them in the desert sand.

And later, even more revealing:

> Hulle diepste hoop is lang verteer,
> Vergaan in rook en as en bloed,
> Hulle sak aanbiddend om my neer,
> Ek voel hulle trane op my voet.
>
> Their deepest hope long ago wasted away
> Perishing in smoke and ash and blood,
> They sink down adoringly round me
> I feel their tears on my foot.

The divinity as a father figure has not been replaced completely. Even now, when he walked in the veld, alone or with his son, lacking reading matter or in fits of despondence, he would recite parts of the old Dutch hymns he had learnt from the Van Rooyens' hymn book – „Vader, vol van mededoogen! Zie op mijn ellende neêr" – and especially those in which he recognised himself so clearly:

O! Gij ziet het, wat ik lijde
Bij 't bederf, dat in mij woont,
Hoe ik worstle, hoe ik strijde;
O! Gij ziet het, wat ik lijde
Bij 't bederf, dat in mij woont,
En Zich telkens
nieuw vertoont.

O! You see how I am made to suffer
By the evil which dwells within me,
How I wrestle, how I struggle;
O! You see how I am made to suffer
In the evil which dwells within me,
And which constantly
reveals itself anew

However, this view of divinity as a father had become secondary. It had been pushed right into the background. It had become a mere convention. Even before his twentieth birthday, God, for Marais, had been nature. In this he had not changed, but in the Waterberg he became convinced that this divinity was not gentle, benign and protective but cruel and merciless – not Wordsworth's Lake District, but his own drought-stricken Middleveld.

That Marais saw nature as a woman was in accordance with the literary tradition in which he had grown up. That to an increasing extent he should see her as the only divinity, a ruthless, cruel goddess, accorded with his own basic approach to women which – while anything but simple – had powerful elements of chivalry, meekness, perhaps even masochism.

Of all the tortures to which nature could subject her defenceless subjects, as Marais gradually came to realise in the Waterberg, drought was one of the most terrible.

The rains had been good in 1907, the year after his arrival in the area. From then on, every new rainy season was drier than before. By 1911 there was enough reason for anxiety, and when rain did not fall for the next two summers either, vast expanses of the Northern Transvaal were transformed into what was virtually a desert.

By this time Marais had long been a true Waterberger. When he had arrived there – one of the Van Rooyen daughters, Cornelia, was to tell this story much later – he knew so little about country life that he tried to barbecue meat on open flames. (The countryman's art of barbecuing was not to become fashionable in the city for decades.) He learnt fast, though. Three years after his arrival he was firmly established. By 1913 there were few things which the ordinary Waterberger knew which he did not know. Only real experts like Jan Wessel Wessels could still teach him surprising new facts about the veld. Eugène, too, kept horses and cattle which had to be fed. The drought therefore affected him personally.

During that period, before the time of the tractor, of fertilizers and of hybrid maize, farming in the Waterberg was completely dependent on rainfall. "In those days you had to wait until it rained," an old Waterberger, Pieter Pistorius, told the author. "You see, the winters are harsh. It gets cold there. And the grass becomes so dry that it has little nutritive value. So the animals become very thin. Now, when it rained – in the old days we used to say that no Dingaan's Festival (16 December) would pass without rain – then you had to wait for the grass to come up, for the oxen to put on some fat, only then could you plough. Sometimes the lands were dry by that time, or it could be too late. In those days we had the old Hickory King maize. It had a grain as big as your thumbnail, but it had to remain on the land for seven months before it was ripe, so it could easily be too late."

In those years one Dingaan Festival after another went by without rain. The farmers were having a hard time. Every winter when Marais and Gys van Rooyen brought their cattle to the Magalakwêna, every time they went hunting, the erstwhile paradise looked more like a desert. Marais suffered personally from drought and thirst:

> What man who has ever experienced some small "thirsts" in the north of our country will ever be able to forget the event? The constant groaning of the oxen – the most heart-rending sound which any dumb animal can make; the glowing heat of the sun; the infinite sand, enveloped in a stifling cloud of dust, which seemed to be the embodiment of Thirst itself, proving that man's most courageous exertions are bound to be useless; everyone looking around him for signs of water – and their hopes constantly dashed!

Scores of conversations with Waterberg farmers convinced Marais that the years before the Boer War were much rainier than those after it. The six years preceding the Jameson Raid, particularly, were excellent years, which had never been equalled since; now he himself saw the entire Waterberg systematically drying out year after year.

The conquering British had brought systematic meteorological observation to the Transvaal. Ever since the early years of the century certain people, especially farmers, voluntarily and in their private capacity, took responsibility for rain gauges belonging to the Weather Bureau, sending monthly rainfall figures to Pretoria. There had been a rainfall station on Rietfontein ever since 1905, and in October 1912 Marais took it over. Rainfall figures, talks with farmers and his own observations led him to write a long, absorbing article which he sent to the Weather Bureau in January 1914. The article, "Notes on some aspects of extreme drought in the Waterberg", consisted of a typescript of seventeen single-spaced foolscap pages. "Enclosed I send you a copy of an article written for the Agricultural Journal which I trust will be of interest to your department," he wrote in the accompanying letter.

It was an impressive article. With an accumulation of facts and figures, Marais made out a convincing case for the theory that the sub-continent was systematically drying out. Ironically, the drought broke before the article could be published and when it appeared in the magazine shortly afterwards the Waterberg was so sodden that Marais could not get to Naboomspruit from Rietfontein.

At any rate, American meteorologists regarded the article as important enough to publish it in the U.S.A. late that year. Although there were no rain gauges in the Waterberg before the Boer War, the memories of the old Waterbergers questioned by Marais had been accurate. Figures which the Weather Bureau supplied in August 1974 make it clear that the thirty years before the Boer War were indeed extremely rainy. In about 1900 there was a sharp drop, and the average for 1900 to 1930 was to be considerably lower than that of the previous thirty years. In addition, the period 1910 to 1914 was indeed the driest decade in the century about which information is available. Marais's anxiety was not unfounded. However, after

1930 the rainfall figures again swung up to a level somewhere between that of the two previous periods.

Thus Marais, who had always regarded the article about drought as one of his most important achievements, was misled by the circumstances of his stay in the Waterberg to expound a theory which was not to be confirmed by the experience of the following sixty years. In 1974 the Waterberg was wetter – not drier – than in 1914. Even so one should perhaps be careful. Such changes come about gradually. It may well be, as happens so often with the weather, that Marais's guess – guided by incomplete information, but also by impressions and intuitions – may have been closer to the mark than the predictions of the experts.

The lengthy drought had other important consequences for Marais. It enabled him to make discoveries regarding the termitary (termites' nest) which would have been impossible under normal circumstances.

13. The Termites of Rietfontein

As Doornhoek was the centre of Marais's baboon research, Rietfontein was the centre of his termite observations. According to eyewitnesses, Marais certainly observed ants and termites in other parts of the Waterberg as well. However, in all his writings about ants and termites we find no other references from the Waterberg period than to Rietfontein. There is in fact little doubt that his serious investigations – or at least the main part of them – were conducted on Oom Gys's farm. The site was a ridge just behind the farmhouse, where no lands had yet been developed.

On the first page of *The Soul of the Ant* he calls his research into the habits of ants and termites part of "a greater investigation into animal psychology" – and so it was.

By the time his observations on Rietfontein began, the baboons had taught him a great deal. He now went to the ant.

Step by step he followed the birth of the nest. Without rain, he found, the flying ants – the future kings and queens – had to wait in the nest for months and sometimes years. This was because they needed moist soil to land on, as this was where they would dig their new nests.

As soon as the first rains fell, the flying ants would emerge from the nests in their thousands.

Once they had started flying, they would scatter like the seeds of a plant, some touching down miles away, others only a few yards from their old nest.

As soon as the female had landed, she would shake off her four wings, point her abdomen at the sky and begin to send out signals, undetectable to man, to lure the flying males to her.

As soon as the male had landed next to her, he in turn would shake off his wings and touch her with his antennae. At this sign she would immediately scuttle away to find a suitable site for a new nest, the male following her.

When the right site had been found, the nest would be dug out. Only then would they mate. The first children to emerge from the eggs would be looked after by the king and queen themselves, but as soon as they were fully grown, the children took over this task.

Marais proved experimentally that every step in this process was essential. In order to mate, the termites had first to fly, even if only a distance of a few inches. When they emerged from the nest, the male and female took no interest in each other whatsoever. If their wings were forcibly broken off before the flight, they would die.

As soon as the first workers were fully grown, they would dig a palace cavity three to six feet below the surface of the ground. This consisted of clay which eventually became extremely tough and in which the queen fitted exactly. When she became too large for this first hole, she would be transferred to a second, more spacious hole. Marais could never establish exactly how this was done. In the end the queen would be six or seven thousand times larger than an ordinary worker.

Marais began experimenting by lightly damaging termitaries. Immediately two kinds of termites would appear: the ordinary workers, white in colour, and a second, yellowish-red insect which had a poisonous sting and which differed so much from the white ants that they looked like two completely different species. While the hornsmen (as Marais called them) defended the "wound", workers would carry grains of soil from the depths of the nest to mend the breach – exactly like the white blood corpuscles in the human body would draw a cordon round the wound while the red blood cells restored it. In his mind's eye Marais may have imagined the white and reddish-yellow termites endlessly pulsing through the shafts and tunnels of the termitary like the red and white blood cells in the veins and arteries of an animal.

Examining the termitary more thoroughly still, he found that it was soft from within but was covered by a tougher outer layer, like an animal's skin.

Gradually, Marais's theory about the unity of the termitary took shape in his mind and he began to wonder: could the queen perhaps be more than – in a completely literal sense – the mother of all the millions of termites in the nest? Could she also radiate a mysterious influence which controlled the movements of each single termite, however far it might be from the nest? Could she, within the protection of the tough palace cavity – like a human brain within the protection of the skull – represent the termitary's control centre? And if this massive white monstrosity, not unlike a human brain in appearance, was the brain of the nest, what was the rest of the nest – and the termites themselves?

Step by step he came to the conviction that the entire termitary formed a unity similar to a highly developed animal, with the single difference that it could not move.

As in an animal, food was absorbed from outside and processed within the body. The workers were the teeth of the termitary. They and they alone had the ability to masticate wood, grass stems and other rough plant material, digesting it to a certain extent. This semi-digested food would then be sent to the so-called "fungus gardens" – the termitary's stomach and liver – where it would be further digested.

What were these "gardens"? They were hollows leading from vertical shafts in which the termites would deposit masticated and semi-digested plant material. They would then irrigate the gardens until they were wet through. After this a kind of toadstool would begin growing in them. To Marais it looked as if the termites brought the toadstool spores to the gardens and planted them there, but he could not be sure of this. All he could state positively was that he did find spores of the fungus on the mouths and feet of the flying termites shortly after they had left the nests.

The fungus gardens contained a variety of digested substances.

The food which was fully digested here was used partly for feeding the termites (the red and white blood cells) and partly – in the form of a sticky substance which kept the grains of earth forming the termitary together – to expand or repair the nests, again rather as in the human body.

The fungus gardens not only acted as digestive organs. The termites did something to the fungi which caused them to give off heat. In the palace cavity, Marais wrote, the temperature was several degrees higher than that of human blood.

Marais had been engaged in his research for some time when a puzzling question occurred to him. Where did the termites get all their water? Each termitary had millions of inhabitants, and each termite consisted of 90% water. The fungus gardens required a constant supply of water. The huge queen, laying 50 000 eggs a day, took nothing but liquids, which the hordes of workers brought to her drop by drop. Where did they find it?

Meanwhile, the great drought which had had the Waterberg in its grip for so long, had assumed such terrifying proportions that a sixty year old orange grove on Rietfontein was completely wiped out. It was the greatest drought in living memory. All the same, although some of the termitaries on top of the ridges behind the farmhouse were already deserted, a large number of them remained sound and well even at the height of the drought.

The air was so dry that no dew was ever seen. In the prospecting furrows on the farm there was no sign of water in the ground at a depth of 40 feet.

Somehow Marais persuaded Gys van Rooyen to help him try to solve the mystery of the termites' water supply, probably pointing out that such information might be useful to human beings as well. Laboriously opening up two of the termitaries, they found both palace cavities six feet below the surface in extremely hard soil. In both termitaries the palace cavity and the fungus gardens were moist. There was water vapour in all the tunnels and shafts. The queen and her subjects looked healthy.

Where did all the water come from?

When Marais's good friend Jan Wessel Wessels was told of the riddle, he thought for a while and then remarked: "Down a well in

Bechuanaland I once saw evidence that termites sink shafts to reach water at great depths."

Marais and Gys van Rooyen found this information very hard to accept. On the ridges behind the farm-house the termites would probably have had to descend to a vertical depth of about one hundred feet in order to reach water. Moreover, Marais found no sign of such vertical shafts when additional termitaries were opened. The riddle was solved by chance. The people of Rietfontein, too, needed water. On the ridge near the termitaries there was a clump of green trees in the barren veld.

"There is bound to be water there," Oom Gys said, and when a water-diviner had confirmed his suspicions, he at once put a gang of labourers to work digging a deep well in the middle of the patch of green. And there, thirty feet from the nearest termitary, they found its vertical shaft, connected to the main nest by a horizontal tunnel thirty feet long.

At a depth of forty feet the well was still completely dry, and Oom Gys stopped the work in disgust. But at the bottom of the well Marais could still see small white termites disappearing into greater depths, while another column of termites emerged from them. He estimated the distance from the termitary to the source of water to be at least a hundred feet.

And now, over a period of months, Marais witnessed a battle for life and death in the termitary. By dyeing the termites blue with indigo, he determined that they never rested or slept but worked day and night. And constantly the rate at which they were working was pushed up. For as the drought persisted, the underground water level sank ever lower, causing the fungus gardens – the organism's digestive system, without which it could not live – to dry out.

During this time Marais suffered badly from insomnia. When he woke at night he would take a pocket lantern and walk to the termitary to study the termites. What he saw and heard there echoed the anxiety in his own besieged mind.

"It was at night, during the hours when the rest of nature was quietest, that the fierceness of the fight gained most frenzy," Marais wrote in *The Soul of the Ant*.

I could hear distinctly the unceasing alarm calls of the soldiers, a

> sound which roused even in me a feeling of terrible anxiety. My electric searchlight revealed the restless stream constantly passing to and fro, as sure and indomitable as fate itself. Nothing could turn them from their purpose, no external terror could distract them. The death of a thousand individuals made not the least impression on that living stream. Vaguely and faintly, I began to realise, as I watched, what the struggle for existence really means in nature.

In this way Marais ended his description of the termitary's struggle for existence. He does not say whether the termites won or lost.

In this conclusion Marais presents his own view of nature, a philosophy which had been growing for some time. He knew now why those two baboons in the crevices of the Hangklip mountain had sprung onto their arch-enemy, the leopard, so fearlessly. They, like the termites, were not acting as individuals but under orders of a group soul, which in the baboons was a subtler concept than in the termitary, as it centred in no particular individual or organism.

Regarding the termite queen which has to live motionless in the darkness of her cell, he makes nature say: "What matters it to me how much or how little is paid for the privilege of my protection? How much happiness is lost and how much misery the new life entails is of no importance. What do I care for the individual? The race is safe, rejoicing, inexterminable. The individual must always pay, and no price is too high."

As early as his London period Marais had written: "Take individuals of the most widely different characteristics ... and place them in such connection with their environment as to form a crowd, a gang, an army, a nation or any of the other methods of herding which distinguish the human species, and immediately all individuality is lost. Hamlet is no longer Hamlet. He is merely ... an inert idiot like one in the trance of hypnotism, that obeys the words of one of its own puny atoms as the machine obeys the movement of its controlling lever ..."

In other words: as soon as the individual has become one of many, its individuality disappears and it then has to act according to orders of a group soul. This applied equally to termite, baboon or man.

The individual was of no importance – only the species had to be preserved. This was a law of nature from which no creature could escape.

14. Twyfelaar and the Rebellion

The drought was to rage throughout 1914. Not before the end of the year was it broken, strengthening the Waterbergers' superstition that rain either fell before Dingaan's Day or not at all. In this year history was to give Dingaan's Day a new, ominous significance.

Early in the year there was another strike on the Johannesburg goldmines, but General Smuts, then Minister of Defence, adopted a hard line and it was suppressed. Reports of disturbances in Europe were so far away and so vague that nobody took any notice. As Justice of the Peace, Marais no longer had quite the same liberty to leave Rietfontein for months on end, but there was always time for the annual winter hunting expedition in the Middleveld. While Marais and his companions were grilling meat in their camp in a clearing on the banks of the Palala that August, a young transport rider arrived and began outspanning his oxen nearby. Marais walked over to his ox-wagon and started talking to him.

They discussed the weather, and the younger man described a recent journey to Bechuanaland, mentioning, too, that he had shortly before been to Pretoria. As Marais was walking away, he added: "Oh yes, they say there is a war abroad, I think between England and Germany, but I'm not sure. I didn't really ask about it."

Only when the hunting expedition had returned to Rietfontein did they hear of the great war in Europe in which England, Germany, France, Russia, Austria, Hungary, Japan and Serbia had by now become involved.

Following Britain, the Union of South Africa had declared war on the Central Powers early in August.

In the Waterberg there were people who felt that the war might give the Boers the opportunity of restoring the independent republics.

Although there was no logic, no rational thinking in this idea, Marais, too, shared this hope.

Dissatisfaction was aggravated by the news that the Union Government had promised Britain that South African troops would invade German South West Africa. It increased sharply when a police bullet, intended for members of the notorious Foster Gang, accidentally killed General de la Rey at a police control point in Langlaagte. Anger and resentment were further fanned by the news that the Government intended commandeering burghers for the campaign against "German West". By October rebellion was in full swing in the Cape Province, the Free State and the Western Transvaal.

All over the Waterberg able-bodied men checked their Mausers, saw to it that their horses were fit and filled their saddle-bags with rusks and biltong. Once more, as they had done fifteen years before, the burghers left their farms and rode to meet the enemy, hoofbeats echoing in the early morning air.

Eugène Marais, Justice of the Peace, did not go with them but he gave his unambiguous support to the rebellion with a much more than symbolic gesture: he presented his best friend, Jan Wessel Wessels, with his beloved stallion, Twyfelaar (Doubter), a tough, fast and spirited horse. Together the two of them would brave the Government bullets.

A foal sired by Twyfelaar was born on Rietfontein the day after the report that Beyers and Botha had clashed for the first time in Rustenburg. In memory of this skirmish Marais called her Valkyrie. One by one the rebel forces were defeated. Beyers' force, in which Jan Wessel Wessels and many of Marais's other Waterberg friends were fighting, was completely scattered at Bultfontein on 16 November and on 8 December the courageous general was drowned in the Vaal river while trying to escape his pursuers. By this time General Christiaan de Wet had been captured. Jan Wessel Wessels was in gaol on a charge of high treason. By Dingaan's Day the rebellion in the Transvaal and the Free State had fizzled out completely. On the same day someone else whom Marais had known for many years was gaoled: Jopie Fourie, who had been a Boer Scout during the Anglo Boer War. In her life-story the Afrikaans authoress, Miemie Rothmann (M.E.R.), tells the story with the immediacy and directness of a contemporary:

(Jopie Fourie) was thirty-five when he happened to be present at the celebration of Kruger's birthday in Pretoria on 10 October 1914. He saw General Beyers being attacked by enraged Englishmen and tried to defend him. This made him come to a decision. He was one of hundreds who took up arms and joined the rebel forces. He headed a small commando and clashed several times with Government troops. He was captured on 16 December. On Thursday 17 December he was taken to Pretoria.

On Saturday 19 December he was court-martialled by three officers. That night, at half past nine, he was woken by an official who told him: "Joseph Fourie, you are condemned to be shot at dawn."

The next morning, 20 December, he was shot dead before the sun rose. That this should happen to a man who was only one of thousands: that was what we all found so strange and terrifying.

And this too:

General Smuts was in Pretoria all the time. A deputation tried to see him on Saturday 19 December to present petitions signed by a large number of people ... In his office ... they heard that he had gone to his house at Irene. They went there. A servant told them that the general had gone for a walk. They waited. After half an hour somebody else came to inform them that the general had been summoned to Pretoria in a great hurry. They returned to Pretoria but were not able to see him, so they handed the petition to a certain Lieutenant Esselen, who telephoned the general. He told Esselen that he would accept the petitions the next morning, Sunday, at 9 o'clock.

All these matters were published in the papers. We were dismayed by what we read.

Eugène Marais had known Jopie Fourie like a relative. Ever since Marais's childhood there had been an intimate friendship between the two families – the Marais' of Pretoria and the Fouries of Wildebeesthoek, beyond Magaliesberg – and there were numerous mutual visits. Smuts's lieutenant, to whom M.E.R. refers, was Louis Esselen, a nephew of Marais's erstwhile hero, Ewald Esselen.

After these events, Marais wrote in his diary:

"Dec 1914: (Twyfelaar) received back from Commandant Geyser at Nylstroom in a sorry state."

This despondent entry reflects the morbid state of mind to which Marais had sunk, as the notes about his attempts to breed horses, broadly speaking, form a barometer of his fortunes on Rietfontein during the previous five years.

The words quoted above were the last he ever wrote about his horse-breeding. At the end of 1914 it seemed as if everything was going to the dogs. The rebellion had been a failure. In fact it had been more than that, demonstrating once more the lack of unity and betrayal among the Afrikaners which had so depressed Marais during the Boer War. Even he now had to admit that his horse-breeding would never be a success.

And in his personal life, that most intimate part of his personal life which had to do with morphine, he was rapidly approaching a new crisis.

15. The Sinking of a Ship

If the year 1914 had been a dark one for Marais, 1915 was to become sheer misery.

At that stage Marais had been dependent on morphine for more than twenty-two years. The drug had become a part of him. What exactly does it mean when we say that "he was approaching a crisis" or when we read in letters written by his friends that "his health had deteriorated a great deal"?

The more generally known example of alcohol abuse, presented here in a brief and simplified form, may help one to understand the phenomenon of morphine addiction, with which it does show certain similarities.

Broadly speaking, in hard drinkers there are two distinct patterns. There is the man who drinks a great deal every day but becomes resistant to it and seldom shows its effects. There is also the so-called dipsomaniac, who does not have to drink every day but has periodic bouts in which he takes more than he can handle. These bouts may eventually develop into a binge, which means that the drinker will start drinking again the next day to alleviate the unpleasant mental and physical consequences of too much drink (a hangover). When these two patterns overlap or merge, the drinker is approaching a serious crisis. When this happens the alcoholic does not only drink every day, but drinks more than he can handle almost every day, while the dipsomaniac does not only get drunk on occasion but virtually every day. The alcoholic forced by circumstances to do without drink completely experiences mental stress and a varying degree of bodily discomfort, including phenomena like insomnia, restlessness and tension. The morphine addict whose supply has been cut off experiences similar symptoms, but in an exaggerated form. These are the withdrawal symptoms, which have been dealt with in some detail.

That a comparable pattern is found in morphine addicts was realised long before Marais's death. In the United States junkies were divided into "users" and "hogs" (those who went on binges periodically).

If morphine is prescribed to a non-addict (e.g. as an anodyne or pain-killer) the dosage is usually a quarter of a grain (15 mg) or a sixth of a grain (10 mg). One grain is sufficient to kill a normal person.

Addiction is established remarkably rapidly. Even more incredible is the increase in the resistance of the addict, who can eventually inject five, ten or even fifteen grains a day. Even twenty or thirty grains a day are not unknown. The dosage increases "automatically". As soon as the addict finds that the old dosage no longer has the required effect, he increases it, up to a certain point. Reaching this point, and it can be a high one, the "user" may often remain there for years without showing outward signs of dependence.

The pattern of the periodic morphine addict is less predictable. His average daily intake may be modest. On the other hand, he may feel a need to get "drunk" from time to time. By periodically taking two or three times as much as his normal dosage – even if this increased dosage is lower than that of the daily intake of the "user" – he may attain a high degree of intoxication. Unlike the periodic drinker, the periodic morphine addict cannot do without the drug for long, even at an early stage. Morphine is too addictive for that. As far as one can judge today, Marais belonged to the second group of addicts. According to what he told his son, his daily dosage did not exceed seven grains for a quarter of a century. One can accept this. Even later there is no evidence that his intake ever exceeded ten grains a day. However, apart from the ordinary dosage, there was a compulsive urge from time to time to take an overdose.

It seems likely that in the early years of his dependence this urge was felt only when his daily dose was reduced below a certain minimum. Not until later in his life does one find firm evidence of periodic excesses, even in periods of uninterrupted supply. But that was to come later.

In the year of this chapter, 1915, extremely little was known about morphine. Even with medical aid it was difficult to reduce the dose systematically. That Marais had managed to do so five years before at Boshof says a great deal for his "willpower". Without medical supervision, as on the farm Rietfontein, it was virtually impossible. Of course he tried, he tried constantly. According to the experts, virtually no morphine addict wants to remain one. Most of them plan constantly to get rid of the painful, constricting fetters which shackle them to the drug. "He searches the literature for advice," writes one researcher, "submits to periods of gradual reduction or complete abstention, and when all has failed tries to maintain functional competency on a minimum of morphine."

That is exactly what Marais tried to do on Rietfontein with the aid of Tamaria van Rooyen. By appointing her as the keeper of his supply, he had asked her to do the virtually impossible. She had now been playing this part for seven years and it was an extremely onerous task.

There is a possible paradox here which should be examined briefly. It is conceivable that Tamaria was deeply attached to Marais and that her death, shortly after he had left the farm a year later, was brought on or accelerated by the fact that she no longer had him to care for, just as Marais's mother had died very soon after his father's death.

These facts should be borne in mind when one considers what was to happen on Rietfontein later.

By this time, 1915, they both knew the routine so well. They knew each crisis so well. On a certain day Tamaria might have a supply for two months in her house, calculated according to Marais's average intake. For a time it would go fairly well, although his body might crave a larger dose. The next stage would be more intense discomfort. He would become irritable and anxious. He would plead with Tamaria to give him more than the amount they had agreed upon. Sometimes she would give way, and then he would find it twice as difficult to return to the previous, smaller doses. Sometimes he would buy opium from Ebrahim Ravat, and in the painful aftermath of over-indulgence he would need more morphine to recover. It was a murderous routine with a hundred variations, in each of which Marais came off worst.

By early 1915 everything in this most important aspect of his personal life was working against him. The financial and other setbacks of the previous year, the failure of the rebellion, perhaps also his friend Jan Wessel Wessels' imprisonment, weakened his spiritual resistance. The nearest doctor was at Warmbaths, fifty miles to the south, and no doctor would in any case have given him enough morphine to meet his present heavy demands for more than a few weeks. The Indians in Nylstroom were becoming more difficult as well. It was no longer as easy to bring in opium, they said. They would have to ask more for it.

"I saw it with my own eyes," Hans Purekrans van Rooyen relates concerning this time. "In Nylstroom Oom Eugène paid Abraham Coolie twenty golden sovereigns for a pound of opium."

Marais was now at Tamaria's mercy, and by this time her patience was wearing thin. In his *Confessions* De Quincey relates – not without a measure of *Schadenfreude* – how the poet Coleridge threatened his servant with dismissal if he did not keep him away from the opium shops by force and how, as the urge grew, he later threatened to dismiss the man unless he got out of the way so that he could buy the medicine he needed to stay alive. Unlike Coleridge, Marais had no hold on the protector of his treasures. On the contrary, he was completely in her power. The Van Rooyens were not more unfeeling or cruel than most people. If Marais had had a serious illness which caused great suffering, they would certainly have been sympathetic. But they had become accustomed to Marais's equally serious withdrawal symptoms and, with the exception of Tamaria, they had little understanding of the condition. The relative who was to tell later how Marais used to follow Tamaria around "like a naughty child", begging for a bit of opium, could have had no idea of the seriousness of his condition. It is true that Maria van Rooyen was doing her duty as a nurse. By restricting Marais's intake, she was in fact doing nothing but carrying out his own expressed request. Or could it be that she secretly delighted in punishing this man whom she had harboured for seven years, for the many times he had abused her hospitality?

One day there was no more opium. Had Maria van Rooyen warned her patient that the supply was getting low?

Or had he, goaded to cunning and despair, succeeded in tracing the remaining supply and taken it all at once?

At that stage, whatever the background, Tamaria was misled into actions which were to sully her good name. While Marais's withdrawal symptoms became increasingly violent, she mentioned that she still had a bottle of Chlorodyne. Chlorodyne was freely available at the time. It was a mixture of chloroform, prussic acid and ether in a peppermint-flavoured syrup. It also contained 0,05 per cent of morphine. Marais knew it well. He knew that one ounce of Chlorodyne contained about a quarter of a grain of morphine.

When Tamaria mentioned Chlorodyne, he grabbed at the opportunity like a drowning man. Could he buy it from her?

"With the greatest of pleasure, Eugène, but what will you give me for it?"

Sister Hotine, the district nurse, who had also witnessed Marais's treatment of tant Hessie van Deventer, was to testify later about the negotiations which followed this exchange of words. A man suffering from withdrawal symptoms is apt to get the worst of a bargain. In the end Marais agreed to pay Tamaria a salted horse (value about £60 to £70) for the bottle of medicine.

In Pretoria Charlie Pienaar, extremely well informed as always, had meanwhile learned that his friend's condition had seriously deteriorated. What was he to do? At this stage Pienaar decided that the son, Eugène Charles, should be told. Incredible as it may seem, the twenty year old young man knew nothing at all of his father's addiction. It was a scene which young Eugène, Eugène Charles, was never to forget. It was dusk. He was standing in the street in front of his stepmother's house. Charlie Pienaar came riding up dusty Maré Street and casually called to young Eugène.

"You know your father is very ill, do you?"

"What's wrong?"

"He's been taking too much morphia."

Almost sixty years later this same son was to say: "It was the first I had heard of it."

Charlie Pienaar got off his horse and explained to the young man that his father had been taking morphine for years, that he was constantly trying to shake the habit, but that he was finding it extremely difficult. However, there was hope. He would see to it that his father was brought to Pretoria to undergo treatment. As usual, Charlie Pienaar kept his promise.

In May 1915, according to the records of the Weather Bureau, the entries for the rain gauge at Rietfontein came to an end (they were never resumed).

It was the same month in which Marais had fled Rietfontein to try and recover at Boshof. This time, too, sick unto death, that is where he fled, travelling by train.

In the same week, by another strange coincidence, the *Lusitania*, a Cunard liner, was torpedoed off the Irish coast by a German U-boat. The huge ship, one of the fastest and largest passenger ships in the world, 785 feet long and with a tonnage of 40 000, sank within 45 minutes.

In fact, apart from the several hundred passengers, the ship, contrary to the Geneva Convention, was also carrying numbers of troops and quantities of arms (not to be revealed until fifty-five years later) and apparently the Germans knew it. But now, in May 1915, the world was told that the Huns had sunk a defenceless passenger ship in cold blood. Among the passengers were 124 Americans and the incident came in for severe condemnation by President Wilson. It was later to play an important part in America's decision to enter the war on the Allied side.

When Marais arrived in Pretoria, the anti-German riots had begun. Among these was an attack on the offices of *Die Volkstem*. These riots were not simply a loyal echo of those which had broken out in London. Among the victims of the attack on the *Lusitania* was at least one Pretorian. She was Cathy Dougall, the attractive, talented daughter of Eugène Marais's sister, Kate. The young girl had been in Canada, where she had taken a course in domestic science.

Charlie Pienaar met Marais at the station and took him to Jess Rex's boarding house, where he spent the night. The room in the same boarding house which had been prepared with such loving care for the returning girl remained vacant. It was to remain like that for weeks, as her parents refused to accept that she would never return. The next day Eugène Marais's brother, Charles, came to collect him in Pretoria and took him to Boshof. This time he did not stay there for long. He was worried about his horses and about the possessions he had left on Rietfontein; he was worried about the police post.

On the way back he spent a night in the room which had been prepared for Cathy Dougall. He was the first person to sleep there.

When he arrived back on the farm he was anything but well. At that stage Charlie Pienaar decided to intervene personally. He knew Marais well. It was he who, in those good old days in Brooklyn, had helped him to get along with a minimum of morphine. He would go to the Waterberg himself and help him to shake the habit once and for all.

Pienaar now arranged to accompany Marais on a hunting expedition in the Middleveld in July. Melt van Niekerk, an official of the Department of Agriculture, a cousin of Marais, was to go along as well.

Pienaar organised the hunting expedition from Pretoria with characteristic thoroughness. On 6 July he wrote Marais a comprehensive letter regarding supplies of food, clothes, ammunition, a keg of beer and even a dog which had been railed to Armstrong, the hotel keeper in Nylstroom.

Marais, meantime, had become increasingly worried about his friend Jan Wessel Wessels who was still in gaol on a charge of high treason for his part in the rebellion. He had written to Charlie Pienaar as Secretary of Justice, asking him to use his influence to have Wessels released.

In the same letter Pienaar replied: "Re Mr. Wessels. I have not been able to go and see him. I cannot write reasons but shall tell you all, but rest assured that my power in doing good and helping him is much greater by not going or attempting any active action at present."

At the end of the letter he mentioned the time and date of the party's arrival at Naboomspruit.

The following day he wrote another short note to confirm a telegram he had sent in connection with the hiring of horses.

At this stage Marais's condition was such that he never read the letters. (For fifty-seven years they were to remain in his son's possession until the two envelopes were cut open by Eugène Charles in the presence of the author in the son's house in Brits for the first time on the evening of 27 November 1972.)

On Tuesday, 13 July, Charlie Pienaar and Melt van Niekerk arrived at Naboomspruit on the 4.15 train from Pretoria. Marais was not expecting them and had made no arrangements for the expedition. Not even the horses had been hired.

While Melt van Niekerk travelled ahead to find a suitable camping site on the banks of the Magalakwêna, Charlie remained with Eugène to look after him and also to make arrangements for the expedition. He hired an ox-wagon and collected the supplies – including maizemeal, salt and condensed milk – from Armstrong in Naboomspruit.

Marais's most important victual, morphine, could not be had for love or money in Naboomspruit or in Nylstroom, however. All they could get was a quantity of Chlorodyne. And Charlie Pienaar decided to help cure his friend by gradually reducing the daily dose during the hunting expedition, when he thought Eugène would be relaxed and happy. The rest of the party followed Melt van Niekerk the day after his departure and found his camp-site on the banks of the river. Marais was to describe it fairly exactly in a magazine article:

> We had outspanned on a fairly high bank ... below which there was water for our animals in the river bed. The bank was at least fifty feet high at this place, but a couple of hundred yards up the river there was a slope which allowed the oxen access to the water. The river banks were densely overgrown with large trees. Our camp was pitched in a small clearing about fifty yards in diameter. In this clearing, just above the steep river bank, was a cone-shaped termitary of about fifteen feet in height.

The expedition began on an ominous note. While the blacks outspanned and led the oxen to the water in the river bed, Eugène, Charlie and Melt van Niekerk strolled over to the large termitary.

> When we were next to the ant-heap, we heard the (black) men in the river, about 300 yards from us, shouting in great alarm. We soon recognized the word "makopa" and within seconds we saw the snake approaching in our direction through the branches of the trees. Mr.

> van Niekerk was in the position of greatest danger, being between the approaching snake and its destination, the ant-heap ... When (the snake) reached the tips of the branches above our heads it shot down into the spout of the ant-heap like an arrow from a bow. Just below this spout was a round hole about six inches in diameter, into which the snake shot with incredible violence. All we could see was a whirling body and tail and a small cloud of dust fuming from the termitary, then all was quiet once more.

It was the prelude to a miserable journey. Marais's son put it extremely concisely: "On that expedition Charlie Pienaar tried to get my father off morphine. He did not succeed."

Notes which Marais made on this expedition described his deprivations. They were not shown to the author.

The supply of Chlorodyne was used up more rapidly than Charlie had intended, and the party had to return to Rietfontein in a hurry.

Soon Charlie Pienaar and Melt van Niekerk returned to Pretoria, leaving a broken man behind them on Rietfontein. Life had no purpose, and he himself was a useless drifter who might as well disappear from the face of the earth.

In that very month, August 1915, six thousand miles to the north, one of the most famous scientists of the time, Dr. Ilya Metchnikov – a man who, according to references in Marais's writings, must have had a certain influence on his thoughts – wrote from Paris to a collaborator in Cuba. This woman, Madame Rosalia Abreu, had kept and studied a number of large and smaller apes on her estate near Havana since the early years of the century. After some observations regarding chimpanzees she had sent him, Metchnikov continues:

> All that you say about the relations between the male and the female, about gestation, and about the birth and rearing of the young is of vital interest. Since you are continuing your observations perhaps it will be possible for you to tell me still more details of the life of your chimpanzees. What is the procedure by which the male arrives at intercourse with the female? How does he behave in taking his particular position and does she manifest any coquetry? Does copulation continue during pregnancy? Or does the female cease to accept the male? Does the latter caress the female before and after the act?

> How many interesting observations will you be able to make on the education of the little one? Does the mother take care of the infant and does she give him some cuffs? How does the male behave face-to-face with his offspring? Does he continue to live maritably with his mate? And does he not make advances to the dry nurse? (The question as to whether the anthropoids are monogamous or polygamous is particularly interesting.)
>
> You thought, Madame, that your letter would appear to me too long. I have read and re-read it many times, but I find it all too short, so vital is the subject of your observations.

When it came to baboons, at least, the forty-four year old wreck of a man who had now remained behind on Rietfontein could have replied to all Dr. Metchnikov's questions. Unlike Madame Abreu he had not observed his specimens in camps and cages but in nature. Everything the distinguished Nobel Prize winner found so intensely interesting was old hat to Marais.

But in South Africa no one – not even Marais himself – realised what important information he had. He was a complete failure, that was all.

Desperately, near the end of his resources, half crazed, he fled to Boshof once again.

16. The Silver Cross

In another world, long, long ago, he had sworn on a ring and a crucifix and in an equally forgotten, other existence, something – a ring, a cross? – had brought him safely through marshes, persecution and malaria. He could get through again, even through this hell, but he would have to find a talisman.

There was an incantation he had to remember. What keeps a man from harm? The silver ring that keeps a man from harm?

From his delirium faces swam before him – his brother Charles; a tender, blonde young woman; a young girl, cool and business-like. The silver cross that keeps a man from harm?

He knew that he was lying in the familiar small back room of his brother's house in Boshof. But for the first time he did not feel safe here either. Danger menaced him here as well. The silver something that keeps a man from harm?

Senator Charles Marais, now sixty-five, was deeply worried. He had never seen his brother so ill. Dr. Stofberg, too, held out little hope this time. Eugène Marais looked like death itself. His skin was transparent. His ears seemed paper thin. What he said made no sense. It was obvious that his mind was wandering.

Since Eugène's arrival, the house on Market Square had been turned into something resembling a hospital. In the room behind Charles's his wife, Emily, was also being treated. A stroke had paralyzed her. A twenty-five year old Danish nurse, Anna Hansen, slept in her room to look after her.

Mrs. Marais did not always treat Anna very politely. In fact she was jealous of her.

Charles discussed Eugène's illness with Anna.

"Something is worrying him, Mr. Marais," she said. "Something keeps turning in his head. It is a magic formula or saying which he can't get hold of – that's what it sounds like to me."

In his legal office Charles now consulted his exceptionally gifted young secretary, Alida Saunders.

Alida was a phenomenon. At a time when most educated girls who wished to work became teachers, she had gone to Cape Town and followed a course in shorthand and typing at the Yost College in Hout Street. When she had started working in Senator Charles Marais's lawyer's office the previous year, she soon discovered that most of the work was in Afrikaans. By taking down the Reverend Malherbe's sermons in the Dutch Reformed Church, she simply developed her own Afrikaans *snelskrif* or shorthand.

As usual Alida did not disappoint her employer. It did not take her very long to find the magic formula which was milling in Marais's mind. It came from Kipling and simply said:

> The little silver crucifix
> That keeps a man from harm.

When Eugène heard the words the spell was broken. His cure could begin. While Dr. Stofberg treated him, Anna Hansen made him well. Women often fall in love with the doctor who has saved them from the depths, men frequently with their nurses. This is what now happened to Marais, at least temporarily. Anna Hansen was a simple Danish girl with a soft heart and capable hands. She was very proud of the knowledge that she had acquired of the Anglo-Saxon world. Ella Wheeler-Wilcox was one of her favourites. In Marais's youth the poetess' work had been regarded as immoral; these days he simply found her verses sentimental. But he was not to disillusion Anna immediately.

Finally, he was well enough to get up. Later still he was allowed to play golf with Alida Saunders on Boshof's golf-course of Kimberley gravel. Anna Hansen remained at home to nurse Mrs. Marais.

Now that Eugène had become more active, the roles were reversed. Anna Hansen fell in love with him and he, although he was still very fond of her, although he still encouraged her, began playing the unconcerned role he had practised on Jane. He teased her, he parodied her beloved Ella Wheeler-Wilcox ("If all my ships came sailing back/With broken masts and tattered sails"), he used her, he rather looked down on her.

He was forty-four. His face showed the interesting, emaciated fatigue, irresistible to many women, of a man who has returned from the tropics or has recovered from a serious illness. He was not equally attractive to all women but he now knew that he could conquer virtually any woman if he went to enough trouble. It was an art, like any other.

Emily Marais was shocked and indignant by the relationship which she saw developing under her roof. Charles was already much too fond of Anna. Eugène's behaviour was completely shameless. Marais took no notice of her. The horrible nightmare from which he had emerged eventually disappeared into the background. The Smithsonian Institution in America had published his article about drought in the Waterberg the previous year. From Boshof he now started up a correspondence with this Institution concerning his baboon observations. Years later Alida Saunders, who typed the letters for him, was to remember that he had, among other information, a list of twenty-five sounds or words which he had heard the baboons use under certain circumstances.

As Eugène had done at Boshof five years before, Alida was now reading Darwin. Eugène devoted part of his time to studying the other great evolutionary thinker, Häckel, to whose work he had been introduced in London. He read Häckel in English. Seventeen years after its first publication, *The Riddle of the Universe* was still a popular book.

"We talked about evolution a great deal," Alida Saunders was to say later in an interview, "but we had to be extremely careful. The children were to know nothing about it. It was a forbidden subject."

And here at Boshof, in the year 1915, Eugène Marais started writing the great philosophical work which he thought would make him world-famous. Although it almost certainly had a different title then, this was the work later to be known as *The Soul of the Ape.*

Darwin had written about physiological evolution. Marais's work, based on his baboon observations and experiments in hypnosis, would treat the evolution of the human soul.

Ever since his stay in London he had been dreaming of a *magnum opus* which would astound the world. Late in 1902, after his return from Europe, he had begun writing it. At that time the title was "An Experiment in Life". He had completed the first paragraph, and it amused him to think back on it now. How conceited he had been. Why, at that time he had thought that a scorpion laid eggs – and that was the least of his deficiencies.

Now he had a study of animals and of animal psychology behind him, stretching over a number of years. Now he could write his book. All that was still lacking were a few field observations and some reading.

Apparently cured, Eugène Marais returned to the Waterberg late in 1915. But the long treatment had not worked. His son said later: "He had hardly arrived back when he relapsed into the old routine with Tamaria and the others. Barely a month had gone by when it was as bad as ever."

The time that remained to him on Rietfontein was very short. Of this last brief period virtually nothing is known. These statements by his son come from a tape-recording made in 1963:

"His only income was then that of Justice of the Peace and even those duties could not be carried out properly. And – that is a part of the story which could perhaps be told later – how he was treated there."

But when Mr. Marais was asked nine years later to elaborate on this remark, he had nothing to add to it.

From the known facts, one must deduce that Maria van Rooyen mercilessly exploited his weakness in these last few months – that is to say, as seen through Marais's eyes and those of his son. From her point of view she might have justified many of her actions. We do not know whether there was ever an agreement that Marais was to pay her rent for his room, but she might well have thought that rent was her due, and from later evidence we know that Marais's rent was frequently paid late or not at all. She might also have thought that he owed her something for the manner in which she had nursed and looked after him. All this may, in her eyes, have justified the fact that during this last short period – as we must surmise – she made as much money as she possibly could from supplying him with Chlorodyne and opium.

There are two sides to every question, but Maria van Rooyen does not emerge as an angel of light from this story.

Marais had arrived on Rietfontein a fairly wealthy man.

At the end of 1915, very close to one of the greatest crises in his life, he was virtually penniless.

17. The Prodigal Father

Sophie Ueckerman, Eugène Marais's sister and his only son's foster mother, had three children: Norma, Carl (or Sonny) and Fay. In 1915, Fay, who was about twenty, and her cousin, Eugène Charles, were still living with her mother in Pretoria. Norma, the eldest child, had long been married. She and her husband, Gustav Fichardt, were farming on the Springbok flats about fourteen miles from Warmbaths. Sonny, twenty-one years old, lived with the Fichardts.

During 1915 it was agreed that Eugène Charles was to go to the farm for a holiday that December.

Before Christmas he packed his bags and caught the train to the north, the same train in which Charlie Pienaar and Melt van Niekerk had travelled to Naboomspruit some months before.

At Pienaarsrivier, the station before Warmbaths, he got off the train and waited for the branch train which was to take him to Settlers, very close to the farm.

At that time a certain Bunting, a jovial, rotund old Englishman, used to be king of the narrow side track between Pienaarsrivier and Settlers. He was the engine driver, he was the stoker, he was the conductor, he was the messenger, he was the bearer of local news and gossip, he was a one-man tourist bureau.

Bunting welcomed young Eugène like an old friend and dropped him at Dandaloo that day, where the Fichardts met him with a cart and horses. In Pretoria Charlie Pienaar had been watching the situation. His information about Eugène was so accurate that one wonders whether he had an informer. As Secretary of Justice it would have been quite easy to ask the officer commanding the police station at Naboomspruit or even the head of the police post at Rietfontein to keep him informed.

On 9 January 1916, Eugène Marais turned forty-five years old. In the same week there was a terrifying deterioration in his condition. Charlie Pienaar was notified, and decided to take drastic action this time. Via the station master at Pienaarsrivier he sent Marais's son a message.

"Your father is very seriously ill. Go and fetch him immediately." Bunting took the message from Pienaarsrivier to Dandaloo and saw to it that it reached the Fichardts' farm from there.

The unexpected announcement left young Eugène thunderstruck. There were hurried discussions. The fastest way of getting to Rietfontein would be to drive from the farm right through the dense bush to Nylstroom. A cart and horses would soon break down, so they decided to attempt the journey on a trolley drawn by four oxen. At six o'clock the following morning young Eugène, Sonny and a black labourer left the farm.

"During the entire trip we found only one small shop where I bought cigarettes and where the oxen could rest for a while," Eugène Charles said later. "They had to trot the whole way."

It was after six o'clock that evening when the exhausted party arrived in Nylstroom. Here Sonny spent the night with a lawyer, Dan Brewis, a good friend of both of theirs, while young Eugène caught the daily train which ran from Pretoria to Naboomspruit. Arriving in the village at a quarter past four the next morning, he woke the hotel-keeper, Armstrong. "Please forgive me," he said, "my father is very ill."

Armstrong nodded sympathetically – he had heard something of the kind. As quickly as possible he organised a cart and horses to take the young man to Rietfontein.

He arrived there later that morning. According to the evidence, one can surmise that Marais had now been without drugs for at least thirty hours, and his condition was terrifying. Not even the shocked realisation that his son was witnessing his withdrawal symptoms enabled him to control the tremors. Without arguing, he agreed to return to Pretoria.

"I packed his possessions for him," Eugène Charles was to say later. "But as soon as I was about to pack something, Tamaria would say: 'Your father gave that to me.'"

One of the last items the son wanted to pack into the bag was his father's "shock fish", the electrical apparatus.

"That is my due as well," Tamaria said.

But Marais, who had so often given away his most prized possessions simply because someone had admired them, protested: "In all fairness, Tamaria, you can't have that as well," and so the apparatus was packed.

By noon everything had been arranged. When they left the farmyard in Marais's cart, he told his son: "My God, I feel as if I'm escaping from prison."

This, about the house he himself had called the Ark.

When they reached Naboomspruit late that afternoon they were received by a certain Anton Goddefroy, an educated young man who farmed near the village and with whom Eugène Marais had become good friends in the past few years.

Marais's condition had meanwhile deteriorated even more. "He was in a devastating state," his son was to say later.

In the hotel room the men discussed what they were to do.

"Doesn't he have something to take?" Goddefroy asked.

"No."

And Armstrong, who had considerable insight into Marais's problems, proposed:

"Give him brandy. That will help."

Later, when a large amount of alcohol – to which he was not accustomed – had pacified Marais, he began protesting that he had to return to the farm. His horses were still there. The police post needed attention.

To young Eugène the most important thing was to get his father back to Pretoria. Goddefroy agreed. "You put his luggage on the train," he proposed. "Once his luggage and possessions have left for Pretoria, he will no longer be able to stay."

Young Eugène accepted the proposal. At 2 o'clock that morning he got on the train at Naboomspruit's little station and arrived in Pretoria four hours later, at 6 a.m. When he sat down to lunch that afternoon, he fell asleep at the table. He had hardly slept at all for three days. Goddefroy would look after his father.

But so passionately did Marais cling to this part of the world that Goddefroy did not succeed in getting him on the next train either. Not before the day after did he return to Pretoria.

He was never to live in the Waterberg again; he was never even to visit it. But all his life, always, always, he was to long for it.

PART 6: INTERLUDES

en as hul wil waarsku en wysheid gee dan praat ek reeds in die woordklank mee	and if they wish to warn, wisdom impart, in the exchange of words already I'm taking part

1. Freud and the Springbok Flats

At that time Dr. Troup was the Ueckermans' house doctor, but in the house next door to them in Maré Street lived David Haylett, a tall, gangling fellow with a cigarette almost permanently between his prominent front teeth. Young Eugène found him a sympathetic person and because he thought that a doctor living so close by would be of greater help, he asked Dr. Haylett to take care of his father. Within half an hour of Marais's arrival at the Ueckermans' house, Haylett gave him his first injection. Discussing the matter with young Eugène, the doctor nevertheless decided to keep his patient on Chlorodyne, to which he had meantime become accustomed, thinking that the daily morphine dosage could be reduced to the minimum much more easily by this method than by using morphine tablets.

The treatment was a success. Eventually, Marais again started showing an interest in life.

At the side of his house, which was called Radyn, Haylett had a croquet court. Here they often played a game in the afternoon and afterwards sat on the small balcony outside Sophie Ueckerman's house to chat. During the eight years he had spent in the Waterberg, Marais had largely lost contact with new trends of thought in the outside world. However, he had managed to read a fair amount at Boshof and now, while he was recuperating, Haylett brought him even more to read – much of the material concerning Freud, the doctor's latest passion. To Marais, Sigmund Freud – who himself was by now about sixty years old – was nothing new. He had been introduced in London to Freud's *Studien über Hysterie* (1895), in which Freud averred that hysteria could be treated by hypnosis. It may have been just this book which had stimulated his interest in the techniques of Freud's mentor, Charcot.

Marais was also familiar with the theories in Freud's *Traumdeutung* (The Significance of Dreams) which had been published as early as the Boer War. After all, he himself had treated patients psychologically by questioning them about their dreams and then discussing their problems in the light of what they had dreamt. He was now introduced to two later works, *Psychopathologie des Alltagslebens* (Psychopathology in Daily Life) and *Drei Abhandlungen zur Sexualtheorie* (Three Treatises concerning the Sexual Theory), for the first time in the English translations.

To his pleasant surprise he found that he could understand Freud's ideas and arguments without undue trouble. The fact was that Marais had just spent nine years, however intermittently, studying animal and human psychology. Understanding by no means meant agreement. His baboon studies, his experiments, hypnosis, his medical and psychological treatment had all convinced him that he had a fairly good idea of human motivation and Freud's theories frequently clashed completely with his own findings. As Darwin had been in a previous generation, Freud was a kind of demi-god to the progressive intellectuals, and Haylett defended him passionately. He and Marais spent whole evenings arguing, sometimes until the early hours.

On the large plot on the corner of Prinsloo and Maré Streets where Sophie Ueckerman used to have her boarding house, she had had another house built, taken sub-division and sold off the portion containing the boarding house. The new house, 350 Maré Street, was not large. Mrs. Ueckerman herself slept in one of the three bedrooms, her daughter Fay in another and young Eugène in the third. After Marais's return from the Waterberg he had moved into his son's room and eventually Sonny Ueckerman, who came back from the Springbok Flats to spend some time in Pretoria once more, also joined them.

Both Haylett and Marais's son were delighted with the progress he was making. Then they discovered that Marais was secretly supplementing his supply of Chlorodyne. After discussing the matter with Haylett, Sonny did the rounds of all the chemists in Pretoria and asked them to give Advocate Marais no Chlorodyne at all.

Their optimism had been considerably dampened.

"We'll have to get him somewhere where he can't buy anything," Haylett said. "But then he'll have to be taken good care of."

Marais could not go to Boshof again. Charles's wife, Emily, was still too upset about his relationship with Anna Hansen. And so it was agreed that he would accompany Sonny when the latter returned to the farm of his sister, Norma Fichardt, on the Springbok Flats.

The dry-land farm of 3 000 morgen where Gustav and Norma Fichardt had now been living for almost eight years, lay about fourteen miles from Warmbaths. Gustav farmed with maize, kaffircorn and enough cattle to plough with. Money was by no means plentiful here. The Fichardts' rondavel house was a simple one, but roomy enough for all who were living there: Norma, Gustav and their three children, Juan (six), Helen (five) and Nielen (two).

Marais had never lost contact with these people completely and he soon felt at home in the rondavel he shared with Sonny. He found two other old friends on the farm as well, Baby and Bakkop, two of his favourite horses and two of the very few who had remained after his unsuccessful horse-breeding. After leaving Rietfontein he had given these two animals to the Fichardts as a present.

On the same farm but in a separate house lived the Hoepners, Gustav Fichardt's sister and her husband. With them lived beautiful, aristocratic Madame Mona von Rapacki-Warnia, whose husband had been interned by the authorities. Hoepner, although a German as well, had somehow managed to escape internment.

For understandable reasons, the general atmosphere on the farm was not very pro-British. Marais was delighted to read in the papers that Tielman Roos, leader of the Transvaal National Party, had interpreted Britain's insistence on the independence of small states literally by asking the British Government to restore the independence of the two erstwhile Boer republics.

This same Tielman Roos was soon to play an important part in Marais's personal life.

Just as everything had worked against Eugène Marais during the last couple of years on the farm Rietfontein, everything on the Springbok Flats now seemed to work for him. His intake had already become fairly low, which meant that the journey to the minimum did not have to be either too lengthy or too laborious.

In this he was assisted by three people: Sonny, who kept the Chlorodyne; Helen, the Fichardts' five year old daughter; and Mona (or Maimie) von Rapacki-Warnia.

Helen was five, the age at which Eugène most loved little girls. She was a bright, attractive, spontaneous child and she loved him unreservedly. When she hurt herself or wept tears of rage or frustration, she would run to him, throw herself into his arms and sob: "Dry my tears!"

By sweetening his life she helped him get along with the relentlessly shrinking dosage.

Fifty-six years later, Marais's son was to describe Mona von Rapacki-Warnia as follows, most likely echoing his father's feelings about her: "She was a lovely girl."

Her husband was in an internment camp and she was lonely. The other men on the farm, Hoepner and Gustav Fichardt, worked hard and had little time for the niceties of social behaviour. Mona was not yet thirty, and attractively plump, according to the fashion of the time. Eugène Marais was more than fifteen years her senior but he was a different person from the man who had returned, sick as a dog, to Pretoria the previous January. He had made a remarkable recovery.

His charm had returned and it was now more than charm. In his relationship with women he had developed a certain recklessness. He knew how to arouse their sympathies and compassion. Then, too, under the velvet of his refined courtesy, there was something tough, something dominating, which he could switch on at will. He knew how to manipulate women and he no longer hesitated to use this ability. Girls like Jane Brayshaw and Anna Hansen, each in her own manner, had taught him a great deal.

Even so, the relationship between him and Mona seems to have remained nothing more than a friendly one.

The Springbok Flats had not been occupied by white men for more than a few years. The material side of life was certainly not much more comfortable than that on Rietfontein, but on the intellectual level there was no comparison. In the Waterberg Marais's reading matter, by choice, was so limited that he had learnt psalms and hymns and entire Shakespearian monologues and dialogues by heart. Thanks to Bunting, books and magazines from the outside world regularly reached them on the Springbok Flats.

Marais's own great work, *The Soul of the Ape*, occupied his thoughts. But in order to write it, he would first have to read very widely. He read sporadically – frequently five or six books at a time – but he read a great deal. As, in spite of his knowledge of German, he had read Häckel in the English translation, he now read the French philosopher, Henri Bergson, in English. After the publication of *L'Evolution Créatrice* ten years before, Bergson had become highly fashionable, not only Bergson himself – for that he was rather indigestible – but the commentaries on his philosophy which had been published shortly before the Great War: Lindsay's *The Philosophy of Bergson*, *Henri Bergson: The Philosophy of Change* by Carr, and especially Elliot's *Modern Science and the Illusions of Professor Bergson*.

Marais completely agreed with him in some respects, for example in Bergson's statement that "intelligence" could not be regarded as the evolutionary apex of "instinct". However, Bergson's finding that instinct and intelligence represented two divergent evolutionary developments clashed directly with Marais's own finding that the instinctive psyche remained in existence on another level next to intelligence. Marais was now reading as if to compensate for his intellectual isolation on Rietfontein. From Freud and Bergson he progressed to Maurice Maeterlinck, the Belgian dramatist and philosopher who had been awarded the Nobel Prize for literature in 1911 for such plays as *L'oiseau bleu* (The blue bird).

Marais was especially interested in Maeterlinck's *La Vie des Abeilles* (The Life of the Bee) and it was probably this famous book which inspired him to begin studying bees on the Springbok Flats. In order to observe the hive without discomfort, he installed one on his bedside table in the rondavel and in the lazy summer afternoons he would lie watching the bees bear pollen to the hive and leave it once more to look for more pollen, apparently ceaselessly.

Marais's writings do not contain a single reference to this study. It may be that he found nothing new, for the bees of Africa – even though they belong to another, much more ferocious species than the European bee – do not differ materially in their social structure from those concerning which other studies, including studies by Henri Fabre, had already been published by then. How many other research projects did Marais tackle of which, for this or for other reasons, we are completely unaware half a century later?

One field of study which he was indeed to describe later concerned the orientation ability or sense of direction. It was Marais's theory that this philetic ability was strongest in birds and then appeared to a decreasing extent in mammals, the lower primates, primitive man and civilised man, in that order.

For an experiment of this kind the Springbok Flats seemed ideal. "The country is so absolutely level," he was to write later, "that it can hardly be said to possess a watershed. It is in addition quite trackless, without a single conspicuous natural feature, and is covered with shrubs and grass all monotonously unvarying."

The nest of a Namaqua partridge was indicated with unobtrusive markers about which only Marais and his assistants knew. Without these markers it seemed impossible to him that any man or animal could again reach the spot. Firstly, he determined that a partridge, driven from the nest in various directions, would always return to it within half an hour, even over a distance of seven miles. Five people who knew the veld intimately could not trace the nest over a distance of only a few hundred yards. One of them was a fourteen year old boy who was subjected to the test three times. The fourth time Marais hypnotised him. This time he traced the nest without any trouble over a distance of a mile.

How was this orientation ability – striking in birds, latent in man – to be explained? Marais found no final reply, but he was soon to formulate one theory as follows:

> An explanation that suggests itself is this: every movement through space, every turning of the body on its axis, is registered in the "subconscious" mentality, so that the animal at the end of the journey, even when it has been shut up in a box, bears in itself a complete psychic chart of the route traversed.

These words are a fair description of the electronic navigational system (inert navigation) by means of which, decades later, American nuclear submarines would manage to stay on course without ever surfacing.

Where could Marais have got this concept from? It was not to become reality for forty years, and in our age of extremely rapid technological development, four decades is a tremendously long time. One is reminded of Jules Verne's apparently magical abilities to predict future scientific developments.

The words quoted about the Namaqua partridge come from *The Soul of the Ape.* In the peaceful and happy months on the farm – months in which one of the most obscene wars in history was raging in Europe – the work constantly occupied his thoughts. He was in fact writing considerable tracts of it.

Apparently cured, Marais returned to Pretoria before the end of 1916, radiantly optimistic and full of self-confidence, to start a new life. He was almost forty-six.

2. The Three Musketeers

In Pretoria Marais again moved into the house of his sister, Sophie Ueckerman, and soon found himself an office: 58 Tudor Buildings. While many Pretorian lawyers had offices in Bureau Avenue ("Buzzard Street") all the advocates were in Tudor Buildings, a short distance from Church Square. Marais had plans to practise as an advocate once more. Legally this was a lean time, and his working day was short. He saw a great deal of his son and in this period of morphine abstention their relationship became closer and more cordial than ever.

Young Eugène who had come of age that year, was doing quite well. While his father had been in the Waterberg, he had been in primary school. His secondary school career was reasonably successful. He excelled in sport, particularly rugby. George Findlay, a grandson of Eugène Marais's sister, Lizzie Niemeyer, had this to say about his academic achievements: "Coming first in class was not something that mattered to him, but he had an excellent and highly individual mind. He was, among us all and in the opinion of the masters, something very special."

After matriculating Eugène had enrolled at the newly founded Transvaal University College. He intended following an arts course. Like his father before him, his academic achievements were little above average. Here, too, he was prominent in sport and in the college's social life. Sixty years later a fellow-student, Louis Hiemstra, was to remember a speech during which, apropos of something completely different, he had burst into a song of praise for woman: "With her feet among the lilies and her head among the stars." Eugène junior may have obtained this image from his father. It is an almost precise echo of the closing lines of the poem Marais was to write many years later: "Star-crowned, in your steps/ Blooms the lily-flower of peace." (The entire poem is quoted in chapter 14 of part 8.) Even so, by about the beginning of World War I, he had dropped out of his course and become a clerk in the Department of Defence.

Young Eugène did not make friends easily, but those friendships he did make were exceptionally firm. One of his closest friends was the juvenile Toon van den Heever, later to become a judge and a well known Afrikaans poet. In Sophie Ueckerman's house, where Eugène senior moved in as well, the two young men had been sharing a room for quite a while. In spite of greater disadvantages and even less money than young Eugène, Toon had persevered and had done considerably better in life. His mother had died when he was two years old. The Boer War had broken out when he was five, leaving him alone on the family farm. Here the English repeatedly came to look for him – he would tell friends how he had aimed at them from the bush with an air gun, wondering whether he should shoot – before they caught him and took him away.

After the war he and his father were reunited. There was no question of school. He had to herd sheep. His father had in the meantime remarried and his stepmother was unsympathetic. When he was fourteen he told his father: "Dad, I am going to school now," and with a lump in his throat (as Toon's widow was to put it later) his father replied: "I'll give you £5. I hope you become a good policeman or swineherd."

The principal at Ermelo, Hoogenhout, must have been a good man. When the simple farm boy came to see him and told him about his great plans, Hoogenhout decided to help the boy. But Toon helped himself as well, collecting spent cartridges from the Boer War in the veld and selling them as brass. Toon matriculated and departed for Pretoria, with neither money nor prospects, to continue his education.

It was at this stage that George Findlay appeared in Toon van den

Heever's life. George had been on his way somewhere in his father's Model T Ford when the forlorn young figure standing next to the railway line caught his attention and he stopped to talk to him.

"Move in with us," said George Findlay's mother when she had heard Toon's story. And so Toon moved into Lyndal, the great, hospitable house in Esselen Street which George's father had built before the Boer War. Erich Mayer, and many others, had lived here on occcasion. By teaching, Toon earned enough money to gain an Honours B.A. in record time. Now, in 1917, he was working as a registrar while taking his LL.B. He had left Lyndal quite some time before to join his friend, young Eugène. These three – twenty-two-year-old Eugène, his slightly older friend Toon, and George Findlay, who was two years younger than Eugène – were virtually inseparable. They called themselves the Three Musketeers.

"Some of Pretoria's streets were very poorly illuminated at the time," young Eugène was to relate later. "At night we used to whistle one of the *Lieder ohne Wörter* when walking in the street in order to recognise each other at a distance."

Without actually being absorbed into the circle of friends, old Eugène (as Toon was soon to call him) nevertheless soon started sharing the three young men's lives. Only four houses from Sophie Ueckerman's lived several young girls and the Three Musketeers would go calling on them.

One of them was Flossie Kay, an attractive young typist of about twenty. Between her and Eugène senior there now developed another of the few great stormy relationships in his life. This one was to last for at least two years. Young Eugène, again, was friendly with Flossie's half-sister, Marjorie van Reenen. Occasionally father and son would take the two girls out together. Sometimes Toon accompanied them – his preference was for "Buttons" Brune – and now and again George Findlay joined the company with his own girlfriend.

It need not surprise one that the forty-six-year-old Eugène senior found it so relatively easy to acquire an attractive twenty-year-old girlfriend. After his stay on the Springbok flats he was looking extremely well and – more important – his self-confidence had not been at such a high level for a long time. The charm he had been refining and honing ever since his London years was now concentrated on Flossie.

He was a man of the world, he could talk about anything.

"I was majoring in philosophy," George Findlay said later, "and I think I knew the subject quite well. I was present when Marais told his son and Toon all about the early Greek philosophers – Heximander, Thales, Anaximenes. One of my handbooks was Ritter & Preller, a collection of texts by the Greek philosophers. I could judge that Marais's facts were accurate, although he liked to embroider."

During this time, with varying degrees of success, all four men wrote poetry – Findlay, Toon and the two Marais'. "George Findlay had numerous original rhymes and thoughts, of which Toon made grateful use," Marais's son was to say later.

Disarmingly modestly, Eugène N. Marais discussed his own work with the three young men, including "Die Lied van die Reën" (Song of the Rain) which was soon to appear as part of one of his Wandering Tales. There can be little doubt that he helped "Antoon" – as he called Van den Heever – even if only by showing him what to avoid in his poetry.

Time passed. It was now 1918, eleven years since the death of Francis Thompson, and five years since the publication of his collected poetry. He was the hero, however obscure they found his poems, of every modern young person who loved poetry.

Years before – when Thompson had tramped the streets of London as an opium addict, tuberculotic, and a hobo – he had submitted some of his work to the magazine *Merry England*, accompanied by a characteristically defeatist request: "Kindly address your rejection to the Charing Cross Post Office."

The editor, Wilfrid Meynell, accepted the poetry for publication, took a great deal of trouble to trace the tattered, dissipated author and arranged for him to be treated in a private hospital. Thompson managed to shake off the opium habit, but he was never "rehabilitated". In his own words, shortly before his death in 1907 (and these words apply exactly to Eugène Marais): "Once step aside from the ways of comfortable men and you cannot regain them. You will live and die under the law of the intolerable thing called romance."

Now, in 1918, Thompson's work was avidly read and excitedly

discussed by the Three Musketeers. What did old Eugène think of it?

To Marais most of Thompson's work was uncomfortably religious. Here and there, as in "Memorat Memoria" (quoted in the chapter about Hillbrow), he found the obscurities of his own soul depicted so accurately that he could hardly read the verse. For others, like "The Hound of Heaven" (echoes of which, decades later, would be found in the work of both W.E.G. and N.P. van Wyk Louw) and still more for "An Anthem of Earth", he had the greatest admiration. He had never been a church-going man. Even so his romantic pantheism was attracted to this long poem with its theme of life as a precious gift, " ... which must, in all the after days, Be craved again with tears, / With fresh and still-petitionary tears".

Even more was he drawn to the last lines of "Anthem", with their longing for peace, for death, the sentiments of his stay at Purekrans on the Palala plateau which he was soon to put down in his own poem "Tebes". Thompson's lines read as follows:

> Here I untrammel,
> Here I pluck loose the body's cerementing,
> And break the tomb of life; here I shake off
> The burr o' the world, man's congregation shun,
> And to the antique order of the dead
> I take the tongueless vows: my cell is set
> Here in thy bosom; my little trouble is ended
> In a little peace.

The idea of peace, of redemption, occupied Marais's thoughts. He frequently discussed religion with Toon and young Eugène. One evening, greatly sceptical, they attended an exceptionally stormy service in "Brother Cooper's" Apostolic Church. Later he told the young men: "They're all looking for a short-cut to salvation – and there isn't one."

During this time, about two years after he had left Rietfontein, Marais was again reminded of the Waterberg when he was visited by one of his young friends from the region. Presumably this was Hannes de Beer who has been mentioned several times before.

Marais welcomed him in his sister's house, but left for the office before breakfast the following morning, leaving Hannes in the young people's care.

Young Eugène, much later: "I told my cousin, Fay, not to come down for breakfast as it would only embarrass both of them. I think I was right. When he saw the array of eating utensils at the breakfast table, he remarked: 'Oh well, one will never get accustomed to all these tools anyway' and he took out his pocket knife and had breakfast that way."

When young Eugène took him into the town later, he was amazed by the tarred streets. "Are ox-wagons allowed to go on them?" he asked.

The young man showed him a lift, a tram and a telephone. He refused to believe that the telephone was not a fake.

This was the same man who, some years before, when they had had no water, unerringly led Eugène N. Marais to a pool in the remote Middleveld between midnight and three o'clock in the morning. In Pretoria he was completely lost.

Before the young visitor returned to the Waterberg, he and Eugène Marais had time to talk a great deal about the old things in the old days.

In this year, 1918, the Waterberg certainly occupied Marais's thoughts a great deal, as he was working on *The Soul of the Ape*. For this he had plenty of time. Only a few of the forty odd advocates in Tudor Buildings were hard at work. The rest of them sat waiting for briefs. "As I remember it," says Advocate Charles te Water, "we spent most of the mornings chatting, not only at tea-times. Eugène's practice was never a large one. In any case law bored him. I cannot remember our ever discussing the work."

For Marais it was more than boredom. For the sterile aspects of this singular profession, Marais was soon to develop the greatest contempt. "No man with a soul above that of a fieldmouse can devote all his attention to this kind of work in the long run," he was to write only a few years later.

(George Findlay, again, remarks about Marais as an advocate: "He had not that quality of forensic insolence that is so essential for getting on at the Bar.")

If they did not discuss law, they certainly discussed literature – especially Marais, Te Water and John Murray – and politics constantly. In these post-rebellion years there was a strong revival of Afrikaner national feeling. According to Government supporters, the Pretoria Bar was a hotbed of nationalism: Danie de Waal, Colin Steyn, Oswald Pirow, Charles te Water, Eugène Marais and – worst of them all – Tileman Roos, leader of the newly founded Transvaal National Party.

Tielman Roos, barely twenty-eight years old, was a dynamic, jovial extrovert. Marais had known him for a long time; in fact he was distantly related to Marais's erstwhile partner, Jimmy Roos. Arriving from the Cape Colony in the Transvaal shortly after the Boer War, he had gained his LL.B. by studying privately. He became a particularly successful advocate and later leader of the Bar. When General J.B.M. Hertzog was expelled from General Botha's Cabinet at the end of 1912 because of his contentious speech at De Wildt, Tielman Roos and Charles te Water were two of the organisers of the "Manure-heap meeting" where 5 000 enthusiastic Afrikaners came together to pay tribute to Hertzog. When the Transvaal National Party was founded two years later, Tielman Roos became its leader. Before the rebellion Roos and his wife were involved in a serious car accident. This had prevented him from taking part in the rebellion but by the next year he had recovered to such an extent that he was elected Nationalist M.P. for Lichtenburg. Tielman Roos knew that Botha's most important support lay in the countryside and in these restless war years he constantly travelled through the agricultural districts in a bid to undermine the Prime Minister's prestige.

During this time he and Marais became good friends but not only for political reasons. Mrs. Roos was a permanent invalid. Tielman had no real married life.

Tielman Roos and Eugène Marais, living the life of bachelors, were soon joined by a third – Advocate William Pitman. "I think Pitman must have been between marriages at the time," George Findlay was to relate later. "He was extremely fond of women – a merry, irresponsible chap with a tremendous intellect."

These three – Marais, Roos and Pitman – were now frequently seen together and sometimes went calling together – even at the boarding house in Maré Street where Flossie Kay and her half-sisters lived. "The Three Senior Musketeers", Toon van den Heever and George Findlay jokingly called them.

For Eugène Marais 1918 was a good year. His connections provided him with "cat's meat" and "guinea pigs". Now and again he was given a brief for which he had to travel into the countryside. A few times he even went to the Appeal Court in Bloemfontein. But his practice was not so large that it seriously interfered with his free time. He worked on *The Soul of the Ape*. He spent whole days talking and arguing with his friends. His girlfriend was an attractive young girl.

At times it almost seemed as if life was again beginning to mean something for him.

3. The Empty Hours

In the eyes of his colleagues of the Pretoria Bar, Eugène Marais was a hardline Nationalist. Was this true?

Then, as later, but to an even greater extent, there were two sets of relationships which dominated politics: Boer/Briton and white/non-white.

One of the factors which had led to the foundation of the National Party in the Transvaal was Afrikaner resistance to the proposed extension of the non-white vote from the Cape to other provinces. People like Advocates Tielman Roos and Charles te Water played leading roles in this resistance, while others – like Marais's ex-colleague, Gustav Preller – cheered them enthusiastically from the side-lines. Marais could not reconcile himself with such vehement resistance. To him the vote was a question of civilisation and education, not of colour. One cannot say whether he would have wanted Old Klaas, the black dwarf who lived in the thornbush, to have the vote, but if Hans Purekrans van Rooyen could have it, then why not Ebrahim Ravat as well?

Marais was a Nationalist because he was a patriotic Afrikaner. And while Hertzog used the word "Afrikaner" at De Wildt and elsewhere to mean "any patriotic white South African" Marais used it in its traditional meaning.

This did not mean that he and his friends wrote Afrikaans or always thought in that language. Their education and background had been English. They were reasonably familiar with Dutch, the second language, but hardly ever spoke it. They did speak Afrikaans, but found it hard to write, as it was still a developing language. Writing to Charlie Pienaar from the Waterberg, Marais complained that he found it so difficult to write the articles he sent him for publication in Afrikaans. Even Marais's son had been prohibited from speaking "the taal" at school. Many of the young Nationalists at the Pretoria Bar frequently spoke English to each other. Even the two great pioneers of the Second Afrikaans Language Movement, Marais and Preller, ironically enough, would often switch to English as soon as they started discussing "deep" matters.

This is the background to the minor clash between Marais and Preller which dates from this time.

Preller was still at the *Volkstem* and when the paper received a copy of Nathan Levi's biography of General Jan Smuts, Minister of Defence in Botha's Cabinet, he asked Marais to review it for the paper.

At that time Smuts was a contentious figure, to say the least. To the English he was proof of their desire for conciliation; after all, like the Prime Minister, he had been a Boer general. To the Afrikaners his harsh suppression of the rebellion and especially the execution of the erstwhile Boer scout, Jopie Fourie, had made him a traitor.

We have seen that there had been close ties of friendship between Marais's family and that of Jopie Fourie. Probably more than most of his fellow countrymen, he must have been moved by the short poem written after the execution by Jan Celliers (son of Marais's friend and mentor in pre-war Pretoria) and then clandestinely passed from hand to hand all over the country, constantly rewritten by hand and passed along:

> Daar trek 'n koeël, met spoed, met spoed;
> hy's nat van Afrikaner-bloed,
> en smart die boodskap wat hy voer:
> hy kom uit Afrikaner-roer …
>
> A bullet speeds, to thud, to thud;
> it's wet with Afrikaner blood,

painful its message as its aim:
from Afrikaner gun it came ...

Marais read Levi's biography of Smuts. Wanting to dictate the review, he went to Law's College to find a shorthand writer. This is how he was to explain the debacle later. Here he was told that there was no Dutch shorthand writer in Pretoria. Although Marais could handle Dutch well, he now dictated or wrote the review in English and gave it to Poutsma of the *Volkstem* to translate into Dutch.

The English review contained a great deal of criticism of Smuts's unrelenting role in the rebellion and of the execution of Jopie Fourie.

"The Afrikander's knowledge of cultured European nations would lead him to believe that no civilised, educated Englishman could possibly have acted in this manner," Marais wrote, "and certainly no patriotic Hollander. It is even inconceivable that a Hun would have found it possible to fight against his own countrymen under such circumstances, and to have had a gallant comrade-in-arms shot in order to pacify the clamours of his recent enemies."

Poutsma's translation was a free one. In fact he took certain liberties which made Marais's review appear even more severely critical. In the Dutch translation the words "to pacify the clamours of his recent enemies" were published as (retranslated from the Dutch) "in order to satisfy the repulsive desires of his erstwhile enemies". Marais saw the translation and noted the inaccuracies, but shrugged his shoulders. It wasn't too bad. When Poutsma asked his opinion, he made no objections.

When the review appeared in the *Volkstem*, the *Pretoria News* launched a bitter attack on it.

The next move did not come from Marais or the *Volkstem*, but from one of Eugène's colleagues at the Bar, Charles te Water. Impulsively and rashly he obtained a copy of the original English review and sent it to the *Pretoria News* with this short letter: "Sir – Your translation from Mr. Eugène Marais's review is not quite fair. The enclosed original English draft will give a better idea of the views expressed and might be of interest to your readers." The *Pretoria News* saw the gap and took it. With an acrimony and relentlessness which rather reminds one of Eugène Marais's own earlier tirades against the Kruger Government, they attacked once more. Charles te Water's note was published together with the original English review, both headed by the following editorial comment:

> It would appear that this mistranslation is due to the pernicious Nationalist habit of thinking and composing and drafting their articles for the press originally in that hateful language English instead of in the beautiful Afrikaner Taal.

Equal language rights had been official policy ever since Union and the Pretoria City Council had recently been criticised for using only English on its noticeboards. In a separate leading article about the incident, the *Pretoria News* now killed several birds with one stone; it discredited Marais and other Nationalists; it discredited the *Volkstem*; and it also made use of the opportunity to reject bilingualism as ridiculous:

> (The review) was written in English because the "educated Afrikanders" who lead the Nationalist Party in Pretoria are not at home in Dutch; they neither think nor talk in Dutch nor do they read Dutch, except perhaps "The Brandwagt" and "The Volkstem", and they cannot express educated ideas in the Taal ...
>
> The incident is very instructive, especially when we remember that a prosecution is at the present moment being instituted by the South African Party and the Nationalists against the Town Clerk because the destination boards on trams and the notices on the fire alarms are not in Dutch as well as English. This prosecution is vexatious and calculated simply to annoy and irritate the English-speaking people of the town ...
>
> The English-speaking people of South Africa are not going to have Dutch jammed down their throats ... by Nationalists who know so little of the language which they are determined to thrust upon other people that when they seek publicity through the medium of a Dutch newspaper they have to draft their articles in English and take them to a Hollander to be translated. Could humbug and hypocrisy go further?

One can imagine the bloodthirsty joy with which Marais would have joined this kind of fray in his *Land en Volk* days a quarter of a century before. But much had happened in those twenty-five years.

For this reason, and probably also because he realised that he and his friends had made some tactical blunders, he said nothing.

Gustav Preller was greatly upset. In a personal letter to Marais he wrote:

> Dear Mr. Marais!
> You have put us all in a painful position by publishing the English original of the review translated by Poutsma.
> I am given to understand that after the publication of the article in the *Volkstem*, you expressed your satisfaction regarding the translation.
> If this is the case it seems to me as if you should stand by the translation.
> In any case, what hurts me and others are the sneers of the English press regarding the ability of Afrikaners to use their own language and you, the author of "Winternag", one of the most beautiful (poems) in Afrikaans should not have left us in the lurch like this.

Marais's reply was subdued. Explaining that Law's College had no Dutch shorthand writer, he said:

> That is the true and only reason why the review was not in Afrikaans or Dutch.
> I deeply regret the publication of the original in the *Pretoria News*, but that is water under the bridge.
> I agree with everything else in your letter.
> What now!

The matter seems to have ended there. Soon Marais and Preller were friends once more.

The incident is an interesting one for various reasons, including one which has nothing to do with the dispute between the *Volkstem* and the *Pretoria News*.

In his review Marais complains that Levi does little to reveal Smuts's hidden motives. What, he asks, is the explanation for Smuts's strange conduct during the rebellion? Rejecting the view that Smuts was a Machiavellian opportunist with no shred of sentiment, he writes:

> There is another explanation, not infrequently heard, and that is that

> the General's opportunism results from an utter despair – a black pessimism which admits of no single ray of light. It is a state of mind not uncommon among educated Afrikanders in these days. It consists of the settled conviction that we are not fit to be a nation, certainly unworthy of being free, and that any political effort which exalts this great ideal to the first rank is foredoomed to failure as far as the Afrikaner people is concerned.

In his review Marais rejects this possible explanation for Smuts's conduct as well. It is quoted here because it may reveal something of Marais's own motives. The words "not infrequently heard" and "not uncommon among educated Afrikanders" may mean nothing more than that these were Marais's personal convictions. Very clearly one finds echoes from the poem "1902" written fifteen years before:

> God van ons Vaders, as U wil bestaan,
> dat ons as Staat en Nasie moet vergaan,
> – besoedel deur verraad, ontrou
> aan alles deur ons vaders opgebou …
> (met) vuile hande, rooi bevlek,
> met bloed van broer en vriend bedek; –
> God van ons vaders, bly U wil bestaan,
> leer ons genadiglik die dood blymoedig in te gaan.
>
> God of our fathers, if it is Your will
> that we must perish as State and Nation
> – polluted by treachery, betraying
> everything our fathers built up …
> (with) filthy hands, stained red
> and covered in the blood of brother and friend; –
> God of our fathers, if that be Thy will
> then in Thy mercy teach us to meet our death with gladness.

Some of the obvious views about Marais's life – that he could never come to terms with his wife's death, that the defeat of his people constantly plunged him ever deeper into an abyss of despair – sometimes seem as if they come very close to the truth.

But unless one is willing to end it all, life goes on. One has to continue eating, one has still to drive oneself to the office, even now the empty hours of the day and night have to be filled (by "writing little verses, or speaking – to whom?" the Afrikaans poet Leipoldt had written, bitterly cynical, some time before). Marais did not "write little verses" during this time, but he did write – and except for *The Soul of the Ape*, he did not write in English.

Virtually all his writing was done for Gustav Preller. The roles of sixteen years before, shortly after the war, when Preller took his editorial instructions from Marais, had now been reversed. Marais wrote a fair amount, including "Enige merkwaardige Afrikaners" (Some remarkable Afrikaners), a long patriotic series of articles from South African history, a theme Preller adored, in which, among other things, he severely criticises John Barrow's views of the Boers.

Apart from his work for the *Volkstem*, Gustav Preller was also responsible for collecting contributions to the *Brandwag*, the Afrikaans magazine which had been founded seven years before. Marais frequently wrote reviews for the magazine. His excellent taste, wide general knowledge and literary integrity made Marais an extremely good critic. An undated letter accompanied one review (of a book by J.R.L. van Bruggen):

> It grieves me to cut down any young Afrikaans writer unnecessarily. But v.B. is no longer a boy and there are other considerations as well. The thing is unutterably bad, in most parts ridiculous. How anything like this could be printed is an inexplicable miracle to me.
>
> To try and give it a boost would simply be a crime against our future taste and literature.
>
> I can tone down the review no more. Do what you think best.

Writing often takes much longer than one thinks it will. That this happened to Marais as well is indicated by these words from another undated letter.

> You must give me until tomorrow evening. I struggled with the thing until five this morning and would like to go through it once more. I would very much like to rewrite it completely (!) but for that I would need a shorthand writer at the least. May I read the first proofs?

It seems that Marais was one of those writers who would have benefited enormously by the use of a tape-recorder. He had no trouble in formulating sentences fluently and rapidly; the problem was to get them down on paper.

But that is by the way. The words quoted above have an ominous ring. Marais was putting everything into *The Soul of the Ape* and at night he would turn to the additional writing which would provide a small income.

A normal forty-seven year old man working in this way might over-exert himself but, given rest, might well recover from it. Eugène Marais was not a normal man. He was a reformed morphine addict. He did not work regularly but at times he worked much too hard. As was so often the case, he had over-estimated his abilities and strength. As so often before, he was overtaxing himself. And once more he reached for the panacea.

4. The Boerevrou

What is it that makes the reformed morphine addict take another dose after he has managed to do without it for so many months, particularly if these months so clearly demonstrated that his ability to work, his energy, his lust for life increased, while the suffering, the misery, the pain and humiliation of his previous state were now spared him? The explanation lies no doubt in man's ability to forget the unpleasant and remember the pleasant; to rationalise; and to delude himself. In the first phase of the patient's abstinence there is a remarkable change in his condition. "His whole appearance is transformed," writes one researcher, Dr. G. Laughton Scott. "His complexion clears, his appetite becomes voracious, a buoyant confidence replaces indifference. The patient feels that he can hardly remember the drug had any charms for him, and to resume it is unthinkable."

But, when six months have passed, perhaps eight months, perhaps a year, the addict discovers that the world has become somewhat drab. He has been freed from the depths, but the highlights, too, as he now remembers them, have departed. The same doctor quoted above writes: "I sometimes find that patients say that the previous treatment never obliterated desire, but that it persisted month after month until at last they yielded."

It is obviously impossible to state exactly which factors played the most important part in Marais's case. However, there is no doubt that every ex-addict is in danger for a long time after his reformation, that for a long time he is hovering on the brink of resumption and that he does not require a very hard push to tip him over the precipice once more. The push which made Marais resume taking the drug in 1918 was probably – as surmised in the previous chapter – over-exertion, the most common cause, or symptoms which accompany over-exertion such as insomnia and increasing nervous tension. It could also have been something very simple like toothache, of which he was to complain later; or even a light attack of malaria.

At about this time he left Sophie Ueckerman's house, where his son was living, and moved into the boarding house of another sister, Jess Rex, who was now sixty-four years old.

Here circumstances brought him into close contact with Jess's youngest daughter, Mabel, thirty-nine. They had always been fond of each other. "Mabel was just about the only member of the family who was not critical of him," the authoress M.E. Rothmann was to say in an interview much later, and Hannie Preller (Gustav Preller's wife) made these comments about a later stage in his life: "His family neglected him, except for Mabel – she tried to draw him closer."

The intense Afrikaner nationalism of these war years had numerous consequences. Marais had got to know Mabel's husband, Kenne Malherbe, a lawyer, just after the Boer War when they were both living in Jess Rex's boarding house. Malherbe and Advocate Tielman Roos, leader of the National Party, were great friends. It seems likely that the idea to start a women's magazine in Afrikaans, the first of its kind, was conceived by these four: Tielman Roos, the Malherbes and Marais.

"Without Eugène Marais's support," said M.E. Rothmann in an interview later, "Mabel (Malherbe) would probably never have founded *Die Boerevrou.*"

While plans went ahead for launching the magazine, in October and November the great influenza epidemic scorched the entire Western world. In South Africa almost 12 000 whites and more than ten times as many non-whites died. Marais and his immediate family were not too adversely affected. The only death was that of Fred Niemeyer – the beloved son of Eugène's sister Lizzie.

In the second month of the epidemic one of the bloodiest wars in history came to an end. Everywhere the cannons and machine guns fell silent. Only in East Africa, where even Jan Smuts could do nothing against him during the war, the German guerrilla leader, Von Lettow-Vorbeck, continued the fight for a few weeks more.

Early in the next year the first edition of *Die Boerevrou* was published. Kenne Malherbe supplied the capital, Mabel became editor, while Eugène had promised contributions.

It was a true family enterprise. Apart from Mabel, the only other permanent employee was Marguerite Pienaar, who was responsible for administration. Like Mabel, she was the daughter of one of Eugène's sisters, in this case Lizzie Niemeyer.

The extremely competent, highly principled Mabel – she was later to become a Member of Parliament and mayor of Pretoria – had very definite ideas about *Die Boerevrou*. The magazine had not been founded to make money, but to help educate and uplift the Afrikaner people. The example of her own father – with whom she had at one time corresponded but whom she had never seen – had made her fully conscious of the destruction drink can cause in a family. *Die Boerevrou* would certainly not accept any advertisements for liquor. Advertisements for medicines, too, were regarded with suspicion. No advertisement for Chlorodyne, still freely available at the time, would ever be published in *Die Boerevrou*. It contained morphine. (Poor Oom Eugène!) And whenever manufacturers of new medicines asked to advertise in the magazine – particularly the so-called Dutch medicines with their high alcohol content – she would first consult a good doctor before allowing the advertisement. In one issue Cooper's Dip was recommended as a disinfectant. Mabel spent a sleepless night pondering the possibility that a child might get hold of the dip and drink it. The next morning she stopped the press and had the six to eight hundred copies which had been printed by that time destroyed.

The magazine was certainly not a financial success. Mabel's advertising policy alone, according to the man who sold the magazine's advertising space, cost them £50 a month in loss of income. Regularly, Kenne Malherbe had to make more funds available to balance the books. Eugène Marais had promised to collaborate, and he kept his promise, even though he was poorly paid for his contributions. In March 1919 his first contribution, the poem "Waar Tebes in die Stil Woestyn..." was published. Mabel had to wait until the middle of the year before she was given another contribution, and a rather mediocre one at that. Not before December was he again to send her something worthwhile, "Die Brief van Nooitgedacht" (The Letter from Nooitgedacht), a sketch featuring the Waterberg types he had got to know so well. Other matters occupied Eugène Marais's thoughts. What was more, 1919 was an ill-fated year for him.

5. I Shall Know Peace There Once Again

What significance should one see in the fact that Marais's first contribution to *Die Boerevrou* – and his first published poem since his departure from the Waterberg – begins with the line: "I shall know peace there once again"?

The possible origin of this poem was quoted in the chapter dealing with Marais's stay with Hans Purekrans van Rooyen and his family on the Palala plateau in the Waterberg.

It is true that moving poems can be written about themes which need not have struck the poet himself so very deeply. But in Marais's case a first line like this one can refer only to his own emotions, and it expresses more than ordinary longing.

In her gripping study of the effects of opium on writers, *Opium and the Romantic Imagination*, Alethea Hayter quotes numerous examples of lines of poetry which came to the poet during an opium reverie, welling up, as it were, from his subconscious.

Morphine, prepared from opium, has a comparable but even more powerful effect. It is conceivable that the first line of "Tebes" either came from a morphine dream or from the painful, semi-delirious after-effects of a binge, and that the rest of the poem was later hung from this nuclear line without the aid of morphine.

Without morphine – for, although the opium or morphine addict may sometimes find themes, insights or phrases in his reveries or dreams – ordered literary work – the kind that Mark Twain had called 99% perspiration, 1% inspiration – has to be done in times of abstinence, temperate consumption or at least sober hours.

It is true that drugs may provide a spark – but, and this is an important reservation, only if the potential is present in the poet. And when the literary work is assuming its final form, even the most gifted poet should shun drugs completely.

Virtually every poet or philosopher who is dependent on one of the opiates will dream of a great philosophical work in which he intends to explain all the unsolved secrets of life, and in almost every case this great work is never written or completed. For while a poem may be built from a spark in a few sober hours, a wide-ranging philosophical work requires intensive, lengthy labour. Only by complete abstention could Eugène Marais work hard enough on *The Soul of the Ape* to complete the greater part – probably the entire manuscript which was to be published in book form fifty years later – by the end of 1918. And now, early in 1919, he was revising it once more and discussing it with his son.

"My father and I often argued about his theories, both verbally and later by letter," his son relates. "According to him all life forms exist in a thin crust of earth. Everything lives as a result of an exterior stimulus, which means through the medium of the senses. The first sense which was stimulated in the primeval form of human development was feeling. From the sense of feeling all other senses – hearing, vision, etc. – eventually developed. All these senses moved to a centre, from which the brain and spinal column developed. This constant stimulus and reaction to stimulus gave rise to what we call instinct. In man a new psyche later came into being which suppressed the old one. In this way man outwitted evolution to such an extent that mankind – as an extreme example – could conceivably develop into a race of hairless, blue idiots.

"Then I would tell my father: 'I agree that there is a new psyche which has suppressed the old one, but to me it is all a question of memory. Tell me what memory is, and I shall be able to explain the origin of the human psyche.'

"No, he would reply, memory was still part of the animal soul and the new psyche gradually pushed the old modes of conduct into the background. Everything man does not want to think about or to remember is submerged in the animal soul, and this soul is guarded by a censor – in that respect I grant that Freud is right."

Early in 1919 Marais handed the completed manuscript to his son, who carefully retyped it. This manuscript was *The Soul of the Ape* as it is known today. When it was published in 1969 with a foreword by Robert Ardrey, it was at least fifty years old.

It is revealing that not everything Marais's son quotes from the discussions in the extracts above appears in the extant form of *The Soul of the Ape.* One can only surmise that Marais kept back portions of the manuscript on which he still wanted to work or with which his son could not agree.

Marais's friend, Advocate te Water, too, refers to a theme which is missing from *The Soul of the Ape* as eventually published: "The role of fear in man and in the higher primates was an important aspect of the book. We often discussed this, agreeing that there was a difference between fear as a biological necessity and cowardice, which was a human degradation of a natural virtue."

Young Eugène gave his father the typescript and kept the copy he had made. Had it not been for that copy, *The Soul of the Ape* would probably have been lost completely.

Marais at once began polishing and changing the typescript. One day, after discussing it with his friend, Flossie Kay, he bought her a typewriter so that she could type a second, revised draft. Very little is known about the relationship between Marais and this girl. Judging by the way in which several friends and relatives spoke about her in interviews – always in extremely careful terms – it was no light flirtation. There seemed to be talk of marriage but something happened which caused it to meet with disaster.

"My father was always seeking the love of a woman," Marais's son said fifty years later, speaking hesitantly and with a sadness he could not completely suppress. "And many of them became extremely fond of him or fell in love with him because he had so much charm. And then someone would write an anonymous letter to warn the girl and everything would come to an end. That terrible thing was always in the background."

There is no doubt about his son's sincerity, but seen in the light of Marais's role in later romantic relationships, one is reminded of the words of Aeschylus: "Who is the slayer, who the victim – speak!"

One of Marais's colleagues at the Pretoria Bar, John Murray (later Sir John Murray, Chief Justice of Rhodesia), tells a story from this time.

"I was in Heidelberg to prosecute in a case. Marais was the advocate for the defence. We were both at an hotel, I think the Royal. Early one morning, at about 7 o'clock, I came down the passage and saw Marais at the telephone. He was in a terrible state, just about completely done for. I could hear that he was talking to a woman and I remembered these words: 'For God's sake, send the stuff over at once.'

"When our case started at about nine-thirty that morning, he was his normal self again."

There is a suggestion that the woman was Flossie Kay. It is not known how soon the break between them came. Marais's son thinks that she may have typed a third draft of *The Soul of the Ape*. At that stage their affair broke up.

Marais never paid for the typewriter. When the suppliers started making trouble, his son had to find the money.

As always, morphine alleviated the worst pain and yet more injections served to wipe out the longing, the shame, the humiliation.

"At the Bar we knew about the morphine of course," says John Murray. "The general impression was that Marais was alright when he had his supply and that trouble only started when he had to do without it."

About this time Marais began using face-powder, completely unfashionable at the time. Morphine discolours and damages the complexion and he had been using the drug for a quarter of a century. The maximum dose to which he had always restricted himself increased as well, as we know by what he told his son: "In the first quarter of a century I never took more than seven grains a day."

That he was using more morphine did not mean that work had become impossible. As far as his *magnum opus* was concerned, he still set the highest standards. Not even the third draft of *The Soul of the Ape* satisfied him. He had shown it to several of his colleagues at the Bar and discussed it with them. "He was constantly changing the manuscript," says Charles te Water, "and every time it was changed, it got worse."

And John Murray: "The manuscript was shown around chambers. One or two fellows at the Bar said it would never be published because Marais had access to some foreign accounts of primate studies and that Marais's experiments were indicative, that they fitted in with the primate psychology which he'd picked up elsewhere."

There is no proof for the suggestion that the theories in *The Soul of the Ape* were second-hand in 1919. But to anyone who has ever tried to write an ambitious book, Te Water's and Murray's recollections should make clear what was actually happening in this case. Marais had written himself into a tangle from which there was no escape. As he wrote he was constantly reading about his theme – and beginning to doubt his own conclusions. In his attempts to substantiate his radical new theories he was merely succeeding – as Te Water realised – in making the manuscript unreadable.

During this period, if he could only have known it, he could say virtually anything he liked about the theme without fear of being challenged. For as far as we know he was the first man in history to have studied such a large group of animals in their natural state for so long and he was certainly the first man to have done so with baboons.

But he got cold feet. It is significant that, while Marais vehemently disagreed with so much of what Freud had written, he never says this in *The Soul of the Ape*. Freud's name was too great. And the other researchers into the behaviour of the higher primates of that time – today mere footnotes in obscure treatises – were, in 1919, professors at some of the most famous universities in the world. Marais would, or so he thought, have to do infinitely more work, both in the field and in the library, before he would be able to disprove their findings.

Once he had started using morphine again, Eugène Marais was not capable of intensive, sustained work in 1919. And even if he was, who would have financed him while he had to give up all other sources of income in order to devote his entire life to an uncertain gamble?

Thus it came about that *The Soul of the Ape* died unsung even before 1920. During the next seven years Marais was to work on it sporadically now and again without making any progress worth mentioning.

6. Back to Sunnyside

After the end of the Great War in 1918, Eugène Marais's son resigned from the Department of Defence to become an attorney, doing his articles first at Pienaar & Marais and then at Marais, Clark & Price.

The young man had long since come of age and as he was having a hard time financially as an articled clerk he decided to sell the remaining portion of the plot his mother had left him in her will. One-fifth of the plot had been sold during Marais's stay in the Waterberg to contribute something to the son's board and lodging. For the remaining four-fifths young Eugène now obtained a good price, as Sunnyside had meanwhile become a coveted neighbourhood.

It was with this income that the young man paid a number of his father's debts, including the typewriter he had bought for Flossie Kay. For himself he bought the motorbike which he had desired for a long time: a brand-new German Brennabor.

Later Aldous Huxley (born the year before young Eugène) was to point out that, in the early part of the twentieth century, for the first time in thousands and possibly tens of thousands of years, mankind had been given a new, previously unknown joy, bright and untarnished. This gift was speed.

Young Eugène's Brennabor was a beauty. It may not have been as powerful, as reliable, as fast as the Rudge-Whitworth belonging to George Findlay (of course George had had a motorbike for years by then), and sometimes he had to push it quite hard to make it start, but even so he could now join George, who had praised the new pleasure in a poem, in crying out: "Of speed I sing..."

The third musketeer, Toon van den Heever, followed his friends' example; all he could afford was a rundown old Harley Davidson, nicknamed "That went" by his friends.

At the time the Ermelo correspondents of Marais, Clark & Price were Bekker & Niemeyer. After Niemeyer's death Bekker needed help, and young Eugène was transferred from Pretoria to Ermelo. It is impossible to say whether there was a connection, but it seems clear that his son's transfer to Ermelo coincided with a gradual decline in the father's condition.

It was no coincidence that all three firms for which Eugène junior worked just after the Great War had been founded by relatives, for in these years the Marais' or their family by marriage played an important part not only in the legal practices of the capital, Pretoria, but also in those of several country towns.

Be that as it may, Advocate Eugène N. Marais, the father, received very few briefs. The truth was that most of his family were by this time strongly critical of him. All things being equal, a lawyer can give a relative briefs but if there was the slightest possibility that the relative might make a mess of the case, one would rather not do so. And in Marais's case such doubts were not unfounded. Not only was he arriving at the office later than ever, on many days he did not arrive at all. His most important source of income were the book reviews he wrote for *Die Brandwag* at Gustav Preller's request. To an increasing extent the three senior musketeers – Roos, Marais and Pitman – were seen together.

When Tielman Roos's invalid wife died, he invited Marais to come and live with him in Sunnyside.

"They agreed to share the housekeeping," Marais's son recollects. "My father told me that it was his responsibility to look after the wine."

At this time Sunnyside was a wonderful place to live: conveniently near the city, but still largely rural. Roos's spacious, imposing house in Walker Street stood on a plot which occupied half a city block. It had vast lawns, huge trees, a tennis court and stables from which cows were driven to the empty plots in the area every day to graze. By chance Marais again came into close contact with relatives who had disappeared from his life in the past few years. Opposite Tielman Roos's house, on the block between Rissik, Celliers, Devenish and Walker Streets, were two large plots on which two sons of Eugène Marais's rich uncle, Piet Marais, had built their homes: Charles, who had inherited his father's financial instincts, and Belfield. Since Ryk Piet's death, "Ryk Charles" had become the wealthiest member of the large Marais family (and also the stingiest, some said). Belfield, too, although he had lost much of his inheritance by investing unwisely, was a wealthy man. He had not been very well for a considerable time and had retired to this house in Sunnyside a while before. He was fifty-one.

Belfield had not always been lucky in love. Years before, when he still lived in the Cape, he had fallen in love with a divorced woman considerably older than he. Ryk Piet not only opposed the marriage, he strictly forbade it. His instincts were proved right soon afterwards. In rage, the daughter of the frustrated woman hid a flask of vitriol in her handbag, arranged to meet Ryk Piet in the Mount Nelson Hotel and flung the contents of the flask in his face. He was to bear the scars until his dying day.

After this episode Belfield remained a bachelor for a long time. Then, in 1910, while he was surveying agricultural land near Cape Town for a new residential area – later to be called Bellville – he met a beautiful young woman, Blanca Borckenhagen, who had been chosen from Bloemfontein's socialites to represent her province at the Union Festivities in Cape Town. They were married not long afterwards. Now, in 1920, they and their two children, Billy (seven) and Yvonne (five), were living in Sunnyside.

Eugène Marais did not have much time for his cousins during this period, perhaps because they had become too important. "He never wanted to make a fixed appointment," says Blanca Marais. "We once had a visitor who wanted to hear his stories at first hand. We invited him to spend the evening with us, but he simply did not arrive. Belfield had to go and fetch him at Tielman's."

The Marais children were a different matter entirely. Quite a number of Ryk Piet's grandchildren were now living in Pretoria – the children of Charles, Belfield and Rupert Marais – and they were constantly visiting each other. To them all he was the most wonderful uncle a child could wish for.

His favourite was Yvonne, Belfield's five year old daughter. Almost every Sunday he took her to the zoo to visit Joe, the chimpanzee.

"The moment Joe heard Oom Eugène's voice," she was to relate many years later, "he began jumping around like a mad thing, gesticulating all the time. And the moment Oom Eugène got into the cage, the chimpanzee would cling to him as if he did not want to let him go. Sometimes we stayed until Joe had to go to bed. Then Oom Eugène would simply say 'Collar,' and Joe would hand it to him, and 'Pliers,' and he'd get them. When Oom Eugène had fastened the iron collar around his neck, he would go to bed quite happily."

Almost every evening he would fetch Yvonne from her house to go with him to call the birds. Her parents, too, had a large, wooded plot. There was an avenue of quince trees, some large loquat trees, a cow-shed, a tennis court, a vegetable garden and stables where two ponies for the children were kept. Behind the house water bubbled from a spring between densely growing reeds.

"He called the birds with a kind of whistling sound," Yvonne was to say. "All kinds of birds came to him. I was terribly at home with him as a child. He radiated a remarkable calmness. I told him things I would tell no other adult, things about my fairies, for instance. Once he brought a magnifying glass and helped me to examine the entire garden, but we found nothing."

To Yvonne, as to all her cousins, he was a magician. He could call not only birds – according to another niece, Stella – but also toads, and under his magical influence the most gruesome creepy-crawlies would become harmless. "There is nothing to be afraid of," he would say, showing Rupert's fourteen year old daughter, Peggy, how to keep scorpions in her hand with impunity. Under his guidance her ten year old brother, Mynhardt, allowed tarantulas to run across his naked arm – without fear and without being bitten.

He told Yvonne stories every night, sometimes carrying on long past her bedtime. The next evening she would have to tell him where he had stopped, because he could never remember.

There are many examples of creative artists who, having written stories or poems under the influence of drugs, would later approach their own writings with some hesitation, like those of a stranger, because they could remember nothing of what they had written. Would it matter if the wonderful stories Marais told young children were frequently inspired by morphine? To the innocent child all things are innocent. The important thing is that for these children – and for scores of other children during the course of his life – he created a magic world which they were never to forget. At God's judgement seat the voices of these children must have borne powerful witness.

His friendship with Yvonne and her little comrades was not one-sided. One of the necessities of his life, as we have seen, was a child or animal to whom he could give love, and one suspects that these children helped him during an extremely difficult period of his dependence to at least maintain the appearance of normality.

7. Joan

At that stage a beautiful serpent appeared in the paradise of children. Her name was Joan. She was about sixteen or seventeen years old, the daughter of Raymond Harley, one of the most eminent Pretorians.

Harley was the Master of the Supreme Court. He was also one of General Hertzog's most loyal followers – both the General and Tielman Roos were on visiting terms with him. Everyone in Pretoria's legal and judicial circles knew him. And all of them, young and old, suddenly realised that he had a daughter who was, to say the least, extremely easy on the eye.

The fashions of the time made Joan's natural beauty even more irresistible. It was late in 1920, the beginning of a permissive decade. The respectable girl or woman was not allowed to use perfume or make up even now, but the latest fashions were more provocative than they had been in living memory. Joan was a bright young thing and she had "it" to the nth degree.

Even Marais's old friend Charlie Pienaar, Secretary of Justice, found her a temptation. "He was very amorous," she was to say later. Tielman Roos, too, found her irresistible. When he went to see her at her parents' house, he took Marais along. With her modern ideas, her provocatively fashionable dress, Joan may have been the predator and Marais her willing prey – as Marais's son was to typify some of the older man's relations with younger girls. Be that as it may, he was soon completely mad about her.

By this time it should be clear how strongly Marais could feel about a desirable woman. "Since her arrival I have been passing through a moral and physical hell on her account," he had written about Lettie Beyers almost thirty years before. "I am just about as dead gone as a man can ever be..."

This – although he was no longer twenty-two, but forty-nine – was how he now felt about Joan.

The young girl was flattered by the attention of two such well known men – Tielman Roos, leader of the Transvaal Bar, leader of the National Party in the Transvaal; Eugène Marais, a member of one of the oldest and best known Pretoria families, a man with a giant intellect, with an enigmatic past, of whom all kinds of strange tales were told. Eugène and Tielman took her out together, watching each other like hawks.

If she had to choose between the two, who would she choose? Tielman was a widower. He had a beautiful house, plenty of money and a great deal of influence. He also had a prominent pot-belly. Many years ago Joan knew, Old Moes, the hobo of Church Square, had tapped Tielman Roos on the shoulder, asking: "Zeg eens, heer Roos, wanneer bevalt u?" (Tell me, Mr. Roos, when is it due?).

Eugène did not have money – she realised this soon enough – but he was still an attractive man. His tales fascinated her and sometimes it felt as if he were mesmerising her with his eyes. Those eyes, his whole face, were to prove unforgettable. "He must have been a very outstanding man to have made such a deep impression on me," she said years later. "I remember his pale face and two small dimples on each side of his mouth. *He had the most extraordinary eyes*. They were a pale, transparent blue, almost like blue glass."

Joan, although she might not have known it, was arousing the Svengali in Eugène Marais.

They went for tea or coffee at Turkstra's coffee house, the great meeting place in Pretoria, sometimes as part of a large group but usually just the three of them.

"We used to get quite gay and happy and talk a tremendous lot, which was the way of doing things in those days. And then afterwards Eugène used to come alone sometimes to see me..."

Joan realised that his courtesy and impeccable manners concealed something sinister. This, too, attracted her to him.

When asked whether her father approved of visits by a forty-nine year old admirer, she replied: "My father approved what my mother said, and my mother liked Eugène."

Did he hypnotise her or try to do so? The question was not asked her. But he did something else in which many psychologists might see clear sexual symbolism: from his collection of knives he gave one to her as a present, a very sharp one, fourteen inches long, with a bone haft. And at her parents' house in Arcadia – a large, imposing house on a double plot – he taught her how to throw it and also how to toss it into the air and catch it by the haft.

"It was quite a feat, and I got quite clever at it, but my mother *loathed* the idea and thought it was an absolutely *lethal* weapon, and one day when it dropped and very nearly cut off the tips of all my fingers, she waited until Eugène came in the afternoon and then she said to him very crossly, 'Eugène, dis 'n *lawwe* soort ding om vir 'n meisiekind te gee. Ek wil hê jy moet dit dadelik terugvat' (Eugène, it's a stupid thing to give a girl. I want you to take it back at once). Eugène took it back and that was the end of *that*.

"Then afterwards, I used to go out driving with him and he used to bring me boxes of chocolates and sometimes flowers."

Not only chocolates and flowers did he give her, but poems as well. Some lines from one of them read as follows:

> Were you but here,
> with tears no more the dreadful night
> would in my soul its sorrows pour
> and through the curtained door
> the wailing of the wind I'd hear no more,
> were you but here.

If this poem had been written especially for Joan Harley, it was a great compliment. If he had written it years before, in his longing for his bride, the compliment becomes an excessive one.

The young girl was playing a dangerous game. Her beauty, her attitude and his state of mind were creating an explosive situation in which he was soon no longer to be satisfied with gallantries like flowers, chocolates and poems. The softening-up phase of his campaign had come to an end. The time for action had arrived.

One day Eugène and Tielman hired a taxi and took Joan to Klapperkop, one of the four hills on which President Kruger's Republican Government had built forts after the Jameson Raid. It was a beautiful day. The mimosas were in full bloom.

"Won't you go and pick me a bunch, Eugène?" she asked.

He flatly refused. Tielman and the taxi-driver could go. When they had left, Eugène embraced her. Joan Harley, in spite of her tender age, was well aware of how to resist approaches which she regarded as premature. When Roos and the taxi-driver came back, the atmosphere was considerably less light-hearted than before.

Marais could not understand it at all: the way she dressed, the way she talked, the things she discussed, gave the impression of sophistication, but when it came to the point she was cool and distant. Her attitude was not only inexplicable. It was also completely unacceptable. Later, at Tielman's house, while Tielman and Joan were standing chatting on the stoep, Marais, passionately jealous, leant through the window of one of the inside rooms, grabbed her arm and pulled her roughly to him.

Even so, her visits did not stop.

She knew about his dependence. She knew that the supply was regularly delivered at Tielman Roos's house. One day she saw him waiting restlessly at the garden gate for a long time, a very long time. But no messenger arrived.

This incident leads one to suspect that not only sexual frustration but also morphine – its use or its lack – played a part in the dramatic climax of this affair.

A supper at Advocate Roos's house. Miss Harley was present but most of the guests were older people, generally rather stodgy company. The party was not going at all well.

When Eugène and Joan stood talking after supper, he invited her to go and see something in his room. It may have been a painting, it may have been a new throwing knife. Years later she could no longer remember what it was.

In the bedroom he turned down the light, fell on his knees before her and declared that he could not live without her. Again she evaded him deftly. But when they returned to the drawing room Marais whipped a pistol from the side table and put a bullet through the ceiling. Realising the danger, the portly Tielman Roos dived under the sofa, whereupon Marais began shooting to either side of it.

Even this was not the last straw for Joan. She still had a number of admirers, but always in the forefront was the enigmatic man with the hypnotic eyes.

She may have loved him after her fashion. A man who was worth his salt should not be put off by other callers.

As far as Marais was concerned, he had become accustomed to success with young women, and this one was of exceptional importance to him. What was more, she was provoking him. She was teasing him. This he could not endure, nor the eternal young men dancing attendance on her. Some time after the shooting incident, they clashed for the last time, she apparently in tears, for she later remembered that he had said these words: "You're just like a stapelia with all those bluebottles flitting around you, you sniffling little hypocrite."

Perhaps he made other remarks in the same vein, remarks which wounded her so much that she was not willing to repeat them later. At any rate, the affair was at an end. In a later interview she said only: "I was so angry and so offended, being adolescent, that I said: 'Eugène, I will never talk to you again as long as I live.' And, actually, I didn't. And the friendship of some months broke up at that stage, and I never saw him again."

Only a few months later she married. She was still extremely young. Could it have been something of a rebound? The poems Eugène Marais had written for her, went with her.

In her husband, too, Joan managed to keep jealousy smouldering. When he later came across the poems in a trunk, he burnt them.

8. The Voice of the Story-teller

The shooting incident in Tielman Roos's house did not cause a complete break between him and Marais but certainly cooled their relations.

Late in 1920 Marais came to the painful realisation that he could have shot one of his best friends; that an outburst of rage had alienated a loved one; and that he was losing all control over morphine.

His son, too, came to talk to him. When things went reasonably well, Marais simply refused to admit the problem or to discuss it with anyone, even his son. But he had reached the depths of despond and he was willing to grab at any possibility of cure.

Father and son agreed that the time had come to call a halt. Perhaps a psychologist could help.

In this year there were about six thousand certified insane people in the Union. Of these about two thousand were in Weskoppies, near Pretoria, by far the largest of the country's eight asylums. It was to this institution that Marais went to discuss his problems with a psychologist.

The psychologist seems to have been a wise man. He was used to far more serious conditions than morphine addiction, and his approach was a practical one. He allowed Marais to get it all off his chest. He agreed with him – for Marais was already firmly convinced of this – that it was essential to eliminate morphine completely by gradual withdrawal, and he gave him the assurance that with the right medical attention, this process would be quite possible.

After all, Marais had done it before.

Marais's courtesy, his soft-spoken manner, his obvious knowledge of medicine and psychology made an excellent impression. At a later visit the psychologist showed Marais and the friend who had accompanied him to Weskoppies around part of the huge complex, including portions not normally shown to the public.

As far as Marais's own problem was concerned, the treatment worked. Early in 1921 he was getting along without any morphine at all for the second time in five years.

By this time young Eugène was back in Pretoria. As before, Marais experienced a remarkable spiritual, intellectual and physical renascence. J.C. Vlok, Eugène junior's "twin brother" – Vlok was born only a month after him in 1895 and his mother, too, had died of puerperal fever – knew nothing about Marais's abstinence, but was to relate later about that year: "It was 1921. Gustav Preller had just appointed me to the staff of the *Volkstem*. I was living in Sunnyside as well, on the corner of Kotze and Bourke Streets. At that time we regularly played tennis at General Botha's house. I would pick up my friend, Zwemmer, on the other side of Tielman Roos's house in Walker Street. I had a Buick. I saw with my own eyes how the women just about fell over themselves to get to Eugène Marais. They would queue up to hear him tell a story or to see him read a girl's future from her hand. It was amazing – remarkable. Isak Olivier said so too: 'The women simply get barmy about Marais.'"

Not morphine but the balsam of female admiration and his friendship with Yvonne and her young cousins helped Marais to forget Joan Harley. His new energies did not bring him noticeably more briefs than before, but 1921 was to be one of his most fertile years as a writer. As early as September 1920 an article about hypnosis had been published in the supplement to *Die Brandwag* and before the end of that year Mabel Malherbe published his articles about the "yellow-bellied" iron-smith whom he had come to know in the Waterberg, as well as "'n Voëlparadys" (A bird paradise), his idyllic article about the old recluse of Geelhoutgrag on the Palala plateau. During 1921 almost thirty of his reviews, short stories, sketches, articles and poems were to appear in various magazines.

The production of this year shows us Marais at his most versatile and illustrates his ability as a teller of tales. Many colourful recollections from his chequered life were now told for the first time: stories about people who had been lost in the bush; about Modjaje, the mysterious rain queen; about snake venom; about the desert flight of the Hereros; about his exciting trip at the mouth of the Save from which we quoted in the last chapter of part 3.

He wrote a popular article about ancient Egypt and in two long articles described the asylum Weskoppies where he himself had gone for consultations.

Another article about psychology, "Verdubbeling van Persoonlikheid" (Doubling of Personality), treats a theme which was to grip the popular imagination a generation or so later in the film "The Three Faces of Eve".

In "Twee Dapper Afrikanermeisies" (Two Brave Afrikaans Girls) he put down in writing, probably for the first time ever, the heroic achievements of Rachel de Beer and Annie Lotrie. He published several poems and adaptations of poems, including "Skoppensboer", a cynical poem which was to become extremely well known in Afrikaans. He wrote about apes for *Die Brandwag* and in the supplement to *Die Brandwag* he published the central theory of *The Soul of the Ape* for the first time, in an article called "'n Nuwe Sielkundige Teorie" (A New Psychological Theory). Two months later this was followed by "Verhoogde Waarneming Onder Hipnose" (Increased Perception under Hypnosis) in which he describes his experiments with Jane and Mary Brayshaw.

This article was a literal translation from the original manuscript of *The Soul of the Ape*. What made him release this important portion of the book for publication before he could complete the book itself? Did he begin to suspect that he would never do so? Or did he think that publication of part of it in an obscure Afrikaans magazine would make no difference to publication of the whole abroad?

In this period of powerful personal revival, Marais's path crossed that of another extremely gifted, versatile and eccentric Afrikaans poet, C. Louis Leipoldt.

Leipoldt, then in early middle-age, was related to Marais's old friend Ewald Esselen on his mother's side. He had a full and varied life behind him. Like Marais he was intensely interested in botany. Like Marais he had, as a young boy, taken part in a long ox-wagon trek through a thinly populated part of the country. Like Marais he had been a newspaper editor at nineteen, in his case *The South African News*. Like Marais he had spent several years in London, where – unlike Marais – he had obtained a medical degree at Guy's Hospital. Like Marais he had travelled a great deal. In 1909 he had spent six months on the luxury yacht of the millionaire newspaperman Joseph Pulitzer, acting as his personal physician. In 1912 he had visited Dutch East India as a ship's doctor and soon afterwards became a war correspondent in the Balkan war between Greece and Turkey. Like Marais he was interested in cooking (but he was a far better cook), in the exotic, in the supernatural and in abnormal psychology. Like Marais he regularly contributed to *Die Brandwag*, *Die Boerevrou* and *Die Volkstem*.

By 1921 Leipoldt had written a great deal: articles in Dutch, Afrikaans and English, scientific publications mainly in English, and poetry in Afrikaans. *Oom Gert Vertel en Ander Gedigte* (Oom Gert Relates and Other Poems) had been published the previous year. Leipoldt had now been in Pretoria for some years. For some time he had been in the Department of Defence. He had also been General Botha's personal physician.

It is not known how Leipoldt and Marais came to be friends. The only real information about their friendship comes from Marais's son, who thinks that they lived together in 1921.

"My father once took me to Leipoldt's house," he said. "I can no longer swear to it that they actually lived together. If that was the case, they did not do so for long."

In fact we know that they did not remain friends. Stephen Eyssen and his wife, a couple Marais was to learn to know only a few years later at Heidelberg, says that the two were bad friends at that time.

One can understand this. Just as considerate and courteous as Marais could be at his best, so brusque, blunt and tactless could Leipoldt be. It may be that Marais made statements regarding his earlier morphine addiction which Leipoldt as a doctor was unwilling to accept or believe. Then, too, they had opposing political views. Since the Boer War, Marais had become less pro-British, and Leipoldt more so.

Whether or not they lived together, Marais moved into another house late in that year. This was 176 Blackwood Street, the spacious dwelling in the shadow of the Union Buildings against Meintjeskop where Gustav and Hannie Preller had been living since the end of the Boer War.

Marais soon became good friends with their three sons – Carl, fifteen, Bob, eleven, and young Gustav, five. He and Hannie Preller, now forty-three, also got along fairly well. They had known each other for a long time. Long before the Boer War she had often heard her father – Marais's old friend, Commandant Henning Pretorius of the Republican State Artillery, a supporter of the opposition against Kruger – speak of him.

Another literary figure whose path crossed Marais's in 1921 was Miemie Rothmann, a middle-aged divorcee who had been appointed to the editorial staff of *Die Boerevrou* the previous year. Her children's book *Kinders van die Voortrek* (Children of the Great Trek), later to be re-issued as *Die Tweeling Trek Saam* had been published shortly before, and Marais was asked to review it. He had not hesitated to criticise Kleinjan van Bruggen previously. Now he did not hesitate to give this unpretentious book the highest praise – and again the literary judgement of a later generation was to prove him correct.

Of her talents as an illustrator he thought less. For her £20 a month at *Die Boerevrou* – a magnificent salary for a journalist in 1921 – she not only had to write and edit contributions, but also do illustrations. Very politely he pointed out that her illustration to his Bushman Wandering Tale "Die Vaal Koestertjie" (The Brown Pipit) was not a pipit but a plover.

In fact all the Wandering Tales, complete with the famous poems which form an integral part of the stories, were published in *Die Boerevrou* from May to August of that year.

It seems unlikely that even Miemie Rothmann, herself a discerning critic, realised the value of these unpretentious tales at the time. That they were published in *Die Boerevrou* as children's stories – and that even in volume form they were never regarded as anything else during Marais's lifetime – does not mean that they were unimportant to him. The spontaneity of the stories – later to be described by the eminent critic Van Wyk Louw as "among the greatest prose in our language" – and of the beautiful poems which form part of them, should not mislead one into thinking that they were written effortlessly. The Wandering Tales were completed in 1921, but from the evidence of George Findlay we know that Marais had been working on them sporadically for four or five years before that time.

Although he was writing a fair amount during this period, he was writing less than he had promised. He had told Mabel Malherbe about his plans to adapt some of the old Afrikaans folk songs and rhymes. He wrote only one. It was his last contribution to be published in *Die Boerevrou* that year, and compared to his previous work it was rather flat. A new phase in his life had begun, one aspect of that phase being that he was again using morphine.

By the end of winter 1921 Marais decided to move to the country once more. In this Gustav Preller again played a part. Marais intended to go into partnership with a friend of Preller's, Fanie van Wyk, an attorney, in Erasmus (later to be called Bronkhorstspruit).

Marais's friends may have thought that as an advocate, dependent on the briefs given to him by capricious lawyers, he would never do well. As a country lawyer he might be more successful. There, in a more peaceful atmosphere, he might even be able to complete *The Soul of the Ape*.

In September 1921 he moved to Erasmus.

9. Die Skepbekertjie

Erasmus lay east of Pretoria on the main road to Delagoa Bay. A small number of houses and several commercial buildings were scattered along the dusty main road. Apart from this there were hardly any streets and no street lights at all. In their houses the inhabitants used candles and paraffin lamps. A feature of the place were the cypress hedges surrounding the plots of the more prosperous inhabitants.

Apart from Marcus' bazaar there were two or three Indian shops and Mr. and Mrs. Vroom's "tin shop" with its corrugated iron walls. Leaving the village, one passed Goodridge's big steam mill. The only entertainment took place in a tiny hall. Concerts were held here from time to time and the more progressive inhabitants could see a shaky silent movie here about once a month. A more important social centre than the "bioscope" was Mrs. Anna Auret-Polderman's boarding house, where Eugène Marais went to live. Other boarders were Attorney van Wyk – Marais's partner in the new firm of Van Wyk and Marais – as well as some of the village's teachers, both male and female.

Mrs. Polderman was an exceptional woman. Born in Scotland, she and her parents had emigrated to Pretoria, where she had become a teacher. She did not remarry after the death of her second husband. At the time of her friendship with Eugène Marais, she was about forty-six, only a few years younger than he. She was exceptionally competent, as well as humane and understanding. And it was she, among others, who in Erasmus helped him to lead the "normal" life which one part of him craved.

During the first few months of his stay he managed to do so. His morphine consumption was under control. In this respect Erasmus had few temptations. There was only one pharmacy, which belonged to the only doctor, Dr. Gerrit Mes, a Dutchman by birth.

Marais worked on *The Soul of the Ape* once again, but not intensively. He seems to have lost interest.

The pile of papers lay in his room. Although he worked at it only sporadically, he spoke about it constantly. In numerous conversations he explained the theory of the book to Louis van Nispen, a son from Mrs. Polderman's first marriage.

He longed to complete it, but the effort required was enormous. As in London, as so often before, he allowed his attention to be divided by half a dozen other interests. He took part in the village's social life. He played a leading role in the foundation of the Afrikaanse Vereeniging (Afrikaans Society). He helped Dr. Mes's wife organise charity concerts. He got to know a fair number of people. Fanie van Wyk's children, Reinoud, twenty-two, and his sister,

Frieda, two years younger, became his good friends. When Frieda went to college Marais gave her the "murderer's watch" which had always hung on his bedpost. "The watch had played an important part in a murder case," she was to say later. "The murdered man's blood had made it stop. In that way they could determine the time of the murder. It was a tremendous honour for me to receive a gift like that."

This "murderer's watch" was typical of Eugène Marais. Whether the story he told about it was true or untrue may have been of less importance to him than the fact that he could please a young female friend by giving it to her.

He got to know all the teachers, including a few who taught elsewhere, like Johannes van Melle, a thirty-four year old Dutchman who had settled in the Transvaal after the Boer War and was later to become a well known Afrikaans novelist.

As always, Marais had numerous child friends.

"I shall never forget those summer evenings out on the grass," one of them, then a ten year old girl, was to say later. "He kept the younger children on his lap and told them fairy tales. The older ones were told everything about the stars."

Some of his friends were farmers in the district around the town. One who became a close friend was Mike Henn of the farm Witklip, about six miles from Erasmus, where he would frequently spend weekends. The Henns had a family of ten children – three sons and seven daughters. His particular favourite was Mara (bitter), born in the rebellion, and now seven years old. But all the children were his best friends. Under his guidance, these children of the veld realised for the first time what riches lay around them. When he went for a walk in the veld he took them along, pointing out the miracles waiting to be discovered.

In this apparently barren land he found the four species of pipits which lived in the area, the cut-throat larks, the quails, the two species of partridge. Marais and the children found the greatest concentration of bird-life on two pans (semi-arid lakes) near the farmhouse. The so-called Great Pan lay near the house. "In a depression near the house there was a large grass pan which never dried up completely. More than half of it was densely overgrown with high reeds and about a quarter of the surface was completely covered in soft water grass which rose above the surface of the water for about a foot. Only about a quarter of the pan was open water ... this was always as blue as the most beautiful gem ...

"The Small Pan lay just over the ridge. One quarter of that was also open water with a rocky bottom. Three quarters was densely overgrown with reeds and rushes, transversed by passages. The small pan would sometimes dry up in winter (the dry season)."

These pans teemed with red-nobbed coots. There were dabchicks, wild duck, moorhen, wild muscovy ducks and occasionally foreign visitors from Europe, cormorants and even a strange looking swan which was not white but brownish-black.

At about this time – it must have been late in 1921 or early 1922 – *Die Boerevrou* advertised a short story competition. "Let me help you," Marais offered one of the Henn daughters, fifteen year old Anna. He not only helped her – he wrote the essay for her. The urge to write which could not find expression in *The Soul of the Ape* was now poured into "Die Skepbekertjie". In his large, hurried but clear handwriting, it comprised more than 140 small sheets of paper.

A "skepbekertjie" is a mug or beaker used to ladle water from a larger container.

The story's theme centred on the birds of Witklip. The title is derived from a tale told by an old Bushman on the farm of the crystal clear magic fountain under a krantz, which had to be sneaked up on and then emptied with one rapid sweep of the mug. If this was not done expertly, it would disappear before one got there. The story, Marais thought, reminded one of the way in which birds were capable of making themselves and their nests invisible.

"Now rewrite it in your own handwriting and send it in," he told Anna when the essay was done.

Nobody ever heard from the magazine. Perhaps there was a mistake. Perhaps Anna had sent it to the wrong address. It may be that *Die Boerevrou*'s adjudicator had preferred a more flowery contribution to Marais's beautifully simple prose, as can happen in such cases. Marais's original manuscript was sewn together into a kind of book and put away somewhere in the house. Only forty-five years later was it discovered and published in book form.

That Marais – at this stage anything but wealthy – could give Frieda van Wyk a watch is understandable. That he persisted in giving away his most valuable possessions to friends must be accepted as part of his generous and carefree personality. But that a writer – that most selfish of all creatures – should give a fifteen year old girl the results of careful field observations and hard writing to submit to a magazine under her name, makes it abundantly clear once more that he lived his life according to a special set of values. "Eugène Marais is not immoral," Toon van den Heever was to say much later. "He is amoral."

10. Lalele

There is a story – in fact it was told by Marais himself – that the poem "Mabalêl", one of the most famous in Afrikaans, was written at Erasmus in one afternoon and evening.

That this is patently untrue is indicated by the pages and pages filled with tentative attempts and deletions, as well as the fact that in these first drafts Marais used three different pens and pencils. It may well be that he managed to integrate and lick into shape the sporadic work he had spent on this long poem of more than a hundred lines in one inspired afternoon and evening. Mechanically speaking, he could write very fast – and in passing one can observe that his writing, except perhaps during withdrawal, never showed the deterioration often found in morphine addicts.

The immediate spur to completing the poem was a request Marais had received from the editor of *Die Burger* for a contribution to the paper's New Year edition, which in the twenties was a literary show-window for Afrikaans writing. The request was made in a telegram, but the editor got more than he had bargained for. Once more demonstrating his contempt for filthy lucre, Marais cabled the entire poem at the newspaper's expense to Cape Town a day or two later. It could not have occupied fewer than ten to fifteen telegram forms. The real Mabalêl, the young daughter of captain Rasithlare, was seized by a crocodile years before in a large "hippo hole" in the Limpopo. The deep pool used to be known as Rakwêna, "father of the crocodile". The incident was described to Marais during his stay in the Waterberg ten or more years before, and had made a great impression on him.

As the poem opens, princess Mabalêl is tripping down the footpath to the waterhole. Young, lithe and beautiful, she is effortlessly balancing the earthenware water jug on her head as she walks. Dusk is falling. In the village far behind her the first fires are being lit. She approaches the wide expanse of water. Unknown to her, Lalele, the giant crocodile, is lurking in its depths.

The maiden has reached the water's edge. She kneels down to fill her jar. She is in no hurry. Dreaming, she stares into the water until she herself becomes part of a beautiful reverie. Slowly the giant crocodile rises to the surface. Mabalêl sees only her own reflection in the water. So absorbed is she in her own thoughts that moments later she also fails to see the "half drowned leaf" floating in the water before her. It is not a leaf at all, in fact, but the ridge of the crocodile's eyebrow, the position it adopts immediately before attacking. Suddenly the huge body breaks from the water. A single cry of agony floats across the river. In the village more fires have now been lit. People have missed Mabalêl. They start calling her name. She will not return.

The crocodile slowly sinks back into the depths.

Mabalêl, as Robert Ardrey has pointed out, represents Marais himself. He had come to Erasmus with great expectations. He had tried very hard, he had made good friends. But in the midst of the relative peace he had found here, Lalele was rising to the surface and soon a desolate cry would shatter the silence of Lake Rakwêna once again.

11. Beauty Bell and Dr. Mes

Beauty Bell was in trouble. To crack a bank in Johannesburg was an expensive business. In the first place he would have to have an acetylene blow-torch for this, together with all the other equipment required for a task of this kind, and the dealers would not let him get away for less than £300. And money was the one thing Beauty Bell did not have at the moment. He would have to try in the countryside. Beauty Bell scouted around for a while and decided to tackle the Netherlands Bank at Erasmus. It was comfortably close to Johannesburg. They would be able to make a quick getaway. In Erasmus the less sophisticated tools of the small safe-cracker would be sufficient: cold chisel, hammer, crowbar and some nitro-glycerine.

On the day of the intended robbery, Beauty Bell and his assistant left early for Erasmus and they spent the entire day there. While the little village went its sleepy way, the two visitors watched everything unobtrusively. They saw the shops being closed and the people going home. They saw an Indian – one Amod – who had a shop and house near the bank, start fixing a new sheet of corrugated iron to his building's roof. The Indian was making a great deal of noise and he obviously intended working late.

Beauty Bell waited patiently. Around the bank several lights were still burning in shops and rooms and just next door there was a garage where the owner and three friends were playing bridge. They seemed to be enjoying themselves so much that he thought they might never go home. At this stage the Indian had stopped hammering. Beauty Bell found a sheet of corrugated iron and ordered his assistant to hit it with a hammer at regular intervals while he broke into the bank. He was inside the building within ten minutes. While his assistant continued to hammer on the corrugated iron, Beauty Bell used beeswax to build a funnel around the keyhole of the safe. Into this he carefully poured nitro-glycerine.

Next to the bank the card players were still at it. The owner had emerged twice to shout at Amod for kicking up such a row, but at this stage they suspected nothing.

At about half past one that morning Beauty Bell and his assistant wrapped the bank's safe in some blankets they had looted from a shop nearby. They then went into a nearby alley to await the explosion, keeping up a constant hammering on the sheet of corrugated iron. When the charge exploded, to some extent muffled by the blankets, the owner of the garage stormed out furiously, shouting, "Amod, if you don't stop your ... noise at once, I am going to call the police." The card players had heard the explosion but had taken it to be a sheet of corrugated iron which had fallen to the ground from the roof.

There was no real danger even now. Beauty Bell and his assistant entered the building once more. To their dismay they saw that the charge had been too small. The outer door of the safe had indeed been destroyed, but they could still not get into the safe itself. Deeply disappointed, the two of them returned to Johannesburg in the early hours without a penny to show for their pains.

However, Beauty Bell's crowbar had left marks on the bank's windowsills, marks which the police recognised. Beauty Bell was arrested in Johannesburg and brought to Erasmus to await trial. Here he met a lawyer, Eugène Marais, who was to act for him.

Marais questioned him and soon gained his confidence. In a strange way the lawyer felt an affinity for the criminal. The man had his own set of values which he would never dishonour.

"The gold and silver of the banks come from the soil," he told Marais. "And the soil belongs to me as much as to Solly Joel." When breaking into the bank – he was one of the best safe-crackers in the country – he never carried firearms. It was against his principles to hurt people. The detectives on the case told Marais about Bell's great love for children and animals. After a successful bank robbery, he would send considerable contributions to the Society for the Prevention of Cruelty to Animals as well as to various orphanages. He took great pleasure in wandering about the slums of Johannesburg and handing out money to street urchins.

This is how Marais described the bank robber in a magazine article:

> A well-built man, as straight as an artillery officer, neatly, even elegantly dressed, with the manner and bearing of a gentleman – a robber and a safe-cracker? Anyone meeting Beauty Bell for the first time would scornfully reject any such suggestion. He was charm itself. There was no subject about which he was incapable of talking intelligently.
>
> The detectives say all this charm is mere hypocrisy; only one weapon in the arsenal of an unmitigated rogue. I do not believe this. I am convinced that his true nature is lovable ... and that this amiability is probably the most important ingredient of a peculiar [psychological] composition.

The sympathy Beauty Bell's lawyer felt for him did not help him in the trial. After so many convictions, he was given the indeterminate sentence.

The bank robbery and the court case remained the main topic of conversation in the small village of Erasmus for some time. Marais could not have failed to discuss it with his doctor and friend, Dr. Mes.

Beauty Bell and Dr. Mes (Dutch or Afrikaans for knife) – names from a surrealistic play, but real people from the period of eight months which Marais spent in Erasmus, and each important in his own way. Gerrit Mes certainly had no sympathy for Beauty Bell, and that was understandable. They were opposites.

Dr. Mes's mother, Margaretha van den Bosch, had begun life as a scullery maid in Haarlem, Holland, a social nobody. But she was a vastly ambitious woman. When she had scraped together enough money, she left her job, qualified as a maternity nurse and became the most famous midwife in Haarlem. Her husband, a bank messenger, was kept firmly under her thumb. Gerrit was their only son. Again they had to scrimp and save. Gerrit was to become a doctor – a successful one. And he managed it. He even managed to marry several degrees above his class. Marie Mes came from the highest circles. Her father, a successful engineer, had been the inventor of the sluice-gates installed at Ijmuiden and elsewhere. Her mother, a Rouwenhorst, was of aristocratic descent.

Gerrit Mes had it made. Then, possibly to escape the mother who had forced him to climb so fast and so far, he emigrated to South Africa. Now he had a beautiful wife, three healthy children, a flourishing practice and a Ford, one of the very few cars in Erasmus.

But all this was not enough. Apart from his practice he was also the district and railway surgeon – useful sources of extra income. His income rose rapidly but his expenditure did not. What good did it do him if his hard-earned money was just frittered away? His consultation rooms were housed in a small separate building next to his house. This building also contained his pharmacy, a minute room of six feet by five, so narrow that one could hardly turn around in it. In this sanctum boxes of medicines were stacked on high shelves. Even higher were two special shelves containing flasks and a small scale. Most medicines were bought ready to be dispensed, but there were certain powders which Dr. Mes himself measured and mixed. When this happened the entire family had to help him fold the powders into parcels and then pack them into boxes: Gerrie, eighteen years old, his sixteen year old sister, Griet, and of course his wife, who, after all, was a qualified nurse.

Everything had to be done extremely accurately. The colours Dr. Mes added to his powders were carefully recorded in a register so that the next mix would have exactly the same colour.

Dr. Mes was equally precise in his dealings with his patients. He knew his job; he also knew his duty. And as far as Marais was concerned it was his duty to reduce the man's dosage of morphine to nil. Anna Polderman watched her lodger's battle. He was smoking more than before. He was using more of the horseradish sauce she kept at the table for him and much more of the peppers he obtained from the Indians, so much that his forehead would perspire freely. In the evenings he was more restless than ever. When there was company he would sit on a chair near his own room, with a cigarette burning in his hand, ready to get away as soon as he could no longer endure the company of others.

"When he was in that kind of mood," Mrs. Polderman said, "nobody saw him leave his room."

He seldom saw the Henns of Witklip anymore. He no longer worked on *The Soul of the Ape*.

The pile of papers gathered dust in his room. When Mrs. Polderman asked him about it, he pointed to her son, Louis van Nispen. "I have told Louis so much about it, he may as well finish writing the book when I am dead."

And week by week his morphine intake was relentlessly reduced. Dr. Gerrit Mes had about as much sympathy for morphine addicts as for bank robbers. The patient was suffering but the treatment was a success.

Of the several people in Erasmus who knew about the withdrawal treatment, only Dr. Mes and one other were experiencing it at close quarters. As an angel of light she now appeared on Marais's landscape of hell. Marie Mes, a qualified nurse, was also a tenderhearted woman. She could no longer bear to see him suffer so dreadfully. One day she began supplementing the patient's supply secretly. To Gerrit Mes all Marais's charm was mere hypocrisy; only one weapon in the arsenal of an unmitigated rogue, as all morphine addicts were.

Marie Mes could not believe this. She was convinced that his true nature was lovable and that his amiability was probably the most important constituent of a peculiar composition.

But it was Dr. Gerrit Mes's opinion which prevailed. He was too precise a doctor not to notice that the morphine supply in his small pharmacy was dwindling.

The day of reckoning dawned. Marie Mes was severely reprimanded. She had betrayed her profession. But it was Eugène Marais who had to bear the brunt.

In this dusty, dour little society it seems as if the "establishment" sided with Marie Mes and Eugène Marais – sided, in a way, with Beauty Bell.

"Of course Dr. Mes saw that the morphine was disappearing and then locked it away carefully," one of the ministers' wives, Mrs. H.C.M. Fourie, wrote in a letter later. "Poor Marais was deprived of the only thing he could no longer do without."

On 30 May 1922, after about eight months at Erasmus, Eugène Marais left the village to settle in Heidelberg.

PART 7: OLD HEIDELBERG

Ek is in jou gevleg, gerank soos 'n wortel in in die donker bank	In you I am twisted and bound like a root in the dark ground

1. The High and the Mighty

When Eugène Marais settled in Heidelberg in June 1922, the town had grown a great deal but it was still completely rural. Not a single road had been tarred and at Nagmaal, held every three months, the farmers of the surrounding districts still came to town in their ox-wagons and spent a few days on Church Square.

The business centre was small but active. There were several hotels – the Grand, the Selborne, the Royal. There were also a number of boarding houses, like the Victoria, and people willing to take in boarders. Apart from being an educational centre, Heidelberg was also the centre of a large agricultural district.

There was enough work for a few legal firms, two chemists and half a dozen doctors.

The Indian quarter lay between one hotel and the river and in the black "location" outside Heidelberg fourteen different religious sects or groups looked after the spiritual needs of about one thousand black inhabitants.

The richest man in Heidelberg was no doubt Connie Pistorius, with whom Eugène Marais was soon to make friends, and the most powerful must have been the Rev. A.J. Louw, the sixty-three year old "Pope of the Highveld", who ruled the town and surroundings from his spacious parsonage on the corner of Van der Westhuizen and Church Streets.

"The village was dead," relates someone who knew it in those years, "and the Rev. Louw helped to keep it that way." C. Louis Leipoldt, allergic to auras of this kind, arrived in Heidelberg in the early twenties as medical inspector of schools and encountered an old acquaintance, Stephen Eyssen, there. "What are you doing here?" he enquired, brusque as always. "Aren't you afraid you'll die from an overdose of the holy ghost?"

For the time being Eugène Marais's path did not cross that of Heidelberg's spiritual leader. Clashes were to come later. Marais stayed in the Grand Hotel. Acting on behalf of Fanie van Wyk of Erasmus, he established a branch office in the Standard Bank Building in Ueckerman Street, taking a young man, Rudolph Coetsee, as a partner. The firm was called Marais & Coetsee.

There was no lack of attorneys in Heidelberg and work was not plentiful. Money was scarce everywhere.

Marais soon left the Grand Hotel for cheaper lodgings, with Mrs. Maria Swart, a widow. She had a spacious double-storey house and Marais was put in one of the two large reception rooms. Although he did not eat with her family – by now his eating habits had long become irregular and the hotel was comfortably close by – he soon got to know them well. Now and again he helped her fifteen year old son, Gerard, with his schoolwork. The other children were all girls: Johanna (thirteen), Dina (eleven), Marietjie (six) and Esperance (four).

"We used to visit him in his room sometimes," the eldest daughter, Johanna, was to relate half a century later. "He had a big desk there and multitudes of books. He made a tremendous impression on us. He could hypnotise people and he could foretell the future. He once read my hand and told me: 'Before you are twenty-seven you will have married three times and been divorced twice.' I firmly believed it."

But the six year old Marietjie was his favourite – she and her cousin, Nitie Pistorius, a daughter of Connie Pistorius, the town's wealthiest man, who lived just around the corner.

At this stage Marais was living rather well. Mrs. Swart was a sister of Mrs. Angenita Pistorius. Although a widow, she was fairly well off. Marais's room created the impression of comparative luxury. He was a frequent visitor at the great Pistorius house and often had meals there. His most important requirement had long been taken care of. There were two chemists in town – the Hollandse Apteek in Voortrekker Street and Harvey's Pharmacy near Marais's office. There were two older doctors, Joubert and O'Reilly, and a much younger and rather brusque Englishman, Nixon. The largest practices were those of a born Dutchman, Frans Daubenton, and a middle-aged Afrikaner, A.G. Visser. At this stage Visser had not yet started writing the popular poetry which was to make him a household name in South Africa.

A.G. Visser; an attractive widow who was not to appear on the scene until later; and Connie Pistorius – these three were to become the most important people in Eugène Marais's life during the four years he spent in Heidelberg.

At forty-eight, Connie Pistorius was some years younger than Marais. His father, one of five German brothers who had settled in the Transvaal in the previous century, died so wealthy that all his numerous children came into sizeable inheritances. Connie was given the farm Wildebeesspruit, as well as a third of the farm Spaarwater, which was more than 7 000 morgen in extent.

Later Connie also bought the largest part of one of his brothers' farms and in the early twenties sold the mineral rights on both portions very profitably, while retaining the farming rights. It was a pattern still frequently found in the Transvaal in those years. One inherited a large farm. One sold the mineral rights, retaining the land. With the money one bought another farm on which gold was soon discovered as well. One sold the mineral rights while retaining the land. With the money one bought ... The Pistorius money was neither elegantly venerable nor so young as to be unseemly. Neither was Connie Pistorius a simple Boer. At about the time when Marais went abroad to pursue his studies – in the 1890's – Connie was sent to Leiden in Holland to become a minister of religion. Shortly before he was to deliver his trial sermon, the young man decided against following a religious career and changed to law. He did not obtain his degree and never practised as a lawyer, but his legal knowledge (combined with legal advice from his attorneys, Meek & Viljoen) certainly helped him to expand his financial empire. And he used some of this money to help others. "He was a man," Sam Joffe, at that time owner of a café in Heidelberg, was to write later, "who showed charity and compassion for his fellowmen in those difficult times. Again and again he would help many of the town's small businessmen financially until they could get along on their own once more. Thinking back on his goodness I do not know whether a father or brother could have given one kinder treatment."

Eugène Marais, who received a great deal of assistance from Pistorius in Heidelberg, was later to give a less flattering impression of him in his long short story "Laramie die Wonderwerker" (Laramie the Magician), which contains interesting autobiographical elements. Pistorius, thinly disguised as "Skat" (Treasure) Pretorius, appears quite early in the story:

> A large limousine appeared from a cloud of dust and a sturdily built, blond giant got out. I at once recognised him as Mr. "Treasure" Pretorius ... He was a very wealthy man, who had grown up in luxury, for he had inherited his treasures from his late father. He was a loud man in all respects, and although one could not really call him a braggart, it was clear that the environment in which he had grown up had affected his character adversely. He was a social tyrant by virtue of his money. He was accustomed to squash anything which offered the least resistance to his wishes with an outburst of words and threatening gestures, like a steamroller would flatten the bush on a new farm ... "Treasure" Pretorius had studied at a European university for a time and although he had never obtained a degree of any kind, he did succeed in gaining a fairly good education, which he never neglected to demonstrate.

Eugène Marais himself had only barely scraped through his legal degree.

According to people who knew Pistorius, the description is not unapt, even if unkind. The "big limousine" which appears so dramatically from a cloud of dust fits the picture perfectly. Connie was mad about cars. And Eugène, although he had never learnt to drive, shared his love of large luxurious sedans, for the sensual fragrance of new leather upholstery and the thoroughbred hum of a powerful engine. Connie wanted a Vauxhall – a car which in the twenties fell into the same class as the Rolls-Royce – and when he could not buy one in the Transvaal, he had it imported. Brought ashore in Durban, the beautiful full-blooded vehicle cost him £1 650. It gave Eugène true pleasure to sink into the soft upholstery of the back seat next to Connie while old Dickenson, the white chauffeur, would move off and eliminate the ruts and corrugations in the gravel road by zooming across them at fifty or sixty miles an hour – to Spaarwater, to Wildebeesspruit, to Johannesburg, to the farms near Nigel where the children of Connie's brother were still farming after they had sold the mineral rights.

Another of old Dickenson's duties was to fetch the Pistorius children and their friends from school during breaks and take them home (a distance of two street blocks) where a table covered in ice-cream, pastries and cakes would await them. If they arrived back at school late this did not matter, for they were the children of Connie Pistorius. When there were complaints that Nita and Willem did not know their work, Mrs. Pistorius sent a message: "The teachers are most welcome to come to our house after three o'clock in the afternoon and give the children extra lessons there."

Marais soon got to know this house intimately, the great Pistorius house on the corner of Market and Strydom Streets. On one side of the broad veranda was the entrance to Pistorius' study. On the stoep itself were several benches where, in these difficult years, supplicants often sat waiting to ask for Pistorius' advice or financial assistance. To the left of the large ornate front door with its small panes of coloured glass was the billiard room and to the right of that the vast dining room.

A long passage led past the other reception rooms to the kitchen, the bathroom and pantry and then brought the visitor to the four large bedrooms, all decorated and furnished at great expense. This was where Connie and his wife, Angenita, slept, and here, too, slept their two surviving children: Nitie and eight year old Willem. The Pistorius' were large, robust people, known for their huge meals, and they radiated self-confidence and abundance. Even so, the early death of three of their five children had cast a shadow over the family. They were in constant fear that something might happen to the remaining two.

The teacher previously quoted may have been unaware of these deaths. In any case she saw the children less than sympathetically. "They were children from a wealthy family, enormously fat and real spoilt brats. At school we had a standing joke that we were the Pistorius' servants. Nita never knew her work and one afternoon she had to stay after school. When Connie came to collect her, I told him, 'She did not know her work and I want her to stay in.' So he replied, 'I demand my child,' and he took her. They were typical Transvaal plutocrats – not from merit, but by inheriting farms on which gold was discovered."

Marais was not blind to the Pistorius' faults, but he had an understanding of the problems of wealth as well as of the problems of poverty. Nita became a beloved young companion, Connie a good friend.

In his first months in Heidelberg, Marais for the first time committed to writing some of his termite observations from the Waterberg period. The article, "Verskynsels van die Dieresiel" (Phenomena of the Animal Soul), was published in the New Year edition of *Die Burger* early in 1923. It was the first time that he had publicised his theory about the unity of the termitary.

At that stage, January 1923, Eugène Marais had been in Heidelberg for about six months and he was compelled to face the fact that things were going far worse than he had hoped. He and Coetsee were not getting along well and there was little work coming in. In addition, he was finding it increasingly difficult to keep his morphine intake within reasonable bounds.

Before it got out of hand completely, he decided he would have to try withdrawal once again.

The physician he selected was Dr. Frans Daubenton, about whom he had heard extremely favourable reports. Here he could expect to receive some of the best treatment available in 1923.

2. Shadows on the Cave Wall

On 17 February 1923, after a series of excavations, the British Egyptologist, Howard Carter, opened a sealed door of the tomb of Tutankhamen, a lesser Egyptian prince of the eighteenth dynasty. Tutankhamen had died at the age of eighteen. His tomb was so small and insignificant that soil excavated during the construction of a neighbouring tomb later almost completely covered it. It was this accident which had preserved this lesser tomb from grave robbers for 5 000 years. The contents of this unimportant treasury – four war chariots, three gilded settees, a magnificent gilded throne, statues, treasure chests, sarcophagi and coffins fitting one into the other, the last of pure gold – gives one an idea, fifty centuries later, of the pomp and splendour with which the really important Egyptian kings must have been buried.

Howard Carter had made his sensational discovery on a Saturday. On the Monday he began investigating the contents of the tomb more thoroughly. And on the same day, on the other side of the same continent, after a bitter weekend, Eugène Marais made his first visit to Dr. Frans Daubenton. A page from the account book of this doctor – three columns of figures and a few words (here translated from Dutch) – gives one an impression, some generations later, of the suffering Eugène Marais regularly endured in the forty-three years of his morphine dependence:

FEB 1923		
19	1X	10.6
20	1 plus med.	10.6
22	1	10.6
23	morning trip (4 or 5 am) 3X	15
24	3	15
25	Night 3X	£1
26	2	10.6
27	3	15
28	2	10.6
MARCH		
1	3	15
2	3	15
3	3	15
4	2	10.6
5	3	15
6	2	10.6
7	2	10.6
8	2	10.6
9	3	15
10	3	15
11	Night X4	£1 5.0
12	5	1 5.0
13	3	15
14	2	10.6
15	2	10.6
16	3	15
17	3	15
18	4	£1 0.0
19	4	1 0.0

20	2 consult. Dr. Moll, psych. Johannesburg.	£1 0.0
21	Night 3X	£1 0.0
22	3	15.0
23	2	10.6
24	2	10.6
25	3	15.0
26	2	10.6
27	2	10.6
28	2	10.6
29	1	10.6
30	1	10.6
APRIL		
3	3	15
4	1	10.6
5	3	15
6	2	10.6
8	1	10.6
9	1	10.6
10	1	10.6
11	2	10.6
12	1	10.6
13	1	10.6
16	1	10.6
17	1	10.6
18	1	10.6
19	1	10.6
22	2	10.6

23	1	10.6
25	1	10.6
26	1	10.6
27	1	10.6
30	2	10.6
MAY		
3	1	10.6
5	1	10.6
6	1	10.6
8	1	10.6
10	1	10.6
11	2	10.6
13	1	10.6
15	1	10.6
16	1	10.6
18	1	10.6
20	1	10.6
21	Night X4	£1 5.0
22	1	1 5.0
23	1	1 5.0
25	1	1 5.0
		£49.8.0

On the wretched Monday morning when Marais was to consult Frans Daubenton for the first time, he again needed a daily dose of several grains just to keep away withdrawal pains. In the candid interview in which Dr. Daubenton, then aged seventy-five, but intellectually still extremely lucid, described his treatment of Eugène Marais in 1963, he said: "I no longer remember how much I gave him at a time, but it was certainly far above the fatal dose of one grain."

Asked whether Marais really wanted to be cured at this stage, he replied with conviction: "He did."

Were the doses reduced too rapidly? Why three visits in the early morning hours of the first Thursday of that week? Another three visits on Friday? Three night visits on the Saturday?

"When I had to see him at night it was often not for injections but for severe palpitations of the heart – a reduction of the dose accelerates the pulse rate – and for nightmares."

Dr. Daubenton briefly summarised the treatment: "I began the treatment with enemas. To bring down the abnormally high pulse rate associated with withdrawal, I gave him injections of digitalis. For insomnia he got Luminal. We also used sodium-bromide freely, as a tranquilliser and a soporific."

The doctor soon realised how serious his patient's condition was. Two stories illustrate this.

"Marais could not bear to be alone. When I went out on calls – I had an open Ford – he often went along. One day we were on our way to a farm; it was summer. Suddenly he called, 'Stop!', and when I stopped he jumped off, plucked the syringe from his pocket, filled it with water from a muddy pool in the road and injected himself. The morphine must have been in the syringe already.

"In the middle of a court case he would sometimes lose track of reality completely. He would not know where he was. The magistrate would then call me to give him an injection. It took only five minutes for him to recover completely and to resume his argument."

It seems as if Dr. Daubenton was applying an adapted form of a withdrawal treatment which had been tested for the first time in Britain fifteen years before. The idea was to keep the patient "high" by means of bromides until his natural withdrawal symptoms had become less severe. In order to intensify the effects of the bromides, the patient first had to receive purgatives. This seems to be in accordance with Dr. Daubenton's statement that he began giving enemas immediately.

The technique had its serious defects. In *The Morphine Habit and its Painless Treatment*, published years after Dr. Daubenton's treatment, the doctor, who himself had been an addict, describes his treatment with maximum doses of hyoscine-hydrobromide. Soon his thoughts were completely confused. Hallucinations and repulsive visions followed. On one occasion gigantic figures approached him menacingly. On their faces were huge, gaping wounds instead of mouths. On another occasion the doctor stood watching his own corpse departing. He saw the coffin being taken away and himself being banished to hell.

In these five months of intensive treatment, Dr. Daubenton also tested heroin as a substitute for morphine. When heroin had been prepared from morphine for the first time years before, many doctors welcomed it as a harmless substitute. Even by 1923 medical science does not seem to have realised that it was in fact a much more addictive drug. Not before 1931 was an international conference on drug control to issue serious warnings against it. In most countries heroin, unlike morphine, was later completely prohibited, even as an anodyne.

"If dagga (marijuana) and tobacco were the first tiny stormclouds to appear in the sky," Eugène Marais was to write later in "'n Paradys van Weleer" (A Paradise of Yesteryear) regarding addiction in the "yellow races" of South Africa, "brandy was undoubtedly the raging thunderstorm itself." A comparison could be made between morphine and heroin. The intravenous injection of heroin "has the violence of a lightning flash and the intensity of an orgasm" writes Charles Duchaussois in *Le grand voyage* (from which we have quoted before), and one is struck by the unconscious echo of Marais's words.

It would be quite wrong to believe that Dr. Daubenton acted irresponsibly by treating his patient with bromides and heroin. He acted according to the latest and most enlightened findings of his time. Even today, half a century later, no infallible treatment of morphine addiction has been found. In 1923, in Heidelberg, Transvaal, failing a miracle, a cure was virtually impossible. And there was no miracle.

The consequence of the combined or alternating applications of bromides, morphine and heroin made Eugène Marais lose all contact with reality for long periods.

"We often spoke about Plato," Dr. Daubenton said in the interview. "Eugène himself no longer knew who and what he was. Two thousand years ago seemed more real to him than the present."

To Eugène Marais, Plato's famous cave had become the here and now. He and his fellow prisoners were chained helplessly in an underground grotto. Behind him there was a fire and the flames cast flickering shadows against the cave wall in front of him. The prisoners, said Plato, were mankind. For them the shadows were the only reality. Of the greater reality outside the cave, in bright daylight, they knew nothing.

And if reality was a shadow, nothing more than a flickering light against a cave wall, why should the shadow – the nightmares, the occasionally divine visions – not be reality?

In this year Eugène Marais began reading hieroglyphics once more. Every week brought new information about the incredible finds in Tutankhamen's tomb, which had aroused tremendous popular interest in Egyptology. Frans Daubenton's wife, Kniera, had lived in Egypt for six years and when Marais visited the Daubentons they often discussed ancient Egypt. "Marais knew a great deal about it," Dr. Daubenton said. "When we were alone, he spoke Dutch to us, very fluently. In the company of others it was English or Afrikaans. He never spoke French. I don't think he could. He'd look at my wife's *Paris Match* now and then."

Apart from being good company, Frans Daubenton was also a conscientious doctor. Within a month after the beginning of his treatment, he told Marais:

"I wonder whether a talk with a psychiatrist might not help you." Marais grabbed the opportunity as he was willing to grab at every new possibility of a cure. He was taken to Johannesburg to see Dr. Marius Moll, an old friend of Frans Daubenton from the Utrecht days. Nothing is known about the interview or about Dr. Moll's questions and findings, except that the treatment was not successful.

After the publication of *Magriet van Laastelust*, a minor play, in 1922, young Eugène – who was still living with Sophie Ueckerman in Pretoria – began collecting and arranging his father's poems for publication in book form. Two of Marais's oldest and best friends, Gustav Preller and Charlie Pienaar, enthusiastically took up the idea. Preller had offered to write an introduction to the volume of poetry and for this he needed biographical details, which Marais was so unwilling to provide that Pienaar prodded him to do so in two letters.

"All the bad things can wait until after my death," Marais wrote to Preller in April, but then proceeded to provide a number of biographical details in several letters, in fact so much that Preller changed his plans. His biographical sketch of Marais – an impressive total of almost ten thousand words – was now to form part of a sizeable volume, *Historiese Opstelle* (Historical Essays), to be published by Van Schaik of Pretoria, while the volume of poetry was to contain only a short appreciative introduction and brief biographical details.

"I always find it somewhat terrifying to see my own name in print," Marais replied when told of the new plans. "Please be merciful with the biography!"

He then replied to all Preller's questions in a long letter, ending with these significant words: "As you say, life is a mosaic of memories – in my case mostly painful ones if I ever allow my consciousness to plunge into the dark stream."

In Marais's life one can in a few cases trace the development of a poem. Here, in the words "dark stream", we find the embryo from which at least part of the poem "Diep Rivier" (Deep River) was to develop in Heidelberg later – a key poem in the search to the enigmas of Eugène Marais's personality.

"The dark stream". To plunge into this dark stream is the whole purpose of psycho-analysis. No wonder Dr. Moll did not get very far.

As far as Frans Daubenton was later to remember, Marais usually had enough work during the five months in which he treated him. However, he and Coetsee were still not getting along very well and before the end of the year he had a new partner, Cecil Lawrance. The firm's new letterhead – Marais & Lawrance – still bore the same address, box number and telephone number, making it clear that Coetsee had been pushed out (or left) and not Marais.

We do not know exactly what had happened here but Marais's old friend, Fanie van Wyk of Erasmus, for whom he was acting when he started the partnership in Heidelberg, lost money in the process.

On the date of the letter to Preller in which Marais referred to the "dark stream", 11 May, he was treated twice by Daubenton and ten days later the doctor had to call four times during the course of one night.

Eugène's seventy-three year old brother, Senator Charles Marais, died only a few days later. Someone who knew Charles well thinks that he no longer wanted to live. "He'd got a fish-bone in his throat and choked. He did not want help. It was virtually suicide."

More than forty years before, Eugène had accepted this brother as his real father. Whether or not his death had anything to do with it is unclear, but in the week of Charles's death, Eugène's account with Daubenton was closed. The doctor, who did not know of Charles's death, said in this regard: "I did not treat him again after that. At that stage I had reduced the dose to half a grain a day. He then started going to other doctors to get more."

The significance of that critical "half a grain" will become clear later.

In the meantime Marais received a neat account for £49.8.0 from Frans Daubenton – a quite staggering amount for 1923, and much more than Marais had. He had great trouble in scraping together £12.10.0.

Later in the year, without consulting Lawrance, he took £20 from the partnership's safe and handed it to his creditor together with Lawrance's .22 Savage.

Frans Daubenton accepted in good faith that the rifle belonged to Marais. Businesslike as always, he estimated the Savage's value at £10. This meant that Marais still owed him almost £7. When the account was not paid within a few months, he wrote off the remaining debt. It was quite a good gun.

3. The Singer of Suikerbosrand

After Frans Daubenton, by about the middle of 1923, A.G. Visser became Eugène Marais's doctor. One must bear in mind that even at that time Marais was something of a celebrity. It was a time of intense national feeling among the Afrikaners. Great pride was taken in the small number of successful poems which had been written in the developing language, Afrikaans. Some of Marais's poems, like "Mabalêl", about the black girl who was killed by the crocodile, Lalele, and "Winternag" were quite often recited in public to prove the potential of the new language.

A.G. Visser on the other hand, was completely unknown outside Heidelberg. In the nineties of the previous century some of his rhymes had been published in *Ons Klyntji*, a pioneering Afrikaans magazine, and from time to time he would write verses to amuse his children and friends. In the six years which remained of his life at that stage, encouraged by Eugène Marais, he was to produce four volumes of poetry and to become a national hero, one of the most popular writers in Afrikaans literature.

The man Eugène Marais came to know in mid-winter 1923 was of average height, exceptionally neat, with refined, aristocratic features. "Crisp" was the word that came to mind when one met him for the first time. He was about forty-four, seven years younger than his new patient.

Like Marais he had studied in Europe. After a clash with the military authorities in the Boer War, he had resigned as principal of the school in Carnarvon in the Cape Colony and gone to Edinburgh to study medicine. Like Marais he was a widower. His wife, also called Lettie, had died in Heidelberg only three years before. Like so many others Visser soon fell under Marais's spell. They were often seen together. When Andries drove to a farm in the district, Eugène would go along. When Andries was waiting for a patient in his rooms, Eugène would sit talking to him. Sometimes Visser would discuss specific cases with him, and he was surprised at Marais's knowledge of medicine.

Visser was a kindly, compassionate man. As a doctor, his great passion was surgery. "If I could not operate, I would not practise," he admitted to a colleague, and he was certainly an extremely able surgeon, his particular pride being his "buttonhole surgery", the ability to remove, for example, an appendix through an incredibly tiny incision. The minute scars he left on his patients enabled other doctors who knew of this ability to recognise his patients twenty, thirty and even forty years later during examinations.

He operated frequently – tonsils, appendices, stomach operations, accidents – and he enjoyed it. According to some of his colleagues, he was rather too fond of it. When his younger colleague in Heidelberg, Frans Daubenton, told him of a nasty accident in which Daubenton had had to take the injured man to a specialist to have an eye removed, Visser asked him: "Why didn't you take out the eye yourself?"

Visser would no doubt have done it himself – because he knew how to do it, because it would have saved time and suffering and because it would have cost the patient less. For Visser the latter was an important consideration. In fact he thought so little of fees that accounts were often not sent out at all and there were quite a number of patients – probably including Eugène Marais – who never paid but were faithfully treated.

Marais often went to see Visser at his house. After Lettie Visser's death in 1920, Visser's stepmother had moved to Heidelberg from Carnarvon to take care of his housekeeping and to look after the three children, Andries, eight years old when Marais met him for the first time, the five year old Annatjie, and the youngest, Willie, after whose birth his mother had died three years before. Eugène very soon made friends with them, as he had already befriended all the children in all the houses he visited: the Swarts, the Pistorius', the Daubentons, and others. When a fascinating tape-recording of childhood memories concerning Eugène Marais was played to Andries thirty years later, he remarked: "It was exactly that kind of magical world which he created for us as well."

As Marais had done long before, Dr. Andries Visser had by now discovered that intense longing for a dead beloved did not exclude interest in others. Lettie – the Laetitia of his poems – had died in 1920. Early in 1921 an attractive young teacher, Marie de Villiers, came to teach at Heidelberg.

Marie was a member of the Afrikaner aristocracy. Her father, nicknamed Japie Helpmekaar (help each other), had taken the initiative in collecting a fund to cover the fines imposed on burghers who had taken part in the rebellion of 1914 to 1915, amounting to several hundreds of thousands of pounds. Oom Japie offered to contribute £500 provided 500 other people gave £100 each. In the event, the contributions greatly exceeded the target figure.

Visser met Marie only a few days after her arrival at a birthday dinner given by the Rev. A.J. Louw. She had not yet come of age. There were mutual stirrings of love even at the first meeting, she herself was to say later.

Now, in 1923, the year in which he got to know Eugène Marais, she and Andries were going steady.

The beautiful Miss Marie was one of about twenty teachers who lived in the Transvalia Girls' Boarding House. Marais regularly saw her in A.G. Visser's house, which was the town's social and musical centre. One of her good friends was Lucy Joubert. Soon the two couples started going out together. Lucy, an able, attractive young teacher of about twenty-eight, had been unlucky in love. "My heart has been broken," she was fond of telling Marie. "Why shouldn't I break men's hearts?"

However, she found it hard to do this to Eugène Marais.

"Eugène, with his beautiful grey eyes, was himself a breaker of hearts," her friend Marie was to relate later. "I remember the way he would look at a woman, as if he wanted to tell her something, as if he had something on his mind which he would not express in words. He had more than charm – one could almost call it magnetism. And he was a magnificent talker, with well-considered conclusions and views on a much higher plane than my young friends and I were accustomed to. But he abused his attractiveness – made young girls fall in love with him and then left them in the lurch."

These words reveal that the cynicism towards young women which had been developing in Marais for many years had become prominent by the time he lived in Heidelberg. At that time Marais was fifty-two but he found no trouble in enchanting Lucy Joubert.

"What will I talk to Eugène about tonight?" Lucy would ask Marie in the boarding house. "He knows so much. What do you and Doctor talk about?"

She thought he was wonderful. When they went for a walk and looked at the falling leaves and he would say something like "'Footfalls silent as the falling leaf' – forgive me for quoting myself," it was not so much what he said that impressed her as the manner in which he said it, effortlessly, without boasting, suave.

Frictions between him and the Rev. Louw were beginning to show by now. The Pope of the Highveld had made a firm rule that the lady teachers had to be home at ten every evening. When they went to the bioscope, as the cinema was called – there were two shows a week – they had to leave before the end of the film. But when Andries and Eugène took the girls to Johannesburg in Andries's Hupmobile, as frequently happened, they were obliged to cheat and then Marie and Lucy – like many other teachers – would slip inside through a window. The Rev. Louw had an agent in the Concordia Male Boarding House, J.P. Malan, who kept him informed of such contraventions of his rules.

Such pettiness annoyed Marais intensely, and he did not hesitate to say so frankly. He was never seen in church. He openly proclaimed his conviction that the dogma of the immaculate conception was a childish one. The Rev. Louw could not stand him.

Visser was no fonder of the minister's inflexible rules, but he knew how to handle him. The parsonage was just opposite Visser's house. While the two of them stood eating peaches one day, the Rev. Louw reprimanded his neighbour for peeling the fruit.

"After all, the best lies just under the skin," he commented.

The next day Visser sent the minister a basket of prickly pears with a message: "I hope you eat these according to your own recipe."

On another occasion the minister, notorious for his endless sermons, consulted Dr. Visser about a sore throat.

"Try to make your sermons shorter," the doctor recommended. "That would be kinder to both your throat and your congregation."

Eugène greatly appreciated Andries' humour, which included his humorous verse. His love poems, on the other hand, were too sentimental for Marais's taste. Encouraged by Eugène, Visser began writing more. They would frequently discuss his attempts and on one occasion they held a competition by each doing an Afrikaans adaptation of the English poem "Peggy Mitchell".

A literary evaluation of Visser's poetry and prose is not relevant here. The incalculable value of his work lay in the fact that it taught Afrikaners to read their own language – and to enjoy it! There is no doubt that Marais, a far greater poet, managed to improve the quality of Visser's poetry by means of hints and advice, if only by removing the worst sentimentalities. On the human level, Visser gave much more than he received. The more Marais saw of him, the greater his admiration became. There were many facets to Visser's personality. He was the perfect gentleman but he could be mischievous at times.

Charles te Water, Marais's friend from Pretoria, was to remember an occasion shortly after the Boer War when he and Visser were students in Edinburgh:

"There were three of us and we were walking to the S A Club in the University Union. On the way an attractive young woman came along pushing a baby in a pram. When the child saw Visser it waved its little hand saying, 'Papa! Papa!' Without hesitation, Visser came to a halt, took off his hat extremely courteously, bowed deeply and said: 'Madame, I have not the pleasure of remembering that exquisite moment. Have you?' She blushed with pleasure."

His humour could be unexpectedly earthy. When a Heidelberg farmer asked him why another farmer had twelve normal sons and a midget, he replied: "While you have timber you cut yokes. When you don't have enough wood left you make yoke-pins."

He delighted in telling of the occasion when he had practised in Steytlerville and had to spend a night on a farm in the company of an English doctor. The drought at the time was so severe that the cows had dried up. The English doctor had noticed this and when he was given coffee with milk the next morning he was greatly surprised. "How is this possible?" he asked Visser.

"Didn't you see our host's daughter nursing her child?"

"How disgusting!"

"On the contrary," Visser replied, "the height of hospitality."

And in that other, dark world in which Eugène Marais could find no room for humour, the world of his dependence, how were relations between him and Andries Visser there?

Visser's knowledge of morphine addiction was no greater than that of the average country doctor. His interests lay elsewhere. But he was a compassionate, understanding man. And when Visser told Marais: "Old boy, we'll have to get you off this thing," Marais resolved to exert himself to the utmost.

And indeed, by the second half of 1923 Visser had managed to do the seemingly impossible: by the end of that year Marais's average morphine intake broke through the barrier of half a grain a day below which he had always found it so difficult to go.

At that stage Visser was felled by an unexpected heart attack.

4. A Vacation in Durban

Frans Daubenton examined Visser thoroughly and diagnosed angina pectoris. Given the right treatment he would probably recover, he told Visser's stepmother and the Rev. Louw, who had come over at once to see whether he could be of assistance.

Then, correct as always, Daubenton called in Andrew Watt, a Johannesburg physician, to supervise the case. Visser was treated in the hospital in Heidelberg.

In the meantime Rev. Louw set about finding a locum. His choice fell on a young medical man, Nico Kestell, who had just completed his medical studies in Holland, and whose parents the minister knew well – he was in fact related to Kestell's mother.

Early in 1924 the twenty-eight year old Dr. Kestell arrived in Heidelberg. By now Visser was over the worst, but he had been ordered to recuperate in Hermanus, a popular seaside resort in the Cape. When Kestell saw him off at the station, Visser said:

"Oh, by the way, I haven't told you about the man who has to get morphine. He's an attorney, a certain Marais. I give him a quarter of a grain a day."

Young Nico Kestell boarded with the Rev. Louw, across the street from Visser's rooms, where he now worked. At five o'clock that afternoon Eugène Marais arrived at the consulting rooms. Kestell had heard that his patient had long been addicted to morphine, and he looked at him with interest.

Marais wore a blue blazer, a neat bowtie, white melton trousers and white shoes – his uniform during the Heidelberg days, remembered by almost everyone who knew him, although most of them mistook his white shoes for tackies.

Kestell had read Visser's notes. He knew that Marais was fifty-two years old and found to his surprise that the man did not look much older than his years. In fact, he seemed quite healthy, although unnaturally pale.

Kestell fumbled a bit awkwardly with his patient's card and then asked:

"You take morphine, don't you, a quarter of a grain?"

"Half a grain."

"But Dr. Visser said ..."

"That's right," Marais replied calmly, "but Dr. Nixon treated me while Dr. Visser was ill, and he gave me half a grain."

Kestell, young and inexperienced, was caught off-guard and said hesitantly: "You'll have to excuse me. I shall have to phone Dr. Nixon."

Eugène Marais shrugged tiredly. "All right."

It took a while to get Nixon on the line. When Kestell had told his story, the English doctor said impatiently:

"Yes, I gave the bastard what he wanted, he was so insistent."

Kestell looked embarrassed but if Marais had heard the words he did not let on. He had already taken off his coat and rolled up his shirtsleeves for the injection.

Now Kestell was fumbling with the flat white tablets.

"May I help you?" Marais asked politely. "You melt the tablets in a teaspoon. Use a match or a Bunsen burner. It is then mixed with water in the syringe. One tablet is half a grain."

By the next day Kestell had regained his composure to such an extent that he refused to give Marais more than a quarter of a grain.

During the ten weeks of Andries Visser's absence, Kestell would sometimes give another quarter of a grain to a black messenger who came to collect it in emergencies. However, he never let Marais have more than half a grain in twenty-four hours.

How Marais survived this harsh regimen is not known. Perhaps he supplemented the doses by going to other doctors or by using substitutes. Chlorodyne could still be bought over the counter and at that time Dover's powder consisted of fifty per cent opium and fifty per cent ipecacuanha.

If Marais regarded it as a humiliation to be restricted to a limited dose by a junior like Kestell, he did not show it. Kestell had very few patients. He was far too young to inspire confidence. A pregnant woman who had booked an appointment with Visser told him roundly that he was too young to deliver her baby and went to another doctor. He thus had plenty of time on his hands and he and Marais would often spend time together chatting.

Marais told him how in the Waterberg he had used ten tablets a day, and had bought additional opium from the Indians. When Kestell asked the inevitable question of how he had become addicted to morphine, Marais told him a story which may have matched his opinion of the inexperienced young doctor.

"We were trekking through East Africa to bring ammunition to the Boer forces. In Lourenço Marques I became severely ill with malaria and the Portuguese simply put a bottle of opium tincture next to my bed and told me to drink as much as I needed. That is how I became accustomed to it."

In the second school quarter of that year Andries Visser returned to Heidelberg. He was far from well, however, and his vision was impaired. With his right eye he could see only straight in front of him, not to the sides.

Young Dr. Kestell departed, and Visser resumed his practice.

His illness had changed him. He had trouble in adjusting to the scotoma in his eye, and he could no longer work as hard as before.

It did not take him long to realize that Marais's treatment was not going according to plan. He was on a low dosage, but he was obviously suffering because of it, and Visser found it impossible to decrease the quantity still further.

At this time, possibly acting on a hint given by Visser, Connie

Pistorius invited Marais to accompany him on a trip to Durban. It was growing cold on the Highveld.

By this time Connie had bought a second Vauxhall. This one was a limousine, larger, more comfortable and more luxurious than the open sedan. It had silver flower vases beside the seats and a magnificent engine. Travelling like royalty they set off for the grand holiday home in Goble Road, Stanford Hill, where Connie spent a few months every winter.

Eugène had by now also lost his second partner, Lawrance, possibly as a result of the incident with the rifle and the £20. He was virtually broke, and Connie had little trouble in persuading him to accept £10 in pocket money.

In Durban, away from the conspiracy devised by Heidelberg's doctors and chemists to deprive him of the one thing worth living for, Marais stepped around the first corner he came to and bought a large supply of morphine, presumably using a prescription form taken from the rooms of one of the Heidelberg doctors.

For months he had been yearning for a decent shot. For months he had been waging the impossible battle day and night. At this stage his nerves had worn so raw that breaking out was essential.

The details of the incident are obscure, but the holiday turned into a fiasco. And – from Marais's point of view much worse – rumours of the débâcle somehow reached Heidelberg. The episode concerning Lawrance's rifle had been kept fairly quiet. Only a few friends knew about it. It is also possible that Marais paid his partner back or that Connie Pistorius did it for him.

But by the winter of 1924 everyone in Heidelberg who knew about Eugène Marais also knew that he was addicted to morphine and soon after his return from Durban it was general knowledge that he had broken loose there and caused a scandal.

At this stage Marais decided to abandon his legal practice completely. It had never really prospered anyway and was now doing extremely poorly.

Apparently he was by now no longer living with Mrs. Swart. In fact, as far as Dr. Nico Kestell could remember, he was by then living "in the worse of the two hotels", a place where the telephone seldom worked and where the lights were switched off at eleven. For some time he also boarded with Edith Goodwin, typist and bookkeeper for a businessman from Johannesburg, Hubert Dale, who visited Heidelberg on business once a week. One of the rooms in the suite had become vacant and she allowed Marais to stay there for a while.

Another old Heidelberger remembers that he also lodged with people called Tullema.

So many moves – and every time his clothes were older and his luggage more meagre. As always he would give away his most prized possessions to people whom he liked, and now there was no longer any money with which to buy replacements.

5. Four Houses

Early in 1925 Connie Pistorius and Andries Visser decided that it would be best for Eugène to live close to his doctor. Eugène duly moved to the house of a widow, Mrs. Roux, in Van der Westhuizen Street, only a few houses away from Dr. Visser.

Not far from Mrs. Roux lived another widow, an attractive and still young woman named Brenda Steyn.

Brenda Steyn's late husband, Paul*, was one of four children. Paul himself had died two years before. His elder brother, Eric, was a notorious criminal, whose misdeeds had a decisive influence on the lives of the other brothers and the only sister.

Was it mere chance that caused the paths of Eugène Marais and Brenda Steyn to cross? Ever since his youth he had been interested in criminal psychology, in the inheritability of criminal tendencies and in the effect which crime could have on innocent people brought into contact with it.

Chance or not, during the next eighteen months four houses were to become his entire world: that of the widow Roux, where he boarded; that of Brenda Steyn; that of Stephen and Adinda Eyssen; and the house next door to theirs, where Dr. Andries Visser lived with his three children and his step-mother. Andries Visser gave him friendship – intelligent friendship – understanding and medical

*In view of the background and further developments of this story, the names in this family have been changed. Certain sensational facts have been suppressed to prevent identification.

care. He also gave him humour. Seldom had Eugène found such a keen sense of humour in anyone. Puns, in both languages, and often so subtle that none but his most intimate friends would catch on – were part of Andries' way of talking. Soon there were a number of private jokes between them. To Eugène, except during times of the greatest misery, humour remained a necessity of life. "A lovely, happy, amused chuckle", was how a young girl-friend described his laugh. And when something really amused him, he could laugh until the tears ran down his cheeks.

The friendship between Eugène Marais and Andries Visser is a famous one in Afrikaans literature, and it has not been exaggerated. "I think of him daily with tears and unavailing regret," Marais was to write to a friend after Visser's death. Never, not even in Haylett, had he had such a friend as a doctor and such a doctor as a friend.

Stephen and Adinda Eyssen gave him Culture. Adinda liked to recite, and she also played the cello; Stephen sang, played the piano and composed. In their eyes Eugène Marais was an important cultural asset to their street. However, his actions could sometimes be extremely peculiar.

He once spent an evening entertaining Eyssen on the similarities between rural Roman and Afrikaans poetry. Eyssen was impressed. Would Eugène not address the school on the subject?

"Certainly," replied Marais, "but only if we can do it on a Saturday morning."

To Eyssen's relief Marais was punctual for once but he flatly refused to address the children inside a hall. "No, we must go outside," he insisted, and when all the children were assembled in the playground in the chilly wind, Marais announced: "Mr. Eyssen is labouring under a misapprehension. I have no intention of discussing the similarities between rural Roman poetry and our own. I shall talk about the Battle of Thermopylae."

At all times Marais (who, according to his son, had no ear for music whatsoever) would insist on listening to musical recitals given by the Eyssens: "The one song after the other," Mrs. Eyssen was to relate later.

One morning he arrived at her house and asked her whether she could invite a number of people for a musical evening that night. "I did so, and all the guests, armed with their music, duly arrived – all except Marais."

The Eyssens were frankly baffled. Something quite unforeseen must have happened.

Then, while they were at supper the next evening, Marais knocked gently at the door. Why had he not turned up the previous evening? He replied: "I no longer felt like it in the end, but I have come early tonight so that you can sing many songs for me."

As we have seen, some of Marais's poems were frequently recited in public.

On the evening of Adinda Eyssen's triumph, when she gave her rendition of "Mabalêl" in the Heidelberg City Hall, Marais himself sat next to Andries Visser, constantly making whispered remarks, holding his head in mock horror: "Oh God, why does she do that? No, no, not that!"

"One must admit that she recited the poem rather melodramatically," relates a young lady who had been sitting next to Andries and Eugène.

But Eugène, always the perfect gentleman, walked to the front of the hall after the recital and helped Adinda Eyssen from the stage.

His landlady, Mrs. Roux, gave Marais little more than lodging. He lived in a one-roomed stone cottage behind the larger house, a rather sombre little place with a cypress on either side of the single door.

It was in the last of the four houses that he found love. Brenda Steyn's husband had left behind several young children, of whom the eldest, Albertus, was now in Standard Five.

One of the few luxuries Eugène Marais had retained was a microscope. When Albertus visited Oom Eugène's little outhouse, he often found him studying ants, flies or other insects. When Marais visited a certain kloof or ravine outside Heidelberg, as he did three or four times a week, Albertus and Andries, Dr. Visser's eldest son, would frequently be invited to come along. Sometimes Marais would break open a termitary and insert several ferocious red ants into the breach. The frail-looking termite warriors would overpower the intruders at once, glue their legs together and drag them away. After a shower Eugène and the boys would follow the flight of the kings and queens and watch how the queen, once she had landed, would shake off her wings, point her abdomen into the air and send out the inaudible, invisible signals which would lure the male to her. Later Marais bought Albertus his first crystal set – an inexpensive early radio receiver – and showed the boy how to receive his own invisible, inaudible signs.

For the other Steyn children, too, he was able to do a great deal to compensate for the death of their father. But in this particular case Marais was more interested in the mother than in the daughters.

Brenda Steyn, born a Morgan, was thirty-five – nineteen years younger than Marais – and an attractive, lively and intelligent woman.

Even now, after all these years, he was still seeking Lettie – or the dream she had become – in every pretty or gentle or sympathetic young woman he met. Brenda was pretty, even beautiful, soft-spoken and refined. However, her self-confidence had taken a few knocks. She had very little money and she was something of a loner. It was not until after she had met Eugène Marais that she began to blossom. It was the 1920's, a time of emancipation in many fields. For the first time in eighty years a respectable woman was permitted to use make-up. Brenda used a little lipstick, a dash of face-powder and a touch of eye-shadow – things which Eugène may last have seen on Susanne and never on women of his own "class". When Brenda dressed up to receive visitors in the evening Eugène could hardly believe that she was the same person he saw working in the house during the day.

Marais himself, to the surprise of many people in Heidelberg, tried to repair the damage wrought by the years by applying talcum powder, and he again started using perfume as an after-shave lotion.

Nineteen twenty-five became a year of hope. The efforts of his friends and son to get his poems into print had not been in vain. During the course of the year the volume was published by the Nasionale Pers in Cape Town. It contained a short foreword by Gustav Preller.

Marais was pleased. The publishers had done an excellent job. In the same year Preller's longer biographical sketch of Marais was published as one of the essays in *Historiese Opstelle* (Historical Essays) by Van Schaik in Pretoria and at about the same time Van Schaik published Visser's debut, *Gedigte* (Poems), containing Marais's rather carefully worded introduction and recommendation. (Only after Visser's death was his appreciation for Visser as a man to affect his literary judgement and was he to refer to the " … poet … whose shoelaces I was unworthy to untie".)

In this relatively peaceful period Marais also managed to get down to recording some of the termite observations he had carried out in the Waterberg more than ten years before. Late that year the first six chapters of *Die Siel van die Mier* (The Soul of the Ant) appeared intermittently in *Die Huisgenoot*, which at that time was as popular a family magazine in South Africa as was the *Saturday Evening Post* in the United States.

Writing now became Marais's only source of income, and he was not writing very much. For the first time in his life his clothes began to look less than impeccable, perhaps ever shabby. For medical treatment and medicine he went to Andries Visser, for food to Brenda Steyn, for pocket money to Connie Pistorius.

His only son, Eugène – Eugène Charles – assisted him financially whenever his father asked him, and he asked only when there was no other way out.

Young Eugène, who was now a young man of thirty, had been practising as an attorney in the small Transvaal town of Brits for some time. He had left Pretoria the year before when his godmother – Eugène Nielen's sister, Sophie Ueckerman – had left her house in Maré Street to move to another part of Pretoria. At that time Brits was no more than a huddle of small buildings in the bush northwest of Pretoria. Here the young man was eking out a precarious existence. So powerful was the influence of his father, according to a close friend of young Eugène, that this gifted and able young man "went to bury himself at Brits … and never begat any children because he did not want any child who might take after his father." (It is certainly true that young Eugène never married or had any children of his own.)

Instead of marrying, he maintained close relations with his godmother and her family. Travelling on the "toot-toot", a bus which ran regularly on the railway line between Brits and Pretoria at the time, he went to the capital every weekend to spend a day or two with them.

Heidelberg never saw him.

6. The Great Yearning

Early 1926, only ten years before Eugène Marais's death, saw the birth of two important relationships in his life.

One was a love affair with the young woman, Brenda Steyn, who lived on his street. The second was a friendship with an extremely wealthy man, eighty years old, whom Marais was never to meet but who was to remain a good friend by correspondence for some years.

The old man was Wilhelm Spilhaus. When Marais's friend Advocate Charles te Water was on his way back to South Africa after a visit to Europe early in 1926, he met the charming old gentleman on board ship – eighty years old but as lively as a youngster with his bright blue eyes, rosy complexion, charming smile and hearty handshake. Spilhaus had arrived in Cape Town from Hamburg in 1869 and started a business which had made him a small fortune.

Was he still working, Te Water asked him.

Yes, two of his sons were partners in the firm Wm. Spilhaus, but he still went to the office every morning. In the afternoons he returned to his farm, Hohenort, in Constantia, to read, write letters and garden.

Te Water found him excellent company. He could talk about virtually anything. Eventually they got onto literature, then onto Afrikaans literature – Spilhaus could speak Afrikaans fluently – and finally onto Eugène Marais. In his cabin Te Water happened to have a cutting of an article written by Marais which he showed to Spilhaus. He also told him about *The Soul of the Ape*.

Spilhaus' interest had been aroused. From his luxurious estate in Constantia he wrote to the impoverished man in the outside room in Heidelberg, so wisely and tactfully that Marais responded:

"The interest you have expressed and your kindly consideration induces me to break a rule I was forced to adopt – not to reply through the post to any communication unless it was of direct value."

Thus began a correspondence, stretching over some years, which was to lead to some of Marais's best known writings in the English language.

Apart from Spilhaus' obvious knowledge and genuine, informed interest in Marais's work, there was one significant reason why Marais found him an acceptable correspondent. They had never met, which meant that Spilhaus – or so Marais could convince himself – was unaware of his morphine addiction.

Spilhaus began sending Marais books which he thought might interest him. They exchanged comments about the work of Charcot, about the Cambridge classification of instinct, about insanity, about evolution, about Freud, repeatedly about Freud.

In clerical circles Marais's free-thinking magazine articles had not gone unobserved. For one thing the Reverend Louw was greatly disturbed by his acceptance of the theory of evolution.

"Wandering Tales is the right name," he told Dr. Andries Visser. "The man's mind is wandering."

Later, when he attacked Marais personally, the latter replied: "Don't argue with me, Dominee, it's a matter between you and the Almighty. I really have nothing at all to do with the creation of the universe."

It gave Marais great pleasure to report this reply in a letter to Spilhaus.

Other influential people, too, were again beginning to take an interest in Marais.

When the prominent Cape Town art critic and author, Bernard Lewis, and his wife, Lizzie, came to visit the Eyssens, they very much wanted to meet Marais. To the Eyssens' relief, Marais kept the appointment but he greatly embarrassed them by hardly saying a word all night.

In April, the month after he had started corresponding with Spilhaus, Prof. Johannes J. Smith, probably South Africa's greatest lexicographer, who had shortly before started working on the standard dictionary of the Afrikaans language, went to see Marais in Heidelberg.

Marais made an extremely favourable impression on him. Writing to Gustav Preller, Smith said: "I found Eugène Marais an extremely remarkable man and his civilised ways as well as his great scientific gifts struck me deeply ... I cannot tell you how glad I am that men like you and Doctor Visser take an interest in Marais. He needs your help."

No doubt Smith did not realise how true these words were. Marais was heading for a new disaster, a disaster which was to strike by the middle of 1926.

Only much later would intimate relations between two people who love each other but cannot marry, or prefer not to do so, become relatively acceptable. In 1926 it was unthinkable in a town like Heidelberg. But of course it happened nevertheless.

There is a story that Eugène Marais wanted to marry Brenda Steyn but that she declined because she would then lose her widow's pension. If her pitifully small income were to fall away as well, how would they live?

However, a woman who knew both Marais and Mrs. Steyn well denies this emphatically: "She would have married him, whatever the consequences. She was madly in love. But I don't think he ever intended to marry."

At about that time Andries Visser's six year old son, Willie, one of Marais's favourites, asked him: "Oom Eugène, will you marry again?"

"Now you're driving me into a corner, old boy," he replied.

Eugène Marais was to remain in Heidelberg for some months more. At this stage the story becomes obscure. It seems as if his morphine consumption increased tremendously, probably past the stage where it had been when Dr. Daubenton had started his treatment.

During these months – January, February, April and June – further instalments of *The Soul of the Ant* appeared in *Die Huisgenoot*. One of the few advantages enjoyed by a young language is that it can constantly produce new "firsts". *The Soul of the Ant* was the first popular scientific work in Afrikaans and it was eminently readable. It was an immediate and outstanding success and it greatly increased the circulation of the magazine. In Cape Town, when the flow of articles from Heidelberg was interrupted, I.D. du Plessis, the young man who had to edit them, worriedly mentioned this to his editor, who replied, fairly close to the truth: "Oh, Eugène Marais must have gone up river with some young widow again."

At this time *Die Huisgenoot* also published three of Marais's recent poems, all of them products of his friendship with A.G. Visser. One of them, "Die Stille Rusplaas", was based on Swinburne's "Garden of Proserpine" and it closed with these characteristic lines:

vergeefs kom weer die Somer	Summer returns in vain
want droomloos is die Dromer,	for the dreamer is dreamless
verdiep in ewig' nag	absorbed in eternal night

The corresponding lines in Swinburne's own poem read:

> Then star nor sun shall waken …
> Nor days nor things diurnal;
> Only the sleep eternal
> In an eternal night.

Proserpine is the goddess of sleep. Eugène Marais himself was living in a dream. He was riding a wave of morphine and love and the inevitable happened.

When he consulted Andries Visser about it and the doctor reacted in a manner which Marais regarded as overly prim and proper, Marais replied: "It's not the first time. I've done it before."

"But, my friend, how on earth can you go and do such things?"

And Marais replied: "Oh, come off it, if it hadn't been me, it would have been somebody else."

These unfeeling, devil-may-care words represent the peak of the cynical approach to women that one sees gradually developing in Marais ever since the oath of chastity he took in 1892.

An old Heidelberg inhabitant says: "Mrs. Steyn got into trouble, but a solution was found." An equally reliable witness confirms this.

The woman as goddess – the woman as possession, as an object: in his relationship with Brenda Steyn it seems as if Marais had completely adopted the latter course. It is possible that he wanted to prove himself: morphine is said to cause impotence at an early age, and by this time Marais was fifty-five. It may be that he had applied the philosophy of life of his other girlfriend, Lucy Joubert, in a perverted sense to himself: "My life has been destroyed, why should I not destroy the lives of others?"

These are all possibilities. But the probability is that he loved Brenda Steyn nevertheless.

"Die groot verlange wat my nooit verlaat" – "The great yearning which never leaves me". These words come from one of Marais's most famous poems, on which he may have started working during his time in Heidelberg. The words refer to more than a woman. But to the extent in which they refer to a woman they also refer to Brenda Steyn, perhaps specifically to her.

Now, in the winter of 1926, Eugène Marais was overwhelmed by the Furies of guilt and remorse. He was injecting ten grains of morphine into his veins every day – forty times more than the minimum he had once attained under Andries Visser's treatment. He was seldom completely himself.

7. Cornered

After breaking off with Brenda Steyn, Eugène Marais, as if willingly subjecting himself to the harshest possible punishment, entered the portals of a torture camp in the district of Heidelberg. The place was called Steenkampskraal, and it was to leave him with such bitter memories, that he was never to speak of it.

In this place his tormentor was not one of the people who cared for him, but the monster he had been nurturing for more than thirty years in his breast, the devil which threatened to tear his insides apart at every attempt to exorcise it.

Andries Visser and Connie Pistorius had decided that Eugène could not carry on the way he was going. Visser went to see Mr. Doors Meyer, owner of the farm Steenkampskraal, about nine miles west of Heidelberg. Would the Meyers take care of Mr. Marais while he underwent the withdrawal treatment which had become impossible in Heidelberg? Oom Doors agreed. He would keep the supply and hand it over only according to Visser's instructions. His two strong sons, Doorsie, thirty-three, and Louis, twenty-nine, were to sleep with Marais in his room to watch over him.

Oom Doors and his wife, Tant Corrie, were very conscious of their responsibility. Dr. Visser had told them: "Advocate Marais can become Chief Justice of this country if you can cure him – otherwise he's done for. He's taking enough morphine every week to kill sixty-five people."

At the beginning Eugène Marais was only vaguely conscious of all these arrangements. During the first two days of his stay on the farm he knew only the inside of the room in which he was kept.

"He seemed to be in a dream," Louis Meyer said. "We tried to get to know him, but he paid no attention at all to us. Mostly, he simply lay on his bed. He was deathly pale, completely without appetite. And when he occasionally came to dinner, my mother always had to coax him to eat something."

As always after great crises in his life, his possessions were now very meagre. He had lost or given away or spoilt most of them.

"There was a sort of box with his stuff in it," said Louis. "I remember some suits of clothes – but he never wore those. His daily dress was a pair of white tackies without laces, a pair of white trousers, a tie which served as a belt and a little black blazer. There were not many books. I remember two – about the monkeys of the world."

During these first few weeks Dr. Visser kept his patient's quota high enough to prevent withdrawal symptoms but much lower than the level on which he had been when he left Heidelberg.

Once a week old Sturie – Stuurman Barry, a faithful Bushman farm labourer of about sixty years old – was sent to Heidelberg on horseback early in the morning to fetch the next seven days' supply from Dr. Visser. He had strict instructions not to take along any notes from Mr. Marais and under no circumstances to bring the medicine to the boss himself but always to take it to the madam.

Very gradually Marais became conscious of the world around him. Steenkampskraal lay on the Suikerbos river and was about eight hundred morgen in extent. It was excellent cattle country. Standing on the high stoep one could see far out over the fields. To the left was the road to Heidelberg and to the right there was a wind-pump and a large patch of eucalyptus trees. Still further over to the right, at the side of the house, were the fruit trees – grapefruit, oranges, tangerines, peaches, apricots, walnuts, almonds – and behind the house the stables and coach-house.

He saw it all, but what did it matter to him? In the foreground of his mind were still those last few nightmarish weeks in Heidelberg:

the humiliation, the shame, the yearning. What mattered to him now was not the farm, nor his books, nor his clothes, but only the white tablets, the syringe, the teaspoon and the candle he used to dissolve the tablets in water. This was what he craved, not only to reduce the suffering of withdrawal but to wipe out all his memories. And for this he was not given enough.

He asked for more, but the reply was always a stern denial. Andries Visser had deeply impressed the importance of the treatment on the Meyers. As the hours passed the craving for oblivion grew, eventually becoming unbearable. What did pride and shame matter if his whole being was crying out for relief? He asked once more, he pleaded, he argued. Finally, he fell on his knees before Oom Doors and begged him for an extra shot.

The Meyers did not have anything like Maria van Rooyen's experience. Doors Meyer could not bear to see so much suffering. The tablets were fetched and handed over.

But now there were not enough for the rest of the week. Again they were begged, beseeched to give him more. Louis and young Doors locked him in his room, but his screams and sobs were so heart-rending that they had to let him out.

For the rest of that week the remaining supply had to be administered in smaller quantities. On the day when the new consignment was expected, Marais's withdrawal symptoms had become so severe that he asked the Meyers to make him a boiling bath of water, so hot that one could hardly keep one's finger in it. He was still sitting in it when the younger son, Louis, brought him the syringe and the tablets.

The new supply brought temporary relief, but it was again less than the previous week. It was hardly enough to keep the suffering at bay. He still craved oblivion. With the cunning born of long experience, Marais found the remaining portion of that week's quota where the Meyers had hidden it behind a family portrait and injected it all at once. This was enough to cause semi-consciousness, but only for a while, and now there was nothing at all left for the rest of the week.

The Meyers had been warned against various possibilities. They took his shoes and hid them away. But in an early summer thunderstorm he slipped away from the farm in his bare feet and started making his way through the wet and muddy veld towards Heidelberg. The Meyers pursued him in a Cape cart and brought him back.

He was in his cell once more. He could take it no longer. He asked Doorsie, the older and more sympathetic of the two brothers, to come and talk to him. "Doorsie, please," he begged, "for God's sake, take your rifle and shoot me. I don't want to live any more. I can't live any more."

But he did live. Again and again in the weeks to follow the Meyers heard his nightmarish pleas: "Oh, dear God, only give me one tablet, I'm dying!" But because they knew that in the end this would only cause more misery, they did not yield again.

Gradually reality returned. There was still a deep and unappeasable yearning. But it was no longer unbearable. Andries Visser was kept informed of what was happening on the farm and he adapted the supply to what he heard. It was reduced gradually, week after week.

To give him something to do, Oom Doors got Marais a still. When it came to distilling brandy Eugène Marais was an expert. After all, he had served his apprenticeship in the Waterberg, where it was a fine art. "He mostly used peaches, prickly pears and apricots," said Doorsie Meyer. "I tasted some of the apricot brandy myself. I remember he had hundreds of empty bottles. He filled them all and sold them to the Kaffirs."

Advocate E.N. Marais, former Justice of the Peace, was contravening the law by the illegal distillation of liquor. He was compounding this contravention by illegally selling liquor to blacks. But who would hear about such things on an isolated farm?

The liquor helped him to subdue the withdrawal symptoms. "He'd get good and high just from tasting the quality of the stuff," Doorsie said. "Then he'd be a very clever man. Sometimes he'd have a whole bottle at a time."

But almost fifty years later Mr. Meyer adds: "He wasn't a drunkard, oh no," confirming that Marais, as always, was using liquor only as a substitute and an emergency measure.

And as he became accustomed to the smaller shots of morphine, his need for alcohol declined. He began to go on walks around the farm. He examined the koppies and ridges, looked at the cattle with the expert eye of one who had bought cattle for Cohen the butcher, studied the termites in their nests.

For months, so it seemed to the Meyers, the struggle raged, and for Eugène Marais, time ceased to exist. In actual fact the worst passed within a few weeks.

Suddenly, miraculously, he was again almost a normal human being.

8. Dialogue between the Writer and His Soul

In Heidelberg Marais had again started working on *The Soul of the Ape* without making much progress. The success of his termite articles, however, had given him the idea of adapting certain portions of the material from his *magnum opus* into a popularised form in Afrikaans. Here on the farm Steenkampskraal he wrote the first article in a series he called "Die Siel van die Aap" (The Soul of the Ape) and which he submitted to *Die Huisgenoot*, where it was published in December that year in two instalments.

This long, well written article dealt with nothing less than euphoric poisoning – in fact, addiction. Seldom in any literature had a writer spoken with such personal and recent experience. A terse opening paragraph introduces the theme:

> Euphoric poisoning is the tendency in man and the higher species of ape to the application of certain kinds of poison (mostly of vegetable origin) to bring about a psychological condition of joy or beatitude (euphoria) absent in the normal condition.

Poisons: his morphine; De Quincey's opium; the peach brandy which the blacks drank; the nicotine on which man and baboon become equally dependent; the cocaine of the South American Indian; the dagga (marijuana) of the farm's Korana shepherd (who had been so steeped in it – so Marais told the Meyers – that he could no longer be hypnotised). Each of these drugs was mentioned in the article except – significantly – morphine. (Nowhere, not even once, in all his writings, private or public, is the word ever mentioned. Only in the most intimate conversations, possibly only in one long discussion with his son, did he allow it to cross his lips. At all other times it was called his plug, his dose, his stuff, his supply, the necessary.)

A single, greatly sublimated reference to his own recent nightmare does appear in the article (the words are important enough to quote for a second time):

> From Tierra del Fuego to the icy plains of Greenland; from the Cape to Vladivostok, the traveller among primitive peoples hears only one beseeching word which echoes forever after in his nightmares: "Tobacco! Tobacco!"

The article became a confession of faith. In it Marais published for the first time his important theory of the inherited and the causal memory. All life, he said, was pain. In the "soul" of inherited memory the pressure and pain of the struggle for existence were distributed over a broad area, but in the primates (like the baboon) and man, with their causal memory, all pain was concentrated on a single point, consciousness. "And it is this perception of inherent psychological pain which man seeks to relieve by (among other methods) euphoric poisoning."

Almost immediately after these words, shortly before the end of the long article, one finds Marais's personal philosophy of life:

> In one of the oldest Egyptian manuscripts, the famous *Dialogue between the Writer and His Own Soul*, the poet comes to the conclusion that the mere existence of the soul is based on stress and pain, and that there is only one perfect solution: to make an end to one's existence!
>
> Much later – twenty centuries before Christ – the harpist of Pharaoh Seti I addresses the king. Life (even for the supreme monarch of all Egypt) is nothing but sorrow and misery, and over it all hangs the shadow of death. There is only one solution: Fill your palace, oh King of the north and south, with the daughters of music and dance; surround yourself with beauty and drink wine and wine again! ...
>
> The Persian poet Omar Khayyám sees the human soul as a city besieged by a black horde of sorrow and fear. But suddenly Mahmud appears, resplendent Allah-breathing Lord, wielding his hurricane-sword and the dark hordes are scattered to the winds.
>
> Resplendent Mahmud, in this case, is Alcohol. De Quincey, in words which for their poetic beauty have seldom been equalled in any literature, describes the endless sorrow and suffering of the soul.

> In all our philosophy echoes an eternal farewell; over all life hangs the shadow of death, the dishonour of the grave. But the blessed being carrying the keys to paradise now appears on the scene, building upon the bosom of darkness, out of the fantastic imagery of the brain, cities and temples beyond the art of Phidias and Praxiteles.
>
> The blessed Being, in this case, is Opium.

Seen against the background of what happened at Steenkampskraal, Marais's drift was clear. There was only one perfect solution: death. And as a surrogate for death there was – in Marais's case – morphine.

In this same period, although perhaps not yet in its final form, he wrote the enigmatic poem in which this philosophy – the coveted death and its surrogate, morphine – was in fact blended in verse:

> O, Diep Rivier, O, Donker Stroom
> hoe lank het ek gewag, hoe lank gedroom,
> die lem van liefde wroegend in my hart?
> – in jou omhelsing eindig al my smart.
> Blus uit, O Diep Rivier, die vlam van haat –
> die groot verlange wat my nooit verlaat.
> Ek sien van ver die glans van staal en goud,
> ek hoor die sag gedruis van waters diep en koud;
> ek hoor jou stem as fluistering in 'n droom
> Kom snel, O Diep Rivier, O Donker Stroom!
>
> O, Deep River, O, Dark Stream,
> how long have I waited, how long dreamed
> the blade of love twisting in my heart?
> – in your embrace is ended all my pain.
> Blow out, O Deep River, the flame of hate –
> the great longing which never leaves me.
> I see from afar the gleam of steel and gold,
> I hear the soft murmur of waters deep and cold;
> I hear your voice like whispering in a dream
> Come quick, O Deep River, O Dark Stream!

That death is meant is quite clear. But it is more than death. The images blend. *The blade of love* – the hated and beloved needle. *The great longing* – the longing for Brenda Steyn, perhaps for Lettie and all the others; but stronger still the unquenchable, ever-present yearning of the morphine addict for his panacea. *The gleam of steel and gold* – the syringe and its amber contents. Twice Marais uses the significant word "*dream*". *Come quick* – for always there was a lack of time, always the urgent desire.

If "This or Death", the motto of Marais's London book-plate in 1898, had dated from his period at Steenkampskraal, one would have interpreted it completely differently. In London it was: *Abstention from morphine in order to escape death, which is the wages of sin.* At the end of his Heidelberg period it was: *Morphine as a second choice after desired but dreaded death.*

One need not be surprised that here at Steenkampskraal Marais was capable of so much creative energy. "Dark Stream", at least, had been taking shape in his thoughts for some years.

And as always after a successful withdrawal treatment, he was full of newly found energy.

From Wilhelm Spilhaus came a letter in which the old gentleman proposed that Marais should publish his termite articles in book form in Germany. For the first time in almost five months Marais now wrote again to Spilhaus. "With reference to the proposed publication in Germany, I shall without question have to revise and recast the articles. They were written primarily for people who knew nothing about these things. I was continuously influenced (while writing them) by the unconscious idea that I was writing for children. This atmosphere will have to be removed for the European edition. There are also some bad errors."

And indeed he went to the ant again at Steenkampskraal, even if unsystematically. Frequently, when he and Doorsie went for a walk in the veld, he would poke open a termitary and show the younger man the nest's magnificent structure. Then he would tell him about the long shaft leading to the queen's hidden cell, and of the soldiers guarding it all.

Another investigation carried out at Steenkampskraal was of greater importance to him. This stemmed from certain theories in his articles about euphoric poisoning. According to Marais, the tiny bony projections on the human lower jaw were somehow related to the power of speech. In the Bushman, he believed, as in the ape, there were tiny holes instead of knobs, which indicated the Bushman's less advanced stage of development. On a Sunday morning he would walk into the mountains, accompanied by one of the black farm labourers, to disinter old graves and remove the skulls of the dead. "He was interested only in Bushman heads," Louis Meyer said. "He would pick up a head and look at it and throw it away – 'No good, it's a kaffir!'"

In the end he found seven Bushman skulls. Dr. Andries Visser (like Marais almost forty years before) took one away with him and had it made into a pen-holder. The skulls Marais kept in the house on Steenkampskraal were reinterred at the insistence of the boys' ninety year old grandmother, who lived with them.

That Eugène Marais was mentally well, that he was fit enough to dig up skulls, that he thought clearly and wrote extremely fluently, did not mean that he was accepting his imprisonment. He was in revolt. He wanted to escape.

The only problem was: where would he go? He had neither money nor prospects. Heidelberg? Andries Visser wanted him to complete the treatment and without the approval of Andries Visser and Connie Pistorius he could not possibly go back there after the fiasco of some months before.

There was no question of going to Fanie van Wyk in Erasmus. Besides, Dr. Mes was there too.

He could go and live with Hans Purekrans van Rooyen in the Waterberg (but how would he buy the stuff there?).

Brits? With his son? No.

Pretoria was impossible – unless Gustav Preller put him up and found him a job.

In the meantime a small ray of hope had appeared on the horizon. The directorship of the Pretoria Zoo had become vacant, an important post. Marais expected nothing of it at first, but Andries Visser and Connie Pistorius thought he might be a suitable applicant. Preller spoke to Tielman Roos about it, and invited Eugène to come and discuss the matter with him in Johannesburg. Connie Pistorius and old Dickenson collected him on the farm and took him to the city.

Tielman Roos had not changed at all. He spoke a great deal. Eugène should not give up hope. Everything would be all right. As far as the post at the zoo was concerned, he could do nothing. He was confident that Preller would look after that side of the business. There would be no problem. And that was the end of the interview.

They returned to the farm. During their visit to Johannesburg, Marais had been carefully watched. There were no incidents. Soon he was back in his cell.

Marais resented the withdrawal treatment because he had lost all hope. He was approaching sixty. He did not believe that he would ever again be able to get along without morphine.

Even so, in spite of his resistance, his health and well-being were steadily improving. So was his self-confidence. Later he again prodded Preller in a letter (the Jeppe to whom he refers was a member of the Zoological Council):

> I would also like to remind you not to forget to see Carl Jeppe. You could give him details about me with which he is probably not acquainted. The Huisgenoot people will also undoubtedly be willing to use their influence with Malan. It might be a good thing if you could write them a letter, if you will be so kind.

Preller, faithful friend that he was, did considerably more. With all his eloquence, he advocated Marais's appointment in a letter to the honourable gentleman Dr. D.F. Malan, Minister of the Interior.

> I venture to offer Your Honour the suggestion because I myself am convinced that you will find no one better suited to the post. Yes, I do not believe that I exaggerate by stating that his appointment will soon draw the attention of the entire world to our zoo and our fauna.

Now it was simply a question of waiting.

With one exception, Eugène Marais got along fairly well with everybody on the farm. He and Louis, who was rather touchy and short-tempered, did not hit it off at all. And the angrier Louis became, the more Marais delighted in pestering him.

In religious matters Louis was somewhat biased. Once, when Oom Doors had left the farm to go and buy trees at Pickstones, Marais conducted the divine service at the table. Although he refused to pray, he read the resounding Dutch text verses beautifully (it was seven years before the first translation of the Bible into Afrikaans) and then embarked on his own exegesis. Sometimes he would discuss the variations in the various translations of the Bible: the original Greek, the Dutch State Bible, the King James Version. In fact the original Greek Bible was itself a translation of the language which Christ and his disciples had spoken. How then could one believe any one Bible? Or he would talk about David and comment: "Now look, David was a man after God's heart, but where would you find a greater rascal?"

Louis would boil with rage, but he bided his time. One summer evening when they were sitting on the veranda, he asked: "Mr. Marais, how can you not believe in God when you look at those stars? Who touched them with his hands and who made the sun and the moon?"

Above them hung the magnificent Transvaal firmament which Eugène had learned to love as a ten year old boy on trek through the Kalahari and which he was later to describe with pantheistic admiration. But now the younger man's aggressive and pious tone annoyed him.

"The sun, the moon and the stars," he replied. "My dear fellow, they all come from a chicken egg." And in the shocked silence which followed, he added, "And I'll tell you another thing. You think you're Louis Meyer and I'm Eugène Marais, don't you? But I'm telling you now, there are no such people."

After this confrontation with Marais, Louis complained to his father. "I no longer want to attend the table service if Mr. Marais is there too," he said. "He delights in perverting the word of God and it is not doing us any good."

After Oom Doors had spoken to Eugène, Louis still attended the table service but Marais did not.

When Louis once asked him about the effects of morphine he replied: "My dear fellow, it's the most wonderful thing there is. You see the most beautiful girls, you see heaven. Never mind heaven – you're in the seventh heaven above the seventh heaven!"

He was not just playing the fool. In Heidelberg, shortly before, he had described the effects of morphine in virtually the same words to Andries Visser's youngest son, Willie.

By this time Eugène Marais had been using morphine for thirty-four years. According to medical findings, he should long since have passed the stage where it could give him any pleasure. He should even have passed the stage at which he could still remember that it had ever given him pleasure. Even so he still praised morphine in verse and lyrical prose. Could he have been the exception, the morphine addict born for the drug, who was spared the worst destruction and could still derive joy from it?

It is more likely that Marais was praising morphine because it could bring oblivion. Morphine relieved the pain of an "existence which had become nothing but suffering". Could he have meant that the mere relief of pain was a seventh heaven?

In his article on euphoric poisoning he lists the methods which mankind had used down the centuries to try and relieve the misery of its own soul. " ... the most important and at the same time the most favourable of these methods ... was undoubtedly supernatural religion, followed by euphoric poisoning. Philosophy was a third and much weaker competitor."

These thoughts occupied his mind. He had become very attached to Doorsie, the elder son. One day he told him: "I wish I could be as devout as you are. My mother died in my arms and I heard her say: 'I see nothing. There is nothing.'"

Even so, when Doorsie inevitably asked him about the origins of his addiction, he gave him a sensational version of the story he had told Dr. Nico Kestell: "We were on an expedition to join the Boer forces, making our way through East Africa. There were thirteen of us, but the malaria there was so terrible that all but two died. Only I and a certain Dr. Schultz survived. Fortunately, we found an Indian there with a supply. He injected and cured us. From that time onwards I have always had to have the stuff."

He tried to befriend the brothers' ten year old sister, Corrie. He called her "Koekie" (little cake). Beneath the house there was a cellar, just big enough to stand up in. In the outer wall there was a small opening. This, he told Koekie, was the door used by the gnomes who lived in the cellar. And when she refused to believe him he cut a small foot from a piece of wood, tied it to a walking stick and made rows and rows of tiny footprints in the dust next to the house while she was sleeping. "The gnomes must have been very busy last night," he told her.

She then believed him implicitly, but she remained suspicious –

one of the very few children in Marais's life who was not drawn to him.

Could there be a connection between this rejection and the experiment he had begun at this stage?

For weeks he would walk to the nearest dam, three hundred yards from the house, every morning. Nobody was allowed to go with him. Finally, after several weeks, he took the Meyers with him. "Now where are the Oubaas's kittens?" he called softly. And to the Meyers' incredulous delight they saw two red-tailed mongooses – shy, extremely cautious animals of the veld, far more difficult to tame than the grey mongoose – emerge from their lairs in the dam wall and eat bread from his hands.

One may wonder what drove a sick man of fifty-six to the almost limitless patience required for an experiment of this kind, waiting for hours on end in the hot sun. Was it merely interest in nature or was it a need to give his love to creatures who could ask no questions?

In any case, no doctor could have prescribed more beneficial treatment than this. By the time he had tamed the mongooses, much of the anxiety in Marais himself had subsided. He even allowed a snapshot to be taken of him on the Meyers' veranda and Koekie, who had always been afraid of him, came to stand by his side.

He was now taking no more than a quarter of a grain of morphine a day, a "normal" quantity – and the proposed reduction to a sixth, to an eighth, to nothing, was no longer as terrifying as before.

"I feel I've got over it," he told the Meyers. And Dr. Visser, highly satisfied, confided a secret fear to Oom Doors: "If only he doesn't get his hands on some of the stuff again."

To Marais himself there was no doubt. In a letter he had received shortly before from Spilhaus, the old German had apparently tactfully made it clear that he knew about Marais's addiction and sympathized with the problem. In his present optimistic mood Eugène was not prepared to tolerate such accusations. Categorically and rather coolly, he reprimanded Spilhaus: "Dr. Visser will have informed you that the affliction to which you so kindly refer is, and has been since before my (postal) acquaintance with you, a thing of the past."

Apparently this was part of the agreement with Visser: as soon as Eugène had "got over it", Visser would personally write to the few people whose opinions mattered to Eugène. These included Spilhaus and Dr. Gustav Preller.

Gustav was most important. He was to see to it that nothing went wrong with Eugène's appointment as director of the Pretoria Zoo. As the weeks passed, optimism turned into certainty. He was well known for his ability to communicate with animals. With his background of natural science research, his popular magazine articles, he would, after all, be able to do extremely valuable work.

And this was not only his own view. Preller, as well as other friends, was virtually certain of his appointment.

It was a time of almost feverish optimism and planning for the new period in which he would be free of the evil goddess, of a strange new euphoria which had nothing to do with the effects of morphine but may have had a great deal to do with the lack of it.

What Andries Visser and even Eugène Marais did not fully realise at this stage – it was not to be proved experimentally until later – was that the danger point in a withdrawal programme sets in when the patient's intake has been reduced to about half a grain a day. And Eugène Marais had long passed this point. The Meyers had long relaxed their vigilance. They felt at ease. During Marais's last month on the farm he set out to waylay old Stuurman as the Bushman was returning from Heidelberg with the weekly quota. Five hundred yards from the farmhouse he stopped the old man and ordered him to get off his horse. Marais's violet eyes were very cold and menacing, like those of a snake. As if in a dream the old Bushman got off his horse and handed Marais the few tablets he had brought with him.

It hardly matters whether this was actually hypnosis or only Marais's strong personality. Too late Stuurman realised his mistake. When he began to plead and threaten, Marais turned on his heel and walked rapidly to the nearest dam – not the dam of the mongooses. The stub of candle and the teaspoon were in his pocket. For such a small quantity of morphine a teaspoonful of muddy dam water would be enough.

The injection he gave himself was seven times as much as the daily quantity to which he had become accustomed. He only just managed to make it to his room, where he lay in a virtual coma for three days and three nights.

At the end of this period he began mumbling like one in a delirium and once Louis heard him laugh aloud and say: "Seven heavens above the seventh heaven."

The Meyers had reached the end of their tether. Before the end of the week Dr. Visser came to the farm to take his friend back to Heidelberg.

9. The Only Gate

On 21 March 1927, from a miserable little room in Heidelberg, came a single agonised cry:

Tell me Gustav: it was only a dream that I ever did anything for the Afrikaans cause and literature?

It was a letter to Gustav Preller. It consisted of only one sentence. The writing, more slovenly than in any other known letter or manuscript written by Eugène Marais, probably reveals the lack of morphine rather than intoxication from it.

He had returned from Steenkampskraal but again found himself in a cell. Not only his lack of presentable clothes but his shame, too, kept him locked up in his room by day. Only once night had fallen did he venture out into the open. In this way about a month went by.

The normal world went its normal way. Earlier that year a young scientist, Dr. Rudolf Bigalke, had returned to South Africa from Germany after being awarded a doctorate *cum laude* at the Friedrich-Wilhelm University in Berlin.

He used the normal channels to apply for the directorship of the Pretoria Zoo and the application was considered according to the normal procedure. And he was appointed in the normal way.

Eugène Marais heard this news in his shabby little room in Heidelberg. Several possibilities have been advanced in order to explain why Marais did not get the post. According to one story, he arrived for an interview under the influence of morphine. A very simple explanation seems more likely: the Zoo's curators, however sympathetic they may have been, had found it impossible to appoint Marais because he had neglected to put in a formal application.

Connie Pistorius had tried to help him. Andries Visser had tried to help him. Gustav Preller had tried to help him. Tielman Roos had spoken a fair amount, if nothing else.

Only Eugène Marais, so it seemed to his friends, had done nothing to help himself.

Now the kindhearted Preller tried again. Perhaps Eugène could come and give him a hand at *Ons Vaderland*, the newspaper where Preller had become editor some time before. He would see.

Eugène Marais found himself in one of the most dejected periods of his life.

From his little room he wrote to Preller:

"I think my time here has so broken me that I shall never be well again. I won't be able to be of much help to you."

And in another letter from the same period:

"I am having a very hard time, harder than ever in my life. It is a constant struggle against the deepest depression which makes work and concentration almost impossible. However, I shall wait and do my best to keep it up."

And another:

"I have to tell you that I find myself in extreme misery. I cannot have my clothes (I have only one or two articles left) washed so that I have to stay in the room almost all day. I am using my last postage stamp on this letter."

At about this time an old friend who had gone to live in East Africa wrote and offered him some sort of job there. Marais decided to accept it – or so he told Preller in a letter: "I can't bear it here for another month ... Everything has been dashed to the ground: hope, ambition, yearning – under the shadow of anxiety and a humiliating struggle for an existence which is nothing but suffering."

Nothing came of the proposed move to East Africa.

In some of these letters there is a tone of self-pity which Eugène sometimes revealed to his most intimate friends. One can hardly condemn this attitude, in view of the almost unimaginable circumstances in which the words were written.

In the meantime Preller had written to Tielman Roos, leader of the Transvaal National Party: did he think it would be a good idea to appoint Eugène to the editorial staff of *Ons Vaderland*? If Eugène found no way out, Preller said, he feared the worst.

This time, writing from the Assembly in Cape Town, Minister Roos acted positively. On 4 April he wrote: "I think it would be a good thing to appoint Eugène Marais. Send him a telegram when you receive my letter. I, too, fear an act of desperation."

Even so Preller did nothing. That strange little note he had received from Heidelberg led to serious doubt. Possibly his wife, Hannie, had her reservations. If Gustav let Eugène Marais come to Pretoria, she might have pointed out, he would have to accept responsibility for him, not only as far as his work was concerned.

In his next letter Preller asked Marais to contribute to the newspaper, but said nothing about an appointment.

In the shabby little room in Heidelberg the weeks dragged by. Finally, late in April, Marais wrote to Preller:

> I received your letter the day before yesterday. Only one thing sticks in my mind – that you said nothing about my coming to Pretoria; but instead of that asked me to continue writing as if the matter had been postponed once more. Gustav, I beg you, I pray you, do not let me continue on this path of misery. I can take no more. Let me know frankly what the matter is – and the truth. If there is something in the way I *have* to go through the only gate still open to me. But give me certainty – whether good or evil.

It was thinly veiled blackmail: look after me or condone my intention to commit suicide.

This letter seems to have decided Preller. Shortly afterwards, in May 1927, he and his seventeen year old son, Bob, met Eugène Marais on the Pretoria station and brought him to the Prellers' house in Blackwood Street. One might say that they had taken over from A.G. Visser.

PART 8: THE LAST LAP

Ken jy my nou? Het jy die spieël gesien, en ken jy jou?	Knows't thou now me? Hast in a mirror looked, and knowest thou thee?

1. Blackwood Street

Hannie and Gustav Preller's comfortable house near the Union Buildings, 176 Blackwood Street, had changed hardly at all since Eugène Marais had lived there for a while some years before. Although built on a spacious double plot, the house itself was not very large. Marais was given a room overlooking Church Street. The three boys, Carl, twenty, Bob, seventeen, and Gustav Jnr., eleven, had to move around to make room for him.

The welcome Hannie Preller gave him was hospitable enough. She was approaching fifty but her soft mouth and beautiful dark eyes made her attractive still. Ever since her childhood days she had heard Eugène Marais's name from her father, Commandant Henning Pretorius, erstwhile head of the Republican State Artillery. Like Marais, he had been a Joubert supporter. Even so, the stories she had heard about Marais lately made her less than enthusiastic about taking him into her house.

It was only Gustav's assurance that Eugène had "got over it" that had made her agree to let him stay in the house for the time being at all. Now that she realised the truth all her reservations returned. Gustav spent most of his time at the office or travelling and she herself, who counted executive membership of the Vrouefederasie (Women's Federation) and membership of the Hospitaalraad (Hospital Board) among her obligations, was frequently away from the house as well. What effect would the constant presence of somebody like Eugène have on the boys?

"I was accustomed to literary people being brought to the house by my husband," she was to say much later. "It was no novelty to have Eugène there, but I am sure I did not think he would stay."

However, Preller knew how to get round his wife. He was a

kindly man, not above using means which justified a humanitarian end. Marais stayed. Eventually, Preller added a new room to the house by having part of the stoep enclosed. This became Marais's room. Again – an outside room.

He was treated by Preller's house doctor, Dr. Gideon Nel, and his partner, Dr. Hendrik Louw. In a way these two were twins. They were cousins, they were partners, both had studied in Edinburgh, both had married Scots girls and both lived in an ultra-modern U-shaped block of flats just below the Union Buildings.

For the rest of his life Marais was to be treated by one or other of these doctors. They were never to "cure" him and probably they realised, being wise men, that at this stage, nine years before his death, it was too late for a cure. But they were to succeed in keeping him reasonably healthy and happy by means of more or less moderate quantities for long periods.

As a Pretorian born and bred, Marais knew many people in the area. Next door to the Prellers lived Charlie Wallach, the printer.

On the other side of the Prellers, at 180 Blackwood Street, lived Dr. Betsy Goddefroy, a daughter of old Dr. M.T. Goddefroy of the Reformed church and a sister of Anton Goddefroy whom Marais had come to know well in the Waterberg. She was destined to play an important part in the last days of his life.

The man we see walking slowly up Blackwood Street and opening the Prellers' gate was not the same man Dr. Andries Visser had known in Heidelberg. In these few years Marais had grown much older, more dejected – and he had a new uniform. After about half a century one sees him clearly through the eyes of one of Bob's young friends, seventeen year old Otto Schwellnus:

"I can see him now, moving up the garden path slowly, almost shuffling, but walking erect in a snow white suit, buttoned up to the neck, with white shoes and a white panama hat, the finely chiselled features, with the slightly bent nose, wax pale, but a fiery, penetrating gaze in the dark eyes."

Marais did not notice the two boys watching him and entered the house.

"Bob then told me that this was Eugène Marais, the author of "Mabalêl" ... To us Oom Eugène was a romantic, almost mysterious figure, and we hero worshipped him as only the young can do."

Preller had invited Marais to have a good rest until he felt ready to leave the house. Even so Eugène soon arrived at the newspaper offices – a single-storey building in Pretorius Street, with the words "Ons Vaderland" in capitals a foot high above the facade. From the editor's office, a room next to the front door, a Remington clattered from time to time like a machine-gun for, using two fingers, Gustav Preller could type faster than most trained typists could using ten.

Marais was introduced to the meagre editorial staff: Ploost van Amstel, assistant editor; Lukas Breytenbach; and Rud. P. Visser, hardly more than a boy.

From the front door the long corridor, with offices to both left and right, led to the back yard. In the front were the editorial offices – far too much space for such a small staff – and at the back walls had been taken out to make room for the typesetting machines and foundry. Preller had plans for expansion at the back of his mind. Behind the foundry, in an equally large hall, a beautiful new German printing press spat out a few thousand copies of *Ons Vaderland* twice a week.

In the back yard Preller showed Marais a small corrugated iron shack. Inside the shack was a writing table and a radio receiver equipped with headphones. Alongside the small building was an impressive radio mast. This was Preller's pride and joy. Here the newspaper's radio operator, Russell Swan, received the signals from the German news service, Transozean, and decoded them for use in the paper.

Eugène soon realised how frustrated Preller was at *Ons Vaderland*. He had spent many years at *Die Volkstem*, a successful daily paper, eventually becoming its editor. But, in Preller's view, *Die Volkstem* had long betrayed the cause of the Afrikaner, and he eventually felt obliged to resign. Now he had to start from scratch, editing a little bi-weekly paper which was so insignificant that he could often produce editorials a week in advance. His greatest ideal was to change it into a daily.

People who knew Marais well later reproached his family for having "put out no hand to him". It was left to the Prellers to care for him. Was this charge well founded and was Mrs. Hannie Preller right when she said, years later, that Marais was "without friends" when he returned to Pretoria?

A large number of Marais's huge circle of friends and acquaintances from the old days had forgotten him, intentionally or otherwise. Many people said that he had been "burnt out". Some, especially those who had been most successful in life, may have been afraid that he would look them up and ask embarrassing favours. But even they, on meeting him again, would often succumb to his charm. To many others he was an object of admiration. It was a time of national pride and Eugène Marais was a pioneer of Afrikaans poetry and language, as one may judge from Otto Schwellnus' reaction.

On a much larger popular front his series of articles, "Die Siel van die Mier" (The Soul of the Ant), readable and readily understandable writings on a fascinating subject, had made his name a household word in thousands of families. This was followed by a second series, "Die Siel van die Aap" (The Soul of the Ape) which was still being published by the time he returned to Pretoria. Marais was not a forgotten figure in 1927. On the contrary, to the Afrikaans-speaking public his name was a famous one.

The public at large were unaware of his addiction. Even people who knew much more about him heard mainly rumours. But in the Marais family, always most concerned about appearances and already beset by a series of family tragedies, his escapades were a source of irritation and embarrassment, while his fame as an Afrikaans poet and author meant little to them. In largely Afrikaans-speaking Pretoria they led such English oriented lives that many of them had hardly heard of *Die Huisgenoot*, and they were certainly not well up on his literary achievements.

Gustav Preller's wife, Hannie, said much later: "His own people never understood him. Let us be honest: they were not Afrikaners. One day I met one of his sisters at the hospital, my husband was ill. Well, I thought she had to wait and I had to wait and then we began discussing Eugène, but I was amazed at how little she knew about him, so I thought, oh well ..."

And indeed many members of his family were severely critical and hostile in these last days in Pretoria. There were those among them who would not even have his name mentioned, and one sister said openly that he might as well be dead.

Marais replied to their hostility by trying to forget them. In this he may have succeeded quite literally, as we shall see in Chapter 15.

Of his three brothers only Henry was still alive in 1927 – he was seventy-five – and of the six sisters, three had died. Four of them had lost their husbands through suicide, divorce or desertion. The exemplary, pious husband of the fifth sister had stayed with her until his death and had then left all his money to the Presbyterian Church. The sixth had married a lovable lame duck. Who can say which of them came off best or worst?

The family of Marais's sister Sophie Ueckerman, with whom his son had grown up, had been struck by more than one tragedy. Young Eugène's beloved god-sister, Fay, had died tragically after a disappointment in love. And now, within months of Eugène Marais's return to Pretoria, much the same thing happened to his god-brother, Sonny.

Young Eugène wanted to visit his father to tell him about the tragedy but did not know where he lived. In the end he managed to trace him to the Prellers.

They met at the door of his father's outside room on the veranda. They had not seen each other in years.

Marais heard the news in shocked silence.

Was he thinking of his own family when, some years later, he was to write these words about a stricken family in the short story, "Die Vlieënde Hollander" (The Flying Dutchman)?

> It was hard to accept that one family could be so chastised by mere coincidence. His scientific training immediately rejected the possibility that a curse could operate over the generations of a family. And yet! ...

Sonny had been thirty-four. Of Sophie's three children only Norma now remained.

2. Maeterlinck vs. Marais

Shortly after Sonny Ueckerman's death, something happened which gripped the popular imagination like few other things in Marais's life. It became known as the Maeterlinck case.

Maurice Maeterlinck's star would wane in later years, but in 1927 he was world famous. As many as sixteen years before, the year of Marais's appointment as Resident Justice of the Peace in the Waterberg, he had received the Nobel Prize for literature for his fantastic fairytale-like plays – particularly *l'Oiseau Bleu* (The Blue Bird).

Later his popularity increased with the publication of a number of popular philosophic writings like *La Vie des Abeilles* (The Life of the Bee).

In 1926, at the apex of his fame, another popular work, *La Vie des Termites*, was published in French. The next year translations in several languages followed. The English edition was known as *The Life of the White Ant*.

Maeterlinck had kept bees himself, and in his book about bees he had written from first-hand experience. But he had never done any termite research and in *The Life of the White Ant* he had simply lumped together a number of theories about the termitary and then applied his own frequently poetic interpretations. And among these theories, without any recognition, featured Marais's central theory about the organic unity of the termitary.

How did this happen? Marais's theory had not been published in book form by that time, and the magazine articles he had written about it were all in Afrikaans – a language of which most Europeans had hardly heard.

However, Maeterlinck was a Belgian, and although he wrote in French, he could understand Flemish – and so Afrikaans as well.

Marais's theory about the termitary was first published in *Die Burger* in January 1923 but it seems more probable that Maeterlinck had somehow got hold of the copies of *Die Huisgenoot* in which the long series of articles "Die Siel van die Mier" (The Soul of the Ant) appeared from 1925 to 1926.

Marais's reaction was one of surprise but Preller was indignant. It was probably at his insistence that Marais got in touch with his old friend F. Paver of *The Star* and with Dr. H.G. Viljoen, editor of *Die Huisgenoot*. Both papers had published a number of Marais's writings and both were eager to run articles about the Maeterlinck case: the fact that the famous Maeterlinck had apparently plagiarised the work of a South African was, after all, hot news. The *Star*'s exposure was published prominently in the newspaper on the day before Christmas. Photographs of Marais and Maeterlinck appeared above an article of two full columns in which Marais explained the whole matter calmly, but without leaving any doubt that, as he put it, "the great Belgian had done me the honour of using my writings without the customary courtesy of acknowledgement."

In *Die Huisgenoot* the story was published early in January 1928 on the magazine's banner page as the week's main article.

After publication of the articles in *The Star* and *Die Huisgenoot*, the indignation in Marais's circle of friends turned into a national indignation. How shameful that a great foreign writer could so unblushingly loot the work of an Afrikaans writer to swell his fame even more! Quite a number of people, including Preller, advised Marais to institute proceedings against Maeterlinck.

In this year, 1928, Marais, who had just turned fifty-seven, tired of life and intellectually broken down, had little left of the fiery spirit which, as a youthful newspaper editor, had driven him to fight against all forms of injustice, both within and outside the courts, even on the highest level. Now Maeterlinck caused a new spark of enthusiasm, and this spark was fanned by friends and colleagues. Marais seriously began thinking about taking legal action.

After Marais's return from the Waterberg, he and Advocate Charles te Water had been colleagues at the Pretoria Bar and had become good friends. Te Water had witnessed the progress of *The Soul of the Ape* at close quarters during that time and it was he who had been responsible for the correspondence between Wilhelm Spilhaus and Marais by showing Spilhaus some of Marais's writings.

Now Marais went to see his old friend in the latter's elegant new house, 852 Arcadia Street. He gave him the facts regarding the Maeterlinck affair.

"Do I have a case?" he asked.

Te Water was still a practising advocate and accepted the brief like any other, although no doubt *pro amico*. Soon afterwards he gave Marais a written opinion. He found that Marais had a case "without a shadow of a doubt." If he sued Maeterlinck, he had a good chance of winning.

Marais soon bewailed his lot to his old friend Spilhaus: "I have been greatly worried lately," he wrote. "Maeterlinck quite calmly loots a theory of mine."

The happy ending would have been for Spilhaus, an exceedingly wealthy man, to help Marais to go and fight the case in Europe. However, a sagacious man and his money are not so easily parted. In the meantime there had been a general election. Te Water lost his seat and the Prime Minister, General Hertzog, decided to appoint him as High Commissioner in London.

Marais again went to see him. He had considered the matter, he said, and he would like to institute proceedings against Maeterlinck. But for that he would have to go to Europe, and that would cost a great deal of money.

Hesitantly, he asked Te Water whether he might be able to persuade the Government to appoint him, Marais, as Te Water's political secretary. This would take him to London, from where he would find it much easier to prosecute Maeterlinck.

Te Water was a courteous man, but he knew where reality ended and fantasy began. No, he said, that would be impossible. He could say so even without consulting General Hertzog. He could not use his office for anything of the kind.

As always in such cases, Marais immediately agreed. "It did seem to me a last hope," he said. "But of course you're right."

Two of the great legends in Marais's life were that his morphine addiction was a result of his wife's death and that the Maeterlinck affair was the *coup de grace*. As late as 1969, Robert Ardrey was to write " … it is fair to surmise, I believe, that the plagiarising of his work by a world famous European author was a major factor in his last collapse."

What grounds are there for such a theory? At this stage no catastrophe could be worse to Marais than a shortage of morphine. Next to this everything was secondary. His self-confidence and self-esteem had taken such a beating during the previous thirty-five years that they hardly existed any more. But he was still a human being, and as a human being, even if he could no longer respect himself, he still yearned for the respect of others.

His poetry had been published in book form only two years before. His greatest work, the four *Dwaalstories* (Wandering Tales), had just been published, but as part of a storybook for children. It was not taken seriously at the time.

His series of articles, "Die Siel van die Mier", on the other hand, had aroused great admiration. If at this stage Marais still hoped to achieve any fame, he saw it as a result of his work in the field of natural science. The fact that one of his central theories had just been published for an international audience had robbed it of its novelty – even if he could prove that the theory had appeared in print years before the publication of Maeterlinck's book.

However, it is doubtful whether he really felt so strongly about it. In any case his priority was indicated in a number of publications before his death. Apart from the articles in the *Star* and *Die Huisgenoot*, his old friend Wilhelm Spilhaus, too, later took up the cudgels for him in a foreign publication. After Marais had expounded his theory in a very long letter to Spilhaus, the latter sent the letter to *Psyche*, a British psychology magazine, in which it was published as an article in 1933.

The article was accompanied by comments in which Spilhaus sided with Marais in no uncertain terms, claiming that there could be no doubt whatever about Eugène Marais's priority.

Marais found this useful when the following year (1934) he had to write a foreword to *Die Siel van die Mier* (the Afrikaans version of The Soul of the White Ant) in book form, although he attributed Spilhaus' conclusion not to his old friend but to the editorial staff of *Psyche*. He adds:

"I am not the least concerned about the determination of this priority for the sake of the honour which it may bring anyone. I would gladly grant it to Maeterlinck – he has in any case already taken it; but I would not like to be exposed to the charge of plagiarism. I think most readers will appreciate this motive."

However, the next year (1935), in a letter to Dr. Winifred de Kok in London, Marais put it much more strongly:

" ... The famous author had paid me the left-handed compliment of cribbing the most important part of my work ... He clearly desired his readers to infer that he had arrived at certain of my theories (the result of ten years of hard labour in the veld) by his own unaided reason, although he admits that he never saw a termite in his life. You must understand that it was not merely plagiarism of the spirit of the thing, so to speak. *He has copied page after page verbally*."

This entire paragraph was much exaggerated. The last, untrue, words may or may not have been underlined by Marais himself. The reason why he put his case so strongly eight years after the incident will be clear when we come to his letters to Dr. de Kok.

At any rate Dr. de Kok, who at this stage wanted to translate *Die Siel van die Mier* into English, soon saw the publicity value in Maeterlinck's plagiarism. In replying to Marais's letter, she said candidly: "Your foreword, giving the facts of the plagiarising, will prove magnificent publicity and will sell the book well."

The truth is not as Robert Ardrey imagined it. When Marais returned to Pretoria after the Heidelberg fiasco in 1927, tired and despondent, the Maeterlinck legend gave a sudden and tremendous boost to his fame and standing. One could probably twist Robert Ardrey's words and say: "It is fair to surmise, I believe, that the plagiarising of his work by a world famous European author was a major factor in prolonging his life."

Such a statement, although no doubt exaggerated, would certainly be closer to the truth than Ardrey's original claim. In spite of deep unhappiness and suffering – no new phenomena in his life – there were several strong intellectual and even physical revivals during the last nine years of life which remained to him.

In regard to the Maeterlinck case there are two ironic twists.

The first of these is that it may have been Maeterlinck's writings which inspired in Marais the idea of the termitary as an organic unity. In the English translation of *La Vie des Abeilles* (The Life of the Bee) Maeterlinck asks: "Where is this 'spirit of the hive' ... where does it reside? It disposes pitilessly of the wealth and the happiness, the liberty and life, of all this winged people; and yet with discretion, as though governed itself by some great duty." Even at this early stage there is reference to a central "soul" (and in passing one may remark that Maeterlinck's philosophical view of the bee society, in which the individual's interests were sacrificed "mercilessly" for the sake of the whole, may be regarded as a precursor to Marais's later theories on this theme).

The second theory in regard to the Maeterlinck affair is that both Maeterlinck and Marais were, in their theory about the unity of the termitary, forestalled by a third thinker. As early as 1911, the year when Marais was appointed Justice of the Peace in the Waterberg, the theory was published in an essay by Dr. W.M. Wheeler entitled "The ant colony as an organism". About seventeen years later – just about the time, in fact, when Marais was considering legal action against Maeterlinck – Wheeler began calling the colony of social insects a "super organism".

It is also necessary to add that the concept of the termitary as an organic unity had not been generally accepted by entomologists at the time of writing.

In the standard work on the subject, *The Insect Societies*, Edward O. Wilson wrote in 1971: "During the later years of his life, Marais claimed that his idea had been stolen by Maeterlinck, and his case has more recently been melodramatically championed by Robert Ardrey in the best-selling book, *The Territorial Imperative*. But it is all just a tempest in a teapot. Wheeler was clearly the architect of the idea, for what it is worth, and neither Marais nor Maeterlinck had any claim for priority or visible effect on later students of social insects."

In the isolation of the Waterberg in 1911 Eugène Marais had never heard of Wheeler's theory. He had arrived at it independently – in itself no inconsiderable achievement. Even in 1928, when the Maeterlinck affair was enjoying great publicity in South Africa, it is probable that neither Marais nor Maeterlinck knew about Wheeler's theory. On the other hand it is fairly certain that Maeterlinck knew about the reaction to his "plagiarism", especially as in the end it was very clearly stated in the foreword to *The Soul of the White Ant*, Winifred de Kok's translation of the original book.

By then Marais was dead, but Maeterlinck was to live for another twelve years. Without implying that the Belgian author felt the Maeterlinck affair as a great blow to his personal prestige, it is just possible that it may have affected him more adversely than it did Eugène Marais.

3. The Magalakwêna and Beyond

At the time when Eugène Marais lived there, the Prellers' home was a hospitable, rather noisy place. In these years there were always guests who lived there more or less permanently – friends of the boys or of the Prellers themselves.

It was the kind of place where a newcomer could soon feel at home. And Eugène soon felt at home. Gustav and Hannie were old friends and he was also getting to know the boys. Soon he made friends with them all.

There was Carl, the eldest, who had just come of age, a great robust fellow who worked at *Ons Vaderland* as an advertising salesman. He was fond of the girls, fond of his drinks, very fond of his Chrysler and he loved company. He had an easy laugh, but when one looked deeper, there was also a shadowy side. Even at this time he was beginning to develop the characteristic posture so many people would remember later: the hat drawn over one eye, one hand in the trouser pocket and a shoulder which sagged sideways.

There was Piet Lub, Carl's best friend, who lived with the Prellers. Piet could charm the most obstinate engine into life.

There was Bob, Hannie Preller's second child, now in Standard Nine, who had an inexhaustible interest in everything which rolled, drove or flew. It was he who was to see to it a year or so later that one of the first electric stoves in South Africa was installed in his mother's kitchen. And it was he, backed by Carl, who saw to it that the Prellers had a "gram-radio" in the dining room, like all modern people should.

There was Gustav Junior, the youngest. He had his father's name and looks, and he was the apple of his father's eye.

To look after the family, the house and the large garden the Prellers had a staff of three. Poul Molefe was the mainstay of the establishment. A good cook, a good gardener, he could organise anything. He could even hand out advice. There was Koos, a tiny yellow imp of distinctly Cape descent, whose main tasks seem to have been to do all sorts of odd jobs for Eugène Marais. There was also Lizzie, who kept the house in order and did the washing.

During this time, when *Ons Vaderland* was published only twice weekly, Marais had an easy life. By the time he got up in the morning everyone had long since left for work or school, and Hannie Preller had gone to a tea party, a meeting or elsewhere. But the breakfast table in the kitchen would remain laid until late in the morning and here he would help himself to bread and chutney or call on Poul Molefe if he fancied something else. At least two days in the week, the days before *Ons Vaderland* was published, he would stroll downtown to see whether he could give a hand. He now had the title of assistant editor, but his main tasks were the translation or adaptation of the reports which Russell Swan received over the radio in the newspaper's back yard.

Quite frequently he would go to the Pretoria Zoo, but for the time being he took care to avoid the new director, Dr. Bigalke. Sometimes he ran into old friends or acquaintances and had a cup of coffee with them at Turkstra's.

Lunch (again in Blackwood Street) was spare. Frequently he skipped it completely.

In the afternoon, after another shot, he went to bed. By the time he woke up Bob and Gustav Junior had already been home from school for hours. He helped both of them with their homework.

"There was a sort of stony cellar underneath the house," Bob was to relate later. "There were shelves against the walls and also tables where one could work. This is where we crammed for our exams. And it was where Oom Eugène came to help me. I had quite a lot of trouble with Latin and he would simply translate the passages just like that. The problem was that my teacher would always ask me the next day: 'Tell me, Bob, is this your Latin or Eugène Marais's?' He helped me just as much with my algebra."

By four o' clock, if the weather was fine, tea was served on the stone table in the garden – a popular rendezvous – and there Eugène and Hannie Preller would often sit and chat under the oak tree before the men returned.

Gustav Preller usually arrived home after five. But there was almost always an hour before supper during which he and Eugène and the rest of the household, wherever they might be, could have a pleasant conversational get-together.

In the evenings everyone went his own way – Marais to his room to read or sleep, Preller to his study to work, Carl and Piet to the cinema, with or without girlfriends, or to visit friends, and the younger boys to bed or to their studies. But the house was seldom empty. They were a sociable lot. Carl and Piet – and Bob when he did not have to study – were great card players, and they could usually persuade their mother to play with them. "Eugène had no interest in cards," Mrs. Preller said later. "All he wanted us to do was to learn to play chess – and eventually he succeeded."

The dining room was the house's social centre. The shiny Pilot gram against the wall would churn out fox-trots and quick-steps, the boys not at all put off by the surface noise; and sometimes they would tune in to Radio J.B. (short for Johannesburg). The broadcasting station – a forerunner of the S.A.B.C. – was in Johannesburg, thirty miles away, but once Carl and Bob had installed a long aerial one weekend, the reception was not bad at all.

When the boys started playing music or settled down to a game of cards, Gustav regularly disappeared, grumbling, into his study. He had a convenient and permanent excuse, for apart from his obligations as a newspaper editor, he was constantly working on further volumes of his vast series on the Great Trek, *Voortrekkermense* (Voortrekker People).

At about this time another of Gustav's old friends joined the family circle. He was Oswald Frank, a dapper little man of Gustav's years, but prematurely old. He was a land surveyor by profession. Until recently he had been prospecting in the north, but at the moment he had no fixed employment. The boys called him "Oom Wal".

Pretorians who had worked with him in the office of the Land Surveyor General years before remembered how he would stroll around the office chatting for hours or suddenly plunge into his work, doing more in an hour than most other people managed in a morning.

By the time Marais made his acquaintance, he no longer had his old working ability. "After his fortieth year he began drinking very heavily," an old friend said, "and he was mostly sober only in the mornings."

Sober or not, Oom Wal's brain was still sound. The interest he took in Afrikaans was one of the links between him and Preller: not only did he translate the quatrains of Omar Khayyám into Afrikaans, but sections of the *Nibelungenlied* as well. But literature was of secondary interest. Oom Wal's consuming passion was Africa and everything connected with it: history, regions, inhabitants, geographical marvels. His bibles were the books of Leo Frobenius, the German ethnologist and Africa traveller, and his prophet Frobenius himself.

After Oswald's return to Pretoria, Gustav would often take an evening off, spending long hours chatting to his old friend while they drank Worcester hock, a sweetish wine with a distinctive grapey taste which Gustav imported from the Western Cape by the barrel.

In the winter evenings Marais frequently joined them in the study, for their interests were his as well.

For the rest of the household the oval-shaped dining room table remained the social centre, and here, one evening, the great plan for the first expedition to the wild north was hatched. A year later Gustav Preller – aided by Gustav Junior's notes and own attempts, and under the latter's name – was to tell the whole story in a charming, unpretentious little book, *Op die Wal van die Magalakwêna* (On the banks of the Magalakwêna):

> The long winter vacation lay before us again, and Mother had said, if we could, we should go away somewhere rather than sit in the cinema every evening or go out.
>
> Dad said nothing at first but one day when he came back from work he told us that Oom Petrus had passed through Pretoria that day on his way to the Bushveld, and had invited him to come along and shoot a few gnu. This was the beginning of our great expedition.
>
> One evening we spread out a large map on the table and Oom Eugène started saying all kinds of foreign names, as if he heard them every day – names like Skimmelperdsepan, Bulkop, and Middleveld and many others.
>
> Mother began baking rusks, and we spent every evening in front of the fireplace making our plans.
>
> Then Oom Oswald arrived on the scene and it was his opinion that the best part of an expedition of this kind was making the plans. Oom Oswald is no longer very young.

When the plans had made a great deal of progress, Carl asked one evening:

"Will Nog-'n-Nash be big enough for us all?"

Nog-'n-Nash was Gustav Preller's pride and joy, a spacious six-seater in which Bob had done more than forty miles per hour on the open road. When he had bought the car, Preller, one of the pioneers and protagonists of the new language, Afrikaans, had been upset to see the English words "Another Nash" unashamedly printed on the canvas cover of the spare wheel. This was soon rectified. Using some black and white paint Carl had painted out "Another" and printed in "Nog-'n" (the Afrikaans equivalent of "another") and since then Nog-'n-Nash had been its name.

"Perhaps we should take Carl's Chrysler too," Bob said. "What do you say, Dad?"

Gustav Preller reared his massive head.

"How many are we?"

"There's dad," began Gustav Junior, "and Oom Eugène and Oom Oswald and Piet Lub, that's four, and we three brothers, that's seven ..."

"And Poul Molefe to make the food."

"Counting Poul, we'll be eight."

"Well, that's all right," said Gustav Preller. "Plenty of tame sheep go into a kraal. I think Nog-'n-Nash will be able to take them all."

"We'll have to use a small trailer to carry the luggage," the ingenious Bob suggested. "I am sure Piet will find one for us."

And so, early one Transvaal winter morning, the long expedition to the north began. At first they lost their way but on the third day they reached Petrus Erasmus' farm, Deadbeat, on the banks of the Magalakwêna. Here they set up camp and Piet and Bob soon had the wireless, bought specially for the hunting expedition, installed, using several car batteries and a long roll of fencing wire. The wire was stretched right across the river to ensure a reasonable reception.

The receiver, complete with horn, was installed on the camp side, just below the fireplace, so that they could hear the music while sitting around the campfire at night.

The reception was excellent, in fact too good, for the "ooms" were not much taken with Radio J.B.'s choice of music. "Oom Wal says the songs which pass for music nowadays are nothing but Kaffir noise," said Gustav Junior's book. "He says everything is going to the dogs and everything is quite inferior to the time when he was a boy – including the boys themselves."

One evening, when a great deal was being said on both sides of the generation gap about the new-fangled music, Oom Oswald accepted the young people's challenge and let them hear how music sounded when he was young – first "A hot time in the old town to-night" and then "Just a song at twilight". Eugène and old Gustav joined in the second, more nostalgic melody.

At that time a wireless was such a novelty that several cars from farms in the environment arrived at the camp the following Sunday to listen to the service broadcast from the church in Irene.

To the extent to which Eugène Marais could still be happy, these were happy days. He was among good friends, his supply was reasonable and he was again in the Bushveld he loved, and – last but not least – he could help and teach others.

He taught the boys how to shoot guineafowl and bustards while in flight – never on the ground. He taught them all how to skin game and how to cut biltong (neatly dissected muscles, later to be turned into dried meat) from the carcass.

He himself no longer felt like hunting. In words which remind one of the environmental consciousness – including the slogans – of half a century later, Gustav Preller was to write about this: "He wanted to be in the veld, out in the wild, and the closer to it the better, but to observe and admire, not to kill."

He showed the boys how the huge droves of game could still, after a drought which lasted for three years, find enough grass and greenery to stay alive on the koppies and in the bush. One night some of the party saw almost a thousand big head of game drinking in the virtually dried up river-bed.

Marais told them what he knew about the honey-bird, after Gustav Jnr. and Poul had followed a bird to the hive one afternoon and had almost lost their way completely.

He showed them how "scouts" would lead a swarm of commando ants to a damaged termitary by means of invisible signs, how the commando ants divided into three separate columns before they attacked the termites, how the termites, which were repairing the breaks in their termitary, disappeared into the interior of the nest at another invisible sign and how their places were taken by thousands of termite warriors, each armed with a bright droplet of poisonous acid on their pointed mouth-parts, ready to beat off the attackers. "We watched the approaching enemy," Preller wrote, "advancing rapidly on the termitary, and saw how the two outermost columns fanned to the left and right as if they were going to surround the termitary." Moments later the ants and the termites were fighting.

It was a perfect demonstration of Marais's theory about the unity of the termitary, which Maeterlinck had adopted by that time: the commando ants as microbes which penetrate an open wound in the body, the workers the red blood cells which cease their activities for the time being so that the white blood cells (termite soldiers) can protect the body against intruders. Marais explained all this to them and more, and he did so in such a way that they were spellbound.

He explained the fertilisation of river reeds, how the wind would pluck plumes from these reeds and blow them away. The plumes would not fall to earth until they had blown across water, the only place where seeds could germinate. A negative electric charge held the plumes open like a parachute, but as soon as they drifted across water or any moist area, the charge was neutralised, the plumes would fold up and the seed would drop where they would germinate most easily.

He even wrote a poem, "Êonone", about these reeds of the desert. The long poem was finished the day before their departure and everyone was impressed – all but Oswald Frank who grumbled a great deal when he was awakened before daybreak the next morning to pack up. It was cold and windy and Oom Wal was most sarcastic about the "merry andantinos of the wind" described by Marais in his poem.

However, later in the day, the old land surveyor had revived sufficiently to be able to measure some of the apiesdorings they found on Professor Andrew Bosman's farm on the way home.

Marais had seen these trees many years before in the company of Jan Wessel Wessels. As Oom Wal had a good knowledge of trigonometry, they could now be measured accurately for the first time.

From these dimensions, as Marais was later to state in an article, it was found that not only was it the largest tree in South Africa, but, including circumference and volume (but not length), it was also larger than the giant trees of California.

(However, either Oswald Frank had made a mistake or Eugène Marais had not remembered the figures, for trees with the measurements which he was to describe in his magazine article some years later have never yet been found in South Africa.)

There were other problems. "Eight people in a six-seater was a tight fit on the way back," Bob Preller recollects. "Oom Oswald's gout had meanwhile become so bad that he would shout out if one merely looked at his big toe."

It was this that made Gustav Preller decide the next winter: "This time we'll take more cars." This time, in addition to the Nash there was the old Chevvie which Bob had inherited from Carl, as well as Carl's own Whippet, the Chrysler's successor. The Chevvie was mainly to transport food and petrol.

After a week Gustav Preller could no longer face the daily diet of gnu meat, always prepared in the same monotonous way by Poul Molefe. They had eaten it for six weeks the previous year. He could not face doing so again.

"Tomorrow morning you will drive back to Pretoria and fetch your mother," he told Carl. "An army marches on its stomach."

This time the expedition went deeper inland than the year before. Their final destination was Kopbeenpan (Marsh of the skulls) near the confluence of the Magalakwêna and the Limpopo rivers.

Here, for the first time in many years, Eugène Marais again stood at the famous hippo pool where princess Mabalêl had been caught by the great crocodile. In the blue depths before him Lalele might still be lurking.

"Is the crocodile still here?" he asked the natives and they replied, "Yes, he is here and he will remain here. He was here when the great-grandfathers of our great-grandfathers were children. He is the biggest and cleverest crocodile in the Limpopo. It is no good trying to ambush him. He is too clever for the white man's bait and the white man's guns."

In this area Eugène Marais now also met for the first time one Du Preez, an experienced white hunter who lived on the banks of the Limpopo. He was to play a strange role in the last days of Marais's life.

Once again the fascination of the veld gripped Marais. As he had been the year before, he was again in his element.

"At night around the leadwood campfire," Gustav Preller was to write about these travels, "as the flames shot high and hyena and jackal howled in the bush, or when the wildebeest snorted and blew close by at the water's edge; or in the languid heat of the afternoon under his beloved apiesdoring trees, where the wood-dove warbled in her melancholy way against the background of the rain locusts' monotonous song – there, in that environment, he could still come out of himself and he would sometimes keep us listening in breathless wonder at the richness of his knowledge of nature. Phenomena which he'd learnt through personal observation and had nowhere set down in writing he generously shared with the circle round the campfire.

"His sense of humour was one of the most subtle I have known. When he was in the mood and once he got going, he could make everyone burst into uproarious laughter and his own infectious laugh contributed not a little to the amusement of the others."

Indeed, the fifteen months or so during which the two expeditions fell, were, generally speaking, happy months for Marais.

He got along splendidly with the four youngsters in the Prellers' house. He gave advice to Piet and Carl, drawing on his own experience, including advice about women and love, themes on which he was an expert. He helped the younger ones with their schoolwork. As one who had known A.G. Visser and his work intimately, the explanatory notes he wrote in Bob's prescribed edition of Visser's *Gedigte* (Poems) were infinitely more useful than anything Bob's teacher could say about the poems.

However, between Marais and the boys' parents matters were not going as smoothly as before.

It galled Preller to see how much of every day his old friend and one time mentor simply slept away; how often he fell asleep with a cigarette smouldering between his lips, burning holes in the bedsheets, and how frequently he would take morphine to excess and be out of action for two or three days. According to him there was only one way out: Eugène had now to leave behind his bad habit once and for all.

Dr. Nel and his partner, Dr. Louw, had, however, come to know their patient well by this time and had reached different conclusions. One could not cure a fifty-eight year old man who had been using morphine for forty years – they thought – at least not this one. According to Dr. Louw the best one could do was to give him the minimum amount to keep away withdrawal symptoms. Dr. Nel carried this even further: "Within reasonable bounds I feel one should give the man as much as he wants. After all, it's all he lives for."

Preller was shocked and indignant, but he could do nothing against all three of them. He would simply have to allow things to carry on as they were. Maybe time would bring a new solution.

Hannie Preller felt even more strongly than her husband, especially regarding Eugène's influence on the boys. There were other grievances as well.

Hannie was not more intolerant than most people, but she was a typical Pretorian, very particular about her husband's prestige and reputation. She had long had to reconcile herself to the fact that Gustav was not a church-goer, and that apart from an occasional funeral or wedding he had last been to church when Gustav Jnr. had been baptised. But she resented Wally Frank's frequent visits and liked even less the fact that Wally and Gustav, occasionally joined by Eugène, had fallen into the custom of no longer drinking their Worcester Hock indoors but now, in the summer months, where passers-by could possibly see and hear them – including Sunday mornings – unashamedly sat out in the garden, drinking hock at the stone table beneath the old tree.

She did not complain about these things; nor did she make a fuss about the chaos in which she often found Eugène's room. But when, for the umpteenth time he fell asleep with a burning cigarette between his lips and burnt holes right through her sheets and blankets, she could take it no longer.

When she really lost her temper Hannie Preller could talk straight from the shoulder and she did so this time. Marais listened quietly, denying nothing. Later on he told Preller that he had decided to look for accommodation closer to the newspaper.

Preller was upset. Eugène must not leave. He was sure Hannie would see sense.

Marais explained that that was not really the problem. Everything she had told him, he said, was in any case completely true. The real reason was that it was more convenient for him to live nearer the newspaper. Virtually next to the newspaper offices there was a house which took in boarders.

Preller secretly suspected that Marais was actually looking for a pretext to live where he and Hannie could not keep an eye on him, but he said nothing.

The place to which Marais had referred was the house of Mrs. Jessie Cross, 371 Pretorius Street, only two houses away from the newspaper office.

4. Edna

When Eugène Marais knocked at the front door of the very ordinary little house, he first heard voices and then silence. Eventually, shuffling steps sounded down the passage and the door opened.

Before him he saw a middle-aged woman dressed in slippers, kerchief and apron, and clinging to her skirt, peering up at him, was a tiny little creature with short straight hair, a runny nose, dirty little legs and a wet nappy. She could hardly have been five years old.

With these people, Mrs. Jessie Cross and her family, Eugène Marais was to spend a large part of the seven or eight years of his remaining life. And during this time Mrs. Cross's youngest daughter, Edna, was probably to become the most important person in his life.

Mrs. Cross's house stood on the corner of Pretorius Street and Arlouis Alley. Marais was given a back room which overlooked the alley.

She had four children: Edna, five, her older sister, Hettie, nine, and two older brothers, Willie and Charlie.

The rather reserved, perhaps even somewhat dour Mrs. Cross could never get along with her husband, a jolly Cockney fellow. They were not divorced but he worked down in the Cape while she took in lodgers to supplement the meagre income she received from him. Edna had never seen her father. In fact she was not to meet him until five years later. Her mother was always too busy to play with her and she was lonely.

In this house Eugène Marais soon felt so completely at home that it could have been made for him. Fate, which had betrayed him so often, had now given him an opportunity to be happy, and he grabbed it with both hands.

To Edna he became the perfect father. Thirty years later, in a long remarkable interview, she would still be able to recall the smallest details about him. "Oom Eugène became my friend," she said, "and much more than my friend. He was my father, my mother, my confessor; he was the man I always most wanted to be with. There is nobody like him today and there will never be anyone like him again. His room was a wonderland. I remember the numerous books, and the skulls on top of his wardrobe – a human skull and an ape skull – and the collection of knives on the table in front of the fireplace.

"In winter he always had a fire going. Every evening when the table had been laid, my sister and I would slip down the passage and knock surreptitiously at his door.

"'May we come in, Uncle Oom Eugène?'

"Then he would sit at the fire and ask us where his story had stopped the night before. There were dozens of stories. There was one about a funny old woman, Tonedou. There was one about cannibals who had a big toe on the one foot and a small toe on the other. They were Wallabies. While he told these stories he would slice biltong, roast it on the fire and feed it to us. In those days we seldom had any appetite for my mother's food. His stories absolutely enthralled us. A single story could last for weeks. There were always new episodes and every night he stopped at the most exciting part.

"Another story was about an old woman who took care of a little girl. The girl's name was Haijeha. She had a doll and she washed the doll's clothes in the river and laid them out on the grass to dry. She then went off to play in the river and while she was gone somebody came along and sprinkled some kind of dust over the clothes which left tiny brown marks. She then washed the doll's clothes again and became invisible."

Eugène Marais paid £8 per month for his board and lodging; out of his salary at *Ons Vaderland* he could usually manage this amount. When he had trouble in paying, Mrs. Cross was as patient as she could afford to be. He virtually lived at his office, and only three or four blocks from the Church Square, so he could reach any shop or chemist in Pretoria on foot.

Mrs. Cross looked after him well. She washed his clothes, she patched his shirts and darned his socks. When he burnt his bedsheets (the tiny brown marks on the doll's clothes?) she would repair them without a word.

What did he do to deserve so much tolerance? He conducted himself like a gentleman, with the utmost consideration.

Thirty years later Mrs. Cross, too, was to have the highest praise for him and in one simple sentence she provided the key to the place he had won in her heart and those of her children: "He was the first man who was ever good to me."

Eugène's supply during this time was tolerable, not too high. Dr. Louw gave him enough to ward off discomfort but he was no longer trying to wean him from it, and it went surprisingly well.

Mrs. Cross was well aware of his affliction. "He injected himself in the mornings," she said later, "always in his left arm, unless he asked me to help him squeeze together the flesh of his right arm. He used a spirit lamp and a teaspoon to melt the tablets."

When Marais arrived at the Cross's there was only one other lodger, Limpret, a German, but all that the Cross's were to remember about him in later years was that he preferred eating his bacon and kippers raw and that he was a rather cruel man. In that house Eugène Marais was the only person of importance.

His friendship with a receptive, imaginative little girl like Edna was the best therapy he could have had at this stage. And to Edna, because he knew and understood children like few other people, he gave much more than a real father could have done.

"He created a dream life for me," she was to say later. "Opposite our house there was a big vacant lot and in the middle a huge sawn-off eucalyptus had begun sprouting new leaves and branches. One evening at dusk we sat looking out of the drawing-room window when suddenly I saw two eyes at the tree. Oom Eugène was with me, but I was scared and I asked him what it was.

"'Oh, a gnome or something,' he said. 'The whole place is full of fairies.'

"And suddenly I saw them too. A beautiful fairy princess was sitting on one of the sawn-off tree trunks on the vacant lot. She was about the size of a girl of twenty. And kneeling in front of her, busy slipping on her shoe, was a page. The street lights had gone on and I asked Oom Eugène:

"'Do you see her?'

"'Of course,' he said. 'Look how shiny her dress is.'

"From then on I never crossed that field again. To me it had become hallowed ground."

In Eugène Marais's own world a cloud had meanwhile appeared on the horizon. The International Opium Convention held in the Hague sixteen years before (1912) had in the meanwhile led to tangible results in South Africa as well.

At that convention all member countries, including South Africa, had agreed to adopt legislation to control the sale and distribution of opium within the next two years. World War I had intervened. Only after the war was a draft bill tabled by the Minister of Health and referred to a Select Committee, which reported six years later. In 1924 legislation was again tabled and again referred to a Select Committee. It was not until 1926, when legislation was returned by a Select Committee for the third time, that Dr. D.F. Malan, Minister of Health, insisted on the adoption of the law.

After a delay of sixteen years South Africa was now following the rest of the world. The new Act for Doctors, Dentists and Pharmacists came into force on 1 January 1929.

In theory all restrictions contained in the new law in the Transvaal had already been in existence from 1909 in a series of ordinances. In practice the new Act would make it more difficult for doctors to prescribe morphine for their patients. No provision at all was made for supplying morphine to addicts; it was to be used exclusively as an anodyne or pain-killer.

If Marais was worried about the new legislation, the magical world in which he and Edna now lived may have helped him to forget it.

One evening when she was already in bed, he knocked at her window. It was no longer summer, about half past seven. Dusk had fallen.

"Come and look," he whispered.

"What is it?"

Next to the fence grew some stunted pine trees. When Edna looked out of the window she saw a fairy, a real fairy, dancing next to the trees. At once she wanted to rush out of the house to look at it but he held his fingers to his lips.

"Don't speak so loudly. She'll get a fright."

At that moment some people came walking down Pretorius

Street. Edna saw the fairy disappear behind a tree-stump but when the people had passed, it emerged again. After dancing and moving around the tree for quite a while the fairy flew up into the branches and disappeared. It was the most wonderful thing that could have happened to her.

"I never doubted that there were fairies," she was to say later. "After all, Oom Eugène and I had both seen them."

One evening he told Edna and Hettie about a little girl with a magic wand which could make her invisible. Edna was immediately mad about the idea. She simply had to have such a wand. Two weeks later he called her: "Squg," – that was his name for her – "come and see what I have found you," and he showed her a twig about two and a half inches long, the front end sharpened and the bark still on the rest.

"What is it?"

"It's a magic wand."

A magic wand! What wouldn't she be able to do with it?

"Keep it in your hand and watch it closely," he said. "Wherever it tells you to go, you should go." He then took her wrist and shook her hand lightly. "Now start walking." Leaving the house, she walked down the steps. She walked around the house and came to the loquat tree.

"Don't look only at the wand," he said, "you have to watch the ground too."

Then she saw a tickey (3d.) lying underneath the tree. The wand had pointed it out.

But when she wanted to keep the stick, he said: "Oh no, it's far too dangerous," and she never saw it again.

"As a child I never knew where fantasies ended and real life began with Oom Eugène," Edna was to say later. "I believed whatever he told me."

Years later, when she was twelve or thirteen, she told Oom Eugène: "People think I am mad because I believe in fairies. But there are fairies, aren't there? Don't you remember that evening when we saw one dancing next to the pine tree?"

Then he laughed, and after all those years he told her that it had been a doll dressed up as a fairy which he had manipulated, using some black cotton. Her brother Charles had helped him with the trick.

When Marais discussed with Dr. Gideon Nel the legislation which was to come into force in the new year, the doctor shrugged impatiently. He had no intention of changing his treatment. Dr. Louw agreed.

Marais was reassured. In any case he had never trusted any doctor completely. He had already arranged for Indian contacts to whom he could go in an emergency.

Meanwhile, he made other friends. Some prescriptions were taken to the Peacock Pharmacy in Church Street, the property of Max Schwartz, who was not yet thirty. But Max was usually too busy to talk and Eugène got to know his apprentice and younger brother, Louis, better.

He took other prescriptions to Freddie Mansfield. Freddie had bought Bones, a well known Pretoria chemist shop, from the founder, Mr. Bones, the year before. Freddie was a fine man, good-looking and athletic. While golf was his great passion, his interests were wide and he and Eugène spent many hours in conversation.

In Church Street, near *Ons Vaderland*, was the Waverley Bar, where Eugène could frequently be seen with one of his newspaper colleagues or some other friend. Here he made friends with the barman, "Bob" Shilling, a sympathetic, animated man and a good talker, and with the proprietors, the Rosenthals, who helped out at the bar from time to time. He still took spirits only when worried by withdrawal symptoms; socially, he usually drank a beer or two.

But always he returned to Edna. In the magic world he was opening before her, he himself was the Great Wizard, lovable and omnipotent. Everything, not only the stories and the fairies, contributed to his charm: the skulls in his room, the curio shop of Mr. Ivy, the taxidermist, where he sometimes took her; the visits to the zoo, where some of the monkeys recognized him even at a distance – all this was part of his sparkling, magical world.

It is possible, although Edna could not have known it, that all these things in actual fact had a great deal to do with an important work which he was trying to complete and through which he was trying to find justification for his life.

At this stage Eugène Marais no longer had the manuscript of *The*

Soul of the Ape. It had been swept away in the deluge of the last few months in Heidelberg.

Perhaps this was in a way a relief. The albatross he had been carrying around his neck for almost fifteen years was no more. He could start from scratch. In Pretoria he was not thinking of *The Soul of the Ape*, but of an Afrikaans version, *Die Siel van die Aap*. By translating the title he had turned it into a new kind of book – not a book which had to take the world by storm, but a less ambitious project, one which might still be within his reach.

The visits to the zoo which Edna remembered may have been aimed at comparing the behaviour and appearance of various primates. The baboon and human skulls which she spoke of (and in their world of fantasy it was quite possibly he who described them to her in those terms) were in all probability the skulls of adult and young baboons. Some time before Marais had written to Hans Purekrans van Rooyen, asking him to get hold of some baboon skulls. Hans and his sons duly went baboon hunting in the mountains and came back with the skulls. As a sequel to "Die Siel van die Mier", Marais wanted to write a second important series of articles in Afrikaans in which he intended dealing with the far more involved theme of the primates.

Just at this time, however, Gustav Preller told him that the board of directors of *Ons Vaderland* had decided to change the bi-weekly paper into a daily. Of course they would have to appoint more people, but good journalists were scarce. It would be a welcome move if Eugène would accept a permanent position there and help them every day. They would need all the help they could get.

"Die Siel van die Aap", too, was never to be completed.

5. Daily and Queen

To change *Ons Vaderland* into a daily had been Gustav Preller's dream for many years.

In this year, 1929, he had been a journalist for at least thirty years. His career had begun during the Boer War when he served as a war correspondent. After his short co-operation with Marais at *Land en Volk* he moved to *De Volkstem* (originally called *De Volksstem* and later changed into *Die Volkstem*). Here he had remained for more than twenty years and he had just been appointed editor in chief of this successful daily when, in 1925, he resigned. After years of frustration, he felt he could simply no longer go along with the paper's political views.

When Preller exchanged the editorship of *Die Volkstem* for that of the struggling *Ons Vaderland* it was done with the tacit understanding that the bi-weekly would ultimately become a daily. This was why the editorial offices were moved from the old house in Blood Street to the more spacious building in Pretorius Street which Marais had seen when he returned to Pretoria – far too spacious for the small editorial staff. At the same time Preller had subscribed to the German radio service Transozean and had bought a new German printing press.

These expenses had been enough to give the Noordelike Drukpersmaatskappy, owners of *Ons Vaderland*, such a financial knock that there was no question of a daily being started in the near future.

It was not until 1929 that the Nationalists, with an eye on the forthcoming general election, started paying rather more attention to the Party's only organ in the Transvaal.

In this atmosphere Preller emphasised the necessity of a daily with even greater vigour than before and eventually it came about: one day he received a telegram from the chairman of the board in Cape Town: "Begin your daily on Monday 15 September."

Neither Preller nor Marais, his assistant editor, was unaware of the problems. *Ons Vaderland* was again about to challenge *Die Volkstem* in its own field. And *Die Volkstem*, backed by the financially powerful Wallach Printing Co. and run by an experienced editorial staff, was a formidable opponent.

But the beehive-like activities which erupted in the tiny offices in Pretorius Street weeks before the publication of the first daily created the kind of euphoria in which all doubt disappears. For every one face in the office there were now two. Apart from the few staff members Marais had learnt to know – Lukas Breytenbach and Rud. P. Visser (as well as Otto Schwellnus, who had been appointed shortly before on Marais's recommendation), the general editorial staff was supplemented by J.C. Fourie, Jan van der Westhuysen and Sollie van Niekerk. Jan Grobler became the political correspondent, Johanna van Broekhuysen (a daughter of the chairman of the board) editor of the women's page and André Huguenet, later to become a prominent actor, was the columnist. Carl Preller was advertising manager, Jurie van As the technical editor and Joan Couzyn, a student at Wits, the Rand correspondent.

Preller was in his element. Now for the first time he could really fill the great, musty editorial offices. For the first time the powerful printing press's reassuring roar could be heard six times a week. For the first time Russell Swan, an ex-sailor, regularly sat down in the little corrugated iron building behind the printing works in the pith helmet he wore summer and winter, put on his earphones and wrote down the reports he received from Germany.

"Our own Afrikaner expert," Preller characteristically called the newspaper's radio operator, without mentioning his English-sounding name and surname. But an expert Swan certainly was.

If there was a lack of local crime news; or when even Preller had decided that a political story had become too mangy to ride even once more; or when advertisements were so scarce that the editorial staff had to supplement the space with additional copy; or if Transozean's reports reached them in a somewhat garbled form, he needed only to give Swan the go-ahead. After all, the whole world's broadcasting systems were within his reach. That this was an infringement of copyright occurred to no one in those naive days.

Even when Russell Swan's technical abilities left them in the lurch, Eugène Marais could on occasion save the situation.

One evening, perhaps in a time of worldwide climatic disturbances, when Swan could hardly hear a trace of Morse code and the only news was a few local crime stories, a main lead had to be found somewhere in a great hurry. All Swan could offer were a few fragments of words from which one could deduce that China had been hit by huge floods.

Marais happened to be at the office at the time. Using one of the numerous hammer-head pens he used to collect, he started writing, standing at the tiny counter in the entrance hall, and wrote an extensive lead story about the terrible misery which had engulfed the Chinese people.

It was a scoop: three days later a similar report appeared in the *Rand Daily Mail*.

The new arrangements suited Marais well. The bi-weekly edition had been published in the afternoon, but as a daily *Ons Vaderland* had become a morning paper. This meant that he could come into the office late – never before his afternoon nap and mostly only towards evening – and then work at night, when he was at his best. Often he was still at the office when one of the printers, Jan Deetlefs, would load up a car with papers and rush to Johannesburg to get the "national message" to the Rand on time. Marais may have gone along once or twice, but it was not a pleasant journey. From Pretoria to Roberts Heights the road was tarred and again from Alexandra to Johannesburg, but for the rest, because of the relatively heavy traffic, the whole route consisted of some of the worst "corrugated iron" roads in the country.

Marais came to work at odd times, and sometimes not at all, but he was mostly available. Often one of the young men would bring Swan's transcriptions to his room in Mrs. Cross's house, which was almost next door to the newspaper offices, where he would be lying reading in bed or sleeping. Frequently, too, the completeness of *Ons Vaderland*'s foreign reports would be determined by his mood. When he was not in a mood for writing, Otto Schwellnus relates, he would summarize the reports in a few lines or dismiss them as "nonsense". On other occasions he would not only translate the service almost in full but add so much editorial comment that the subeditors had a hard time deciding what to cut.

He worked intermittently but he worked well, and sometimes he worked hard. For this his colleagues gave him full approval, and this did not only come from Preller, who was later to write: "The greatest evolvement of his journalistic abilities after the Boer War came when *Ons Vaderland* was published as a morning paper and he worked with us daily and gave his best, sometimes rolling up his shirt-sleeves to help with the daily routine."

Preller himself, relates Rud. P. Visser, then the newspaper's subeditor and proofreader, seldom saw the newspaper go to bed.

"He was never there at night, but at about ten o'clock he would phone and ask, 'Is the paper filling up after all?' One could phone him until two or half past two in the morning to consult him."

The daily paper also brought Eugène new friends. More than thirty years later, Rud. P. Visser was to remember how Marais encouraged him to write. He and André Huguenet, the paper's columnist, who stayed in the boarding-house just across the way from Mrs. Cross's, spent hours in conversation. Marais tried to persuade him, too, to start writing seriously.

Another new friend was Kathleen Mansfield, Frikkie's sister, who was helping her brother in Bones the Chemist.

Marais and his colleagues now turned up more frequently in the Waverley Bar and he became one of the special clients for whom "Bob" Shilling kept shrimps in aspic under the counter. In the Waverley he also became acquainted with a brilliant young reporter from *Die Volkstem*, Anton Malga.

Although he no longer wished to live with the Prellers since his clash with Hannie, he still visited their house regularly. At about this time Gustav received an honorary doctorate from the University of Stellenbosch, an achievement of which Hannie was extremely proud.

Bob was doing his B.Sc. at the Transvaal University College. Gustav wanted him to complete the degree and then to specialize in chemical technology, "the thing of the future." But Bob had only half completed his degree when he followed the example of his college friends, Louis Pepler and Mauritz Kruger, and joined the Transvaal Training Squadron.

"Every morning at half past five," he was to say later, "the old military Crosleys called at all the university hostels and then rumbled down Park Street – that was where I had to get aboard. About twenty of us went to Swartkops every morning to fly before breakfast. We had to go two or three days a week – and more if we wanted to. My father didn't like this at all, but Oom Eugène encouraged it."

In these busy days something happened which was to be of great importance to Eugène Marais and which also indicates the extent of Preller's patience with his fickle, unreliable friend.

The last of Marais's fourteen articles in the series "Die Siel van die Mier" had been published in *Die Huisgenoot* four years before. The series had excited great interest; even so, he had written it without ever having seen the queen termite in her palace cavity. Even at Rietfontein, when he had been able to follow the underground shafts to great depths, he had never found her.

It is ironic that he was to find her in central Pretoria.

Ons Vaderland's offices lay in a fairly backward residential area from which the "better people" had long since moved away. The houses were old, sometimes musty (as were *Ons Vaderland*'s offices) and many had fallen into disrepair. On the corner of Du Toit and Pretorius Streets, only half a block away from Mrs. Cross's house, the Sprawson family lived in an almost derelict old place which had been infested with termites for years. All attempts to exterminate them had been unsuccessful.

In 1930 the City Council of Pretoria decided to attempt the task itself. Work had hardly begun when Marais arrived on the scene. For days he watched the labourers unsuccessfully looking for the palace cavity. When he offered to point out the cavity to them, provided he would be allowed to observe the live queen for some days, the foreman agreed.

His extremely tolerant editor, Gustav Preller, agreed to give Marais several days' leave, as, according to Marais, the termites would have to be watched day and night. Marais and a friend, Victor Foster, had the dining room cleaned out and swept, and they soon discovered the three most important termite tunnels.

At the place where these tunnels crossed – underneath the fireplace – he asked the labourers to lift up the floor. After this he and Foster started opening the palace cavity in earnest.

"When we reached the outer walls of the cavity," Marais described the entire series of observations in a letter to Wilhelm Spilhaus, "I softened the cement work by drenching it repeatedly with a gentle spray of water. When it was quite moist we sliced away the outer wall with a sharp knife until the hollow itself was disclosed. By means of occasional flashes from the electric torch we located the queen cell in the centre of the cavity. We could see that up to the present we had occasioned very little disturbance. The work of the egg carriers and feeders seemed to be proceeding normally.

"The opening of the queen's cell itself was a far more delicate operation and took several hours to accomplish, but even here we were successful eventually. We cut away more than half of the thick cell within which the queen was enclosed. After that we kept her under constant observation for more than two days."

For Marais it was a great moment, and not only because for the first time he could observe the queen in her inner sanctum. Surgery was one of his dreams, and his contact with Dr. A.G. Visser had strengthened this urge. Four years before, writing about the cure of certain mental conditions by surgery, he had told Spilhaus in a letter. "If I were a great surgeon I would not hesitate to operate in certain cases. I would lift the top of the skull."

Now, in that dilapidated old house, this was exactly what he did. Like a surgeon he exposed the brain without damaging the organism, for in the rest of the termitary activities carried on in a normal way.

Before their observations came to an end Marais and his friend witnessed the "brain" being dramatically damaged. A lump of hard clay dropped from the wall of the palace cavity and fell onto the queen.

Throughout the termitary there was an immediate reaction. The workers stopped their work in the palace cavity. The circle of guards broke up and most of them disappeared into the undamaged passages behind the palace cavity.

Next a dense mass of workers entered the cavity, covered the queen's body and began taking fluid from her body, assisted by the king. In the remoter parts of the nest, where work had still been in progress before the accident happened, all activities came to a stop within a few minutes.

Now the restoration began: the queen, who had been waving her head frantically from side to side, quietened down. The circle of guards again took up their positions. The feeding of the queen was accelerated and soon her body was back to its normal size.

By the following day all activities throughout the vast kingdom had returned to normal, but it was only a respite. *The Soul of the White Ant* ends on a sad note: "The workmen had occupied themselves with excavating and removing the breeding gardens in other rooms, but now the time allotted to us had come to an end. The queen was removed from her half-cell and taken away, captive; and after that the activities and life of this nest ceased for good."

Mrs. Jessie Cross was to remember how Marais brought the queen home in a jar.

"A repulsive looking thing," she said.

These observations enabled Marais to complete the series of articles called "Die Siel van die Mier". After an interruption of more than four years, the fifteenth and final article in the series was published in *Die Huisgenoot* the next year – which says a great deal not only for Marais's reputation but also for the flexibility of the period.

Some time later Wilhelm Spilhaus was to send the letter in which Marais had described his observations to the English psychology magazine *Psyche*, where it was published as an article titled "The Termite Queen as the Brain of the Organism". This explains why some of the observations in that article are stated much less guardedly than in the last chapter of *Die Siel van die Mier*: the English version had been a letter, written not for the public but for a friend and admirer.

In the decrepit old house Marais had noticed that the heads of the queen's bodyguards had all pointed north. Could there be a connection between magnetism and the activities of the white ants? Would magnetism also have an effect on other organisms?

He borrowed two powerful magnets from Piet Haak of Haak's Garage and began experimenting.

"He would take two bricks," Mrs. Cross said later, "and cover them with straw, putting the magnets between them. The termites would then begin building on one side, but as soon as the magnets were removed they would stop. 'Why do you do that?' I asked. 'Oh,' he replied, 'one never knows. One might find out something.'

"One morning I brought him coffee in bed, and I saw that he was sleeping with the magnets on his chest. When I asked him about it later he said that he wanted to see whether they had an effect on the heart. On another occasion he took a morning glory and tied the magnets to the spot where the new bud would come out. It never came out. At first I thought he had pinched it to kill it, but he convinced me that it had been the magnets only."

Marais also conducted experiments with magnetism when he accompanied Gustav Preller on a hunting expedition to the Magalakwêna later that year. This time only *Ons Vaderland* people went along: Preller, Marais, Carl Preller, Joan Couzyn and E. Haslem.

Joan Couzyn (his first name was pronounced like Johan, but without the "h") was soon to become one of Eugène's most faithful friends and admirers. He was a young man with an unhappy past but many ideals. Couzyn's mother had died when he was fourteen.

He ran away from home and went to work on a farm but after three years he returned to Pretoria to continue his schooling. Here he met Bob Preller and, through Bob, Gustav Preller. The kind-hearted editor had given him the job of translating the Transozean reports after school.

After matric Joan won a bursary and went on to the University of the Witwatersrand. He was not only *Ons Vaderland*'s Rand correspondent, but also worked in the offices during the holidays.

The fifth member of the company, E. Haslem, also fitted the Preller pattern perfectly: he, too, was a friend of the Preller boys; he, too, had been given an appointment at *Ons Vaderland* (as an illustrator) and he, too, boarded in Blackwood Street.

"During that expedition Eugène watched the ants for hours," Joan Couzyn was to say later in an interview. "I remember very well how he tried to establish whether the direction followed by a column of termites would be affected by strong magnets. Haslem and I made some sketches. His articles about the Soul of the Ant had by that time been published in *Die Huisgenoot* and I was amazed that he was still so interested."

On this expedition Marais also read German poetry, including Schiller and Goethe. When his German failed him, he asked Couzyn to help him.

It was only a short holiday. Gustav Preller could no longer, as he had been able to three years before, stay away from work for six weeks.

Marais returned to Pretoria with an Afrikaans adaptation of Goethe's "Der Fischer". Joan Couzyn returned to the Rand, where he attended lectures in the morning and assisted the elderly sculptor Anton van Wouw in his studio during the afternoon. The others immediately returned to their jobs at *Ons Vaderland*. Gustav Preller and Carl, especially, had no time to waste – Carl to see whether he could increase the newspaper's meagre advertising revenues and Gustav to see whether he could save the paper's life.

Hardly ten months after its founding it was clear that *Ons Vaderland* was having an extremely hard time. Even in its bi-weekly form the newspaper had not produced enough income to pay the staff's salaries every month, and now there were twice as many people. Preller, who had always insisted that they would be able to make money if only they could become a daily, had to admit that there was no room for two Afrikaans daily newspapers in Pretoria. It was true that *Die Volkstem*'s circulation was adversely affected by the publication of *Ons Vaderland* as a daily, but its circulation was still five thousand copies more than that of Preller's newspaper and its financial resources infinitely greater.

Marais had no doubt about the outcome. Early in 1931, after a series of painful and protracted negotiations with the board of directors, Preller, to his great humiliation, had to announce to the editorial staff one morning that *Ons Vaderland* would from now on again be published only twice a week.

Even more painful were the interviews with the loyal members of staff whose services would no longer be required. More than half of them would have to seek work elsewhere.

Some of the staff were retained conditionally. Rud. P. Visser was allowed to remain provided he accepted the job of proofreader. Marais could continue on a part-time basis. He must have accepted this decision with mixed feelings. After all, he could now devote more time to Edna.

6. The After-Effects

Even before the demise of the daily, Marais, Mrs. Cross and her family had moved to Vermeulen Street, a street running parallel to Pretorius Street but two blocks further north.

Mrs. Cross was glad to move on. During the past two years the area had deteriorated markedly. Recently a number of Indians had moved in across the road, noisy people whose radio was turned full blast all day and much of the night.

The new house, 420 Vermeulen Street, was much larger than the old one. It had six bedrooms and a spacious plot. For Edna it was a new world. Behind the house stood a row of old stables and inside them a huge water-tank. This was more of a residential area than the part of Pretorius Street where they had lived before and it teemed with children.

"They made me mad," Edna Cross said. "Oom Eugène had a sort of magic quality – an amazing attraction for birds and animals and children. Within two days in Vermeulen Street the wagtails and sparrows were eating from his hands. And he had only to walk out of the gate and every child in the area would come running along and hang onto him. When he came back from his office or from town it was the same. But I was an agile brat, and I could frequently get to him first. When the others came crowding around him and grabbing at him, I would get angry, throw off his hand and walk alone. Then he would say: 'Don't worry about Edna. She's just got a little black devil on her shoulder again.'

"I punched those kids when I could get them. He was to belong to me and to me alone. One day he said: 'I may like other children, but you're mine.' That consoled me. They could have him as he walked in the street, but I had him to myself as soon as we got into the house. In this way he taught me never to be jealous and lose my temper.

"At about six in the evening I was supposed to lay the table and then I would run to Oom Eugène and ask him whether we might go for a walk. Then he would tell my mother: 'Mrs. Cross, Edna and I are going for a short walk, to the Market Square and back. There'll be plenty of time to lay the table when she gets older.'

"On Market Square I was allowed to walk only on the cobbles and on the way there only on the cement blocks of the pavement – if I happened to tread on the lines between them, a catastrophe would happen. We didn't really walk, we marched. And then he would recite rhymes to accompany the rhythm: 'There was a young lady who was tall and fair, Her eyes were yellow and blue was her hair, she looked around with a terrible stare, And it served her jolly well RIGHT, yo-ho!' Or otherwise: 'My mother said it served you RIGHT, You had a good home and you LEFT!'"

In Vermeulen Street Marais started a secret society, the Whoa-Bill Club, for the girls and their friends and noted the details in his diary: "President E. Marais, 1st Vice President Pierre, 2nd Vice President Hettie, 3rd Vice President Edna. Rules: 1. Regular meetings once a week Friday 4.30-5 p.m.; 2. Other meetings called by the President; 3. Every member must know password, grip and signal; 4. Members pledge themselves to help any member who needs help at any time."

In this year, 1931, Edna was eight years old. Hettie, her twelve year old sister, was the club's secretary.

These words Eugène Marais could apply directly to himself. To others – thus he had felt for many years, and now more than ever – his talents, his charm, his abilities were of no importance. To them it was his morphine addiction – the morphine in his veins – which counted, and this made him a pariah. For him, too (in how many anonymous letters had it not been said in so many words), love was forbidden.

Earlier in this book it was assumed that next to death, the most desirable state, the words "Dark Stream" also refer to the substitute death, morphine. Seen against this background, Juanita could hardly meet her end in any other way than to be struck by a snake and that is what happens in the story.

The poem and the story were quite probably written independently, but by using the poem in the story, and moreover in the mouth of the doomed young girl, it is given a new significance. It reflects Marais's own fate, exactly as does another poem, "Die Towenares", (The Witch, subtitled "The Song of the Exiled Young Girl"):

> Sy hoor net die stem van die wind alleen
> en die wind treur altyd
> om hy alleen is.
>
> She hears only the voice of the lone wind
> and the wind mourns always
> because he is alone.

It strikes one how, in one poem after another, the character with whom Marais may be associated is in the first place a woman and in the second, dark-skinned: in the two mentioned above, in "Mabal-êl", in the songs of the Bushman girl, Nampti (who, insignificant though she may be, tenderly cares for the desert lark as Marais cared for Edna Cross – "all I have in the world").

For decades Marais had felt drawn to those of another colour – in London, in the Waterberg, in Pretoria – they who, in these times and places, were pariahs like himself.

11. Drought

In 1933 the greatest drought "in human memory" reached its climax in South Africa. The drought was the theme of two articles and one remarkable short story which Marais wrote during that year.

In "Die Verwoestingsgang van Droogte" (The Destructive Course of Drought) Marais commits a serious scientific blunder, for reasons which will soon be made clear. He refers to his article on drought published in *The Agricultural Journal* in 1914 and then continues: "The theory accepted by the author was supported from the most unexpected sources. The world famous French astronomer, Flammarion, among others, based a stunning prediction on it – that the entire earth was drying out because an incredible amount of water was being lost for ever every year through the evaporation of subterranean waters in the central fires and the disappearance of the vapours into space."

In fact, Flammarion's theory was a great deal older than 1914 and Marais had referred to it in the article he wrote in that year. "In Asia and Africa, the two 'dry' continents, the disappearance of water annually is so great it seems to justify the prediction of the French astronomer, Flammarion, that within a measurable space of time the human race will find its final eclipse in this cause."

Some months later Marais again commemorated the drought with a long story, one of the weirdest in Afrikaans, which was published in three instalments as "Die Ondergang der Tweede Wêreld" (The Downfall of the Second World).

This was the climax of his lifelong interest, virtually an obsession, with drought. Some critics have suggested that this interest had something to do with the desiccation and barrenness of Marais's own soul as a result of his addiction. The theory sounds superficially acceptable, but the theme appeared in his work many years before he had taken to morphine, in the poem "There shall be no more sea", written as a Paarl schoolboy. The closing lines went beyond all his later writings on the theme of drought and in fact contain the embryo of the story he was to write almost half a century later at the peak of the great drought of the thirties: "While night, with livid lightning lit, hangs dark upon thy troubled waters, and to Him we'll flee for refuge when there shall be no more sea."

In the story "Die Ondergang der Tweede Wêreld" Marais takes his theory (and that of Flammarion) of the desiccation of the earth to its extreme consequences: as a result of incredibly violent volcanic activities, all rivers start running into fissures in the earth, and eventually so does the sea. In scenes of total break-down and collapse, misery and cruelty, all inhabitants of the earth die of thirst, with the exception of a few survivors. But, unlike the poem written half a century earlier – for a great deal had happened to Eugène Marais in those fifty years – there was no God from whom salvation could be sought. The story reminds one rather of Edgar Allan Poe (also an opium addict) at his most gruesome, and in fact gives the impression of a morphine nightmare.

It is not pleasant reading. In the year of Hitler's rise to power, 1933 (and shortly before the first of Stalin's series of bloody "liquidations"), Marais describes in his science fiction story how the municipality of Pretoria lures all non-whites in the city, under false pretences, to an open patch of ground where they are then murdered by twenty thousand armed whites. The description of this scene is at least equalled, if not surpassed, later in the story by a description of a young white girl cold-bloodedly shooting dead a black man grovelling on his knees in front of her and pleading for his life.

In passing one might point out that the image of an attractive girl with her slaves or subjects at her feet is a recurrent one in Marais's writings and fantasies. One finds it in the vision suggested by Marais to Edna Cross: the fairy queen, who looks like a twenty year old girl, with her page kneeling in front of her and slipping on her shoes. Echoes of the theme are found in Marais's poem about the merciless goddess he sees as nature: "Adoring round me all are prone/I feel their tears upon my feet." It may not be coincidence that when first encountered the girl in the short story mentioned above, like Sacher-Masoch's *Venus in Furs*, is wearing, over short pants and stockings, a fur coat – in this case one looted from a Pretoria shop during the general chaos. As the dying black man sinks down in front of her, his head comes to rest on her foot.

Both scenes are described without a vestige of moral disapproval. A greater contrast with the sentiments displayed in the short story "Diep Rivier" – which reveals great sympathy for people of colour and which was not to be published until some month *later* – can hardly be imagined.

Examining these various examples of stories, one is tempted to surmise, to borrow a phrase from religion, that a battle between good and evil was being waged in Marais during the last years of his life. If so, evil had by no means gained the upper hand. Even now he was to Edna still the perfect father.

"When he was still in bed on Sunday mornings, I would always bring him the *Sunday Times*," she was to say later, "and then creep into bed with him. We would read the comics together. There was one thing I could never understand. It was all right if I got into bed with him and put my head on his shoulder, but he never wanted me to get beneath more than the first blanket. I found this very strange. It was not until much later that I realised that it had been the correct thing to do and what a great man he had been."

There seems little doubt that the varying subject matter and quality of the stories written by Marais during this period bear a relationship to the degree of his morphine consumption. In some of the stories one seems to be able to see directly into the dark stream of Marais's subconscious, with the Freudian lid lifted off, so to speak, for the protective action of what Freud called the "censor" was frequently suppressed by morphine during the process of creation. Not only themes from his own life well up spontaneously from the depths, but also themes from books which he had read long ago. His story "Die Ondergang der Tweede Wêreld" shows marked similarities to a science fiction story by Flammarion, *La fin du monde*, published in 1894 – the year of Marais's marriage – and translated during the same year into Dutch as *Het vergaan der wereld*.

In this book the "first world" collides with a comet, while the "second" is destroyed by drought. The degree to which Marais may have used undigested memories here – quite possibly unconsciously – is clear from his use of the Dutch genitive "der" instead of normal Afrikaans "van die". There is little doubt that the story was written under the influence of morphine and that there was not enough time for editing before publishing it in the newspaper. Only when it was published in *volume* form later was the title changed to *Die Ondergang van die Tweede Wêreld*. Moreover, without a knowledge of Flammarion's book the word "tweede" (second) in the title has no meaning, as it is never mentioned in Marais's story.

During this time a political meeting led to a third piece on drought, one of Marais's best known articles: "'n Paradys van Weleer" (A Paradise of Yesteryear). As a reporter on *Die Vaderland*, Marais accompanied P.G.W. Grobler, Minister of Lands and leader of the Transvaal National Party, to a political meeting near Brits, where Marais's son lived.

When they reached Brits, Marais took his leave of the Minister, who travelled the rest of the way alone. He then went to look up his son.

"Don't you have to attend the meeting, father?" young Eugène asked.

And Marais replied: "Oh no, it would be much too tedious. Anyway, I have the whole speech in my pocket."

By that time the young man had his own car and so father and son could take a long drive through the countryside north of Brits. "The veld was so bare," the son was to relate later, "that we could see mongooses running through the veld up to five hundred yards from the road."

On the road to Brits Marais had visited that part of Agter-die-Berg (Behind the Mountain) where the Fouries of Wildebeesthoek and many other family friends from his childhood days had lived. In animated prose he was to describe the misery and humiliation he witnessed during this journey.

> I visited Agter-die-Berg again some time ago – naturally not for the first time – and, involuntarily, recollections from the days of my childhood crowded into my mind, excluding all other thoughts. And it all caused a feeling of indescribable longing. How will one ever be able to put into words the difference between what I saw yesterday and the glorious days which – alas – now exist only in memory.
>
> The paradise of yesteryear had become a barren desert of stone ... of all the well known bubbling mountain streams no drop remained ... This is the third year of the greatest drought which has visited Magaliesberg within the memory of man.
>
> We came across numerous descendants of old Magaliesberg families, numbering among the aristocracy of the Transvaal. In tattered, dust-covered clothes, they were working on the roads with shovels and pick-axes for four shillings a day.

The complete title of this article, as it was published in the newspaper, was "A Paradise of yesteryear lost in the cruelty of drought". It was not only a clever piece of journalism about a devastated landscape, but also a yearning for Marais's own unspoilt youth, a paradise lost which he was never to regain.

During this intensely creative period (which does not mean that anything like a majority of his writings was on an acceptable level) Marais was continually looking for new themes. One theme which had long fascinated him was that of the Flying Dutchman. Some of the information for the long story he wrote about it he found in the house of a good friend of his at the time, G.O. Lunnon.

It was Lunnon who had persuaded Marais the year before to address the S.A. National Society about Bushman stones and he was frequently seen in Lunnon's company during this time in the Waverley Bar.

The Waverley in Church Street was still Marais's favourite haunt. From the street a long, narrow passage led past the public and private bars to the restaurant and here Marais and Lunnon whiled away many hours.

"During the oyster season he would frequently ring me up to say that he had ordered oysters and stout for two and that it was ready and waiting for me. It was only by trickery that I would ever be able to pay my whack. I used to enjoy these little meetings. Frequently, he would bring something of interest for us to discuss: a plant, a book, a scientific or historical article, a tortoise with unusual markings, or some other object that he thought would amuse or interest me."

Years later Lunnon himself was to end his life on his smallholding near Somerset West by blowing himself up with dynamite.

Marais's regular visits to the Waverley and his friendship with the barman, Bob Shilling, make it seem as if he had now begun drinking more. One of his colleagues at *Die Vaderland*, Rud. P. Visser, said: "I often saw him go into the Waverley at ten o'clock for a hair of the dog. If the child was with him, she would wait outside."

This statement, implying a fairly advanced stage of alcoholism, is not confirmed by other testimony.

Neither did he need the extra support of drink during this time. His supply was sufficient, but within bounds. The fact that his doctors – Louw and Nel – could maintain this extremely delicate balance may have had something to do with the fact that they were not only his doctors but also his friends and – last but not least – his partners in a bright new world which now, as it had done forty years before, was opening before him.

12. The Glitter of Gold

Edna was only vaguely aware of this new world in which Oom Eugène was moving. She does remember:

"Early one morning Dr. Nel's car came to fetch us. It was a big luxurious car driven by a chauffeur. We were taken to some place in Johannesburg, I don't know where. I only have a vague recollection of shrubs and a beautiful garden."

To Edna it was an exciting outing. To Eugène Marais and his fellow entrepreneurs it was a serious matter.

In September 1931 General Hertzog's refusal to go off the gold standard along with Britain had caused serious criticism of his Government. As we have seen, it may have contributed to Hertzog's decision to obtain a stronger mouthpiece in the Transvaal by means of *Die Vaderland*.

During the next year, while Marais, spurred on by Fasie de Wet's two wonder-boys, was experiencing a remarkable revival in his journalistic output, criticism of the Government kept mounting. In a Dingaan's Day speech near Lichtenburg, Marais's old friend Mr. Justice Tielman Roos of the Appeal Court made it clear that he was planning to enter politics again, and that his platform would be departure from the gold standard. This announcement caused tremendous excitement throughout the country. Although General Hertzog had said that he would stand or fall by his decision to stay on the gold standard, public pressure became so intense that, hardly two weeks after Tielman Roos's speech, the General was forced to yield to pressure and leave the gold standard.

This announcement, in the last days of 1932, happened to coincide with Eugène Marais's return to an active writing life after a slough of almost four months.

With the departure from the gold standard, following on the previous pessimism, a period of hope, optimism and new life began early in 1933 – exactly what was happening to Eugène Marais in these months.

The Johannesburg Stock Exchange had been closed when the Government made the announcement, so there was some time to think the matter over. Leaving the gold standard would immediately cause a 30% rise in the price of South African gold. Shares in the best gold-mines would rise by about the same percentage. But the low grade mines, which had been unprofitable or only just profitable up to 29 December, would be able to start making a whopping great profit as a result of the higher gold price – and their shares would at least double in value.

The Stock Exchange was to reopen on 3 January. Anyone who could invest £1 000 in a weak mine on that day would be able to sell his shares for £2 000 to £3 000 only a few weeks later. It was so beautifully simple. The only snag was that the Exchange could not handle all the applications – more than 200 000 new investors wanted gold shares.

Then the idea occurred to someone that worked-out mines might be reopened, as the price of 142 shillings a fine ounce would make them profitable, too.

Suddenly the depression flowered into a boom. The increase in the price of gold was followed by the founding of about 200 new mining companies. Eugène Marais knew just about everything there was to know about gold mining. He himself had lived through the early growth of the Rand industry; he was the confidant of the legendary mining kings; his own family, Oom Ryk Piet for example, had made fortunes from gold. Now the pattern of the 1890's was being repeated. When Eugène Marais spoke about gold, Dr. Gideon Nel listened to him, and so did Dr. Louw and Dr. van Reenen, the dentist, and the chemist, Max Schwartz, and the friend in Germiston who had been sending him parcels by mail.

Soon a syndicate was formed to invest money in gold and other minerals. Marais became one of its members. Apart from his own special knowledge, he also had a number of acquaintances and contacts.

"These people had the most fantastic plans for getting rich," Mrs. Cross said much later. "They used Mr. Marais because he knew all the right people, Ministers and things like that. They were constantly driving around, then they would come to ask me to make them some food to take along. They were to supply the money and he the contacts and they would share the profits equally. And of course they also helped him to get hold of his stuff."

Expensive chauffeur-driven cars began picking up Marais in Vermeulen Street early in the morning, worked-out mines in the countryside were visited, great plans were made, glorious dreams dreamt.

Eugène Marais relived the days of his youth when he, Dr. Nel and the other partners arrived in Barberton, the old gold ghost town, one Saturday morning on the trail of yet another proposition and astounded the sleepy population of the village by ordering ice-cold French champagne.

The investment possibilities were not restricted to minerals. As always in times of a gold fever, everything eventually began to look promising.

"Once they wanted to invest money in a sugar estate," said Mrs. Cross. "It was a well known place, but I can't remember the name any more. Their biggest scheme was to buy land in Namaqualand. The Government owned one portion in the centre, and they wanted to buy that from the Government. They said they were going to pick up diamonds from the ground. Fourie, the Minister, was willing to approve the transactions.

"'We're all going to be millionaires,' Mr. Marais said one evening when he told us about the scheme.

"Then I asked him: 'What are you going to do with all your millions?'

"'I'm going to send your sons to any university, Mrs. Cross,' he replied, 'and your daughters to school in Germany.'

"So I told him: 'Now you have taken care of my family, what about me?'

"'Oh, the mother. No, Mrs. Cross and I are going to take a trip around the world.'

"'And what about Mr. Cross?'

"'Oh,' he said, 'forget about him.'"

As Mrs. Cross remembers it, the Minister of Mines, A.P.J. Fourie, was suddenly called away. Oswald Pirow would have had to sign in his place, and he was not prepared to do so.

In any event they could not forget Mr. Cross. In August 1933 he asked his family to join him in Clanwilliam in the Cape, where he was helping to build the big new dam.

It may have been a coincidence, but during this month no single contribution by Eugène Marais was published in *Die Vaderland* – the longest break that year.

In the same month, Wilhelm Spilhaus sent Gustav Preller a copy of *Psyche*, the English psychology journal in which Marais's letter about the queen termite in her cell had just been published in article form. Writing from Cape Town, Spilhaus told Preller that he was writing to him rather than to Eugène Marais – "on account of the fate of my last letter to him" – which had apparently gone astray and to which he had received no reply.

Preller handed the magazine over to his friend, but to Marais Spilhaus's action was an accusation and a reproach. In fact, he had not written to Spilhaus for two years. In the light of the old man's present attitude, he did not feel inclined to resume the correspondence. It had long been clear to him that Spilhaus knew about his problem.

Marais had, in his mind, long since taken leave of his aged friend. Now he also had to take leave of his young girl-friend, Edna. They were to move in September. Edna had just turned ten.

Everything one knows about Eugène Marais would make one suspect that a deep slough of despond was to follow these developments. It did not and the most likely reason – apart from the spiritual injection of the activities of the gold syndicate – was that Eugène Marais had found an ingenious way of maintaining contact with the family in a more than symbolic manner.

Gustav Preller, in spite of everything that had happened, had meanwhile again invited him to move into Blackwood Street. Now Marais persuaded Mrs. Cross to leave Hettie, Edna's attractive fourteen year old sister, behind in Pretoria in order not to interrupt her schooling. At the same time, he persuaded the Prellers to take her into their home as well.

Gustav Preller arranged for all Marais's earthly possessions to be collected from Mrs. Cross's house in September. By this time he had hardly anything: a large yellow suitcase, two blankets, burnt full of holes, a bag of old papers, a few books and a medicine chest.

And yet, when Mrs. Cross and her two sons and youngest daughter left for the Cape soon afterwards, he was, judging by the barometer of his regular weekly contributions to *Die Vaderland* – in fine fettle.

Forty years later, Hettie Cross was asked whether, in view of these circumstances, she thought that Eugène Marais might have been a little in love with her. "That's out of the question," she replied. "Edna was the one he was mad about." And when the theme was again broached later during the conversation, she added: "If that should be true, I would feel extremely flattered."

Regarding the move, Preller wrote to Spilhaus in 1933: "Mr. Marais ... allowed himself to be persuaded by me to come and share our humble abode."

The words reveal a degree of irritation.

Preller could never understand why Eugène Marais had not wanted to return to Blackwood Street before now and why he seemed to prefer Mrs. Cross's house to his. After all, the Prellers belonged to the Pretoria establishment; they were among the best people.

To Hannie Preller such matters were of even greater importance. To her the fourteen year old girl who was now boarding with them at Eugène's insistence was not quite their class. She gave her all kinds of jobs about the house and every Saturday afternoon she made Hettie do her hair – quite a time-consuming task in the 1930's.

Unfortunately, Oom Eugène had never encouraged her to know her place. "If Tollie Preller can write a book," he had told her once regarding *Op die Wal van die Mahalakwêna*, "you can do it too."

Forty years later Hettie was to say of Hannie Preller: "She was a great snob, terribly arrogant." And she added: "During the few months I was there there was a quite tangible tension."

Even so, during these months things were going quite well with Eugène Marais. His contributions were appearing regularly in *Die Vaderland*; he and the other members of the syndicate were paying regular visits to the countryside to investigate new propositions. When the first heavy rains broke the drought that summer he celebrated the occasion with a lively poem: "Wanneer dit reën op Rietfontein" (When it rains on Rietfontein). Parts of this poem have been quoted before. However, to understand the poem, it should be seen not only against the background of the Waterberg during

World War I but against that of Pretoria in November 1933.

By writing this poem, Marais, sick and run-down as he was, had jumped back nineteen years in time and had recaptured the atmosphere of those wonderful, rainy days in December 1914, fresh, sparkling days, fragrantly beautiful days, in spite of the setbacks of the rebellion.

Here one could see Oom Gys sitting on the stoep; there was Cohen dismounting at the front door. One could even see Sammy with his bales of goods. And Tamaria? She is referred to as Tant Malie.

It is true that it is extremely difficult to fit Tamaria, as the name is pronounced, into the rhythm and rhyme scheme of the poem. However, the real Tant Malie was the mother of Hans Purekrans van Rooyen. Could it be that Marais here, as he had done before, was unconsciously trying to avoid unpleasant facts from the past by simply immersing them in the dark stream of his memories and (perhaps literally) forgetting them?

At about this time he made a young friend who was to remember him all his life with great affection: Gideon Louw, two years and ten months old, a son of Marais's doctor, Dr. H.J. Louw. Like his cousin and partner, Dr. Nel, Dr. Louw was still living in the U-shaped block of flats next to the Union Buildings. Every day Marais walked across for his supply. It soon became a routine. Quite late in the morning he would visit the flats, and, taking little Gideon by the hand, walk around the Union Buildings' gardens until lunchtime. Then he would lunch at the flat. If Dr. Louw happened to be going to the countryside that afternoon, he would go along, be dropped in the veld to study plants and insects and be picked up again later.

"Despite my tender age," Louw's son was to say forty years later, "it is my personal theory that my outings with Eugène Marais definitely influenced me to become a zoologist instead of a doctor, although I grew up in a city."

He was only one of numerous children who had come under Marais's magical influence at an incredibly early age. And in his relations with children this seemed always to be a wholesome and beneficial influence.

When this book was written, Dr. Louw had already died. Regarding his treatment of Marais, the doctor's son said: "According to my father, he had succeeded in reducing his intake from a very high one to a quantity which kept him going day by day. My father used to say that Eugène Marais could have reached a great age on the dosage he was taking, and that he was quite well adapted to the problem."

This view is in accordance with the known facts. Although Marais did occasionally supplement Dr. Louw's supply from other sources, his consumption never got quite out of control in 1933.

Between Marais and Preller, too, relations were quite cordial during this time. If Eugène did not go in to the office every day, he did turn up fairly regularly. He was an ally, if only in a moral sense, against what Preller called the "carpet-baggers" from the South.

To an increasing degree, Preller was embittered by the fact that so many important decisions were taken without consulting him. He was terribly disappointed over the loss of his beloved German news service, Transozean. Under the new regime, he was to write later, "a new management in Cape Town who thought they knew better cancelled the service and played into the hands of an Israeli concern, allowing the newspaper to be used for covert anti-German propaganda from time to time."

On this and other matters Preller clashed with Fasie de Wet, and after each clash De Wet was even more inclined than ever to regard Willem van Heerden as the real editor and Preller as nothing but the leader writer.

Apart from De Wet's heavy guns, Preller also had to contend with a number of sharp-shooters. These included "joiners". The main issue was the use of the Afrikaans language.

In a newspaper every report should be read by a second person. Anyone can make a mistake and it is no disgrace for an editor if a younger member of the editorial staff reads through his pieces and occasionally asks him whether a sentence could not perhaps be phrased slightly differently. However, to change the boss's language and style without his permission was unheard of.

Unfortunately, the Afrikaans language had changed during Preller's working career. A great many things which would have been quite correct during the transitional stage from Dutch to Afrikaans had now become anachronistic and old-fashioned. Apart from their work on the magazine, Van Schoor and Schwellnus were responsible for editing certain important reports. How were they to deal with the language crisis? They soon found a simple solution by appointing a language commission. Schwellnus was to be the northern representative and Van Schoor was to be responsible for the southern point of view. Now when Preller wrote "Die man't gesteel en werd gestraf" (using the apostrophe t because he detested that clumsy "het" and using "werd" because "is" made no sense to him at all), the north-south language commission would unanimously change it into: "Die man het gesteel en is gestraf" – which did not, of course, prevent Gustav Preller from changing it back into *'t* and *werd* on the proofs.

In language questions Marais sided with Preller. After all, they literally spoke the same language and were in complete agreement. But if the boy wonders elected to chop and change his style, what difference did it make? Once he had rushed through an article or a short story, its fate was a matter of complete indifference to him.

But to Gustav Preller, an individualistic editor in chief of more than thirty years' experience in journalism, these were anything but minor matters. "Pseudo-improvers" he was to call Schwellnus and Van Schoor. "Pedantic blue-pencil tinkerers who have no respect for the work of others and in many instances understand no rap of it."

There were other, more important, points of friction. Fasie de Wet realized that there was no money to change *Die Vaderland* into a daily newspaper in Pretoria. By appointing the very best people he could find, he wanted to make the bi-weekly paper self-supporting and profitable as soon as possible so that it could be moved to Johannesburg.

Most of the editorial staff, including De Wet's Young Turks, had rather welcomed this goal. Preller did not. On the contrary, he was intensely irritated by the constant refrain: "Within three years we'll be in Johannesburg."

Preller could not understand such thinking. Why Johannesburg if the heart of the Afrikaner people had always been Pretoria and would remain so?

In the meantime Schwellnus and Van Schoor were still having great problems in extracting Oom Eugène's contributions from him in time for their magazine division. In all newspapers this division goes to bed (i.e. is printed) long before the news sections. Page 1, containing the main news reports, is held open to the very last so that unexpected news developments may still be inserted.

When Schwellnus and Van Schoor discussed their problem with Fasie de Wet, he thought up a simple solution which was enough to give most newspapermen a fit.

"Put page 1 to bed first and leave the magazine page open till Marais has completed his contribution," he advised.

And, as usual, he was completely right. Eugène Marais's stories did much more for *Die Vaderland*'s circulation than even the hottest news, which would in any case be lukewarm or cold by the time it reached the platteland. De Wet showed his appreciation by paying Eugène Marais such high rates for his work – by journalistic standards, of course – that eyebrows were raised in certain quarters.

For this, in the long run, he was not to receive great thanks or appreciation.

13. "The Leeches"

A newspaper does not change its entire way of doing things for the sake of one man unless there are very good reasons for doing so and of this both Preller and Marais were quite aware.

"The truth is," Preller was to write about Marais later, "that his meagerly compensated short stories and other contributions increased the newspaper's circulation to such an extent that a mercenary management regarded it as a matter of the highest priority to keep him going as long as they could."

Preller's disapproving attitude may to a considerable extent have been caused by his feud with the carpet-baggers. Willem van Heerden was later to deny that Marais's remuneration, according to the standards of the time, was meagre. "On the contrary," he said, "De Wet paid Eugène Marais amounts that were almost irresponsibly lavish, paying fees and advances which were in fact hard to justify. But Eugène was bitter; he could misinterpret even the best of intentions."

It is said that there are people who know the price of everything and the value of nothing. At this time one could perhaps have said just the opposite about Eugène Marais. In his eyes the relatively high amounts he received for his contributions made no difference to the fact that he was being used by the paper. The money paid for his work could be earned by an advocate in a short consultation or by a broker just by his signature.

But he, with his much rarer talents, was shaken awake when he was so ill that he would rather have died. And then, agonisingly, he had to put down chunks of his own life on paper for them to huckster with, his own life-blood. In his eyes all newspaper bosses, all publishers, eventually became leeches.

This point of view was probably aggravated by the fact that his writings were published in book form by three publishers, Nasionale Pers in Cape Town, the Afrikaanse Pers, and Van Schaik in Pretoria. Up to 1932 all Marais's books had been published by the Nasionale Pers in Cape Town. There were five altogether. After this date a tussle arose between Fasie de Wet and Van Schaik for Marais's work.

In 1933 J.L. van Schaik was the most prominent Afrikaans publisher. The technical production of his books was excellent, and he saw to it that manuscripts were edited by capable people.

From Marais's point of view, there was another advantage: Van Schaik was willing to pay cash for every acceptable manuscript.

In literary circles this custom has on occasion been frowned upon. The accepted agreement is, after all, that the publisher pays the author a royalty of the total retail price of the work. However, if the publisher has money and the author does not, it may be an attractive proposition to both of them for the publisher to buy the full copyright for cash. With this system one of the two parties will always be the loser – if the book sells poorly, the publisher will lose, but if the book does well the writer will lose. On the face of it, this sounds fair enough. But, in practice, the publisher usually has a better feel for the kind of book which should succeed. And, in practice, the writer, who was only too grateful to receive a purse full of money at the time, gets unhappy when one edition after another is reprinted without another penny coming his way.

This was what happened to E.B. Grosskopf when he sold the manuscript of the famous Afrikaans juvenile novel, *Patrys-hulle*, to Van Schaik for £75 in 1926. It was one of the best investments a publisher had made in South Africa. By the 1980's the book had been reprinted almost 40 times.

For Eugène Marais, on the other hand, this sort of agreement was exactly what he wanted. He was 62. To him cash was everything, long-term benefits nothing.

Judging by the evidence, one suspects that Van Schaik was willing to publish certain of Marais's writings which he knew would not be a great success in order to obtain the rights for others. However, he drew the line at *Die Swart Verraad* (Black Treason), a play performed in Pretoria in June 1933. Plays in book form were not a proposition at the time, as both Van Schaik and Fasie de Wet knew.

On 3 July 1933 Marais wrote to Helène Gündelpfennig, director of the play:

> I have offered it to several publishers and the best I can get from them is an amount which hardly pays for retyping it. Somebody is making the money, but heaven knows it is not the author. Why should we always remain dependent on these leeches?

With radiant optimism he continues:

> After we have produced it all over South Africa we can sell the publication rights, in which I am willing to offer you a share. What do you think of the proposal? I must say at once that I shall not be able to contribute anything to financing the production. You will have to find somebody to take the risk. But I do not think there will be the least danger. The first performance in Pretoria will bear all the costs of advertising etc. and then it should be able to run before the wind all the way to Cape Town.
>
> If you can take care of the financial side, I can almost guarantee that there will be a great deal of money to be made from it. Think of Danie Smal who made a fortune from his abominable recitations.
>
> Come and see me if the proposal seems acceptable.

Nothing ever came of these ambitious plans. Danie Smal's tours, on which he recited well known and popular Afrikaans poetry in a melodramatic manner, had been a roaring success precisely because they had such low-brow appeal. Unlike them, *Die Swart Verraad* would never make a fortune. In the end Fasie de Wet agreed to publish the volume, provided he might also publish a collection of Marais's short stories from *Die Vaderland*.

This fairly voluminous book, published the following year, consisted of stories clipped from old instalments of *Die Vaderland* and reset for the book, without Marais ever having seen them again.

Not that he wanted to see them. His own work, like virtually everything else, had become of no importance at all to him.

Van Schaik was most perturbed about the publication of *Die Huis van die Vier Winde*. How could Marais allow Afrikaanse Pers to publish such a volume while Marais had solemnly promised him, Van Schaik, the year before that he might publish all his short stories?

Of such a promise Marais remembered nothing, but he did give Van Schaik permission to compile a volume of short stories which had not been included in *Die Huis van die Vier Winde*. (It was to be published later as *Die Leeus van Magoeba*, The Lions of Maguba.) This news in turn infuriated Fasie de Wet. Marais was working for *Die Vaderland*. He was paid for every story he submitted. Surely it went without saying that the Afrikaanse Pers had the right to publish these stories in book form?

And so it went. Not that Marais did much to discourage the tug-of-war.

Being permanently in need of money, Marais was constantly trying to transmute his writing or even promises into gold. If the work had not yet been written, he would ask for an advance. "He would promise anything just to get hold of a bit of money," said Otto Schwellnus. "Yes, the story would be at the office the next day. But once the money had been paid over, nothing happened."

When *Die Vaderland* no longer saw its way open to paying him additional advances, Marais turned to Van Schaik, who was known as a hard businessman. Disappointed authors often related how their pleas for advances had been met with a reply which might amuse only another publisher: "Sir, I am a publisher. If you want to borrow money – the Netherlands Bank is only a few buildings away."

Marais was a different matter. He was the most successful Afrikaans writer of the time. His contributions had increased the circulation of a struggling newspaper like *Die Vaderland*. His books would sell. He was the one man with whom Van Schaik was willing to negotiate. At a later stage he would sometimes open a drawer and show more than one visitor the stacks of IOU's which Eugène Marais had signed on his regular visits.

In a letter to Spilhaus, with whom Marais had by that time long stopped corresponding, Preller wrote:

"No, you were not wrong, I regret to say, about our friend Eugène. He lives with us and is, I am sorry to say, steadily going downhill. Of course, there has never been a cure. If he could have stayed with Dr. Visser, this might perhaps have eventuated but here he has worked for years for the chemist."

One can only surmise that it must be Van Schaik about whom he adds (as De Wet had no shop):

"At present he is in the hands of a rather unscrupulous publisher who uses him, among other things, to boost the books he has published for him, by dictating letters to the press ... He comes down daily for the few shillings, sits down in the store of this man and does anything he requires of him."

(The "few shillings" was no exaggeration. Cheques drawn by Marais during this time are often for eight shillings, six shillings and even five shillings.)

Preller continues his letter with a remarkable statement:

"Recently, two books of his appeared of which he, Eugène, assures me he did not even know and for which, he says, he got nothing in return."

In that year, 1934, two of Eugène Marais's books had been published by Van Schaik, *Die Leeus van Magoeba,* (The Lions of Maguba), a collection of short stories, and *Die Siel van die Mier* (The Soul of the White Ant).

Preller, faithful friend that he was, did not leave this at words. He went to see Van Schaik.

"I have been much troubled about it," he wrote to Spilhaus, "but I am powerless. On speaking to the person in question, I was told that Eugène was working off advances that had been made to him, while Eugène assures me that his publishers owe him money."

Van Schaik was not the only one to come under fire. Marais's grievances concerning Fasie de Wet of the Afrikaanse Pers are obvious from a letter he wrote to Dr. Winifred de Kok later regarding the translations of certain of his work:

" ... De Wet, the manager of Afrikaanse Pers, has begged of me to leave the matter in his hands and to allow him to arrange terms. He thinks I am too big a fool to be entrusted with any transaction of a financial nature. Well, he should be able to judge, since he has fathomed all the depths and shoals of my soul in this particular respect – always to his own pecuniary advantage."

The most sober and perhaps most objective view of these charges is given by Eugène Marais's own son, in one of the many letters he had to write after his father's death to clear up the chaos of his financial affairs.

" ... in (his) physical and spiritual struggle all business sense, or the acceptance of what are the normal behaviour values, had to take a secondary place. It was inevitable, then, that his business affairs were frequently in a chaotic state."

After this brief view of the intricate world of Marais's publication rights and his conviction that he had been cheated and misused, we resume the story in the first month of 1934.

14. The Goddess

Late in January 1934, the unprecedented period of thirteen months in which articles and stories by Eugène Marais were published in *Die Vaderland* as regularly as clockwork came to an end. For this there was probably more than one reason.

One cannot guess how important a factor it was, but at about this time Hettie Cross left the Prellers' house in Blackwood Street and went to live elsewhere. At about the same time Dr. Hendrik Louw, who had been keeping Marais on a reasonable level of consumption over the past year, left for East London. He was in fact not a GP, but a radiologist, and opportunities in this field were limited in Pretoria. And at about the same time Eugène Marais came to the conclusion that he was dying.

It was early in the year, his son said. "I was visiting him in Blackwood Street in the Preller house. He was in a terrible mood. You know, this popular image of my father as the great lonely, melancholy man is a lot of bosh. As a rule he was very jovial. His sense of humour was remarkable and if something really amused him he could almost kill himself laughing. But when he was depressed –

and this virtually always had something to do with morphine – it was pitiful to see him. When I went to visit him in Blackwood Street that day, he gave me a terrible picture of his life. He told me how he would shuffle around the town, up and down, to Van Schaik for a small advance, to some old friend for a chat. His money was almost gone and then he said, 'Eugène, I have a sore in my throat. I think it's the beginning of the end. It's throat cancer.'

"In fact this should not have surprised one, as he was still smoking so much. What is peculiar is that he never coughed a great deal. We then arranged for an operation, but the doctor could find nothing malignant in his throat."

This operation was paid for by his son, as he paid so many of his father's expenses in the last years of his life. And then, on top of the encouraging outcome, something completely unexpected happened, something just short of a miracle. Dr. Gideon Nel's "fantastic schemes" had borne fruit after all. A company which had belonged to the syndicate was sold to the Greyhound Racing Company, and suddenly Eugène Marais found himself with £600 in his hands.

One might say that it was a gift to Marais from his old friend Tielman Roos.

By the previous year Roos had become such a formidable power in South African politics that both Hertzog and Smuts feared him. His influence was not effectively neutralized before the coalition between the SAP (South African Party) and the Nats. The "coalition of the people", which he had dreamed would happen under his leadership, took place without him. The political party which he founded in 1934 was doomed to extinction from the start and was in fact dissolved before his own death the following year.

Eugène Marais watched his old friend's vicissitudes impassively. As the possession of cages filled with chickens and ducks had given him the feeling of "inexhaustible riches" when he was ten years old, he now felt the same way about the £600. To him it was a fortune – more than he could at this stage earn from the creative writing of several years.

Suddenly he blossomed. Soon he was sporting an elegant new suit of clothes, dark brown, with a fine white stripe. There was an expensive new winter coat, there were new shirts and shoes.

There was a two-seater car and, because he had never learnt to drive, there was also a chauffeur, John. There was a silver cigarette holder with his name engraved on it. There were two thoroughbred terriers (and they must have cost him more than the £25 he had paid in Brooklyn thirty years before).

His writing stopped completely. His consumption shot up, for now he could afford the outrageous prices the Indians in Pretoria asked for illegal morphine. As always, he regarded these people not only as a necessary evil but as his friends too. Everyone who could relieve his suffering was his friend, and if one happened to ask a rather higher price for it than another, the commodity – within very liberal bounds – was always a bargain in his eyes. Only one person, Tamaria van Rooyen, had exceeded these bounds long before on lovely Rietfontein.

At this stage another farm – Pelindaba, eighteen miles west of Pretoria – began to play an important part in this story.

After the Boer War, Henning Pretorius (Hannie Preller's father) and his two brothers had farmed on a fifteen hundred morgen farm, Welgegund. Hannie's father owned the central portion. When the Hartebeespoort Dam started filling up and flooded part of the property the brothers decided to sell up and move elsewhere. Hannie's father was dead by then, but she kept prodding Gustav into trying to obtain a part of the ground which would then be theirs for posterity.

"At first he was most unenthusiastic," she was to say later. "In the rainy season the water was everywhere. All the orchards which were still alive, lay below the highwater mark. Eventually, he agreed, but we could only buy the place provided we occupied it. This was at about the end of World War I. My husband could not get away so I and our youngest, Gustav Junior, lived on the farm for about a year.

"Shortly afterwards, Dr. Reitz had the idea of developing a township there. A competition to choose a name was held and it was given the name Pelindaba.

"Nothing could ever become of the township. People preferred Johan Schoeman's township below the Hartebeespoort Dam."

However, the Prellers were allowed to select six hundred morgen. Here they built rondavels and in the early thirties it became their weekend retreat.

"Those weekends were extremely pleasant," says Bob Preller, who had returned from Britain after his officer's course about the middle of 1933. "When I returned from England, I brought along Eric Coates' London Suite, which we played there. Our family had a Philips battery radio and an old-fashioned gramophone which one had to wind up."

His yearning for the country, which he identified with innocence, with his own lost paradise, had never left Eugène Marais. Pelindaba, relatively close to Pretoria but still largely unspoilt, became a refuge for him.

When the Prellers went there in summer he preferred to sleep out in the veld, under the starry sky he loved and knew so well.

"I slept in the open next to the fire," the main character of *Laramie die Wonderwerker* says in Eugène Marais's short novel, and here one can clearly hear Marais's own voice, "and night after night I could contemplate the magnificent spectacle of the Milky Way crossing the heavens – that glory of which the lowliest, the most miserable creature cannot be deprived."

Major Lood Pretorius, one of Hannie's brothers (and later to be Otto Schwellnus' father-in-law) lived about a mile from the rondavels in his own house. His wife and children were living in Pretoria. He and Eugène Marais were about the same age. Lood had been a member of the Republic State Artillery and he was an excellent shot. The Afrikaans expression "skote Petoors", meaning more or less "well shot, old man", is said to have been derived from his name. The two of them had many things in common. Both of them knew the old Transvaal and could talk about its people and past. Lood loved animals and the veld and he had a special fondness for dogs. They soon became friends.

Now that Marais was well-to-do, he frequently went to Pelindaba, sometimes staying there for several days. He learnt to know the environment well.

Across the river lay the village of Broederstroom (literally, stream of brothers). Like Swaershoek (valley of the brothers-in-law), another favourite area from his past, the name of the place indicated the close family relationships so prevalent in the Transvaal at the time. There was a post office, a couple of shops, a garage and an Afrikaans-medium primary school.

"Many Pretoriuses lived there," Mrs. Preller was to relate much later, "and they came to visit when we went to the rondavels over a weekend. Eugène loved children, but he also loved old people – the real typical old Boers. Those Boer types with their naive, almost primitive language. I could always see how he enjoyed the way in which they expressed themselves."

The tiny school at Broederstroom was run by two teachers. As one might expect, one of them was a Pretorius, Andries. The other was Chris Roos, and he and Marais became firm friends. Chris was not much over thirty. He had grown up in Brits. Their common interests were animals and the veld.

It was in his company that Marais had witnessed a remarkable scene on Dingaan's Day (16 December) the year before (1933). As they were strolling from one ant-hill to another

> ... we simultaneously noticed a surreptitious movement in the grass about us. The hillside here consists of bare, stony patches interspersed with clumps of young green grass. For several minutes it was indistinct and uncertain. It seemed as if the earth itself had suddenly come alive and manifested itself as a general gruesome crawling. I do not think it was exactly a relief when we realized that the movement was due to countless numbers of scorpions which had suddenly appeared from nowhere ... a few minutes before we had not observed a single one but within those few minutes the veld was simply alive with these terrible killers of the insect world ... it was fully forty minutes before the mystery of the scorpions' appearance was explained. Over the southern hilltops a dense swarm of locusts appeared, moving in our direction. They settled at Pelindaba, dropping into the grass around our feet, their wings glittering, and there was hardly a scorpion for whom a locust did not come to rest conveniently within reach.

Virtually the entire swarm was relentlessly attacked and killed. By what mysterious "wireless signals", asked Marais, in this article, did the scorpions become aware of the locusts' approach almost three quarters of an hour before?

With his observation of insects, with his experiments in hypnosis on an old Bushman – who then seemed to become clairvoyant – Eugène Marais was, during this period, repeating old patterns from his past in more than one respect.

As he had done years before, he bought a typewriter for a young girl-friend – only this time he paid for it himself.

We do not know the name of the girl. Hannie Preller thinks that she must have been about twenty, that he was in love with her and she with him.

"One day the two of them accompanied me and Gustav to the farm. When we came back, they sat in the back seat and my husband and I in front. A number of piglets crossed the road in front of us. As I glanced around to look at the piglets more closely, I saw him touching her chin and calling her by some name of affection or other.

"'You remind me so much of one of those darling little pigs,' he said.

"But it all came to nothing, like everything else."

Soon everything began drifting to the dogs, as he had said many years before. Bob was given the expensive terrier he had bought, as well as the silver cigarette case; Hannie Preller was given the fox-terrier bitch.

But even the familiar and beloved old patterns were now wearing thin – hypnosis; the possession of well-bred animals; the joy of gold and silver; even the admiring twenty year old girlfriend. Tomorrow and tomorrow and tomorrow creeps in this petty pace from day to day (and even these words from *Macbeth* which he had always been so fond of quoting, no longer moved him, but had become weary, stale and unprofitable).

Eight years before Eugène Marais had written at least part of the poem "Diep Rivier" (Deep River), with its central theme of a dark stream, on another farm, Steenkampskraal. There is a second, less famous poem, never printed in book form, about death and the substitute death, morphine. It is called "Die Nag" (The Night). The date of its origin is not known. This author surmises that it was written during the very last years of Marais's life, quite possibly during a lonely sojourn on Pelindaba. In this poem the references are far more explicit than in "Diep Rivier". One is struck by the number of elements from De Quincey's famous paean to opium, but Marais goes further than De Quincey did. "Die Nag" is a love poem and the beloved – the goddess, for he calls her "u", a word used only to superiors – is either morphine or death:

Stille moeder van erbarme
Droomgevuld u sagte arme.
Uit u donker oge straal
Heling vir die felste kwaal
Leniging van alle smarte
Balsem in gewonde harte.

Soeter, sagter, O Beminde,
Dan van sneeuverkoelde winde
Op geskroeide lippe strelend
Raak u sagte hande helend.

Diep vergetelheid, u duurste gawe,
Breek die kettings van die slawe,
Was die bloedskuld van bevlekte harte
Neem van snoodste onreg al sy smarte.

Ster-gekroonde, in u skrede
Bloei die leliekelk van vrede!

Quiet mother of compassion
Dream-filled are your tender arms.
From your dark eyes there streams
Cure for the cruellest disease,
Easing of all pain,
Balm for wounded hearts.

Sweeter, softer, O Beloved,
Than snow-cooled winds
Caressing scorched lips
Touch your soft hands in healing.

Deep oblivion, your dearest gift,
Breaks the chains of slaves,

Washes the blood guilt from defiled hearts
Takes from the basest injustice all its pain.
Star-crowned, in your steps
Blooms the lily flower of peace!

The pendulum had swung back. Marais was again adoring a goddess, only she was no longer a woman. The girl mentioned by Hannie Preller was to be the last in his life. Henceforth he would remain true to his one, his first, his only indestructible love.

At this time Hannie Preller and Eugène Marais had a strange relationship. In the old days, although Eugène was much younger, he and Hannie's father, Commandant Henning Pretorius, had been equals. Now Hannie was 56, six years younger than Eugène. She had become a true *volksmoeder* (mother of the people), highly conscious of her dignity and her prestige. In her eyes Eugène Marais was a kind of poor relation. While he called Gustav by his first name, he addressed her as *"mevrou"* (equivalent to the French *madame*). Rather unpleasantly submissive is the tone of a note he sent her from the rondavels during that year: *"Geagte Mevrou,"* (Dear Madam) it began. "Please be so kind as to hand bearer two shirts with collars and one pair of flannel trousers – only to go to town with, if that should ever be necessary. (I went in today to consult the doctor, but intend going back at once.)"

And, like a prelude to his death two years later, he adds: "A huge snake lives near the fowl-run. I have not yet been able to take a shot at it."

The truth was that Marais, in spite of his two-seater and his chauffeur, in spite of his money, was living on the Prellers' charity. He could perhaps still have gone to live in a cold hotel or boarding house at this stage if he had wanted to, but there was almost nobody who would accept him into his house as a friend.

When Mrs. Cross and her family returned from the Cape to Pretoria in November that year – Mr. Cross having stayed behind in the Cape once more – Marais asked her whether he could come and stay with them again.

She was sorry, Jessie Cross replied, but that would not be possible.

"At that time both boys had left the house," she was to say later regarding this decision. "Only I and the two girls were left. So I told him, 'Listen Eugène, if Willie or Charles had still been here, it would have been a different matter. I know there is nothing, you know it, but what must the neighbours think?'"

At this time, suddenly, his money ran out. There was not even enough left to keep on the car and the driver. His new suit was starting to show signs of wear and his winter coat was spotted. Once again the man with the broad-brimmed hat began to put in an appearance from time to time at *Die Vaderland*, trying to sell a review or an article.

Marais was now back in Blackwood Street.

In a letter to Spilhaus, Preller describes how Marais's condition had deteriorated lately. Only a short while before, in September, he said, he had taken Eugène to the Kruger National Park which he, Preller, was obliged to visit as an honorary member of the Board. But the visit had turned into a fiasco, for Marais had laid his hands on his entire supply and taken it all at once. Preller had to rush back to Pretoria with him, "spoiling everything."

Then he adds: "One forgives and forgets everything, however, he is such a real 'good sort'. Latterly, however, he forgets a lot, sleeps most of the time and is not much of a companion ... Generally I see him at home for about an hour in the evening. The remarkable thing to me is that his appetite remains apparently unimpaired and that outwardly during that one hour before dinner, you would never say that there is anything wrong with him. Then he vanishes (goes to bed) and one does not see him again until the next evening, though he comes to town regularly for the necessary."

Even now, eighteen months before his death, the terrible words later to be used about him by Willem van Heerden were an apt description.

"There was no longer much to die, only a weak, flickering little flame dancing hesitantly on a burnt-out log."

15. The Dregs

Nineteen thirty-five, the year before Eugène Marais's death, began with a remarkable interview in the house of Dr. Gustav Preller in Blackwood Street, Pretoria.

A young student, F.G.M. du Toit, who had worked as a reporter on the staff of *Die Vaderland* for some years, was doing his master's degree. As the theme for his thesis he had chosen (in Afrikaans): "Eugène N. Marais – his contribution to Afrikaans literature".

Marais was 64. He lay in bed in the Prellers' veranda room while Tooitjie – as Marais called him – sat by his bed and took down what he said, almost word for word. For somebody who had been using morphine for 43 years Marais was remarkably lucid. Nevertheless, Du Toit wrote down statements which were later to lead to great misunderstanding and confusion.

I was born on 9 January 1872 in Daspoort, Pretoria.

According to Marais's son, the correct year was 1871; the correct place Pretoria itself.

My parents were Jan Christiaan Nielen Marais of Stellenbosch and Sophia van Niekerk of the district of Malmesbury.

It is possible that Marais's mother was for some reason called Sophia on occasion but her baptismal names were certainly Catharina Helena Cornelia.

(In Paarl) I matriculated in the middle of 1877 when I was fifteen.

In 1887 Marais was sixteen.

I took part in the Jameson Raid and at Doornkop I fought against the invaders.

Although Marais had technically been on commando, it is improbable that he actually took part in the fighting or that he fired a shot.

The Government – the President and Executive Council – summoned me and the President asked whether I could speak English well. I was then sent (to Johannesburg) to meet the Reform Committee.

When General Joubert had sent Marais and his son-in-law, Abraham Malan, to Johannesburg for the first time, the President and the Executive Council were completely unaware of the mission.

I met them (the Reformers) the next night at two o'clock in the morning again and told them that the Government was willing to listen to their grievances if they surrendered unconditionally. After some hesitation they accepted these conditions.

These facts are not correct, as has been indicated.

In 1896 I went to Europe where I studied medicine for a time. I attended a private clinic in London ... While I was there, I received a letter from

Ewald Esselen from the Transvaal in which he encouraged me to study law instead. I allowed myself to be persuaded and qualified as an advocate at the Inner Temple.

In fact Marais entered the Inner Temple immediately after his arrival in London.

When I had finished my exams ... I went to Antwerp where, after a long series of difficulties, I succeeded in contacting certain members of the expedition ... we sailed as far south as Tanga, the most northern port in German East Africa, on a German ship.

It is likely that Marais was confusing Brussels and Antwerp during this interview. In any case he did not leave Europe with the expedition but only met Burger in Dar-es-Salaam and Schultz in Beira.

(In the Waterberg) General Hertzog, then Minister of Justice, appointed me as a special Justice of the Peace.

In fact Marais was appointed by his friend Charlie Pienaar, Secretary of Justice.

I resigned my post when General Hertzog left the Cabinet (1912).

In fact Marais was still a Justice of the Peace when he left the Waterberg early in 1917.

In 1910 I was the first person to write a long brochure claiming that South Africa was drying out: the effects of extreme drought on animal and plant life.

The correct year is 1914 and the correct title "Notes on some effects of extreme drought in the Waterberg".

Since 1912 I practised as an advocate until after the war. In the twenties I again went to the Waterberg to continue my termite and baboon studies, but my health was poor. I then spent a long time at Boshof, where I lived with my brother.

Marais left the Waterberg in 1917 and never returned there. His sojourn in Boshof dates from an earlier period.

I am the youngest child of a family of seven.

There were thirteen children, of whom three died young. (Which of his meddling sisters had Marais hurled into the dark stream of his subconscious – and forgotten?).

A few days after the first interview, Frans du Toit again went to Blackwood Street to supplement this interview with some details.

"Mabalêl" was written at Erasmus and took from just after supper until

11 p.m. "Wanneer dit reën op Rietfontein" was written in one hour in the offices of Die Vaderland.

Both these statements are incorrect.

I twice studied hieroglyphics in Egypt – as well as in the British Museum, where I translated one original papyrus, "The Travels of an Egyptian".

Marais visited the pyramids only as a tourist, and only once. The tickets of admission to the British Museum's reading room – as far as is known the only part of the museum in which a visitor was allowed to work during the nineties – show that he was never there.

During the second interview Frans du Toit noticed that a book by Rex Beach was lying on Marais's bedside table, as well as two American "pulps": *Master Detective* and *Startling Detective*.

Quite a number of the more serious mistakes in the two interviews were later corrected by Gustav Preller or by Marais's son; quite a number were not.

Taking into account that Marais's memory for dates had always been weak, that Frans du Toit could have made mistakes in his hurried notes, that one does not always relate events chronologically during an interview and that anyone's recollection regarding facts from one's own life may become unreliable, even the possibility that some facts in this book may be wrong and Eugène Marais right – taking all this into account, the two interviews still present a shocking picture of intellectual decline in an exceptionally gifted man.

"In Oom Eugène's company," Edna Cross pays him the tribute of a young child, "I never knew where truth ended and fantasy began."

The dream world which he had created for so many young children was one of the most precious things Marais was to leave behind him. But by February 1935, little more than a year before his death, he himself was moving in a dream where he could frequently no longer distinguish truth from fiction.

In the month after the second interview, one of the hardest blows fell.

With the utmost difficulty, Marais had managed to produce another short story, "Spore in die Sand" (Footsteps in the Sand) and delivered it to *Die Vaderland*'s magazine division. But the paper was published without the story.

Someone in the department had had doubts concerning the quality of the contribution and had referred it for a decision to the assistant editor, Willem van Heerden. And it was Van Heerden who had to tell Marais the news.

"When his dark figure entered the doorway," Van Heerden was to write, "the face on which I so seldom saw a smile, accentuated and lightly shadowed by the broad-rimmed hat he always wore, only the inexorable facts of the situation gave me the courage to tell him the bad news. The story could really not be used. I explained as tactfully as I could that it did not quite come up to the quality of his previous work, that it was in his own interests as a writer not to have it published and other excuses which the reader may be able to imagine ... As I had expected, he made no attempt to refute what I had said. When he turned to go, I could have cursed myself a thousand times ... He who had been besieged his whole life by letters and telegrams from every magazine in South Africa which meant anything, whose name alone was enough to make editors rush his copy into print."

Later, after Marais's death, Preller was to comment bitingly on these events:

"It is noteworthy ... that the last story written by Marais and rejected so ostentatiously on the grounds of being inferior work – this after the bothersome 'encouragement' of before – was immediately published by another journal."

"Immediately" is a slight exaggeration. It was only several months later that the story was eventually published in *Die Huisgenoot*. (The real irony was to come later. After Marais's death, the Afrikaanse Pers was not only to include the same story in a collection of short stories, but was to give the volume the title of the story: *Spore in die Sand*.)

For the rest of his life Marais was never again to submit anything to Die Vaderland.

It now seemed as if the end must be near, but it had not yet arrived. Even now Marais continued to drag his worn, patched clothes from house to doctor, to chemist, to house.

At this stage Gustav Preller, the generous and faithful friend who had housed and looked after Eugène Marais when no one else would take him in, who had protected his reputation as a man and an author – at this stage even Gustav Preller starts to appear in a less favourable light.

It was inevitable. Anyone this side of an angel who has dealings with a morphine addict must start making mistakes sooner or later. Give him as much as he wants and you destroy him. Try to cure him and you might well be accused of cruelty.

To Gustav Preller his friend's decline had become too much. He was a generous, kind-hearted man but there was a second side to his personality, not necessarily contradictory to the first. As he used a filing system at home to create order out of the thousands of facts and letters he had collected through the years, so Preller wished to see order in the world around him. It had gladdened his heart when Mussolini had succeeded in building a modern state from the chaos of Italy. He was even more overjoyed to witness the order which was now being reborn from the disorder of the Weimar Republic in Germany. In that state a gifted man like Eugène would not be allowed to commit suicide by taking morphine. It was time for action.

It is virtually certain that Dr. Nel, who took care of Marais after Dr. Louw's departure, disapproved most strongly of Preller's point of view. From notes he left behind, it is clear that Preller regarded Dr. Nel as a bad influence on Marais.

Now, in 1935, Preller thought he could handle the situation himself. He persuaded Eugène Marais to subject himself to yet another withdrawal programme at Pelindaba.

The hill was very steep now, and the road was coming to an end.

The previous year Lood Pretorius, Hannie's brother, assisted by black farm labourers, had built the Prellers a solid, comfortable farmhouse, four hundred yards above the rondavels, where they could spend their weekends and where they would later be able to retire. Eugène was welcome to sleep in the house, but he always had preferred the rondavels.

Now Lood Pretorius was keeping the supply, and week after week it dwindled away. Sometimes Lood was not there. In a less violent form the nightmare patterns of Steenkampskraal were repeated here on the beautiful farm Pelindaba. True, the reduction of his dosage was more gradual than it had been on Steenkampskraal, but Marais was much older now, and far less resistant to it.

"In the year before his death, I learnt to know him well," Mr. Chris Roos, the teacher from the school at Broederstroom, was to say later. "Our house was not very far from the rondavels, across the road but on this side of the river. He had a very hard time. A few times he arrived at our house hungry. Two or three times I had to take him to Pretoria in my Chev to go and fetch his supply.

"He was very lonely, and mostly he only wanted company. He had a yellow boy, called Koos, and he used to send Koos with a message to my house: 'Please come and see me,' or something of the kind. He never wanted me to bring my wife along."

Hannie Preller confirms that Marais disliked the company of certain women during this time.

"I can remember that he got up and walked out when strange women entered the room," she said.

As the weekly quantity dropped still further, the deprivation became harder to bear.

"His hands and face would turn blue if he had to do without his shot," Chris Roos said.

One weekend when the Prellers were on the farm Marais rebelled.

"I cannot take it any more," he said.

And Gustav replied: "But you must. It's your only salvation."

It was dusk, and raining.

"There was an open clash," Otto Schwellnus revealed in an interview later. "Eugène threatened to return to Pretoria on foot if Preller refused to give him more. Maybe Preller didn't believe him but suddenly he was gone. Preller and perhaps one of the boys went after him in a car but Eugène followed footpaths and they could not find him."

It was not until the following week that the Prellers traced Marais to some Indians with whom he had sought sanctuary.

At this stage even Gustav Preller was losing hope. If Pelindaba was no good either, Eugène might as well come back to Blackwood Street.

He would no longer offer work to *Die Vaderland*. How then could he earn the meagre amount of money he required to keep going? In the end it was *Die Volkstem* which helped him out – the Volksmet (blemish of the people), as he had called it more than forty years before in *Land en Volk*, the newspaper of the enemy, from which Gustav Preller had indignantly resigned as editor.

Here, like Oswald Frank, journalistically speaking, he lived on charity, and here, in the last months of his life, he became an intimate friend of J.C. Vlok, a forty-one year old journalist on the staff of *Die Volkstem*.

Once again chance played a role, for Vlokkie, as Marais called him, was a son of his old friend A.C. Vlok, the boy who had been born only five weeks after Eugène Jr. in 1895 and under exactly the same circumstances. The same doctor had delivered the babies and Vlokkie's mother, too, had died of puerperal fever shortly after his birth.

J.C. Vlok had been a civil servant and later a teacher, but now, in 1935, he had been on the staff of *Die Volkstem* for fourteen years, having been appointed by Gustav Preller in 1921.

"In those last few months," he said in an interview, "I learnt to love Eugène as I have loved few people in my life. He used to pitch up at the office at about nine o'clock and by half past ten a yellow boy would bring him his plug. He was two people, two personalities, and the man I learnt to know there early in the morning was really worthwhile. But once the syringe had appeared on the scene, he was a completely different person."

During these months Marais's social circle dwindled even more and his days became shorter than ever. For an hour and a half he would chat and work at *Die Volkstem* in the morning; after his afternoon nap he spent an hour or so before supper chatting to the Prellers. To Edna he was still like a father, and he went to see the Cross family whenever he could. Edna had turned twelve that year and for the first time she was beginning to wear her hair long. The ugly duckling was changing into a swan.

In the second half of the year somebody took a snapshot of Marais and Edna in the backyard of 733 Arcadia Street, where Mrs. Cross now lived. Later Markus Viljoen, editor of *Die Huisgenoot*, would say that in his old age Marais had become "fairly corpulent" and "virtually unrecognizable". The picture does not confirm this. Naturally, he is older. But his clothes look shabby and the winter coat he had bought in his comparatively wealthy period was spotted.

People whom he used to count among his best friends, like the chemist, Frikkie Mansfield, whom he now owed more than £30, were no longer willing to advance him a few shillings. All prescriptions which he took there had to be paid in cash. (Later the soft-hearted Mansfield did relax this rule.)

Bitter experience had taught Marais's son not to send him money but to pay his bigger debts directly.

At one stage during these last months, friends only just succeeded in preventing Marais's arrest on a charge of debt.

Marais had hit rock bottom and no humiliation was spared him. Somebody who worked at a legal office as an articled clerk in Pretoria at the time was to relate: "A man came to the office and asked for money. I gave him half a crown. When he had left one of the others asked me: 'Don't you know that's Eugène Marais? Don't give him money, give him food.'"

Flash back forty years to Gustav Preller's classic image of Eugène Marais: elegant and sophisticated with his cane and red-lined cloak at the opera, a citizen of the world.

Marais's own comment, perhaps unconsciously, appears during this time, shortly before his death, scribbled on a piece of paper in between other notes: "Hoe zyt gy gevallen, Lucifer, zoon des dageraads!" (How have you fallen, Lucifer, son of dawn!)

Even now he was incredibly tough. One is struck by the thought that his time had come and that fate, in a fruitless effort to end his suffering, was dealing him one blow after the other.

One of the cruellest blows was dealt in the early summer of 1935: because one of her sons was in Johannesburg Mrs. Cross and her daughters decided to move to the Rand as well. They left early in January 1936.

"I cannot tell you how miserable and lonely I felt after I had realized that you were actually gone," he wrote to her after the move. "I do miss you all terribly and I avoid the street as the devil is said to avoid holy water."

Even so, incredibly, that same period brought a short but intense spiritual revival. The reason lay in a brief but extremely important correspondence Marais conducted with a South African woman in Suffolk, England towards the end of 1935.

16. Winifred de Kok

This woman was Dr. Winifred de Kok, born in Bethlehem in the Free State, where her father had for years been a magistrate. She went to England to qualify as a doctor and had then spent six months in Vienna to specialize in psychology, studying under Stekel. She was married to Alfred Edward Coppard, a highly regarded author in the thirties.

Because Coppard hated London, they now lived in Suffolk, where she was unable to practise. She spent her time looking after her two children, and on journalism and writing. A book she had written on child psychology – based on her observations of her own children – had been fairly successful.

She was an energetic, intelligent woman with a lively mind and an excellent sense of humour. In 1935 she was 42. Her letters somehow give one the impression that life was no longer looking as bright as before. Then she received a copy from South Africa of *Die Huis van die Vier Winde* by Eugène Marais. At that stage she was looking for something to occupy her time. Why not try to translate the stories into English?

Preller handed Marais the letter she had written to the Afrikaanse Pers, publishers of the book, in July or August. Not until 11 September did he write Dr. De Kok a letter, sixteen large pages long. It was the start of a remarkable correspondence.

In the course of this correspondence the man who, in the eyes of many Pretorians, had become a tramp, was to give a picture of his ideal self; and he was to do so in the most lucid prose and in a steady hand. He was to do all this so convincingly that not only was he to delude the intelligent, perceptive Winifred de Kok but, more than thirty years later, also the American author Robert Ardrey, who dedicated his book *African Genesis* to the memory of Eugène Marais, partly on the basis of these letters.

If Eugène Marais was no more than a weak, flickering little flame dancing hesitantly on a burnt-out log only six months before his death, late in 1935, what was it that fed the sustained, bright flame of these letters? It was this: that Winifred de Kock admired him as an author, that she accepted him as a human being and not as a morphine addict. It was a similar reaction, but this time even more magical, as the reaction to Wilhelm Spilhaus years before.

If he deluded her deliberately in one sentence after the other, who can blame him in the light of all we know about him now?

In his first letter he accepts her proposal to translate the book and tells her something of his life and work:

> In later years I studied in England and was called to the bar in the Inner Temple – after abandoning the results of a four year's medical course. As a boy I took part in the last war against the English. You will perhaps be astonished to learn what my psychological "reactions" were to this jumble of circumstances. The most enduring result was that it made me far more bitter than men who took part in the war at a more advanced age and who had had less to do with the English before the war. It was for purely sentimental reasons that I refused to write in any language except Afrikaans and notwithstanding the fact that I am far more fluent and more at ease in English.

Took part in the war, and as a boy? This was important, as it made him younger than he really was. It was true that he wrote English more fluently than Afrikaans but it was also true that Fasie de Wet – if not Willem van Heerden – was willing to accept lower standards than Paver of the *Star*.

While giving Dr. de Kok permission to translate the stories from *Die Huis van die Vier Winde*, Marais also proposed that she should examine *Die Siel van die Mier* (The Soul of the Ant), published in book form the previous year, with a view to translation. He told her about the Maeterlinck affair and here again the facts are inaccurate.

> He (Maeterlinck) clearly desired his readers to infer that he had arrived at certain of my theories (the result of ten years hard labour in the veld) by his own unaided reason, although he admits that he never saw a termite in his life. You must understand that it was not merely plagiarism of the spirit of the thing so to speak. He has copied page after page verbally ...

He continues later in the letter regarding *Die Siel van die Mier*:

> I want you to translate this book. You will be assured of my unstinted assistance. The [Afrikaans edition] is a worthless jumble, with no

apparent effort to disguise the fact that it consists of a series of disconnected magazine articles. But it could quite easily be knocked into shape. I still have all my field books.

At that stage there could no longer have been "field books". That there had ever been much in the way of "field books" was doubtful. After all, Marais prided himself on being able to get along without making notes. His offer to rewrite this "worthless jumble" before she began translating it, was a dream.

Finally, he mentioned a third possibility:

> Thereafter we might consider my greatest work, *Die Siel van die Aap*, which has not yet appeared in book form, although (Fasie) De Wet worries me continuously and has made me the most tempting offer ever received by a South African writer. But I just can't get up sufficient enthusiasm to arrange this particular material in an *Afrikaans* book.

This paragraph confirms the supposition that Marais had by this time lost the manuscript of *The Soul of the Ape*. But could his inability to complete the English work have been such a painful disappointment to him that he had flung the mere existence of the manuscript into the dark stream of his memories – that by the time of his letter to Winifred de Kok he had literally forgotten about it?

These are moving letters and, in the real sense of the word, tragic letters because they give an idea of what could have been. They give one a glimpse of the soul of a dying man, a man still yearning for admiration and esteem, even if this involved a woman as far as six thousand miles from Pretoria, in England. By the end of the first letter, like the first suggestion of a theme in a great orchestral work, we find a reference to his death, which was by then only six months away.

"Would you kindly note the following in case I forget or die ..."

Winifred de Kok had no reason to doubt any of Marais's statements and she replied at once, writing him a long, enthusiastic letter which she sent by airmail (an expensive luxury in 1935).

> Dear Mr. Marais,
>
> I have just had your very interesting letter. I wish I could spirit my-

self straight to Africa to talk to you. There are so many things in your letter that interest me enormously and damn it letters take so long. It is nearly a month since you wrote yours. But I'll send this by air. To come to business at once. I am tremendously pleased & honoured that you would like me to translate "Die Siel van die Mier"; I know Maeterlinck's book of course, and never dreamt he had pinched it from you. I am sure it ought to be translated (yours) & it ought to be a best seller – not that that is the most important – & I'd like to expose Maeterlinck for his beastly trick. I'd simply love to translate it. I am very much interested in psychology & "Die Siel van die Aap" certainly ought to be done too. My idea is to let "Die Huis van die Vier Winde" drop for the moment & get straight down to "Die Siel van die Mier".

I particularly want to do this because of what you wrote of your health. Please tell me, what is the matter? I don't like your reference to being in pain and what you said about dying. But if you are seriously ill, then all the more it is important for me to get to work straight away so that the English translation can be published soon ...

I can't think why you have honoured me with letting me do the translation but I'll do everything in my power to co-operate with you & do it well. You need not apologize for the length of your letter, every word was of great interest to me, particularly the biographical details.

It does seem to me your publishers have done you down. Publishers are the worst vampires on earth. My husband, who is really a good writer, has never had justice from his publishers (Cape) and is now going to Macmillan for his next book.

The very next day she wrote again, having left so much unsaid in the first letter. The references to his health show what a good doctor and psychologist she must have been.

Eugène Marais, for goodness sake, don't go and die just when we are beginning all this exciting work. Please assure me when you write that you are not going to die for years and years.

You have told me enough in your letter for me to feel that I have known you for years and years, but I want to know you much better and if I can't meet and talk to you some day & if we can't carry out this work to a good & satisfactory conclusion for you, I shall always go about with a sense of something unfulfilled ...

If you really are very ill (which God forbid) will you please let me know how I could get hold of your papers in case anything happened to you. But really Eugène Marais, I hate writing this and I can assure you, although I would do my best all the same it would not be half the thrill doing this work if you are not there to see the results ...

I am sure that after you have read my two long letters you will have no doubt that I have a very kind feeling for the writer of such a very lovely letter, and I feel very sad to think you are ill and in pain.

With many kind thoughts & wishes.

Winifred de Kok's enthusiasm had infected Marais. This time he replied at once to her two long letters, telling her in fascinating detail about his baboon research in the Waterberg.

By this time the sympathetic and intelligent woman was beginning to realize, however, that although her correspondent could write beautifully and fluently, he could not be moved to deeds very easily. Her next letter, written shortly afterwards, was mainly devoted to tactful encouragement to make him send her *Die Siel van die Mier*. She then adds: "I am glad your health is not as bad as it sounded in your former letter. You sounded very ill."

And indeed at the end of this correspondence – and largely as a result of it – he was healthier than he had been for many months.

On 11 December he wrote his last letter to her: "I am sending you a rapidly revised Siel van die Mier in a few days."

And contrary to what one might have expected, the promise did not go unfulfilled. Before the end of the year he posted her a copy of the book, with copious and meaningful notes in every possible white space on the first few pages.

There were now only three months left.

17. Taking Leave of Edna

From out of the depths Winifred de Kok had raised him, and his spirit shone once more.

Shortly after he had posted her the complete annotated copy of *Die Siel van die Mier*, he was spending the Christmas holidays at Pelindaba with the Prellers. He wanted to return to Pretoria early in the new year in time to take his leave of Mrs. Cross and her daughters before they moved to Springs on the Witwatersrand.

Near Pelindaba the Jukskei river runs into the Crocodile, and in times of heavy rain – like that December – the river came down in rapids and the Crocodile would lap against the face of a high krantz, Baviaanskrans, on the farm. Here the river would surge against the rocky barrier and stream over the boulders on the right.

Hannie Preller and Eugène Marais visited the spot one afternoon.

"We were sitting on a flat rock next to the river," she says. "Well, when the river was full, it was violent, it would fling its water here and there. Eugène found it all too beautiful for words. There was also a wild gardenia – he found this kind of thing terribly attractive, the wild flowers and rocks and dassies. Then I said:

"'When the river runs deeply and swishes its water to this side and that, it reminds me of a lady dancing in a silk taffeta dress.'

"Suddenly he asked: 'Why don't you write?'

"'But I can't.'

"'Well,' he said, 'I'll do the writing. Just give me the theme.'"

They worked it out together. The climax of the story was to occur at the Makapaans Cave. A young man, his fiancée and her girl-friend were climbing up a steep krantz bound together by a rope. The fiancée's foot slipped and while the young man and the other girl were safely on top of the krantz, she hung over the abyss on the end of the rope. Would the girl-friend – who was in love with the man – cut the rope? This was one of the questions, Gustav Preller was to remember later on.

Marais was still riding on the wave of his correspondence with Winifred de Kok. Early in the new year, when the Prellers had already returned to Pretoria, he had to take leave of Mrs. Cross and the girls. It was only once they were gone that he realized that he would have to do without her. Even so his spirits were still high.

On 9 January he turned 65. From Springs came a letter from Edna, a letter from Mrs. Cross and a telegram from the whole family – probably the only congratulations he received by mail.

The very next day he wrote to Mrs. Cross to tell her how he missed them. And he referred to the novel. "I am starting a novel in English today. I shall try to make it as good as anything I have ever written in Afrikaans. The plot is a story told me by Mrs. Preller.

She takes a great interest in the work and will translate it simultaneously into Afrikaans."

He sent Hettie greetings and love and added a footnote for Edna: "Dearest Squg, I'll write you a separate letter in a day or two. I have a little story to tell you. Love, Uncle."

And again, surprisingly, the letter actually was written the very next day – a long, fluent letter about a dream which he had had the evening of Edna's move to Springs.

Once, long before, Eugène Marais had promised to bequeath all his earthly possessions to Edna. Probably he had completely forgotten all about the promise. But this letter can be said to be something of a testament. At the same time it was a sort of confession, by the man whom she had regarded as her father confessor. One feels that it cannot but be authentic, that it must contain truths concerning his own aspirations and ideals now dead which can be unlocked provided one has the right key.

In a certain sense it was also a love letter. In any case, it was a very personal and intimate one, and thus Edna regarded it. For almost twenty years she showed it to nobody except her mother.

Dearest Squg,

Thanks so much for your terrible little scrawl, & don't spell Squg – "Squge". Surely you ought to know how to spell your own name! Now I want to tell you the story: It was really a remarkable & very vivid dream I had the night after you left. I suppose I was rather nervous & upset and that was the cause of it. Well I dreamt that I was at the foot of a very steep hill. I could see a footpath winding through rocks & trees right up to the top of the hill. It was all just as real as if I was awake. As I strolled along the foot of the hill I suddenly came face to face with a little old lady. She was short & stout & in her right hand she had a walking-stick of heavy black wood with a cross handle of solid silver. (It is funny but just such a walking stick appears in one of my stories: "Die Vliegende Hollander" – "The Flying Dutchman".) The little old woman had a very cross face & glared at me as if I had done her some great wrong. I forgot something else: She had on a big white pinafore. She had rolled something up in the bottom part of the pinny & she was carrying this something under her left arm. She glared at me from head to foot without saying a word until I felt as awkward & shy as a little schoolboy who doesn't know his lessons. I know I blushed furiously & shuffled about on clumsy feet, trying hard to think of something to say to the angry old dame. And I couldn't think of a single thing. I forgot even to take off my hat & say "Good Morning". And then I noticed that all about her on the ground were lying a number of clumsily tied parcels, – in brown paper. Most of them were broken & the contents ready to drop out. Then at last the old dame said very sarcastically – speaking *at* me, you understand.

Old lady: "Although we seem to have lost our tongue, & have forgotten to take off our hat & say 'Good morning', – still we may be sufficient of a gentleman to carry these parcels to the top of the hill for a lady who has an impediment in her walk." I then noticed that when she moved she was a little lame & that was why she used the black stick. "Rheumatism" – I said to myself. To the old lady I said: "Certainly Madam – with the greatest pleasure in the world." And then I began to scramble those d-d parcels together & tried to carry them. I was never in such an awful jam in my life. As soon as I picked up one parcel another would drop & they were becoming more & more undone & broken up. At length I had them stacked up under both arms & commenced crawling up the hill with the old Dame just behind me. She kept on making the most sarcastic remarks about my clumsiness – every now & then she would give me a hard poke in the back with the walking stick & pretend to apologise with a sarcastic grimace: "So sorry! I intended that to press back a parcel that was slipping." I knew, of course, that that was a fib & she knew that I knew! All the time I was very much interested in the thing she had rolled up in her apron. Once or twice when I had to stop to pick up a dropped parcel I studied it very carefully & I was sure that I had seen something wriggle inside that apron & once I heard a peculiar little squeak. I said to myself: "From the shape of the parcel it ought to be either a kitten or a puppy but now I know it is a little pig." That squeak had betrayed it! You know the little squeak a piglet makes; – there is no other noise in the world faintly resembling it. Well at length we got to the top of the hill, with the perspiration streaming down my face. Old Lady: "Well, my dear man, I did not expect you to do this for nothing. Our ways part here. You turn back & I go on. And here is your reward." And then she unrolled her apron & quickly shoved into my arms a week-old human baby.

(I had just before that stacked the damned parcels in a heap on the ground.) The little beggar wriggled & kicked & bawled to beat the band! The old lady looked on beaming all over her face. "Listen to those lungs," she said. "She is going to be a big singer one day. Good Heavens but you are clumsy. Try to hold the little angel more comfortably." All the time I was staring at the face of the little demon but it was so puckered up that she might just as well have been a chimp as a human being. I was trying to say: "Damn it, Madam, I don't want this nightmare. Take it back at once." But she took no notice of me. She was chirruping at the squawling kid & making all sorts of funny noises at it. And then suddenly it stopped yowling. It opened its eyes wide, staring up at my face. And then, all at once, I saw what it was that had interested me in the kid. I had seen that face before. It was *you* – Edna Cross; only you were 8 days old. I said angrily to the old lady: "Where on earth did you get this child from?" She replied, still very sarcastically: "Where do you think I got it from? I stole it, of course. And now you can have it all for your very own & you need pay me nothing more than the service you have already done me." And then the old Dame grew mistier & mistier & at last melted into nothingness together with her parcels. And there was I standing on the top of the hill "shushing" a terrible kid.

I woke up damp with perspiration.

Goodbye, Sweetheart! No more pages. Love to Hettie & your Mom,

Uncle E.

What significance has a dream of this kind? For Freud's theory of dreams in which dreams are interpreted according to fixed formulae and in which a locomotive might represent death, a box the womb and a king the father figure, Eugène Marais had always had the greatest contempt. On the other hand, he believed no less firmly that dreams did have a deep significance.

Like his Ex Libris, a great deal can be said about this letter. The following comes to mind.

A twisting footpath is a very common symbol for a human life. In the dream the footpath becomes extremely difficult for the dreamer, more especially towards the end, and while his road ends that of the old woman continues.

Mrs. Cross's name is never mentioned in the letter, but immediately after the dreamer meets the old lady the word "cross" is used twice ("cross handle" and "cross face").

In the story to which Marais refers in the letter we find the "walking stick with a cross handle of silver" in the hand of a rather sinister old lady, who is trying to keep a family secret and protect the family's honour – an old lady who reminds one of some of Eugène's own sisters as they were to develop in later years.

What were the jumbled, half-open parcels the dreamer had to carry? In a literal sense it reminds one of Hannie Preller's description of the parcel of books, dust-covered and partly opened, which lay untouched in his room in Blackwood Street for many months. On another level it can represent all the ambitious but virtually untouched projects which Eugène Marais began during his life and never completed. Even now he must have known that the great new English novel about which he had been so enthusiastic the day before, would remain only an idea.

Why a pig? The twenty year old typist in the car on the way to Pelindaba?

In *Alice in Wonderland*, written by a brilliant but lonely man for a little girl with whom, according to some observers, he was in love, the baby which Alice receives from the monstrous Duchess turns into a piglet. In Eugène Marais's dream the piglet turns into a baby.

In the dream the baby at first looks like a chimpanzee. In London, Marais tended a baby chimpanzee as if it was his own baby daughter, attaching so much importance to the episode that he was to repeat the story all his life.

Lewis Carroll and his Alice have to be mentioned for more than one reason. In spirit and atmosphere Marais's dream reminds one of the opening chapters of *Alice in Wonderland*, about which A.M.E. Goldschmidt was to write, at least two years before Eugène Marais's letter, in a psychoanalysis of Carroll: "We have (Carroll's) own word for it, that he simply said the first thing that came into his head. The story of Alice was begun in the course of a river party, the author telling it, quite impromptu, to three of his girl-friends. The story is in the form of a dream, and it has the strange spontaneity of a dream ... The incidents and images are suggested by the subconscious, and their nature is erotic." (In other words, the psychoanalyst may expect to find clues to the writer's personality in these passages.)

The theme of pursuit begins very early in *Alice* and it is the dominant theme in Eugène Marais's letter to Edna. "It is worth noting," remarks Goldschmidt, "that Stekel interprets the pursuit in dreams of something we are unable to catch as representing an attempt to make up a disparity in age." (This was the same Dr. Stekel, internationally famous during the thirties, under whom Eugène Marais's friend Winifred de Kok had studied in Vienna.)

For psychologists of the school of Freud or Jung, climbing a hill or mountain represents the sexual act.

In his psychoanalysis of Carroll, Goldschmidt adds (and this should be stressed in connection with Marais as well): "There can be no doubt, historically speaking, that (the erotic) emotion was completely repressed and that (his) relations with his child-friends were of the most harmless and delightful kind."

"Freudian" interpretations, with their often exaggerated and sometimes unbalanced accent on sex, are given here for interest's sake. Even if they are completely discounted, Eugène Marais's farewell letter to Edna still contains a wealth of potential symbolism.

How did the dream end? After the tedious, winding footpath on which he had to drag his broken and confused parcels he is rewarded with the gift of a child. Edna was eight days old again and this time she could not be taken from him because she belonged to him.

Or does the child in the dream not ultimately represent Edna but instead his own flesh and blood?

Eugène Jr. was eight days old when he was left in his father's care forty years before.

18. The Signs of Grace

During the last few months of the previous year the entire editorial staff of *Die Vaderland* had been discussing more enthusiastically than ever the move to Johannesburg, scheduled for 1936.

In December 1935 Fasie de Wet rented another office across the way from the old editorial offices in Pretorius Street and founded a school for journalists, the so-called crèche, which he filled with young, recently matriculated boys, including C.E. Boshoff, Jac. Botha, Hint Hyman, R. Hendriks, Paling le Roux, Donald McDonald, Sep Smidt and Jo Spies. Young Uys Krige, too, just returned from Spain, was soon to join them. After an intensive period of training these boys were to form *Die Vaderland*'s junior editorial staff when the newspaper moved to Johannesburg in June 1936 and became a daily.

The Eugène Marais era in the history of *Die Vaderland* had passed. The move to Johannesburg meant that that of Gustav Preller would come to an end as well.

Gustav Preller had turned sixty in October 1935. He was still active enough to continue as editor in chief, but he had always been opposed to the move to Johannesburg and, moreover, Fasie de Wet wanted a younger, more progressive editor for his dynamic new Johannesburg daily.

One does not know whether this problem was solved peaceably. The bitter remarks Preller later made about his successor, Willem van Heerden, leads one to suspect that there was some disagreement. However, if unpleasantness did indeed threaten to raise its head, Dr. Preller's appointment as State Historian prevented it. He was to leave *Die Vaderland* at the end of February 1936. Could it have been that General Hertzog, the Prime Minister and one of the newspaper's founders, played a part in the solution?

At about this time, in the early hours of 15 January 1936, eleven weeks before Eugène Marais's death, something happened which does not seem as if it should belong to real life.

An astronomer provided the date. The story was told by Hannie Preller (repeated here verbatim from a tape recording made in 1963):

"One of our little dogs became very ill. The vet came, but he said the dog was dying, he could do nothing for it. Even Eugène agreed and said: 'Yes, it seems the best thing to do will be to put the poor thing down.'

"Gustav was typing in his study that evening and I think Eugène was lying on his bed. I don't know where the children were. I put the dog on a chair in the dining room and folded a blanket around it. But as I walked out I heard a crash and looking around I saw the dog lying in front of the chair in its own blood.

"I called out, and Eugène came along. The dog was dead. Eugène himself fetched an old rag and wiped up the blood. Then he said, 'We'll have to go and bury him.'

"By that time we already had the tennis court – it was built when Bob was in England – and next to the tennis court we had a refuse pit, mostly for paper. I sometimes wonder whether valuable documents weren't buried there.

"Well, Eugène and I put the dog on a rug and carried it to the tennis court. Eugène did all the work – dug the hole and filled it. And then he said, 'Look up there, you can see the double morning star. One sees it very seldom. It's Venus and Jupiter next to each other. And tomorrow night you'll see Jupiter is a bit further away, the two stars will be a bit further away from each other. It's not something one sees often.'"

The occlusion of certain heavenly bodies, according to centuries old superstition, is often the prelude to great or stirring events.

The blood and the star were the first sign.

Within a few days after this event, the Prellers decided to let their house in Blackwood Street and to go and stay at Pelindaba from March onwards.

"After more than thirty years in Arcadia, we had to move to the farm in the summer of 1936," Gustav Preller wrote. It was "completely unexpected", thereby strengthening the impression that his departure from *Die Vaderland* had been a recent decision.

Was Eugène to go along?

One of Preller's colleagues at *Die Vaderland* thinks that Preller wanted his old friend to go with them but that Hannie had serious doubts about this. And it may be this period that Mrs. Preller referred to when she later said the following words in an interview with a magazine:

"It did not often happen that my husband became really angry, but that day he was furious.

"'Do you also want to turn against Eugène now?' he cried.

"And so Eugène stayed with us until his death."

According to Preller, the matter was soon discussed with Marais.

"Under the oaks in the garden of our house (in Pretoria), where we sat chatting after work every evening, we came to a mutually satisfactory solution, while the bobo-shrike gave its mocking call from the telephone wire and the bokmakieries called to each other in the trees. Naturally he was to go along, that was our idea."

As always, Marais said little that evening.

What could he say? How could he ask the Prellers to change all their plans for his sake? And if he refused the offer, who else would house him?

But, and it was a terrible but – at Pelindaba his supply would again be threatened, as had happened only a few months before, when he had had to run away from the farm.

He had to choose and he could not do so for it was a choice between two kinds of death. This conflict spawned despair and the beginning of mental disintegration.

"I saw him frequently in Pretoria," his son was to write later that year in a letter, "and noticed at the beginning of this year a shocking change for the worse. I personally came to the conclusion that the end of the year would not see him alive and I have since heard that when my aunt, his sister (probably Eugène Jr.'s godmother, Sophie Ueckerman), met him in the street sometime in January and commented on the fact that he did not look well, he said he was feeling very bad and wished he could put an end to it all."

These words had not been heard since Heidelberg, after the fiasco of Steenkampskraal. "When he stayed with us," Mrs. Cross said, "we used to discuss, the question of suicide from time to time and then he would say, 'Someone who kills himself must be a complete coward.'"

But in the weeks after the decision to move to Pelindaba, he began to think differently.

"Almost every day at *Die Volkstem* he spoke to me about suicide," J.C. Vlok relates. "I always told him I thought it was a coward's way out and he would grant this, but he would also add: 'Yes, Vlokkie, but my God, there is one thing to justify it and that's loneliness. That is the most terrible thing in the world.

"'And what's more, what will I do on the farm?'"

"Then I realized," Mr. Vlok said, "that he was afraid he would have to do without his supply."

The Prellers could see that Marais was depressed but he told them nothing or perhaps they were too busy, during this important transitional stage in their lives, to worry about it.

The large farm-house which Hannie's brother, Lood Pretorius, had started building for them at Pelindaba two years before was not yet completely ready and had to be finished in a hurry. Their own house in Blackwood Street was provisionally let until they could find the right buyer.

"I do feel," Mrs. Hannie Preller said late in her life in a taped interview, "and I am not sure whether I should say this or not, that we rather left him in the lurch, both my husband and I, but we were so busy with our new house."

In their two different worlds the weeks passed for the Prellers and for Eugène Marais. They were to leave for the farm on a Friday, 19 March.

And now, only a few weeks before his death, something out of the ordinary happened again.

One day a huge crocodile skin was delivered to Blackwood Street.

"A friend had sent it to him," Mrs. Preller said, "a Mr. du Preez, I believe, who lived on the Limpopo. Eugène was entranced and he wanted us to take a snapshot of him with the skin to show how large it was. And then our black boy, Alfred, got such a fright that he decided to leave us completely. That was shortly before we left for the farm.

"And then, a month or so after Eugène's death, I came to town and saw Alfred in the street. I stopped the car and asked him, 'Alfred, you know Mr. Eugène is dead, don't you?'"

"He said yes, he knew he was going to die. But he would say nothing more."

The coming of the crocodile was the second sign.

The name of the farm to which they were going, Pelindaba, is a Zulu word which means, more or less, "the exchange of words is complete, the argument has been settled". Now, with the end approaching so rapidly, Eugène Marais feverishly began seeking other possible ways out. He wrote a letter to Hans Purekrans van Rooyen, nephew of the late Oom Gys van Rooyen, with whom he had maintained contact through the years and asked him whether he could come and stay with the Van Rooyens.

He probably contacted his son, but found no solution for his problem there. Then he asked Gustav Preller whether, after the Prellers had moved to the farm, he could stay in the house in Blackwood Street for another few days. Neither Preller nor the tenants of the house had any objection. In the meantime Marais arranged to meet Mrs. Cross at Bones the chemist on Saturday, 20 March, the day after the Prellers' departure.

He told Gustav and Hannie nothing about this. On the day of their departure he stood watching their furniture being loaded onto the ox-wagons which were to take everything to the farm.

He intended to ask Mrs. Cross the next day whether he could not go and stay with her and her family in Springs, even though she had refused this before.

"From deductions we made later," J.C. Vlok was to relate, "I now realize that Eugène knew his doctor was going away. As he was going to the farm, he asked for a two week supply. And when Nel left, he went to his locum and asked him for the same. He then had enough for a month."

Even so it does not seem to have been morphine which prevented him from keeping his appointment with Mrs. Cross at the chemist.

On the Saturday morning after the Prellers' departure, Marais arrived later than usual at Frikkie and Kathleen Mansfield's chemist shop to get his morning shot. It was just after nine and at that same moment a venerable 83 year old gentleman was eagerly searching for Eugène.

This old man, a Mr. Beyers, was an uncle of Lettie, Eugène's late wife. He had last seen Eugène after Lettie's death in 1895, about forty years earlier. At the moment he was visiting his daughter in Brooklyn. And there was a good reason why he wanted to see Eugène Marais once more after so many years.

The injection Kathleen had given Eugène was taking effect while he was still chatting to her behind the curtain in Bones's.

According to his agreement with Mrs. Cross, she was to call at the chemist during the course of the morning to find out at what time she should meet him at the Black Cat corner.

The aged Mr. Beyers and his chauffeur had meanwhile, after a considerable search, arrived at Bones's.

Eugène was to come with him, he said – he wanted to introduce him to his family in Brooklyn. His car and driver were waiting outside.

"Gladly," Eugène said and mumbled something about his appointment later that morning.

"Yes, yes," the old man replied, and so they left for Brooklyn, the suburb where Eugène had shared a house with Charlie Pienaar more than thirty years before.

Here he walked into a dream.

Lettie – his dead wife, Aletta Beyers – came forward to greet him.

He was introduced to her. This was the old man's granddaughter. The similarity was incredible.

In Brooklyn the hours passed.

In the meantime Mrs. Cross had arrived in Pretoria from Springs. She called at Bones's and asked Frikkie Mansfield whether Eugène had left a message. Frikkie asked Kathleen. No, there was no message.

Mrs. Cross waited until almost one o'clock, went to visit the other friends she wanted to see in Pretoria and arrived home late that afternoon, disappointed and saddened, to tell Edna and Hettie that Oom Eugène had stood her up.

In Brooklyn it was already after one o'clock when Eugène Marais, to his shock and dismay, noticed the time. The old man's driver took him through to town and dropped him at Bones's. The shop was already closed, but Pringle, Mansfield's assistant, opened the door to his knock.

Was there a message?

"No," said Pringle, "Mrs. Cross was here, but she spoke to Mansfield and I do not know what they discussed."

Marais stood around outside the shop for a while. Then he hurriedly walked to 733 Arcadia Street, the house Mrs. Cross had left shortly before. He hoped to find her here, visiting one of the lodgers she was friendly with.

But she was not there either. He went to *Die Volkstem* and found nobody he knew. The editorial staff were not due to come in until the next day to start working on Monday's edition. The caretaker knew nothing about a message.

He even went to *Die Vaderland*, and here, too, the place was deserted.

Until after six he wandered up and down Church Street. Every now and again he returned to the Square to see whether Mrs. Cross was perhaps waiting at one of the bus-stops. By evening he managed to get hold of some paper and a pencil, perhaps from Bob Shilling at the Waverley Bar, and wrote Mrs. Cross a letter to apologize. If his statements deviate from the strict truth in certain respects, this is understandable.

"I left no message at Bones because I had decided to wait for you at the Black Cat corner from twelve until you arrived, at whatever time it might be. Just before I left Bones an old uncle of mine turned up in a car and insisted that I accompany him to Brooklyn to meet a married daughter of his ... He promised to bring me back whenever I wished. The old man is eighty-three and when we got to his daughter's he was taken ill and when I next thought of the time it was past one. I got his driver to rush me down to Bones in the hope that you had left a message. But only Pringle was in ..."

No coincidence could have been worse and he wrote: "It seemed as if fate itself intervened."

The appearance of Lettie was the third sign.

19. Whisperings in a Dream

Once he had posted the letter he felt better. But later that evening, or that night, in his little room in Blackwood Street, all the loneliness returned. And he used the only thing he still had left.

Were there beautiful dreams? Oblivion, in any case, and when oblivion was followed by bitter awakening, a new wave of oblivion. Later J.C. Vlok wrote to Dr. Winifred de Kok in England to tell her about Marais's death and he mentioned: "He had managed to get a month's supply of morphine and he had a terrible binge. He looked too ghastly for words."

By the middle of that week Eugène was strong enough to send Hans Purekrans van Rooyen a telegram, something like: "Please meet me at Naboomspruit."

He had never received a reply to his earlier letter.

He still visited *Die Volkstem* several times. There were certain things he still wanted to attend to – even at this stage. Shortly before he had asked Chris Roos at Pelindaba to try and obtain for him a young ape for certain experiments he planned to conduct.

This may have been why he wanted to write to the Director of the Pretoria Zoo later that week:

Dear Dr. Bigalke,
Regarding your letter.
Yours sincerely
Eugène Marais.

"That was the last letter he wrote on earth," says J.C. Vlok. "He was virtually in a coma. I had quite a job to see that his cigarettes did not set anything alight. I can see him to this day sitting there, his face like marble."

By this time his supply had been used up.

He dared not go to his doctor's locum again. None of his chemist friends would help him. Neither Max nor Louis Schwartz, nor George Steer of the Tudor, nor Pringle, nor Mansfield, nor even lovable Kathleen. For the Indians he did not have nearly enough money.

"I think Mansfield pitied him terribly at times," J.C. Vlok said. "I think he probably helped him on occasion. No, I can't say that. They were all very careful – especially after the police threatened to act. And after that week's binge nobody would have dared."

While his withdrawal symptoms intensified minute by minute, Eugène crossed and re-crossed the city of his birth in search of salvation. He found it only when he was almost on his last legs, from Dr. Betsy Goddefroy, who was still living next door to the Prellers' old house in Blackwood Street.

In the meantime Mrs. Cross had discussed his letter with her daughters in their new house in Springs. They were deeply moved.

"I then told my youngest son Charles he should go to Pretoria the next morning, a Saturday, to fetch Mr. Marais so that he could come and live with us. We had no choice."

In the meantime Piet Pretorius, Hannie's brother, who was to keep an eye on Marais after the Prellers had moved to Pelindaba, decided that he should no longer stay in Pretoria. Piet's son, Henning, and his friend Jannie Shegog were asked to take him to Pelindaba on the Saturday afternoon.

When Eugène arrived at *Die Volkstem* on the Saturday morning to say farewell to Vlokkie, he had been to Mansfield with his prescription.

"He already looked much better by then," Mr. Vlok says, "but he was very depressed.

"'It's no good,' he said. 'There is nothing I can do. Do you know what they want to give me on the farm – two grains a day. If I have to get along with that, I might as well be dead.'

"I then felt terribly sorry for him and started insisting that he should come and stay with me, however difficult that would be, as my wife had just broken her back and we had four young children. He refused: 'It's bad for them to see me when I'm, you know, sleepy,' as he said.

"Eventually I lost my patience and from where he was standing in the doorway he said:

'I only wanted to tell you that I love you just as much as your twin brother.'"

The "twin brother" was Marais's own son, who at that stage was either in Brits or visiting his godmother in Pretoria.

In the meantime, on that rainy, subtropical Saturday morning, Charles Cross, Edna's youngest brother, had arrived in Pretoria from Johannesburg to take him to Mrs. Cross and her daughters in Springs.

"He looked everywhere," said Mrs. Cross. "The last place he went to was Bones the chemist. There Frikkie Mansfield told him, 'No, Oom Eugène has his supply but I think he's gone to Pelindaba.'

"Charles had to be back in Johannesburg at one o'clock that afternoon. He couldn't go out to the farm to go and get him there."

Just before the two young men collected Eugène Marais in Blackwood Street, he went to Dr. Betsy Goddefroy for the last time. And for the last time she helped him.

Then they were off. At about lunchtime the car left Pretoria, one of the young men driving, with Marais next to him in the front seat. He said not a word. Near the graveyard a funeral procession passed them. Marais took off his hat and mumbled: "Lucky bastard."

At Pelindaba the Prellers were not there to welcome him – apparently they did not even hear him arrive. He immediately moved into the rondavels and lay down on the bed on the veranda with some blankets over him, his pile of Abdullahs on the chair next to him, books and newspapers at hand.

While he lay smoking, he looked through the soft rain which was falling, across the fields to the river and the mountains.

"It had rained a great deal that March," Gustav Preller was write later, "and the dismal weather had a depressing influence ‿ him. Magaliesberg was covered in fog for days on end and in the ev enings the mist spread up the river and streamed like a white veil in the moonlight."

If Gustav Preller could have had his way he would have preferred posterity to know nothing about Marais's addiction. It was certainly not the rain alone which made him depressed that last weekend. Years later Hannie Preller said in an interview: "We didn't know he had arrived at the rondavels. Somebody told us. Well, we were so busy. My husband was then writing the history of Andries Pretorius. He was constantly involved with his books, and the house had not been finished. He wanted his room ready to work in and I had to scrape off the cement they had spilled there and Eugène was in the rondavels and I really think we left him in the lurch there. Thinking back on it now, he must have had a very bitter time."

Marais had supper in the main house that night. Lood Pretorius had built the house from dolerite and slate and had given it a thatched roof. Marais had frequently admired the building's natural style, which blended with the surroundings.

He was taken back to the rondavels by car early that evening, because it was dark and rainy (Gustav Preller wrote later, but, as always, he suppresses all reference to morphine).

And morphine was the one thing Eugène Marais had to have that night. After the great binge of the past week he needed it more than ever but Gustav Preller had been busy with his own affairs lately. However incredible it may sound, he had neglected to provide even for his old friend's minimum requirements.

Eugène Marais had been afraid that he would have to make do with two grains a day at Pelindaba. In fact, there was absolutely nothing here. On the windowsill of the rondavel, like a mockery, lay a few aspirins.

That is why this evening and night became such a bitter one. Not even Dr. Betsy Goddefroy, with all her sympathy, had given him something to take along. After all, Dr. Preller kept his supply at the farm. Hence the anxiety, the restlessness, the tremors, the cramps, the nausea.

J.C. Vlok had made a mistake. Eugène Marais was not to write his last letter in life until that evening, a last pathetic letter in a feeble, scratchy hand. He told one of the farm labourers to take it across the road to the house of his old friend, the teacher Chris Roos.

> Dear Mr. Roos,
>
> I have suddenly become seriously ill. Can't you take me in please? I have to have medicine at once. I shall compensate you for the two trips. Please come quickly.
> Your friend,
> Eugène N. Marais

Two trips? According to Chris Roos, he had had to take Marais to Pretoria a short while before as well.

It was a dark and rainy Saturday evening. Moreover, Chris knew that both Lood Pretorius and Gustav Preller were on the farm. If Eugène was approaching him it meant they had refused him and then he was not allowed to have anything.

The black man returned through the wet grass to bring Marais the news.

Marais was lying curled up on his bed in one of the rondavels when he had been given the message. He tried once more:

"Then please ask the boss for a bottle of brandy."

This too was refused.

While his friends slept – at Pelindaba, in Pretoria, in Springs, in Brits and in the Waterberg – this became Eugène Marais's longest night.

When he did not arrive at the farm-house the next morning to have breakfast, one of the Prellers' sons came to inquire how he was. They talked for a while and Marais pointed to a drinking trough he himself had built in front of the door out of dolomite, stone and cement.

"There's a snake in the thorn-tree which catches the little birds," he said. "Ask your father whether he can lend me a gun."

At half past one that afternoon, when Eugène had not arrived for lunch either, Gustav and Hannie Preller themselves went down to see him.

Once more Marais asked for a gun.

He had a gun, said Preller, but no cartridges.

"He was in bed," Mrs. Preller said later. "So I asked him whether I couldn't send him down some food. No, he said, he would come for supper that evening. He had no appetite right now."

There does not seem to have been much said.

"Some way from the rondavels," Gustav Preller was to write later, "a number of milking cows stood ruminating listlessly, their backs bent and their tails turned to the softly falling rain and while we discussed the excessive rain for that time of year he, who could usually be so exuberant about rain, remarked in a manner which struck me as rather impatient: 'Even the poor animals have had enough of it by now.'

"If the rain continued, we agreed, we would send down the car to bring him to the house for supper. If it stopped raining, he would walk up to the house."

Gustav and Hannie returned home.

Eugène Marais got up, wearily put on his shoes and jacket and set off through the veld, the Magaliesberge faintly visible in the distance through the fog and mist and the river gleaming dully to his right. Stumbling and struggling through the knee-high wet grass, he walked about a mile before he saw the tall eucalyptus tree on the right-hand side of Lood Pretorius' house, then the kitchen chimney and eventually the simple farm-house itself with its corrugated iron roof, its thickly plastered and grooved walls and long veranda.

Again the talk was a short one. Could Lood give him a drink?

No, he was sorry, he had nothing.

Where could he get a car (for he longed for the healing hands of Dr. Betsy Goddefroy)?

No, said Lood, he knew of no car except those belonging to Gustav and Chris Roos.

Did he have a rifle? There was a snake near the rondavels.

"Then take a shotgun," Lood Pretorius said. "You should know you can't shoot a snake with a rifle."

These two men understood each other well. Lood Pretorius – this, more than forty years later, goes almost without saying – knew that Eugène Marais did not want to shoot a snake, at any rate not a real snake.

From his gun-rack he took one of his best guns, a twelve-bore double-barreled shotgun. On another occasion Eugène and Lood, both experts, might have discussed the gun's appearance and qualities.

Lood walked a short way with him before returning home. Who can blame him if, shortly afterwards, when the first shot rang out, he pretended to have heard nothing?

Only a hundred yards from the farm-house, in the wet sour-grass beneath a karreeboom, Eugène Marais had come to a halt and had tried, in spite of the jerking of his hands, to shoot himself in the heart. It was a pitifully glancing blow. Did he still hope for another way out?

Then he hesitated no longer. Putting the second barrel into his mouth, he made quite sure.

Then that, too, was done.